ACT Prep
by Mag✔✔sh

RTC Team   Publisher **Corey Michael Blake**
President **Kristin Westberg**
Editor **Geoff Campbell**
Content Coordinator **Keli McNeill**
Designers **Sunny DiMartino, Christy Bui**
Illustrators **Brent Metcalf, Analee Paz**
Proofreaders **Adam Lawrence, Carly Cohen**
Project Manager **Leeann Sanders**

Magoosh Team   Project Leads **Rita Kreig Neumann, Maizie Simpson**
Content Specialists **Lucas Fink, Kristin Fracchia,**
   Rachel Kapelke-Dale, Chris Lele, Mike McGarry,
   Rita Kreig Neumann
Copy Editors **Jeff Derrenberger, Kristin Fracchia,**
   Samuel Kinsman, Tony Le, Adam Lyons, Wyatt
   McDonnell, Rita Kreig Neumann, Michele Roberts,
   Cydney Seigerman, Carolyn Shasha, Sarah Stricker,
   Kat Thomson, Jessica Wan, Matt Weinstein,
   Andrew Wessels
Proofreader **Rachel Kapelke-Dale**
Student Feedback Coordinator **Anne Bercilla**
Cover Designer, Illustration **Mark Thomas**

Copyright © 2018 Magoosh

Writers of the Round Table Press
PO Box 511, Highland Park, IL 60035
www.roundtablecompanies.com

Printed in the United States of America

First Edition: July 2018
10 9 8 7 6 5 4 3 2 1

Library of Congress Cataloging-in-Publication Data
Magoosh.
ACT prep by magoosh: act prep guide with study schedules, practice
questions, and strategies to improve your score / Magoosh.—1st ed. p. cm.
ISBN Paperback: 978-1-61066-069-3
ISBN Digital: 978-1-61066-070-9
Library of Congress Control Number: 2018907311

ACT Prep
by Mag✔✔sh

ACT Prep Guide with Study Schedules, Practice Questions, and Strategies to Improve Your Score

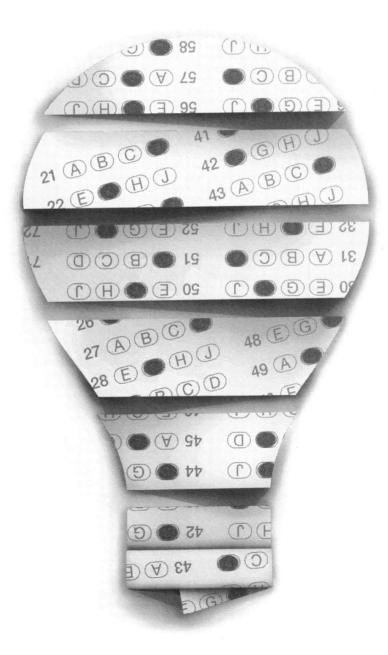

Contents

Chapter 7

313 ACT Reading Test

Chapter 8

351 ACT Science Test

Chapter 9

423 ACT Writing Test

Chapter 10

469 Full-Length ACT Practice Test

Chapter 11

535 It's Test Day!

Introduction

Welcome to ACT Prep by Magoosh!

We want to take this opportunity to thank you wholeheartedly for picking up this book. We truly poured our hearts into it and hope that it helps you achieve your test prep goals.

Who are we? Magoosh is a team of education nerds who have been helping students improve their test scores (and get into their dream schools) since 2009. We're very happy to meet you!

What you're holding in your hands is a companion guide to the Magoosh ACT prep program offered online at act.magoosh.com. You'll soon discover that the content of this book, combined with our online test prep, packs a gigantic ACT wallop.

Fair Warning: You're not just going to find a random assortment of practice questions in these pages. Rather, this book aims to provide you with an astounding number of practical strategies and tips for every test (and moment) of the ACT exam.

We hope you're getting the sense that we *really* care about your success because, well . . . we do! Our aim is to offer you the best overall guide to taking the ACT exam. That's where this book comes in.

One day, our team of educators started wondering how Magoosh could help students around the globe study more effectively, and we realized that an actual book might come in handy. Sometimes books can go places laptops and phones can't. You can toss this book in your bag and study whenever you find yourself lacking an internet connection, wanting to take some handwritten notes, or feeling like you might learn something better by reading it in a physical book. This book amplifies Magoosh's online ACT content to help you study whenever and wherever is convenient for you.

Speaking of studying online . . . our online ACT platform provides additional tools to teach you exactly what to expect when you sit down to take the ACT. In addition to the hundreds of ACT practice questions we offer online, we also provide a video and text explanation for each one. Yes, every single one! And we don't just offer practice questions. To help you cover all the ACT basics, we also provide more than 200 video lessons covering every topic on the exam. With the help of this book, and all the useful features included in the Magoosh online platform, you are going to rock your ACT.

And, in case you didn't know, Magoosh isn't just about practice questions and tests. We also offer free resources to improve your study experience. Be sure to check out our High School Blog (magoosh.com/hs), which offers even more great study tips and resources. In fact, some of our most popular blog posts have been incorporated into this book.

Still looking for more fun ways to prep? Study on your phone with the free Magoosh ACT Test Prep and Magoosh ACT Flashcards apps. Both can be found in the iOS and Google Play stores. Love your Amazon Echo? Try the Magoosh Vocabulary Builder and Magoosh Spelling Game skills.

Whether you're taking the ACT for the first time or studying for a retake, we hope you're getting the feel for just how many resources you have at your disposal. Not only that, but we love hearing from students. So, if you have questions or comments or just want to send us a virtual high five, please get in touch with us at help@magoosh.com. Our awesome test prep experts respond to all emails in a timely manner.

We hope you find this ACT guide useful. Happy studying!

The Magoosh Team

Meet Magoosh

We're a team of passionate educators based in Berkeley, California. We like word games, video games, and helping students do really well on standardized exams so that they can achieve their educational dreams.

This is Bhavin Parikh, our CEO and founder. He has a BS/BA in economics and computer science from Duke University and an MBA from the Haas School of Business at University of California, Berkeley. Now, he's on a mission to change the way people learn and how they think about learning, which is why he started Magoosh in 2009. Fun fact: when he's not hard at work with our team, you'll usually find Bhavin playing ultimate Frisbee or Smash Bros.

And here's the rest of the fantastic Magoosh team!

The Magoosh Experts

These are the Magoosh ACT experts who helped write this book. All the tips and lessons contained in these pages came from the brilliant minds of these educators. If you have any questions for them, send an email to help@magoosh.com. Magoosh test prep experts are always happy to speak with students, parents, and fellow instructors!

Kristin Fracchia

Kristin is the ACT Expert at Magoosh who creates awesomely fun lessons and practice materials for students. With a PhD from UC Irvine and degrees in education and English, she's been working in education since 2004 and has helped students prepare for standardized tests, as well as college and graduate school admissions, since 2007. She enjoys the agonizing bliss of marathon running, backpacking, hot yoga, and esoteric knowledge.

Rita Kreig Neumann

Rita helps high schoolers find Magoosh, improve their SAT/ACT scores, and get into their dream schools. She earned both her BA and Master of Pacific International Affairs from UC San Diego, where she also studied Spanish, French, and Portuguese. Rita loves education and community development just as much as she loves vinyasa yoga and baking chocolate chip cookies.

Mike McGarry

Mike creates expert lessons and practice questions to guide students to success. He has a BS in physics and an MA in religion, both from Harvard, and over 20 years of teaching experience specializing in math, science, and standardized exams. Mike likes smashing foosballs into orbit, and despite having no obvious cranial deficiency, he insists on rooting for the New York Mets.

Chris Lele

Chris is one of the creators of Magoosh's online ACT and SAT prep lessons and practice questions. For the last 10 years, Chris has been helping students excel on the ACT and SAT exams. In this time, he's coached five students to a perfect SAT score! Rumor has it he does a secret happy dance when his students get a perfect score.

Lucas Fink

Lucas is Magoosh's resident grammar nerd. Since tutoring his first ACT student in 2008, he has moved around the world to teach; from running English classes for non-native speakers in the Czech Republic and South Korea to teaching ACT and SAT students in California, he has taught students at every level and age. Unsurprisingly, he's a big fan of word puzzles, including Scrabble, *New York Times* crosswords, anagrams, Balderdash, and Codenames … you name it!

Rachel Kapelke-Dale

Rachel is a high school and graduate exams blogger at Magoosh. She has a BA from Brown University, an MA from the Université de Paris VII, and a PhD from University College London. She has taught test preparation and consulted on admissions practices for over eight years. Currently, Rachel divides her time between the US and London.

Our Mission

We create products that give students everywhere access to enjoyable, affordable, and effective test prep.

Our Core Values

Accessible > Exclusive	⇨	We're open to ideas from everyone, inside and outside of Magoosh.
Challenge > Comfort	⇨	We challenge ourselves to learn new skills by tackling tasks we've never done before.
Friendly > Formal	⇨	We always show respect and kindness to our teammates, customers, and partners, whether online or offline.
Wow > Profit	⇨	We go above and beyond in our work and never say, "It's not my job."
Done > Perfect	⇨	We have a bias toward action and won't delay for perfection tomorrow what can be done well today.
Data > Intuition	⇨	We run experiments to test ideas and gather data.
Passion > [Something]	⇨	We love what we do! Helping students is too much fun to be considered work.
Communication > Efficiency	⇨	We set clear expectations, communicate when we've completed a task, and follow up when necessary.
Change > Status Quo	⇨	We adapt to difficult situations and reevaluate our priorities, so we'll always be a work in progress.

Our Products

Magoosh offers test prep for the ACT, SAT, GRE, GMAT, LSAT, TOEFL, IELTS, MCAT, and Praxis. And we're expanding to new exams soon!

What Is Magoosh ACT Prep?

Magoosh ACT Prep is an online course that offers:

- 200+ unique lessons on all ACT subjects
- 900+ English, math, reading, science, and writing practice questions, with video explanations after every question
- Access anytime, anywhere from any internet-connected device
- Email support from experienced ACT tutors
- Customizable practice sessions and quizzes, plus up to three full-length practice tests
- Personalized statistics based on your performance
- Study schedules to help keep you on track
- +4-point score guarantee for retakers
- Free ACT Flashcards app and ACT Test Prep app, available in iOS and Google Play app stores

Why Our Students Love Us

Think of us as your cheerleaders, here to reassure you throughout your ACT journey. Trust us when we tell you that this support goes a long way! Take a look at what some of our current and former ACT students have said about us below and on magoosh.com/stories and act.magoosh.com/testimonials.

John L. scored 28 (+5 points)	**Amelia C.** scored 21 (+4 points)	**Nicholas B.** scored 33	**Ashtyn V.** scored 30 (+4 points)
"Magoosh has a user-friendly interface and was very effective for me. The practice problems gave me an estimated score, which helped me know what subjects to focus on."	"I loved being able to see video explanations of the problems that I missed. I also really felt that I had individualized help through Magoosh's study plans and helpful test tips."	"Often the ACT is about confidence, and Magoosh gave me the advice and tips tailored to my weakest topics to give me a cool head for my first test day."	"Magoosh had helpful video lessons and explanations for questions. Usually when I miss a problem I don't know what my mistake was, but Magoosh helped explain things."

A Quick Pep Talk Before We Dive In . . .

We know that taking the ACT can feel like a daunting task. You've probably heard whispers about it in the hallways of your high school, but when it comes time for you to sit down and begin studying, you may find it difficult to know where to start.

There's a pesky, yet persistent, myth circulating out there that standardized tests like the ACT and the SAT measure your intelligence, and that practicing for such tests is futile.

As tutors, we know that nothing could be further from the truth.

The ACT requires a skill set that can be learned. In that way, it's no different than learning to play soccer. Like any other skill set involving some talent, there may be limits to the level you can ultimately attain—you may never become a professional soccer player—but you can improve your accuracy. Everyone has the potential to make improvements! And your training starts now.

Here's how to get started:

- **Spend some time with the free resources at act.org.** This is the official ACT website, and yet it's amazing how many students take the ACT without ever having visited it! This should be the first stop in your ACT test prep journey. You'll find ACT basics plus free practice tests and advice from the test-makers themselves.

- **Use reputable study sources.** Every ACT student should get *The Official ACT Prep Guide* (affectionately known as "The Red Book"), which includes a handful of old official exams.

- **Get inside the heads of the test-makers.** Try to develop an understanding of what the test-makers "prefer" in terms of answer choices. For example, after studying the ACT English Test for some time, you'll notice how the ACT test-makers generally prefer answer choices that employ economy of language—they're concise, clear, and correct. Chapter 3, "General ACT Tips and Strategies," has a lot of strategies that will help you make better educated guesses on difficult problems.

- **Plan out a reasonable study schedule.** To make sure you get the ACT test date and test center you want, register early—at least three months before the exam. That way, you can create a study schedule, working backward from the test date. When you do this, be realistic with yourself. How much time can you commit each week to ACT practice questions, lessons, and exams? It's better to study for 20–30 minutes a day than for a four-hour block once a week. Aim to work on ACT material at least four days a week to keep your mind sharp. Flip forward to chapter 4, "ACT Study Schedules," to learn how to plan your prep schedule (or use the Magoosh study plan).

- **Take timed, full-length practice tests.** If you aren't taking timed, full-length ACT practice tests, then you're not *really* preparing yourself for the experience of taking the ACT. You wouldn't train for a marathon by running a few hundred-yard dashes and then calling it a day. And make no mistake—the ACT exam is an academic marathon. Sitting down for four hours to take an entire practice test is the best way to determine what you already know and what you need to learn before test day. Plus, practice tests work with every type of study plan and strategy. You'll find the Magoosh ACT Practice Test in chapter 10.

- **Learn the concepts tested the most often.** The reality of standardized tests is that they are, well, standardized. There are a finite number of concepts that the ACT will test. To perform well, you will need to figure out what you already know and what you need to work on. The good news: the questions are predictable! Once you learn the concepts, you'll see them pop up over and over again, and you will know exactly what to do when you see them on the official exam. Talk about a confidence booster! Flip to chapters 5–9 to learn the specific concepts covered in each test on the ACT.

- **Pinpoint your weaknesses and improve them.** Know which subjects you'll need to work on more than others, and plan to address them first. Understandably, you'll need to dedicate more study time to your weaknesses than to your strengths. So as you're working through the practice problems in chapters 5–9, take note of which concepts you don't understand very well. Then, don't put off studying for a test subject just because you dread it!

- **But don't forget your strengths are particularly valuable on the ACT.** This is especially true for the ACT (in comparison to the SAT). Though college admissions committees will look at your test scores (English, Mathematics, Reading, Science, and Writing), most colleges will focus more on your overall ACT composite score. Because this ACT composite score is the average of all your individual test scores, doing even better on your strongest areas can help make up for your weakest tests when everything averages out. Learn all about ACT scoring in chapter 2.

- **Don't stress!** This is arguably the most important piece of advice in this book. Months of hard work can be forgotten, all because your anxiety kicked in and you panicked on test day. Remember that test-taking is a learned skill, not an inherent gift. Some people may seem to be "naturally" good at the ACT, but even if you're not one of them, you can still learn how to earn a good score! Think positively, breathe, and focus on your personal progress throughout your ACT test prep. Recognize that making mistakes is a necessary part of the learning process. Incorrect practice questions will help you home in on the concepts that need more work, so welcome them!

And don't forget that this book is here to help you along your test prep journey. If you have any questions, we're real people (not robots), ready to help! You can sign up for online prep at magoosh.com, download a Magoosh app, check out our blog, or even email us at help@magoosh.com. Friendly Magoosh experts are always around to help you succeed.

How to Use This Book

We designed this book as a journey. Unless you're already well into your ACT prep, we recommend that you work through this book in order, from start to finish. You'll begin with basic information, plan your prep timeline, learn about each ACT test individually, practice what you've learned, assess your practice, and then move on to the next steps in your college application process. Here's what you can expect from the following pages:

Chapters 1–3

The first three chapters of this book focus on teaching you the basics. This is the "bare minimum" information: what the ACT is used for, when you should take it, how it's scored, and some general strategies. If taking the ACT is like planning a trip, then these chapters are your road map.

Chapter 4

Now that you know the basics, it's time to strategize your plan of attack. How long do you have to prep for the ACT? What should you do to maximize the effectiveness of that time? The study schedule in this chapter will help you break your prep into manageable pieces that won't leave you cramming (never fun) or forgetting everything you already studied (never effective).

Chapters 5–9

Each of these chapters tackles one ACT test: English, math, reading, science, or writing. This is the meat of the book. Here, we go into detail about what to expect from each test. You'll get general information about the test (timing, strategies for success) as well as specific information on each and every concept and question type you'll encounter on the ACT. Plus, each chapter offers practice questions to help you master all of our proven tips and strategies. This is where you'll be spending the most of your time with this book … so get comfortable!

Chapter 10

After learning and practicing all of the strategies you'll need to know for ACT test day, it's time to take a timed, full-length practice test. First, you'll read about how to maximize the benefit of your practice test, then you'll grab a timer and sit down for a four-hour mock-exam. This is the first big test of your endurance and pacing skills, so be patient with yourself. Let's face it, you wouldn't swim across the English Channel without first doing some practice laps in a pool. And taking a four-hour test may be just as challenging as a 21-mile doggy-paddle if you've never tried it before!

Chapter 11

By this point, you'll be well-versed in everything related to the ACT. You'll know your strengths and weaknesses and what you need to do to improve your score. The bonus resources in this chapter will provide you with strategies to help you make the most of your ACT test day.

Chapter 1

Meet the ACT

The ACT: A History Lesson

How much do you know about the origins of the ACT? What do those three letters even stand for? Time for a pop quiz! (Just kidding ... we'll provide the information this time around.)

The Origins of the ACT

Prior to 1959, the SAT served as the United States' only national, standardized college entrance exam. However, as more students decided to pursue higher education and universities responded to the demand by opening up more seats, the need for another measurement system emerged. Say hello to the American College Testing Program (or ACT for short)!

Fun fact: In 1996, the ACT acronym became the official name for both the test and the company behind it, meaning it no longer "stood" for anything. So if you didn't know what "ACT" means, you were actually technically right: today, the letters don't stand for anything!

Originally, the ACT was designed to assess college-bound students' specific knowledge of content they learned in high school: English, mathematics, reading, and science reasoning. This multiple-choice exam measured a student's ability to recall the fundamentals and formulas of these subjects. It consisted of four 35–40-minute tests. Sound pretty familiar? That's because it is.

Unlike the SAT, which has undergone many formatting, grading, and timing changes over the years, the ACT has remained largely the same—a trait that has made it very attractive to some modern test-takers. Though there have been some small changes to the format and question types over the years, the only big change occurred in 2005, with the addition of the ACT Writing Test.

Today, more students are choosing the ACT over the SAT. This gives you all the more reason to invest in your ACT prep. Read on to gain an edge on the competition!

How Hard Is the ACT?

How hard is it, *really*? Well, difficulty is a relative term. On a difficulty scale that ranges from learning your ABCs to learning rocket science, the ACT probably ranks about here:

Compared to your ABCs and a typical state standardized test, the ACT probably ranks about here:

Of course, this is just an example. For some people, learning the alphabet is hard—maybe they are non-native English speakers or struggle with a learning difference such as dyslexia—but multivariable calculus might be a piece of cake. The point is that it is ultimately impossible to answer the question "How hard is the ACT?" because the answer is going to be different for everyone.

But we know you aren't reading this for that very unsatisfying answer. So here are some things we can tell you about what some students think makes the ACT "hard":

- **It's hard because there is a lot of time pressure.** The ACT gives you three hours and 35 minutes to answer 215 questions and write an essay. Granted, certain questions take longer than others to answer, but many ACT test-takers end up feeling that they could have done much better if they'd only had more time.

- **It's hard because of the concentration and amount of reading demanded by the test.** The ACT has a lot more reading than the SAT—there are longer reading passages, more math word problems, and more complex science scenarios to sort through. This can really tax your attention span, which is why taking full-length practice tests is so important. You're going to need to develop the endurance and focus that the test demands.

- **Relatively speaking, the ACT has gotten "harder" over the years.** As students started to do better on the ACT, the test-makers gradually adjusted the difficulty level of the test. In 1970, the average composite score nationwide was 18.6. In 2016, it was 20.8. Although this may initially seem to show that the test has gotten easier, the opposite is actually true. The ACT has more than compensated for the fact that the average student has gotten better at the test by creating more difficult questions and passages that ensure only a small number of students are at the tippy-top of the scale. (Before you start raging at the test-makers, you should know that this is true of all standardized tests, not just the ACT.)

- **But the ACT is NOT hard because it is "tricky."** The ACT is a pretty straightforward test. No matter how you feel about problem x, y, or z, the test is not trying to play mind games with you. The ACT requires you to be very detail-oriented so you don't make silly mistakes, but the answer is always in plain sight. And that's actually good news! There's no *Matrix*-style "the answer was inside me the whole time" twists. The answer is right there on the page. The whole time!

Above all, the ACT is specifically designed so that not everyone can ace it. Only a small number of students will achieve a top score. This means that, for the vast majority of students, the ACT is going to be a "hard" test. On the other hand, because it is a *standardized* test, every test-taker does have the exact same opportunity to ace it (standardized = same problem types, same difficulty level). The best advice we can give you is to be prepared and go into the ACT knowing exactly what's in store.

ACT Basics

What can you expect from the ACT? Let's start at the beginning and work our way through the exam step by step.

The ACT exam is made up of four required multiple-choice tests and one optional timed essay. The required tests are (in order): English, Mathematics, Reading, and Science. The optional essay is called the ACT Writing Test.

Note that the ACT doesn't use the word "section" when describing these components. Rather, the ACT calls them "tests," and that's the word we'll mostly be using in this book. So, yes—you can expect tests within a test. It's the Russian nesting doll of standardized assessments.

Prefer a visual to a metaphor? We've got you covered. Check out the chart below to learn basic information about the structure, format, timing, and scoring of the ACT.

Test	Required or Optional?	Number of Questions	Timing	Scoring	What to Expect
English	Required	75 questions	45 minutes	1–36	Assesses your mastery of English grammar conventions
Mathematics	Required	60 questions	60 minutes	1–36	Tests algebra, geometry, and some trigonometry
Reading	Required	40 questions	35 minutes	1–36	Evaluates your reading comprehension skills
Science	Required	40 questions	35 minutes	1–36	Measures scientific reasoning and your ability to interpret and analyze data
Writing	Optional*	One essay prompt	40 minutes	1–12	Assesses the composition skills that you'll need in your first-year college classes

Note that the ACT Writing Test is technically optional. However, it is not optional when applying to certain schools. If you're unsure about where you're applying, it's usually better to take the Writing Test. We'll talk more about this test in chapter 9.

An Overview of the ACT

Who Takes the ACT?

Will you be applying to attend college or university in the United States? Yes? That's perfect, because most US universities require that students submit either ACT or SAT scores as part of their college application. And all of those colleges that require a college admissions test as part of the application accept ACT scores. So if you are planning to apply to college sometime in the near future, then the ACT exam is for you!

Of course, you also have the option of taking the SAT exam ... but that's a different book. It's important to know, though, that neither exam is better or easier. Some students find that they tend to score higher on one over the other, so if you're not sure which to take, we recommend taking a practice ACT and a practice SAT and seeing if you naturally perform better on one.

Note: If you need help funding your college years (honestly, who doesn't?), ACT and SAT scores may help you qualify for certain scholarships. Do your research to learn more about scholarship requirements before you take your ACT. Then, use that information to determine your target score and motivate yourself to study!

Does Your State Require the ACT?

If you're not sure whether to take the ACT or the SAT, here's some helpful news: your state may already have decided for you! That's right—as states begin to use college admissions tests to meet the national standards required of public high schools, they're starting to make the ACT or SAT mandatory.

One upside of this? Because of this change, some states have already begun to provide the ACT or the SAT free to all juniors.

So just where do the lucky students who experience (or will experience) mandatory college admissions testing live? Which states require the ACT? And which of those offer it for free? Because state requirements change all the time, we recommend that you check with your guidance counselor to confirm state requirements and subsidies.

How Long Should You Study for the ACT?

Once you've decided (or been informed) that you definitely need to take the ACT, either for your college applications or to meet state requirements, the natural next question is: "When should I start my prep?"

The answer is different for everyone, so let's figure out where you fall on the spectrum of ACT test-takers. A handful of questions can help clarify this:

1. **What are the average scores of admitted students at your target/dream schools?** Do some research on the scores of admitted students at the colleges you are most interested in (or a sampling of colleges you *might* be interested in). Determine the average and above-average scores of the recently admitted class to see the ACT score range that you need to hit to confidently apply to those colleges. (Some schools refer to this as the "middle 50 percent," meaning that 25 percent of admitted students scored below this threshold and 25 percent scored above it.) The high end of the middle 50 percent is your target score range.

2. **How far are you from your goal score?** Take a diagnostic test (or analyze your PreACT test, if you took one) to figure out your baseline ACT score. Determine how many points you'd need to improve that baseline score to get it within the target-score range of the colleges you want to apply to. Also consider where you're losing points: if one particular test score is significantly lower than the others, you may actually have an easier time raising your overall score than you would if you needed to bring up your score on all four (or five) tests.

3. **How much time do you realistically have to study?** Consider how much time you have to devote to studying on a daily and weekly basis—taking into account school, work, extracurricular activities, and general life obligations. If your schedule is chock-full of things to do, you may need a longer study timeline to achieve the score increase you need.

Remember that everyone is different, and it takes some students more time than others to see the score improvement they want. The categories below should give you some indication of approximately how long you need to hit the books to achieve your goal. As you follow these general guidelines, keep track of your progress to determine if you should increase or decrease the prep time needed to get your goal score.

Three-Point Composite Score Increase = One to Two Months

A three-point increase (say, from a composite score of 26 to 29) is reasonable to achieve with a month or two of studying. To make those score gains, you'll need to devote yourself to prepping for a couple of hours three times a week and taking at least two full-length practice tests (and preferably more) on weekends over the course of the study period. The ACT is a very predictable test, and with good study materials, you can quickly learn the strategies that can help you achieve this goal.

Five-to-Six-Point Composite Score Increase = Three to Four Months

This is a loftier goal, but it is certainly an achievable one for many students. You can achieve this point gain through disciplined self-study ... but you're not allowed to slack! You'll need to take practice tests at least every other week and build the ACT into your life, just as you would if you were adding another subject at school.

Seven-to-Ten-Point Composite Score Increase = Six Months to One Year

Once you start talking about this kind of score increase, you need a much longer-term prep plan. This comes with its own pitfalls: notably, the *score plateau*, in which you might not see your score rise for a significant period of time. If you find yourself hitting a score plateau, you may need to devote extra time to conquering issues that are affecting your performance, such as test anxiety and time management. You'll need a good, structured test-prep program you can rely on, and, if you qualify, you may want to apply for testing accommodations, such as extra time. Do this as early as you can and allow time for an appeal if necessary.

A Note about Significant Score Improvements

The higher your baseline score, the harder it is to make a seven-to-10-point jump. It's impossible to make a 10-point increase if you are starting at a 29, of course, but even a seven-point increase from 29 to 36 may not be possible. Getting a 36 on the ACT is extraordinarily difficult to do, because on some versions of the exam, that means answering Every. Single. Question. Correctly. And like it or not, there may always be a handful of questions that just stump you, no matter how hard you've studied. Not many—but a few.

In this case, start with baby steps. Begin by aiming for a three-point increase, then a five-point increase, and only then a seven-point increase if you are still chugging along. Three points may not sound like a lot, but on the ACT scale, it is a significant improvement.

For the 32+ Club . . .

Let's say you're starting at a 32, which already puts you in the 98th percentile, and you want to claw your way up to a 33, a 34 ... maybe even a 35. At this level, there's almost no room for error. You may need anywhere from six weeks to six months to make these jumps, and we would suggest that you take a practice test every single weekend. You'll also want to personalize your prep and carefully control what you study. At this level, you need to figure out exactly what your weaknesses are and target them.

Remember that ACT prep always works best when it's comfortably built into your life like any other class or activity. Cramming is a terrible idea—but so is starting your prep in preschool! Figure out your target score, determine how long you need to prep, and then start to sort out the logistics (like when to take the test).

Guide to Your Best ACT Test Date

If you're able to choose your own ACT test date, feel lucky! Though the test date options may seem overwhelming, you have control here, and that can make all the difference.

Currently, the ACT is offered seven times each school year: September, October, December, February, April, June, and July (though these months are subject to change). Depending on your individual circumstances (grade level, high school courses taken, college application type, schedule), any of these options might work for you. Let's dive into some specific circumstances to try to help you choose your best test date.

Seniors

If you're going into your senior year, then you basically have four ACT test dates that you could potentially use for college admissions: July, September, October, and December.

Early Decision or Early Action deadlines and ACT test dates

If you're a rising senior looking to apply Early Decision or Early Action (meaning, for the most part, that you'll be targeting application deadlines between November 1 and December 15), you only have three possible ACT test dates: July, September, and October. Important note: October is pushing it for the November deadlines. Most schools with Early Decision or Early Action options will allow students to submit October scores, but keep in mind that you may have to submit your application before you get your scores, and it will be incomplete until your scores arrive. So don't count on October as anything but a backup if you are applying early; **September is the ACT test date for you.**

Of course, when you sign up for the September test date, it's not a bad idea to sign up for the October test date at the same time. Registration deadlines for October will have passed by the time you get your September scores, and you don't want to have to worry about signing up late or testing standby if you find you need (or want) to take the October ACT as well.

Typical Regular Decision deadlines and ACT test dates

This is the bucket most rising seniors are going to fall into, and it means **you have four realistic ACT test dates left: July, September, October, and December.** This is because most Regular Decision college application deadlines are between January 1 and January 15, ruling out February as an option.

Later Regular Decision deadlines and rolling admissions

There are some colleges that have application deadlines that run into February, or that have rolling admissions policies (which means they make decisions on applications as they come in and may continue evaluating applications into the late spring and summer). **For the most part, schools with later application deadlines tend to be less competitive institutions than those that have earlier deadlines, and many of them will accept February ACT scores from seniors.** But if you are applying to a school with rolling admissions, you don't want to wait until the last minute, even if you technically can. Admissions get increasingly competitive as spaces get filled, so get your testing done and your application in as soon as you can.

Rising seniors who have already taken the ACT: should you take it again?

The answer to this depends on your college list. If your ACT test scores are within or above the middle 50th percentile for all of the colleges on your college list, your time may be better spent focusing on your schoolwork, activities, and applications than studying for the ACT again.

If your scores fall within the middle 50th percentile for your dream school, that's a great start and means you have a good chance of acceptance, but you'll be even better off if you can push your score above the 75th percentile for admitted students. This generally means that your test scores won't be a determining factor (or at least, not a reason for rejection) in the admissions process. A retake in September after a summer of ACT test prep could be a very good idea if this applies to you.

If you've already taken the ACT three or more times, however, you might want to do some serious thinking about whether or not you can still improve your score. Maybe you didn't prep enough the first time, you got sick during another test, your calculator died on another, and a rampaging yeti attacked the test center during the fourth (that would be awful!). In these cases, your odds of an improved score on a retake are good.

Juniors

Juniors! We're glad you are thinking about the ACT, because you should be. Most students will have taken the coursework necessary to be ready for the ACT by **spring of junior year**. Ideally, you'll have taken algebra, geometry, biology, and chemistry before you take the ACT. But note that these courses aren't essential to ACT success, since you can fill in your knowledge gaps with test prep (and set yourself up for awesome grades in next year's science class while you're at it!).

For top scores, you should at least have a semester of algebra II/trigonometry and physics under your belt. Even though the ACT does not significantly test science knowledge, familiarity with the material will help your scores. That's why we're including the science subjects here, although they are probably the least-essential actual content to learn for the ACT. A solid basis in algebra and geometry is important, though: the ACT Math Test is 30–40 percent algebra and 35–45 percent geometry.

In addition, familiarity with standardized tests in general can help boost your scores. Chances are good that by winter of junior year, you will have already taken the PSAT or PreACT at least once. These tests will help prepare you for the structure and rigor of the ACT.

Early birds

If you've done test prep for the PSAT (say for National Merit consideration) or PreACT, you probably fall into this category. **This means you might be ready for the ACT in December or February of junior year.**

Why is taking the ACT this early a good idea (if you're ready)? Well, for one, it allows you plenty of time for a retake or two in the spring of junior year, meaning you can likely wrap up testing by the end of the school year. It also allows you time to focus on SAT subject tests (if required) and/or AP tests in the spring.

Most juniors

Most juniors will do their best on the ACT if they take it in the spring of junior year. This means the April and/or June test dates. As of 2018, you also have the option of taking it in July! By this point, you'll be wrapping up crucial third-year courses, improving your reading comprehension for both the ACT English and Reading Tests, covering what you need for the Math Test, and getting more comfortable with material for the Science Test.

Following the principle that it's always better to take care of testing as soon as you're ready, we suggest that you plan to sign up for both the April and June ACT dates: April for a first go, and June for a possible retake. For those of you who are rising juniors, you'll also have the July test date to choose from. In other words, April, June, or July: pick two.

Sophomores

A quick note before we begin: If you're a sophomore who is taking the ACT as part of your application to a competitive high school, then the score requirements probably aren't the same as if you were applying to college—so please don't be discouraged! This next part applies to students taking the ACT for college admissions.

First of all, we can't stress this enough: *You shouldn't take the ACT before you are ready for it.* While some students have acquired all of the knowledge they need for the ACT by the beginning of junior year, it's rare for students to accomplish this by sophomore year, so don't take the test too early.

If you'd like to begin your prep during sophomore year, then there is a lot you can do. We recommend taking the PreACT if your school offers it. Plus, advanced reading and math practice will help train your ACT brain.

The takeaway? Don't take the ACT before you're ready. At the end of the day, it's highly unlikely that you'll get your best score during sophomore year.

Freshmen (or Earlier)

If you're a freshman looking to map out your high school career, props to you! The earlier you start thinking about college applications, the better. If you're just trying to figure out when you should take the ACT, plan on targeting the exam junior year. Also, make sure you map out your classes accordingly so that you are ready for the ACT by that time. Specifically, take the most advanced classes you can handle. Ideally, you'd plan to be in algebra II/trigonometry or precalculus during junior year.

How to Register for the ACT

Now that you have an idea of *when* you'll be taking the ACT, let's get into the logistics of signing up for the test.

Most students prefer to register for the ACT through the online form on act.org. It's easy and pretty quick (much faster than registering through the mail). Note that you only have to register by mail if you're under 13 years old or if you are not paying with a credit card.

If you don't already have an account with act.org, you're going to need to sign up for one. Have a photo file ready, because they'll ask you to upload one for identification purposes. Also, make sure you use login information (username and password) that you can remember! You'll need it to print your admission ticket and, ultimately, to check your scores.

Once you've created an account, you'll be able to choose your test date and test center. Make sure to select the test center that's closest to your home. During the registration process, you will be asked to take a survey about your high school grades and interests. Not all of the information is required, but you might want to set aside some extra time for registration if you plan to answer every question.

ACT prices can vary depending on whether you're taking the ACT Writing Test, when you're registering (on time or late), and where you live (in the US or abroad). Prices often change from year to year, so you'll want to check the current pricing on act.org. Fee waivers are available for students who qualify, so be sure to find out if you might be eligible before you register for the ACT!

Once you've registered, you'll receive a confirmation. Keep it in a safe place! You'll need to bring your admission ticket on test day.

End of Chapter Review

Okay, let's check in. You now know that you (almost definitely) need to take the ACT. You understand:

- The origins of the ACT exam
- How hard the ACT really is
- ACT basics, like the exam's format and timing
- How long you'll need to study
- The best test date for your circumstances
- The basic registration process

So what's next? Let's learn all about ACT scores!

Chapter 2

ACT Scoring

Introduction to ACT Scores

Someday, in the not-too-distant future, many of your friends are going to be staring at their ACT score report and wondering what it all means.

But not you! You're going to be prepared. In fact, you're probably reading this book because you want to accomplish one crucial task: improving your ACT score. So first, you need to understand what that means and what the most important ACT "scores" to focus on are. Oh yes—your ACT score report is going to include a lot of different numbers. So let's break down what's important and what you need to know about those scores.

Composite Score

Your overall, or composite, score is the most important number on your report. Your **composite score** can range from 1 to 36. It's an average of the individual scaled scores you received on the four multiple-choice tests, each of which are also scored on a scale from 1 to 36.

Let's say you scored a 24 on the ACT English Test, 19 on Math, 23 on Reading, and 18 on Science: your overall composite score would be a 21. If you want to practice your math, that's: $\frac{24+19+23+18}{4} = 21$.

The ACT does round its averages up. So if the exact calculation of your average worked out to 20.5, you're in luck: the test would round your score up to a 21. If your average worked out to 20.25, however, you would receive a 20.

Scaled Scores

But what do these numbers even mean? How do you get an 18 or 21 or 36?

This is where everything gets a little bit more complicated.

When scoring your exam, the ACT takes your **raw score** (the exact number of questions you got right) on a test and converts it to a **scaled score** of 1 to 36.

The exact relationship between raw scores and scaled scores varies slightly between tests given on different days. So, for example, a raw score of 54 (meaning you answered 54 questions correctly) on the English Test might get you a 22 on one ACT and a 24 on another. Why? Because each ACT exam is unique and therefore difficulty can vary from test to test.

To make sure that students are graded fairly (you wouldn't want your friends to get a better score just because they took the test a month before you!), the ACT uses complex math to scale each student's raw score into a score that can be objectively compared to any other ACT score from any other ACT exam.

This math is done through a process known as "**equating**," which takes a raw ACT score and turns it into a scaled ACT score. In other words, equating measures your results against the results of all the other students who took the same test, as well as against some other factors. This process is designed to ensure one thing: that you are scored fairly, no matter what day you take the exam, so that you don't need to worry if your test felt particularly hard or easy.

Using scaled scores instead of raw scores or percentages means that the ACT can assure colleges that your score can accurately be compared to the scores of students taking any other version of the test. A 28 on one test will mean the same thing as a 28 on another test (even if this equates to a raw score of 63 questions correct on one test and 64 on another).

Unless you order the Test Information Release service (available in December, April, and June), the ACT won't tell you what your raw score was, so, ultimately, the precise relationship between the actual number of questions you got right and your 1 to 36 score will probably remain a mystery to you. Don't stress too much about this process—it's designed to ensure that your score is fair.

Percentiles

The percentages you see next to your scores compare your scores to those of other students who have taken the ACT, so you can see where you rank among other test-takers. If your **percentile ranking** is 73 percent, that means you did the same or better than 73 percent of test-takers (not too shabby!).

Subscores

The ACT will also provide you with **subscores** on the English, Math, and Reading Tests. Subscores tell you how well you did on different question types within these tests. The ACT has its own formula for calculating these subscores, so the numbers provided are relatively useless to students.

What is useful, however, are the percentiles that go with these subscores. If you scored better than 88 percent of test-takers on pre-algebra/elementary algebra, but only better than 37 percent of test-takers on plane geometry/trigonometry, well, then you know you need to work on your advanced geometry and trig. You don't need to worry about subscores very much at all, but they can be useful to diagnose where you should focus your energy if you're planning on retaking the ACT.

Writing Score

If you take the optional ACT Writing Test, you'll receive an **essay score** between 1 and 12, which is the average of scores from two different graders, who score you on four different "writing domains" from 1 to 6.

That's a little confusing in theory, so let's look at an example:

Sample Suzy's ACT Writing Score

Writing Domain	Grader 1	Grader 2	Sum
Ideas and Analysis	3	4	7
Development and Support	5	5	10
Organization	3	2	5
Language Use and Conventions	4	3	7
Overall Writing Score (rounded average of sums of four writing domain scores)	7		

ELA and STEM Scores

If that's not enough ACT scoring for you, have no fear—we are not finished yet.

Your **ELA score**, or "English Language Arts" score, is the average of your scores on the ACT English, Reading, and Writing Tests. It's only reported if you take the optional essay. You don't need to worry about this one too much; it's primarily there in case colleges want to have a way to compare ACT scores to SAT scores more directly (since the Reading and Writing Test scores are now combined on the SAT). Some language arts-heavy universities will look at this score during the admissions process.

Similarly, your **STEM score** is the average of your Math and Science Test scores. If you're applying to an institution or major with a heavy STEM focus, this score may factor into the admissions process.

Scoring Your Practice Tests

If you're using official practice tests from the ACT, you should find a chart at the back of your test that shows you how to convert your raw score to a scaled score specific to that test. If you don't have that chart, you can use the raw-to-scaled ACT score chart in the next section of this book to give you a rough idea of your score. But be aware that tests from other companies don't always match up exactly with the ACT in terms of difficulty, so take any results you obtain this way with a grain of salt.

Receiving Your Score Report

When will you get your ACT score report? The short answer is two to eight weeks after you take the test. Yep, you read that right. Sometime between two weeks and two months from when you take the test. Don't worry too much: to be honest, you'll probably receive your scores within a month, and most students receive their scores the first day that scores are available. The ACT just gives you a long range of dates in case something weird happens.

The Difference Between Your Score Report and Your Schools' Reports

The **score report** you receive will be different from the report that gets sent to your high school, which is different from the one that's sent to the colleges or scholarship programs that you're applying to. There are three types of ACT score reports:

1. **Student Report:** The report that you'll receive from the ACT is called a Student Report. You'll be able to access it online through your ACT web account. It'll include your ACT scores (by test and combined), as well as college and career information.

2. **High School Report:** The report that your high school receives is called a High School Report. Not a very inspired name, but it gets the job done. This report includes all the same information that's in the Student Report, plus an image of your essay if you chose to take the ACT Writing Test.

3. **College Report:** Finally, there's the College Report, which you'll eventually need to order and send to each university or scholarship agency that you apply to. Most students order reports through their online ACT account. There are a few options for sending ACT score reports to colleges, which we will discuss in the next section.

    The ACT College Report is a bit different from the Student and High School Reports, in that it contains additional information. Not only does it include your ACT scores, but it also comes with an image of your ACT Plus Writing essay and the additional information that you report when you register for the ACT (like the grades you reported for your high school courses). It also includes predictions for your performance in specific college programs and courses. It's a pretty serious document!

Sending Score Reports

You have a few options when it comes to sending your score reports:

1. **Four Free Score Reports:** When you register for your ACT, you may opt to send four score reports to colleges that you select. The advantage of this option is that these first four score reports are free. The disadvantage is that you are committed to sending these scores before you know how well you did on the test. If you have the means to pay for score reports, we recommend foregoing this option and waiting for your Student Report before sending anything to colleges. That way you can retake the test if you need to and only send reports once your scores are ready. This gives you more control over your applications.

2. **Regular Report:** You may order this report once you've received and reviewed your scores. There is a small fee for each Regular Report that you send to a college or university. This is a great (and very popular) option, because you can order and send these reports once you have your scores and college list in hand.

3. **Priority Report:** If you're running out of time and need to get your applications in quickly, you can send Priority Reports for an additional fee. These rush orders will make sure that your ACT scores get to the colleges on your list within a few days.

Good news: If you take the ACT more than one time, you can choose which scores to send to colleges and universities. The ACT records each of your tests separately and only sends the record from the test date that you choose. Some colleges require that you submit all of your scores, but this is pretty rare.

Good (and Average) ACT Scores

In such a numbers-obsessed world, it's easy to become preoccupied with comparing your "numbers" to the numbers of others. Who has the better GPA? Who has more Instagram followers? Who can eat the most marshmallows in 30 seconds? (We're not recommending you try that last one. There's no winner in that game … except maybe your audience? Moving on …)

The point is, it's easy to understand why you'd want to know whether or not your own test scores are "good." On the one hand, this isn't an easy thing to figure out. On the other hand, there are a few numbers we can use to put your scores in context. Let's start by looking at average ACT Scores.

Average ACT Scores by the Numbers

In 2016, US students averaged a composite score of 20.8 on the ACT, broken down like this:

Composite	English	Math	Reading	Science
20.8	20.1	20.6	21.3	20.8

However, keep in mind that these numbers are being drawn from an incredibly large pool of students (more than two million) each of whom is taking the ACT for different reasons: because it counts as their high school assessment, because they're trying to get into Harvard, because their parents made them, because they couldn't think of anything better to do on a Saturday morning …

So, although this is a good start to understanding average ACT scores, it's not incredibly helpful.

To get a better idea of how your scores compare to an average ACT score, it's better to look at a smaller pool of students.

1. **You can look at average ACT scores for your state.** Although you will find that scores don't vary drastically between states, you may live in a slightly more or less competitive one.

2. **You can look at average ACT scores for your school.** Many students can access this data on their high school's "Profile" sheet. This might be posted on your school's website, or, if not, you can ask your college counseling department for it. This is a really crucial piece of paper. Did you know that this is the same sheet many colleges use to understand how your high school compares with other high schools, and how you compare with your fellow students?

3. **You can look at how your ACT scores compare to the average ACT scores at the colleges or universities you are targeting.** This last one is particularly important for the college-bound. You can typically find average test scores directly on admissions websites. But if you don't have a college list yet (or even if you do),

we highly recommend doing some exploratory searches online or at your high school's college admissions office.

Some colleges are still stuck in the Stone Age and only publish their average SAT scores … but if this is the case, you can easily convert this score into an ACT score to see how your scores compare. Use the chart later in this chapter!

And don't forget the most important person to be comparing yourself to is … you. If you studied hard and increased your ACT score from a 16 to a 20, that is a huge win, and to heck with any charts on average ACT scores!

Good ACT Scores by Grade Level

Now, let's say you're getting an early start on your prep (or you've taken the PreACT and you want to know if your scores are on target with your goals)—you may be wondering what a good score is for the grade you're in.

We've crunched some numbers and come up with the following figures, based on your ultimate goals.

One caveat: The numbers in the following ACT score chart are loose projections—as we mentioned earlier, students with lower scores may still get into their dream schools! Still, these scores provide a good start for students at different grade levels with the following goals.

Good ACT Scores by Grade Level and Goal

	Only Ivy League for me!	I'm going for schools ranked between 25–50	I'm going for schools ranked 50–75	I'm going for schools ranked 75–100	I'm going for schools ranked above 100
Sophomore	24+	21+	17+	16+	13+
Junior	28+	25+	21+	20+	17+
Senior	32+	29+	25+	24+	21+

Keep in mind that we constructed this table under the assumption that you'll keep studying and pushing yourself in your ACT prep as you move through high school.

If you do this, then a rise of four points a year is within your grasp. However, if you let everything drop until the last minute, you may not see an appreciable rise at all. (To be fair, the more advanced coursework you're encountering should still help give your scores a bump.)

What Is a Good ACT Score for Scholarships?

A strong ACT score can put you in the running for scholarships. As with ACT scores for college admissions, there's no one magic number that can win you a scholarship. But there are a few guidelines we can look at.

If you're scoring in the 30s, that's a great place to start. After all, if you score above 30, you're in the top 10th percentile of all ACT test-takers.

On the other hand, you can still get a scholarship even if you're scoring in the mid-20s.

The main variables here? Which scholarships you're applying for, and which schools you hope to attend.

How Much Money Will You Get?

In almost every case, the higher your score, the bigger the payout. Want an example? In recent years, Baylor University has offered scholarships of up to $41,996 a year to students getting a perfect score of 36 on the ACT. But knock that score down a few points, to 29, and suddenly that scholarship becomes $27,996. (Okay … that's not too shabby either.)

Also in recent years, Oklahoma State University has given students scoring 24 on the ACT (with a 3.0 GPA) up to $7,000 a year. Six points more, though, and students scoring 30 are eligible for up to $12,500 annually. It's important to note that universities increase scholarship gifts based on specific score guidelines of their choosing. You'll need to do your research to find the exact score numbers required for each scholarship.

As these cases show, some scholarships will also have GPA requirements, or even additional applications to fill out, so be sure to check before assuming that money's in the bank. Good sources for scholarship information include your high school's admissions counselor and university admissions offices. Educators love students who think ahead, so don't be nervous about asking for help!

And remember—figuring out scholarship requirements is only half the puzzle. If you're wondering how much money your ACT scores can help you get, the first thing you'll need to do is figure out your scaled ACT score.

Score Conversion Charts

As you take full-length ACT practice tests, you'll need to find a way to convert your raw scores on each section into the type of scaled score that you'll receive on the actual ACT. That way, you can compare your practice test scores to your goal ACT score and see how much you're improving.

Every official ACT test has its own chart that converts raw scores to scores on the 1- to 36-point scale, but if you find yourself in need of a rough estimate for a practice test, or if you simply want an estimate of how many questions you need to get right to get a certain score, the following official ACT test score chart can help!

The chart below presents the raw scores on the four ACT Tests (English, Mathematics, Reading, and Science), with their equivalent scaled scores in the left column. Again, remember this will vary slightly between tests!

Raw ACT Scores and Scaled ACT Scores

Because the Reading and Science Tests have fewer questions, sometimes you'll find that missing a question causes your scaled score to go down two points instead of one, hence the dashes on the chart. Similarly, because all of the tests have more questions than there are scaled scores, you'll often find that there are two different raw scores that match up with a scaled score. This is true on all ACT tests.

Scaled Score	Raw Score English	Raw Score Math	Raw Score Reading	Raw Score Science
36	75	60	40	40
35	72–74	58–59	39	39
34	71	57	38	38
33	70	55–56	37	37
32	68–69	54	35–36	—
31	67	52–53	34	36
30	66	50–51	33	35
29	65	48–49	32	34
28	63–64	45–47	31	33
27	62	43–44	30	32
26	60–61	40–42	29	30–31
25	58–59	38–39	28	28–29
24	56–57	36–37	27	26–27
23	53–55	34–35	25–26	24–25
22	51–52	32–33	24	22–23
21	48–50	30–31	22–23	21
20	45–47	29	21	19–20
19	43–44	27–28	19–20	17–18
18	41–42	24–26	18	16
17	39–40	21–23	17	14–15

Scaled Score	Raw Score English	Raw Score Math	Raw Score Reading	Raw Score Science
16	36–38	17–20	15–16	13
15	32–35	13–16	14	12
14	29–31	11–12	12–13	11
13	27–28	8–10	11	10
12	25–26	7	9–10	9
11	23–24	5–6	8	8
10	20–22	4	6–7	7
9	18–19	—	—	5–6
8	15–17	3	5	—
7	12–14	—	4	4
6	10–11	2	3	3
5	8–9	—	—	2
4	6–7	1	2	—
3	4–5	—	—	1
2	2–3	—	1	—
1	0–1	0	0	0

SAT to ACT Score Conversion

How do I convert my ACT scores to SAT scores?

With every major college and university in the US accepting both SAT and ACT scores for admission, there has to be a way for schools to compare the scores of their applicants. Although some schools have their own systems, in general, most educational institutions use the following conversion table (also known as a concordance table) to compare ACT and SAT scores.

Note that between 2005 and early 2016, the SAT was scored out of 2400 (it's currently scored out of 1600). If you're looking to compare your ACT score to an SAT score from that timeframe, you can also use the chart below! Just refer to the third column instead of the second column when looking for your SAT score.

ACT Composite Score	New SAT Total (400–1600)	Old SAT Total Score (600–2400)	ACT Composite Score	New SAT Total (400–1600)	Old SAT Total Score (600–2400)
36	1600	2390	33	1510	2190
35	1590	2380	33	1500	2170
35	1580	2350	33	1490	2150
35	1570	2330	32	1480	2130
35	1560	2300	32	1470	2110
34	1550	2280	32	1460	2090
34	1540	2260	32	1450	2080
34	1530	2230	31	1440	2060
34	1520	2210	31	1430	2040

ACT Composite Score	New SAT Total (400–1600)	Old SAT Total Score (600–2400)	ACT Composite Score	New SAT Total (400–1600)	Old SAT Total Score (600–2400)
31	1420	2020	20	1030	1400
30	1410	2000	20	1020	1390
30	1400	1990	19	1010	1370
30	1390	1970	19	1000	1360
29	1380	1950	19	990	1340
29	1370	1930	19	980	1330
29	1360	1920	18	970	1310
29	1350	1900	18	960	1300
28	1340	1880	18	950	1280
28	1330	1870	18	940	1270
28	1320	1850	17	930	1250
28	1310	1840	17	920	1240
27	1300	1820	17	910	1220
27	1290	1810	17	900	1210
27	1280	1790	16	890	1200
26	1270	1780	16	880	1180
26	1260	1760	16	870	1170
26	1250	1750	16	860	1150
26	1240	1730	15	850	1140
25	1230	1710	15	840	1120
25	1220	1700	15	830	1110
25	1210	1680	15	820	1090
25	1200	1670	15	810	1070
24	1190	1650	14	800	1060
24	1180	1640	14	790	1040
24	1170	1620	14	780	1030
24	1160	1610	14	770	1010
23	1150	1590	14	760	990
23	1140	1570	13	750	980
23	1130	1560	13	740	960
22	1120	1540	13	730	950
22	1110	1530	13	720	930
22	1100	1510	12	710	910
21	1090	1490	12	700	900
21	1080	1480	12	690	880
21	1070	1460	12	680	870
21	1060	1450	12	670	860
20	1050	1430	12	660	850
20	1040	1420	12	650	840

ACT Composite Score	New SAT Total (400–1600)	Old SAT Total Score (600–2400)
12	640	830
12	630	820
11	620	810
11	610	800
11	600	790
11	590	780
11	580	770
11	570	760
11	560	750
N/A	550	740
N/A	540	730
N/A	530	730
N/A	520	720
N/A	510	710
N/A	500	700
N/A	490	690
N/A	480	680
N/A	470	670
N/A	460	660
N/A	450	650
N/A	440	640
N/A	430	630
N/A	420	620
N/A	410	610
N/A	400	600

ACT Scoring

How to Avoid Score Drama

Obviously, studying for the ACT is no piece of cake. But the drama that surrounds the whole process can make it uncomfortable. Here are our top tips for how to avoid awkwardness, gossip, and more:

- **Don't check scores around your friends.** We can advise against this from personal experience: tears because one person got a lower score than their friends, guilt over higher scores. It's always a bad scene.

  Moral of the story: make sure you are in a private place when you check your scores. And don't feel pressured to share your score with friends if you don't want to.

- **Don't judge people's responses to their scores.** If you find yourself in a situation where you have to be around your peers when everyone is checking scores, try to focus on yourself. Don't worry about their responses, happy or sad. Everyone is different, so everyone will have different reactions.

  If someone is enthusiastically happy with what you think is a low score, let them be. If someone is sobbing over a score that's higher than yours, let them sob. That's also their prerogative. You never know how much work a student put in or what kind of emotional stress they are under.

- **Don't spread scores around.** To many people, ACT scores are private information. Just because someone tells you their score doesn't mean they want it to become common knowledge to the whole student body.

  News of various students' scores can become a big source of gossip in high school. But you don't need to get involved, because other peoples' scores have nothing to do with you and your college chances.

- **Understand context.** It doesn't make sense to compare yourself to others, because everyone prepares for the test differently. If a classmate got a higher score than you did, it could mean that they've been secretly studying since seventh grade. Or maybe they got lucky and studied the exact right things. You never know!

In the end, it's important to remember that your intelligence and abilities as a student can't be boiled down to a set of ACT scores. But if you do want to improve your score, know that everyone has the ability to improve their ACT skills to some degree. In the next chapter, we'll discuss general strategies and study skills to help you study for the ACT.

Chapter 3

General ACT Tips and Strategies

How to Study for the ACT

Let's say it's winter break of junior year. For the holidays, your parents have gifted you a stack of ACT prep books with a card that says, "Get started."

Or maybe it's the Friday before the test, and you suddenly remember you can't go to a movie with your date because tomorrow you'll be holed up in a testing room with nothing but your No. 2 pencils to hold tight.

Or maybe it's seventh grade, and you're thinking about ACT prep just for fun. (Hi, middle schoolers! You deserve a special shout-out just for being here.)

No matter where you are in your test-prep timeline, standardized test preparation can essentially be boiled down into three categories:

1. Knowledge Review
2. Test Prep Strategy
3. Practice Tests

Let's take a look at each of these in a little more detail:

Knowledge Review

There are going to be concepts tested on the ACT that you haven't studied in a long time, haven't ever studied, or never fully understood when you did study them. Some of these might be quick fixes ("Oh right, *that's* the formula for the area of a trapezoid"); some might take a lot more work ("The last time I read a book was … uhh?").

As you begin your ACT prep, you should start by diagnosing your weaknesses. Take care of as many "quick fixes" as possible, and then put in extra work on the bigger issues that require more time to improve, like reading comprehension and time management. Depending on how much study time you have, you may need to prioritize based on what is fastest and easiest for you to tackle. And nothing boosts confidence like a quick uptick in your score!

Test Prep Strategy

There's a reason why there are so many prep options for this test. It's because the ACT is something that **can be learned**. You can learn more than just the concepts—you can also learn a lot about the test format. In other words, to get your best score on the ACT, you need to know not only *what* it tests, but also *how* it tests those concepts.

Prep resources can teach you how to use the structure of the test to your advantage. You can learn how to substitute numbers to make an algebra problem easier to solve. You can learn to recognize answer choices on the ACT Reading Test that are too broad or too narrow. Treat the ACT like any other subject or skill you want to master and study specifically for this unique test.

If adding another subject to your study schedule seems overwhelming, take heart: this is good news! It actually *minimizes* the amount of material you'll need to study. For example, knowing the limited scope of ACT Math topics allows you to narrow down the math you have to study from the past 11 years of classes to the specific topics you'll see on the ACT.

Practice Tests

There's no getting around it. You *must* practice under conditions as close as possible to those you'll experience on the real test. Whether you are taking complete practice tests (which you should definitely do) or individual timed sections, it's crucial that you learn the endurance that the ACT requires, how to manage your time, and the best ways to deal with distractions. The only way to truly feel prepared for the test is to (surprise!) take the test.

Studying for the ACT won't be overwhelming if you break this large task up into manageable sessions. So make sure your prep plan includes knowledge review, test prep strategy, and practice tests. By using all three tools, you're bound to see your score improve!

The one thing that these three strategies all have in common is that they are proactive. But you'll need to play defense, too! With that in mind, let's take a look at a few of the most common pitfalls on the ACT: pacing, avoidable mistakes, and using practice materials the wrong way (not just by using them as a paperweight ... though that is definitely a wrong way to use them). Let's go, defense!

How to Master Pacing on the ACT

One of the most important test prep skills you need to master is pacing. The ACT exam actively tests your ability to do a lot of work within a very limited time frame. This is why having a strong time-management strategy is crucial to picking up as many points as possible during each test.

Here are our top five general tips to make sure you can complete all of the multiple-choice questions on ACT test day!

1. **Don't leave any questions blank.** You won't lose any points for an incorrect answer on the ACT. So if you feel the clock ticking down and you still haven't gotten around to looking at the last few questions, that's okay! Always bubble something in on your answer grid. Once you hear the proctor announce that there are five minutes remaining, eliminate any obviously wrong choices (like math answers that are way too big or way too small) and then guess on the remaining questions. After all, you might guess correctly and pick up some free points!

2. **Don't let tricky questions bring you to a halt.** Students often find that time starts to run away from them when they come across a hard question that they refuse to give up on. Don't let a few tough questions stop you from answering as many questions as possible! If you're spending more than two minutes on a single question, it's time to guess and move on. You can always come back to the tricky question if you have time at the end. Main lesson: don't get stuck on one tough problem when you can move on and collect more points!

3. **Memorize the instructions.** The instructions for each ACT test don't change, so if you memorize them before test day, you won't have to read them during the actual test. Boom! We just saved you valuable minutes that you can use to answer questions and pick up points.

4. **Know each test's format like the back of your hand.** The number of questions per test never changes, which means that you can always be aware of how many questions you have left. Keep track of where you are at all times so that you know if you need to pick up your pace or slow it down. Memorize this:

English Test	75 test questions
Mathematics Test	60 test questions
Reading Test	40 test questions
Science Test	40 test questions
Writing Test	one essay prompt

5. **Even if you finish an ACT test early, DO NOT close your booklet!** This is the time to go back and check your work, not to take a nap! Don't second-guess yourself to the extreme but do check your work on the medium- and hard-level questions, and

on the questions that you weren't 100 percent sure about in the first place. Start practicing this tactic when you take ACT practice tests, and you will be more likely to naturally apply this strategy on test day.

These five tips pertain to the ACT as a whole, but some students find pacing a struggle on certain tests and don't have a problem on others. For strategies to improve your pacing on specific tests, refer to chapters 5–9.

How to Keep a Record of Strengths and Weaknesses as You Study

As you prep for the ACT exam, you may find that you're struggling to measure your progress. Should you amp up your practice before the big exam, or are you on track to get your target score?

Whether you're practicing with timed practice sets or taking a full-length practice test every week (ideally, you'll be doing both), you should have some evidence of which questions you're consistently getting right and wrong.

Our suggestion? Get a notebook to use exclusively for your test preparation. Buy one—it'll be a small investment with a big payoff!

ACT Prep Notebook

This is where you will record all of your scratch work and mark down all of your answers as you do your ACT practice. If you prefer to mark down your answers in this book, that's fine, too! The point is to have a record of all your work in one place.

Weekly Check-In

Each week that you prep for the ACT, mark the following information in your notebook:

1. **The date:** This is so that you can track your progress over time and keep yourself honest as you move through your chosen study schedule.

2. **Your practice test score for the week:** Comparing your scores over time will allow you to monitor your progress (and celebrate your wins!). If you didn't take a practice test during the week, mark down the percentage of practice questions that you answered correctly.

3. **How many points your score went up or down compared to last week:** Celebrate positive improvements, and don't get hung up on score decreases—learn from your mistakes and move on.

Then, create a table containing a list of the questions that you're answering correctly and incorrectly on each ACT test. Keep track of how many questions of each type you're getting right and wrong, and figure out which question types you're repeatedly missing. Then, make a note to focus your efforts on those question types next week. Note that using Magoosh ACT prep online will help you stay on track by identifying which types of questions you're missing and which types you're getting right.

The table might look something like this:

Test	Notes
English	
Math	
Reading	
Science	
Writing	

By checking in with yourself on a weekly basis, you'll be able to maximize the efficiency of your studying. After all, it doesn't make sense to spend more time practicing the concepts that you've already mastered. Score improvement comes from getting more and more questions right every time you answer ACT practice questions. But how do you find the time to take all of these practice tests?

In the next chapter, we'll talk about how to develop a study schedule to help you realistically and efficiently organize your prep time.

Review: Top 10 Tips for Prepping for the ACT

We've already discussed a lot of general strategies that you can use to improve your ACT score. You know that you need to become a master of time management and work to collect as many points as possible. Now, let's review our top 10 tips.

1. **Keep the test in perspective.** Getting a great score on the ACT will certainly help you achieve your college goals. But it's important to remember that scoring a few points lower than you had hoped doesn't mean that you won't achieve your academic dreams. College admissions officers will think of you as a student and potential community member, not as a score. Remember that your ACT score is just one part of your application portfolio—your grades, extracurricular activities, personal statements, and recommendation letters are also incredibly important.

2. **Remember that test-taking is a learned skill, not an inherent gift.** Some people may seem to be "naturally" good at the ACT, but even if you're not one of them, you can still learn to do well! Think positively, and focus on beating your personal best scores as you progress through your prep.

3. **Know that mistakes are necessary for improvement.** Incorrect answers on practice ACT questions help you home in on areas that need more work, so welcome them! Just make sure you understand why you got those questions wrong, so you can learn new skills and avoid repeating the same mistakes in the future.

4. **Plan a reasonable study schedule.** Register for the ACT at least three months before the exam, so that you can follow a reasonably paced study schedule. Be realistic with yourself, and make sure to factor in your extracurricular activities and regular coursework. Remember that short, regular periods of study time are way better than the occasional marathon session. See chapter 4 for more help planning your study schedule.

5. **Pinpoint your weaknesses and attack them.** Are you a slow reader? Is your math knowledge so-so? Know which concepts need work and address them first. Learn the strategies, then answer those questions with confidence!

6. **Learn the most frequently tested concepts.** There are a finite number of concepts tested on the ACT. Figure out what you already know and what you need to work on. The questions are predictable—you'll see the same types pop up over and over again.

7. **Use the entire time for each section.** Yes, this applies even if you're a naturally fast test-taker! It's important to read carefully and to be extra alert when marking your responses on your answer sheet. If you finish early, go back and check for silly mistakes or incorrect bubbling. Even the smartest students make mistakes when rushing.

8. **Get inside the heads of the test-makers.** Learn which types of answer choices the testmakers "prefer." For example, they love concise answers, or "economy of language," on the English Test (see chapter 5). Knowing this preference allows you to focus energy on the shorter answers, upping your odds of answering correctly, even when you're running out of time.

9. **Spend some time on act.org.** This is the official ACT website, yet it's amazing how many students never take advantage of the free resources offered here! Sure, the offerings are not as thorough as what we offer in this book, but the full-length practice tests alone are worth a visit.

10. **Mimic test conditions when you practice.** When you take a practice test, imitate test conditions as much as possible. Be sure to sit down for a minimum of one full-length test at the beginning (this is your diagnostic test), in the middle (to gauge your progress), and at the end (to calm your nerves before test day) of your prep!

Break time after strategizing?
Enjoy this ACT-themed crossword.

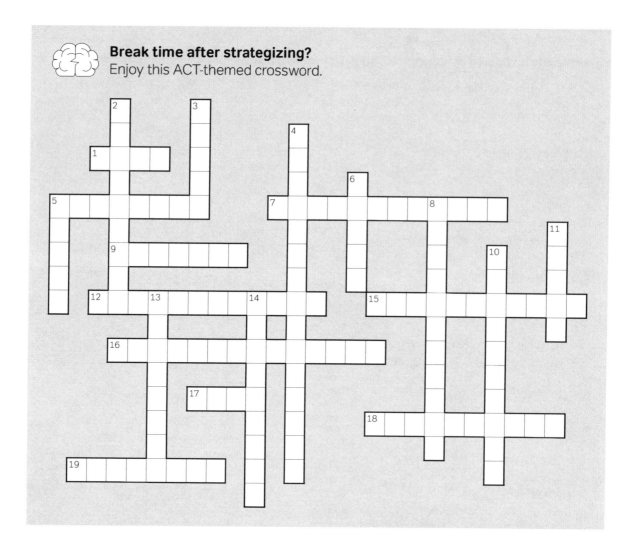

ACROSS

1. Where you'll live freshman year (abbr.)
5. A group of atoms that are bonded together, like H_2O
7. A course you must complete before signing up for the next level
9. You dissolve a solute in this to form a solution
12. Sin, cos, and tan are all part of this branch of math
15. What you submit to potential colleges
16. A special quality of a person, thing, or group
17. To intentionally leave something out
18. College "_____": process of getting into college
19. ACT Math subject involving lines and shapes

DOWN

2. What you'll call most of your teachers in college
3. For the ACT, it's on a scale from 1–36
4. "_____" activities: Ex: volunteering, student government, or the debate team
5. Your main academic focus in college
6. What you need to do before the ACT so you don't get too anxious
8. Money awarded based on your academic achievements
10. The official record of all your high school grades
11. Ex: "raining cats and dogs" or "hit the road"
13. When you "_____" high school, you will become a high school "_____."
14. Optional courses that you will take for college credit

Answers can be found at the end of the book.

Chapter 4

ACT Study Schedules

The first challenge of studying for the ACT is finding the time and energy to get started. The second challenge? Committing to your study plan.

If you haven't already noticed, high school is an enormous exercise in time management: completing all your homework, studying for your tests, finishing your projects, managing all your extracurricular activities, sleeping, and maybe even having some time left over for yourself (wouldn't that be nice!).

Then, you throw standardized tests into the mix, and your well-organized schedule falls apart at the seams. **But you don't need to be overwhelmed!** Take a deep breath and remember that all this hard work is temporary and worthwhile. One day, in the not-so-distant future, you'll be wearing your college sweatshirt, decorating your dorm room, and all of this studying will be a fuzzy memory. For now, there are ways to make juggling all of these tasks manageable.

Finding an ACT study plan that you can stick to will help you stay organized and self-motivated while keeping procrastination at bay. With a good study plan, you can break up your prep across several days each week, preventing the weekend-long cram sessions that mess with your sleep pattern and social life.

Magoosh offers various study schedules that are integrated with our online prep. This chapter is devoted to our most popular study plan: The One-Month ACT Study Schedule. If this schedule doesn't fit your timeline, please visit our site for other options.

How to Use an ACT Study Guide

There's no such thing as a one-size-fits-all study schedule. That's why our study plans are designed specifically so that you can adapt them to your own personal needs. Here's what you do:

1. **Honestly assess your ACT strengths and weaknesses.** There are a few ways to assess your ACT skills. If you've already taken the ACT (or even the PreACT), you can use your test subscores as a guide. Alternatively, you can take a timed, full-length practice test and use it as your diagnostic. Then be honest with yourself: do you always struggle with a certain section of standardized tests or with certain ACT question types? Almost everyone has specific skills or question types that throw them for a loop. Once you've assessed your strengths and weaknesses, factor them into your study schedule. Add extra time and practice materials to the days of your schedule devoted to your weaker topics.

2. **Determine how much time you can realistically devote to your ACT prep.** If you're working, playing sports, volunteering, and maintaining your course load all at the same time, you probably can't commit to an hour of ACT prep every day. In this case, you might want to break the One-Month ACT Study Schedule that we've included in this book into smaller units and tackle it over two or three months. Try to set healthy and realistic goals for yourself—it's important that you have time to sleep!

3. **Always check your work and understand where you are making mistakes.** While following the One-Month ACT Study Schedule to a T will get you through most of the material you'll see on the test, just reading about strategies and breezing through practice questions won't drastically improve your ACT score. You need to figure out *why* you're missing questions so that you can avoid making the same mistakes later. (This is where your ACT prep notebook will come in handy!) In truth, it's better to complete fewer practice problems and actually learn from the experience than to answer a ton of questions in order to check a box on your task list. There's no use in making the same mistakes over and over during your ACT prep—it just means that you'll get the same types of questions wrong when they show up on the ACT.

4. **Incorporate ACT prep into the rest of your life.** Answering practice questions and learning new strategies are key for improvement, but if you only think about ACT skills during your designated prep time, then you're missing out on a larger opportunity. Practice the ACT skills you are learning during the rest of your day, too. For example, look carefully at the structures of sentences in your history homework to understand the grammar rules they follow (or don't). When you're buying lunch, quietly tally up the cost with tax to speed up your mental math and improve your number sense. If you're reading a novel, ask yourself regularly why the author included various details. Any time you're dealing with words or numbers, there's an opportunity to fit in some ACT prep.

5. **Take care of your overall well-being!** Achieving your goal score on the ACT takes more than just studying. Be sure to eat right, exercise, and get enough sleep. If your body and mind are healthy, especially during the week of your actual ACT exam, you'll be much calmer and more confident heading into the challenge. So give yourself permission to take some meaningful study breaks! Hang out with your friends, watch your favorite show on Netflix, or go on a leisurely jog … all in the name of test prep.

Which Strategy Will Work Best for Me?

It's okay if your ACT study plan is unique! In fact, it should be. Making the most of your ACT study schedule requires adapting it to your particular needs, and you'll learn more about what those needs actually are as you go along. Be patient if you don't see your scores shoot up immediately. The strategies you'll learn in this book and on act.magoosh.com may slow you down or even mess you up at first, but practicing them will give you extra tools on test day that will boost your score.

How Do I Know If My Prep Is Working?

Focus on what you've learned, and don't be upset if your first couple practice tests aren't as high-scoring as you'd like. Preparing for a test takes organization, practice, and a positive mental attitude. There is no such thing as a "good" or a "bad" test-taker. Some students are just more familiar with the content areas and strategies than others. Test-taking is a learned skill, so don't be discouraged. Check assignments off of your study schedule as you go so you can reward yourself for a job well done!

Finding and Using High-Quality ACT Resources (Besides the One You're Holding!)

A great place to begin learning about the test itself is at act.org. If you can, order a copy of *The Official ACT Prep Guide* in addition to this book. Although it's pretty lacking in the strategy department, the official guide includes full-length practice tests as well as answers and explanations.

Free ACT practice materials abound online, but many are of pretty questionable quality. For help finding more great ACT resources online, head to act.magoosh.com/resources.

Study Schedules

In the upcoming pages, we're going to walk you through our one-month, four-days-per-week schedule. The One-Month ACT Study Schedule printed in this book is a modified version of the same schedule you'll see on your dashboard if you're studying online with Magoosh, and it uses that online material in addition to the book you're holding now.

Many of our Magoosh ACT study schedules are organized by duration, and students choose based on how long they have to study (two months, three months, etc.). We also offer subject-focused study schedules that allow students to focus more time on their weaknesses (math-focused, English-focused, etc.). We're only including the one-month version here because that's our most popular plan, but you can access our additional schedules through your dashboard at act.magoosh.com or on the Magoosh High School Blog at magoosh.com/hs/act.

We highly recommend using the online version of your study schedule to keep track of your progress. But don't worry if you don't have access to the internet; the study schedule in this book will also offer you offline assignments so you can study without a computer.

If you're studying for a shorter or longer time than the schedule provides, it's a good idea to modify the schedule to fit your time constraints! There's no harm in splitting one day into two if needed. Just make sure you're not neglecting any one part of your prep: reviewing wrong answers is just as important as doing practice, and reading up on science strategies is, for many students, just as important as watching math videos. Know your weaknesses and focus on them, but don't completely neglect any one section of the test.

If you have any questions about adapting a schedule or getting started with Magoosh online, email us at help@magoosh.com for help!

One-Month ACT Study Schedule

Time Requirement

First of all, we recognize that this schedule may appear overwhelming at first glance. Take a deep breath, and remember that you'll be taking this one day at a time.

This schedule assumes that you have at least four days a week to devote to ACT study and about three to four hours on each of these days. It also assumes that you'll be able to set aside four to five hours on a couple weekends for a practice test, plus schedule some review time. (If you're taking the test with extra time, you'll need to build in more time based on whether you have received time-and-a-half or double-time /multi-day testing.) Hopefully, this is a manageable amount of study time when balanced with your schoolwork and activities.

If it seems like too much, you can adjust the plan to focus primarily on reviewing your weaknesses via lesson videos and answering practice questions, or you can divide each schedule day between two actual days, so that you're doing about an hour to an hour and a half of prep a day. If you're unable to set aside a four-to-five-hour chunk of time on the weekend, you can split this up into two sessions. It's not ideal, but it's better than nothing.

Often, the same topics will be covered in lesson videos and in the book you're holding now. If you're already somewhat comfortable with those topics, it's not necessary to spend hours reviewing the information in both places. Choose your preferred format for review—book or video lesson—and stick to that. If information is completely new to you, though, we recommend using both resources because you'll better remember the advice and concepts if you take it in both ways.

Accessing Lesson Videos

This study schedule includes lesson videos that are hosted online at act.magoosh.com. The videos cover each and every topic that you'll encounter on the ACT exam. You can absolutely use this study schedule without ever going online, but we do recommend watching online lesson videos whenever possible. To access these videos, you'll need to sign up for, and log in to, your Magoosh ACT online account.

Additional Video Lessons

There are several ACT video lessons in the online version of Magoosh ACT (act.magoosh.com) that this plan doesn't have time to cover. This is particularly true in math. There are also many math video lessons that provide more fundamental reviews or take a more advanced look at topics. When you have extra time, watch the lesson videos on the topics you feel you need the most practice with. For extra practice, you can also always work through additional questions on Magoosh or use the practice questions on the official ACT student website.

Week One, Day One: Introduction and Math | Time: three hours

Note that the times listed in this schedule are estimates. For some students, completing these tasks may take a little bit more or less time.

In This Book

◯ Read chapters 1 through 3.

◯ Get familiar with the resources listed in chapter 11.

In Magoosh Online

Watch these lesson videos:

◯ Math – Introduction to ACT Math

◯ English – Introduction to the ACT English Test

◯ Reading – Introduction to the ACT Reading Test

◯ Science – Introduction to the ACT Science Test

◯ Math – Strategy: Backsolving

◯ Math – Assumptions & Estimation (Geometry)

◯ Math – Three lessons of your choice, focusing on your weak areas

Do the following practice:

◯ 30 math questions

◯ Watch the explanation videos for all of your incorrect answers from those 30 math questions, and note how to avoid the same mistakes in the future.

In This Book

○ Start chapter 5, on ACT English. Read up to "Usage and Mechanics Questions."

○ Start chapter 8, on ACT Science. Read up to "Passage Types."

In Magoosh Online

Watch these lesson videos:

○ English – ACT English Question Types

○ English – Commas

○ English – Apostrophes

○ English – Dashes

○ English – Semicolons

○ English – Colons

○ English – Other Punctuation

○ Science – Introduction to Science Test Passage Types

○ Science – Introduction to Science Question Types

○ Science – Using Key Terms

Do the following practice:

○ Two English passages

○ Watch the explanation videos for all of your incorrect answers from those two English passages, and note how to avoid the same mistakes in the future.

○ Three science passages

○ Watch the explanation videos for all of your incorrect answers from those three science passages, and note how to avoid the same mistakes in the future.

Week One, Day Three: Reading and Writing | Time: three and a half hours

In This Book

- ○ Start chapter 7, on ACT Reading. Read up to "Question Types on the ACT Reading Test."

In Magoosh Online

Watch these lesson videos:

- ○ Reading – ACT Reading Passage Types
- ○ Reading – ACT Reading Question Types
- ○ Reading – Approaching Passages
- ○ Writing – Introduction to the Essay
- ○ Writing – How to Wow the Graders
- ○ Writing – Scoring
- ○ Writing – Time Management

Do the following practice:

- ○ Three reading passages
- ○ Watch the explanation videos for all of your incorrect answers from those three reading passages, and note how to avoid the same mistakes in the future.
- ○ Write one essay, following the official time constraints. Keep your essay in a safe place! You will review this essay on Week 2, Day 7.

Week One, Day Four: Weekend: Mock Test | Time: four hours

In Magoosh Online

- ○ Take a full practice test. You will grade and review this exam on Week 2, Day 8.

Week Two, Day Five: Math | Time: three and a half hours

In This Book

○ Start chapter 6, on ACT Math. Read up to "The Dreaded Exponent."

In Magoosh Online

Watch these lesson videos:

○ Math – Calculator Use and Mental Math

○ Math – Mental Math: Estimation

○ Math – Mental Math: Dividing by 5

○ Math – Mental Math: Doubling and Halving

○ Math – Three lessons of your choice, focusing on your weak areas

Do the following practice:

○ 40 math questions

○ Watch the explanation videos for all of your incorrect answers from those 40 math questions, and note how to avoid the same mistakes in the future.

Week Two, Day Six: English and Science | Time: four hours

In This Book

○ Continue chapter 5, on ACT English. Read from the start of "Usage and Mechanics Questions" up to "Rhetorical Skills."

In Magoosh Online

Watch these lesson videos:

○ Science – Pacing on the ACT Science Test

○ Science – How to Read the ACT Science Test

○ Science – The Conflicting Viewpoints Passage

○ English – Grammar Basics

○ English – Subject-Verb Agreement

○ English – Verb Tense

○ English – Adjectives and Adverbs

○ English – Pronoun Cases

○ English – Idioms

○ English – Run-On Sentences and Comma Splices

○ English – Misplaced Modifiers

○ English – Parallelism

Do the following practice:

○ Three English passages

○ Watch the explanation videos for all of your incorrect answers from those three English passages, and note how to avoid the same mistakes in the future.

Week Two, Day 7: Reading and Writing | Time: three and a half hours

In This Book

- ◯ Continue chapter 7, on ACT Reading. Read from the start of "Question Types on the ACT Reading Test" up to "Pacing for ACT Reading."

- ◯ Read chapter 9, on ACT Writing.

In Magoosh Online

Watch these lesson videos:

- ◯ Reading – Trap Answer Choices
- ◯ Reading – Example Passage
- ◯ Reading – Basic Strategies
- ◯ Reading – Using Key Words
- ◯ Reading – Comparison Passages
- ◯ Writing – Example Essay Prompt
- ◯ Writing – Planning the Essay
- ◯ Writing – The Thesis
- ◯ Writing – Coming Up with Examples
- ◯ Writing – Structuring the Essay

Do the following practice:

- ◯ Two reading passages

- ◯ Watch the explanation videos for all of your incorrect answers from those two reading passages, and note how to avoid the same mistakes in the future.

- ◯ Return to the essay you wrote on day three. Edit the essay carefully for grammar and add any extra detail it would need to achieve a higher score. Learn more about grading your practice essays in chapter 9.

In This Book

○ Continue chapter 6, on ACT Math. Read from the start of "The Dreaded Exponent" up to "Plugging In and Ball-Parking."

In Magoosh Online

Review your wrong answers from the practice test you took one week ago. Watch explanation videos and/or related lessons from any questions that you aren't confident you would be able to answer correctly if they were on your actual ACT.

Do the following practice:

○ Two reading passages

○ Watch the explanation videos for all of your incorrect answers from those two reading passages, and note how to avoid the same mistakes in the future.

○ Two English passages

○ Watch the explanation videos for all of your incorrect answers from those two English passages, and note how to avoid the same mistakes in the future.

○ 30 math questions

○ Watch the explanation videos for all of your incorrect answers from those 30 math questions, and note how to avoid the same mistakes in the future.

Week Three, Day 9: Science and Writing | Time: three and a half hours

In This Book

○ Continue chapter 8, on ACT Science. Read from the start of "Passage Types" up to the start of the "ACT Science Practice Questions."

In Magoosh Online

Watch these lesson videos:

○ Science – Understanding Tables, Graphs, and Figures
○ Science – Finding Trends and Patterns
○ Science – Linking Tables and Graphs
○ Science – Unfamiliar Terms
○ Science – Science Knowledge on the ACT Science Test
○ Science – Math Problems on the ACT Science Test
○ Science – The Scientific Method
○ Writing – The Introduction
○ Writing – The Body Paragraphs
○ Writing – The Conclusion
○ Writing – The Importance of Style
○ Writing – Top Grammar Rules for the Essay
○ Writing – Proofreading Your Essay

Do the following practice:

○ Seven science passages
○ Watch the explanation videos for all of your incorrect answers from those seven science passages, and note how to avoid the same mistakes in the future.

Week Three, Day 10: Math | Time: four hours

In This Book

○ Continue chapter 6, on ACT Math. Read from the start of "Averages" up to "Matrices."

In Magoosh Online

Watch these lesson videos:

○ Math – Intro to ACT Data Interpretation
○ Math – Types of Graphics
○ Math – Timeplots for Motion
○ Math – Other Timeplots
○ Math – Histograms
○ Math – Tables of Values
○ Math – Three lessons of your choice, focusing on your weak areas

Do the following practice:

○ 60 math questions
○ Watch the explanation videos for all of your incorrect answers from those 60 math questions, and note how to avoid the same mistakes in the future.

Week Three, Day 11: Reading and English | Time: four hours

In This Book

○ Complete chapter 7, on ACT Reading, starting from "Pacing for ACT Reading."

In Magoosh Online

Watch these lesson videos:

○ Reading – Line Reference

○ Reading – Meaning of Words

○ Reading – Main Idea

○ Reading – Inference

○ Reading – Author's Method (Purpose)

○ Reading – Author's Voice

○ English – Comparatives and Superlatives

○ English – Neither/Nor

○ English – Singular and Plural

○ English – Who vs. Whom

○ English – Word Choice

○ English – Dependent and Independent Clauses

○ English – Conjunctions

○ English – Parenthetical Information

○ English – Sentence Fragments

○ English – Pronoun Agreement

Do the following practice:

○ Three reading passages

○ Watch the explanation videos for all of your incorrect answers from those three reading passages, and note how to avoid the same mistakes in the future.

Week Three, Day 12: Weekend: Mock Test | Time: four hours

In This Book

○ Take the full practice test (chapter 10).

Week Four, Day 13: English | Time: three and a half hours

In This Book

- ◯ Complete chapter 5, on ACT English, starting from "Rhetorical Skills."

In Magoosh Online

Watch these lesson videos:

- ◯ English – Writer's/Essay Goal
- ◯ English – Adding or Deleting Sentences
- ◯ English – Best Illustration Questions
- ◯ English – Least Acceptable Questions
- ◯ English – Introducing and Concluding Paragraphs
- ◯ English – Ordering Sentences and Paragraphs
- ◯ English – Transitions
- ◯ English – Redundant Meanings
- ◯ English – Ambiguous Pronouns
- ◯ English – Concision and Wordiness
- ◯ English – Clarity in Phrasing
- ◯ English – Tone
- ◯ English – Passive and Active Voice

Do the following practice:

- ◯ Three English passages
- ◯ Watch the explanation videos for all of your incorrect answers from those three English passages, and note how to avoid the same mistakes in the future.

Week Four, Day 14: Science and Math | Time: four hours

In This Book

○ Complete chapter 6, on ACT Math, starting from "Matrices."

In Magoosh Online

Watch these lesson videos:

○ Science – Answering "Yes/No, Because" Questions

○ Science – Finding Clues in the Answer Choices

○ Math – Three lessons of your choice, focusing on your weak areas

Do the following practice:

○ Seven science passages

○ Watch the explanation videos for all of your incorrect answers from those seven science passages, and note how to avoid the same mistakes in the future.

○ 20 math questions

○ Watch the explanation videos for all of your incorrect answers from those 20 math questions, and note how to avoid the same mistakes in the future.

Week Four, Day 15: Final Review | Time: one and one-third hours

In This Book

○ Complete chapter 8, on ACT Science, starting from "ACT Science Practice Questions."

In Magoosh Online

○ Review your wrong answers from all four sections of the test. Rewatch explanation videos and/or related lessons from any questions that you aren't confident you would be able to answer correctly if they were on your actual ACT.

○ Make yourself a "cheat sheet" of final reminders to review the morning of the exam. This can include things like "Watch out for run-on sentences!" and "The area of a trapezoid is (base 1 + base 2) ÷ 2 × height."

The Day Before Your Test

○ Review last-minute test-day tips (page 531) once more and pack your bag (see test day checklist below).

○ Do something you enjoy, and be sure to go to bed early and get good rest before the big day.

TEST DAY!

It's test day, which means no last-minute prep! Do some light exercise, eat a full breakfast, and give yourself plenty of time to get to the test center. Don't forget:

○ No. 2 pencils (not mechanical)

○ good eraser

○ calculator

    ○ Check act.org for a list of calculators you're allowed to use.

    ○ Make sure that you're familiar with how the calculator works.

    ○ Make sure that the calculator is charged or has brand-new batteries.

○ watch (old-school, silent watches only; no smart watches or anything that beeps!)

○ drink

○ snack

○ admissions ticket

○ photo ID

○ jacket or sweatshirt

Review your list of last-minute pointers before you go into the test center. You've put in a month of hard work, so walk into the test with confidence!

Chapter 5

ACT English Test

Intro to ACT English

Before we get into the nitty-gritty, let's just point out that the "English" Test isn't a test of any old English: it's a test of the rules of standard American English writing. There are plenty of ways of writing and speaking English that are completely legit in other places, but not on the ACT. That's an example right there: the word "legit." We'll keep it here because we like the sound of it, but the ACT doesn't include slang like that. The ACT is all about the same type of English you use in school essays (big surprise!).

In order to measure those skills, the test basically puts you in the shoes of an English teacher grading essays. You'll get a set of five short passages, each containing a number of errors or places where the style could be improved. Luckily for you, the locations of those errors are all marked. For most questions, you'll choose the best replacement for the underlined section (or whether to replace it at all). There isn't actually a question, per se—just that bit of underlined text in the passage and a few answer choices off to the side, like this:

When Geoffrey Chaucer wrote *The Canterbury Tales*, he was choosing one of the many variants of the then-new language of English. By William Shakespeare's time, English had become standardized as the language we all know and love today.

Halfway through peeling her soft-boiled egg, <u>and having been growing</u> increasingly exasperated with the chunks of white coming away with the shell, Adrienne gave up and hurled her snack at the window.

A. NO CHANGE
B. having grown
C. although, she was growing
D. grows

But not all questions lack a … well, a question. There are also a handful that ask about sentences to add, delete, or rearrange, and a few that ask about the purposes of certain parts of text.

We can also break up the English Test by content rather than format. There are two broad categories of questions:

1. Usage and Mechanics
2. Rhetorical Skills

We'll go into more depth on those two categories throughout this chapter, but roughly speaking, you can think of the first as questions on what's *correct* and the second as questions on what's *good*. The egg-zample above (we couldn't help ourselves!) may be grammatically correct, but it's awkward and wordy. Choice **B** is shorter and clearer. The original isn't written as well as it could be, so it falls into the "Rhetorical Skills" category.

All in all, the English section is one that you can improve quickly on, given some review of the content that the ACT likes to test. You'll probably be a bit pressed for time, but you can shave down the time you take on each question as you learn to systematically check for the types of errors you can expect from the test-makers.

But enough with the generalizations—let's get down to business with some hard facts!

At a Glance

What to know

- English is the first section of the ACT.
- You have a 45-minute time limit.
- You will see 75 multiple-choice questions. (Yeah, that is a lot!)

What to study and practice

- Punctuation (commas, apostrophes, colons …)
- Grammar (subject-verb agreement, verb forms, pronouns, adjectives vs. adverbs …)
- Sentence structure (independent and dependent clauses, misplaced modifiers, run-on sentences …)
- Style (wordiness, redundancy, word choice …)
- Organization (rearranging sentences, choosing transition words, introductions and conclusions …)
- Relevance (when to add, remove, or change a phrase, sentence, or paragraph)

What not to study

- Spelling (except for commonly confused words and their meanings: "here" and "hear"; "there," "they're," and "their")
- Vocabulary
- Rote memorization of grammar rules (You will be asked to correct grammar but not asked to explain why. You'll need to know the grammar rules, but in order to apply them to examples—not just for the sake of knowing them.)
- Slang (urbandictionary.com isn't going to help you here!)

Top Three Tips to Improve Your ACT English Test Score

Sometimes you just want the quickest and most effective ways to give your ACT score a boost—maybe it's the week before the test or maybe you just need a surge of confidence early on in your test prep. Well, we hear you. Here are three tips for fast improvement on ACT English:

1. **Read well before and after the underlined portion.** This is both a rookie mistake and a veteran one (heck, even we do it when we're not being careful). Many times an answer choice will seem just fine in the part of the sentence where it is, but it's not fine in the grander scheme of things. Something earlier in the same sentence, or—even trickier—something later in the following sentences may make this answer choice incorrect. So make sure you're vigilant!

2. **Learn punctuation.** There are so many punctuation questions on this test. Around 20 percent of the questions have something to do with commas alone, so you can see huge gains by studying the major punctuation marks: commas, semicolons, colons, apostrophes, and dashes.

3. **Be concise.** The correct answer is often the shortest one, particularly on questions that provide different phrasing options for a portion of a sentence. It's not always correct, so you need to be careful to check for errors, but when in doubt, keep it short and simple. Generally speaking, the ACT really likes answers that state things in the simplest, most direct way.

Usage and Mechanics Questions

The word "mechanics" says a lot about what these types of questions want from you. For the most part, they don't get at the deeper ideas that the author is trying to communicate. Instead, they're all about how the words and phrases fit together to create meaning, instead of what that meaning actually is.

In other words, these kinds of questions have little to do with reading comprehension. That's an important distinction to make: when we go through Rhetorical Purpose questions later, we'll look at some questions that *do* touch upon reading comp. But these guys—the Usage and Mechanics questions—they're in a class of their own.

There are three types of Usage and Mechanics questions, though there's some overlap among them: sentence structure, grammar, and punctuation. In order to answer them well, you need to know a handful of rules. This is one part of the ACT where memorization will pay off in spades. For example, let's say you didn't realize that colons have to follow independent clauses. Learn that quick fact. Then, every time you see a colon in the English section, look back to see if the clause before could work as a full sentence. And the points will come rolling in!

Not sure what we mean by "independent clause"? Great! That'll be where we start.

Sentence Structure: The Basics

Clauses

Here's a quick run-down on clauses, phrases, and the differences between the two. Don't worry: it's (mostly) painless.

- Phrases are groups of related words that don't have both a subject *and* a verb. (*Examples:* "over the rainbow," "singing in the rain," "a tale as old as time," and other non-musical related words)

- Clauses are groups of related words that *do* have a subject and verb. There are two types:

  Independent clauses, which can be used as complete sentences (*Examples:* "I think I'll try defying gravity," "The sun will come out tomorrow," etc.)

  Dependent clauses, which have a subject and verb but aren't complete sentences (*Examples:* "as if it were butter," "if I only had a brain," etc.)

Sentence fragments

Sentence fragments are like fish without gills, birds without feathers, sneakers without shoelaces: incomplete. Sometimes they're dependent clauses that are sitting alone, and sometimes they're not even full clauses but rather just verb phrases, noun phrases, or other similarly incomplete strings of words. Here are a few examples:

While she was biking through the wilderness.

The great wizard of the west.

Without a dream to hold on to.

For example, chocolate-dipped strawberries.

Sentence fragments are usually missing either a subject or a verb (and sometimes both). To fix a sentence fragment, we need to add the missing element(s):

While she was biking through the wilderness, **my girlfriend saw a mountain lion**.

The great wizard of the west **broke the spell**.

I am like a drifter *without a dream to hold on to.*

For example, chocolate-dipped strawberries **are her favorite breakfast**.

On the ACT, you particularly want to watch out for -ing words.

⊗ *Having finished his lab experiment before the rest of the class, then deciding to leave early.*   ⇦ Sentence fragment

⊘ *Having finished his lab experiment before the rest of the class,* **he decided** *to leave early.*   ⇦ Add a subject and change the verb form.

You also want to watch out for sneaky sentence fragments that seem to be connected to the previous sentence but can't stand alone grammatically.

⊗ *She was a wonderful professor. The* best *professor.*   ⇦ Sentence fragment

⊘ *She was a wonderful professor. In fact,* **she was** *the* best *professor.*   ⇦ Add a subject, "she," and a verb, "was."

Sentence fragments pretend to be sentences, but they're lacking an element of independent clauses. By turning them into independent clauses (with subjects and verbs) or attaching them to independent clauses, we can fix these guys up.

Conjunctions

Conjunctions are the mediators of the grammar world. They bring words and phrases together and say,

"Hey, you guys go together like peas **AND** carrots."

Or they agree to disagree: "You're cool, **BUT** we have really different opinions."

Or they sometimes get feisty and issue ultimatums: "We're going to have to break up **UNLESS** you come up with a really amazing proposal."

In short, conjunctions bring words and phrases to the table to talk and tell us how they relate to one another.

The ACT loves conjunctions. It tests not only that you know how to use conjunctions correctly but also that you know which one to use to convey the writer's intentions.

There are two major categories of conjunctions you need to be familiar with: coordinating conjunctions and subordinating conjunctions.

Coordinating Conjunctions

Coordinating conjunctions are the FANBOYS: *for, and, nor, but, or, yet,* and *so.*

We need to be careful here, because the meaning of "for" that's included in that list—meaning "because"—isn't very common nowadays, but ANBOYS just doesn't have the right ring to it.

These are the conjunctions used to create compound sentences when combined with a comma, but they can also just connect simple words or phrases to show how they relate. ("I like pizza **and** ice cream." "I like pizza **but** not ice cream.")

Subordinating Conjunctions

Subordinating conjunctions provide a transition between ideas and *subordinate* one clause to another main clause. Unlike the FANBOYS coordinating conjunctions, there are many subordinating conjunctions. Here are a few common ones:

after, although, because, if, than, that, when, where, while, before, as soon as, since, though, unless, until, once

For example, "I plan to launch my career as a poet **once** I finish this novel I am writing, **because** my English teacher told me **that** I could do it for extra credit."

In that example, the main clause is "I plan to launch my career as a poet." The subordinating conjunction, "once," gives us more information about when the speaker plans to launch her poetic career. The second subordinating conjunction, "because," gives more information about why the writer is writing a novel first. Then, "that" sets up the final clause as what the teacher said. These subordinating conjunctions make the clauses they lie within *dependent* on the main clause. "Because my English teacher told me" is not a sentence by itself, nor is "That I could do it for extra credit." All of this depends on that independent clause at the start: "I plan to launch my career as a poet."

So before we dive into the info you'll need to get punctuation questions right, let's recap sentence structure so far. A string of words with a subject and a verb is a **clause**. A clause that includes a **subordinating conjunction** (like "because") can't stand alone as a sentence, because it's **dependent** on something else—an independent clause.

If either a subject or verb is missing from a string of words, it's a **phrase**, not a clause, and if a phrase is standing by itself as a sentence, that's a **fragment** that needs to be fixed. If we want to combine two or more clauses, we're going to need a **conjunction** to act as the glue. But conjunctions on their own don't quite do the trick: we also need punctuation. That's what we'll cover next.

Practice Questions: Sentence Structure: The Basics

Count the number of clauses in each of the sentences below. Mark the subject and verb in each clause. Note whether the sentence is a correct, complete sentence or not.

	Number of clauses	Subjects and verbs of clauses	Correct, complete sentence?
1 When she cooks it, Aunt Mei's roast pork is, without fail, the fattiest, messiest dish at the table.			
2 Failing math, desperate for help, and tired of studying, Monique started looking for ways to cheat, against her better judgment.			
3 Until the end of the week, or by Monday at the very latest, depending on the severity of the snowstorm this Friday.			
4 And the curtains fell.			
5 After the tree's leaves had fallen fully away, having died from the blight, with winter drawing near.			

Check your answers below.

Answers

1 **Two** clauses (*subjects:* **she, roast pork**; *verbs:* **cooks, is**). This is a **correct** sentence!

2 **One** clause (*subject:* **Monique**; *verb:* **started**). Also **correct**.

3 **Zero** clauses (*subject:* **none**; *verb:* **none**). **Incorrect**. This is one big adverb phrase, but it doesn't connect to a verb. That means it's a fragment by itself.

4 **One** clause (*subject:* **curtains**; *verb:* **fell**). This is technically **correct**. Although not everybody agrees that it's good style to start a sentence with "and," a coordinating conjunction doesn't make a clause dependent, so the clause can technically stand alone as a sentence.

5 **One** clause (*subject:* **leaves**; *verb:* **had fallen**). **Incorrect**, because there's no independent clause here. "After" makes the only full clause dependent. "Having died from the blight" is a *phrase* describing the leaves, and "winter drawing near" is a *phrase* describing the weather. "With winter drawing near" is a prepositional *phrase*. (We'll see more of these later in the chapter!)

Once you know the rules for combining phrases and clauses, questions on punctuation can be some of the fastest on the ACT English Test to answer. Why? Pretty often, the only difference between the answer choices is the punctuation mark used and/or a conjunction or two. That's in contrast, say, to a question that asks about the structure of an entire clause, or one that asks about the purpose of a 100-word paragraph.

Even better news? There are only a handful of punctuation marks that really matter for the test, and for each one, there are a couple of rules to follow.

Commas

In real life, the rules governing commas can be tricky because often there's some flexibility for your personal style. On the ACT, the "style" rules *have to* have just one right answer. "Style" rules with more than one possible right answer are just not tested.

Instead, you can bet on commas being used incorrectly in a few predictable ways. And once you know how to pick apart a sentence into clauses and phrases, you're already halfway there …

Comma Splices

We have a friend who likes to put commas everywhere in his sentences; he jokingly calls them "artistic commas." And while artistic commas might be fine when you're writing poetry, a diary entry, or an email to your friend, they aren't okay when they're breaking a fundamental English grammar rule—one of the biggest there is. **This offending error is called the "comma splice."** Dun-dun-DUUNNN.

You might be familiar with splicing from horror films (though they use it, uh, a little differently than the ACT does). To splice is to join two things together by interweaving their parts. In everyday life, you might splice together two cable wires. In horror movies, sometimes two scary beasts are spliced together to create one ultra-scary beast. A grammatical comma splice is almost as bad. Maybe worse. In other words, comma splices join two independent clauses that would really rather be apart.

Here's an example:

I run five miles along the river on Saturdays, I use a treadmill at the gym when it's raining.

That little offending comma in the middle is creating a comma splice.

"I run five miles along the river on Saturdays" is a complete sentence (an independent clause).

"I use a treadmill at the gym when it's raining" is a complete sentence (an independent clause).

And we can't join them with just a comma. To fix a comma splice, we can do one of four things:

1. We can separate these two disagreeable independent clauses with a period.

   I run five miles along the river on Saturdays. I use a treadmill at the gym when it's raining.

2. We can keep the comma and join the clauses together with a friendly coordinating conjunction that says, "Hey, guys, let's hold hands." There are seven of these happy mediators we can choose from: *for, and, nor, but, or, yet,* and *so.* Sound familiar? Yup—those are the good ol' FANBOYS.

   I run five miles along the river on Saturdays, but I use a treadmill at the gym when it's raining.

3. We can stitch the clauses together with a semicolon. Semicolons are sophisticated, so sometimes this makes for a rather elegant solution.

   I run five miles along the river on Saturdays; I use a treadmill at the gym when it's raining.

4. We can subordinate one clause to the other, so that it becomes a dependent clause instead of an independent clause.

   I run five miles along the river on Saturdays, although I use a treadmill at the gym when it's raining.

In other words, don't let the horror of comma splices keep you up at night. They're *all over* the ACT, and they often appear in far more complex sentences, but the basic rules always apply. So if you see two independent clauses spliced together with only a comma, make sure you bring in some reinforcements so they can live in harmony.

Run-On Sentences

Run-on sentences have the same problem as comma splices, except there's no comma. A run-on sentence mashes two independent clauses together, like this:

I had a hard childhood my mother was constantly forcing me to do extra homework.

"I had a hard childhood" can stand alone as a sentence, and so can "my mother was constantly forcing me to do extra homework," so we have a run-on sentence. To fix this run-on, we can actually use any of the same four fixes we used for the comma splice.

Lists

Of course, commas aren't just for combining whole clauses. Sometimes they're placed between individual words. Here, the commas separate individual items in a list of three or more items:

Othello didn't realize that Iago was conniving, two-faced, and evil.

See those commas there? They're pointing out all of Iago's finer qualities, which Othello is unaware of. We have to use commas to separate them, or the end of the sentence would be a bit of a mushy mess.

Note: The comma before the "and" is called the "Oxford comma" or the "serial comma." Some writers include it, but others don't. In real life, the Oxford comma is largely a matter of personal preference, but it can make certain sentences clearer. On the ACT, **always include the Oxford comma in a list.** It won't be the only difference between two answer choices, but the ACT prefers it, so, as far as the test is concerned, you should, too!

Adjectives

We also use a comma to separate two adjectives when the word "and" could be inserted between them. One way to check this is to switch the position of the adjectives and see if the sentence still makes sense.

Romeo's choice to take poison was a rash, foolish decision.

It was a rash and foolish decision. It makes sense for a decision to be foolish and rash. The comma is necessary.

The quirky English teacher was the student's favorite.

Is the teacher from England? If yes, then a comma makes sense. Otherwise, it would be strange to have an English quirky teacher, so omit the comma.

Additional (Parenthetical) Information

Let's say we're telling you a story about a guy named James. Here's the beginning:

James is rather fond of Slim Jims.

A simple enough sentence, no? But it leaves us with a major unanswered question: *who is James?* Clearly, he must be someone we know, or we wouldn't be able to discuss his dietary preferences, but we haven't told you who he is or how we know him.

Well, James is our cousin. We know he likes Slim Jims because we're family. We need to put that information into the sentence to satisfy our readers' burning curiosity about James. We could rephrase it to say "My cousin James is rather fond of Slim Jims," and it would be 100 percent grammatically correct. On the other hand, we could also do this:

The common phrase "green-eyed jealousy" comes from Shakespeare's *The Merchant of Venice* and *Othello*. The common phrase "a fool's paradise" comes from Shakespeare's *Romeo and Juliet*. The common phrase "there's method to his madness" comes from Shakespeare's *Hamlet*.

James, my cousin, is rather fond of Slim Jims.

The difference here is one of style, and neither one is "more right" than the other. However, if we're going to include the information that James is our cousin *after* we introduce his name, we need to separate it with commas.

The two-commas rule works in many cases. If the extra information isn't grammatically necessary in the sentence, you can offset it with two—*only and always two*—commas. (You can also use dashes or parentheses for a similar effect. Again, it's a style-preference thing, and differences in style preferences won't be tested on the ACT.)

Here's another example:

James is rather fond of Slim Jims. My aunt, however, would rather starve than eat them.

The sentence would be perfectly understandable without the word "however," but we wanted to include it anyway. It's additional information, a non-essential word. Therefore, we surround it with two commas.

Introductions

This point is closely related to the last one. If you're starting a sentence with a transition or other introductory word or phrase, separate it from the rest of the sentence with a comma.

In my life, I've made many mistakes. Very few of them were grammatical.

Colons

The colon (:) is a fairly straightforward punctuation mark. The rules for colon usage are clear-cut and don't leave much room for error. Master these, and the day is yours!

Colons are used after *independent clauses* (a.k.a. "complete sentences") in three situations. You can remember them using the letters "LEQ."

L   The *L* stands for *list*. You use a colon after an independent clause to introduce a series of items.

   I have three things on my to-do list for this summer: sitting, loafing, and goofing off.

E   The *E* stands for *explanation*. You can use a colon after a complete sentence to expand on what you're talking about.

   This, I know: Do or do not. There is no "try." —Yoda

   While I was in Ireland, I had heaven in a cup: a Cadbury "Flake" bar in vanilla ice cream.

Q   The *Q* stands for *quote*. You can use a colon to introduce a quotation.

   It's like Emerson once said: "I hate quotations."

And above all else, remember that bit about the independent clause. The ACT loves to throw in colons where they don't belong.

Here are some examples of how L, E, and Q can *all* be made incorrect by putting a fragment before the colon:

The three things on my to-do list for this summer are: *sitting, loafing, and goofing off.*

If we took out the colon, we'd be fine! We need those "things" in the clause for it to be complete. "The three things are" alone is not a complete sentence.

What I know is: *Do or do not. There is no "try."*

This is pretty much the same as the last one. We can't end this sentence with "is." Let's bring "this" back into the sentence so it can be complete: "What I know is **this:** …"

Emerson once said: *"I hate quotations."*

Switch that colon out for a comma, and this sentence would be fine. We can only use a colon to introduce a quotation if removing the quotation would still give us a grammatically correct sentence. "It's like Emerson once said" may not be very insightful by itself, but it *is* a complete sentence. "Emerson once said" is not.

Semicolons

Semicolons are great. They're our favorite punctuation mark—no, seriously. They're sophisticated; use them properly, and people will be impressed at your mastery of the English language.

Use a semicolon to separate two closely related independent sentences. When we say "closely related," we mean that they are *clearly part of the same thought.* The two sentences are grammatically complete but make much more sense when joined together.

With educated people, I suppose, punctuation is a matter of rule; with me it is a matter of feeling. But I must say I have a great respect for the semi-colon; it's a useful little chap.
—Abraham Lincoln

Use a semicolon to separate listed items that *already* contain commas. In the following example, the narrator is meeting with *three people.* If we hadn't used semicolons, you might think the narrator was meeting *five* people.

I have a meeting with Donna Jones, the school principal; Ms. Hawkins, my daughter's English teacher; and Jim Jackman, the volleyball coach.

Unclear version: *I have a meeting with Donna Jones, the school principal, Ms. Hawkins, my daughter's English teacher, and Jim Jackman, the volleyball coach.*

Dashes

Before we start talking about this, we need some clarity of language. A *hyphen* (-) is often used to join words. We'll talk about those later in this section. A *dash* (—) is a versatile and often dramatic punctuation mark. Because it's more fun to talk about, we'll discuss it first.

There are actually two different kinds of dashes. The *en dash*, which is slightly shorter, and the *em dash*, which is the one you can see in the previous paragraph. The good news is that the ACT isn't going to test you on the differences between the two. You will only be tested on the three rules of the em dash:

1. **Use an em dash to show a change in flow in the middle of a sentence.** Here, a pair of em dashes sets off additional information in the same way commas or parentheses would.

   > *Critics of the* Pokémon *video game franchise—also known as people who have no fun—say that each game in the series feels exactly the same.*

   Note: The use of the em dash instead of commas here is a matter of personal preference, so you won't have a question on the ACT that will ask you to choose among dashes, commas, or parentheses. But you may be asked to make sure that they're used in pairs or that the additional information really needs to be separated from the rest of the sentence.

2. **Use an em dash to introduce an explanation in the same way you would use a colon. Always make sure you have an independent clause before the colon or em dash!** Again, though, remember that the ACT won't test you on what punctuation point to use if it's a matter of style. In other words, it won't ask you to choose between a color and an em dash if either would be acceptable in a sentence.

   > *I'm not a big fan of* Skyrim*—if I can't figure out where the story is going in the first hour, then I don't want to play the game!*

3. **Use an em dash to indicate a change in thought or a humorous or dramatic addition to the sentence.**

   > Pac-Man, *at its core, is a game about consuming food pellets and pieces of fruit while trying to outrun beings who are out to destroy you—sounds like a typical school day to me!*

Wait! What about hyphens?

Oh, right. We promised you we'd talk about those.

Well, to be honest, the ACT isn't really going to test you on hyphen usage. We'll outline the rules here anyway because we're grammar nerds, but if you're not interested, go ahead and skip this bit!

Use a hyphen to join two or more adjectives together when they act as a single idea and come before the noun they modify.

a five-page paper

a one-year-old girl

an all-too-common mistake

a friendly-looking dog (remember, even though it ends in -ly, "friendly" is an adjective!)

Don't use a hyphen when you have an adjective and an adverb. Adverbs can't modify nouns, so the sentence should already be clear without the hyphen.

*Katie was **terribly tired**.*

*I deleted the **clearly problematic** sentence.*

Use a hyphen for all spelled-out numbers from *twenty-one* to *ninety-nine* and fractions.

one-third of high school students

seventy-six trombones

Use a hyphen for most compound last names.

Lady Guinevere Hopkins-Drake will attend the soirée.

Use a hyphen for some compound nouns.

sister-in-law

master-at-arms

commander-in-chief

Apostrophes

Want to find out which of your friends is a bit of a jerk? Use "they're" in place of "their" a few times in writing and wait to see who corrects you. For whatever reason, misuse of the humble apostrophe attracts more disdain, and more nitpicking, than most of the other marks we've talked about here. But even if they're jerks (correct usage, BTW), those friends who chime in to correct a misplaced apostrophe are rarely wrong. That's because the rules are so simple!

- Use an apostrophe **before** an "s" to show that somebody or something has possession of something else.

  James's haircut looks like it was cut with a busted weed whacker instead of the stylist's scissors.

- If the owner's name or description already ends in "s" because it's plural (more than one), put the apostrophe **after** the "s" and don't add another. If it ends in an "s" but is singular, follow the first rule above.

  Many colleges' admissions offices are very small, with just a few people going through thousands of students' applications.

- Pronouns made possessive in the same way don't take an apostrophe, except for "one's."

me ⇨ my	her ⇨ her	it ⇨ its
you ⇨ your	we ⇨ our	one ⇨ one's
him ⇨ his	they ⇨ their	

- Contractions use apostrophes.

it + is ⇨ it's	should + have ⇨ should've
they + are ⇨ they're	could + not ⇨ couldn't
you + are ⇨ you're	

Get those last two rules down, and you'll score mega-points on the ACT: most apostrophe trouble stems from confusion between pronouns used for possessives and in contractions. Pronoun contractions get the apostrophes; pronoun possessives don't! It can help to remember that in contractions, apostrophes show where the missing letters are. In other words, if you can plug the two original words back into the sentence and it makes sense, the apostrophe is most likely used correctly.

Practice Questions: Punctuation

There's one necessary punctuation mark missing from each sentence below. Add the missing punctuation.

1 My fathers attempt at grocery shopping for the two of us was laughable.

2 He brought home two loaves of bread but not a single lunchmeat or spread although we had nothing at home to eat with the bread.

3 I hate bananas even so, he bought nearly a dozen of them.

4 Even if he were planning on making banana bread we'd have extra, and there were no such plans.

5 The rest speaks for itself a package of cookies, prune juice, toothpaste we didn't need, and a nearly rotten cantaloupe.

Check your answers below.

Answers

1 Apostrophe: My father's attempt at grocery shopping for the two of us was laughable.

2 Comma: He brought home two loaves of bread but not a single lunchmeat or spread, although we had nothing at home to eat with the bread.

3 Semicolon: I hate bananas; even so, he bought nearly a dozen of them.

4 Comma: Even if he were planning on making banana bread, we'd have extra, and there were no such plans.

5 Colon: The rest speaks for itself: a package of cookies, prune juice, toothpaste we didn't need, and a nearly rotten cantaloupe.

Parts of Speech

This part of the Usage and Mechanics category is a little less well defined than the ACT's punctuation category. We're using "parts of speech" as an umbrella term, a bucket where we can throw some of the miscellany that has to do with verbs, subject-verb agreement, and other various problems. There are many ways a sentence can be well-structured, with all the right punctuation, but still be the least correct.

Yes, that was on purpose, so you can see what we're saying. "The least correct" doesn't make sense, does it? Because there's no real comparison in that sentence, there's no reason to use the superlative form. We should have said just "incorrect." Many "parts of speech" questions on the ACT hinge on similar mistakes: single words or short phrases that don't have quite the right form, needing only a small tweak in tense, number, or case to be corrected.

When you see an underlined portion of an ACT English passage, you should immediately go through a quick list of how that punctuation mark or part of speech can be used incorrectly. For each part of speech, there are a few ways it might be used incorrectly. If you see a pronoun underlined, look for the ways pronouns can be used incorrectly. It's the same with verbs, adverbs, etc.

Verbs

Subject-Verb Agreement

When working on any type of ACT English question, keep an eye out for verbs that are underlined. Of course, part of the reason for that is that the ACT tests verb tenses, but there's also the matter of subject-verb agreement.

What does subject-verb agreement mean?
Let's look at some simple examples. Which is correct?

> *Rihanna win hot-dog eating competitions all the time.*

> *Rihanna wins hot-dog eating competitions all the time.*

The verb "win" has to match up with the subject of the sentence, Rihanna, which means it has to have an "s" at the end, like in the second sentence. Even if you think these sentences sound fine in conversation without the "s," they're not standard American English; you can't write them like that—at least not on the ACT.

If the subject is singular (*he, it, the horse, white-pepper ice cream*), then it needs a singular verb (*does, was, is prancing, has congealed*).

If the subject is plural (*they, we, Rick and Morty*), then it needs a plural verb (*do, are speeding, have mutated*).

Of course, there's a caveat here: even though the word "I" is singular, and the word "you" can be singular, those words don't use the typical singular verb forms ("has been," "does," "sparkles"). Instead, we have "I/you **have been**," "I/you **do**," and "I/you **sparkle**." But we don't need to memorize which pronouns take which verb forms. Just make sure you match them up the way that sounds the most correct. But that may be trickier than it sounds, because the ACT doesn't necessarily give you such simple sentences to work with …

Subjects separated from their verbs

On more complicated questions, the verb may not be next to its subject like it is in the examples above. Instead, it might be separated by a pretty big chunk of text.

> *The results of the contest, hotly debated by the members of the audience, was announced soon after the first contestant became sick.*

If you didn't notice the problem there, take a look at the verb "was announced." Can you find the subject that it refers to? It's all the way back at the beginning of the sentence.

Since that subject—"the results"—is plural, the verb should be "were announced."

Neither, either, everyone, everything, and each are singular

Some nouns aren't so clear in number. "Everything" sounds like a lot, right? So it should be plural, right? Well, no.

All of the words listed above refer to the individual pieces of a group. The verbs that get paired with them will also be singular to reflect that.

> ⊗ *Neither of us think that competitive eating is a good career choice for pop singers.*
>
> ⊘ *Neither of us **thinks** …*
>
> ⊗ *Everyone who watched the show were simultaneously entranced and disgusted.*
>
> ⊘ *Everyone who watched the show **was** …*

These can be especially tricky, so keep an eye out.

"My team is" or "my team are"?

Now we're getting to the good stuff! This is a very subtle grammar point, and to be fair, it's unlikely you'll ever see it on an ACT. But let's be safe, just in case. Generally, when we have a noun that refers to a *group* of people, like "team," "staff," or "jury," sometimes the verb should be singular, and sometimes it should be plural. It depends on the meaning of the sentence.

> *The restaurant's staff **is** small, considering how popular the restaurant is.*
>
> *The restaurant's staff **are** small, with nobody weighing over 110 pounds.*

In that first example, we're talking about the group as a whole. There's no need to think of the individual staff members. We use the singular there because it's referring to a small group, not small people. Words for groups take the singular verb most of the time.

Occasionally, we want to talk about all the individuals within the group, *as individuals.* In that case, we're really talking about many people, not the group as its own entity. In the above example, because there are many staff members who are small, we use the plural "*are*" to refer to them.

Automatically check for matches

Every time you see a verb whose subject isn't immediately obvious, go back and find that verb in the sentence. Do it again and again until it's second nature. It should only take a fraction of a second by the time you're doing it on your official ACT.

Verb Tenses

The basics: verb tenses on the ACT

Are you a native English speaker? If you are, then forget the ACT for a moment and just be grateful that you don't have to learn English, because it's riddled with some really complicated verb patterns. Whereas some languages are happy enough to live simpler lives and only use a few verb patterns to indicate the past, present, and future, English has flashy tastes and likes to overindulge. Take, for example, this sentence:

That stadium will have been being built for three years come May.

There are five words in that verb construction. *Five.* It's like a gaudy necklace of helping verbs. And they're mostly just there to show when the main verb ("built") happens. Happened. Has happened. Uh … you get the idea.

The good news is that you don't need to know the names or explanations of English tenses for the ACT. And there's no bad news! Instead, there's actually some more good news.

You already know which tenses are right in ACT English.

To be fair, that's only really true if you are a native speaker. If you're not, then we won't lie: you do have an extra obstacle to overcome.

But the point is that for native English speakers, the different times that different tenses signify are already hard-wired into your thought patterns. All you have to do on the ACT is to make sure that the times given in the sentence are consistent and logical. Any time you see a verb underlined on the English section, you should check that the given tense feels natural with the time period(s) that the rest of the sentence presents.

For example, do you smell anything fishy in the following sentence?

Ernest Hemingway's short stories, including the favorite "Indian Camp," continue to be highly influential pieces of fiction despite the fact that they have been written over 50 years ago.

If you do, then you might be onto something. It might be rotten.

The time period "over 50 years ago" sounds pretty strange when put next to "have been written." You can train your ear to hear this to answer the question quickly, but you can also think it through logically: "have been written" suggests that they are still being written, while "over 50 years ago" tells us that they aren't still being written. This is just another reason that, when you see a verb underlined, think twice about the time period it refers to.

Similarly, if there's a sequence of events, make sure their tenses put them in the right logical order. *"Having just been swimming, Maria smelled like chlorine"* makes much more sense than *"Having just been swimming, Maria had smelled like chlorine."*

The "chlorine" regularly used in most swimming pools is actually sodium hypochlorite, because chlorine itself, the standard ingredient of toxic mustard gas, would react pretty badly with human skin and hair!

Trusting Your Ear

Practice reading aloud the sentences on the ACT English Test. No, you can't actually read them aloud on test day (that might get you removed from the test center for disturbing the peace), but you can move your lips and pronounce each word. That can help your inner "ear" catch errors that just "sound wrong"—errors that your brain might otherwise miss or automatically correct for you. Don't worry about looking silly! Everyone's eyes will be on their own tests!

The Perfect Tenses

Before we get into a definition of "perfect," let's look at a couple of quick sentences:

Nic Cage didn't see The Wicker Man.

Nic Cage hasn't seen The Wicker Man.

Nic Cage hadn't seen The Wicker Man *until just last year.*

Now, think about the timeline each of those sentences describes. The first one is pretty simple: we're talking about the time when *The Wicker Man* was released (2006). It's clearly in the past, and we're treating it as if it's completely finished. It sounds as if he missed his chance and as if he'll never see the movie.

The second sentence is a bit more like something you'd actually say. Sure, Nic didn't subject himself to watching his movie right when it came out, but he could still if he wanted. He just hasn't done it *yet*. We're now talking about a time period that starts in the past and that runs right up to the present. This is what the "has/hasn't seen" form does: it compares some timespan in the past to the present. We're really talking about two time periods at once.

The third sentence is interesting, because it brings in a second time period from the past: "just last year." But the helping verb "hadn't" is doing the same thing that "hasn't" did in our second example, by comparing two time periods. We're now talking about all the time *before* last year when Nic didn't watch the movie, plus the specific time when he did watch the movie.

The second and third sentences are "perfect" tenses, made of [have] + [main verb]. That main verb has to be in a particular form, though. It's not "have did" but instead "have done." That form ("done," "eaten," "been," etc.) is called the "past participle," if you're interested in stuffy grammar terms. For most words, the past participle is actually the same as the past tense. "I walked" and "I have walked" are both correct. But English is crammed with irregulars, such as (shown as infinitive / past tense / past participle)

swim / swam / swum

ring / rang / rung

forget / forgot / forgotten

forgive / forgave / forgiven

lie / lay / lain

rise / rose / risen

swing / swung / swung

There are countless others, most of which you wouldn't think twice about. But some of them can be tricky to remember and it's not uncommon for people to make them up in everyday conversation (e.g., "I would've swang if I'd known he was going to keep throwing strikes"). Careful, though, because the ACT won't stand for that kind of nonsense.

To recap, when you see a perfect tense—a verb form using "have" before the main verb—check two things:

1. Does it make sense on the timeline? ("Nic Cage hadn't seen *The Wicker Man* until next year" doesn't make sense, because "next year" isn't in the past.)
2. Is the participle correct? ("Nic Cage hadn't saw *The Wicker Man* until last year" is incorrect because we need "seen," not "saw," to make the perfect tense.)

The Continuous Tenses

Once again, let's take a look at a couple of example sentences:

Blood is dripping from the ceiling of my room.

Blood drips from the ceiling of my room.

The first could be about a murder scene (not a pleasant image, but it's definitely memorable). The second is straight-up haunted-house territory. But here's the thing: why do the sentences have such different meanings?

"Is dripping" refers to something happening at a particular point in time. It was happening before that point, and it will continue to happen after. That's the present *continuous* form, because it's repeated or, well, continuous.

"Drips," on the other hand, is just a general statement. It doesn't have any specific length. It's just what the ceiling does as a rule. We call that the present *simple*.

If we took both sentences and put them in the past tense, we'd have a similar distinction:

Blood was dripping from the ceiling of my room.

Blood dripped from the ceiling of my room.

In the first sentence, we're describing a particular point in time when the blood was dripping. We can imagine a person in the room, watching the droplets form. In the second sentence, the event is totally (and thankfully) in the past. We're not concerned with what happened during it, at least grammatically, so we don't care if it was continuous or repeated. As with the present simple, this past simple is more general: it's not as focused on a moment within that time period in which repeated dripping took place.

These distinctions aren't always neat and tidy, though. There are some verbs that almost never become continuous, such as "love." It's not grammatically correct to say, "I'm loving Neil deGrasse Tyson," regardless of how you feel about him, even though it's (in a sense) happening now. It would be, "I love Neil deGrasse Tyson." And sometimes, when telling a story, we do use the simple present "drips" to describe a ceiling that's currently dripping.

So the important takeaway for the ACT isn't, "Use continuous when X and use simple when Y," because there would be too many cases when the rules didn't hold. Instead, think about what *sounds* right; in most cases your ear will lead you in the right direction. But in order for that to work, you need to look at the rest of the sentence—identify the time periods, using the other verbs for context. Mapping out the timeline can be really helpful for non-native speakers, too.

Tips for Verb Questions on the ACT

- **Find the subject.** The thing that does the verb has to match the verb itself. But be careful: sometimes that subject is far away from the verb!

- **Look for time periods in the sentence.** "Until last year," "when the phone rang," and "in 1940" can all indicate what form a verb somewhere else in the sentence should take.

- **Look for other verbs in the sentence and consider their relationship.** When in doubt, keep the verb tense consistent. On the other hand, if you have a more complex sentence, create a timeline. If you see "had sunk" in part of the sentence, the other verb is probably plain-ol' past tense to show the time comparison.

- **Don't complicate things.** Once you've looked at the subject and any other mentions of timing in the sentence, your ear will guide you. Trust it!

Adverbs

If you played Mad Libs as a kid, you might already know your parts of speech. But in case you didn't, let's make the distinction between adjectives and adverbs clear.

Adjective: Modifies a noun. "Big," "smelly," and "friendly" are adjectives.

⊘ *The big, smelly, friendly dog was named Killer.*

⊗ *The dog, Killer, greeted us big, smelly, and friendly.*

Adverb: Modifies a verb, adjective, or adverb. Some examples are "completely," "carefully," and "soon."

⊘ *Students say they'll do their homework completely, carefully, and soon.*

⊗ *Her homework was completely, carefully, and soon.*

How to Tell the Difference Between Adjectives and Adverbs

So how can we fail to spot the proper use of the adverb? Well, consider the following examples:

> Mary yelled to Tina, "Drive safe—it's wet out there."

> The new PC was the most clever designed computer the market had seen in years.

If you rely on your ear, you may think that both sentences are fine as is (they're not—both are incorrect). This brings us to our main point: when looking for an adverb in a sentence, see if there are any words modifying a verb (or another adverb).

In the first sentence above, the verb is "drive." The word that modifies "drive" is "safe." "Safe" is an adjective, and you cannot modify a verb with an adjective—you need an adverb. To make "safe" an adverb simply add "-ly": *Drive safely*.

For the second sentence, we need an adverb to describe how a computer is designed. "Clever" is an adjective. So by adding "-ly," we get an adverb: *the most cleverly designed computer.*

The easiest way to spot the difference between adjectives and adverbs is to look for the *-ly* construction. Adverbs usually end in *-ly*, and adjectives don't. But wait a minute … if you look back at our earlier examples, you'll see that's not always true. "Friendly" is an adjective; at the same time, "soon" is an adverb. That's why you should use *-ly* just as a rule of thumb. To be certain, you have to check what the words modify.

Once you identify the modified words, correcting the sentences becomes a whole lot easier.

Adjectives with Sensation Words

The ACT uses adverbs after sensation verbs to make the errors in modifier problems harder to spot. If we write, "She put her hand on mine because she felt badly," there's a grammatical problem with that sentence, however subtle.

In this case, "badly" doesn't describe the action of feeling. Instead, it describes her emotions. Or at least, it should. But if we want that to be the case, we have to change "badly" to "bad."

If you use the words "feel" and "badly" together, it actually describes the action of physically feeling something, i.e., touching.

So what does this mean for the ACT? If any of the words "smell," "feel," "taste," and "look" is followed by an adverb, think twice. Is the verb supposed to be an action or not?

> Allen looked quick. (Allen seemed fast.)

> Allen looked quickly. (Allen glanced at something.)

Subconscious Error Correction

Sometimes ACT English problems about parts of speech are hard to see not because of anything as tricky as sensation words, but rather because of our own reading habits. Because the difference between a correct and incorrect answer is often just two letters (*-ly*), we sometimes read the sentence wrong, substituting the correct word for the error.

You may know that "heavy loaded" is wrong, but if you read quickly, you might think it says "heavily loaded" and miss the problem.

This is why you should always read ACT English questions again if you don't see a problem the first time around. Go through systematically, checking each word for the problems it could create.

If, while going through piece by piece, you come to an adverb or adjective, link it to the word it should modify and check whether or not you want the *-ly*.

Pronouns

On the surface, pronouns are very simple. You start with a noun (like "shoe") and replace that with a pronoun later ("it") so you don't write the same word over and over. There are just a handful of rules:

1. If the original noun is singular, use a singular pronoun. ("Shoe" becomes "**it**.")
2. If the original noun is plural, use a plural pronoun. (The word "shoes" becomes "**they**" or "**them**.")
3. If it's the subject of the sentence, use the subject pronoun. ("The shoes were" becomes "**They** were.")
4. If it's the object in a sentence, use the object pronoun. ("Mary stole my shoes" becomes "Mary stole **them**.")

If you check the number and case of a pronoun that the ACT's testing, you're almost set. But there are a couple of tricks to watch for.

Ambiguous Pronouns

The ACT actually categorizes these as "style" questions (we'll talk about those later, when we get to "Rhetorical Skills"), but as long as we're on the topic of pronouns, we thought now would be the best time to cover them!

> *Samantha is less interested in her calculus homework than in her English reading, so she sometimes neglects it.*

Now, maybe you're thinking that "it" refers to Samantha's calculus work because she's less interested in it. That would make sense—we're more likely to neglect something we're less interested in, after all. But this isn't good enough for the ACT. In this sentence, we actually have two things that "it" could be referring to—calculus homework or English reading assignments—so we need to clarify what "it" is referring to. Here's one way to do it:

Because Samantha is more interested in her English reading, she sometimes neglects her calculus homework.

This way, we've avoided the pronouns entirely.

Otherwise, we could replace the pronoun with a different way of referring back to the calculus homework:

Samantha is less interested in her calculus homework than in her English reading, so she sometimes neglects the math assignments.

Because "the math assignments" clearly refers to calculus instead of English, we've done away with the problem.

Bottom line? Don't assume you know what word a pronoun's referring to on an ACT English question. Double-check to make sure that you've considered all possibilities!

My friend and I? My friend and me?

The stereotypical English teacher has a few favorite grammar rules, some of which aren't even real rules. "And I" is one of the best examples. Too often, English teachers correct "and me" to be "and I" without considering the phrase's placement in the sentence. And you know what? Sometimes, they're wrong.

There is, admittedly, plenty of truth in one rule touted by your eighth-grade English teacher: when you're listing other people as well as yourself, "I" or "me" should come last. Think of it as being polite and holding the door for the other names.

However, on the ACT, it's important that you get the "I" or "me" part right. They're not interchangeable, even though we often use them that way when we're talking. But the ACT wants us to show that we know what's correct. When the names are the subject (they're the main actors in the sentence), use "I." If they aren't (and are being acted *upon* by someone or something else)—a notable example being after prepositions—then use "me," the object form. If we always used "I" when making lists of people, we'd be wrong, well, a lot.

⊘ *My pinkie toe and I have been through some hard times.*

⊗ *The world is against my pinkie toe and I.*

⊗ *A polar bear ate my pinkie toe and I.*

That second example comes after a preposition (*against*) and should take the object form, *me*. "And I" can be wrong even without the preposition, however, as long as those two or more people or things are objects in the sentence, as in the third example above. The correct forms are

⊘ *The world is against my pinkie toe and me.*

⊘ *A polar bear ate my pinkie toe and me.*

Isaac Newton was the first to discover calculus when he was in his early twenties but initially kept it to himself. Newton later published his work at the encouragement of his friend, the astronomer Edmond Halley, who discovered Halley's comet.

75

By the same token, don't start a sentence with "… and me."

⊗ *My pinkie toe and me fought off a polar bear.*

⊘ *My pinkie toe and I fought off a polar bear.*

Just focus on whether or not the preposition is the subject of the sentence. If that distinction isn't clear for you, then take out the other player (e.g., "my pinkie toe") and see how it sounds. That's the quickest and best method to decide. Saying "A polar bear ate I" sounds good to approximately nobody, so don't write it—even if there's a pinkie toe that comes first.

And if it's still a bit unclear, then you can generally assume that *I* is more likely correct near the beginning of the sentence, while *me* is more common at the middle or end.

Practice Questions: Grammar

Do you know your present perfect from your past tense? Can you link pronouns to the nouns they refer to? Test your grammar chops by fixing the error in each sentence below!

1 Neither Maria nor her mother were fond of the house they ended up buying together, but it was the best they could afford.

2 Be careful: if you don't read the sentence slow enough, you're bound to miss the mistake.

3 Mr. DeWard was absolutely furious with Albert and I, even though we had apologized profusely for the prank.

4 Each time a needle dropped from the cactus, a small bird was swooping down to collect the material for its nest.

5 After you have beat the eggs, add a quarter cup of milk and stir well before pouring the mixture into the frying pan.

Check your answers below.

Answers

1 were fond ⇨ **was fond**. The two nouns in a "neither ... nor" construction are regarded separately, so we use a singular verb.

2 slow ⇨ **slowly**. "Read" is a verb, so we need an adverb to modify it. The adverb of "slow" is "slowly."

3 I ⇨ **me**. After the preposition "with," we need the object form "me." If you remove Albert from the story, the problem becomes very clear. It sounds wrong to say, "Mr. DeWard was furious with *I*." Albert being included doesn't change that.

4 was swooping ⇨ **swooped**. Even though the bird was swooping repeatedly, this verb has to make sense with the earlier part of the sentence, "each time a needle *dropped*." The "each" means that the verb "dropped" refers to a single past event (similar to how you would say "each muffin **is**," not "each muffin **are**"). We need the later verb, "swooped," to match that and refer to each instance of swooping, not the many repeated instances.

5 have beat ⇨ **have beaten**. The past participle of beat is "beaten," not "beat." (Although we sometimes use "have beat" or "got beat" in conversation, the ACT wouldn't accept that.)

Sentence Structure: A Bit Trickier . . .

Now that we've covered almost all the parts of a sentence, from the clause to the comma, from the verb to the adverb, we can talk a bit more about how *logic* comes into the picture. Grammar isn't just a set of rules some random person made up centuries ago; a lot of grammar is about what makes sense (and what makes a sentence make sense)! But questions that hinge on these kinds of rules can be a bit tough, because they're often very subtle.

We'll start back in on sentence structure with a topic we touched on earlier in this chapter: conjunctions, or words that combine clauses. Here's a quick refresher: coordinating conjunctions—the FANBOYS—connect two independent clauses, while subordinating conjunctions (like "because") make one clause dependent, so it can't stand alone.

The logic of conjunctions

Often, the ACT will check to make sure you understand the underlying message a sentence is trying to convey and that you can pick the conjunction that makes it make sense.

Take a look at this example:

*The first few months have been relatively dry **because/although** weather forecasters predicted a rainy year.*

Should it be "because" or "although"?

"Because" doesn't quite make sense, because if forecasters predicted a rainy year, we wouldn't expect the first few months to be relatively dry. And they definitely aren't dry *because* forecasters said they would be rainy.

"Although" correctly sets up the contradiction between the two parts of the sentence. And that's exactly what the sentence is trying to convey: even though forecasters said it would be rainy, it's actually been dry so far. It can get a little more complicated on the ACT, but the important thing when it comes to conjunctions is that you're on the lookout—not only for places to apply grammar rules, but also for places where the sentence can make more sense.

Misplaced modifiers

Caused by a fatal error in design, the airship SS Doanblowup *met its tragic end in 1915 in a sudden explosion.*

If you see a sentence like this on the ACT English Test, you definitely want to make a correction. If you haven't spotted what the problem is already, take a look at the first part of the sentence, up until "airship." Then, ask yourself: what exactly was "caused by a fatal error." Was it the airship? No.

Everything that comes before that first comma is supposed to modify, or give details about, one specific noun in the main sentence. If we go back and try to find that noun, we'll come to the word "explosion," which makes the most sense (after all, a fatal error would likely cause something bad to happen). Those two pieces—the noun and the modifier—have to be placed near each other in the sentence for the reader to make sense of it easily. As it is now, the sentence is incorrect, and the ACT English section is going to test whether you know that.

Any time you see an introduction like that set off by a comma, check to see if it should modify one specific noun in the sentence. Then check whether that noun comes soon after the comma. If it doesn't, and there's another noun there instead, then you've found an error.

How to Fix the Problem

There are two ways to fix this. First, we can move the modifier.

> *The airship SS* Doanblowup *met its tragic end in 1915 in a sudden explosion caused by a fatal error in design.*

The other option is to rearrange the main part of the sentence (the independent clause).

> *Caused by a fatal error in design, a sudden explosion brought the airship SS* Doanblowup *to its tragic end in 1915.*

In both cases, that modifier now falls next to the noun it's meant to give details about, and that noun is the explosion.

Modifiers Everywhere!

Introductory phrases are prone to setting up misplaced modifiers, but the truth is that these logic slips can fall anywhere in a sentence.

> *The airship SS* Doanblowup *met its tragic end in a sudden explosion in 1915, which was caused by a fatal error in design.*

This is really no different than our first airship example in terms of the problem with the sentence. What was caused by the fatal error? It definitely wasn't 1915. We need to bring "which was ..." next to the noun that it describes. In order to do that, we may need to move "in 1915" to somewhere else in the sentence—and that's okay! As long as all the modifiers end up as close as possible to the things they modify, we're free to do as much rearranging as we need.

Parallelism

In this section, we're going to take a look at errors in parallel structure, how to find them, and examine how to correct them on the ACT.

Did you catch the mistake we made in the above sentence?

If you did, gold star to you. If you didn't, that's completely okay. It's a subtle mistake, but it'll become way more obvious once you know what to look for. So let's get to work!

The real airship *LZ 129 Hindenburg*, a blimp filled with flammable hydrogen gas, exploded in 1937 New Jersey, killing 36 people. The blimp was named for German president Paul von Hindenburg, the man who made the unfortunate choice of appointing Adolf Hitler as chancellor of Germany in 1933.

Lists of Items

When two or more items are given equal weight in a sentence, they should be written as similarly as possible. The simplest example of this is a list of items:

For breakfast, I like to eat cereal, fruit, and I also like yogurt.

"Yogurt" is getting a little extra love there with that "I also like," and grammatically speaking, that's a no-no.

To correct the parallel structure, we need to get rid of the stuff in front of "yogurt" so we have a list of three nouns, and only nouns:

For breakfast, I like to eat cereal, fruit, and ~~I also like~~ yogurt.

Lists in a sentence don't necessarily have to be a group of nouns; they can be verb phrases, for example.

⊗ *To escape the wicked witch, the boy ran out of the gingerbread house, rolled down the hill, and he jumped across a river of fire.*

⊘ *To escape the wicked witch, the boy ran out of the gingerbread house, rolled down the hill, and ~~he~~ jumped across a river of fire.*

So let's go back to the sentence we started with:

In this section, we're going to take a look at errors in parallel structure, how to find them, and examine how to correct them on the ACT.

See that extra verb in the third part? All of the items in the list should go with our original verb phrase, "take a look …" We're "taking a look" at (1) errors, (2) how to find them, and (3) how to correct them.

Here's the smoothed-out version, using only noun phrases in the list:

In this section, we're going to take a look at errors in parallel structure, how to find them, and how to correct them on the ACT.

Parallel Comparisons

Lists are easy enough to spot once you get the hang of it. Comparisons can be trickier; we tend to pass them by without even seeing them. But we need to watch for them for exactly the same reason we watch for lists! Two things being compared need to be logically—and grammatically—equivalent.

Take a look at the following sentence.

Danny's test scores weren't as good as Bryan.

In this case, the sentence's meaning is pretty clear, so you might not give it a second thought if somebody said this to you. But on the ACT English Test, you need to have eagle eyes. A closer look at the sentence reveals that the parallel structure is faulty. We should actually be comparing Danny's test scores to Bryan's *test scores*, not to Bryan, the person:

Danny's test scores weren't as good as Bryan's test scores.

So when you see comparisons on the test, make sure they are comparing apples to apples and not apples to oranges.

Prepositional Phrases

Sometimes, even trickier parallel-structure questions have to do with prepositional phrases.

Take a look at the following sentence:

I wasn't informed or interested in the after party.

You may have a feeling something's off here but may not be sure what. Well, let's take out "or interested" for a moment. Then we just have "I wasn't informed in the after party," which doesn't make sense. We need a preposition to go with "informed" that works with that verb and sets up a parallel structure with "interested in."

Here's one solution:

I wasn't informed of or interested in the after party.

So when it comes to parallelism on the ACT English Test, make sure you watch out for three specific scenarios:

1. Lists of items that are supposed to be weighed equally (nouns, verb phrases, etc.). Remember that a "list" can just be two items!
2. Comparisons of two or more items. Make sure that, grammatically speaking, the lists are comparing the same type of thing.
3. Multiple prepositional phrases in the same sentence. Take care that a preposition essential to understanding the meaning (and maintaining elegant parallel structure) isn't dropped!

Practice Questions: Sentence Structure: A Bit Trickier . . .

Four out of the five sentences below have errors. Find the four errors and explain why they are wrong. (Since there are multiple ways to correct each error, there's no need to make the correction yourself.)

1 Having lost his grip on the cliff's edge, Ryan's screams echoed across the canyon while he plummeted to the bottom.

2 Only five years earlier, Darryl had been working as a barista while in college for minimum wage.

3 We drove through the night on Sunday, despite the rain, the sleet, and the hellish winds, even if we were exhausted from our hike.

4 Jada was clearly bright, but her sister Jasmine was an even better student, having skipped two grades and finished high school at 16 years old.

5 Though not nearly as much of an eccentric as many of his historical peers, Einstein did have a few personal quirks, including a great disdain for socks, which he never wore, and he slept for nearly 10 hours each day.

Check your answers below.

Answers

1 **Misplaced modifier.** The phrase before the first comma all refers to Ryan, not his screams, but the subject of that independent clause is the screams (they're what echoed—not Ryan).

2 **Misplaced modifier.** "[F]or minimum wage" describes how Darryl worked, but as is, the phrase is placed next to "in college." That makes it sounds like he's "in college for minimum wage," which definitely isn't the case! We need to move the "for" phrase closer to its verb.

3 **Misused conjunction.** The phrase "even if" should set up a *possibility*, not a fact. We could talk about what we'll do tomorrow "even if we are exhausted," but not about what we did yesterday. The conjunction the author wanted was likely "even though" or "although."

4 **Correct!** The comparison between Jada and Jasmine might have tricked you, but since we didn't include the "than . . ." part of the comparison, there's no room for a parallelism error there. "Having *skipped* . . . and *finished*" is also parallel as is.

5 **Parallelism error.** The two examples of Einstein's quirks following "including" are in different forms: "a disdain" is a noun, but "he slept" is a full clause. We could fix this by changing "he slept" to "sleeping," which can work as a noun and be parallel to "disdain."

Rhetorical Skills Questions

Let's do a little thought experiment. Imagine you have a passage from an ACT English Test, but you cut off the side of the paper that has all the questions. Then you go through the passage and correct all the grammar errors; you add commas, change pronouns, and move misplaced modifiers—all that good stuff. What's left? Is it an A+ essay?

By now, you've probably gathered that the answer is "no." The essay you'd be left with would have weird repetitive sentences, sudden breaks from formal to informal tones, and maybe even paragraphs that seem totally irrelevant. Even when it follows all the rules, writing can still be, well, *bad*. So let's tape those questions back on to the page, because they're going to point out exactly where the writer went wrong—be it a quick style faux pas, a set of poorly organized sentences, or a giant flop of a concluding paragraph.

Strategy Questions

Strategy questions are all about the choices a writer makes in order to communicate the main ideas clearly and effectively. That means that, on the ACT, you have two jobs, in a way: understand what the author wrote and understand what the author wanted to say. The gap between them isn't going to be all that wide; you don't have to be a mind reader, but you do have to be skeptical of everything you're reading. The most common type of strategy questions asks you to determine the effect of adding, revising, or deleting a phrase or sentence. Question the purpose of every detail, whether it's already in the text or being added to it.

Let's start with a couple examples. There are two excerpts from passages below (real ACT English texts are much longer, of course), each with a common type of strategy question to illustrate what we're facing:

The following winter, a blizzard shut down banks in the city for days, and ATM usage suddenly increased by 20 percent. This blizzard also launched Citibank's long-running "The Citi Never Sleeps" campaign, <u>with posters and billboards showing customers trudging through snow drifts to get to Citibank ATMs</u>. After Citibank's success, other banks followed suit, and ATMs popped up in every major city in the world.

1. If the writer were to delete the underlined portion, deleting the comma and ending the sentence with a period, the paragraph would primarily lose:

   A. an explanation of why so many people used ATMs during the blizzard.

   B. descriptive detail about the imagery of the advertising campaign.

   C. a restatement of an idea expressed earlier in the paragraph.

   D. an explanation of why ATMs became necessary in the late 1970s.

What made Angelina and Sarah unique and defined within abolitionist circles was neither their oratorical and literary talents nor their energetic commitment to the causes of racial and gender equality. Rather, it was their firsthand experience with the institution of slavery and its negative effect on slaves. [2] Abolitionists such as William Lloyd Garrison, editor of *The Liberator*, and Theodore Weld, who Angelina married in 1838, could give stirring speeches about the need to abolish slavery. However, they could not testify from personal knowledge to either its impact on African Americans or on their masters.

2 At this point in the text, the writer wishes to add the following sentence:

> The Liberator *was founded in 1831 and was published in Massachusetts.*

Should the writer make this addition here?

F. Yes, because it gives the reader specific information regarding *The Liberator*.

G. Yes, because it helps the reader understand why Garrison could not speak about slavery from personal knowledge.

H. No, because the reader can infer the date *The Liberator* was founded from the paragraph.

J. No, because it distracts the reader from the focus of the paragraph.

We'll dive into how to get the answers to these kinds of questions in just a moment, but if you've got a burning desire now to find out whether you were right, we won't torment you. The answer to the second example is **J**, and the first example is discussed below.

Now, let's talk strategy. Your strategy for the strategy questions, that is.

How to approach ACT English strategy questions

1. **Read well before and after the referenced portion.** ACT English questions are often best answered as you go through the passage. Read through the passage until you get to a question, answer it, and keep moving—pretty simple. But with strategy questions, you need to be very careful that you're reading well before and after the underlined or excerpted portion. Sometimes, what comes after the section in question will give you the clues you need to answer the question correctly. And if a question specifically says, "In the context of the passage as a whole," be extra careful that you're actually considering the entirety of the passage!

2. **Focus on whether or not an underlined portion is on topic.** Most of the answers to the strategy questions on the ACT will revolve around adding sentences that help clarify a point or support the development of an important point and deleting those that don't. If a paragraph is missing an introductory or concluding sentence,

the test may be looking for you to add one. If it's missing a connection between ideas or a supporting detail that would help a reader understand the content, the test will be looking for you to add that as well. If there's information that's off-topic or unnecessary, the test will be looking for you to get rid of that excess.

3. **For "Yes/No Because" questions, make eliminations based on the rationales in the answer choices first.** Strategy questions—especially those that ask whether an author should add, remove, or adjust a specific sentence—often have answer choices in a predictable pattern:

   A. Yes, because ...
   B. Yes, because ...
   C. No, because ...
   D. No, because ...

On these questions, ignore the "yes" or "no" at first and just focus on the "because ..." parts of the answers. You can eliminate reasons that give false info without worrying about what the author should do. So, for example, let's look at the above question on *The Liberator* again:

What made Angelina and Sarah unique and defined within abolitionist circles was neither their oratorical and literary talents nor their energetic commitment to the causes of racial and gender equality. Rather, it was their firsthand experience with the institution of slavery and its negative effect on slaves. [2] Abolitionists such as William Lloyd Garrison, editor of *The Liberator*, and Theodore Weld, who Angelina married in 1838, could give stirring speeches about the need to abolish slavery. However, they could not testify from personal knowledge to either its impact on African Americans or on their masters.

2 At this point in the text, the writer wishes to add the following sentence:

> The Liberator *was founded in 1831 and was published in Massachusetts.*

Should the writer make this addition here?

F. Yes, because it gives the reader specific information regarding *The Liberator.*

G. Yes, because it helps the reader understand why Garrison could not speak about slavery from personal knowledge.

H. No, because the reader can infer the date *The Liberator* was founded from the paragraph.

J. No, because it distracts the reader from the focus of the paragraph.

Without even reading the passage, we can eliminate answer choice G, because the sentence the question is asking about says nothing about Garrison or why he couldn't speak about slavery from personal knowledge, so it cannot possibly be the answer.

After reading the whole paragraph, we can eliminate answer choice H, because there's no reference to when *The Liberator* was founded elsewhere in this paragraph.

So now we're down to F and J, and need to apply the principles in point 2 above and decide whether or not the proposed sentence is on topic and helps develop the paragraph. Since this paragraph is focused on two women named Angela and Sarah and their contributions to the abolitionist movement, it's not crucial to this paragraph that we give a ton of specific info about *The Liberator*. It's simply mentioned in passing, and so our answer is **J**.

4. **Don't overthink the question.** If a question asks you what a sentence will lose or gain by deleting or adding certain information, think to yourself, "This sentence will lose/gain exactly the content in the underlined phrase." That means on our first example above, we should think to ourselves, "This sentence will lose the fact that posters and billboards showed customers trudging through snow drifts to get to Citibank ATMs." That alone is not an explanation, a summary, or an argument of any kind, as the wrong answers suggest; it's only descriptive imagery. That means the answer is **B**: the paragraph would lose specific descriptive detail of the campaign (what's on the posters and billboards). Be careful not to overthink a question and end up rationalizing why one of the other answer choices could be true. If you think an image is actually serving as an explanation, pin down concretely why it's an explanation before you choose an answer choice that says so. Be very literal.

5. **Summarize paragraphs for the big picture.** This is an important variation on point 2 above. Since relevance is key for strategy questions, summarizing helps us get an overarching understanding of what the author is trying to say. When you're reading a single sentence or paragraph, it's easy to get lost in the details. By zooming out a bit to look at the main ideas of whole paragraphs, you can get a more accurate picture of the main point of the passage. That, in turn, can make it clear if a particular thought needs to be added, removed, or adjusted to fit within the big picture.

Once you get the hang of them, strategy questions can start to seem repetitive, because the ACT repeats the same patterns over and over. That's great news for us, because we can figure out the correct answers based on those patterns. Knowing what to look for is more than half the battle!

Organization Questions

ACT English passages are written by organization freaks (your English teacher would love them). If the passages don't have clear topic sentences, they want one. If sentences aren't in chronological order, they flip out. When you keep their quirks and preferences in mind, though, those organization freaks will reward you with a massive boost to your score. So here are the most important things you need to know about organization questions on the ACT English section.

There are three particularly common types of organization questions:

1. Ordering sentences or paragraphs
2. Choosing the best introduction or conclusion
3. Choosing the best transition word or phrase

Ordering sentences or paragraphs

If a question asks you to reorder sentences or paragraphs to present the most "logical" order, you are looking for one of two things: (1) chronology or (2) coherence.

Chronology is pretty straightforward. If the passage is describing a famous person's life, starting with their childhood and ending with their death, then you want to make sure a paragraph about their college years doesn't appear at the end. Sometimes, chronology questions will be about putting seasons or other things with a clear order in sequence.

Coherence means that every sentence should follow logically from the previous one in terms of how it adds to the content.

Take a look at this challenging example:

[1] Many scholars believe that Thomas Kyd wrote a play about Hamlet a decade before Shakespeare's famous play. [2] Although Kyd's "Ur-Hamlet" is now lost, it is believed that it probably bore many similarities to Kyd's *The Spanish Tragedy* or rather that *The Spanish Tragedy* bore many similarities to it. [3] This is a revelation that surprises many fans who believe that *Hamlet* was solely a product of Shakespeare's imagination.

What is the most logical placement for sentence 2?

Explanation

This is a tricky question, and you need to look closely at it. The best way to tackle a question like this is to paraphrase the essence of each sentence in your head. Sentence 1 tells us Kyd wrote a play about Hamlet before Shakespeare. Sentence 2 tells us it bore many similarities to *The Spanish Tragedy*. Sentence 3 tells us that the fact that Kyd wrote a play about Hamlet surprises many Shakespeare aficionados.

Aha! There's the kicker. Take a look back at sentence 3: it starts with the word "this." But what does "this" refer to? It's the fact that Kyd wrote a play about Hamlet—it's not the stuff about *The Spanish Tragedy* (sentence 2) that surprises Shakespeare's fans. So that means sentence 3 should follow sentence 1. **And sentence 2 should be moved to after sentence 3.**

Choosing the best introduction or conclusion

In order to answer these types of organization questions correctly, it's important that you review the main idea of the paragraph and make sure you pick an option that best accomplishes two things:

1. Summarizes the main idea of the paragraph
2. Connects what comes before and after it

Be wary of answer choices that are too broad or too narrow: basically, this means anything that seems to encompass more than what the paragraph talks about or that only gives one specific detail.

Choosing the best transition

Let's jump right into an ACT example for this one. See if you already know the best transition word for the underlined portion of the following sentence.

As she got older, Katerina did not find ice skating as appealing as she once did. <u>On the other hand</u>, she cut back on her practice time and spent more time on other activities.

A. NO CHANGE
B. Therefore,
C. In fact,
D. Furthermore,

Explanation

On a question like this, we need to pick the transition that best communicates the relationship these sentences are trying to express. One way to handle this is to temporarily put a blank in the sentence where the transition is supposed to go, ignore the answer choices, and try to come up with your own connection: *Katerina did not find ice skating appealing. _____, she cut back on her practice time and spent more time on other activities.*

The connection between these two ideas is one of *cause and effect* (Katerina didn't like ice skating so much anymore, **so** she cut back on her training), so we need a cause-and-effect transition. "So," "as a result," or "consequently" would do that! Answer choice **B**, "Therefore," also fits the bill, and so that's the answer.

Style Questions

Style questions are a bit different from the Rhetorical Skills questions we've gone through so far because they can ask about relatively small-scale issues. An organization question about a single transition word requires you to think about the main ideas before and after it; in contrast, some style questions are really just about a single word. In a way, that makes them similar to many Usage and Mechanics questions. They're about the nitty-gritty of the writing itself, not floating high on the author's main ideas. But, as with all the other Rhetorical Skills questions, they're not about what's "right." Strictly speaking—they're about what's … well, stylish. Editorially speaking, that is. So your job in these questions is to help the writer out with his or her style. Not everyone can be as cool as you!

That all sounds a bit vague, so let's break it down into some more digestible bits. There are only a few types of style errors you'll be on the lookout for during your ACT English Test.

Style error #1: redundancy

If you don't know to look out for redundancy, these types of problems can slip right under your radar. But once you know to watch out for them, it's points galore!

For example, choose the clearest version of the following sentence.

I donate annually to the scholarship fund each year.

Annually, I donate to the scholarship fund each year.

I donate to the scholarship fund annually each year.

I donate to the scholarship fund annually.

Since "annually" means every year, we don't need to say "each year," too. That's kind of like putting sandals on over your sneakers. What's the point? The final sentence is the best version.

Redundancy questions can be hard to spot: make sure you read before and after the underlined portion in case there's something underlined that's redundant with a phrase that's *not* underlined. A **big clue** to look out for is an answer choice that says, "OMIT the underlined portion." That doesn't always mean that you should, but it is a big flashing signal that you very well might be dealing with a redundancy question and that omitting the underlined portion would fix it. The correct answer to a redundancy question is often OMIT.

Style error #2: tone

Sometimes, an underlined portion will be in the wrong style for the essay in which it appears. Maybe it's too formal for a personal narrative about the writer's first pet. Maybe it's too informal for a serious biographical study. Most of the tone errors on the test fall into the second category—too conversational for formal writing. When in doubt, choose the phrase you would include in a paper for your English teacher.

This question type isn't incredibly common on the ACT, but you should be aware of it. Here's an example:

Instead of presenting a rebuttal to my argument, she simply nodded and <u>went</u> that it sounded fine.

Some people use "went" in informal conversation describing a dialogue they had with others, but it's not standard written English. We need to replace the word with something along the lines of "muttered," "replied," or simply "said."

Style error #3: vague phrases

Quite often on the ACT, you'll be asked to pick the phrase that best illustrates a certain situation. In this case, you're always looking for the most specific, vividly detailed response. Take a look at the following ACT example:

> The weather forecast prepared us for a deluge of rain; instead, we emerged from our vacation <u>tired of</u> sunshine.
>
> Which choice most effectively uses ironic imagery to emphasize that the weather was the opposite of what was expected?
>
> F. NO CHANGE
> G. satisfied with the
> H. having seen plenty of
> J. saturated with

Because we're looking for "ironic imagery," our best and most vivid descriptor is answer choice **J**, "saturated with." You can't literally be saturated with sunshine, but that's what makes it ironic. And most importantly, it's the most vivid expression of the bunch.

Style error #4: wordiness and awkward expressions

One of the most common types of style questions asks students to choose the clearest version of a phrase. Sometimes these questions can be easy: three of the answer choices are noticeably confusing or awkward. At other times, they can be quite tricky because, again, this is a matter of trusting your ear rather than finding specific grammatical errors.

Here's an ACT test example:

> No one meteorological model <u>has the quality of being able to fully account for</u> the sweltering summers that have brought nearly 50 consecutive days of triple-digit highs to some parts of the country.
>
> A. NO CHANGE
> B. is able to be accountable to
> C. can fully account for
> D. has demonstrated the ability to account fully for

Explanation

We're looking for a phrase that uses as few words as possible, avoids the passive voice (if possible), and makes logical and grammatical sense. When making a tough choice between two options, just choose the shorter answer choice. But **be careful**. Just because an answer choice uses fewer words, that doesn't mean that there isn't an error in it. Avoid the temptation to always choose the shortest phrase; first, check it thoroughly for grammar mistakes. But, as in this case, sometimes there's no error in that shortest option: the answer is **C**.

Putting It All Together

ACT English isn't a straightforward test. There are many different types of questions, and the skills they test aren't always closely related, even if they all fall under that wide umbrella of English writing skills. But that doesn't mean it isn't systematic! For every question type, and for every topic, there are only a handful of ways the test-makers will cook up wrong answers. It takes time and practice to get familiar with every question type on every topic, but with experience and patience, you'll start anticipating what will be in the answer choices—as well as what the right answer will be.

In the next section, you'll get a chance to put your skills to the test. As you go through these sample questions, think about not only what the answer is but also how you would categorize the question. What topic or skill is the test-maker quizzing you on? And, based on everything you've read so far, what types of errors might you expect in the wrong answers?

ACT English Practice Questions

In the passages that follow, certain words and phrases are underlined and numbered. In the right-hand column, you will find alternatives for the underlined part. In most cases, you are to choose the one that best expresses the idea, makes the statement appropriate for standard written English, or is worded most consistently with the style and tone of the passage as a whole. If you think the original version is best, choose "NO CHANGE." In some cases, you will find in the right-hand column a question about the underlined part. You are to choose the best answer to the question.

You will also find questions about a section of the passage or about the passage as a whole. These questions do not refer to an underlined portion of the passage but rather are identified by a number or numbers in a box.

For each question, choose the alternative you consider best and fill in the corresponding oval on your answer document. Read each passage through once before you begin to answer the questions that accompany it. For many of the questions, you must read several sentences beyond the question to determine the answer. Be sure that you have read far enough ahead each time you choose an alternative.

PASSAGE 1

The Smile in Portraiture

[1]

Today when someone points a camera at us, we smile. This is the cultural and social reflex of our time, and such are our expectations of a picture portrait. In the long history of portraiture, however the open smile has been largely, pun aside, frowned upon. [A] A walk around any art gallery for a very long time will reveal that the image of the open smile was deeply unfashionable.

1 A. NO CHANGE
   B. portraiture however
   C. portraiture; however,
   D. portraiture, however,

2 The best place for the underlined portion would be:

   F. where it is now.
   G. after the word reveal.
   H. after the word unfashionable.
   J. after the word walk.

[2]

Such is the field upon which the mouth in portraiture has been debated: an ongoing conflict between the serious and the smirk. Such a subtle and complex facial expression may convey almost anything—piqued interest, contentment, mild embarrassment, or satisfaction.

3 A. NO CHANGE
   B. debated, ongoing
   C. debated. An ongoing
   D. debated, and an ongoing

4 F. NO CHANGE
   G. contentedness
   H. gratification
   J. DELETE the underlined portion.

The *Mona Lisa* was not widely known outside the art world until it was stolen in 1911. Vincenzo Peruggia stole the Italian masterpiece because he believed that it rightfully belonged in Italy, the country of its creator. Peruggia was eventually caught trying to sell the painting, and it was returned to the Louvre in 1914.

ACT English Test

[B] The most famous and enduring portrait in the world takes advantage of this very conflict. [C] So many words, likely in the millions, have been devoted to the *Mona Lisa* and her smirk—more generously known as her <u>"enigmatic smile"—that</u>[5] today it's difficult to write about her without sensing that we are at the back of a very long and noisy line <u>in which no one would ever want to wait.</u>[6]

[3]

Prior to the invention of the camera, people might expect that their portrait would only be recorded once, maybe twice, <u>in they're lifetime.</u>[8] [D] Nowadays, however, each of us <u>are recorded</u>[9]

5 **A.** NO CHANGE
   B. "enigmatic smile" that
   C. "enigmatic smile," that
   D. "enigmatic smile;" that

6 If you were to replace this underlined phrase with a phrase that most dramatically illustrates that a significant number of people have tried to write about the *Mona Lisa*, which would you choose?

   F. NO CHANGE
   G. that stretches all the way back to 16th-century Florence.
   H. in which many have tried and failed to wait.
   J. that many people have been in before.

7 Which of the following, if inserted at the beginning of paragraph 3, would provide the best transition from paragraph 2 to paragraph 3?

   A. The rise of open smiling in portraits may have originated with the development of the modern camera.
   B. Many people are concerned that cameras do not accurately reflect their range of emotions.
   C. The woman in the *Mona Lisa* was thought to be a prominent figure in Florence at the time.
   D. The camera allowed for the capture of many emotions, unlike the painting of the *Mona Lisa*.

8 **F.** NO CHANGE
   G. in their lifetimes
   H. in their lifetime
   J. in they're lifetimes

9 **A.** NO CHANGE
   B. is recorded
   C. was recorded
   D. would be recorded

across <u>hundreds or thousands, of images, and</u>₁₀ many of us are smiling broadly. Together, they represent us in all our moods and modes, so we no longer have to worry <u>about if we are being defined by one picture.</u>₁₁

[4]

This is exemplified in how prominent figures try to ensure that a number of photographs are available that capture the gamut of their emotional range, from troubled solemnity to enthusiastic joy. Royal families, <u>additionally,</u>₁₂ have been recorded either in carefree, knockabout <u>moments; or in</u>₁₃ stately, respectful poses. In the 21st century these people must be all things to all people, and the modern camera allows for these figureheads to connect with their populace to a much greater degree than they could in 16th-century Florence.

Adapted from Jeeves, Nicholas. "The Serious and the Smirk: The Smile in Portraiture." *The Public Domain Review*. 18 Sept. 2013. http://publicdomainreview.org/2013/09/18/the-serious-and-the-smirk-the-smile-in-portraiture.

10 F. NO CHANGE
   G. hundreds, or thousands of images, and
   H. hundreds, or thousands, of images and
   J. hundreds or thousands of images, and

11 A. NO CHANGE
   B. about one picture defining us.
   C. about having one picture define who we are.
   D. about having been defined by one picture.

12 F. NO CHANGE
   G. therefore
   H. for instance
   J. on the one hand

13 A. NO CHANGE
   B. moments or in
   C. moments, and in
   D. moments and in

14 Upon reviewing the essay, the author wishes to add the following true statement:

> *Painting a portrait was no easy matter and often took hours to complete in a single sitting.*

Where should the author make the addition?

   F. Point A in paragraph 1
   G. Point B in paragraph 2
   H. Point C in paragraph 2
   J. Point D in paragraph 3

15 Suppose the writer had intended to write an essay that explained the effect of the modern camera on how people represented themselves in portraits. Would this essay accomplish that goal?

   A. Yes, because it illustrates how the camera enabled people to be captured in multiple moods.
   B. Yes, because it describes how the *Mona Lisa* inspired people to smile more in their photos.
   C. No, because it does not describe how the camera was invented in early 16th-century Florence.
   D. No, because it does not explain how the camera affected people's poses while their picture was taken.

Imaging Snow Crystals

[1]

In 1885, at the age of 20, Wilson Alwyn Bentley, a farmer who would live all his life in the small town of Jericho in Vermont, gave the world its first ever photograph of a snowflake. Throughout the following winters, until his death in 1931, Bentley would go on to capture over 5,000 snowflakes—or, more correctly, snow crystals on film. Despite the fact that he rarely left Jericho, thousands of Americans knew him as "The Snowflake Man" or simply "Snowflake Bentley."

[2]

It started with a microscope his mother gave him at age 15 that opened the world of the small to young Bentley. Being a lover of winter, he made plans to use his microscope to view snowflakes. To Bentley's surprise, his father purchased a camera for his son, and combining it with his microscope, Bentley went on to make his first successful photomicrograph of a snow crystal in 1885, which ended up being pretty cool.

16 F. NO CHANGE
   G. first, ever photograph
   H. first initial photograph
   J. first photograph

17 A. NO CHANGE
   B. correctly, snow crystals—on film.
   C. correctly snow crystals, on film.
   D. correctly—snow crystals on film.

18 F. NO CHANGE
   G. Bentley being a lover of winter,
   H. Him, as a lover of winter,
   J. A lover of winter,

19 Which of the following choices would best indicate that the father bought a camera for Bentley a significant period of time after his mother bought him the microscope?

   A. NO CHANGE
   B. Eventually,
   C. Concurrently,
   D. Additionally,

20 F. NO CHANGE
   G. which looked really neat.
   H. and the micrograph had cool features.
   J. OMIT the underlined portion, ending the sentence with a period after "1885."

[1] <u>In addition to the development of this imaging routine,</u> Bentley also had to devise a protocol to capture a snow crystal and transport it with minimal damage to the camera's field of vision. [2] What he found worked best <u>was to capture, on a cool velvet-covered tray, the crystal.</u> [3] Taking care not to melt the crystal with his breath, he identified a suitable subject, lifted it onto a pre-cooled slide with a thin wood splint from his <u>mothers' broom, and</u> nudged it into place with a turkey feather. [4] The back-lit image was then focused using a system of strings and pulleys he devised <u>to accommodate his mittened hands.</u> [5] The slide was then carried into his photographic shed and placed under the microscope.

21 Which of the following would provide the best transition from paragraph 2 to paragraph 3?

   A. NO CHANGE
   B. While Bentley was grateful to his parents,
   C. In addition to obtaining the right equipment,
   D. Having experimented with snow crystals,

22 F. NO CHANGE
   G. was, to capture on a cool, velvet-covered tray, a crystal.
   H. was, on a cool velvet tray, to capture a crystal.
   J. was to capture a crystal on a cool, velvet-covered tray.

23 A. NO CHANGE
   B. mothers broom, and
   C. mother's broom, and,
   D. mother's broom, and

24 If the author were to delete the underlined portion, the paragraph would primarily lose:

   F. descriptive material that reminds the reader of the need for a cold environment.
   G. an unrelated detail that distracts from the focus of the paragraph.
   H. important information that describes the system of pulleys and strings.
   J. an indication that it was difficult to develop the crystal images.

25 For the sake of the logic and coherence of paragraph 3, sentence 5 should be placed:

   A. where it is now.
   B. after sentence 1.
   C. before sentence 3.
   D. after sentence 3.

GO >

[1] With 70–75 photographs per snowstorm and notes on the conditions <u>on</u> which they were collected, Bentley <u>accrued</u> a considerable understanding of snow. [2] In 1897, together with Professor George Perkins, a professor of geology at the University of Vermont, <u>he prepared</u> the first paper on snow crystals published in the May 1898 issue of *Appletons' Popular Science* entitled "A Study of Snow Crystals."

Adapted from Heidorn, Keith C. "The Snowflake Man of Vermont." *The Public Domain Review.* 14 Feb. 2011. https://publicdomainreview.org/2011/02/14/the-snowflake-man-of-vermont.

26 F. NO CHANGE
  G. inside
  H. under
  J. for

27 Which of the following alternatives to this underlined portion would NOT be acceptable?

  A. developed
  B. amassed
  C. increased
  D. acquired

28 F. NO CHANGE
  G. prepared
  H. he had been preparing
  J. he was prepared to publish

29 Which choice most effectively concludes the essay?

  A. The paper was a testament to a career initiated by a simple gift from a boy's mother.
  B. Perkins even agreed that the paper was an excellent feather in Bentley's cap.
  C. Both Perkins and Bentley worked day and night to get the paper finished.
  D. The paper was positively reviewed by critics, and Bentley's career finally began.

This question asks about the passage as a whole.

30 Suppose the writer had intended to write an essay about the history of the development of the photomicrograph. Would this essay fulfill that goal?

  F. Yes, because it discusses how one man published a research paper regarding snowflake imaging.
  G. Yes, because it describes how Bentley and Perkins contributed to the field of photomicrograph imaging.
  H. No, because it does not discuss how Bentley became interested in imaging snowflakes.
  J. No, because it only focuses on one person's contribution to the imaging process.

During the test, you will need to wait until instructed to turn the page. STOP

ACT English Answers and Explanations

Answer: D

1   Generally speaking, conjunctive adverbs such as "however" need to be set off with commas if used in the middle of the sentence. This comes from the even larger rule that we should set off unnecessary information with commas. Notice that you could remove "however," and the meaning of the sentence wouldn't be changed (even though it would lose a bit of connection to the previous sentence). Also notice that the word could have been placed at the beginning of the sentence ("However, in the long history …"). That's a good clue that this word is an add-on adverb, so to speak—a word that's not part of the main sentence structure—and that we can separate it with a pair of commas. Option A creates a comma splice because the first comma isn't paired with another to close the "extra" information. C is very tempting, because the semicolon does often come before a conjunctive adverb with a comma, but it uses the semicolon incorrectly because the part of the sentence before the semicolon cannot stand alone as a sentence. If a semicolon is tempting, check to see if it could be replaced by a period. If not, then we shouldn't use a semicolon, either. B, by not using commas at all, fails to offset the introductory phrase "in the long history …" from the main independent clause "the open smile …" The answer is **D**.

Answer: H

2   This is a great example of a question that's easiest to answer if you keep the author's overall purpose in mind. Answer choices F and J make some sense, but they don't match the meaning intended by the author. Why would you need to walk around the museum "for a very long time" to understand that smiling was unfashionable? That would imply the information is hard to find; it would fit better with the author's point if it were a short time. But that's not an option, so we need to check the other placements: G doesn't work since there's no logical time limit on how long the information would be "revealed" for. But H matches the author's overall meaning very well! Throughout much of history, smiling in portraits was unfashionable. Because it transitions well to the next paragraph, we can be confident that **H** is correct.

Answer: A

3   The phrase before the colon is an independent clause, which is good, because colons need to come after complete thoughts. The phrase following the colon is a noun phrase that explains what comes before the colon, so the punctuation here is correct as is. Answer B introduces awkward phrasing by removing the word "an." Answer C creates a sentence fragment: the phrase after the colon can't stand alone as a sentence. And for the same reason that it can't be a sentence on its own, the phrase after the colon can't be joined to the first clause as a compound sentence, so D is wrong. The answer is **A**.

4 There's nothing grammatically incorrect here, but we should always be on the lookout for a style error when the answer choices include "OMIT" or "DELETE." In this case, if we look carefully, we can see a redundancy problem: the list already contains the word "satisfaction," which is roughly synonymous with "contentment." Always remove redundancy. Gratification and contentedness are also very close in meaning to the original word, so we should be suspicious about them even before seeing the redundancy. The test-makers would not create a correct answer that has the same meaning as a wrong answer! If "contentment" were acceptable, then "contentedness" would be, too, and that's not possible for an ACT question. The answer is **J**.

Answer: **J**

5 As is often true for punctuation questions, looking at the sentence as a whole is key. This dash comes after a bit of extra information about Mona Lisa's smile. If we removed that phrase, starting instead with "more generously," the sentence would make perfect sense. Any time we have a phrase that adds extra information like this, the punctuation setting it off from the rest of the sentence should be paired—two commas, two dashes, or two parentheses. So the correct answer must include a dash, because the beginning of the parenthetical information was set off with a dash. B, C, and D all mix punctuation marks, so they're incorrect. The answer is **A**.

Answer: **A**

6 The question asks us to pick the choice that "most dramatically illustrates" the list of people. Pay careful attention to adjectives used in questions similar to this one! One of the answers will have a dramatic illustration. **G** presents the most specific detail and creates an image of a line of people extending back five centuries—clearly a long time and so a very long line—which fits. Answer choices F, H, and J all use far less descriptive wording, making them less dramatic.

Answer: **G**

7 We're looking for an appropriate introduction to paragraph 3, so first, we should check what the main idea of that paragraph is. There are only a couple of sentences here, and they set up a contrast between portraits before cameras and after cameras. Our introduction should mesh with that contrast in the rest of the paragraph. The answer is **A**, which introduces the invention of the camera and the change in portrait style that it caused. B fits with part of the paragraph, but it doesn't connect either to the following sentence or back to the main idea of the passage: the smile. C references the previous paragraph but not the paragraph it's supposed to introduce, providing unnecessary detail about the *Mona Lisa*. D has a flaw, because the passage does imply that there are many potential emotions captured in Mona Lisa's smile. The transition from "the painting of the *Mona Lisa*" to "the invention of the camera" in the next sentence is also awkward.

Answer: **A**

8 Any time there's a pronoun underlined, it helps to first look back at what the pronoun refers to. In this case, "they" refers to "people," with no ambiguity. And both words are plural, which is great, but we need a possessive pronoun before "lifetime" so the answer needs to be "their." When you see an apostrophe in a preposition, it's not acting as a possessive but instead making a contraction: "they're" is short

Answer: **G**

for "they are," which makes no sense here. That rules out F and J. Between G and H, the only difference is whether "lifetime" should be pluralized. Since we're talking about the plural "people," it makes sense to use the parallel plural, "lifetimes." The answer is **G**.

Answer: **B**

9 Because this underlined section is just a verb phrase, we should first check it against the subject of the sentence, then make sure the tense works with any other indications of time in the sentence or paragraph. Looking back for the subject, it's tempting to stop at "us." But that word is after a preposition ("of")—the real subject of this sentence is "each," and that's singular, as counterintuitive as that may be! Any time you see "each," "everybody," or "either," think twice about verb number—even if they sound plural, they are all singular. As for the tense, the sentence starts with "nowadays," so we need a verb in the present tense. C and D use the wrong tenses. The answer is **B**, which uses the singular form of the present tense of the verb "to be" ("is").

Answer: **J**

10 As the sentence is, "of images" seems to be a parenthetical—information that we can just take out of the sentence if we wanted. But doing that would leave us with "hundreds or thousands and many," with no idea what there are hundreds of. So F is wrong. Similarly, if we took the information between commas in G out, we would have "hundreds and many." That's the same problem as in F. Meanwhile, choice H actually makes a grammatically correct parenthetical, since removing "or thousands" would leave us with a correct sentence. But the FANBOYS conjunction "and" must be preceded by a comma, so H is incorrect. The answer is **J**, with no parenthetical and a comma placed correctly between the independent clauses linked with "and."

Answer: **B**

11 There are two red flags in this sentence as is: first, the construction "about if," which would be more natural as "whether," and second, the passive "we are being defined by one picture" instead of the active "one picture is defining us." If we spot either of those points, we can be fairly confident that the error is stylistic: remember that the ACT wants the clearest and most concise wording. The meanings of B, C, and D are similar, but B is the shortest, with no loss of meaning and no grammar problems. If you can say the same thing in fewer words on the ACT, do it! **B** is correct.

Answer: **H**

12 When we see a transition word underlined like this, we need to check how the surrounding sentences relate to each other. In this case, we have a sentence about "prominent figures" photographed in a full "emotional range," and then a sentence about "royal families" in "carefree, knockabout moments" or "respectful poses." The first sentence makes a general statement, and then the second gives a more concrete example. Choice F, "additionally," doesn't match that relationship; we need a word that shows the second sentence is an example of the earlier point. Choice **H** matches, while both G and J create incorrect relationships of other types (cause/effect and contrast, respectively).

13 The vast majority of the time, a semicolon joins two independent clauses—think of it as a milder version of a period. If we put a period here, we would have a sentence made up of only the words "Or in stately, respectful poses." That has neither a noun nor a verb, so it can't be a sentence. That means it can't follow this semicolon, either. So A is out. The word "and" isn't appropriate because the paired idiom here is "either … or." "Either this and that" would never be correct; both C and D are out. The answer is **B**.

Answer: **B**

14 The addition should be made at point **J** in paragraph 3, because at that point, the author is discussing how people would only have had one or two portraits painted in their lifetimes. The sentence about painted portraits being difficult and time-consuming helps to explain that point. Points F, G, and H are all placed awkwardly between sentences that should be closely connected. F is between two sentences about smiling in portraits, though the sentence we're adding has nothing to do with smiling. G is between two sentences about the complex emotions conveyed by smiles, and again, the new sentence isn't about smiling. H is between two sentences that refer to the *Mona Lisa* specifically, but the new sentence is about painted portraits generally and isn't at all connected to da Vinci's famous portrait.

Answer: **J**

15 Starting from the information after the "yes" or "no," we can quickly rule out a couple of options that give information that's unrelated to the question being asked or, even worse, information that's just plain wrong. B is wrong because the essay doesn't describe how the *Mona Lisa* inspired people. The *Mona Lisa* is only mentioned to illustrate the complex emotions a smile conveys. Besides that, the question is asking about "the effect of the modern camera," and the *Mona Lisa* is clearly not a camera. C is also factually incorrect—though you don't need to know that—and has a problem similar to B, because the time and place that the camera was invented isn't connected to the impact it has had on portraiture. D is much more tempting, because it would match the question we're asked, but it doesn't match the passage: the author explains how people posed differently with cameras, including "all our moods and modes" in both "stately, respectful poses" and "carefree, knockabout moments," in contrast to the unsmiling solemnity common in painted portraits. Choice **A** matches the passage for the same reason that D is incorrect: the camera allowed people to be captured in a wider range of moods.

Answer: **A**

16 The sentence as it stands isn't grammatically incorrect, but a glance down at the answer choices gives us a hint that there may be a style issue here, since choice H replaces "ever" with "initial" and J omits the word entirely. Any time deleting a word or phrase is an option, we need to ask, "Is it necessary?" In this case, it's not—"first photograph" conveys the exact same meaning in fewer words, and that's what the ACT prefers. **J** is correct. Choice H creates a redundancy, since "first" and "initial" are synonyms. Meanwhile, the comma added in choice G suggests that you could put the word "and" between "first" and "ever," but clearly "first and ever photograph" would be wrong, so that comma doesn't work either.

Answer: **J**

17 This is a great example of a punctuation question that requires you to look at the other punctuation in the sentence before the underlined section. Before the word "or," there's a dash that starts a parenthetical phrase. Remember that whatever we set off with dashes (or parentheses or commas) in a situation like this needs to be able to be lifted out of the sentence, and the sentence should still read fine. (Be careful here: there's a second parenthetical, "more correctly," inside a larger parenthetical. It helps to remove that for easier reading.) As is, the sentence would end with "over 5,000 snowflakes" if we removed the text after the dash, because there's no second dash to end the parenthetical. But the sentence shouldn't end there, because Bentley didn't capture the snowflakes—he photographed them. So A is wrong. What would logically follow "capture 5,000 snowflakes"? Scanning the rest of the sentence, we find the phrase "on film." That makes sense: Bentley captured the snowflakes on film. Everything in between is just an aside, providing more detail on "snowflakes." The only answer choice with a dash before "on" is **B**, the correct answer. C has the same problem as A, since there is no second dash. D places the second dash in an odd position: removing the text between the dashes in that version would leave us with "5,000 snowflakes snow crystals on film." That's no good.

18 The word "being," when underlined in an ACT English question, should set off alarm bells in your head, because it's one of the most common indicators of a wordiness problem. In some cases, like this one, we can simply remove it. **J** has the same meaning, is grammatically correct, and is shorter, so it's the best answer. G has the same wordiness problem that makes F incorrect. H creates an entirely new problem, since we don't need the "him."

19 Pay careful attention to this sort of question when you're given one. In this case, the test-makers want you to pick the choice that indicates "a significant period of time." The original phrase "To Bentley's surprise" doesn't involve time, so A is out. In fact, only B "eventually" and C "concurrently" are time related, so we can also eliminate D. And again, since we want a word that implies a "significant period of time," meaning a long time, **B** must be the answer. "Concurrently" means at the same time, which wouldn't be a long time at all.

20 "Pretty cool" is a problem—we definitely can't have such informal vocabulary in an essay like this. Answer choices F, G, and H don't get rid of that problem. "Really neat" in G is just as informal as "pretty cool," even though it sounds like we're back in the 1950s. And any time we see "OMIT" or "DELETE" as an option, we should question the phrase's necessity. In this case, it's really not necessary. The phrase doesn't add any essential information to the sentence, and so it should be deleted. The answer is **J**.

21 Because the question asks for "the best transition," we should start by looking at the main ideas both of the previous paragraph and of the paragraph the author is introducing. The previous paragraph discusses Bentley obtaining the microscope and camera he needed to produce images of snow crystals. The paragraph being introduced talks about the specifics of his imaging setup and the difficulty of capturing snow crystals. A is very tempting, but "imaging routine" doesn't fit the previous paragraph nearly as well as "obtaining the right equipment." There's no mention of a process in the previous paragraph, just of the equipment. In fact, the author moves on to describe the process in this new paragraph. Answer choice **C** better captures the previous paragraph. The incorrect choices B and D don't link back to the previous paragraph and so don't make good transitions.

Answer: **C**

22 By placing the phrase between commas, this sentence structure makes "on a cool velvet-covered tray" a parenthetical—unnecessary information. But what happens if we remove that phrase? We're left with "What he found worked best was to capture the crystal." That's supremely uninformative. Of course he captured the crystal, but how did he do it? F and H both make this mistake, making them wrong. We need to move the information about the velvet-covered tray to its logical place in the sentence. Choice **J** does so and is correct. There are many problems with G, meanwhile, but the comma after "was" should be the biggest tip to avoid it. Just as a comma in "He was, old" is wrong, so too is a comma in "the best way was, to capture."

Answer: **J**

23 Scanning the answer choices, we see two pieces of punctuation at play here: the apostrophe and the comma. The apostrophe has fewer rules and uses, so let's start there. Because Bentley had only one mother, we can rule out A. "Mother" is singular, so the apostrophe should go before the "s." Choice B isn't possessive at all, so that must also be incorrect. C and D both correct the apostrophe problem, but C adds an unnecessary comma after "and." **D** is the best answer.

Answer: **D**

24 First, let's imagine the text without this underlined portion. The sentence becomes "The back-lit image was then focused using a system of strings and pulleys he devised." That sounds interesting, but it's a bit strange. Why did he devise this system of strings and pulleys? Why not just focus the camera normally? The underlined portion lets us know that the strings and pulleys were used because Bentley had to wear mittens in the cold shed—we need it to understand other information in the text. Choice F works, because we need to remember the cold environment in order to understand the system of pulleys. Answer choice G is incorrect because the details aren't off-topic: the paragraph is a description of Bentley's photography setup. H is incorrect because the underlined portion is about his hands, not the pulleys. J is wrong because there's no info about developing these images. Instead, this paragraph is all about taking the photo in the first place. Be careful not to infer too much on this one! The answer is **F**.

Answer: **F**

Answer: D

25 This paragraph details a process in chronological order. To find the best place for sentence 5, we need to think about that process and what's happening in each step. At what point does Bentley put the slide under the microscope? Well, first he gets a snowflake (sentence 2), then he places the snowflake on a slide (sentence 3), and we can imagine that he then places the slide under the microscope. So this is where sentence 5 should be moved to: after sentence 3. It also helps that the slide referred to in sentence 5 was specifically mentioned in sentence 3. We can't say "the slide" before the slide is introduced—it would be "a slide" when first mentioned. "The slide" must come after the first mention of "a slide," which is again in sentence 3. Sentence 4 mentions focusing the image, and this logically would take place after the slide is placed under the microscope as discussed in sentence 5, so sentence 5 also needs to come before sentence 4. The answer is **D**.

Answer: H

26 This is an idiom question testing prepositions, so you mostly have to trust your ear. It may help to rearrange the sentence a bit to place that preposition before the word it's introducing ("conditions"). If we simplify the phrase to "they were collected _____ conditions," we can then try each answer choice to find the one that sounds best. In this case, the crystals were collected "under" certain conditions, not "on," "inside," or "for" certain conditions. Therefore, the answer is **H**.

Answer: C

27 A question that asks you to find the one answer choice that does NOT work sets you up to play "which one of these is not like the other," in a way. Three of the answer choices will all be similar in some way that makes them acceptable. One will be different. In this case, the three answer choices that work will all be similar in meaning to the original word "accrued." "Amassed" and "acquired" are both very similar in meaning, so neither B nor D is the answer. If we look back at the sentence, we can also pair "developed" with "accrued" in context—Bentley gained an understanding of snow from studying it. On the other hand, "increased" doesn't fit the meaning of the sentence; he didn't "increase" his considerable understanding, which would imply he already had that understanding. "Increased" is the answer choice that is least like the others in meaning. The answer is **C**.

Answer: F

28 Without "he," this sentence is missing a subject, so G is incorrect. Because the preparation of the paper was an event completed in the past (and not something that went on over a period of time), we need the plain past tense and not an "-ing" continuous form, so H doesn't work either. J changes the meaning of the sentence slightly and is unnecessarily wordy—keep things short and sweet whenever possible on the ACT! The answer is **F**.

29 If a question asks you how to best conclude a passage, it makes sense to go back and look at the passage as whole. One quick and effective way to do that is to briefly think about the point of each paragraph. In this case, the first paragraph introduced us to Bentley and explained why he was important. The second paragraph explained how Bentley's study of snowflakes began. The third paragraph explained his photographic process. And the final paragraph described the outcome of his studies. If we want to conclude this essay well, we need a sentence that relates to more than just the last paragraph, but answer choices B, C and D all only mention topics discussed in the last paragraph. D is tempting, but it would work better as a transition to a new paragraph that continued the story of Bentley's career, which we don't have. Because this is the end of the essay, it's better to conclude with a sentence that relates to the essay as a whole. Only **A** reaches back to the introduction to help conclude the essay by connecting the beginning and the end.

Answer: **A**

30 Before we even get to the answer choices, think about the exact wording of this question. We want "an essay about the history of the development of the photomicrograph." When answering these types of questions—about whether authors achieved their goal—be acutely aware of whether the essay is too general or too specific for that purpose, because that's usually why they don't accomplish a goal. In this case, the essay is far more specific than the phrasing in the question: it's all about one person! There's no other history of the photomicrograph. So immediately, we can cross off F and G, because the essay doesn't fulfill the proposed goal. Choice H, on the other hand, doubles down on being too specific. If the goal is a history of the photomicrograph, why would Bentley's interest in snowflakes be so significant? It wouldn't, so we can eliminate H. Choice **J** is correct because the passage is indeed too specific.

Answer: **J**

Common Mistakes on the ACT English Test

Avoiding "No Change." Some students think answer choices like "No Change" are traps, but this is not true, particularly on the ACT English section. "No Change" is just as likely to be correct as any other answer choice.

Not reading the entire sentence. The ACT often asks a question about one small part of a really long, complex sentence. Make sure to read your answer choice in the context of the entire sentence—there may be a punctuation mark that doesn't work with your answer, or your answer may inadvertently create redundancy or a sentence fragment.

Answering questions on the entire passage or paragraph too soon. Sometimes questions that pertain to a whole paragraph or passage appear before you've gotten through the entire thing. Skip these questions and save them for last, after you have read everything.

Chapter 6

ACT Math Test

Introduction to ACT Math

Okay, we're going to talk about math! As soon as you read that, did you get up to do the happy dance? It's okay if you didn't. While a small percentage of people are totally cool with math, a much larger percentage are not so comfortable with it, even though we use it all the time. (Notice that we had to refer to some math even in that sentence!) Some people even feel that "being good at math" is an exclusive club they were never invited to.

Here's what we would say to anyone who is not jumping-up-and-down excited to do math: believe it or not, math rewards hard work and practice. If you're willing to put in the effort and go on this ride, then you can improve! You don't need to be Einstein. Your progress starts from wherever you are now, and if you continue to build on what you know, you can do this!

Albert Einstein was, as physicists go, not very good at math. His special theory of relativity involves not much more than high school math, and for his general theory of relativity, he needed the support of more mathematically talented colleagues. As Einstein said, "Imagination is more important than knowledge."

At a Glance

The ACT Math Test assesses the mathematical skills students are expected to obtain before grade 12 (meaning through advanced algebra and basic trigonometry but not calculus).

What to Know

- It's the second section of the ACT.
- You have a 60-minute time limit.
- You'll face 60 multiple-choice questions.
- You get to use a calculator for the whole test (but it must be an approved one).

What to Study

- Backsolving (page 116)
- Number Basics (page 118)
    - numbers, positive and negative numbers, zero
- Multiples, Divisors, and Factors (page 120)
    - prime factorization, GCF and LCM
- Fractions (page 123)
    - algebraic operations, improper fractions vs. mixed numerals, compound fractions, decimals, percents
- Exponents and Roots (page 132)
    - basics, zero exponents, negative exponents, roots, fractional exponents, the distributive property, simplifying, scientific notation
- Geometry (page 147)
    - evaluating points and lines on a graph, angles, parallel lines, polygons, triangles, area, formulas, perpendicular bisectors, quadrilaterals, parallelograms, trapezoids, pentagons, circles
- Three-Dimensional Geometry (page 170)
    - prisms, pyramids, cylinders, cones, spheres
- Coordinate Geometry (page 174)
    - parallel and perpendicular lines in the xy-plane, midpoints, parabolas, distance, circles, reflections
- Elementary Algebra (page 183)
    - factoring, solving quadratics, inequalities on the number line, picking numbers
- Word Problems (page 198)
    - solution and mixture problems, proportions, direct and inverse variation, strange operators, money, problem sets
- Intermediate Algebra (page 208)
    - symbols, absolute value, quadratics, powers and roots, rational expressions
- Statistics and Data (page 218)
    - range, modes of displaying data, charts of numbers, probability and counting, expected number, combinations of events, counting

Top Tips to Improve Your ACT Math Test Score

1. **Think realistically.** Many of the ACT's word problems are based on real-world situations, and they usually present realistic scenarios, so make sure the answer you get makes sense in the context of the problem. Thinking realistically also applies in a slightly different way to the geometry problems on the test. Unlike the SAT, the ACT's figures are drawn (relatively) to scale. So even if you don't know how to solve a problem, you can visually estimate the answer to narrow down the answer choices, sometimes even to the correct answer, without doing any additional work. Don't let the pressure of the exam make you stop using your common sense—you know a lot that can help you, even in a pinch. Let's say an $80 dress is on sale for 20% off. If you do the math and get an answer of $96 … well, that sounds like a really bad sale. That couldn't possibly be the answer, so don't pick it!

    Do you think you're ready? Quick, pop quiz!

    Approximately how long is a new, standard, unsharpened No. 2 pencil?

    A. 7 centimeters
    B. 7 inches
    C. 7 feet
    D. 7 yards

    You may not know the exact length of a standard pencil, but we bet you could take a REALLY good guess from among the above answer choices just by using a little common sense (the answer is **B**). It is easy to get caught up in the calculations and to forget to measure our answer against the original problem to see if it checks out. And that's why being realistic is our first tip to help you improve your ACT Math Test score.

2. **Use the answer choices.** On every single ACT Math Test question, the correct answer is literally sitting right in front of your face. Sure, it's hidden in a multiple-choice lineup, but it's still there. This means the ACT is giving you the tools to plug in answer choices and test them instead of finding the answer from scratch on your own! Don't forget about strategies like working backward on ACT Math Test questions—many questions are just begging to be solved this way. And if you aren't familiar with strategies like this one, don't worry. We have plenty of content here to help you master those approaches.

3. **Move quickly and efficiently.** The questions on the ACT Math Test aren't arranged precisely from easy to hard. Keep in mind that the concepts do tend to get more advanced as you move through the section, but most students find there isn't an exponential increase in the difficulty of questions. If you recently

studied identities in your trig class, for example, you might find question 59 easier than question 12. This means you can't let yourself get stuck on any one problem, because you'll most likely find problems that are easier for you elsewhere in the section. Make quick decisions to skip and come back to problems if there is time. It's so frustrating to spend three minutes wrestling with a question you ultimately get wrong—and then find that you've run out of time when you see a problem you could absolutely get right.

How to Use Your Calculator Wisely

Here are some tips to help you get the most out of your calculator on test day.

- Remember that you can only use the calculator on the ACT Math Test—not Science (or English or Reading, for that matter).
- Make sure that your calculator is allowed. You can use any four-function, scientific, or graphing calculator, unless it has prohibited algebra software on it. For full details, check out The ACT Calculator Policy on act.org.
- Make sure to use a calculator you're familiar with. Don't go out and buy or borrow a new calculator the night before the test. You need to know how to use it, and you need to be comfortable with all of the functions you might need.
- Replace your calculator's batteries the night before the test, even if they're not that old; the last thing you want is a dead calculator in the middle of your math section.
- Don't be tempted to use calculators for problems with fractions and radicals; these problems are often solved faster with mathematical reasoning, and the calculator can lead you astray.
- Pick up your calculator only when you're sure of how to solve the problem and how the calculator will help you do so. Using it any other way is … you guessed it … a waste of time!
- Remember that ACT problems are meant to be solved quickly. If you're picking up your calculator to try to solve $\sqrt{597}$, you've probably made a mistake somewhere. Double-check your work up to that point. This is key: ACT Math Test questions are designed to be solved without a calculator, so if you really do need one, that's a hint that you're off track.
- Keep in mind that, at the end of the day, you're the one taking the ACT. Your calculator is not. The ACT Math Test is testing your math skills, not how well you can use a calculator.

Calculators on the ACT

You Do Get to Use a Calculator, But . . .

. . . it's potentially a trap. Don't get us wrong: the calculator is an amazing tool, and it's true that you get to use one on the ACT. But it's also true that you should practice a ton with the calculator you're going to use beforehand, so that you're intimately familiar with its quirks long before you walk into the test. And you should also be familiar with good and bad uses of that same calculator.

For example, a good use of a calculator would be finding 17^5. A bad use of a calculator would be finding 5×8. If you use the calculator for every simple arithmetic action, then you're using it as a crutch—and this slows you down significantly. It is tempting to check everything, but don't give in to temptation! To be most efficient on the ACT Math Test, it's actually really important to be good at mental math.

By the way, mental math is definitely, 100 percent, a skill you can develop. In addition to your practice for the ACT Math Test, practice adding, subtracting, multiplying, and dividing in your head every day. Have a friend hold a calculator and quiz you, checking your work. Practice arithmetic with fractions in your head. Race your friends to calculate a tip at a restaurant. Notice the geometry in all the shapes and buildings around you. If you're not comfortable with mental math, it's all the more important to practice it consistently! It's not a skill that develops overnight, but it is one that you can build up over time. If you are comfortable identifying math applications in your daily life, you won't be overwhelmed on the ACT.

Yes, we admit, taking the mental math route will make you slower in the beginning—but trust yourself, and trust the process. As you practice, you'll gain speed and confidence. Ultimately, you'll find that your own brain can be much faster than stopping to use the calculator.

Your Calculator and PEMDAS

Now, there's one final thing we want you to do. If you have the calculator you want to use for the ACT, we'd like you to enter this problem into your calculator:

$$1 + 2 \times 3$$

If you get 7, congratulations! Your calculator follows the standard order of operations. All of the math problems you'll be dealing with on the ACT will follow this order, and your calculator already takes that into consideration automatically. That makes things easier for you.

If you entered the problem into your calculator and it gave you 9, then your calculator does not follow the order of operations. This means a little more work for you; you will have to separate problems out into the proper order yourself before entering anything into your calculator. So, to get the right answer, you would have to enter the above problem into your calculator like this:

$$2 \times 3 = 6$$
$$1 + 6 = 7$$

So what is going on here? You might have learned this as PEMDAS, or by the phrase "Please Excuse My Dear Aunt Sally." It's the order that you're supposed to follow when solving an equation, and each letter of PEMDAS stands for an operation: Parentheses, Exponents, Multiplication, Division, Addition, and Subtraction. To be totally accurate, we should call this process GEMDAS, where the "G" stands for "Grouping symbols," or the symbols that make a set of numbers and operations "go together." Certainly, parentheses are one common set of grouping symbols. Others include all the numbers and operations in the numerator or denominator of a fraction, absolute values, radicals, and all the numbers and operations in an exponent.

So how do we interpret this? There are four "levels" of importance when you are solving a math problem. Level 1 is the most important and Level 4 is the least important.

- **Level 1:** Grouping symbols
- **Level 2:** Exponents
- **Level 3:** Multiplication and Division
- **Level 4:** Addition and Subtraction

This means that we have two pairs of operations (multiplication and division are one pair; addition and subtraction are the other pair) that are equal, so if you have something like $5 + 4 - 1$, you should solve this from left to right. Neither of the operations takes precedence over the other. Here are some practice problems:

$$\frac{24}{2 \times 4 - 5} =$$

$$|2 \times 4 - 5| + 12 =$$

$$\sqrt{2 \times 4 - 5} =$$

$$2^{2 \times 4 - 5}$$

In all four of those math expressions, the $2 \times 4 - 5$ part is "grouped" and should be done first, before anything else. To reiterate, multiply the 2 and 4, then subtract the 5, before doing any other operations in any other part of the expression. That means in each case the $2 \times 4 - 5$ part will become $8 - 5$ and then just plain 3 in whichever context it's in. Like this:

$$\frac{24}{2 \times 4 - 5} = \frac{24}{3} = 8$$

$$|2 \times 4 - 5| + 12 = 3 + 12 = 15$$

$$\sqrt{2 \times 4 - 5} = \sqrt{3}$$

$$2^{2 \times 4 - 5} = 2^3 = 8$$

It's important to recognize the "higher status" of all grouping symbols in math, and the ACT will certainly provide answer choices that improperly use the order of operations. If you are armed with this knowledge, you'll be in great shape!

Number Sense

As you work on developing your mental math skills, you'll also work on developing the skill known as "number sense." Number sense is that seemingly magic ease with numbers that people who are really good at math have. It's a keen intuitive capacity for numbers and how they behave. Number sense involves using patterns to "see" shortcuts to solving some problems that appear, at first glance, to require more laborious calculations.

One common aspect of number sense is estimation. For example, what's 97 × 41? Well, we'd need a calculator (or at least a few minutes with some scratch paper) for an exact answer. But we also know that 97 is close to 100, and 41 is close to 40, so whatever this product is, it would have to be close to 100 × 40 = 4000. (The actual answer, if you're wondering, is 3977.) Many times, making that simple calculation in your head is sufficient to narrow the answer choices down to one, and it's much, much faster than using the calculator to find an exact answer when that level of certainty is not needed. Well-practiced number sense makes approximately a third to half of all the questions on the ACT Math Test go faster: strong number sense gives you a huge advantage!

So as you practice mental math, here are some examples of mathematical patterns or tendencies you can look for and practice using.

1. Making the numerator of a fraction bigger makes the whole fraction bigger.
2. Making the denominator of a fraction bigger makes the whole fraction smaller.
3. (big positive) + (small negative) = something positive
4. (small positive) + (big negative) = something negative
5. Multiplying by a positive decimal less than one makes something smaller.
6. Dividing by a positive decimal less than one makes something bigger.
7. Any positive number is larger than any negative number.

There are also tons of patterns of divisibility. For example, one pattern works with 3's: the digits of a number add up to a multiple of 3 if and only if the number itself is divisible by 3. Take the number 2,018 (2 + 0 + 1 + 8 = 11), which is not a multiple of 3, which means the number 2,018 can't be a multiple of 3. By contrast, with the number 2,019 (2 + 0 + 1 + 9 = 12), which is a multiple of 3, so this means the number 2,019 also must be a multiple of 3. (We can verify this: 2,019 ÷ 3 = 673.) These types of patterns can help you infinitely!

While there's no "complete list" of these mathematical tendencies, that's actually not important at the end of the day. You shouldn't try to build your number sense by memorizing lists, anyway. Instead, do it by practicing problems and observing patterns, even by playing with numbers. Get curious about observing how numbers work on your own. What patterns do you observe in multiples of 17? In fractions that have 7 in the denominator? This analytical mindset will help you on the ACT and beyond.

Divisibility Rules

2: A number is divisible by 2 if the units digit is 0, 2, 4, 6, or 8.

3: A number is divisible by 3 if the sum of its digits is divisible by 3.

4: A number is divisible by 4 if the number made by the tens and units digit is divisible by 4.

5: A number is divisible by 5 if the units digit is 0 or 5.

6: A number is divisible by 6 if it is divisible by both 2 and 3.

7: This one's a bit tricky. A number is divisible by 7 if the absolute difference (positive or negative) between two times the units digit and the number left by the rest of the digits is divisible by 7.

8: A number is divisible by 8 if the number made by the hundreds, tens, and units digits is divisible by 8.

9: A number is divisible by 9 if the sum of its digits is divisible by 9.

Backsolving

Mastering the ACT Math Test requires thinking a little differently than you do in math class. For example, your algebra teacher would want you to assign variables, set up equations, and solve the problem algebraically. If you know how to do all of that to solve a given ACT problem, that's great! But that's not the only way to solve the problem—and it's almost never the quickest way.

There's an alternate method of solving multiple-choice problems: *backsolving*, which is a fancy way of saying that we are going to work backward from the answers. This is always an option if the five answer choices are all numbers.

How does it work? Use the numbers from the answers and plug them into the variable(s) in the question stem. This brings us to the second requirement for backsolving: the question stem needs to have a variable in it (in other words, it needs to use some kind of algebra). When you plug the correct answer into the equation, it will make the equation work.

In backsolving, it always makes sense to start with the middle value. If the answers are listed from smallest to biggest or biggest to smallest, we would start with answer choice C, since it's right in the middle. One-fifth of the time, we'd be lucky and get the answer on our first try.

Even if that doesn't happen, we get valuable information. If C is too big, then D and E are also going to be too big. Conversely, if C is too small, then A and B are also too small. This way, we can eliminate three answers all at once. After that, we just have to pick one of the two remaining answer choices, backsolve one more time, and we've solved the problem for good.

How might that look? Let's say C was too low. Then A, B, and C are all out. Next, we can try either D or E. Let's say we try D. Either D works, making D the answer, or D doesn't work, which means that E has to be the answer. Problem solved!

Let's take a look at an example. Suppose we saw this problem on test day:

If $3 + \sqrt{\frac{2}{3}x^2 + 1} = 8$ what is the value of x?

- A. 5
- B. 6
- C. 8
- D. 10
- E. 12

If you didn't know how to solve that algebraically (or you wanted a faster way to do it), you could try backsolving.

As always with backsolving, we'll start with the middle value, $x = 8$. Plug this into the left side of the equation, wherever you see x.

$$3 + \sqrt{\frac{2}{3}x^2 + 1} = 8$$

$$3 + \sqrt{\tfrac{2}{3}8^2 + 1} = 8$$

$$3 + \sqrt{\tfrac{2}{3}(64) + 1} = 8$$

$$3 + \sqrt{42.67 + 1} = 8$$

$$3 + \sqrt{43.67} = 8$$

$$\sqrt{42.67 + 1} = 5$$

We know that 43.67 isn't a perfect square, and definitely isn't equal to 5 × 5, so we know that C is not the correct answer. Using logic, we know that we want the solution to be $\sqrt{25} = 5$, which means that answer choice C is too large of a number: $\sqrt{43.67} > \sqrt{25}$. We want our answer choice to be smaller than 8, which means that we can already eliminate C, D, and E.

To solve the problem, we need to backsolve one more time. We can choose to plug in answer choice A or B. For the sake of this example, let's go with B. We'll plug in 6 wherever we see an x in the equation:

$$3 + \sqrt{\tfrac{2}{3}6^2 + 1} = 8$$

$$3 + \sqrt{\tfrac{2}{3}(36) + 1} = 8$$

$$3 + \sqrt{24 + 1} = 8$$

$$3 + \sqrt{25} = 8$$

$$3 + 5 = 8$$

$$8 = 8$$

B is the answer. We solved it without having to do any complex algebra!

Before we look at other strategies, remember that we set algebra aside when looking at this question. But what if you're really strong in algebra? Which is faster: straightforward algebra or backsolving? The frustrating answer is that it depends: it depends on you, and it depends on the kind of problem.

At the end of the day, here's how to decide what to do. When you're practicing and reviewing ACT Math Test problems, practice using all applicable strategies to solve each problem. If you know more than one way to solve a problem, you really understand it. If you use both algebra and backsolving on a variety of problems, you'll develop a really good sense of which is faster for you in a given situation.

Number Basics

Developing (and using!) your number sense and backsolving skills will give you a big boost on test day. But we've only seen the tip of the iceberg when it comes to content. So let's take a deeper look: what do you need to know for the ACT Math Test at a basic level? Here are some important fundamentals/terminology that you should know before walking into the test.

Numbers

Pop quiz: How many numbers are greater than 3 and less than 7?

How you answer that question depends on what comes to your mind when you hear the word "number." It's true that 4, 5, and 6 are between these two numbers, but so are a bunch of fractions and decimals. In fact, the real answer to this quiz question is: infinitely many!

It's important to remind yourself that the word "number" can always include everything on the number line. This includes the following "families" of numbers:

1. counting numbers or positive integers = {1, 2, 3, 4, 5, ...}
2. integers = {... −3, −2, −1, 0, 1, 2, 3, ...}
3. rational numbers, i.e., fractions (which can be both positive and negative)
4. real numbers, i.e., decimals (which can be both positive and negative)

The official math name for counting numbers (think: the numbers you'd use while counting down in hide-and-seek) is *natural numbers*. These are also positive *integers*, or whole numbers. By the way, zero is an integer, as are all positive and negative whole numbers.

Rational numbers are called that because they can be expressed in terms of ratios: each rational number can be written as a fraction in the form "integer over integer" (i.e., $\frac{x}{y}$). This is in contrast to some decimals, such as $\sqrt{5}$ or π, which cannot be written as integer-over-integer fractions: instead, these *irrational numbers* are decimals that go on forever. *Real numbers* are all the numbers on the number line. So, as you can see, the word "numbers" isn't as precise as we might want it to be.

Evens and Odds

A few key facts to note for the ACT Math Test:

- Positive and negative integers can be either even or odd.
- Zero is an even number.
- The terms "even" and "odd" do not apply to fractions or decimals.
- There are a few principles governing the addition of odd and even numbers:

  odd + odd = even
  odd + even = odd
  even + even = even

It would be good to have this information on the tip of your tongue, but in a pinch you can pick a random even and random odd number to test the relationships. They hold true for any set of numbers.

Positives, Negatives, and Zero

- Integers, decimals, and fractions can be either positive or negative.
- Zero is the only number that is neither positive nor negative.
- Anything multiplied by zero is zero, and it is always 100 percent illegal to divide by zero.
- There are a few principles governing the multiplication of positive and negative numbers:

$$\text{positive} \times \text{positive} = \text{positive}$$
$$\text{negative} \times \text{negative} = \text{positive}$$
$$\text{negative} \times \text{positive} = \text{negative}$$

- The same principles govern the division of positive and negative numbers:

$$\text{positive} \div \text{positive} = \text{positive}$$
$$\text{negative} \div \text{negative} = \text{positive}$$
$$\text{negative} \div \text{positive} = \text{negative}$$

Prime Numbers

- A *prime number* is a positive integer divisible by just two positive integers: itself and 1.
- 1 is *not* a prime number because it is only divisible by one positive integer: itself. (You don't have to remember the exact reason why; you only have to remember that 1 is *not* a prime number.)
- 2 is the lowest prime number and the only even prime number. It is good to be familiar with the prime numbers up to 30, though you don't have to memorize them. The prime numbers up to 30 are {2, 3, 5, 7, 11, 13, 17, 19, 23, 29}.

While Euclid is more famous for his contributions to geometry, his book *The Elements* also contains a section on number theory, which includes a famous, concise proof that there are an infinite number of prime numbers. This was the very first mathematical fact about prime numbers proven in the history of mathematics.

Multiples, Divisors, and Factors

A *multiple* of n is what you get if you multiply n by any positive integer. For instance, if n = 3:

1. 3 × 1 = 3
2. 3 × 2 = 6
3. 3 × 3 = 9
4. 3 × 4 = 12

The products above {3, 6, 9, 12} are all mutiples of 3. We could repeat this process with any number we choose and find its multiples.

A *divisor* is a number that divides into an integer evenly, meaning it leaves no remainder or decimal. It perfectly divides. So if we take the multiples we just found above, 3 is a divisor of all those multiples {3, 6, 9, 12}. Likewise, 4 is a divisor of 12, 2 is a divisor of 6, and so on. The idea of a divisor is very related to our next concept: factors.

A *factor* is an integer we can multiply by another whole number to create a certain, larger integer. Imagine we have positive integers a, b, and n. If a × b = n, then we can say that a and b are factors of n. We can also say that n is divisible by a and by b.

Let's look at 24 as an example. What numbers can we say are factors of 24? One such pair of factors is 12 and 2. That gives us 12 × 2 = 24, which fits our a × b = n format we just discussed. This reinforces our definition that factors are the integers that form a larger whole number when you multiply them together. Factors can be positive or negative, but on the ACT, you will be dealing mainly with *positive* factors. We aren't finished yet, though! 2 and 12 aren't the only factors of 24. The entire set of positive factors of 24 is {1, 2, 3, 4, 6, 8, 12, 24}. (Note that 24 is both a factor and a multiple of 24. That's because, in math terms, for every integer n, n is both a factor and a multiple of itself.)

So, to recap, we can say all of the following:

- 24 is a multiple of 1, 2, 3, 4, 6, 8, 12, and 24.
- 1, 2, 3, 4, 6, 8, 12, and 24 are divisors of 24.
- The factors of 24 are 1, 2, 3, 4, 6, 8, 12, and 24.

Prime Factorization

Prime factors are prime numbers that are also factors of a certain number. The *prime factorization* of a number includes all of the prime factors we would need to multiply together to create our starting value. Think of prime factors as the smallest building blocks of that larger number. Finding prime factors involves breaking the number down further than just finding normal factors. Let's look at this using 24 as an example. Start by first identifying any pair of factors you wish. We can use 4 and 6 to get started (4 × 6 = 24). Now that we have broken 24 into smaller parts, we can break those smaller parts into even smaller parts. So we break 4 into its smallest parts (2 × 2 = 4) and 6 into its own smallest parts (2 × 3 = 6). Here's what this process looks like:

$4 \times 6 = 24$

$2 \times 2 \times 6 = 24$

$2 \times 2 \times 2 \times 3 = 24$

This shows us that the prime factors of 24 are {2, 2, 2, 3} and the prime factorization of 24 is $2 \times 2 \times 2 \times 3$. We can also write the prime factorization as $2^3 \times 3$. The prime factorization of each positive integer is unique: it's the number's "fingerprints." More than that, though, it also allows us to see which numbers could or couldn't be factors of another number. Let's break down another number:

$3900 = 39 \times 100$

$3900 = 3 \times 13 \times 10 \times 10$

$3900 = 3 \times 13 \times 2 \times 5 \times 2 \times 5$

$3900 = 2^2 \times 3 \times 5^2 \times 13$

From this factorization, we can see that 3,900 is divisible by $15 = 3 \times 5$, or $65 = 13 \times 5$, or $12 = 2^2 \times 3$. Any combination of those prime factors will give us a factor of 3900. On the other hand, 3,900 wouldn't be divisible by any multiple of 7, by any multiple of 11, etc. This is because we don't have any of those prime factors represented in the prime factorization of 3,900.

Greatest Common Factor (GCF) and Least Common Multiple (LCM)

Here are two abbreviations you might not have thought about in a while: GCF and LCM. While they may not have come up in math class for a while, they are vital concepts to know for the ACT. So what are these things? Well, they're not Roald Dahl characters (you might be thinking of the BFG!). The GCF is the *Greatest Common Factor*, and the LCM is the *Least Common Multiple*. Understanding these two interconnected concepts will give you a big hand when approaching ACT Math Test questions involving fractions and some word problems.

Let's start with some simple numbers: 4 and 6. The factors of 4 are {1, 2, 4} and the factors of 6 are {1, 2, 3, 6}. This means the GCF of 4 and 6 is 2 (the largest factor they share) and their LCM is 12 (the lowest integer that's a multiple of both 4 and 6). As you might imagine, it's often easier to find the GCF and LCM for smaller, rather than bigger, numbers. But what if the numbers *are* bigger, as they can be on the ACT? For example, what about 60 and 96? Here's a system you always can use to find the GCF and LCM.

Step #1: Find the prime factorization of each number.

$60 = 2 \times 2 \times 3 \times 5$

$96 = 2 \times 2 \times 2 \times 2 \times 2 \times 3$

Step #2: Identify all the prime factors the two numbers have in common; multiply these to get the GCF of those specific numbers.

$$60 = \mathbf{2} \times \mathbf{3} \times 2 \times 5$$
$$96 = \mathbf{2} \times \mathbf{3} \times 2 \times 2 \times 2 \times 2$$
$$\text{GCF} = 2 \times 3 = \mathbf{6}$$

Step #3: Once we have the GCF, we can use the following formula to find the LCM:

$$\text{LCM} = \frac{(number\,1) \times (number\,2)}{\text{GCF}}$$

In other words, we multiply the two original numbers and then divide by the GCF. Remember to cancel BEFORE you multiply because this will make the calculation work much simpler (but if you forget, you'll still get the right answer).

$$\text{LCM} = \frac{60 \times 96}{6} - 10 \times 96 = \mathbf{960}$$

This is the system you always can use if you can't eyeball the numbers and come up with the GCF and LCM. (Don't worry—few of us could do that with numbers like 60 and 96!)

Fractions

As you may already know, a fraction is a way of showing division. The top of a fraction is called the *numerator*, and the bottom of a fraction is called the *denominator*. To look at an example, the fraction $\frac{2}{7}$ means "the number you get when you divide 2 by 7." The fraction $\frac{2}{7}$ also means the following. Imagine dividing something whole into seven equal parts—one of those parts is "one out of seven" or $\frac{1}{7}$ of the whole, $\frac{2}{7}$ is two of those parts $\left(2 \times \frac{1}{7}\right)$, etc. This diagram will probably call up dim memories from your elementary school math classes of talking about dividing pies or cookies. Now look at the following diagram.

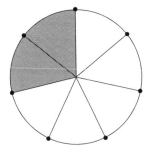

That, visually, represents the quantity $\frac{2}{7}$. Whenever we deal with fractions, we are thinking both about the mathematical idea of parts and division and about the visual perspective of what those parts look like compared to the whole.

There are other values equivalent to $\frac{2}{7}$. If you look at the fractions $\frac{4}{14}$ or $\frac{10}{35}$, they both reduce down to $\frac{2}{7}$. **Canceling reflects the process of division.** That's a big idea—a concept that should be second nature during the ACT Math Test. In the case of $\frac{4}{14}$, we have 4 or 2 × 2 in the numerator and we have 14 or 2 × 7 in the denominator. We can reduce both by eliminating the shared factor of 2; in other words, we divide both the numerator and denominator by 2, leaving 4 ÷ 2 = 2 and 14 ÷ 2 = 7 for a reduced fraction of $\frac{2}{7}$.

Adding and Subtracting Fractions

First of all, let's address what you **can't** do: when you add fractions, you can't simply add the two numbers in the numerators and then add the two in the denominators. (This is the kind of mistake people make when mechanically performing a rule that isn't right for the situation.) In mathematical form, this means:

$$\frac{a}{b} + \frac{c}{d} \neq \frac{a+c}{b+d}$$

The only time you can add or subtract across the numerator is **when you have a common denominator.** But why is that true? Think about what we just said above. When we have something like $\frac{3}{11} + \frac{5}{11}$, we are really just saying $\left(3 \times \frac{1}{11}\right) + \left(5 \times \frac{1}{11}\right)$. Basically, we're adding three of this "$\frac{1}{11}$ thing" plus five more of this same "$\frac{1}{11}$ thing." Just as three pencils and five pencils add up to eight pencils, three elevenths and five elevenths add up to eight elevenths.

When the denominators aren't the same, say, $\frac{3}{8} + \frac{1}{6}$, then you can't add them as is, but you can take advantage of your knowledge of fractions to manipulate them. With fractions, any number over itself is the same as 1. So $\frac{3}{3}$ is 1 and $\frac{125}{125}$ is also 1. Also, if you multiply anything by 1, that does not change the value. With this knowledge, we can change the way we write those fractions above without changing their value, and that will make it easier to add them. So we want to multiply $\frac{3}{8}$ by something and $\frac{1}{6}$ by something else that will make their denominators the same (so we can add them).

The simplest way to do this is to find the least common denominator (LCD), which is exactly the same concept as the LCM discussed above (just in the denominator of a fraction). Here, the LCM of 8 and 6 is 24, so this is how we add the two fractions. First, we need to create our common denominators:

$$\frac{3}{8} + \frac{1}{6} = \frac{3}{8} \times \frac{3}{3} + \frac{1}{6} \times \frac{4}{4}$$

Next, we complete the multiplication to reveal our new fractions:

$$\frac{3}{8} \times \frac{3}{3} = \frac{9}{24}$$

$$\frac{1}{6} \times \frac{4}{4} = \frac{4}{24}$$

Finally, we do the addition:

$$\frac{9}{24} + \frac{4}{24} = \frac{13}{24}$$

The same basic process also works with subtraction. If you get the same denominator in your fractions, you can solve these types of problems much easier.

Multiplying and Dividing Fractions

Multiplication involves the easiest of all fractions rules. (Yay!) To multiply fractions, just multiply across the numerators and multiply across the denominators.

$$\frac{5}{7} \times \frac{2}{3} = \frac{10}{21}$$

What's a little tricky about multiplication is knowing what you can cancel. If we're multiplying two fractions, of course we can cancel any numerator with its own denominator, but we can also cancel one numerator with another denominator. (To reiterate, this is only true because we are multiplying!) Sometimes, people call that "cross-canceling," but we think that just reinforces mechanical thinking. We don't need to memorize a separate rule for each case of what we can or can't do. It's much more effective to remember that when we multiply fractions at all, **we can cancel any numerator with any denominator**. Here's a horrendous multiplication problem that simplifies elegantly with the liberal use of canceling:

$$\frac{26}{48} \times \frac{18}{56} \times \frac{64}{39}$$

Notice that at this point it would be a disaster to multiply all the numbers in the numerators and all the numbers in the denominators. Even with a calculator, it's a bit of a pain! Instead, we should begin by simplifying, which typically means we **begin by canceling**. Cancel the factor of 8 that 56 and 64 share.

$$\frac{26}{48} \times \frac{18}{\mathbf{56}} \times \frac{\mathbf{64}}{39} \quad \Rightarrow \quad \frac{26}{48} \times \frac{18}{7} \times \frac{\mathbf{8}}{39}$$

We can then cancel the factor of 13 that 26 and 39 share.

$$\frac{\mathbf{26}}{48} \times \frac{18}{7} \times \frac{8}{\mathbf{39}} \quad \Rightarrow \quad \frac{\mathbf{2}}{48} \times \frac{18}{7} \times \frac{8}{\mathbf{3}}$$

Now, we can cancel the factor of 8 that 48 and the 8 share.

$$\frac{2}{\mathbf{48}} \times \frac{18}{7} \times \frac{\mathbf{8}}{3} \quad \Rightarrow \quad \frac{2}{\mathbf{6}} \times \frac{18}{7} \times \frac{\mathbf{1}}{3}$$

Then, we can cancel the factor of 6 that 6 and the 18 share.

$$\frac{2}{\mathbf{6}} \times \frac{\mathbf{18}}{7} \times \frac{1}{3} \quad \Rightarrow \quad \frac{2}{\mathbf{1}} \times \frac{\mathbf{3}}{7} \times \frac{1}{3}, \text{ or } 2 \times \frac{3}{7} \times \frac{1}{3}$$

And then, we can cancel the 3's.

$$2 \times \frac{3}{7} \times \frac{1}{3} \quad \Rightarrow \quad 2 \times \frac{1}{7} \times 1 \text{ (notice that we can reduce that to } 2 \times \frac{1}{7}, \text{ or } \frac{2}{7}\text{)}$$

In other words …

$$\frac{26}{48} \times \frac{18}{56} \times \frac{64}{39} = \frac{2}{6} \times \frac{18}{7} \times \frac{1}{3} = \frac{2}{1} \times \frac{3}{7} \times \frac{1}{3} = \frac{2}{1} \times \frac{1}{7} \times \frac{1}{1} = \frac{\mathbf{2}}{\mathbf{7}}$$

The entire product of these three fractions with big numbers reduces to just $\frac{2}{7}$. The big moral here is to **cancel before you multiply**. If you make the numbers smaller at the outset, you don't have to work with big numbers, which can mean skipping the calculator—or using it for fewer operations—and saving a bit of time.

All that was about multiplying, but division isn't all that different, thankfully. First, it is important to know another term for fractions: *reciprocal*. This is just another way of saying the opposite fraction, or a fraction flipped upside down. The reciprocal of $\frac{1}{2}$ is $\frac{2}{1}$, and the reciprocal of $\frac{7}{6}$ is $\frac{6}{7}$. When we divide fractions, we take the reciprocal of the fraction that we're dividing by and then use the same process we used to multiply, remembering to cancel first.

$$\frac{5}{12} \div \frac{3}{8} = \frac{5}{12} \times \frac{8}{3}$$

Remember to cancel before multiplying! In this case, we can cancel a factor of 4 from 12 and 8.

$$\frac{5}{12} \times \frac{8}{3} = \frac{5}{3} \times \frac{2}{3}$$

Finally, multiply:

$$\frac{5}{3} \times \frac{2}{3} = \frac{10}{9}$$

In other words,

$$\frac{5}{12} \div \frac{3}{8} = \frac{5}{12} \times \frac{8}{3} = \frac{5}{3} \times \frac{2}{3} = \frac{10}{9}$$

That answer is an improper fraction (the numerator is larger than the denominator). Should we automatically convert this to a mixed numeral (rewriting the fraction using whole numbers and fractions)? Not necessarily. On the ACT Math Test, always check to see the form of the answer choices before changing a number to one form or another. Don't do more work than you have to!

And finally, what happens if we want to divide a fraction by an integer? As you may recall, any positive integer n can be written as a fraction of the form $\frac{n}{1}$. Dividing by this integer n is the same as multiplying by $\frac{1}{n}$. Here's an example of equivalent expressions:

$$\frac{\frac{6}{13}}{3} = \frac{6}{13} \div \frac{3}{1}$$

Then, divide the fractions by multiplying by the reciprocal of the fraction we're dividing by.

$$\frac{\frac{6}{13}}{3} = \frac{6}{13} \times \frac{3}{1}$$

Reduce by factoring 3 from the 6 and the 3:

$$\frac{6}{13} \times \frac{1}{3} = \frac{2}{13} \times 1$$

And notice that you've solved the problem!

$$\frac{\frac{6}{13}}{3} = \frac{6}{13} \div \frac{3}{1} = \frac{6}{13} \times \frac{1}{3} = \frac{2}{13}$$

Once again, this is really the same idea: dividing by 3 means the same thing as multiplying by $\frac{1}{3}$.

Improper Fractions vs. Mixed Numerals

When a fraction is greater than 1, we know that the numerator will be larger than the denominator. We have two options at this point: we can write the number as an **improper fraction** (a fraction that leaves the form as we just described, with the numerator larger than the denominator, like $\frac{10}{7}$) or a **mixed numeral** (a different expression of the same value that uses both whole numbers and fractions, like $1\frac{3}{7}$). Which is better?

You may have been told that all improper fractions have to be changed to mixed numerals, but you can just erase that notion from your mind. What you need to do depends on the specific question you're answering. The form of the answer choices should inform you what is right. Aside from that, what are the relative strengths of the two forms?

Mixed numerals are much more useful when we have to locate the number on a number line, perhaps to compare it to another number. The way we locate, say, $\frac{83}{6}$ on a number line is to convert it to 13 and $\frac{5}{6}$. That is somewhere between 13 and 14 on the number line, which is more obvious when it is a mixed numeral than an improper fraction. Meanwhile, for addition and subtraction, it's usually a wash: one form doesn't necessarily have a clear advantage over the other. And if we need to multiply or divide or raise the fraction to a power, we need to use improper fractions, because for these operations, mixed numerals require a lot more effort to use.

Compound Fractions

Sometimes a fraction has smaller fractions in its numerator and denominator. That type of beast is called a *compound fraction*. Here's an example:

$$\frac{6+\frac{2}{3}}{\frac{4}{3}+\frac{3}{4}} = ?$$

Who put all those little fractions inside a big fraction? This looks more intense than it is. The trick is to multiply both the numerator and denominator of the larger fraction by the LCM of all the denominators of the little fractions. It also may help to remember that the integer 6 can be thought of as the fraction $\frac{6}{1}$. So if we include that 1, the denominators of those little fractions are {1, 3, 3, 4}, and the LCM of those four numbers is 12. Multiply the big fraction by $\frac{12}{12}$.

$$\frac{6+\frac{2}{3}}{\frac{4}{3}+\frac{3}{4}} = \frac{6+\frac{2}{3}}{\frac{4}{3}+\frac{3}{4}} \times \frac{12}{12}$$

We can do this because $\frac{12}{12}$ is equivalent to 1, so we are not actually changing the overall value of our expression. We need to now multiply that 12 in both the numerator and denominator, giving us the following:

$$\frac{6+\frac{2}{3}}{\frac{4}{3}+\frac{3}{4}} \times \frac{12}{12} = \frac{(6 \times 12)+\left(\frac{2}{3} \times 12\right)}{\left(\frac{4}{3} \times 12\right)+\left(\frac{3}{4} \times 12\right)}$$

It's okay if this looks like a lot! Just keep going forward, simplifying all that multiplication.

Remember that in the case of something like $\frac{4}{3} \times 12$, there will be some canceling you can do (because the 12 contains a factor of 3 that will cancel with the denominator) so $\frac{4}{3} \times 12 = \frac{4}{1} \times 4 = 16$.

Here's what happens to our entire fraction:

$$\frac{(6 \times 12)+\left(\frac{2}{3} \times 12\right)}{\left(\frac{4}{3} \times 12\right)+\left(\frac{3}{4} \times 12\right)} = \frac{72+8}{16+9}$$

Finally, we can add and simplify.

$$\frac{72+8}{16+9} = \frac{80}{25} = \frac{16}{5}$$

We can use that same basic approach to simplify both numerical compound fractions or algebraic compound fractions.

Here's a practice problem along these lines:

Practice Question

$$\frac{1}{1+\dfrac{1}{1-\frac{1}{3}}} =$$

F. $\frac{2}{5}$

G. $\frac{4}{7}$

H. $\frac{2}{3}$

J. $\frac{3}{4}$

K. $\frac{5}{6}$

Answer and Explanation

Start with the smallest part of the expression. That's $1 - \frac{1}{3}$. Remember, we can rewrite 1 as $\frac{3}{3}$. $\frac{3}{3} - \frac{1}{3} = \frac{2}{3}$. This gives us:

$$\frac{1}{1+\dfrac{1}{\frac{2}{3}}}$$

That looks messier at first, but by taking the reciprocal, we can turn that into:

$$\frac{1}{1+\frac{3}{2}}$$

So that we can add those numbers in the denominator, let's make the denominator's fractions use like terms. Turn 1 into $\frac{2}{2}$:

$$\frac{1}{\frac{2}{2}+\frac{3}{2}}$$

Now that we have fractions, we can add:

$$\frac{1}{\frac{5}{2}}$$

Let's take the reciprocal again to solve; you'll end up with $\frac{2}{5}$, or answer **F**.

Fractions and Decimals

Let's look at a random decimal number:

1.61803398887499 …

It's important to understand place value to the right of the decimal point. That 6 is in the tenths place. The 1 to the right of that 6 is in the hundredths place. The 8 to the right of that 1 is in the thousandths place. The zero to the right of that 8 is in the ten thousandths place. This pattern continues on forever, with the denominators increasing by a multiple of 10 each time.

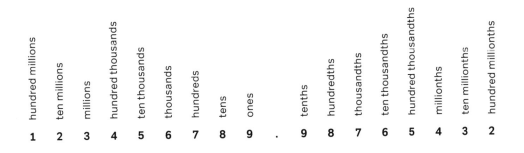

If you understand place value, it's very easy to change any decimal into a fraction (or vice versa). We put the decimal over the appropriate power of 10 and then reduce.

$$0.35 = \frac{35}{100} = \frac{7}{20}$$

$$0.032 = \frac{32}{1,000} = \frac{16}{500} = \frac{8}{250} = \frac{4}{125}$$

Above, we transformed 0.35 (thirty-five hundredths) into $\frac{35}{100}$ based on our knowledge of decimal places. And we were then able to reduce it by a factor of 5 in both the numerator and denominator. Likewise, we took 0.032 (thirty-two thousandths) and created $\frac{32}{1,000}$, which we were able to reduce overall by a shared factor of 8, but we did it by reducing by 2 each step.

While you can always reason through a conversion, you should know how to convert the basic fractions to decimals. (The bars over digits below mean that those digits repeat forever.)

$$\frac{1}{2} = .5 \qquad \frac{1}{4} = .25 \qquad \frac{1}{6} = .16\overline{6} \qquad \frac{5}{8} = .625$$

$$\frac{1}{3} = .3\overline{3} \qquad \frac{3}{4} = .75 \qquad \frac{1}{8} = .125 \qquad \frac{7}{8} = .875$$

$$\frac{2}{3} = .6\overline{6} \qquad \frac{1}{5} = .2 \qquad \frac{3}{8} = .375 \qquad \frac{1}{9} = .1\overline{1}$$

If you have a choice, which should you choose to work with, fractions or decimals? People who are overly calculator dependent usually use decimals, but students with strong number sense often choose fractions (especially if the problem gives you values as fractions). To build up that general number sense and comfort with the ACT Math

Test, we would encourage using fractions as your default, but on the test, remember to check the format of the answer choices first!

Think about it. What's $1.875 \div 0.375$? Almost no one can do that as a purely mental calculation, and typing it into a calculator would take a few moments. Now, think about the same problem with fractions. Notice that we're going to change the first into an improper fraction.

$$\frac{\frac{15}{8}}{\frac{3}{8}} = \frac{15}{8} \times \frac{8}{3} = \frac{5}{1} = 5$$

If you are flexing your mental math muscles, the above is completely doable without a calculator. And you're less likely to make a mistake if you do it by hand, too. So don't be afraid to roll up your sleeves and practice fractions a lot.

Percents

The word "percent" means "per 100." (The Latin word *centum* means "one hundred." This is the root of the word "century" as well as the root of the value of a penny, one "cent.") Changing a percent to a fraction simply means putting the number over 100, and then simplifying (if applicable). So here is a starting example:

$$40\% = \frac{40}{100} = \frac{4}{10} = \frac{2}{5}$$

We start by putting that 40 over 100 and then we are able to simplify it down to its final form of $\frac{2}{5}$. The fractional form of percents is very useful in algebraic problems; often you will need to translate a value from $P\%$ to the fraction $\frac{P}{100}$. Knowing how to switch back and forth between fractions, decimals, and percentages will be very useful to you.

Similarly, changing a percent to a decimal means sliding the decimal place two places to the left.

$$37\% = 0.37$$

One useful skill is knowing how to find 10% "pieces" and determining what multiples of 10% would be, too. For example, what's 60% of 300? Don't reach for your calculator! We know that 10% of anything is $\frac{1}{10}$ of it, so 10% of 300 is 30. And 10% times 6 would be 60%, so just multiply that 30 by 6. So 60% of 300 is $30 \times 6 = 180$. We recommend that you practice finding multiple-of-ten percents (like we did above) of multiples of 100 or 1,000, too.

It's also important to distinguish 40% *of* a number from a 40% *increase* or a 40% *decrease*. For example, 40% of 200 is 80 (verify that you can find that in your head!)—therefore, if we increase 200 by 40%, we add 80 to it, to get 280, and if we decrease 200 by 40%, we subtract 80 from it, to get 120.

It's easiest to express percent increases and decreases as decimals using **multipliers**. Here are three related but different values we might express:

1. If we want 40% of *N*, we multiply *N* by 0.40.

2. If we want to increase *N* by 40%, we multiply *N* by 1 + 0.4 = 1.4.

3. If we want to decrease *N* by 40%, we multiply *N* by 1 − 0.4 = 0.6.

We get the multiplier for a percent increase by adding 1 to the percent as a decimal, and we get the multiplier for a percent decrease by subtracting the percent as a decimal from 1. That 1, by the way, stands for 100% of our starting value. Again, this is very important to understand when the percent is a variable in an algebra word problem—for example, questions that involve compound interest (see page 281).

Exponents and Roots

Exponent Basics

Exponents can seem scary; the word *exponent* alone might make you imagine huge numbers, but never fear! Even though exponents can make crazy large numbers, learning a few simple rules will make you the master of exponents. In particular, there are two basic aspects of exponents that can be especially tricky: (1) it seems like there are a ton of rules to remember with them; and (2) they tend to behave in ways we don't automatically expect. This leaves us with a choice to either take:

Approach #1: Blindly memorize exponent rules.

Approach #2: Carefully understand *why* exponent rules are true.

What are the pros and cons of these approaches? Well, if you take Approach #1 and then get flustered and forget the rules on test day, there's not a lot of wiggle room to help you recover from a memory lapse. But if you use Approach #2 and forget the rule, you just might be able to reason your way back to it because you are on friendly terms with exponents and their wily ways. Even under pressure, you'll be able to get to the answer you need. With this in mind, we'll take an "understanding why" approach to exponents.

What is an exponent?

An exponent tells us how many factors of a number get multiplied together to make that value represented by the number and exponent. For example: $5^7 = 5 \times 5 \times 5 \times 5 \times 5 \times 5 \times 5 = $ something big that we don't care about right now. Just notice that the exponent of 7 tells us we have to multiply 5 together by itself *seven* times. In the expression b^k, b is called the **base**, k is called the **exponent**, and the whole expression b^k is called the **power**. These words will make learning about exponents and powers easier, but ACT Math won't test you on these terms.

It's good to know the **perfect squares** of single-digit numbers cold. A perfect square is just the product of any rational number multiplied by itself. (Quick refresher: Raising something to the power of 2 is called "squaring" it, and raising something to the power of 3 is called "cubing" it.) So if you know automatically that 2^2 is 4 or that 7^2 is 49, your life on the ACT will be a little easier. Try to know up to the square of 12, if you can. It's also important to know that 10 to the power of n is equal to 1 followed by n zeros. Thus:

$$10^2 = 100 = \text{a hundred (two zeros)}$$
$$10^3 = 1{,}000 = \text{a thousand (three zeros)}$$
$$10^6 = 1{,}000{,}000 = \text{a million (six zeros)}$$
$$10^9 = 1{,}000{,}000{,}000 = \text{a billion (nine zeros)}$$

Basic rules of exponents

It probably won't surprise you to learn that there's a rule for the multiplication of powers.

$$(b^m) \times (b^n) = ?$$

Even if you know the formula, let's think about this problem concretely by thinking about actual numbers. Suppose we have $(6^3) \times (6^4)$ and we want to know what that means. Well, what does 6^3 by itself mean? That means three factors of 6 are multiplied together. Similarly, 6^4 means four factors of 6 are multiplied together. So, really, $(6^3) \times (6^4)$ is an expression in which we multiply three factors of 6 times four factors of 6.

$$(6^3) \times (6^4) = (6 \times 6 \times 6) \times (6 \times 6 \times 6 \times 6) = 6 \times 6 \times 6 \times 6 \times 6 \times 6 \times 6$$

If we multiply three factors of 6 by four factors of 6, we get $3 + 4 = 7$ factors of 6 in total. Thus,

$$(6^3) \times (6^4) = 6^{3+4} = 6^7$$

Is your vision swimming with sixes? Go to your happy place for a moment and then come back so we can repeat that more abstractly. Now, we want to multiply the powers $(b^m) \times (b^n)$. We know that b^m means we have m factors of b, and similarly, b^n means we have n factors of b. If we multiply these, we put all these factors together in one big product, so we would have $(m + n)$ factors of b altogether. We write that as b to the power of $(m + n)$:

$$(b^m) \times (b^n) = b^{m+n}$$

Multiplying powers means adding the exponents. If you understand the logic of that argument, then you really understand this rule. (If you're not sure, that's what we modeled with all those 6's above!)

Next up, division of powers:

$$\frac{b^n}{b^n} = ?$$

We'll assume, for the moment, that $n > m$. Again, let's begin by thinking concretely. Suppose we had 2^{17} divided by 2^8. That would be a fraction with seventeen factors of 2 in the numerator and eight factors of 2 in the denominator. Of course, we'd be able to have a cancellation festival here! In fact, each one of the eight factors of 2 in the denominator would cancel one factor of 2 in the numerator. Therefore, the denominator would cancel down to 1. In the numerator, we'd be left with $17 - 8 = 9$ factors of 2.

Thus,

$$2^{17} \div 2^8 = 2^{17-8} = 2^9$$

Again, let's repeat that process with variables. Now, we're thinking about b^n divided by b^m. The numerator, b^n, has n factors of b. The denominator, b^m, has m factors of b. Since there are so many of the same factor in both the numerator and the denominator, these common factors cancel. (Remember, at the moment we're assuming that $n > m$, so there are more factors of b in the numerator.) This means that all m factors of b in the denominator will be canceled: the entire denominator will be canceled down to 1.

Since m factors of b were canceled in the denominator, we had to cancel m factors of b in the numerator. This means that m factors of b have been removed from the numerator. There were n factors of b in the numerator originally, and m were canceled. That leaves $n - m$ factors of b in the numerator, all over 1 in the denominator. Thus,

$$\frac{b^n}{b^m} = b^{n-m}$$

Dividing powers means subtracting the exponents. Again, if you understand the logic of that argument, then you really own this rule.

Notice that with both of these rules, it's absolutely crucial that the two powers have the *same base*. If the bases are different, all bets are off and these rules don't apply.

The final of the three basic exponent rules is the power rule.

$$(b^n)^m = ?$$

Once again, let's start concretely. Suppose we had to simplify $(7^3)^5$. Let's start on the outside, with the $(\ )^5$ part. Raising anything to the fifth power means multiplying it by itself 5 times. Since we're raising 7^3 to the fifth power, we'll multiply 7^3 by itself 5 times. From there, we can substitute what 7^3 really is: three factors of 7 multiplied together.

$$(7^3)^5 = (7^3) \times (7^3) \times (7^3) \times (7^3) \times (7^3)$$
$$(7^3)^5 = (7 \times 7 \times 7) \times (7 \times 7 \times 7) \times (7 \times 7 \times 7) \times (7 \times 7 \times 7) \times (7 \times 7 \times 7)$$

What we have here are five "groups," each with three factors of 7, which gives us $3 \times 5 = 15$ factors of 7 altogether.

$$(7^3)^5 = 7^{3 \times 5} = 7^{15}$$

Let's repeat that reasoning with variables.

In the expression $(b^n)^m$, we're raising something to the power of m, so we have m different factors of it. What we're raising to the power of m is b^n, which is n factors of b multiplied together. Thus, we have m "groups," each with n factors of b. The total number of factors of b would have to be $m \times n$.

$$(b^n)^m = b^{n \times m}$$

So, finally, we see that **raising a power to an exponent means multiplying the exponents**.

These are the three fundamental exponent rules—and we're big fans of understanding the arguments, rather than simply memorizing them, to help maximize your ACT Math Test score.

Zero Exponents

So those were positive integer exponents. But what happens if something has an exponent of zero?

There are a couple ways to think about this. To start out, let's think about this chart, which has exponents in the top row and corresponding powers of 2 in the bottom row.

Exponent	1	2	3	4
Power	2	4	8	16

Math is all about patterns, so let's look at the patterns. In the top row, we're just adding 1, using ordinary counting, as we go to the right, and subtracting one, counting backward, as we go to the left. If we wanted to fill in the top-row space to the left of 1, it would hold 0 (because it is the integer 1 less than 1).

Now, look at the pattern of the bottom row. For each step we take to the right, we multiply by 2, and for each step we take to the left, we divide by 2. If we extend this pattern one step to the left of the entry 2, we would get $2 \div 2 = 1$. Thus, the entry would look like the following:

Exponent	0	1	2	3	4
Power	1	2	4	8	16

So we see that extending this pattern suggests that $2^0 = 1$. Here, the base of 2 was arbitrary: we could have chosen any other base. And it holds up! **For any base, $b^0 = 1$.**

We can also think about it this way: suppose we want to divide b^n by b^n. On the one hand, we could use standard division:

$$\frac{b^n}{b^m} = b^{n-n} = b^0$$

But we can also take a minute to think about it, realizing that in terms of ordinary common-sense thinking, anything over itself equals 1. (We talked about this earlier in the fractions section.) Therefore,

$$b^0 = 1$$

For any base (other than a base of zero), that base to the power of zero equals 1. (A base of zero is not particularly interesting, since all the powers of zero are just zero.)

Negative Exponents

First, let's bring back our fancy chart.

Exponent		0	1	2	3	4
Power		1	2	4	8	16

We found that in the top row, we are adding 1 each time we step to the right and subtracting 1 each time we step to the left. In the bottom row, we multiply by 2 for every step right, and we divide by 2 for every step left. Now, think about how we can use this pattern to extend everything to the left. The top row will just go down into the negative integers, and in the bottom row, we'll just continue to divide by 2, producing fractions with powers of 2 in the denominator.

Exponent	−3	−2	−1	0	1	2	3	4
Power	$\frac{1}{8}$	$\frac{1}{4}$	$\frac{1}{2}$	1	2	4	8	16

Notice that the bottom row also has a kind of symmetry around the number 1: if we take pairs starting with $\frac{1}{2}$ and 2 and move outward, we end up with pairs of numbers that are reciprocals of each other (like $\frac{1}{4}$ and 4, which is $\frac{4}{1}$). For the positive exponent, we have 2 to a power, and at the corresponding negative exponent, we have 1 over 2 to that same power. Using this reciprocal pattern, we can write the following rule:

$$b^{-n} = \frac{1}{b^n}$$

Let's verify that this is consistent with the quotient rule above.

$$\frac{1}{b^n} = \frac{b^0}{b^n} = b^{0-n} = b^{-n}$$

Perfectly consistent! Notice that we can also think of b^{-n} as the fraction $\frac{b^{-n}}{1}$, so we can also see that when a negative exponent in the numerator "moves" to the denominator, the exponent changes from negative to positive. It also works the other way around: when a negative exponent in the denominator moves to the numerator, the exponent changes from negative to positive. (This can be very helpful in simplifying algebraic problems, by the way.)

$$\frac{1}{b^{-n}} = b^n$$

Ready to put it all together? Here's a hairy-looking practice problem you can use to test out some of those ideas.

Practice Question

$$\frac{(x^{-5})^2(x^4)^4}{x^3 x^{-5}}$$

For all values of $x \neq 0$, the above expression simplifies to which of the following?

A. x^2

B. x^3

C. x^4

D. x^5

E. x^6

Answer and Explanation

Although this looks a little tricky (you may still have had the "AHH, EXPONENTS!" reaction), we can use exponent rules to simplify. A lot.

First, use the power rule on both factors in the numerator. (*Hint:* You have two separate instances where you can apply the rule.)

$$(x^{-5})^2 \, (x^4)^3 = (x^{-10})(x^{12})$$

Then, use the product rule in both the numerator and, separately, in the denominator.

$$\frac{(x^{-10})(x^{12}) = x^2}{(x^3)(x^{-5}) = x^{-2}}$$

Move the negative exponent up to the numerator, and multiply with the product rule.

$$(x^2)(x^2) = x^4$$

Overall, the process looks like this:

$$\frac{(x^{-5})^2(x^4)^3}{(x^3)(x^{-5})} = \frac{(x^{-10})(x^{12})}{(x^3)(x^{-5})} = \frac{x^2}{x^{-2}} = (x^2)(x^2) = x^4$$

Answer: **C**

Square Roots

The most common roots are square roots, and these (kinda) undo squaring. Everything looks straightforward enough if we're only dealing with positive numbers: with all positives, square roots undo a square, plain and simple. For example:

$$5^2 = 25 \qquad \sqrt{25} = 5$$
$$25^2 = 625 \qquad \sqrt{625} = 25$$
$$85^2 = 7225 \qquad \sqrt{7225} = 85$$

Everything so far is correct. Notice, though, that when we square a negative, or multiply a negative by a negative, we get a positive number.

$$(-5)^2 = 25$$
$$(-25)^2 = 625$$
$$(-85)^2 = 625$$

So there are two different numbers on the number line, +5 and −5, that, when squared, have an output of 25. But in the table above, each square root had a single, positive output. What's going on? If we're "undoing" the square of 25, when do we take just the positive result and when do we consider both roots? This is a subtle issue, and some of it revolves around this symbol:

$$\sqrt{}$$

What's this symbol called? In everyday life, we call this simply the "square root symbol," but the real and technical name is the "principal square root symbol." You might also hear it called the *radical*. Here, the word "principal," in the sense of "main," means **only the positive root**. In other words, when a positive number is under this symbol, the output is always positive.

In terms of test day, here's the important distinction. When the folks who write the ACT use the $\sqrt{}$ symbol as part of the problem, then this always, 100 percent of the time, means that you should take the positive root *only*.

On the other hand, if the problem prints a variable squared (e.g., x^2) or presents some other set of conditions that leads to the square of a variable—and you yourself have to take the square root as part of your problem-solving process—then always, 100 percent of the time, you must consider *both* roots, positive and negative. Thus, $\sqrt{25}$ has only one output ($\sqrt{25} = 5$), but the equation $x^2 = 25$ has two solutions ($x = +5$ and $x = -5$).

Speaking of square roots, keep in mind that the square root of a perfect square comes out to a nice neat integer, but the square roots of most positive integers are ugly decimals. For example, $\sqrt{19} = 4.3588989435407$. In other words, this is one of those times when you might want to break out your calculator if you need an exact number, but make sure you really do. Nobody expects you to know $\sqrt{19}$ in your head, but the ACT may expect you to see that because $16 < 19 < 25$, it must be true that $4 < \sqrt{19} < 5$ (the square roots of those numbers). Also, it's good to know rough approximations for two particularly common roots:

$$\sqrt{2} \approx 1.4$$
$$\sqrt{3} \approx 1.7$$

There are a few things other things you need to know about square roots. For instance, it's very important to appreciate the fundamental definition of a square root. For example, $\sqrt{5}$ is the number which, when multiplied by itself, has a product of 5. (In other words, $\sqrt{5}^2 = 5$.)

So far, we've only talked about positive numbers under the square root. But can we take the square root of zero? Yep! $\sqrt{0} = 0$ and the equation $x^2 = 0$ has only one solution, $x = 0$.

What happens if there's a negative under the radical? For example, what does $\sqrt{-25}$ equal?

In this case, we have to be precise with wording. There is no *real-number* output for the square root of a negative. A little more concretely, there is no number on the real number line that could be the output of this expression. Nevertheless, technically, it's not correct to say that $\sqrt{-25}$ has "no answer" or "no solution" (even though this may be what your calculator says).

The correct answer to this is an **imaginary number**. We'll discuss these in a little more depth later, but here's what you need to know for solving square roots. In the equations below, *i* is the fundamental imaginary number: the square root of negative one. (Once again, we will discuss this in the advanced topics on page 274, so don't worry if it's a little confusing at first.)

$$\sqrt{-25} = 5i$$

So $x^2 = -25$ has two solutions, $x = +5i$ and $x = -5i$.

Other Roots

The ACT sometimes asks about cubes and cube roots. Cube roots undo cubing, but the rule for negative numbers differs from the rule for square roots.

$$3^3 = 27$$

$$(-3)^3 = -27$$

$$\sqrt[3]{27} = 3$$

$$\sqrt[3]{-27} = -3$$

The cube of a positive is positive, and the cube of a negative is negative. That means that the cube root of a positive is positive, and the cube root of a negative is negative. Notice something important here: the pattern is completely different from what it was for square roots.

We can also find the cube root of any number on the number line—positive, negative, or zero.

The definition of a cube root is that it is the inverse of cubing. In other words, $\sqrt[3]{5}$ is, by definition, the number which, when cubed, equals 5. We can generalize that pattern for any root: for any integer $n > 2$, $\sqrt[n]{m}$ is the number which, when raised to the nth power, equals m.

We can also generalize the sign difference between squares and cubes. A negative to the power of *any even* number is positive, so we can't take an even root of any negative number. On the other hand, a negative to the power of *any odd number* is negative: odd powers and roots preserve signs, so it is perfectly possible to take an odd root of a negative number—this would have a negative answer.

Sound good in theory? Great! Let's put that into practice:

Practice Question

Which of the following expressions, for some values of $x \neq 0$ and $y \neq 0$, could have an output that is less than zero?

F. $\sqrt[4]{x^4}$

G. $\sqrt[7]{x^4}$

H. $\sqrt[4]{x^7}$

J. $\sqrt[5]{x^2 + y^2}$

K. $\sqrt[5]{x^2 - y^2}$

Answer and Explanation

When approaching this problem, spend a minute thinking about what it's asking you to find before doing anything else. To get a negative output, we would need something negative under an odd root. Right away, choices F and H are out, because the fourth root of a positive would have a positive output. What if x^7 is negative, though, because it's an odd power? Remember, we can't take an even root of a negative number! These don't work.

In G, the fourth power of any number is positive, never negative, so the output can't be negative. This doesn't work.

In J, each square will be positive, and the sum of two positives will be positive, so what's under the radical always will be positive and the output can't be negative. This doesn't work.

In K, each individual square still will be positive, but it is possible for the difference of two positive numbers to be negative. For example, if $a = 5$ and $b = 7$, then $a^2 - b^2 = 25 - 49 = -24$. Thus, in this situation, we could have a negative under the radical; since 5 is an odd number, the fifth root of negative would have a negative output. This is the only answer choice that works.

Answer: **K**

Fractional Exponents

From time to time on the ACT, you'll see something that might look a little wonky: a fractional exponent. This is exactly what it sounds like, an exponent in the form of a fraction, rather than an integer. When you see a fractional exponent (for example, $x^{\frac{1}{y}}$), the product of the whole expression will actually give you one of the roots of the base (a root of x). Why is this?

Well, suppose we really didn't know what the exponent of x would be when we have $\sqrt{x}$. In other words, x to the something equals $\sqrt{x}$, and we'd like to figure out that something. Give it a variable: we can't use x, because we are already using that, so we will use p for power.

$$x^p = \sqrt{x}$$

Well, go back to the fundamental definition of a square root: $\sqrt{x}$ is the number which, when squared, equals x. So we'll square both sides:

$$(x^p)^2 = x$$
$$x^{2p} = x$$

Well, x by itself has an exponent of 1, so it must be true that

$$2p = 1$$
$$p = \frac{1}{2}$$

Thus, x to the $\frac{1}{2}$ is $\sqrt{x}$. By a similar argument, x to the $\frac{1}{3}$ is $\sqrt[3]{x}$. In fact, we could make the generalization that

$$x^{\frac{1}{n}} = \sqrt[n]{x}$$

We know what you're thinking: what happens if the fraction has an integer other than 1 in the numerator? For example,

$$x^{\frac{2}{3}} = ?$$

Well, think about how fractions work. Fundamentally, the fraction $\frac{2}{3}$ is a product of the integer 2 and the fraction $\frac{1}{3}$, and we can express that product in either order.

$$\frac{2}{3} = 2 \times \frac{1}{3} = \frac{1}{3} \times 2$$

We can think of either factor as coming first. That means that we can think of x to the $\frac{2}{3}$ as an x^2 inside a cube root, or the cube root of x, squared. This is slightly easier to visualize:

$$x^{\frac{2}{3}} = \sqrt[3]{x^2} = (\sqrt[3]{x})^2$$

We can generalize this, too:

$$x^{\frac{a}{b}} = \sqrt[b]{x^a} = \left(\sqrt[b]{x}\right)^a$$

Exponents and the Distributive Property

If the term "Distributive Property" is a fuzzy memory from math class, let's do a quick refresher on what it means in terms of the ACT Math Test:

$$P(Q + R) = (P \times Q) + (P \times R) \qquad (Q + R) \div T = (Q \div T) + (R \div T)$$
$$P(Q - R) = (P \times Q) - (P \times R) \qquad (Q - R) \div T = (Q \div T) - (R \div T)$$

The basic idea is that when you have multiplication or division in the same problem as addition or subtraction, the multiplication or division applies to each of the terms in the addition or subtraction part of the problem. In other words, multiplication and division distribute to addition and subtraction. Notice that, in all four of those equations, when we go from left to right, that's called "distributing," but when we go from right to left, that's called "factoring out."

And here's an important mathematical analogy: addition has the same relationship to multiplication that multiplication has to exponentiation. If we ask you to tell us what eight 7's added together is, you can tackle it by dutifully saying $7 + 7 + 7 + 7 + 7 + 7 + 7 + 7$ or you can use multiplication and find 7×8. In a very similar way, exponentiation allows us to more efficiently tackle a lot of multiplication. If we asked you to multiply eight 2's together, you could find $2 \times 2 \times 2 \times 2 \times 2 \times 2 \times 2 \times 2$ or jump immediately to 2^8. It is also worth noting that, in the same way that multiplication distributes over addition, exponents distribute over multiplication.

At this level, exponents and roots do distribute over multiplication and division, and it looks like this:

1. $(a \times b)^n = (a)^n (b)^n$

2. $\left(\dfrac{a}{b}\right)^n = \dfrac{a^n}{b^n}$

3. $\sqrt[n]{a \times b} = (\sqrt[n]{a})(\sqrt[n]{b})$

4. $\sqrt[n]{\dfrac{a}{b}} = \dfrac{\sqrt[n]{a}}{\sqrt[n]{b}}$

Let's put each of these rules into a statement.

1. The power of a product is the product of the powers.
2. The power of a quotient is the quotient of the powers.
3. The product of roots is the root of the product.
4. The quotient of roots is the root of the quotient.

If you find reading about these rules confusing, don't worry: the important thing is that you know how to use them! On that note, we have to warn you about a very tempting mistake. Multiplication distributes over addition and subtraction, and powers distribute over multiplication and division, but we can't "jump" a level—we're not allowed to distribute powers or roots over addition or subtraction.

$$(a + b)^n \neq a^n + b^n \qquad \sqrt{a+b} \neq \sqrt{a} + \sqrt{b}$$
$$(a - b)^n \neq a^n - b^n \qquad \sqrt{a-b} \neq \sqrt{a} - \sqrt{b}$$

These are very tricky, and believe us: test-takers make these mistakes *all the time*. Even when a teacher covers why these are wrong, and everyone gets it in that moment that these are wrong, the next day, those same students will make these mistakes again. When students are stressed or under pressure, they are more likely to make these mistakes, too. So these exceptions are really important to remember! Remind yourself several times that these are wrong. Plug in numbers to verify that they don't work. Do whatever you have to do to remember these exceptions.

Simplifying Square Roots

Suppose you solve a question correctly and find that the answer is $\sqrt{200}$. Why might it be that, even though you have done everything correctly, you can't find $\sqrt{200}$ among the answer choices? If this happens to you, it is probably because the ACT sometimes lists radicals in simplified form.

What exactly does it mean to simplify a radical? Well, if the number under the radical is a perfect square, we can take the square root and simplify it. What's less clear is that we still can simplify the expression somewhat, even if the number under the radical is not a perfect square *but has at least one factor that is a perfect square.* For example, 8 is not a perfect square, so $\sqrt{8}$ is not an integer. Nevertheless, one factor of 8 is 4, and 4 *is* a perfect square. If we write 8 as 4 × 2, then we can use the laws discussed above to re-express the root of a product as the product of the roots (it's not just a fun saying!):

$$\sqrt{8} = \sqrt{4 \times 2} = \sqrt{4} \times \sqrt{2} = 2\sqrt{2}$$

The square root of 8 is simply two times the square root of 2: the latter expression is considered a simplified version of the square root of 8, because the numbers (2) are smaller than the original number (8).

Returning to our earlier example, 200 is divisible by 100, which is a perfect square.

$$\sqrt{200} = \sqrt{100 \times 2} = \sqrt{100} \times \sqrt{2} = 10\sqrt{2}$$

Notice that $5 \times 2\sqrt{2} = 10\sqrt{2}$. We wouldn't necessarily notice this when the radicals were in their unsimplified form, but noticing that kind of relationship can be incredibly helpful when solving more complex ACT Math Test problems.

Ready to put your knowledge to the test? Try it out!

Practice Question

$$\sqrt{45} + \sqrt{80} =$$

A. $5\sqrt{5}$
B. $7\sqrt{5}$
C. 11
D. $25\sqrt{5}$
E. $\sqrt{125}$

Answer and Explanation

Not to be all negative, but first of all, let's review what we CANNOT do (because a lot of people end up doing it). We can't add through the radicals: $\sqrt{a} + \sqrt{b} \neq \sqrt{a+b}$. In other words, we definitely can't add the 45 and 80 in any way.

Instead, we have to simplify each radical separately, writing each number under the radical as a product in which one of the factors is a perfect square. (If you're stumped regarding where to start, peeking at the answer choices can help in a problem like this: notice that a lot of them contain $\sqrt{5}$ which does end up being an important part of the solution! Also consider how your prime factorization skills can help you.)

$$\sqrt{45} = (\sqrt{9})(\sqrt{5}) = 3\sqrt{5}$$
$$\sqrt{80} = (\sqrt{16})(\sqrt{5}) = 4\sqrt{5}$$
$$\sqrt{45} + \sqrt{80} = 3\sqrt{5} + 4\sqrt{5} = 7\sqrt{5}$$

Answer: **B**

Scientific Notation

Now that you're an exponent master, let's start untangling *scientific notation*. Scientific notation is used as a convenient way to denote numbers of a very large or very small size. Rather than waste a lot of space with a long string of placeholding zeros, scientific notation gives us a way to write these numbers compactly. For example,

> mass of an electron = 9.109×10^{-31} kg
> mass of the planet Jupiter = 1.898×10^{27} kg

Those are two extreme numbers, one inconceivably small and the other inconceivably big, and yet scientific notation allows us to print each with fewer than a dozen characters. That's efficiency!

So how does scientific notation work? So glad you asked! A number in the form $A \times 10^p$ is in proper scientific notation if

1. p is an integer, and
2. $1 \leq A < 10$

When we multiply or divide, we can treat the A parts and the 10^p parts separately and then combine the results. When we raise ($A \times 10^p$) to a power, we distribute the exponent to the two factors and follow the laws of exponents.

Notice that if A is greater than 10, then the number is not in proper scientific notation form. Sometimes, as a result of calculations you make, the A figure (the number out in front) might wind up greater than 10. If this happens, we have to adjust: we have to move one or more powers of 10 from the A to the 10^p. For example,

$$(4 \times 10^6)(6 \times 10^{11}) = (4 \times 6) \times (10^6 \times 10^{11}) = 24 \times 10^{17} = 2.4 \times 10^{18}$$

Finally, you may have noticed that in science class, folks make a big fuss about the difference between 4×10^6 and 4.000×10^6. This is an issue of "significant digits": while this is a big deal in the sciences, the ACT Math Test does not test the rules of significant digits, so you don't have to worry about them for the moment.

Here's what an ACT Math problem using scientific notation might look like:

Practice Question

$$\frac{3 \times 10^{15}}{6 \times 10^{-7}} =$$

 A. 5×10^7

 B. 2×10^8

 C. 5×10^{21}

 D. 2×10^{22}

 E. 1.8×10^{23}

Answer and Explanation
While this looks complicated at first, it gets a lot simpler if you treat this fraction as the product of two separate fractions: a 3 over 6 fraction times a fraction of the powers of ten.

$$\frac{3}{6} \times \frac{10^{15}}{10^{-7}}$$

Let's look at the first fraction.

$$\frac{3}{6} = \frac{1}{2} = 0.5$$

As it is, that's less than 1, so we'll have to change that to put it into proper scientific notation. But before we know how we can change it, we'll have to deal with that second fraction.

$$\frac{10^{15}}{10^{-7}}$$

In the second fraction, remember that dividing by a negative power is the same as multiplying by a positive power, so 10^{15} divided by 10^{-7} is the same as 10^{15} times 10^{7}. When we multiply powers, we add the exponents, so this product is 10^{22}.

$$\frac{10^{15}}{10^{-7}} = 10^{15} \times 10^{7} = 10^{15+7} = 10^{22}$$

Multiply these quotients and convert to proper scientific notation.

$$0.5 \times 10^{22} = 5 \times 10^{-1} \times 10^{22} = 5 \times 10^{21}$$

Answer: **C**

Common Mistakes on the ACT Math Test

Not answering the right question. It's easy to get caught up in calculations and forget that the question asked you to find the value of $2y$ instead of y. Circle what the question is asking for and double-check it before you answer.

Not using your calculator enough. You are allowed to use a calculator, so use it for all but the simplest calculations. It's easy to make a mistake dividing 84 by 6 with long division; you are less likely to do that on a calculator. If you have a graphing calculator, you can also use the graphing function to solve some coordinate geometry problems, or use the sin, cos, and tan buttons to solve trig problems. However, there is such a thing as using your calculator too much! Obsessively checking your calculations can waste precious time, especially when some calculations can be accomplished using mental math.

Not writing down your work. If you are using hypothetical numbers to help solve a word problem, make sure to write down the numbers you're using. The last thing you want to do is get to your solution and forget the original numbers you used. Similarly, if you're plugging negative numbers into an algebra equation, make sure to use parentheses so you don't forget about the signs. For example, if you know $x = -6$ and $y = 14 - x$, write $y = 14 - (-6)$. Use your scratch paper to your advantage!

Geometry

The word "geometry" comes from "geo" (Earth) and "metry" (measure). Geometry is the study of shapes, and the ACT loves the topic! Why? Look around! There's geometry everywhere! Look at all of the shapes different objects and materials can form. Whether you plan to be a scientist, engineer, designer, or any kind of visual artist, principles of geometry can play a role in your work.

One of the reasons math teachers and people who write math tests absolutely love geometry is that it's loaded with terms that are dense with information. If the test tells you, say, that *ABCD* is a square or that *JKL* is an equilateral triangle, either one of these facts already implies a large number of other facts. A deep part of understanding geometry is to recognize what's already implied in any geometric statement.

Lines and Angles

First of all, let's talk about points and lines. In geometry, a *point* is a location, and we use a dot to indicate a point. A *line* is a straight path that goes on forever in both directions. When we cut off a line in one or both directions, we don't have a line anymore. Rather, a *ray* is a straight path that goes on forever in one direction and has one endpoint, while a *line segment* has two endpoints.

An *angle* is formed where two lines meet. More precisely, an angle is composed of two rays leaving a point. The point where the angle originates is called a *vertex* (plural "vertices"). Oftentimes, you'll see an angle represented by the ∠ symbol.

Angles are often measured in degrees (denoted by the ° symbol). They can also be measured in radians, which we'll talk about in more detail in the section on trigonometry. For now, we'll stick to degrees. Here are four types of angles you should be familiar with:

1. acute angles (less than 90°)
2. right angles (equal to 90°)
3. obtuse angles (more than 90°)
4. straight angle (equal to 180° and is a straight line)

Whenever two lines intersect, they create four angles. The angles opposite each other are called "vertical" angles—not because they're up-and-down but because they only touch at their vertices. **Vertical angles are equal.**

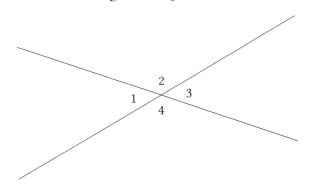

Two lines are
considered
perpendicular to
each other when
they meet at a
right angle (90°).

In this diagram, (∠1) = (∠3) and (∠2) = (∠4). Why? These are the two pairs of vertical angles. The only time that all four angles would be equal would be if the lines were perpendicular: that would produce four 90° angles.

Some of the most fundamental geometry facts have to do with the special properties of parallel lines. But while there are a number of special geometry facts that are true for parallel lines, absolutely none of them are true for lines that are *almost* parallel. This is important to remember when you're looking at diagrams. While we mentioned earlier that the figures on the ACT are drawn relatively to scale, we have to be careful. The instructions on the ACT tell us, "***Illustrative figures are NOT necessarily drawn to scale.***" So, while you can generally use figures to estimate relationships, if two lines simply *look* parallel, you cannot assume they *are* parallel. In order to apply any of the great parallel-line facts, you have to be told that the lines are parallel.

If Two Lines Are Parallel

When the test-makers guarantee us that the lines are parallel, and another line intersects these parallel lines, what do we know? We can actually figure out a ton. We'll use the following diagram to summarize everything you need to know about the relationships between parallel and intersecting lines.

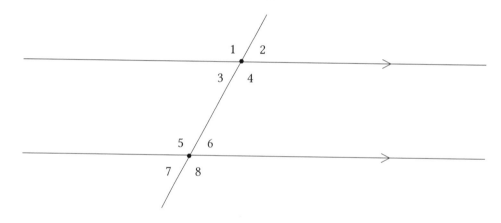

First of all, notice that these lines create eight angles. Also, we could divide these eight angles by size into big angles (angles 1, 4, 5, and 8) and small angles (angles 2, 3, 6, and 7). Here's some more info about what's happening up there:

1. All the big (obtuse) angles are equal.
2. All the small (acute) angles are equal.
3. Any big angle plus any small angle equals 180°.

There are all kinds of fancy geometry names for these angles—for example, angles 3 and 6 are "alternate interior angles"— but for the purposes of the ACT, you don't need to know those technical terms. Rather, you'll want to focus on understanding the relationships between these eight angles mentioned above.

Polygons

Polygons are closed "geometric figures" (shapes) with all sides made of line segments. When we say polygons are closed, we mean that the line segments form an unbroken chain. In a *polygon*, two line segments come together to form a vertex or point with a certain angle measure. A polygon has an equal number of sides, vertices, and angles. It's also good to know that all polygons are two-dimensional, which means we can draw them on a piece of paper. While polygons must have at least three sides, there is no limit to the number of sides a polygon may have!

Ordinary Triangles

A *triangle* is the smallest type of polygon. Every triangle has three straight sides and three angles. The sum of the three angles of any triangle is 180°. This property can be referred to as the *angle sum theorem.*

A triangle can have three acute angles (e.g., 50°, 60°, and 70°), or a right angle with two acute angles (e.g., 30°, 60°, and 90°), or an obtuse angle with two acute angles (e.g., 10°, 20°, and 150°).

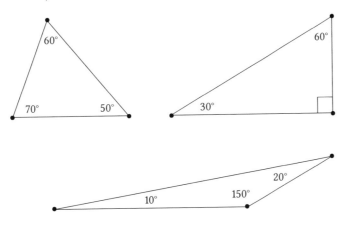

We'll get into more on that 30-60-90 triangle below. Many not-so-interesting triangles have three different side lengths and three unrelated angles. Things get more interesting when there are more patterns inside a triangle.

Isosceles Triangles

An *isosceles triangle* has two *congruent*, or identical, sides.

Euclid's theorem

Euclid's theorem, proved over 2,200 years ago, applies directly to isosceles triangles. The theorem states the following:

If the two sides are equal, then the opposite angles are equal.

and

If the two angles are equal, then the opposite sides are equal.

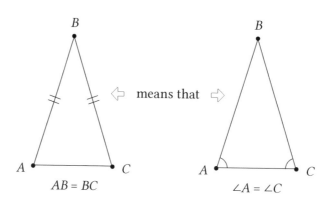

AB = BC $\quad\quad$ ∠A = ∠C

Isosceles triangles and the 180° Triangle Theorem

If you're told that triangle *ABC* is isosceles, and one of the bottom equal angles (called a *base angle*) is 50°, then you'll also know that the measure of the other base angle is also 50°. That means the top angle, or the *vertex angle*, must be 80°. Knowing the measure of one base angle of an isosceles triangle is sufficient to find the measures of all three angles. Thanks, Euclid!

In an isosceles triangle, we call the two sides of equal length "legs" and the third side the "base." The two angles formed by a leg and the base are the "base angles." These two angles are equal in measure. The third angle, which is formed by the two legs, is the vertex angle.

Let's take it a step further: suppose the problem tells you that triangle *ABC* is isosceles and the vertex angle is 50°. Well, you don't know the measures of the base angles, but you know they're equal. Let *x* be the degrees of each base angle; then

$$x + x + 50° = 180°$$
$$2x = 130°$$
$$x = 65°$$

So each base angle is 65°. Knowing the measure of the vertex angle of an isosceles triangle is sufficient to find the measures of all three angles.

Right Triangles

A *right triangle* is any triangle that has one right (90°) angle. In a right triangle, the other two angles have to be acute—in fact, they have to have a sum of 90°. The longest side will always be opposite the right angle and is called the *hypotenuse*; the other two sides are called *legs*.

Pythagorean theorem

Excuse us while we geek out a bit, but there's a reason the *Pythagorean theorem* is the most famous theorem in mathematics! This remarkable theorem is one of the most versatile and highly adaptable formulas in existence. It states: For any right triangle, $a^2 + b^2 = c^2$.

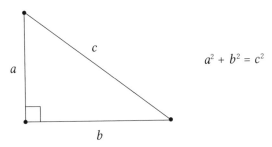

$$a^2 + b^2 = c^2$$

You can use this formula when a question on the ACT gives you two sides of a right triangle and asks you to find the third. This remarkable theorem will show up in many places on the ACT Math Test: in geometry, coordinate geometry, trigonometry, and complex numbers.

There are triplets of integers that satisfy the Pythagorean theorem. These are called *Pythagorean triplets*, and they refer to the ratio of a triangle's sides. The most fundamental is {3, 4, 5}. Other common ones you should know are {5, 12, 13}, {8, 15, 17}, and {7, 24, 25}. These are useful, first of all, because they save you the work of doing calculations. If you know that the hypotenuse is 17 and one leg is 8, you don't have to square 17, then square 8, then subtract; instead, you simply know the other leg has to be 15. Furthermore, any multiple of these also works. Thus, from the {3, 4, 5} triplet, we also get {6, 8, 10} and {9, 12, 15} and {12, 16, 20}, etc. If you spot a ratio of this sort among larger numbers, it can save lots of time. It often pays to look for common factors in the measurements of a right triangle's legs, precisely because they can reveal this kind of pattern.

For example, try this practice problem *without a calculator*:

Practice Question

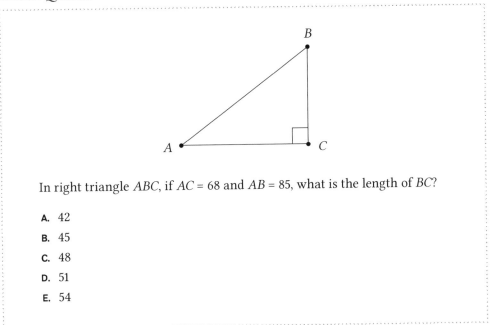

In right triangle *ABC*, if *AC* = 68 and *AB* = 85, what is the length of *BC*?

   A. 42

   B. 45

   C. 48

   D. 51

   E. 54

Answer and Explanation

It would require a big chunk of time (especially without a calculator!) to directly apply the Pythagorean theorem, by first squaring 85, then squaring 68, then subtracting them and finally trying to take the square root of this four-digit difference. Instead, notice how all of the side lengths we're given in the prompt and answer choices are all integers. That means that we are working with a Pythagorean triplet! So, we can save time by looking for common factors. It turns out that $85 = 5 \times 17$ and $68 = 4 \times 17$, which means that this triangle is simply the {3, 4, 5} triangle multiplied by 17. While multiplying by 17 may not be your favorite thing in the world to do, it's way more fun than squaring 85. The short side of this triangle, *BC*, would have to be $3 \times 17 = 51$.

Answer: **D**

That is an example of proportional thinking, which can save you a ton of time on the ACT Math Test.

Special right triangles

In all the Pythagorean triplet triangles, the sides are "nice" but the angles aren't "nice"—they're irrational numbers, and we would need trigonometry to figure out their exact values. Alternately, most right triangles with "nice" angles—say the 20°-70°-90° triangle or the 40°-50°-90° triangle—don't have "nice" side lengths; again, we'd have decimals we would have to find with trigonometry. There are two special right triangles, though, for which we can find all the angles and all the side lengths purely from geometric reasoning: the 30-60-90 triangle and the 45-45-90 triangle. The ACT Math Test expects you to know these two triangles cold, because it loves testing you on their niceness.

We use the word "symmetrical" to describe a shape that looks the same when we transform or move it in some way, like rotating, flipping, or sliding it. For example, when we rotate a square 90°, it looks the same as before we moved it. That is one testament to the symmetry of a square!

The 45-45-90 triangle

Let's start with the square, a magically *symmetrical* shape that we will talk about in more detail on page 160. Assume the square has a side of 1. Cut the square in half along a diagonal and look at the triangle that results.

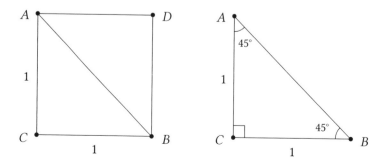

We know $\angle C = 90°$ because it was an angle from the square. We know $AC = BC = 1$, which means the triangle is isosceles, so $\angle A = \angle B = 45°$. Let's call hypotenuse $AB = x$. By the Pythagorean theorem,

$$(AC)^2 + (BC)^2 = (AB)^2$$
$$1 + 1 = x^2$$
$$x^2 = 2$$
$$x = \sqrt{2}$$

The sides are in the ratio of 1-1-$\sqrt{2}$ (this can also be expressed as 1:1:$\sqrt{2}$). We can scale this up simply by multiplying all three of those by any number we like: a-a-$(a\sqrt{2})$.

The three names for this triangle, which are very useful to remember because they summarize all its properties, are

1. The Isosceles Right Triangle
2. The 45-45-90 Triangle
3. The 1-1-$\sqrt{2}$ Triangle

The 30-60-90 triangle

Let's start with an equilateral triangle, another magically symmetrical shape. Of course, by itself, an equilateral triangle is not a right triangle, but we can cut it in half and get a right triangle.

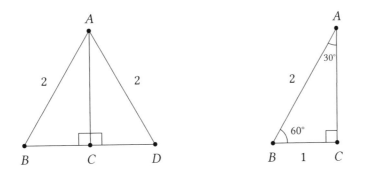

Let's assume ABD is an equilateral triangle with side lengths of 2. We can draw a perpendicular line from A down to BD, which intersects at point C. Because of the highly symmetrical properties of the equilateral triangle, the segment AC (1) forms a right angle at the base, (2) bisects the angle at A, and (3) bisects the base BD.

So in the triangle ABC, we know that $\angle B = 60°$ because that's the old angle from the original equilateral triangle and it hasn't changed. We also know that $\angle C = 90°$ because AC is perpendicular to the base. We know $\angle A = 30°$ because AC bisects the original 60° angle at A in the equilateral triangle. Thus, the angles are 30-60-90. We know $AB = 2$ because that's a side from the original equilateral triangle. We know $BC = 1$ because AC bisects the base BD. Call $AC = x$: we can find it using the Pythagorean theorem.

$$(AC)^2 + (BC)^2 = (AB)^2$$
$$1^2 + x^2 = 2^2$$
$$1 + x^2 = 4$$
$$x^2 = 3$$
$$x = \sqrt{3}$$

The sides are in the ratio 1-$\sqrt{3}$-2. This also can be scaled up by multiplying by any number, which gives the general form:

$$a\text{-}(a\sqrt{3})\text{-}(2a)$$

So the three names for this triangle, which are useful to remember because they summarize all its properties, are

1. The Half-Equilateral Triangle
2. The 30-60-90 Triangle
3. The 1-$\sqrt{3}$-2 Triangle

It's particularly important to remember the "half-equilateral" aspect of this triangle because all the other properties flow from that fact and you'll be able to use this trick on many an ACT problem.

Here's a practice problem.

Practice Question

In a 30-60-90 triangle, the hypotenuse has a length of $24\sqrt{3}$. What is the length of the leg opposite the 60° angle?

F. 12

G. $12\sqrt{3}$

H. 24

J. 36

K. $36\sqrt{3}$

Answer and Explanation

In a 30-60-90 triangle, the ratio of the longest leg (i.e., the leg opposite the 60° angle) to the hypotenuse is $\sqrt{3}$ to 2. Set up a proportion, and call the unknown leg x.

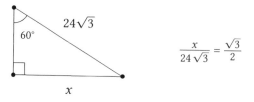

Cross-multiply and solve for x.

$$2x = (24\sqrt{3})(\sqrt{3})$$
$$x = (12\sqrt{3})(\sqrt{3})$$
$$x = 12 \times 3 = \mathbf{36}$$

Answer: **J**

Triangles and Exterior Angles

Another triangle topic the ACT Math Test loves to ask about is *exterior angles*. What are exterior angles? For any shape, an exterior angle is the angle formed between a side of that shape and a line extended from the next side. For example, suppose we extend each side of a triangle as a ray, so that we get three angles outside the triangle.

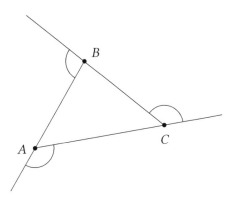

These angles outside the triangle are exterior angles. It turns out that the sum of all of the exterior angles of a triangle (and of any polygon) is 360°. Think about it this way: if you were a bug walking along the perimeter of the triangle, when you got to each vertex, the exterior angle would be the amount you would have to turn to face in the correct direction to go along the next side. When you went all the way around, you would wind up facing the same way as you began, so the total amount that you turned would have to be 360°. That argument can be repeated for any higher polygon: for any polygon, the sum of the exterior angles has to be 360°.

For triangles, there's one more special theorem involving an exterior angle. Suppose we extend only one side of a triangle and get one exterior angle, as in this diagram.

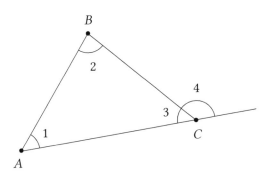

We know that $\angle 3 + \angle 4 = 180°$ because they form a straight line. We also know that $\angle 1 + \angle 2 + \angle 3 = 180°$ because those are the three angles of a triangle. Rewrite those in the following way:

$$\angle 4 = 180° - \angle 3$$
$$\angle 1 + \angle 2 = 180° - \angle 3$$

Because both of those lines are equal to the same thing, they are also equal to each other:

$$\angle 1 + \angle 2 = \angle 4$$

That's a powerful pattern, and the ACT Math Test loves it! The **exterior angle theorem** summarizes the pattern: *The measure of any exterior angle of a triangle equals the sum of the two non-adjacent interior angles.* That's a mouthful to state, but thankfully, you won't have to state it on the ACT (though you definitely need to be able to recognize this pattern).

Areas of Triangles

How can you find the area of a triangle? You may remember the refrain from math class …

$$\text{Area} = \tfrac{1}{2}(\text{base} \times \text{height})$$

But there's something deceptively tricky about this formula: what exactly *is* a base or a height? We might say that the "base" is the flat side, the bottom … but if a triangle looks like this, what's the base?

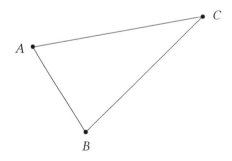

Not every triangle in the universe comes with a standard-issued horizontal side! In fact, *any of the three sides* of a triangle can serve as the base. And if any side can be the base, what's the height? The height associated with any base is a segment called the *altitude*: it is perpendicular to that base and passes through the opposite vertex. Just as a triangle has three bases, it has three altitudes, one corresponding to each base.

So to be more specific, the area of a triangle is (actually) one-half the product of the length of the base and the length of its corresponding altitude.

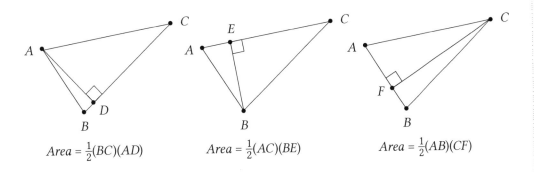

$$Area = \tfrac{1}{2}(BC)(AD) \qquad Area = \tfrac{1}{2}(AC)(BE) \qquad Area = \tfrac{1}{2}(AB)(CF)$$

All three of these triangles have the same area. In practice, the ACT Math Test would make one (and only one) base and its corresponding altitude clear. Notice a couple caveats in odd cases. If the triangle is a right triangle, then if either leg is the base, the other leg is the altitude. Also, if the triangle is an obtuse triangle, then two of the altitudes will lie *outside* the triangle:

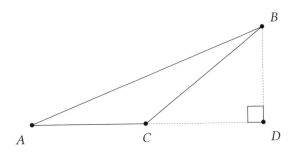

The area of this triangle, *ABC*, is one-half of the product of the base *AC* and its associated altitude, *BD*, the segment passing through *B* and perpendicular to the *line containing AC*. Remember that sometimes altitudes have to go outside the triangle to do their job!

Perpendicular Bisectors

Poor perpendicular bisector. It's really an underestimated geometric idea—so underestimated that we thought it'd be important to review it here. Given any segment, the *perpendicular bisector* of this segment is the line which (a) goes through the *midpoint* (the exact middle point) of the segment and (b) is perpendicular to the segment.

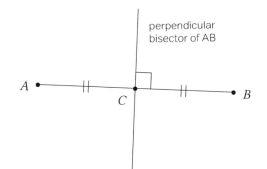

What's the big deal about a perpendicular bisector? First of all, every single point on the perpendicular bisector is equidistant from *A* and from *B*. Thus, we could pick any random point *C* on the perpendicular bisector and *ABC* automatically would be an isosceles triangle. For example,

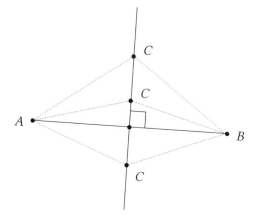

Also, if we reflected point *A* over the perpendicular bisector (or, to put it another way, took its mirror image), its image, or where it would end up being reflected, would be point *B*. That's why we can think of the perpendicular bisector as a "mirror line."

In fact, any time we reflect a point over a mirror line, the mirror must be the perpendicular bisector of the segment connecting the original point to its reflected image.

So whenever a geometric shape is symmetrical when it's reflected, there *must* be perpendicular bisectors as mirror lines, regardless of whether they're explicitly drawn.

Quadrilaterals

A **quadrilateral** is a polygon with four sides and four angles. For all quadrilaterals, the sum of the four angles is 360°. This means that if you know three of the angles, you always can find the fourth. Two special categories of quadrilaterals are parallelograms and trapezoids.

Parallelograms

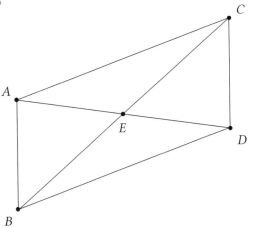

A *parallelogram* is a quadrilateral with two pairs of parallel sides. All parallelograms have the following properties, sometimes referred to as the "Big Four":

1. Opposite sides are parallel (*AB* ∥ *CD* and *BC* ∥ *AD*).
2. Opposite sides have equal length (*AB* = *CD* and *AC* = *BD*).
3. Opposite angles are equal (∠*A* = ∠*D* and ∠*B* = ∠*C*).
4. Diagonals bisect each other (*AE* = *ED* and *BE* = *EC*).

Those four properties always go together: it's impossible for any one of them to be true without the other three being true as well. Remember, all parallelograms automatically have all four of these properties, including the special parallelograms we're going to look at now: the rectangle, the rhombus, and the square.

Rectangles

Because opposite angles are equal in a parallelogram (#3 of the "Big Four" above), if a parallelogram has one right angle, all four of its angles have to be right angles. A parallelogram with right angles is called a *rectangle*. Figure *ABCD* in the diagram below is a rectangle. A rectangle is equiangular (its angles are equal), but it doesn't necessarily have to be equilateral (with equal sides). The diagonals of a rectangle are congruent (or identical).

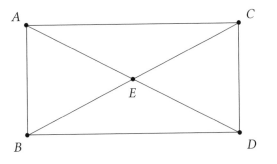

We mentioned before that *ABCD* in this diagram is a rectangle. So, we can say of the two diagonals that *AD* = *BC*. Because the diagonals of any parallelogram bisect each other, we also know that *AE* = *ED* = *BE* = *EC*. That's always true for a rectangle.

Rhombuses

A quadrilateral with four equal sides is a *rhombus*. Because opposite sides are equal, a rhombus must be a parallelogram and have all the properties of a parallelogram. Sometimes, when a rhombus is turned to stand on a vertex (as below), non-mathematicians call it a "diamond," although that's not an official math term. The diagonals of a rhombus are always perpendicular, and they always bisect the vertex angles.

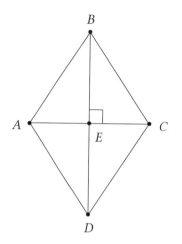

Thus, if $AB = BC = CD = AD$, then $AC \perp BD$; also, $\angle ADE = \angle CDE = \angle ABE = \angle CBE$ and $\angle BAE = \angle DAE = \angle BCE = \angle DCE$. All this is true for all rhombuses.

Squares

Squares are the most symmetrical of all quadrilaterals (and in our opinion, pretty special). However, because it's one of the first shapes anyone learns as a toddler, many people don't appreciate how extraordinary the square is. A *square* is, simultaneously, a parallelogram, a rectangle, and a rhombus, and it has the properties of all three. If the ACT Math Test tells you that a shape is a square, you immediately know that at least a dozen properties are true. For example, we know that the diagonals of any square must (1) bisect each other, (2) be equal in length, (3) be perpendicular to each other, and (4) bisect the right angle at each vertex into two 45° angles. We get all that information and more when we're told a shape is a square. Conversely, it takes a great deal of information to establish that something *is* a square if you aren't given that fact, because a shape has to meet so many different criteria to be a square.

Areas of parallelograms

Ah, the parallelogram. Or rather, the parallelo*grams*—there are lots of them. We'll start with the rectangle. The area of a rectangle is the measure of its base times its height or ($A = bh$), where either side can be the base and the other will be the height.

We can simplify this even more for squares: for a square of side s, the base is s and the height is also s, so the area is simply $A = s^2$. In fact, raising any number or variable to the power of 2 is called "squaring" precisely because this is the operation used to calculate the area of a square.

The area of a rhombus or a general parallelogram is also just $A = bh$, but we have to be careful here. As with triangles, any side can be the base, but the height is an altitude, perpendicular to two bases.

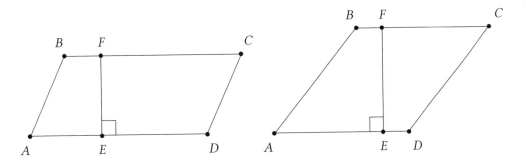

In either of those diagrams, area = (*AD*)(*EF*). Remember that the slanty lengths, such as *AB*, **do not** "count" as the parallelograms' heights. A height *must* be perpendicular to the base.

Trapezoids

Parallelograms are one category of special quadrilaterals; the other is trapezoids. These two categories are mutually exclusive, meaning that you can be a parallelogram or you can be a trapezoid, but you can't be both. A *trapezoid* is a quadrilateral with exactly one pair of parallel sides. The two parallel sides are called the bases, and the two non-parallel sides are called the legs.

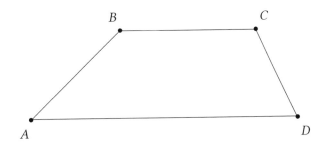

In this diagram, sides *AD* and *BC* are the parallel bases, and *AB* and *CD* are the legs. Because of the rules about parallel lines, the pair of angles along a leg always have a sum of 180°.

$$\angle A + \angle B = 180° \quad \text{and} \quad \angle C + \angle D = 180°$$

Isosceles trapezoids

The ACT Math Test has a particular fondness for isosceles trapezoids. These are trapezoids with two equal legs.

These are completely symmetrical around an imaginary mirror line down the middle (top to bottom) of the shape. Thus, the legs are equal, and the angles along either base are equal: $AB = CD$, $\angle A = \angle D$ and $\angle B = \angle C$. The diagonals of an isosceles trapezoid are the same length.

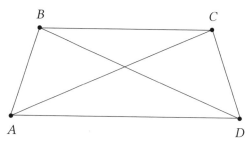

Again, the shape is completely symmetrical about an imaginary vertical midline. Not only does $AC = BD$, but triangles ABD and DCA are also congruent, as are triangles ABC and DCB. All the symmetrical pairs of lengths and angles are equal.

Area of a trapezoid

In practice, the most efficient way to find the area of a trapezoid is often to subdivide it into right triangles and a rectangle.

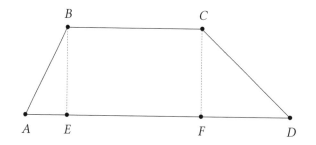

Thus, (area of trapezoid $ABCD$) = (area of triangle ABE) + (area of rectangle $BCFE$) + (area of triangle CDF).

But there's also a one-shot formula for the area of a trapezoid. If the height (the altitude) between the two bases is h, and the lengths of the bases are b_1 and b_2, then the area is given by

$$A = \left(\frac{b_1 + b_2}{2}\right)h$$

Think about this formula for a second: one way to name that term in parentheses is to call it the "average of the bases." That would be the length of a "midline," the line parallel to the bases that connects the midpoints of the two legs.

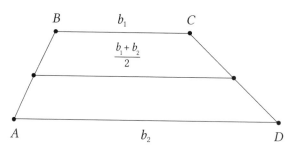

Why is that line pertinent to finding the area? Well, imagine that we drop perpendicular segments from each of those midpoints to make two little right triangles. Then, we could cut these off and flip them around to turn the trapezoid into a rectangle:

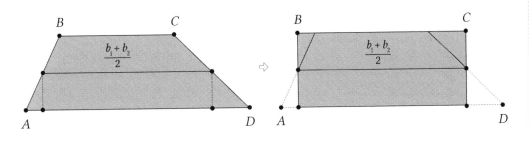

The resulting rectangle, with the same area as the trapezoid, has the same height as the trapezoid and a width of $\frac{b_1 + b_2}{2}$, the average of the bases. If you can remember the logic of this diagram, you can remember the formula for the area of a trapezoid!

Pentagons

A three-sided polygon is called a triangle. A four-sided polygon is called a quadrilateral. A five-sided polygon is called a *pentagon*. A pentagon has five sides and five angles. The sum of the five angles in any pentagon is 540°. We can use the angle sum theorem—that the sum of the angles of a triangle is 180°—to show this!

Here's the logic: we can divide any pentagon into three triangles.

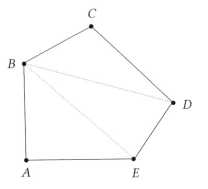

The angles in each one of those triangles would have a sum of 180°, and 3 × 180 = 540. That's why the sum of the angles in a pentagon has to be 540°.

In fact, that rule generalizes to an *n*-sided polygon, where *n* is the number of sides.

Sum of angles in *n*-sided polygon = $(n - 2)180°$

That rule covers the triangle ($n = 3$), quadrilateral ($n = 4$), and pentagon ($n = 5$) cases, as well as all higher polygons.

Regular Polygons

Let's spend a minute with *regular polygons.* In ordinary language, the word "regular" means "ordinary, commonplace, or usual." But in geometry, this word takes on the opposite meaning: it refers to the most perfectly symmetrical shape possible in any category. Any regular polygon has all equal side lengths and all equal angles: it is both equilateral and equiangular.

The "regular triangle" is the equilateral triangle. The "regular quadrilateral" is the square.

The Regular Pentagon

Here are the regular pentagon and the associated star you get when connecting any point contained within it to any other point (pretty, right?):

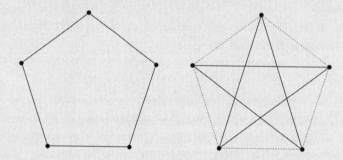

Of course, 50 of that particular kind of star adorn the United States' flag. If needed, we could find the measure of each angle by dividing the sum of the angles, 540°, by five: 540° ÷ 5 = 108°. The lengths of the sides here are not anything the ACT Math Test would expect you to know, so we're not going to worry about those.

Regular polygons have high levels of symmetry. We can do different transformations to these shapes without looking like we did anything. For example, when we rotate a regular polygon by the number of degrees that its angles measure, it looks like we didn't change anything! Also, when we cut these shapes in half, the two pieces are mirror images of each other.

Circles

Now that we've talked about the most symmetrical polygons, it makes sense to talk about the only *infinitely* symmetrical geometric shape: the circle. For the ACT Math Test, you'll need to know a few of the old favorites:

$$c = \pi d = 2\pi r$$
$$A = \pi r^2$$

The former is the formula for the *circumference* or the distance around a circle. That latter formula, for the area of a circle, was proven by the great Greek mathematician, Archimedes (c. 287–212 BCE). In both formulas, *r* is the *radius*, the distance from the center of the circle to the circumference in any direction. Any line segment with both endpoints on the circle is a *chord*, and the longest possible chord is the *diameter*, which is twice the length of the circle's radius. The diameter is the only chord that passes through the center of the circle.

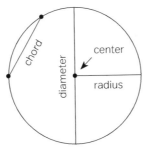

<aside>
Archimedes used an elaborate polygon construction to derive one of the best ancient approximations of π. No one was able to derive more than a few dozen digits of π until advances of calculus in the 18th century. As of November 2016, the record for the most digits of π calculated is over 22 trillion digits.
</aside>

Circles, Radii, and Triangles

All *radii* (plural of radius) of the same circle have the same length. One consequence of this—which the ACT Math Test is a big fan of, by the way!—is that if two sides of a triangle were radii of the same circle, that triangle would have to be isosceles.

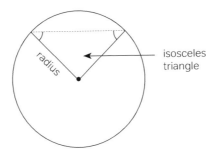

Angles and arcs in circles

An *arc* is a piece of the circumference of a circle. We can talk about the size of an arc in two different ways—in terms of angle, the *arc measure*, and in terms of length, the *arc length*. For the moment, forget all about arc length as we focus on arc measure.

For any arc, we could draw two radii that terminate at the endpoints of the arc.

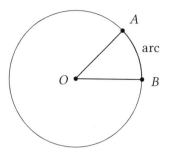

In this diagram, *O* is the center of the circle and arc *AB* is bound by radii *OA* and *OB*. Because angle *AOB* has its vertex at the center of the circle, it is called a *central angle*. Any arc has exactly the same arc measure as the measure of its central angle. If ∠*AOB* = 41°, then arc *AB* has a measure of 41°. As mentioned above, if we were to connect points *A* and *B* with a line segment, we would create an isosceles triangle with the central angle as its vertex angle.

What gets tricky about this is when the angle is not between two radii but rather between two chords, so that its vertex is on the circle.

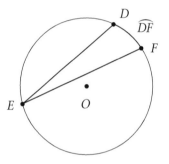

This kind of angle is called an *inscribed angle*. It makes sense that, since we've pushed the vertex farther away, the inscribed angle is smaller than the central angle would be. This means that the inscribed angle is smaller than the arc measure. The astonishing fact is that **the measure of an inscribed angle is always exactly half the arc measure**. For example, if ∠*DEF* = 16°, then arc *DF* has a measure of 32°.

Why is this true? Consider this diagram.

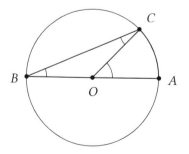

This shows the special case in which one of the chords forming the inscribed angle is a diameter. We want to establish the relationship between angle *B* and arc *AC*.

What do we know? We know that triangle *BOC* has to be an isosceles triangle: *BO* = *CO*, so angle *B* = angle *C*.

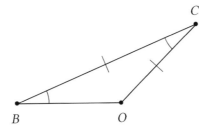

We know that angle *COA* = arc *AC*.

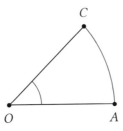

Here's the really crucial part: we can use the exterior angle theorem we introduced in the section on triangles. The theorem states that the measure of any exterior angle of a triangle equals the sum of the two non-adjacent interior angles.

From that theorem, we know ∠*COA* = ∠*B* + ∠*C*.

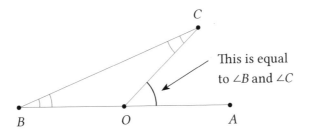

This is equal to ∠*B* and ∠*C*

Since ∠*B* and ∠*C* are equal, we can say that *COA* = 2(*B*).

Since *COA* equals the arc, we can substitute

$$2(\angle B) = \text{arc } AC$$

$$\angle B = \frac{1}{2}(\text{arc } AC)$$

That's a simplified argument about *why the measure of the inscribed angle equals half the measure of the arc it intersects.* You don't need to reproduce this argument on the ACT Math Test, but remembering this argument will help you remember this fact, and you definitely need to remember the fact itself for the ACT.

Arc length and sectors

Now we can talk about arc length! If we know the radius and the size of a circle's central angle, we can figure out the arc length by setting up a proportion in the form part-over-whole. The central angle is "part" of all the way around the circle, which is 360°. The length of the arc is part of the whole distance around the circle; that is, the circumference, given by $c = 2\pi r$. Here's the proportion.

$$\frac{central\,angle}{360°} = \frac{arc\,length}{2\pi r}$$

The arc is a piece of the circumference, a piece from the outside of a circle. If we say the arc is like the crust on a slice of pizza, then the area of the slice itself would be a *sector*.

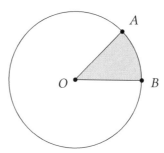

A circular sector is the area bound by an arc and two radii. That's our slice. Just as we did with arc length, we use a part-over-whole proportion to find the area of the sector. Once again, the central angle is part of the full 360° around the circle, and the area of the sector is part of the area of the circle.

$$\frac{central\,angle}{360°} = \frac{area\,of\,sector}{\pi r^2}$$

How could this show up on test day? Have a look!

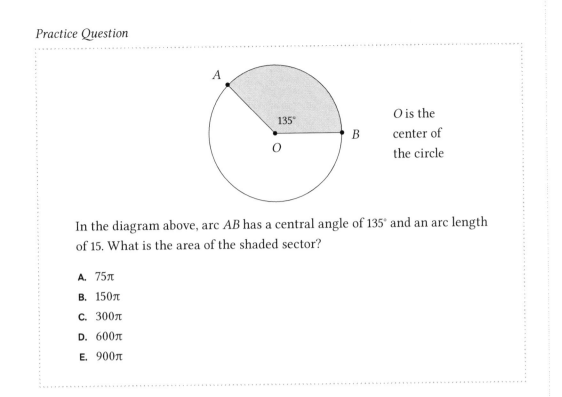

O is the center of the circle

In the diagram above, arc *AB* has a central angle of 135° and an arc length of 15. What is the area of the shaded sector?

A. 75π

B. 150π

C. 300π

D. 600π

E. 900π

Answer and Explanation

The shaded sector makes up a fraction of the entire circle. We can find the area of the shaded circle by first using the angle of the arc to determine what fraction of the circle is shaded. Then, we will need to find the area of the entire circle in order to calculate the area of the shaded section. So, first, think about 135°: it's 3 times 45°. A 45° angle is half of 90°, a quarter of 180°, and an eighth of the whole 360°. Thus, 135° is $\frac{3}{8}$ of the whole 360°—that's the fraction of the circle involved here. That means that this arc length, 15π, is $\frac{3}{8}$ of the circumference: $15\pi = \frac{3}{8}c$. Now we can find the whole circumference in a few, simple steps. First, divide by 3: $5\pi = \frac{1}{8}c$. Now, multiply by 8: $40\pi = c$. We see that the whole circumference must be 40π. We can use that to find the radius. (As a general rule, in almost all circle problems, a very good strategy is to find the radius first—even if you don't know what you're going to do with it yet—because you need that to find everything else!)

$$c = 2\pi r$$
$$40\pi = 2\pi r$$
$$r = 20$$

Now that we know the radius, we can find the area of the entire circle.

$$A = \pi r^2 = \pi(20)^2 = 400\pi$$

The shaded sector has to be $\frac{3}{8}$ of this. $\frac{1}{8}$ of 400 is 50, so $\frac{3}{8}$ is 150.

$$\text{Area of sector} = 150\pi$$

Answer: **B**

Three-Dimensional Geometry

If you think of the geometry we've been looking at so far as about "shapes," 3D geometry's about "objects." Because of its symmetry, we'll start by looking at the cube. If a *cube* has side s, the volume is given by $V = s^3$. Of course, the very reason why raising any number or variable to the third power is called "cubing" is because of this formula. Each side of the cube is a square with area s^2. Since there are six identical sides to a cube, the total *surface area* is $SA = 6s^2$.

Rectangular solids (i.e., boxes) work in a similar way. All faces (sides) of the solid are rectangles, and all meet perpendicularly. If the rectangular side has a height h, a width w, and a depth d, then the volume is given by $V = hwd$.

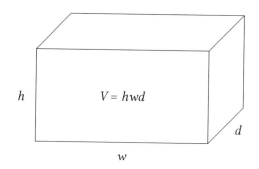

To figure out the surface area, we would figure out the areas of the six faces and add those, remembering that opposite faces have to be congruent rectangles.

Prisms and Pyramids

A *prism* is a solid object with two bases that are the same shape and size. The most common kind of prism is a *triangular prism*, which has a triangle base, an identical congruent triangle as the top, and three rectangle sides connecting these two triangles, linking corresponding sides of the two triangles. Think of a tent or a triangular block of cheese. They're good everyday examples of triangular prisms, both having approximately this shape:

The triangle at the top and bottom could be any triangle at all. In practice, it's often either a right triangle or an equilateral. If B is the area of the triangle base and h is the height, then the volume is given by $V = Bh$. (But if the ACT Math Test wanted us to figure out the area, it would have to give enough specifications about the triangle base first.)

Technically, the base could be a higher-order polygon (a polygon with more sides). A "rectangular prism" is called a cuboid and is simply a box, a rectangular solid. Theoretically, a pentagonal prism would be fair game on the ACT, too, but that is an exceedingly unlikely topic.

A *pyramid* is somewhat like a prism: it has a polygon bottom, but it comes to a point at the top. The base could be a triangle, but more commonly it's a rectangle, and the most common base is a square (such as the Great Pyramid of Giza, the only Ancient Wonder of the World still standing!).

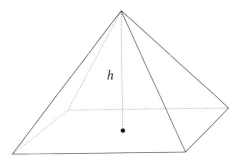

The volume of a pyramid is

$$V = \frac{1}{3}Bh$$

In that formula, B is the area of the base, and h is the height, an altitude that is a line rising perpendicularly from the center point of the base to the top vertex. A problem could ask you to calculate various lengths associated with the pyramid using the Pythagorean theorem.

How might the ACT test this? Take a look.

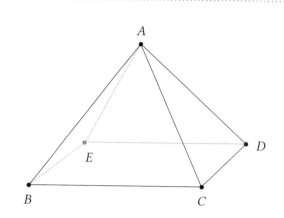

A pyramid has a vertex at A and a square base. The area of the square base is 144 square units. The combined area of the four triangular faces is 240 square units. What is the volume of the pyramid in cubic units?

F. 288

G. 384

H. 768

J. 864

K. 1152

Answer and Explanation

We know that the sides of the square are 12. The solid has four triangular faces, so the area of each one would be $\frac{240}{4}$ = 60. We know the base (b) of the triangle would have a side of 12, so we could use the area of the triangle to find the altitude or height (h) of the triangle.

$$A = (0.5)bh$$
$$60 = (0.5)(12)h$$
$$60 = 6h$$
$$10 = h$$

The height of each triangle face is 10. This is NOT the height of the pyramid: this is the slanted height up the face of the slanted triangle. In the diagram below, let's say that the triangular face we're examining is ACD. Let F be the midpoint of CD. We've just found that $AF = 10$. That's the height of the triangle, but the height of the pyramid is AG, where G is the center of the square base.

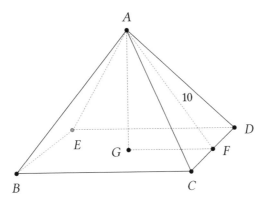

So, to find the volume of the pyramid, we need to find *AG*. We've just found, from the area of the triangular faces, that *AF* = 10. Notice—and this is the big insight the problem requires!—that *AGF* is a right triangle. We know the hypotenuse *AF* = 10, and because *G* is the center of the square, *GF* must be half the side of the square: *GF* = 6. This is just the {3, 4, 5} triangle multiplied by two to get {6, 8, 10}. Since *AF* = 10 and *GF* = 6, it must be true that *AG* = 8. *That's* the height of the pyramid.

$$V = \tfrac{1}{3}Bh = \tfrac{1}{3}(144)(8) = 384$$

(While it's important to be stingy with your calculator use, it's perfectly fine to use a calculator for that kind of multiplication!)

Answer: **G**

Cylinders, Cones, and Spheres

Archimedes, who proved the area of a circle, also figured out the volumes of cylinders, cones, and spheres. He found that a cylinder is like a prism with a circular base, and a cone is a pyramid with a circular base. In each case, the area of the base is the area of the circle, πr^2. Thus, the formulas for these volumes are

Volume of a cylinder = $\pi r^2 h$

Volume of a cone = $\tfrac{1}{3}\pi r^2 h$

The final formula, the volume of a sphere, is a hard one. Archimedes' sophisticated argument from which he derived this formula anticipated the work of integral calculus (*not* a subject the ACT will touch with a 10-foot pole). That makes this one of the very few mathematical formulas for which we will say: forget about understanding the argument. Just memorize it.

volume of a sphere = $\tfrac{4}{3}\pi r^3$
(where *r* is the radius of the sphere)

Coordinate Geometry

What do you need to know about the *xy*-plane for the ACT Math Test? You need to understand that the *x*- and *y*-axes are simply number lines, and these two number lines cross perpendicularly at their zero points. That crossing point, (0, 0), is called the *origin*, and it's a special point in many ways. The two axes divide the plan into four *quadrants*, and these are numbered in a counterclockwise arrangement, as seen below.

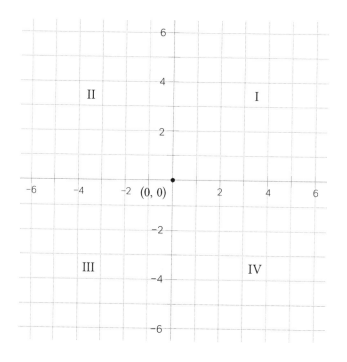

For the ACT Math Test, you'll need to know the quadrants by their numbers. *Why are they numbered counterclockwise?* you might ask. Well, in unit circle trigonometry, all the angles are measured counterclockwise from the positive *x*-axis. This makes the two systems consistent. Still, why do both systems orient things counterclockwise? Maybe because *x* comes before *y* alphabetically? Maybe because most people are right-handed, and when you point your right thumb at yourself, your curled fingers curl in the counterclockwise direction? ("Right-hand rules" are common in physics, especially in electricity and magnetism.) We could speculate further, but it's pretty unnecessary. The point is, for the ACT Math Test, you need to know the quadrants of the *xy*-plane—and you need to know them cold!

Every point in the plane is denoted by a pair of coordinates, and the *x*-coordinate always comes before the *y*-coordinate. Thus, the point (3, 5) means, starting at the origin, go to the right (along the *x*-axis) 3, and then up (along the *y*-axis) 5.

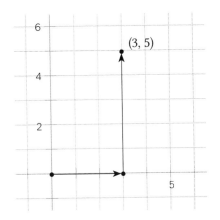

Of course, the *x*- and *y*-coordinates can be any type of numbers: positive, negative, zero; integers, fractions, decimals. Most of the time, when the *xy*-plane appears on the ACT Math Test, the *x*- and *y*-coordinates will be integers.

Those are the basics; time to kick it up a notch.

Parallel and Perpendicular Lines in the XY-Plane

The ACT Math Test could—and very well might—ask you about parallel and perpendicular lines in the *xy*-plane. The rule for parallel lines is 100 percent predictable and easy to remember: **parallel lines have the same slope.** That means that two parallel lines have the same steepness and will go on and on forever without ever intersecting.

It's perpendicular lines that typically give people a little more trouble. Let's think about this. Suppose Line #1 has a certain slope, *M*. We can think of slope as "rise over run" (or the difference in *y*-coordinates over the difference in *x*-coordinates). But what happens if we take that slope triangle and rotate it 90°?

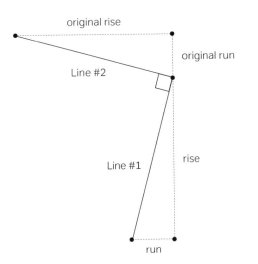

The rotated line, Line #2, is perpendicular to Line #1. Notice that a couple things happened when we did that. First of all, the slope changed sign: originally a positive slope became a negative slope; similarly, an originally negative slope would become a positive slope. Furthermore, the "rise" and the "run" swapped places: the old rise is the new run, and vice versa. This means that, in the slope fraction, the numerator and denominator would swap places. Of course, when we change from $\frac{a}{b}$ to $\frac{b}{a}$, that's called a *reciprocal*. So to go from the original slope to a perpendicular slope, we must change ± signs and also take a reciprocal; more concisely, **the perpendicular slope is the opposite reciprocal of the original slope**.

Applying this to an ACT Math Test problem, this means that if Line #1 and Line #2 are perpendicular, and Line #1 has a slope of $\frac{P}{Q}$, then Line #2 must have a slope of $-\frac{Q}{P}$.

Midpoint of a Segment

This is another predictable rule. Suppose you have a segment with endpoints (x_1, y_1) and (x_2, y_2) and we want the coordinate of the midpoint. The rule is to average the x-coordinates and average the y-coordinates.

$$\text{midpoint} = \left(\frac{x_1 + x_2}{2}, \frac{y_1 + y_2}{2} \right)$$

For example, what's the midpoint of a segment with endpoints (−5, 4) and (7, 2)? The sum of −5 and 7 is +2, so their average is +1. The average of 4 and 2 is 3. Therefore, the midpoint is (1, 3).

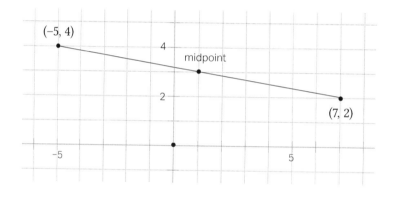

Parabolas in the XY-Plane

When we have an equation in the form $y = ax^2 + bx + c$, the graph is a parabola; this form is sometimes called "standard form." In the standard form, a, b, and c are constants and each one gives us a tremendous amount of information about the parabola. If $a > 0$, the parabola opens upward, like a U; if $a < 0$, the parabola opens downward, like … an upside-down U. If $|a| > 1$, then the parabola looks narrow with steep sides; if $|a| < 1$, the parabola looks wide and flat. In fact, just as there's one circle-shape (though individual circles can be bigger or smaller), so too is there only one parabola-shape—a zoomed-out parabola looks narrow and when we zoom into the vertex, it looks wide. Every parabola in existence is a zoomed-out or zoomed-in version of this same fundamental shape.

The c in the equation $y = ax^2 + bx + c$ is the y-intercept of the parabola. The b is the most interesting—at least as far as the ACT Math Test is concerned. On its own, if we can say that $b > 0$, then the vertex is to the left of the y-axis, and if $b < 0$, vice versa. Even more specific and more important than this is the equation for the line of symmetry. This is the equation for the line that runs up the middle of a parabola and right through the vertex.

$$x = -\frac{b}{2a}$$

Notice that if, in the quadratic formula, we set everything after the ± sign to zero, this is what would be left.

$$x = \frac{-b \pm \sqrt{b^2 - 4ac}}{2a} \quad \Rightarrow \quad x = \frac{-b \pm 0}{2a} = \frac{-b}{2a}$$

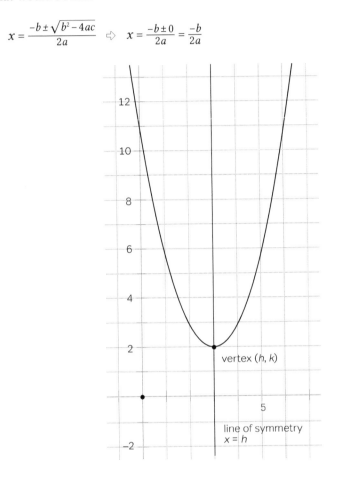

Let's say that the vertex has coordinates (h, k). The value of h, the x-coordinate of the vertex, is the same as the x-value for the line of symmetry: $h = \frac{-b}{2a}$. Once we have that number, we can plug that in for x in the equation, and the value of y would equal k. That allows us to rewrite the equation in "vertex form":

$$y = a(x - h)^2 + k$$

The a here is the same as in standard form, and (h, k) is the vertex.

A third form is "root form." The roots are the *x*-intercepts of the parabola.

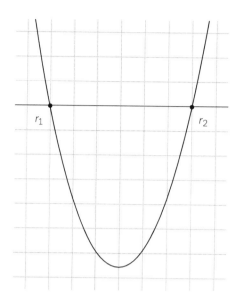

Let's consider this parabola, which has two roots or *x*-intercepts, r_1 and r_2. The root form to describe this parabola would be: $y = a(x - r_1)(x - r_2)$.

Again, the *a* here is the same as in the other two forms, and r_1 and r_2 are the two roots.

If you understand all three ways to describe a parabola, and how to change back and forth among them, then you're on your way to mastering how they show up on the ACT Math Test.

Does every parabola have two distinct real roots? No. If the parabola intersects the *x*-axis in two different places, it has two distinct real roots. If the parabola is tangent to the *x*-axis at the vertex, it has just one real root; for example, $y = x^2$, the simplest of all parabolas, has just one real root at $x = 0$. If the parabola never intersects the *x*-axis, then it has no real roots, only complex roots (we'll discuss complex numbers on page 285).

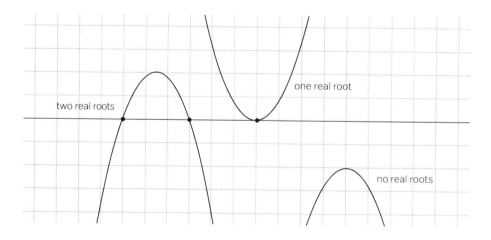

Keep an eye out for cameos that the *xy*-plane—this truly astonishing mathematical tool—makes a few times later in this chapter!

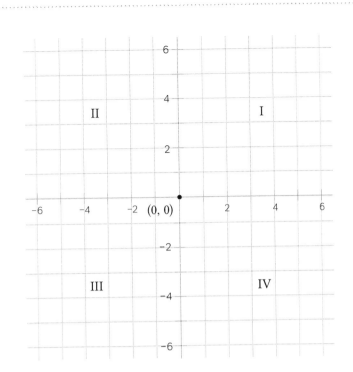

A parabola has a vertex at (–2, 9) and one root at (4, 0). Through which quadrants must this parabola pass?

A. I and II only

B. I, II, and III only

C. I, II, and IV only

D. All four quadrants

E. Cannot be determined from the information given

Answer and Explanation

From the two points we're given, we know that the vertex is above the root (9 is larger than 0), so this is a downward-facing parabola: it would have a negative value of *a*, although we don't need to find that. We also know that the axis of symmetry must be $x = -2$. Thus, we know the vertex is in Quadrant II. One root, (4, 0), is six units to the right of this line, so the other root must be six units to the left of that line, at (–8, 0). The parabola must cross the *y*-axis and travel through I to get to (4, 0). From the root (4, 0), the parabola moves down into IV, and from the root (–8, 0), it moves down in III. Thus, it must move through all four quadrants.

Answer: **D**

Distance in the XY-Plane

Somewhere along the line, you may have run into a monstrosity known as the distance formula. We regard this formula as an unholy abomination (which is a fancy way of saying that we don't like it one bit!).

Rather than memorize a gargantuan formula with a thousand moving parts, it's much better to **understand** how distance works in the *xy*-plane. Of course, by far the easiest distances we can find in the *xy*-plane are purely horizontal and vertical distances. Any two points on the same horizontal line have the same *y*-coordinate, and we find their distance by subtracting their *x*-coordinates. Similarly, any two points on the same vertical line have the same *x*-coordinate, and we find their distance by subtracting their *y*-coordinates. That's easy.

However, for most pairs of points, they will not have a purely horizontal or purely vertical separation: instead, the line from one to the other will be slanted. Here's the really clever insight (if we do say so ourselves). Remember the slope triangles we created to find slope earlier in the Coordinate Geometry section? We can construct one here. The rise and run, easy-to-find vertical and horizontal distances, are the legs, and the hypotenuse of this right triangle is the distance we want to find. What world-famous theorem allows us to find the hypotenuse from the two legs? The Pythagorean theorem. We can find any slanted distance in the *xy*-plane by using the Pythagorean theorem!

For example, suppose we need to find the distance between (−6, 6) and (9, −2). Well, we can find the rise and run using ordinary subtraction: we'll subtract the leftmost point from the rightmost point.

$$\text{run} = 9 - (-6) = 15$$
$$\text{rise} = (-2) - 6 = -8$$

Now, normally we would have to square these, add them together, and find the square root to find the distance between them. But wait! This is an ordinary Pythagorean triplet, {8, 15, 17}. Keep in mind that when dealing with distances, we are only looking at the positive values of the run and rise. That's why even though we got −8 for the rise, we can consider the rise +8. Thus, without any more calculations, we see immediately that the hypotenuse is 17, and this is the slanted distance between those two points.

Circles in the XY-Plane

Fundamentally, what is a circle? It's the set of all points equidistant from a fixed center. Let's say that the origin is the center of the circle, and say that the radius is *r*.

For any point (*x*, *y*) that's on the circle, it must be true that its distance to the origin is *r*. For a point (*x*, *y*), its run is *x* and its rise is *y*, so when we do the Pythagorean theorem, using a triangle to find the slope, we get

$$x^2 + y^2 = r^2$$

Any point that obeys that equation lies on a circle centered at (0, 0) with a radius of *r*.

Pythagoras was the leader of a mysterious religion to which initiates were sworn to secrecy. The members of this religion were strict vegetarians, and, for some reason, Pythagoras expressly prohibited his followers from eating beans. Why he had that particular rule is anybody's guess!

Now, let's up the ante. Let's say that the center is a random point (h, k), and the radius is still r. The run would be $(x - h)$ or $(h - x)$, but the order doesn't matter, because the circle formula means that we're going to square this difference anyway. The rise would be $(y - k)$ or $(k - y)$. Now, applying the Pythagorean theorem to the slope triangle gives us:

$$(x - h)^2 + (y - k)^2 = r^2$$

That's the general formula for a circle in the xy-plane. Notice that this is a direct consequence of the relationship that the Pythagorean theorem has to finding distance in the xy-plane.

Reflections in the XY-Plane

The ACT Math Test loves to ask about reflections in the xy-plane. Most often, the "mirror" lines it asks about are either the x- or y-axes. Think about reflections this way: the axis (or the line across which a point is being reflected) acts as a mirror. So if you were looking at an object in the mirror, where would it appear on the "other side"?

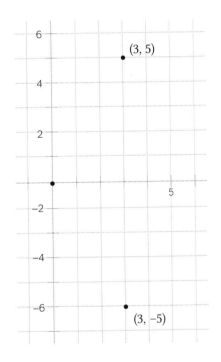

Let's think about reflection over the x-axis. The point $(3, 5)$ is in QI. When we reflect it over the x-axis, its x-coordinate stays the same, and the height above the x-axis becomes a depth below it: the $+5$ becomes -5. The reflected image is $(3, -5)$, which is now in QIV.

Now, let's think about reflection over the *y*-axis. Again, we'll start with (3, 5) in QI. When we reflect it over the *y*-axis, its *y*-coordinate stays the same, and the distance 3 units to the right of the *x*-axis becomes 3 units to the left: the +3 becomes –3. The reflected image is (–3, 5), which is now in QII.

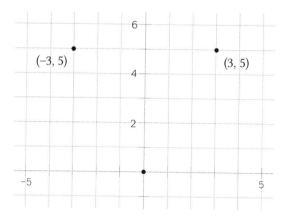

Elementary Algebra

Factoring

A *quadratic* is a polynomial with up to three terms, in which the highest power is x-squared. To factor a quadratic is to express it as the product of two binomials, such as $(x + a)(x + b)$. Technically, we can factor any quadratic, but often the result would be two binomials with horribly ugly numbers—radicals or even non-real numbers. As a general rule, factoring is not your best bet when the roots aren't integers. For the purposes of this section, we'll say a quadratic is "factorable" if, when we factor it, the resulting equation contains only integers.

For the ACT Math Test, you would ideally be comfortable enough with factoring that you can determine relatively quickly whether a quadratic is factorable into integer roots. It's an essential algebra skill to have, but there's no one-size-fits-all tool to determine this. (Later, we'll discuss other solution methods for unfactorable quadratics.)

Solving Quadratics

Now that we've discussed that quadratics can be factored into two binomials, we have discussed the biggest part of solving quadratics. We just have to clarify all the steps of getting to a solution, because the ACT Math Test definitely will expect you to know how to solve a quadratic.

Here is the general recipe for solving a quadratic.

Step #1: Before anything else, always, always, always get everything on one side of the equation equal to zero. Everything else in this procedure depends on having a quadratic that equals zero.

Step #2: Once the quadratic equals zero, factor it. (What if it's unfactorable? We'll discuss those solutions on page 211.)

Step #3: Once we have a product of two binomials that equals zero, we'll use what mathematicians call the "zero-product property" (though you don't need to know that name). This says

$P \times Q = 0$ if and only if ($P = 0$ **or** $Q = 0$)

… in which P and Q are the factors of the quadratic set equal to zero.

Step #4: Once we have each binomial equal to zero separately, we solve those equations.

Here's an example. Suppose we're given the quadratic equation $x^2 + x = 6(x + 6)$ and we have to solve this. Of course, right away, the very fact that there's an x^2 is what makes this quadratic and what demands that we follow the four-step procedure.

Step #1: Here, the problem is a little inconvenient: we have to do a few steps to get everything equal to zero.

$$x^2 + x = 6(x + 6)$$
$$x^2 + x = 6x + 36$$
$$x^2 - 5x = 36$$
$$x^2 - 5x - 36 = 0$$

Step #2: Now that everything equals zero, we can factor. We need a pair of numbers, one positive and one negative, that has a product of –36 and sum of –5. These would be +4 and –9.

$$x^2 - 5x - 36 = 0$$
$$(x + 4)(x - 9) = 0$$

By the way, it's very important not to confuse the numbers we get at this stage—the two numbers we need to factor to find the roots—with the answers. We don't have our answer yet: we're only halfway through the process.

Step #3: Apply the zero-product property.

$$(x + 4)(x - 9) = 0$$

means

$$(x + 4) = 0 \quad \text{or} \quad (x - 9) = 0$$

Step #4: Solve each one of these two easy equations separately. (Don't lose the "or"!)

$$(x + 4) = 0 \quad \text{or} \quad (x - 9) = 0$$
$$x = -4 \quad \text{or} \quad x = +9$$

Those are the solutions!

Other types of quadratic equations

The ACT Math Test may simply hand you a quadratic and say, "solve it," but it really loves to tweak a more straightforward question into something more complex. For this reason, understanding the three forms of a quadratic, discussed on page 176 above, is really helpful.

For example, suppose the ACT gives us a quadratic in the standard form, $ax^2 + bx + c = 0$, with a mix of numbers and variables for the coefficients a, b, and c, but it also tells us one of the roots. For example, suppose the test tells us that the quadratic equation $x^2 - 11x + c = 0$ has $x = 4$ as one of its roots: the test could then ask you to find either the value of the other root or, more typically, the value of c. Since we know one root, it would make sense to set the standard form equal to the root form. To do this, we'd have to write out the root form first, using $x = 4$ as one root; let r be the other root.

$$x^2 - 11x + c = (x - 4)(x - r)$$
$$x^2 - 11x + c = x^2 - rx - 4x + 4r$$
$$x^2 - 11x + c = x^2 - (r + 4)x + 4r$$

Any two forms of the same quadratic must be true for all values of x, so all the coefficients are equal to each other. Setting the coefficients of x equal, we get

$$-11 = -(r + 4)$$
$$11 = r + 4$$
$$r = 7$$

Now, we can set the constants' coefficients equal:

$$c = 4r = 4(7) = 28$$

This is just one way in which it's important to be familiar with all three forms of quadratics and be able to use them to solve problems.

We mentioned in our discussion of parabolas on page 178 that some quadratics have two roots, some have only one, and some have none. The ones that have no real solutions have complex number solutions (involving the imaginary number i), and it's rare that the ACT Math Test expects you to find complex number roots. In contrast, the ACT *loves* to ask about the single root case.

If a quadratic has only one root, then it absolutely must be the square of only one binomial. It will be the square of a sum or the square of a difference.

square of a sum: $(x + p)^2 = x^2 + 2px + p^2 = 0$

square of a difference: $(x - p)^2 = x^2 - 2px + p^2 = 0$

So ***every single time*** **there is only one root, the quadratic equation will take one of these two forms.** This is precisely why it's crucially important to be deeply familiar with these algebraic patterns. Familiarity with these two equations can save you a ton of needlessly complicated calculations on such questions!

Ready to put your knowledge to the test?

Practice Question

The quadratic $x^2 + bx + 25 = 0$ has a single root that is a positive number. What is the value of b?

F. 10
G. 5
H. 0
J. −5
K. −10

Answer and Explanation

If the root is positive, then the expression to get this factor for must involve subtraction. For example, the expression associated with $x = +3$ would be $(x - 3)$. Therefore, we need the square of a difference pattern.

$$(x - p)^2 = x^2 - 2px + p^2 = 0$$

We know that $p^2 = 25$, and we need a positive root, so we will choose $p = +5$. This would result in the equation:

$$(x - 5)^2 = x^2 - 10x + 25 = 0$$

From this, we can see $b = -10$.

Answer: **K**

Inequalities on the Number Line

We've seen quite a few of the ACT Math Test's favorite things so far: in addition to bright copper kettles and warm woolen mittens, the test loves problems with inequalities represented as number lines. It may give you the picture of a number line that you have to match to the correct inequality, or it may give you the inequality and you have to match it to the correct picture. Knowing how to go back and forth between algebraic statements of an inequality and its pictorial representation is key.

Let's think about a couple basic inequalities: first of all, $x \leq 4$.

Notice that the endpoint, $x = 4$, is included in the inequality, so this is represented as a solid dot (in other words, this is a "less than or equal to" situation). Now, here's the number line of $x > -5$.

Here, the endpoint, $x = -5$, is **not** included, so this is indicated by an open circle. In other words, the region $-5 < x$ includes every point down to, but not including, $x = -5$. It includes $x = -4.9$, $x = -4.9999999$, and $x = -4.99999999999999999999$. In fact, how many more numbers between that last number and $x = -5$ are included? Infinity! That's one of the mind-boggling things about the real number line.

The ACT Math Test is usually interested in combinations of inequalities. For example, let's solve this compound inequality:

$$-7 < 3 - 2x < 11$$

We can treat this exactly the same as we treat an ordinary inequality. First, subtract 3 from all three places.

$$-10 < -2x < 8$$

Now, we'll multiply everything by –1 to change the signs; this will entail reversing the direction of the inequalities.

$$10 > 2x > -8$$

Finally, we'll divide by 2.

$$5 > x > -4$$

Of course, we could have combined the last two steps by dividing by –2, but we separated out the sign and dividing by the number for clarity. The graph of this solution would be:

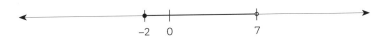

The endpoints aren't included on this number line because the equation didn't give us an "equal to" scenario. We could write this algebraically either as the compound inequality $-4 < x < 5$ or with the powerful logical word "and":

$$-4 < x \quad \text{and} \quad x < 5$$

This is a good point at which to discuss these incredibly powerful words, "and" and the other logic word "or." (We will discuss "or" in a short bit!) These words are not decoration, like parsley on your plate. These are bona fide mathematical operators, every bit as important as $+$, $-$, $\times$, and $\div$.

When the allowed region is between two endpoints, we can use either a compound inequality or the word "and." For example, this region

we could denote either as $-2 \le x < 7$ or as

$$-2 \le x \quad \text{and} \quad x < 7$$

Think about why the "and" makes sense here. Every point in that included region is simultaneously *both* greater than or equal to –2 and less than 7. It wouldn't make sense to use "or" because every number on the number line is greater than –2 or less than 7: the number +100 is greater than –2, and the number –100 is less than 7. Every number on the number line satisfies at least one of those two conditions, so "or" would denote the entire number line, not simply the set we desire.

Now, think about this region:

What's included here is all the real estate outside the two endpoints. For this kind of region, we have to use "or," and we absolutely cannot use a compound inequality. The *only* way to write this is

$$x \le -2 \quad \text{or} \quad 7 < x$$

We can't combine these expressions into one big compound inequality with x in the middle because that would imply that +7 is somehow less than –2. Why is this an "or" case and not an "and" case? Some folks look at the two regions that form the solution and think, "Well, it's this one *and* that one," but that's not the best way to conceptualize it. Think in terms of an individual x-value—after all, all the mathematical statements here are about individual values of x. Any x that works satisfies either one condition *or* the other. No single value on the number line could simultaneously be both less than –2 and greater than 7.

Inequalities in the *XY*-plane

Inequalities with two variables, x and y, are often displayed in the xy-plane, and, you guessed it, the ACT Math Test loves asking about this. In the xy-plane, **equations** denote individual lines and curves, and **inequalities** represent regions in the plane.

For example, both $x > 0$ and $x \ge 0$ denote everything to the right of the y-axis, all of quadrants I and IV. What's the difference between those two? The latter includes $x = 0$, which is the equation of the y-axis, and the former excludes it. Graphically, for $x \ge 0$, we draw the boundary line, the x-axis, as a solid line to indicate that it is included; for $x > 0$, we would draw the boundary line as a dashed line to show that it's not included.

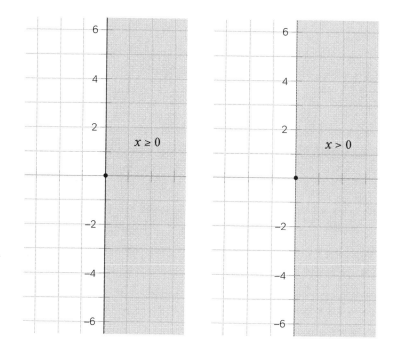

Most boundary lines are neither simple vertical nor horizontal lines but, instead, slanted lines described by the equation $y = mx + b$. If y is greater than x, then the shaded region is above the line, and if y is less than x, the shaded region is below it. The $\leq$ and $\geq$ signs indicate that the boundary line is included and should be drawn as a solid line, whereas the $<$ and $>$ signs indicate that the line is excluded and should be represented by a dashed line. If the inequality is not solved for y, we have to do some algebra to get y by itself.

For example, suppose we have to graph the region $x + 2y < 7$. First of all, isolate y by subtracting x and then dividing by 2:

$$y < -\frac{1}{2}x + \frac{7}{2}$$

Now, we graph the line as a dashed line because there's no "and equal" sign and the shaded region has to be below the line.

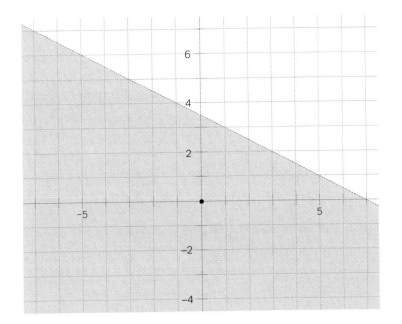

Graphing inequalities with individual lines is level 1. To kick it up to level 2, we'll look at the *compound* of two inequalities. What we've been shading so far have been the "allowed" regions, the regions that show all the points that work in the inequality. If two inequalities are in effect, the shaded region should be only the overlap, that is, only those points that work in *both* inequalities simultaneous.

For example, the very basic compound inequality

$x < 0$
$y > 0$

represents Quadrant II. Notice that these are not the "and equal to" kinds of inequalities, because technically, the axes are not included in the quadrants.

Next, we'll see how the ACT might test you on this concept.

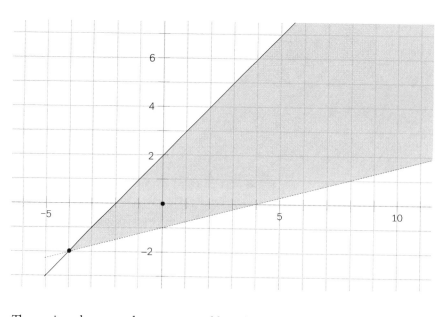

The region above can be represented by which set of inequalities?

A. $(y \leq x + 2)$ and $(y \geq \frac{1}{4}x - 1)$

B. $(y < x + 2)$ and $(y > \frac{1}{4}x - 1)$

C. $(y \leq x + 2)$ and $(y > \frac{1}{4}x - 1)$

D. $(y < x + 2)$ and $(y \geq \frac{1}{4}x - 1)$

E. $(y \leq x + 2)$ and $(y > \frac{1}{4}x - 1)$

Answer and Explanation

First, we need to determine the equation of the top boundary line by looking at its slope and y-intercept; here, that equation is $y = x + 2$. Since this line is solid, it must be represented by an "and equal to" inequality. The allowed region is below this line, so the correct inequality for this boundary line is

$$y \leq x + 2$$

We can eliminate B and D.

The lower boundary line is dashed, so it's not included in the equation. We can't have the "and equal to" kind of inequality. We must have an ordinary > sign. This eliminates A. To distinguish the two remaining answers, though, we'll need the exact equation of that line.

From the graph, we can see that the intersection point is (−4, −2), and both lines go through that point. The lower line then goes through the y-intercept of (0, −1). Consider the slope triangle between these two points. The run from −4 to 0 is +4, and the rise from −2 to −1 is +1. This makes rise over run $\frac{1}{4}$. Thus, the lower boundary line is represented by the equation

$$y > \frac{1}{4}x - 1$$

Answer: **C**

In later sections, we'll discuss graphing higher-order polynomials and functions on the xy-plane. For the moment, we can make some blanket statements. Suppose the boundary line is given by the equation

$$y = \{\text{something with } x\}$$

Then

$y > \{\text{something with } x\}$ ⇨ curve is dashed, region above curve is shaded
$y \geq \{\text{something with } x\}$ ⇨ curve is solid, region above curve is shaded
$y < \{\text{something with } x\}$ ⇨ curve is dashed, region below curve is shaded
$y \leq \{\text{something with } x\}$ ⇨ curve is solid, region below curve is shaded

That covers almost anything you will see with inequalities in the xy-plane, with one exception: **circles**.

Remember from the Coordinate Geometry section that the general equation of a circle in the xy-plane is

$$(x - h)^2 + (y - k)^2 = r^2$$

What happens if we replace that equal sign with the various inequality signs? As with the other situations we've looked at, the "and equal to" signs include the circle's perimeter (it would be solid), and the not-equal-to signs would not include the circle's perimeter (it would be dashed). If the side with the x's and y's is *less than* the radius squared, this means they have a smaller radius than r and would be *inside* the circle. If the side with the x's and y's is *greater than* the radius squared, this means they have a larger radius than r and would be *outside* the circle. For example, this is the graph of $x^2 + y^2 < 16$.

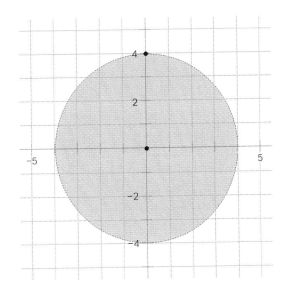

This is how you might see this concept come up on the official ACT Math Test ...

Practice Question

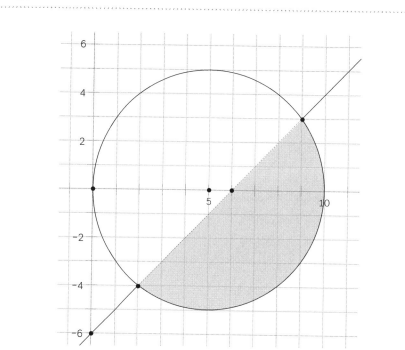

In the diagram, the circle has a center at (5, 0) and passes through the origin. The line has a *y*-intercept of –6 and an *x*-intercept of +6. Which of the following sets of inequalities describes the shaded region?

A. $y < 6x$
$(x - 5)^2 + y^2 > 100$

B. $y > x + 6$
$(x + 5)^2 + y^2 \leq 100$

C. $y \leq 6 - x$
$(x - 5)^2 + y^2 \geq 25$

D. $y \geq 6x - 6$
$(x - 5)^2 + y^2 < 25$

E. $y < x - 6$
$(x - 5)^2 + y^2 \leq 25$

Answer and Explanation

Let's look at the circle first. The circle has a radius of $r = 5$, so $r^2 = 25$. Also, the center is (5, 0), so the equation of the circle itself should be

$$(x - 5)^2 + y^2 = 25$$

The circle is included in the boundary of the region, and the region is inside the circle, so that equal sign should be replaced with a ≤ sign. Here, the only answer that works is **E**. Let's make sure that the line also works there.

The equation of the line in the graph is $y = x - 6$, a line with a slope of 1 and
y-intercept of -6. The shaded region is below the line and the line is not included, so
the correct inequality is

$$y < x - 6$$

Which is what we can see in choice **E**, as well. The answer is **E**.

Picking Numbers

Now that we've discussed a lot of algebra, let's return to strategy for a moment and
talk about a particular strategy that's vital to ACT algebra. Suppose the ACT Math
Test gives you a hard algebra problem. Of course, your algebra teacher might want you
to do this problem the "official" algebra way, using all the laws of algebra to solve it.
That's great, but when you're taking the test, what any teacher might want you to do is
irrelevant—it's just you and the test! Furthermore, the ACT doesn't really care *how* you
get the answer: all it's concerned with is whether you choose the correct answer from
the five choices.

All of this means that if an alternate strategy is more efficient, don't hesitate for a
moment to use it. We already discussed backsolving on page 116. Now, let's discuss
picking numbers.

Suppose the ACT gives you some complicated algebraic expression and wants to
know what this equals when simplified. Well, of course you can use pure algebra to
solve it, but it may help to pick numbers or choose numbers to use instead of variables
in a problem. Here's an example problem.

Practice Question

Given that $0 \le y \le x$, $\dfrac{x}{x^2 - y} + \dfrac{\sqrt{y}}{y - x^2} =$

A. $\dfrac{1}{x - \sqrt{y}}$

B. $\dfrac{1}{x + \sqrt{y}}$

C. $\dfrac{x - \sqrt{y}}{x + \sqrt{y}}$

D. $\dfrac{x\sqrt{y}}{x^2 - \sqrt{y}}$

E. $\dfrac{x\sqrt{y}}{x^2 + y}$

Answer and Explanation

If you want to do the full-on algebra solution, that's great! Don't let us stop you! But if
you look at this and have doubts about doing it algebraically, this would be a perfect

time to practice picking numbers. (Even if you don't, humor us for a minute.)

We have two variables, x and y, and since there's a square root of y in the problem, we want to pick a value of y that will have a square root that's an integer. The big idea behind picking numbers is that we can use this strategy to eliminate answers. In order for an algebraic equation to be true, it has to work for all values. If we can pick values of x and y that make, for example, choice E not equal the original expression, then we can eliminate that choice. Conversely, if we pick values that make an answer choice equal to the prompt expression, we can conclude nothing definitive: that *could be* the correct answer. We need to eliminate four choices by picking numbers, so that the correct answer remains by process of elimination. Ideally, we hope to be able to eliminate four answers all at once with one choice of numbers. To establish that some answer is correct or always true on its own, we'd need to use algebra or logic: picking numbers can only eliminate answers. It can't give us the correct answer alone.

This raises another good point: there's an art to picking numbers well. The ACT knows that folks use picking numbers as a strategy, and sometimes incorrect answer choices are designed to work for the most obvious choices of numbers; thus, students who pick these obvious choices will not be able to eliminate such incorrect choices on the first go. It can be helpful to pick something a shade different from the most obvious choice. This problem gives us the stipulation that $0 \leq y \leq x$. The most obvious choice for numbers might be $y = 1$ and $x = 2$. Just to be a shade different from the most obvious choice, let's pick $y = 1$ and $x = 3$. That's still easy enough for simple calculations, but just a little different from the most obvious choice. Believe it or not, this one subtle change will save us time in this problem.

Part of the art of picking numbers includes thinking about all categories of numbers: positive and negative integers, zero, fractions between 0 and 1, fractions between -1 and 0, very large positive numbers, and very large negative numbers. Number sense, discussed on page 114, plays a large role in the art of picking numbers well.

Okay, plug those values, $y = 1$ and $x = 3$, into the prompt expression of this question.

$$\frac{x}{x^2 - y} + \frac{\sqrt{y}}{y - x^2} = \frac{3}{9 - 1} + \frac{1}{1 - 9} = \frac{3}{8} - \frac{1}{8} = \frac{2}{8} = \frac{1}{4}$$

That's the value of the prompt equation, given the numbers we picked. Any answer that has a chance of being the correct answer has to match this value when we plug in these variables: if we get a value other than $\frac{1}{4}$, then we can eliminate that answer.

A. $\frac{1}{x - \sqrt{y}} = \frac{1}{3 - 1} = \frac{1}{2}$ ⇨ doesn't work!

B. $\frac{1}{x + \sqrt{y}} = \frac{1}{3 + 1} = \frac{1}{4}$ ⇨ works

C. $\frac{x - \sqrt{y}}{x + \sqrt{y}} = \frac{3 - 1}{3 + 1} = \frac{2}{4} = \frac{1}{2}$ ⇨ doesn't work!

D. $\frac{x\sqrt{y}}{x^2 - \sqrt{y}} = \frac{3(1)}{9 - 1} = \frac{3}{8}$ ⇨ doesn't work!

E. $\frac{x\sqrt{y}}{x^2 + y} = \frac{3(1)}{9 + 1} = \frac{3}{10}$ ⇨ doesn't work!

We got lucky with this choice, because we were able to eliminate four answers all at once. This is more likely to happen when we make a non-obvious choice of numbers, but don't worry if you need to pick more than one set of numbers: the more you practice, the faster you'll get, and the more efficient and correct you'll be in the long term.

Answer: **B**

(While you shouldn't waste time on this on test day, a good algebraic exercise to use in practice is to verify why the right answer actually works. The difference-of-two-squares pattern, discussed on page 197, will help you understand this one!)

We also can use picking numbers to solve algebraic inequalities. Here's another sample problem.

Practice Question

> If $0 \leq q \leq p$, then for all possible values of p and q, p must be greater than which of the following?
>
> A. $\dfrac{1}{p+q}$
>
> B. $\dfrac{1}{p-q}$
>
> C. $\dfrac{p-q}{p+q}$
>
> D. $\dfrac{p^2-q^2}{p+q}$
>
> E. $\dfrac{pq+q^2}{p}$

Answer and Explanation

Let's pick some numbers! Our goal for each of the five answer choices will be to find some choice of p and q that won't fit the inequality, so that we can eliminate this choice. In order to do this, we'll have to keep in mind all categories of numbers: ordinary positive integers, fractions less than one, and very, very large positive and negative numbers. In all cases, we're trying to find numbers that will make the answer choice *greater than p*, so that the inequality doesn't work and we can eliminate the answer choice.

In choice A, $\frac{1}{p+q}$, if p and q are integers, then the reciprocals of integers will always be smaller than any positive integer. Those choices satisfy the inequality. But what happens if we made both p and q fractions less than one? Let's say,

$$p = \frac{1}{10} \quad \text{and} \quad q = \frac{1}{20}$$

Then,

$$p + q = \frac{1}{10} + \frac{1}{20} = \frac{2}{20} + \frac{1}{20} = \frac{3}{20}$$

So,

$$\frac{1}{p+q} = \frac{20}{3}$$

Whatever the value of that is, it's bigger than 1, and p is smaller than 1, so we've found numbers that make this expression bigger than p. We can eliminate choice A.

Option B give us $\frac{1}{p-q}$. Similar to the choices in A, we need fractions smaller than 1. Again, we'll use

$$p = \frac{1}{10} \quad \text{and} \quad q = \frac{1}{20}$$

Then,

$$p - q = \frac{1}{10} - \frac{1}{20} = \frac{2}{20} - \frac{1}{20} = \frac{1}{20}$$

So,

$$\frac{1}{p+q} = \frac{20}{1} = 20$$

Well, 20 is certainly bigger than $p = \frac{1}{10}$, so we can pick numbers to make this choice bigger than p. We can eliminate B.

Choice C is tricky: $\frac{p-q}{p+q}$. Again, ordinary integers will make a fraction smaller than one. Here, using a little number sense, we'll pick a fraction for p and then a very, very small fraction for q. For example,

$$p = \frac{1}{2} \quad \text{and} \quad q = \frac{1}{1,000}$$

Then,

$$p - q = \frac{1}{2} - \frac{1}{1,000} = \frac{500}{1,000} - \frac{1}{1,000} = \frac{499}{1,000}$$

This leads to

$$\frac{p-q}{p+q} = \frac{499}{501}$$

This is a fraction very close to one. Also, this is much larger than $p = \frac{1}{2}$ because 499 is much larger than whatever half of 501 is! Therefore, we've picked values that make this expression larger than p. We can eliminate C.

There's no obvious numerical choice for making D larger than p. Come back to this one.

There are lots of q's in the numerator of option E's $\frac{pq+q^2}{p}$, so make $p = 1$ and make q a large number such as $q = 100$.

$$\frac{pq+q^2}{p} = \frac{100 + (100)^2}{1} = 100 + 10{,}000$$

That's certainly bigger than $p = 1$. Therefore, we've picked values that make this expression larger than p. We can eliminate E.

At this point, we were able to eliminate four answers, and are left with D. That means that **D** would have to be the correct answer. To see *why* this MUST BE less than p, again, we need to use a little algebra. Specifically, we need to use the difference-of-two-squares formula.

$$\frac{p^2 - q^2}{p + q} = \frac{(p-q)(p+q)}{p+q} = p - q < p$$

Any positive number gets smaller when we subtract another positive number, so $(p - q)$ is always less than p.

Answer: **D**

Word Problems

Solution and Mixture Problems

This is a relatively rare problem type, but it's definitely possible that one will crop up on your ACT Math Test. The problem will involve mixing some quantity of some solution #1 of one concentration with some quantity of solution #2 of another concentration to get some quantity of a resultant solution of yet a third concentration.

Let's think for a moment about "concentration"—not the mental quality but in the chemical solution sense. What does it mean to say we have 400 units of a 6% phosphoric acid solution? Whatever those units are, the total amount of mixture—of solution—we have is 400 units. Of that, 6% is pure phosphoric acid. Well, 6% of 400 is 24, so we know we have 24 units of pure phosphoric acid. That is the amount of solute we have in our solution (though that's not a word you need to know for the ACT Math Test). The rest of the solution is the solvent (another word you don't need to know): typically, the solvent in most chemical solutions on the ACT is simply water.

(We know that "phosphoric acid" sounds highly scientific, technical, and abstruse, but it's actually one of the ingredients in every can of a number of popular soft drinks!)

The secret to any mixture or concentration problem is to use two equations. The first equation is about the amount of stuff or the total volume. This is called the volume equation. The basic idea is this:

> *volume of solution #1*
> + *volume of solution #2*
> ———————————————
> = *total volume of the resultant solution*

This makes sense when you think about it: the volume of the resultant solution had to come from the volumes of the two things we mixed.

The concentration equation is similar. This concerns, specifically, the amount of concentrate of whatever the chemical or substance is of which we have a solution. For example, in one problem, the concentrate could be phosphoric acid and, in another problem, it could be sugar. The amount of concentrate that winds up in the resultant solution must come from somewhere; it comes from the amounts of concentrate in the two solutions mixed together.

> *amount of concentrate in solution #1*
> + *amount of concentrate in solution #2*
> ———————————————
> = *total amount of concentrate in the resultant solution*

As in the section above, the amounts of concentrate will always be equal to (the concentration percentage as a decimal) × (the total volume of the solution concerned).

Typically, the problem will give us most of the numbers we need; by assigning variables to what we don't know, we can solve for those unknowns.

Here's a practice problem.

A scientist has 400 liters of a 6% phosphoric acid solution and an unlimited supply of 12% phosphoric acid solution. How many liters of the latter must she add to the former to produce a 10% phosphoric acid solution?

A. 200

B. 400

C. 500

D. 600

E. 800

Answer and Explanation

We could backsolve from the numerical answer choices, but let's use a more direct algebraic approach for practice. Let X equal the liters of 12% phosphoric acid solution we use, and let Y be the liters of 10% phosphoric acid solution that result.

The **volume equation** is

$$400 + X = Y$$

In the first solution, we have 6% of 400 or 24 liters of phosphoric acid. In the second solution, we have 12% of $X = 0.12 \times X$ liters of phosphoric acid. In the resultant solution, we have 10% of $Y = 0.10 \times Y$ liters of phosphoric acid.

The **concentration equation** is

$$24 + 0.12X = 0.10Y$$

Multiply this by 100, to clear the decimals:

$$2{,}400 + 12X = 10Y$$

Everything is even, so divide by 2 to simplify:

$$1{,}200 + 6X = 5Y$$

We want X, so let's multiply the volume equation by −5 and add that to this equation we just got:

$$1{,}200 + 6X = 5Y$$
$$-2{,}000 - 5X = -5Y$$
$$-800 + X = 0$$
$$X = 800$$

Answer: **E**

Word Problems with Proportions

We know, we know—we've already discussed proportions. Everything about proportions, though, becomes a little trickier when variables are involved. Part of the trick of doing proportions with variables is simply not to get flustered. You know the rules of proportions when everything is a number, so just do the same thing with variables!

To give you a sense of how variables up the ante, here's a practice problem.

Practice Question

> Walking a constant pace on flat ground, a hiker can cover M miles in 5 hours. On another day, if she walks again, at this same pace on flat ground, how many miles can she cover in $(1 + M)$ hours?
>
> A. $\frac{M}{5} + \frac{1}{5}$
>
> B. 6
>
> C. $\frac{M}{5} + \frac{5}{M}$
>
> D. $\frac{5M}{M+1}$
>
> E. $\frac{M^2 + M}{5}$

Answer and Explanation

This problem is a great example of how the "bookkeeping" aspect of math—just keeping careful track of all the details, keeping everything organized—plays a big role in getting the right answer. There are a lot of steps to this question!

To answer it, we'll set up two ratios, each in the form (miles)/(hours), then set these two equal to each other. The first will be M miles over 5 hours, or $\frac{M}{5}$. The second has an unknown number of miles, so let's introduce the variable x. Then, this second ratio has x miles over $(1 + M)$ miles. Set these equal.

$$\frac{M}{5} = \frac{x}{M+1}$$

We want to solve for x, so multiply both sides by $\frac{M+1}{1}$ to isolate x.

$$\frac{M(M+1)}{5} = \frac{M^2 + M}{5}$$

Answer: **E**

Direct and Inverse Variation

Very roughly and approximately, direct variation means that two things go up together or go down together. Inverse variation means that as one thing goes up, the other goes down. There are *many* mathematical ways either of those rough scenarios could play out, so let's go ahead and make that more complicated. Here are more precise statements.

Direct variation means that the two variables in question are always multiplied by the same factor; for example, if one triples, the other triples as well; if one is divided by 5, the other is as well; etc. If A and B vary directly, we can create the equation $A = kB$ for some constant k. If we graph A vs. B, the graph will be a straight line through the origin.

Inverse variation means that when one variable is multiplied by a factor, the other is divided by the same factor; for example, if one tripled, the other is divided by 3; if one is divided by 5, the other is multiplied by 5; etc. If A and B vary inversely, the product AB will always equal a constant; in fact, we can create the equation $AB = k$ or $B = \frac{k}{A}$ for some constant k.

We can combine the relationships of a few variables into one problem. For example, if A varies directly with B and inversely with C, then one possible equation for A would be

$$A = \frac{kB}{C}$$

Anything directly proportional goes into the numerator of the fraction on the opposite side, and anything inversely proportional goes into the denominator of the fraction on the opposite side.

Ready to try your hand at it? Here's a practice problem.

Practice Question

In a certain physical system, $(V - 10)$ is inversely proportional to the square of R. If $V = 20$ when $R = 6$, what does V equal when $R = 3$?

A. 50

B. 60

C. 70

D. 180

E. 190

Answer and Explanation

We're told that $(V - 10)$ is inversely proportional to the square of R. From this, we can set up the equation:

$$V - 10 = \frac{k}{R^2}$$

Now, plug in the starting values, $V = 20$ and $R = 6$, to solve for k.

$$20 - 10 = \frac{k}{36}$$

$$k = 10 \times 36 = 360$$

Now, with this value for k, we have the equation

$$V - 10 = \frac{360}{R^2}$$

Plug in $R = 3$.

$$V - 10 = \frac{360}{9}$$

$$V - 10 = 40$$

$$V = 50$$

Answer: **A**

Strange Operators

Sometimes the ACT Math Test will introduce a brand-new symbol that no one's ever seen before and the test writers will define what it means. Many students who see this unfamiliar symbol think, *"The teacher must have covered that the day I fell asleep in the back of the room! I have no memory of it!"* These students panic and skip the problem.

You are not going to be one of these students!

In fact, everyone is seeing this strange symbol for the first time, so it's an entirely level playing field—nobody has any kind of "previous experience" advantage that you don't have! Furthermore, the rule that the symbol stands for is often relatively simple, and if you follow the process step by step, you'll get the right answer.

For example …

Practice Question

A new operator, _♣_♣_, is defined for an ordered set of three positive integers {a, b, c} as follows:

$a ♣ b ♣ c = \frac{ac}{b^2}$

If $12 ♣ b ♣ 27 = 1$, then b equals which of the following?

A. 12
B. 18
C. 36
D. 54
E. 72

In this case, we plug numbers into the "recipe" provided.

$$a \clubsuit b \clubsuit c = \frac{ac}{b^2}$$

$$12 \clubsuit b \clubsuit 27 = \frac{(12)(27)}{b^2} = 1$$

A huge mistake would be to perform the multiplication of 12 times 27. This would complicate the next step in finding the square root! Leave that product in this unmultiplied form.

$$b^2 = (12)(27)$$

$$b = \sqrt{(12)(27)} = \sqrt{(4)(3)(3)(9)} = 2 \times 3 \times 3 = 18$$

Answer: **B**

Problems about Money

Many problems about money on the ACT Math Test just involve ordinary percents or simple algebra. (One exception to this is compound interest; for more information about this advanced topic, see page 281). You do have to remember that 100¢ = $1.00, but that's pretty much all you need to have memorized. Sometimes the test presents a complicated real-world scenario, and it takes a little interpreting to figure out exactly what is being asked. Always remember to take such a problem step by step, piece by piece. No one step will be all that difficult, and if you can just keep it organized, you won't have any difficulties.

Here's a practice problem.

Practice Question

> George bought a large electronic item with a 15% off coupon and paid a total bill. When he got outside, he studied the receipt and realized that he mistakenly had been given double the discount of the coupon, even though there was no double-coupon offer in effect that day. He went back inside and pointed this mistake out to the manager, offering to make up the difference between what he paid and what he should have paid. The manager was so grateful for George's honesty that he allowed George to pay just half that difference, so George paid him $40.50. What was the original price of the item, before any coupons? Assume that there was no tax at all in this scenario.
>
> A. $135
> B. $270
> C. $405
> D. $540
> E. $810

Answer and Explanation

Good old honest George! We want the original price before any coupons. Call that *P*. He used a 15% coupon, so the discount of the coupon is 0.15*P*. To find the price after the coupon, we want to find (1 − 0.15*P*), or 0.85*P*. So with the coupon, George should have paid 0.85*P*, but instead he paid just 0.70*P*. These have a difference of 0.15*P*. This is the difference George offered to pay, but the manager told him to pay just half of that. Half of that is 0.075*P*, or $40.50.

$$0.075P = 40.05$$
$$P = (40.50) \div (0.075) = \$540$$

(That division would be a perfectly legitimate use of the calculator, in case you were wondering/feeling guilty.)

Answer: **D**

Geometry Word Problem Sets

The ACT Math Test always has a set of word problems that go together, usually three questions but sometimes four, and that accompany some kind of chart or diagram. Every ACT Math Test has one such set, and about half the time, it has two. Some of these involve spatial diagrams, for which we can use geometry or coordinate geometry. Others involve charts displaying data, which we'll discuss in the Statistics section. Occasionally, there's a set that involves an advanced formula of some kind. We'll discuss the Geometry sets here, the Data sets on page 220, the Advanced Formula sets on page 251, and then another Advanced Formula set on compound interest on page 281.

We can split these up relatively easily, because there's no new material to learn for these Geometry Word Problem sets. This is just a matter of using your geometry skills or coordinate geometry skills in some real-world context.

Use the following information to answer questions 1–3.

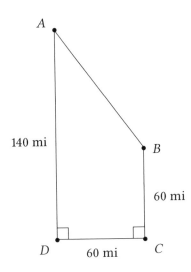

In a certain country, the District of Tetragon has four straight-line borders, as shown; AD = 140 miles and BC = CD = 60 miles. Border CD is perpendicular to borders AD and BC. The District of Tetragon has land borders on all sides, bordered by other districts.

1 If 40% of the land in the district is dedicated to agriculture, and the Agricultural Department expects 50,000 bushels of produce per year from each square mile dedicated to agriculture, approximately how many bushels of produce per year would the entire District of Tetragon yield?

   A. 8.4×10^7

   B. 1.2×10^8

   C. 1.68×10^8

   D. 2.4×10^8

   E. 3×10^8

2 A single railroad line follows the border of the District of Tetragon from A to B, then from B to C. How many miles of track are there along the route from A to C?

   F. 100 mi

   G. 120 mi

   H. 160 mi

   J. 220 mi

   K. 360 mi

3 The Department of the Interior wants to publish a map of the District of Tetragon and wants it to fit on a 12 × 25-inch area of a piece of paper. Which of the following is the smallest number of "miles per inch" such that, with this scale, the entire District of Tetragon still would fit in this area?

  A. 1 inch = 3 miles
  B. 1 inch = 4.2 miles
  C. 1 inch = 5 miles
  D. 1 inch = 5.6 miles
  E. 1 inch = 7.5 miles

Answers and Explanations

1 The District of Tetragon is a trapezoid. The average of the bases is $\frac{60 + 140}{2}$ = 100 mi, and the "height" between those bases is 60 mi. Area = (60)(100) = 6,000 sq mi. We know that 40% of this is dedicated to agriculture; well, 10% is 600, so 4 times that is 2,400 sq mi. Now we want to multiply this by 50,000 bushels per sq mi.

bushels = $(2,400)(50,000) = (2.4 \times 10^3)(5 \times 10^4) = 12 \times 10^7 = 1.2 \times 10^8$

Answer: **B**

2 Notice that we could draw an imaginary line through *B* parallel to *CD*.

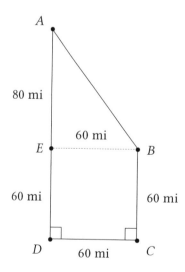

Call the intersection with *AD* point *E*. We see that *BCDE* must be a square, so *DE* = *BE* = 60 mi. This means that the remainder of *AD* must be *AE* = 80 mi.

Now, we have two legs of the right triangle *ABE*. Notice that this is simply a multiple of the {3, 4, 5} triangle: it's {60, 80, 100}. Thus, *AB* = 100, and *AB* + *BC* = 160 mi.

Answer: **H**

3 The District of Tetragon has a length vs. width ratio of $\frac{140}{60} = \frac{14}{6} = \frac{7}{3}$. How does this compare to the length vs. width ratio of $\frac{25}{12}$? Multiply the former by $\frac{4}{4}$, and it becomes $\frac{28}{12}$. Thus, the District of Tetragon is longer in the north-south direction than the area on the piece of paper. It appears that this 140 mi length will be the limiting factor.

Indeed, if we had a scale of 5 miles per inch, we'd neatly fit the 60-mile width into the 12-inch width of the area, but the 140-mile length would require a length of 28 inches, more than the area on the paper can accommodate. This scale does not work.

What would the scale need to be to accommodate that length?

We can calculate (140 mi)/(25 in) with a calculator to find the scale of 5.6 miles per inch. This scale fits in the area on the paper, and any larger number of miles per inch would also fit.

Answer: **D**

Intermediate Algebra

The Subtraction/Minus Sign

You know when you think you know something, but then you find out something that blows your understanding of it out of the water? In this section, we're going to take a look at something along just those lines.

What is the meaning of the − symbol?

You may have rolled your eyes, but this symbol actually has three different meanings.

1. **The subtraction sign:** This is an operator that can appear between numbers or variables (e.g., $5 - 3$, $x - 4$, or $x^2 - y^2$). This should be super-familiar: you learned this one way back in grade school.

2. **The negative sign:** This appears exclusively before numbers and denotes a number that is less than zero (e.g., -10). This one also should be pretty familiar. This use of the symbol arises from the subtraction sign, because $0 - 5 = -5$ and because subtracting $+5$ is the equivalent of adding -5.

3. **The opposite sign:** This appears exclusively before variables, and it changes the $\pm$ sign of the variable. For example, consider the expression $-x$. If x is positive, then $-x$ is negative. If $x = 0$, then $-x = 0$ as well. But—and this is the part that blows a lot of students' minds—if x is negative, then $-x$ is positive!! This use of the symbol arises from the negative sign, because $(-1) \times x = -x$.

Always be very careful when you see the − sign, and don't automatically assume that its appearance means that everything is negative. Once again, when x is already negative, then the − sign is precisely what can make it positive!

Absolute Value

Now that we have discussed the distinction between subtraction, negative, and opposite signs, we can discuss absolute values.

$$|3| = 3$$
$$|0| = 0$$
$$|-7| = +7$$

The way absolute value is taught in middle school is that it "makes things positive." Of course, it doesn't make zero positive: it leaves zero as zero, which is neither positive nor negative. That's just one of the limitations of this explanation, which is a simplistic numerical way of thinking about absolute value. A more sophisticated understanding involves two more perspectives: absolute value as a measure of distance, and the piecewise function definition of absolute value.

The absolute value of any number is that number's distance from the origin. Distance can be only zero or positive, so this is why the absolute value doesn't have any negative outputs. This perspective seamlessly extends to variables: $|x|$ is the distance from wherever x is on the number line to the position of zero. Similarly, $|x - p|$ is the distance between x and point p, regardless of their arrangement on the number line. This will become particularly important when we discuss absolute value inequalities in the next section.

Finally, the formal definition of absolute value is as a piecewise function. By definition,

$$|x| = \begin{cases} x & x \geq 0 \\ -x & x < 0 \end{cases}$$

In ordinary words, when x is positive or zero, then $|x|$ is equal to x. When x is negative, $|x|$ equals $-x$. That's the opposite sign we discussed above, which turns the negative value of x into a positive value. This definition is important in graphing absolute value in the xy-plane, which looks like this:

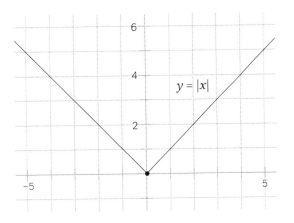

The absolute value graph will always have that characteristic V-shape, so keep an eye out for it on the ACT Math Test.

Absolute Value Inequalities

Let's go back to the distance definition of the absolute value, remembering that $|x - 7|$ means the distance from x to 7. Thus, this inequality

$$|x - 7| \leq 5$$

means that the distance from x to 7 is 5 or less. This is the set of points close to 7, up to and including a maximum distance of 5 away from 7. Thus, this region would have included endpoints at $7 + 5 = 12$, and $7 - 5 = 2$. 7 would be the midpoint of this region.

We also could denote this unit as $2 \leq x \leq 12$ or as

$$2 \leq x \quad \text{and} \quad x \leq 12$$

For the ACT Math Test, it's best to be comfortable switching back and forth between all the algebraic representations of such a region, both with and without absolute values.

Here's a problem with bigger numbers: more specifically, the inequality

$$x < -120 \quad \text{or} \quad 280 < x$$

How would we find the absolute value inequality representation of that region? Recall that the point from which we were measuring the distance was the midpoint between the two endpoints. Here, the endpoints are −120 and +280. The midpoint would be $\frac{-120 + 280}{2} = \frac{160}{2} = 80$. The point $x = 80$ is exactly between those two endpoints. Each endpoint is exactly 200 units from $x = 80$, and so every point in the included region is more than 200 units from $x = 80$. The distance from $x = 80$ can be written as $|x - 80|$, and this distance should be more than 200.

$$|x - 80| > 200$$

Notice that this required no major calculations, other than averaging two numbers. If you understand the distance definition of absolute value, then you can convert from an ordinary inequality system to an absolute value inequality with minimal effort.

Finally, notice that we get easy, extreme cases when negative numbers are involved. For example, which x's solve the inequality $|x - 78| > -17$? The numbers might make you think it involves a long, complicated calculation, but whatever the output of the absolute value is, it must be positive or zero, so this will always be bigger than any negative. Another way to say it is that every number on the number line has a distance to the point $x = 78$ that is greater than −17, because distance can only be positive or zero. The solution is simply all real numbers, or every number on the number line.

Similarly, the inequality $|x + 289| \leq -23$ can be dispatched quickly. The output of absolute value is always positive or zero, so it can never be less than a negative number. This is an example of an inequality that has no solution. Notice what a time-trap it would have been to start doing calculations with those numbers. As soon as you see an absolute value less than a negative, your logical antennae should go up: you should look for the quick and easy solution.

Practice Question

Which of the following is equivalent to $-13 \leq 8 - 7x \leq 85$?

A. $|x + 4| \leq 7$

B. $|x - 4| \leq 7$

C. $|x + 11| \geq -3$

D. $|x - 36| \leq 49$

E. $|x - 49| \leq 36$

Answer and Explanation

First, we have to simplify the inequality, so that it is simply in terms of x. Subtract 8 from all three expressions, and then divide by –7, reversing the inequality.

$$-13 \leq 8 - 7x \leq 85$$
$$-21 \leq -7x \leq 77$$
$$3 \geq x \geq -11$$

That's a much neater expression for the region. Notice that the midpoint is –4, which is exactly 7 units away from each endpoint. The distance from $x = -4$ is less than or equal to 7.

$$|x + 4| \leq 7$$

Answer: **A**

More on Quadratics

Earlier, on page 183 we discussed factoring as a method to get the solution of a quadratic. That's fine if the quadratic is factorable. But what if it isn't?

One very handy trick to solve a quadratic is called "**completing the square.**" This is based on the fundamental algebraic pattern known as the square of a sum/difference (you can review these on page 185).

$$(p \pm q)^2 = p^2 \pm 2pq + q^2$$

Let p be x and let q take on the first few integer values:

$$(x \pm 1)^2 = x^2 \pm 2x + 1$$
$$(x \pm 2)^2 = x^2 \pm 4x + 4$$
$$(x \pm 3)^2 = x^2 \pm 6x + 9$$
$$(x \pm 4)^2 = x^2 \pm 8x + 16$$
$$(x \pm 5)^2 = x^2 \pm 10x + 25$$
$$(x \pm 6)^2 = x^2 \pm 12x + 36$$

Notice a pattern? Now suppose we have to solve the quadratic

$$x^2 - 10x + 23 = 0$$

Don't worry if you're scratching your head—this is utterly unfactorable as written. Notice that the part on the left looks awfully close to the correct expression for $(x - 5)^2$; it's a little incomplete, so we have to complete it. If we add 2 to both sides, the expression for the perfect square is completed.

$$x^2 - 10x + 25 = 2$$
$$(x - 5)^2 = 2$$

Now, we simply take the square root. Remember, we need a ± when we take a square root on our own.

$$x - 5 = \pm\sqrt{2}$$
$$x = 5 \pm \sqrt{2}$$

That's the correct solution. We matched the variable expression to one of the perfect square patterns, added a number to both sides to "complete" the square, and took the square root.

We're on a roll! Let's solve the equation

$$x^2 + 12x - 39 = 0$$

Hmm, this looks a little far from complete. The complete square pattern with the same variable part would be $(x + 6)^2 = x^2 + 12x + 36$. What would we have to add to −39 to get +36? We would have to add +75. But we can do that, so let's go ahead.

$$x^2 + 12x + 36 = 75$$
$$(x + 6)^2 = 75$$
$$x + 6 = \pm\sqrt{75} = \pm 5\sqrt{3}$$
$$x = -6 \pm 5\sqrt{3}$$

That's the solution. The whole trick of completing the square is to be very familiar with the numbers in the $(x + q)^2 = x^2 + 2qx + q^2$ pattern. If you can spot the matching pattern quickly, then completing the square can be a lightning-fast way to solve an unfactorable quadratic.

Then, of course, there's the method of last resort, the **quadratic formula**. Quite often, the ACT Math Test supplies this to you when you need it, but there's no guarantee that they will. It's a very good idea to have this memorized—for the ACT and in life (you never know when there'll be a lull at a dinner party). For a quadratic in standard form, $ax^2 + bx + c = 0$, the solution is

$$x = \frac{-b \pm \sqrt{b^2 - 4ac}}{2a}$$

That's the quadratic formula. By the way, rather than rote memorization, it's an excellent exercise to start with the standard form of a quadratic, $ax^2 + bx + c = 0$, and follow the completing the square pattern with variables to derive the quadratic formula. If you can derive this formula from scratch, then you really understand it! We want to emphasize, once again: do not make this formula your primary mode of solving quadratics. This is a strategically poor approach that stunts your mathematical growth. Instead, factor absolutely every quadratic that you can factor, and practice the completing the square procedure on unfactorable quadratics until you get quick at it; if you do these two things, you'll have very little use for the quadratic formula. Other than those aforementioned dinner parties, of course.

Quadratic Inequalities

This is a relatively infrequent topic on the ACT Math Test, but that doesn't mean it won't show up. Quadratic inequalities look really intimidating, but the process of solving them is straightforward. Here's a sample problem.

What are the values of x, such that $x^2 + 4x - 11 > 10$?

When they see this, many students get wigged out and start trying to do things with the inequality. Instead, you can follow this simple procedure.

Step #1: Get zero on one side, as we always do with a quadratic.

$$x^2 + 4x - 21 > 0$$

Step #2: Change the inequality to an equation, and factor to solve (if the ACT gives you this kind of question at all, then it's dollars to doughnuts that they'll give a completely factorable quadratic!).

$$x^2 + 4x - 21 = 0$$
$$(x - 3)(x + 7) = 0$$
$$x - 3 = 0 \quad \text{or} \quad x + 7 = 0$$
$$x = 3 \text{ or } x = -7$$

Step #3: Think about the quadratic: is it a "happy" quadratic (U-shaped) or a "sad" quadratic (upside-down U)? Remember, the sign of the x^2 coefficient tells us this.
   This quadratic is happy!

Step #4: Sketch a number line and put the two roots on the number line; these divide the number line into three regions. A "happy" parabola will be negative between roots and positive outside of the roots; a "sad" parabola will be positive between the roots and negative on the outside.

Also, a parabola with no real roots will be always positive or always negative, with no sign changes ever. A parabola with exactly one real root will be zero (neither positive nor negative) at one point, and then the same sign everywhere else—either all positive or all negative everywhere besides the root.
   In this problem, this parabola is a "happy" parabola with roots at 3 and −7, so it will be positive outside these roots. The solution to the inequality is

$$x < -7 \quad \text{or} \quad x > 3$$

Equations with Powers and Roots

The ACT Math Test won't give you many equations with radicals that you have to solve. The basic strategy to solving any algebraic equation with a square root is (1) get the square root on one side and set it equal to everything else, and (2) square both sides. For example, suppose we had to solve the equation

$$7\sqrt{2x-7} + 9 = 44$$

We need to get that square root by itself. Everything under the square root stays the same during this phase of the solution.

$$7\sqrt{2x-7} = 35$$
$$\sqrt{2x-7} = 5$$

Now, simply square both sides. Squaring "undoes" the radical, so what had been under the radical is now "freed" from it.

$$2x - 7 = 25$$
$$2x = 32$$
$$x = 16$$

That's the answer!

For most equations with powers, it's enough to be familiar with the laws of exponents. In particular, it's good to be familiar with the patterns of positive and negative signs, and how they play out with even vs. odd roots. The practice problem on page 140, about which expression could be negative, is an example of this.

Rational Expressions

When we make a fraction in which both the numerator and denominator are algebraic expressions, we have made a *rational expression*. The following are examples of rational expressions.

$$\frac{x+3}{x-7} \qquad \frac{1}{x^2-36} \qquad \frac{x^3}{x-2}$$

Some rational expressions can be simplified by canceling—sort of. You see, if a rational expression has the same factor in both the numerator and the denominator, then *usually* these can be canceled to simplify the radical. Why are we hedging here? Here's the thing. If your job is only to "simplify" the rational expression, then cancel away. But if this is part of an equation or inequality, and you're solving for the value or range of a variable, then you have to consider what happens when the factor in both the numerator and the denominator has a value of zero. Remember that zero over zero is mathematical nonsense: it is something so off-the-charts wrong that it doesn't even deserve to be connected with an equal sign!

For example, consider the following problem.

$$3 < \frac{x^2 - 3x - 10}{x - 5}$$

What is the range of x's that satisfies that inequality?

Whenever a quadratic appears in either the numerator or the denominator of a rational expression, step #1 is to factor that quadratic. Here's the same inequality with the numerator factored.

$$3 < \frac{(x+2)(x-5)}{x-5}$$

Before we cancel anything, notice that the value $x = 5$ turns the expression into the nonsense expression $\frac{0}{0}$, which of course cannot be greater than or less than or equal to anything because it has no well-defined value at all. For the moment, we'll just file this in our memory banks: $x = 5$ is most certainly NOT a solution to this inequality.

With that stashed in our memory banks, we can go ahead and cancel the factors of $(x - 5)$.

$$3 < x + 2$$
$$1 < x$$

Once we canceled, that was pretty simple. It would seem that every value above $x = 1$ works. But wait! Recall that we found out that $x = 5$ doesn't work! Thus, the solution is everything greater than $x = 1$, *except for $x = 5$*. In other words, the solution range is

$$1 < x < 5 \quad \text{or} \quad 5 < x$$

Canceling in algebraic expressions is not as worry-free as canceling numbers! Canceling algebra has logical stipulations and logical consequences, as we saw in this example problem. Here's a practice problem on the same theme.

Practice Question

$$0 \le \frac{(x-1)(x^2 - 12x + 36)}{x - 6}$$

What is the range of values for which the above inequality is true?

A. $x < 1$ or $6 < x$

B. $x < 1$ or $6 \le x$

C. $x \le 1$ or $6 < x$

D. $x \le 1$ or $6 \le x$

E. $1 \le x \le 6$

Answer and Explanation

First of all, we need to recognize the second factor in the numerator as the square of a difference (see page 185).

$$x^2 - 12x + 36 = (x - 6)^2$$
$$(x - 6)^2 = (x - 6)(x - 6)$$
$$(x - 6)(x - 6) = 0 \le \frac{(x-1)(x-6)(x-6)}{(x-6)}$$

After factoring the quadratic expression in the numeration, we get factors of $(x - 6)$ in both the numerator and the denominator. When $x = 6$, we get the nonsense expression $\frac{0}{0}$, which has no meaningful value. Thus, $x = 6$ can't be a part of any solution.

Putting that value aside for the moment, we can cancel an $(x - 6)$ on the numerator with the $(x - 6)$ on the denominator, getting

$$0 \le (x - 1)(x - 6)$$

What we have on the right is a quadratic, an upward-facing parabola (because the x in each term is positive), in root form. We know this because if we expand the expression $(x - 1)(x - 6)$ using the FOIL method (reviewed on page 299), we get an upward-facing parabola that is less than zero between its roots, greater than zero outside of the roots, and equal to zero at the roots. Thus, it would seem that the answer would be

$$x \le 1 \text{ or } 6 \le x$$

In fact, that would be exactly the solution range if we were just dealing with this already canceled form. We have to remember, though, that we discovered earlier that $x = 6$ cannot be a part of any solution because it produces the nonsensical $\frac{0}{0}$ form. Thus, we have to exclude $x = 6$, which leaves us

$$x \le 1 \text{ or } 6 < x$$

Answer: **C**

Finally, anything that the ACT Math Test might expect you to do with compound numerical fractions (discussed on page 127), it could ask you to do with rational expressions. Here's a challenging sample problem on this.

$$\frac{1+\frac{4}{x-2}}{\frac{4}{x^2-4}+\frac{1}{x+2}}$$

The above expression simplifies to which of the following?

F. $x + 2$

G. $x - 2$

H. x^2

J. $x^2 + 4$

K. $x^2 - 4$

Answer and Explanation

This problem gets a whole lot simpler when you notice that all the denominators of the smaller fractions are factors from a familiar difference of two squares expression.

$$x^2 - 4 = (x + 2)(x - 2)$$

Thus, this expression is the LCM of all the little fractions. Multiply by this in the numerator and denominator.

We know, it's not as simple as it sounds! We'll have to approach it first piece by piece. Notice that, in some instances, we will multiply by the factored form to make canceling more apparent.

When the 1 in the numerator is multiplied by $(x^2 - 4)$, it will just become $(x^2 - 4)$.

When the $\frac{4}{x-2}$ in the numerator is multiplied by $(x + 2)(x - 2)$, the factors of $(x - 2)$ cancel, and we get $4(x + 2)$.

When the $\frac{4}{x^2-4}$ in the denominator is multiplied by $(x^2 - 4)$, it will just become 4.

When the $\frac{1}{x+2}$ in the denominator is multiplied by $(x + 2)(x - 2)$, it will just become $(x - 2)$.

Now, put all that together in the big fraction.

$$\frac{1+\frac{4}{x-2}}{\frac{4}{x^2-4}+\frac{1}{x+2}} = \frac{(x^2-4)+(4(x+2))}{(4)+(x-2)} = \frac{x^2-4+4(x+2)}{4+x-2} = \frac{x^2-4+4x+8}{x+2} = \frac{x^2+4x+4}{x+2}$$

You may recognize that numerator as the square of a sum:

$$(x + 2)^2 = x^2 + 4x + 4$$

$$\frac{x^2+4x+4}{x+2} = \frac{(x+2)^2}{x+2} = x + 2$$

That's the simplified expression.

Answer: **F**

Statistics and Data

Range

One statistics term you need to know is *range*. The range of any set of numbers is just the maximum, the largest number in the set, minus the minimum, the smallest number in the set. For example, if we had the set {1, 2, 3, 4, 58, 604, 1729}, then the range would simply be 1729 – 1 = 1728. Biggest minus smallest: that's it! Of course, the ACT Math Test is unlikely to hand you something as easy as "Here's the set. Find the range," but knowing about the range could play into a more complicated question.

For example, you might see range in a problem like the following.

Practice Question

> In a set of four positive integers, the range is 60 and the median is 50. What is the highest possible value of the largest number in the set?
>
> **A.** 105
> **B.** 108
> **C.** 109
> **D.** 110
> **E.** 111

Answer and Explanation

This is a tricky problem that involves some number sense. (For more on number sense, see page 114.)

We want to make the largest of the four numbers as large as possible. Let's say that from smallest to biggest, the numbers are {P, Q, R, S}. We know

$$60 = S - P, \text{ so } S = 60 + P$$

In other words, if we're going to make S as large as possible, we also have to make P as large as possible. In order to have a median of 50, Q and R must be symmetrical around 50. Let's say each is a distance D from 50.

$$Q = 50 - D$$
$$R = 50 + D$$

What's the largest we could make P? Well, P can't be greater than Q, if the numbers are listed in order, but P certainly could equal Q. In this case.

$$P = Q = 50 - D$$
$$R = 50 + D$$
$$S = (50 - D) + 60 = 110 - D$$

The limiting factor is D. What is the smallest we could make D? Well, we could make $D = 0$. Then:

$$P = Q = R = 50$$
$$S = 110$$

The set is {50, 50, 50, 110}. That set has a median of 50 and a range of 60. Furthermore, since those lower three numbers are already locked at the value of the median, we can't move the set any higher, so 110 is the highest that fourth number can be.

Answer: **D**

Modes of Displaying Data

The ACT Math Test sometimes asks about pie charts. A pie chart uses the size of the "slice" of pie to indicate the percent of a group or population that something is. Remember that the proper geometric name for such a "slice" is a sector: see the discussion about the area of sectors on page 168. The ACT Math Test will want to know that you can go back and forth between the degrees of the sector and the percent of the population. For example, if a group were represented by a filled-in semicircle on a pie chart, it would be half the population. If a group were represented by a quarter-circle slice, it would be 25% of the population. We can set up a part-to-whole proportion, similar to one we set up to find the area of a sector.

$$\frac{degree\ of\ slice}{360°} = \frac{percent\ of\ population}{100\%}$$

Remember that what we're calling the "degree of slice" here is known in geometry as the central angle.

Here's a sample problem using this concept.

Practice Question

In the Newhouse Company, there are 36 engineers, 67 customer service representatives, 7 HR employees, and 10 other employees. If this information about all 120 employees were converted to a pie chart, then the central angle of the sector for engineers would measure how many degrees?

F. 48°

G. 72°

H. 96°

J. 108°

K. 120°

Answer and Explanation

If you're comfortable with shortcuts, we can simplify $\frac{36}{120} = \frac{3}{10}$, so the sector for engineers should occupy $\frac{3}{10}$ of the pie chart. We know that $\frac{1}{10}$ of 360° would be 36°, so $\frac{3}{10}$ would be three times this, which is 108. If you prefer to apply the formula and use your calculator, set up your equation: $\frac{36\text{ engineers}}{120\text{ employees}} = \frac{x°}{360°}$. From here, cross-multiply to solve for $x°$: $120x° = 36 \times 360$. Divide both sides by 120, and $x° = 108$.

Answer: **J**

Charts of Numbers

The ACT Math Test often gives numbers in charts. For example, the numbers given in the previous practice problem about Newhouse Company also could have been presented in a chart.

Employees at Newhouse Company	
Engineers	36
Customer service reps	67
HR employees	7
Other	10
Total	120

Sometimes the ACT Math Test will present only one column of data in a chart. More often, the charts will show how two different numerical scales relate. For example,

Acme Set of Nails	Ounces Per Nail	Nails Per Set
One-inch	1	100
Three-inch	7	50
Four-inch	9	40
Six-inch	25	20

With this data set, we could figure out the weight of each of the four nail sets. The box of one-inch nails weighs only 100 ounces, but the box of six-inch nails weighs 25 × 20 = 500 ounces, which is five times more!

A chart may also present a "schedule" of different prices or rates for different conditions.

Pony Express Horse Transport Service		
Number of Horses to Be Moved	Fee	Price Per Horse
1–5	$100	$100
6–20	$300	$80
21+	$1000	$50

Depending on the number of horses that we want to move from one place to another, we'd have to pay both a different fee and a different rate. For example, if we moved 5 horses, we'd pay the $100 fee plus $100 for each of the 5, for a total of $100 + $500 = $600. If we moved 6 horses instead, we'd have the new fee of $300 plus a rate of only $80 for each of the 6, for a total of $300 + 6($80) = $300 + $480 = $780.

Charts of data can accompany single problems or can provide the information for a set of three questions. As we've seen, most of the problems on the ACT Math Test are single stand-alone problems, but you will have at least one set of three problems, all revolving around the same information. Geometric diagrams or data sets seem to be by far the most frequent prompts for these sets. We discussed the Geometry Word Problem Sets above on page 204. Here's an example of a Data Word Problem Set. Still to come are Advanced Formula Problem Sets on page 251 and an additional Advanced Formula Problem Set on Compound Interest on page 283.

Practice Questions

Use the following information to answer questions 1–3.

The graph shows the profits of TCA Corporation during the period 2006–2015 inclusive. The vertical scale is in millions of dollars.

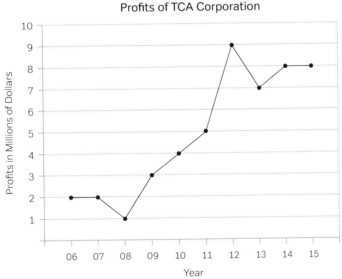

1 In 2013, TCA would have had the same profit as in 2012, but there was a special federal tax in 2013 that was the only cause of the difference. What was the amount of this special federal tax?

- A. $1 million
- B. $2 million
- C. $3 million
- D. $4 million
- E. $5 million

2 In which year did the profits of TCA Corporation increase *by the greatest percentage* of the previous year's profits?

   F. 2009

   G. 2010

   H. 2011

   J. 2012

   K. 2014

3 If the point (2005, $0) is the origin, if *x* is the number of years after 2005, and if *y* is the profit, then which of the following lines best models the region of the graph from 2008 to 2012?

   A. $y = x - 2$

   B. $y = 2x - 1$

   C. $y = 2x - 5$

   D. $y = 3x - 12$

   E. $y = 4x - 19$

Answers and Explanations

1 Profits in 2012 were $9 million, and profits in 2013 were $7 million. If the profits in 2013 were going to be $9 million, and they were knocked down to $7 million by the tax, that's a difference of $2 million. This must mean it was a $2 million tax.

Answer: **B**

2 We want the biggest percentage increase, not the biggest numerical increase. Clearly, 2012 had the biggest numerical increase, but that was an increase of less than 50 percent from the previous year.

   If something starts small and has a big increase, those are the conditions for a very big percent increase. In 2008, the profits were at the low point, only $1 million, and in 2009, they went up to $3 million. That's an original of $1 million plus an additional $1 million (100%) plus yet another $1 million (100%)—that's a 200% increase! No other upward segment on the graph produces anything even close to that kind of percent increase. Thus, 2009 had the biggest percent increase.

Answer: **F**

3 Notice that the points (2008, $1 million), (2009, $3 million), and (2012, $9 million) are all collinear or on the same line. If we consider (2005, 0) the origin, then these three points are (3, 1), (4, 3), and (7, 9). A line through these points would have a slope of 2. If we follow this slope to the left (left 1, down 2) from (3, 1), that brings us to (2, –1) ⇨ (1, –3) ⇨ (0, –5). That's the *y*-intercept. The equation is $y = 2x - 5$. This line goes through three of the five points during the time period from 2008 to 2012, and it is very close to the other two.

Answer: **C**

Probability and Counting

What are the odds that the ACT Math Test is going to ask you about probability? Pretty good! In fact, we'd bet good money on it! Chances are, though, with a few simple rules, you can master the majority of these problems.

Many probability problems on the ACT Math Test give you a larger set of various groups and ask you the probability of selecting a member of one of those groups. Here, the probability is simply a part-to-whole fraction. Another way to think of that is as follows.

$$\text{probability of a desired outcome} = \frac{\text{number of desired outcomes}}{\text{total number of outcomes}}$$

In some probability questions, all we have to do is compute that numerator and denominator. Here's a straightforward practice problem.

Practice Question

> In a high school in a small town, there are 12 freshmen, 14 sophomores, 15 juniors, and 19 seniors. If a student is selected at random, what is the probability that this student will be a freshman?
>
> A. $\frac{1}{4}$
>
> B. $\frac{1}{5}$
>
> C. $\frac{1}{6}$
>
> D. $\frac{3}{8}$
>
> E. $\frac{1}{12}$

Answer and Explanation
The first thing we need to do is to find out the size of the whole group—in this case, that's the entire student body.

$$12 + 14 + 15 + 19 = 60$$

The probability is a part-to-whole ratio. The part is 12, for the 12 freshmen. The whole is 60, the size of the student body. We'll need to reduce that fraction.

$$\frac{12}{60} = \frac{1}{5}$$

Answer: **B**

Probability from Ratios

Ratios and probabilities are often expressed as fractions. In fact, if a ratio is set up in the part-to-whole form, then it could be a probability as well. Many ratios, though, are given in part-to-part form. If, in a certain set, the ratios of P elements to Q elements to R elements are 1:3:5, then the whole is $1 + 3 + 5 = 9$, and Q to the whole is $\frac{3}{9} = \frac{1}{3}$. This would also be the probability of picking a Q element if we picked one element from the set.

Things gets a little trickier if we're given a few different kinds of ratios in the problem, though. Here's a practice problem.

Practice Question

On a county-wide baseball team, the best players were sent from each high school. The players are grouped into 3 categories: infielders (including catchers), outfielders, and pitchers. If the ratio of infielders to outfielders is 7:4, and the ratio of pitchers to outfielders is 5:3, then if we pick one player at random from the county-wide baseball team, what is the probability that we will pick a pitcher?

- **F.** $\frac{1}{3}$
- **G.** $\frac{4}{13}$
- **H.** $\frac{5}{16}$
- **J.** $\frac{20}{33}$
- **K.** $\frac{20}{53}$

Answer and Explanation

First, we have to reconcile and combine the two ratios given. The common term is the number of outfielders, which is 4 in one ratio and 3 in the other. The LCM of 3 and 4 is 12, so we have to multiply each ratio so that the number of outfielders is 12 in both ratios. In the first, infielders:outfielders is 7:4—multiply this by 3 to get 21:12. In the second, pitchers:outfielders is 5:3—multiply this by 4 to get 20:12. Thus,

infielders:outfielders:pitchers = 21:12:20

Notice this doesn't mean that there are exactly 21 infielders, 12 outfielders, and 20 pitchers, but just that the numbers fall into those ratios. If we have 21 parts, 12 parts, and 20 parts, the total number of parts is $21 + 12 + 20 = 53$. The fraction of the whole that are pitchers would be $\frac{20}{53}$. This is a part-to-whole ratio, so this is also the probability of picking a pitcher at random from all the players.

Answer: **K**

Expected Number

Sometimes, when the ACT Math Test gives a probability as a ratio or a percent, it'll ask for what is known as the "expected number." (But be careful: the ACT Math Test won't necessarily use that particular term.) Here's a sample question of this sort—just the prompt itself:

> *A poll found that 30% of the people randomly sampled in Brower County are in favor of the proposed new sales tax in the county. If this poll is representative of the 2,000 shoppers at the largest mall in Brower county, which of the following would be the best estimate of the number of shoppers at the mall we would expect to support this new sales tax?*

A few things are noteworthy here. We're given a percentage of the population; remember that a percent is also, essentially, a probability, a kind of part-to-whole ratio. We are told it is "representative"—in other words, we can treat this piece of mathematical information as relevant. If we picked one person at random from the whole county, then we would have about a 30% chance of picking someone in favor of the new tax. You don't need to know this detail for the ACT Math Test, but a randomly selected sample of a population is, for most intents and purposes, statistically representative of the population, so you often will see that detail mentioned in these problems. Finally, we're given a particular group and we want to know the "expected" number from this group that hold the position. Of course, we would know the actual real number of people in the mall who support the new tax only if we did the work to ask all 2,000 of them. We don't want to do all that—we just want a quick estimate. The "expected" number is an estimate we can make, from the percentage given, of the "part" of the population that holds the position.

Here's the basic logic we need to solve this problem. We discussed above that we can think of probability in terms of the following formula:

$$probability = \frac{part}{whole}$$

Well, if we multiply both sides by "whole," we get

$$(probability) \times (whole) = part$$

That's the key to our strategy right there. To find the "part" of the 2,000 shoppers who support the new tax, we simply multiply the whole 2,000 by the percent given as a decimal. In other words, we want 30% of 2,000. We know that 10% of 2,000 is 200, so we can multiply that by 3: 30% of 2,000 is 600. That's the answer: we would estimate that about 600 shoppers of those 2,000 would be in favor of the new tax.

Ready to try it on your own? Here's another practice problem you can use to put this concept to the test.

Practice Question

The Dairy Manufacturers of Bovitaur County conducted a random survey in the county for favorite ice cream flavors. They asked, "Do you eat ice cream?" and if the answer was "yes," they asked the respondent to name her favorite flavor. In the survey, 20% said they didn't eat ice cream. Among the ones who answered "yes" to that first question, here is a table of the responses, in order of popularity:

Flavor of Ice Cream	Number of Respondents
Plain vanilla	38
Plain chocolate	24
Fruit flavored (e.g., strawberry)	7
Something containing nuts	3
Something containing raisins	2
Other	2

Assuming that all these numbers are representative, the Dairy Manufacturers can expect that how many of Bovitaur County's 20,000 residents like plain vanilla?

A. 2,000

B. 4,000

C. 6,000

D. 8,000

E. 10,000

Answer and Explanation

First of all, 20% of people don't like ice cream, so 80% like it. That 80% is represented by the numbers on the chart. We have to add those numbers up to get a total: we'll be clever about *how* we add them to make the arithmetic a little simpler.

$$(38 + 2) + 24 + (7 + 3) + 2 = 40 + 26 + 10 = 76$$

The proportion of folks who prefer plain vanilla is $\frac{38}{76} = \frac{1}{2}$. Thus, half of that 80%—or 40%—of the population of the county likes plain vanilla.

Now, we need to find 40% of the 20,000 residents. We know that 10% of 20,000 is 2,000, so multiply this by 4: 40% of 20,000 is 8,000. That's the estimated number of residents in Bovitaur County who prefer plain vanilla.

Answer: **D**

Combinations of Events

Sometimes, the ACT Math Test will ask about the probability of two events happening at once. Here, we will share a down-and-dirty trick: as a very rough-and-ready rule, in probability the word "AND" means **multiply**. For the ACT Math Test, that's all you need to know. (We'll add that if you study probability in any depth anywhere else—for example, in an AP Statistics course—then you'll learn about all sorts of stipulations and exceptions to that rule, but all of that additional information doesn't matter on the ACT Math Test.) The probability of event *A and* event *B* happening at the same time is just the probability of *A* times the probability of *B*.

The probability of rolling a fair six-sided die and getting a 5 is $\frac{1}{6}$. The probability of picking one card at random from a standard shuffled deck and drawing a heart is $\frac{1}{4}$. Therefore, the probability of rolling the die and drawing the card simultaneously and getting both a 5 on the die and a heart card, would be $\frac{1}{6} \times \frac{1}{4} = \frac{1}{24}$. We multiply the probabilities for two simultaneous events. Try it out in the following problem.

Practice Question

For a certain classroom game, the teacher will pick a student who is learning Spanish and a letter of the alphabet. There are 10 students learning Spanish in the class, and one of these 10 is Alan. The teacher put tiles with the 26 letters of the alphabet in a bag. The teacher will pick one tile at random and then one of the 10 students at random. What is the probability that teacher picks both Alan and the letter Z?

F. $\frac{1}{16}$

G. $\frac{1}{36}$

H. $\frac{1}{260}$

J. $\frac{5}{13}$

K. $\frac{9}{65}$

Answer and Explanation

The probability of picking Alan at random from the 10 Spanish learners is $\frac{1}{10}$. The probability of picking the letter Z from the 26 letters of the alphabet is $\frac{1}{26}$. To find the probability of both of these events happening together, we have to multiply the probabilities.

$$P(\text{picking Alan and Z}): P = \frac{1}{10} \times \frac{1}{26} = \frac{1}{260}$$

Answer: **H**

Counting

This may seem like a funny topic, because, of course, everyone (even someone who absolutely hates math) still knows how to count. This is a little different, though: the ACT Math Test will ask you to count the number of combinations of different things or the number of different ways to do something. For example, suppose a restaurant offers 4 different kinds of salads, 10 different entrees, and 6 different desserts. All of these choices can be mixed and matched in any combination. If we consider a meal a salad plus an entree plus a dessert, how many different possible meals are there at this restaurant? In other words, we have to "count" the number of different possible meals. This is the sort of scenario that you'll come across on the ACT Math Test.

One idea that simplifies a large number of such "counting" problems is the *fundamental counting principle* (FCP). Suppose task #1 can be done in N_1 number of ways, task #2 can be done in N_2 number of ways, and task #3 can be done in N_3 number of ways. Suppose a "job" consists of these three tasks, and any combination of them counts as a different "job." Then the total number of different "jobs" would be $N_1 \times N_2 \times N_3$. The FCP says that we simply multiply the number of ways to do each of the individual tasks, and this product is the total number of combination of the tasks.

For example, in the restaurant problem above, there are 4 different kinds of salads, 10 different entrees, and 6 different desserts. Thus, the total number of meals is $4 \times 10 \times 6 = 240$, meaning that from these choices, we can create 240 different possible meals.

Remember that in any problem in which there are such-and-such ways to do one thing, and varied ways to do the next thing, etc., all we have to do is multiply all the numbers together to find out the total number of options.

Harder Counting Problems

The majority of the counting problems in the ACT Math Test follow the above pattern and can be dispatched quickly with the FCP. Every once in a while, often on one of the last 10 questions, the ACT Math Test presents a harder counting problem, one that involves number sense and thinking outside of the box. If you see one of these problems, don't use the FCP or any other formula, because a formula won't help you. You'll have to use logic to think about the situation, recognizing the full range of possibilities in the scenario presented.

That sounds a little scary, we admit, but here's what it looks like in practice (not so bad!).

For a school outing, the school has 20 small ice chests, each of which can hold up to 6 cans of soda. At the beginning of the day, 10 of the ice chests are full, with 6 cans each, and 10 are empty. The teachers are going to rearrange where the cans of soda are stored. If every can of soda must be in an ice chest, and each ice chest must have at least 1 can and not more than 6, then what is the largest number of ice chests that can have exactly 4 cans?

A. 10
B. 12
C. 13
D. 14
E. 15

Answer and Explanation

We know that there are 60 cans of soda. If these were distributed evenly, there would be 20 ice chests with 3 cans each. Consider that our starting point: 20 ice chests with 3 cans each. Let's remove 1 can each from 10 of the ice chests and give the other 10 ice chests 1 can each: then we'll have 10 ice chests with 4 cans each and 10 with 2 cans each. Put those 10 ice chests with 4 cans aside: they're done.

Now, let's look at the 10 ice chests with 2 cans each. We want to see whether we can get any more chests with 4 cans. We could take 3 of these ice chests, take 1 soda away from 2 of them, and give these 2 soda cans to the third, so that we create 1 more ice chest with 4 cans. In this set of 3 ice chests, we go from {2, 2, 2} to {1, 1, 4}. We can do this 3 times with this set of 10 ice chests, so the set of 10 goes from {2, 2, 2, 2, 2, 2, 2, 2, 2, 2} to {4, 4, 4, 2, 1, 1, 1, 1, 1, 1}. Thus, we get 3 more ice chests with 4 cans each, for a grand total of 13 altogether.

Answer: **C**

Functions

What's another thing the ACT Math Test loves? You'll definitely see at least a few questions about functions on any given ACT Math Test.

A function is a mathematical rule that assigns an input to an output. The set of all possible inputs is the *domain*, and the set of all possible outputs is the *range*. Often, a function is represented in algebraic form. For example:

$$f(x) = x^3 - x - 1$$

Any number on the number line could be the value of x, the input. Notice that this means that the domain of this particular function is all real numbers. We would plug a given value (the input) into x in the above expression, and the value of the entire expression on the right side would be the output. While this might not be obvious, this function also has a range of all real numbers: with the right choice of x, we could get any output on the number line.

That was an example of a function given in algebraic form. Here's one given in graphical form.

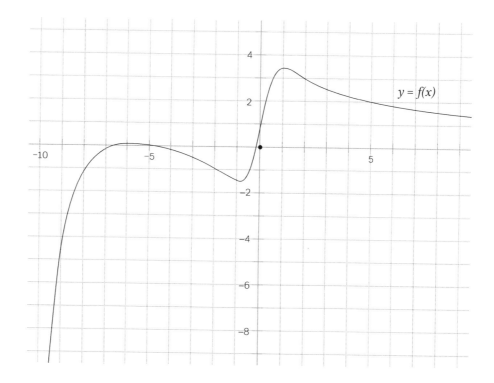

This unusual function appears to have a domain of all real numbers—a value for each possible x-value. It looks like it comes up from negative-infinity values of y, but it only goes as high as between $y = 3$ and $y = 4$ and then decreases, so it doesn't have a *range* of all real numbers. (The ACT Math Test would **not** expect you to approximate the value of this maximum y-value!) How might you see this on test day? The ACT Math Test could give you just the algebraic formula, or just the graph, or both, and ask you questions about it.

One of the most straightforward questions the test might ask is for you to evaluate the function at a point. Suppose we are given this function again, $f(x) = x^3 - x - 1$, and we're asked to evaluate $f(-2)$. That means we have to plug $x = -2$ for x in the expression on the right side.

$$f(-2) = (-2)^3 - (-2) - 1 = -8 + 2 - 1 = -7$$

The ACT Math Test often asks this question as one of its earlier, "easier" questions.

One really big idea that you should keep in mind is that **every (x, y) point that satisfies the algebraic equation $y = f(x)$ is a point that is on the graph of $y = f(x)$.** For example, if the value $x = 3$ produces $f(3) = 7$, then it must be true that the graph of the function passes through and contains the point $(3, 7)$. This idea has some immediate consequences. Suppose we have a diagram that shows the graph of two functions, as below:

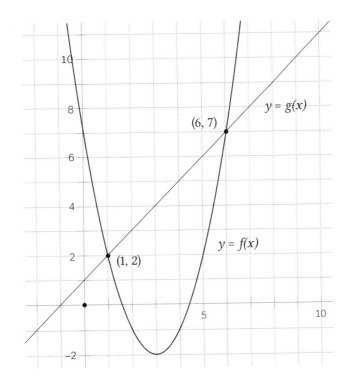

Here, $y = g(x)$ is a straight line and $y = f(x)$ appears to be a parabola. We know from that graph that the functions $f(x)$ and $g(x)$ have the same output at $x = 1$ and again have the same output at $x = 6$. We also can see that the graph of $f(x)$ is below the graph of $g(x)$ between the two intersection points, so we can say that $f(x) < g(x)$ for the interval $1 < x < 6$, and $f(x) > g(x)$ to the left of $x = 1$ and to the right of $x = 6$. All of this is the type of information the ACT Math Test might ask you to deduce from a graph.

Polynomial Functions

A polynomial function is a function that has one or multiple terms. Each term either is a constant or has positive integer powers of x. Sound a little abstract? Let's take a look at a few of them. The following are polynomial functions.

1. $f(x) = 7$
2. $f(x) = 3x + 5$
3. $f(x) = x^2 - 8x + 16$
4. $f(x) = x^{75} - x^{35}$

The highest power of x is called the *degree* of the polynomial function. Any function with just a number, no x, is a constant function, as (1) is, and has a degree of zero. Any function in of the form $ax + b$, like (2), is a linear function and has a degree of one. If the highest power is a square, as in (3), it is a quadratic function and has a degree of two. Don't worry about the names of anything beyond that, because the ACT Math Test won't hold you responsible for the names of higher degree polynomials (cubic, quartic, quintic, etc.).

Although you won't have to know the names, you will have to know the pattern of the shapes. A linear function, with degree 1, is just a straight line. A quadratic second-degree function, turns around once: we'll call that one "bend." (This term, "bend," is our own term, not one the ACT will use!) A polynomial function of degree 3 could have as many as two "bends."

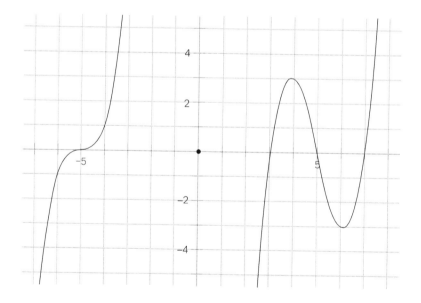

Importantly, though, while it may have two "bends," it could also have no "bends"—two is just the maximum number of "bends" a third-degree polynomial can have.

A polynomial function of degree 4 could have as many as three "bends."

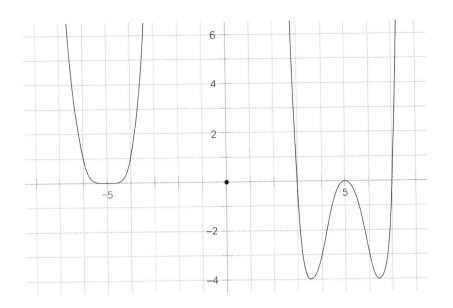

Again, it may only have one "bend," but three is the maximum number of "bends" that a fourth-degree polynomial can have.

You're probably beginning to see a pattern here. If the degree of a polynomial is n, then the maximum number of bends would be $(n - 1)$. Here's a sample problem.

Practice Question

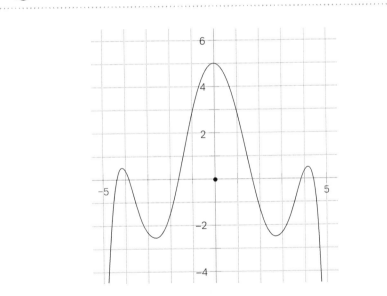

Above is the graph of a polynomial function. What would be the minimum degree required to produce a graph of this sort?

A. 3

B. 4

C. 5

D. 6

E. 7

Answer and Explanation

We count 5 "bends," so the degree must be one higher than this. This could be produced by a sixth power, a polynomial with degree 6, or it could be produced by a higher power polynomial. 6 is the minimum possible degree.

Answer: **D**

Transformation of Functions

Given the equation of a function and its graph, we can construct new functions that are simply this original function shifted—up or down, right or left. When we shift one function to produce another, we have performed a *transformation* of the function.

To discuss this, we will distinguish the "inside" and "outside" of the expression $f(x)$. Any operation that takes place inside those parentheses, acting on the x before it gets fed into the function, is an "inside" transformation, and any operation that acts on the outside on $f(x)$ as a unit, acting on the output after it has been through the $f(x)$-machine, is an "outside" transformation. As a general rule, we make vertical changes in the graph with "outside" transformations and horizontal changes in the graph with "inside" transformations.

Suppose we want to shift the graph of $f(x)$ up 5 units, making a vertical change. In this case, we add 5 to the outside.

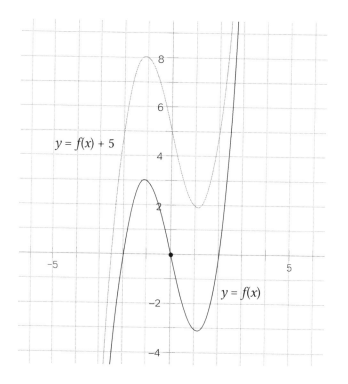

Similarly, if we want to shift the original function 4 units down, we subtract 4 from the outside.

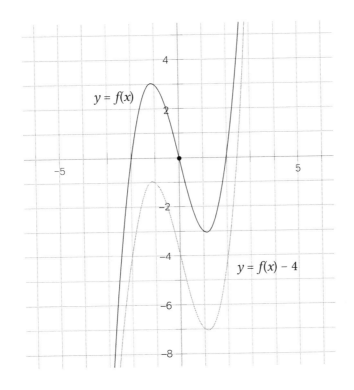

Adding on the outside moves the function up, and subtracting on the outside moves the function down. So far, so good.

What happens in the horizontal direction is not so intuitive. Suppose we want to shift the function 5 units to the right. That's the positive direction, so we might think that some kind of addition would result in a movement in the positive direction. In fact, **the opposite is the case**. We have to *subtract* 5 inside to move the function 5 units to the right!

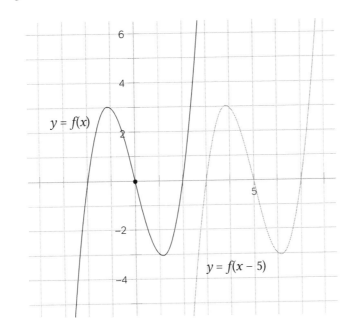

Now, why does this follow an anti-intuitive pattern? That is, why does *subtracting* on the inside move the function in the *positive x*-direction? Think about it this way. When $x = 5$, then $y = f(x - 5) = f(0)$; in other words, $f(x - 5)$ has the same output at $x = 5$ that $f(x)$ has at $x = 0$. Similarly, when $x = 0$, then $y = f(x - 5) = f(-5)$; in other words, $f(x - 5)$ has the same output at $x = 0$ that $f(x)$ has at $x = -5$. This pattern continues:

The output of $f(x - 5)$ is at this *x*-value:	Equals the output of $f(x)$ at this *x*-value:
0	–5
3	–2
5	0
8	3
10	5
12	7
etc.	etc.

Thus, whatever $f(x)$ does, $f(x - 5)$ does the same thing 5 units to the right! Similarly, adding on the inside moves the function to the left.

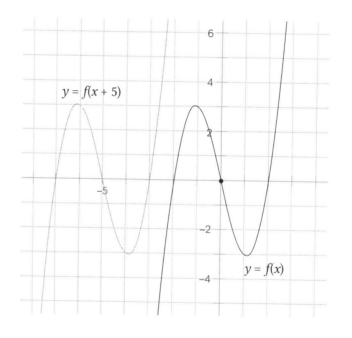

A completely different kind of transformation that the ACT Math Test might ask you to do involves taking the absolute value of the entire function. Since the absolute value is outside the entire function, it acts on the output, the *y*-values, affecting the graph vertically. Everywhere that $f(x)$ has an output that is either positive or zero, $|f(x)|$ has exactly the same output and overlaps the original graph in those regions. If you're wondering about the regions where $f(x) < 0$ are reflected over the *x*-axis by the absolute value, see the section on reflections in the *xy*-coordinate plane on page 181.

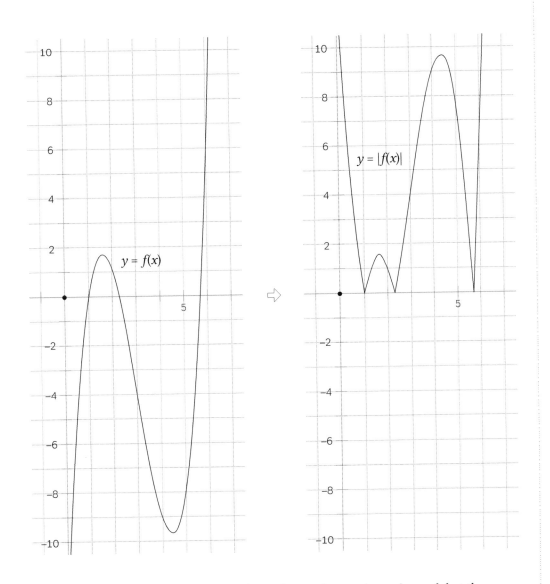

Notice that the pieces of $f(x)$ that are above the x-axis remain unchanged, but the pieces of $f(x)$ that are below the x-axis get reflected over the x-axis, so that every output is either positive or zero.

Here's an example of a function transformation question that you could see on the ACT:

Practice Question

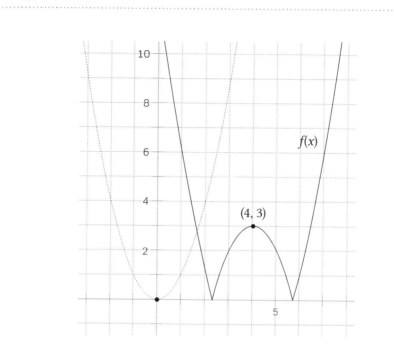

In the diagram above, the graph of the parabola $y = x^2$ is shown as a gray dashed line. The graph of $f(x)$ has been transformed from this parabola shape. Which of the following could be the equation of $f(x)$?

F. $f(x) = (|x^2| - 4) + 3$

G. $f(x) = |x^2 + 4| - 3$

H. $f(x) = |x^2 - 4| + 3$

J. $f(x) = |(x + 4)^2 + 3|$

K. $f(x) = |(x - 4)^2 - 3|$

Answer and Explanation

First of all, an absolute value has been applied to the function—the bottom of the parabola has been reflected up over the *x*-axis (if you don't see this right away, a quick glance at the answer choices would also have showed you that there had to be an absolute value in there *somewhere*). Let's imagine how that parabola looked before we applied the absolute value. The vertex, which has been reflected up to (+4, +3), would have been below the *x*-axis at (+4, −3). We know, either from the discussion of vertex form of a parabola on page 177 or from the rules of transformation above, that the original parabola has been shifted 4 to the right and 3 down, so it would have had an equation of

$$y = (x - 4)^2 - 3$$

To reflect the bottom of this parabola up above the *x*-axis, we'd take the absolute value of the whole expression.

$$f(x) = |(x - 4)^2 - 3|$$

Answer: **K**

Composition of Functions

When we write $f(x)$, we are imagining that x is the input that is put into the "machine" of a function, and the value of $f(x)$ is the output of this machine. Ordinarily, we put a number into the machine and get another number out. For example, suppose that

$$f(x) = x^2 - 6x + 7$$

Then, certainly we could plug in a number like 2:

$$f(2) = 2^2 - 6(2) + 7 = 4 - 12 + 7 = -1$$

We also could plug in another variable:

$$f(t) = t^2 - 6t + 7$$

Essentially, we're writing the same algebraic rule with a different symbol. It doesn't actually change anything except the superficial appearance of the algebra.

We also could plug in an algebraic expression. In each case, the "*x*" of the function formula is replaced by the expression in the parentheses.

$$f(2x + 7) = (2x + 7)^2 - 6(2x + 7) + 7$$
$$f(x^2 - 5) = (x^2 - 5)^2 - 6(x^2 - 5) + 7$$

What that means for us is that, in order to understand functions completely, we have to learn to see the original expression like this:

$$f(\square) = \square^2 - 6(\square) + 7$$

Essentially, the "*x*" is a box in which we can put just about anything, any algebraic expression, any number. Whatever may get put into the parenthesis following the "*f*," this gets squared, and from this square we subtract 6 times whatever was in the parenthesis and, after that, we add 7. That is the consistent rule we follow (for this particular function), regardless of whether the input of $f(x)$ is simply a number or some complicated algebraic expression.

Let's just stay with this for a minute: **we can plug an algebraic expression into a function**. For example, we could plug the expression $(2x^2 - 5)$ into some function $f(x)$.

Well, this expression could be the expression of *another* function, like $g(x) = 2x^2 - 5$. This means we can plug one function into another: that process is known as the *composition of functions*.

Let's use these two functions.

$$f(x) = x^2 - 6x + 7$$
$$g(x) = 2x^2 - 5$$

The expression $f(g(x))$ tells us that the function $g(x)$ has been plugged into $f(x)$. In other words, in the expression for $f(x)$, every x on the right side should be replaced with the expression for $g(x)$.

$$f(g(x)) = (2x^2 - 5)^2 - 6(2x^2 - 5) + 7$$
$$= (2x^2 - 5)(2x^2 - 5) - 12x^2 + 30 + 7$$
$$= 4x^4 - 10x^2 - 10x^2 + 25 - 12x^2 + 37$$
$$= 4x^4 - 20x^2 - 12x^2 + 25 + 37 \quad \text{(reorganize like terms)}$$
$$= 4x^4 - 32x^2 + 62 \quad \text{(combine like terms)}$$

Here, we took a couple extra steps to simplify the terms, but that's not always necessary. An answer on the ACT Math Test may be unsimplified or simplified.

Notice that if we compose the functions in the other order, we get a different result:

$$g(f(x)) = 2(x^2 - 6x + 7)^2 - 5$$

As a general rule, unless the functions are extremely simple, it almost never will be the case that $f(g(x))$ and $g(f(x))$ are equal.

The ACT Math Test will expect us to recognize the algebraic expression for the composition of two functions, but it might also want us to evaluate the composed function at a particular point—say, $f(g(2))$. (We'll continue to use these two example functions for simplicity's sake.) When we're evaluating the composition at a single point, we do NOT need to do all the algebraic work of combining the functions. We simply can treat the two functions separately. What $f(g(2))$ means is that, first, we will simply plug $x = 2$ into $g(x)$, get an output, and then **this output of g(x) will be the input of f(x)**.

$$g(x) = 2x^2 - 5$$
$$g(2) = 2(2^2) - 5 = 8 - 5 = 3$$

That numerical value, 3, is the *output* of $g(x)$, so this becomes the *input* of $f(x)$.

$$f(x) = x^2 - 6x + 7$$
$$f(g(2)) = f(3) = (3)^2 - 6(3) + 7 = 9 - 18 + 7 = -2$$

That's the value!

Here are two practice problems: one has a numerical value, and the other involves the full algebraic expression for the composition.

Practice Questions

1 Given that $f(x) = 3x - 5$ and $g(x) = x^3 - x$, what is $f(g(2))$?

   A. 0

   B. 1

   C. 7

   D. 13

   E. 19

2 Given that $f(x) = 2 - 3x$ and $g(x) = x^2 - 5x - 2$, which of the following is an expression for $f(g(x))$?

   F. $3x^2 - 15x - 4$

   G. $-3x^2 + 15x + 8$

   H. $3x^2 + 15x + 6$

   J. $-3x^2 - 15x - 6$

   K. $3x^2 - 5x$

Answers and Explanations

1 Since $g(x)$ is inside $f(x)$, we first have to plug $x = 2$ into $g(x)$, and then the output of $g(2)$ will be the input of $f(x)$.

$$g(x) = x^3 - x$$
$$g(2) = (2)^3 - 2 = 8 - 2 = 6$$

That's the output of $g(2)$, so that's what we plug into $f(x)$.

$$f(g(2)) = f(6) = 3(6) - 5 = 18 - 5 = 13$$

Answer: **D**

2 We are plugging $g(x)$ into $f(x)$. The x in the $f(x)$ expression gets replaced by the expression for $g(x)$.

$$f(g(x)) = 2 - 3(x^2 - 5x - 2)$$

Also, we have to remember to distribute that negative sign across all terms in the parentheses.

$$f(g(x)) = 2 - 3(x^2 - 5x - 2) = 2 - 3x^2 + 15x + 6 = -3x^2 + 15x + 8$$

Answer: **G**

Inverse Functions

This is a rare topic, but that doesn't mean that the ACT Math Test won't ask about it! As we've seen, a function is a rule that goes from an input x to an output y. An inverse function "undoes" the original function: the outputs of the original function are the inputs of the inverse, and the inverse maps these to outputs that were the inputs of the original function. In other words, if for the original function $f(5) = 17$, then it must be true for the inverse function that $f^{-1}(17) = 5$. Notice that we use the notation $f^{-1}(x)$ for the inverse of $f(x)$. Be careful: **the negative-one superscript does not mean that anything is to the power of negative one here**; instead, it very specifically means the inverse of the function.

If we back up for a moment, this idea of an inverse is common in math. Subtraction, for example, is the inverse of addition. (And vice versa!) Multiplication and division are one another's inverses, too. Returning to functions, if the function is a single simple mathematical operation, then the inverse function is the inverse that *undoes that operation*. Here are some actual examples:

if $f(x) = x + 7$, then $f^{-1}(x) = x - 7$

if $f(x) = x/5$, then $f^{-1}(x) = 5x$

if $f(x) = x^2$, then $f^{-1}(x) = \sqrt{x}$

Notice that, in the first two examples, both functions have a domain of all real numbers, but in the third example, while $f(x) = x^2$ has a domain of all real numbers, $f^{-1}(x) = \sqrt{x}$ does not. The main takeaway here is that a function and its inverse do not necessarily have the same domain.

If there are multiple operations, one way to think about the inverse is according to what some math teachers call the "shoes and socks theorem." When you get dressed, you put on your socks first, then put on your shoes second, but you can't follow this same order in the "inverse operation" of getting undressed. (Imagine trying to take your socks off but leaving your shoes on!) So, to take everything off, you have to take off your shoes first, then your socks second. In much the same way, the order of operations is reversed in the inverse. For example,

if $f(x) = 3x - 5$, then $f^{-1}(x) = \dfrac{x + 5}{3}$

The original function had us multiply by 3 first, then subtract 5. In the inverse, we have to do the inverses of these actions in the opposite order: add 5, and then divide by 3.

One way to simplify the process of getting the formula for the inverse is as follows: we can replace the $f(x)$ with y in the formula of any function: that's what we would do to graph the function any way. Well, we can find the inverse by swapping the x's and y's in that formula: replace the y with an x, and replace every x with a y. Finally, we'd have to solve the resultant equation for y. Let's use the function we used above:

original: $f(x) = 3x - 5$

$y = 3x - 5$

inverse: $x = 3y - 5$

$x + 5 = 3y$

$\frac{x+5}{3} = y$

$\frac{x+5}{3} = f^{-1}(x)$

Here's a practice problem for you to try your hand at.

Practice Question

Given that $f(x) = \frac{2x+3}{x-5}$, which of the following expressions is equal to $f^{-1}(x)$ for all real numbers?

A. $\frac{0.5x - 3}{x + 5}$

B. $\frac{x + 5}{2x - 3}$

C. $\frac{2x - 3}{x + 5}$

D. $\frac{2x + 5}{x - 3}$

E. $\frac{5x + 3}{x - 2}$

Answer and Explanation

Remember that we can replace the $f(x)$ with a y, as we would do if we were to graph this function.

$y = \frac{2x+3}{x-5}$

Now, replace each x with a y and vice versa. This is now the inverse.

$x = \frac{2y+3}{y-5}$

Next, we have to solve for y. First, multiply by the denominator and distribute.

$x(y - 5) = 2y + 3$
$xy - 5x = 2y + 3$

Now, move all the terms with y to the left, and all the terms with no y's to the right.

$xy - 2y = 5x + 3$

Factor out the y on the left side.

$$y(x - 2) = 5x + 3$$

Now, divide by the term in parentheses to isolate y.

$$y = \frac{5x + 3}{x - 2}$$

That's the function expression for $f^{-1}(x)$.

Answer: **E**

Sequences

It's entirely likely you'll come across sequence questions on the ACT Math Test. In basic terms, a sequence is a list of numbers following some kind of pattern. While we conversationally refer to things like a "sequence of events," the test only cares about *sequences of numbers*. There are many kinds of numerical sequences, but luckily the ACT will ask you about only two of them.

Arithmetic sequences

The first is an *arithmetic sequence*. This is a sequence in which we move from one term to the next by adding a constant amount, also known as the *common difference*. In other words, if we subtracted any two adjacent members of the arithmetic sequence, the result would always be this common difference. Here's an example.

$$7, 10, 13, 16, 19, 22, 25, 28, 31, \ldots$$

Notice in that sequence, the common difference is 3: from any term, to get to the next (larger) term, we add 3. And to move in the opposite direction, we subtract 3.

One way to talk about the sequence is to show it all at once, as we just did. Another way involves a system: we pick a letter (often a) for the whole sequence, and then we use a subscript to denote the position of an individual term. For the sequence above, $a_1 = 7$, $a_5 = 19$, and $a_9 = 31$, because the first term is 7, the fifth term is 19, and the ninth term is 31. Sometimes, this number that gives the place in the sequence is called the *index number* (a term you don't need to know for the ACT, though you do need to know the concept!). In $a_9 = 31$, the subscript 9 is the index number. We'll return to this idea in the next section.

In that first example, all the terms were positive integers, but terms can also be negative numbers or fractions. Even the common difference doesn't have to be an integer.

Notice that if we knew only the numerical value of the first term and the common difference—just two pieces of mathematical information—we could generate the entire sequence. Similarly, if we knew just the common difference and the numerical value of any term, or if we knew just the numerical value of any two different terms, either of these also would be enough to generate the entire sequence. If we don't know the common difference, that's often easy to figure out, and from there, we can figure out everything else about the sequence.

Here's a practice question.

Practice Question

What is the third term of an arithmetic sequence in which $a_6 = 10$ and $a_{20} = 16$?

A. 5

B. $6\frac{2}{3}$

C. $7\frac{3}{7}$

D. $8\frac{5}{7}$

E. $9\frac{1}{10}$

Answer and Explanation

The first thing we need to do is calculate the common difference. Between $a_6 = 10$ and $a_{20} = 16$, there are 14 "steps"—we would have to add 14 times the common difference to 10 (our a_6 value) to get 16 (our a_{20} value). Thus, the size of the common difference should be the difference of our two values divided by the number of steps: $16 - 10 = 6$, divided by 14.

$$\text{common difference} = \frac{6}{14} = \frac{3}{7}$$

To get from $a_6 = 10$ to a_3, we have to subtract three of those common differences (remember your order of operations!).

$$a_3 = 10 - \left(3 \times \frac{3}{7}\right) =$$

$$10 - \frac{9}{7} =$$

$$10 - 1 - \frac{2}{7} = 8\frac{5}{7}$$

Answer: **D**

Geometric sequences

The other sequence pattern is a *geometric sequence*. Just as arithmetic sequences are based on addition, geometric sequences are based on multiplication. After a starting term, we multiply by a fixed *common ratio* to get from one term to the next. Here's a simple geometric sequence:

$$3, 6, 12, 24, 48, 96, 192, 384, \ldots$$

In that geometric sequence, the common ratio is 2. Notice that, unlike arithmetic sequences, geometric sequences get big in a hurry!

As with arithmetic sequences, we need very little information to determine everything about a geometric sequence. If we know any specific term and the common ratio, or two specific terms, then we can solve for the whole sequence.

If two terms are adjacent, then we call the ratio between them *the common ratio*, or *r*.

$$a_2 = 6, \ a_3 = 42 \quad \Rightarrow \quad r = 7$$

If the terms are separated by one, say a_5 and a_7, then there are two "steps" from one to the other, and each "step" involves multiplying a factor of the common ratio. That means the ratio of a_7 over a_5 will be the common ratio squared!

$$a_4 = 4, \ a_6 = 36 \quad \Rightarrow \quad \frac{a_6}{a_4} = \frac{36}{4} = 9 = r^2 \quad \Rightarrow \quad r = 3$$

Similarly, the ratio of two terms three "steps" away, say a_{11} and a_8, would be the cube of the common ratio.

So far, for simplicity, we've only looked at geometric sequences in which the common ratio and all the terms are positive integers. If the common ratio is negative, then the signs of the terms will alternate between positive and negative. Check it out: $(-2)^2 = 4$, $(-2)^3 = -8$, $(-2)^4 = 16$, etc. If the common ratio is a positive fraction less than one, then terms will get smaller. For example: $\left(\frac{1}{2}\right)^2 = \frac{1}{4}$, $\left(\frac{1}{2}\right)^3 = \frac{1}{8}$, etc. All of these are cases that could arise on the ACT Math Test, so being familiar with these relationships will be helpful to you.

Practice Question

In a geometric sequence, $a_6 = 5$ and $a_8 = 20$. If every term is positive, what is the value of a_3?

A. 2

B. 2.5

C. 1

D. 1.25

E. 0.625

Answer and Explanation

First, we need to find the common ratio. It's two "steps" from $a_6 = 5$ to $a_8 = 20$, so we multiply the former by the common ratio squared to get the latter.

$$5r^2 = 20$$
$$r^2 = 4$$
$$r = 2$$

We divide by 2 to go down a term.

$$a_6 = 5$$

$$a_5 = \frac{5}{2} = 2.5$$

$$a_4 = \frac{2.5}{2} = 1.25$$

$$a_3 = \frac{1.25}{2} = 0.625$$

Answer: **E**

Types of Functions and Modeling

Notice that if we were to graph the numbers in an arithmetic sequence against the index number, we would get a straight line. A straight line is the graph that rises by a constant height on each x-unit to the right. Here's the first example arithmetic sequence we showed on page 244.

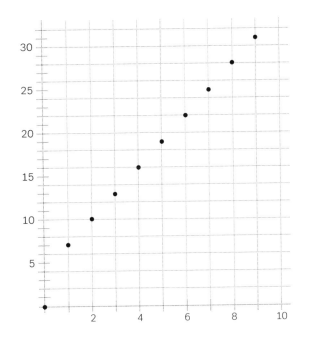

By contrast, a geometric sequence graphed against the index number would **not** form a straight line. It would form a sharply rising curve. Here are the first few terms of the introductory geometric sequence given on page 245.

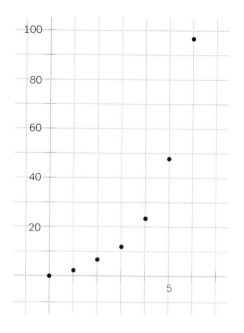

This is the shape of an exponential graph, a graph of the form $y = b^x$, for some positive base b. This is a good shape to know; for example, it's the shape of population growth.

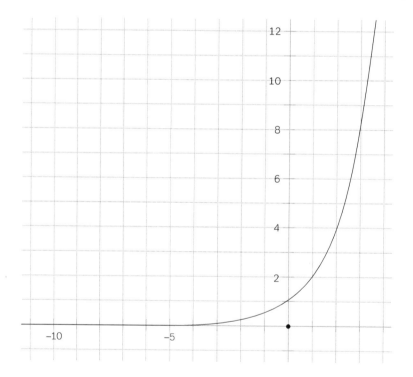

Reversed left to right, it also can be the graph of radioactive decay and some other patterns of decrease, such as cooling.

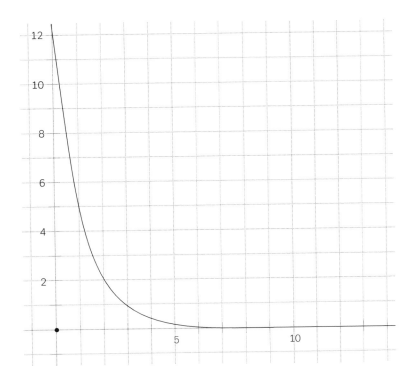

That graph would have a pattern of $y = A(p^x)$, for some $0 < p < 1$.

The ACT Math Test may give you points, either in graphical or numerical form, and ask you what kind of graph would fit these points. We've already talked about the shapes of various orders of polynomials; modeling points with a parabola is far more common on the ACT than modeling with any higher-order polynomial. Still, it's possible that the test could ask you to model something that follows a general exponential pattern or even a trigonometric pattern, which we will discuss below. Most frequently of all, the points are simply linear, and we're asked to find a line that fits them well.

Here's a practice problem.

Experimental data is represented on the standard *xy*-coordinate plane below.

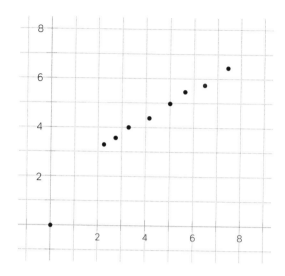

Which of the following functions best fits the experimental data?

F. $y = 0.15x + 3$

G. $y = 0.6x + 2$

H. $y = 1.5x$

J. $y = (x - 2)^2 - 4$

K. $y = -(x - 8)^2 + 4$

Answer and Explanation

First of all, we need to eyeball the points. There's really no discernible curve there; except for a few odd wiggles, these points lie in what is essentially a straight line. When we scan the answer choices, there are three lines—F, G, and H—and two parabolas—J and K. Those parabolas would have way too much curvature to model these points, so eliminate J and K immediately.

Now, which line is the best fit? There are a few ways to go about finding this. If we had exact coordinates, we could take the endpoints and estimate the slope. Here, we would have to estimate the coordinates. Instead of doing that, though, let's think about each line. Since the points start around $x = 2$ and end around $x = 8$, we'll plug in the points $x = 2$, $x = 5$, and $x = 8$ to get a sense of where these three lines go. This chart summarizes the *y*-values of these three lines at those three *x*-values.

x	Line (F) $y = 0.15x + 3$	Line (G) $y = 0.6x + 2$	Line (H) $y = 1.5x$
2	3.3	3.2	3
5	3.75	5	7.5
8	4.2	6.8	12

All three of them start out reasonably close to (2, 3), which is around where the points seem to begin. Notice that Line F stays low: by $x = 8$, it's still down at 4.2, whereas the data points are above 6 at that point. Line F is not steep enough. Meanwhile, Line H takes off like a rocket, and is already off the chart at $y = 12$, way above the top of the graph here, by the time we get to $x = 8$. Line H is way too steep.

This leaves Line **G**. Notice that this goes through (5, 5), which appears to be a data point, and at $x = 8$, it's at 6.8, very close to the final point on the right. This line is a very good fit.

Answer: **G**

Advanced Formula Problem Sets

Once again, we revisit our Problem Sets, those sets of three (or maybe four) problems that all revolve around the same given information. We discussed Geometry Problem Sets on page 204 and Data Problem Sets on page 221. Here, we'll look Advanced Formula Problem Sets; after this, we'll see the last example of a Problem Set on page 283.

Very rarely, the ACT Math Test will give an Advanced Formula Problem Set, a set of three problems asking specifically about a complex formula. Such a set is usually the second set of problems on that ACT Math Test, after, say, a Geometry or Data Problem Set. It's a very good idea to have your calculator handy for these problems, as you'll see when we look at this example set.

Practice Questions

Use the following information to answer questions 1–3.

The predicted number of cars traveling on a certain stretch of freeway at a particular moment in time is given by the following formula.

$$C = \frac{40,000L}{s^2 + 1,200}$$

In this formula, C is the number of cars, L is the number of lanes, and s is the average traffic speed in miles per hour.

1 If there are 3 lanes, and the average traffic speed is 60 mph, then how many cars does this formula predict to be on this stretch of freeway?

   A. 7

   B. 25

   C. 64

   D. 120

   E. 250

2 Which of the following shows the formula solved for s?

   F. $\sqrt{40,000LC - 1,200}$

   G. $\sqrt{40,000LC - 1,200}$

   H. $\sqrt{40,000LC} - \sqrt{1,200}$

   J. $\sqrt{\frac{40,000L}{C} - 1,200}$

   K. $\sqrt{\frac{40,000L}{C}} - \sqrt{1,200}$

3 For a given number of lanes, how does C change when s increases from 10 mph to 40 mph?

   A. C is multiplied by 4.

   B. C is divided by 4.

   C. C is increased by 15%.

   D. C is decreased by 14%.

   E. C is decreased by 54%.

Answers and Explanations

1 For this one, we have to plug in $L = 3$ and $s = 60$

$$C = \frac{40,000(3)}{3,600 + 1,200} = \frac{120,000}{4,800} = \frac{1,200}{48} = \frac{100}{4} = 25$$

Answer: **B**

2 Start with the formula and multiply both sides by the denominator to get started:

$$C = \frac{40{,}000L}{s^2 + 1{,}200}$$

$$(s^2 + 1{,}200) \times C = \left(\frac{40{,}000L}{s^2 + 1{,}200}\right) \times (s^2 + 1{,}200)$$

This cancels the denominator, so we end up with

$$C(s^2 + 1{,}200) = 40{,}000L$$

Next, divide by C:

$$s^2 + 1{,}200 = \frac{40{,}000L}{C}$$

And then subtract 1,200:

$$s^2 + 1{,}200 = \frac{40{,}000L}{C} - 1{,}200$$

We are almost there. Now, take the square root of everything on both sides, which will isolate s for us.

$$\sqrt{s^2} = \sqrt{\frac{40{,}000L}{C} - 1{,}200}$$

$$s = \sqrt{\frac{40{,}000L}{C} - 1{,}200}$$

Answer: **J**

3 For this one, we **definitely** will need a calculator! The value of the numerator doesn't matter for this one, so make the value of the numerator some big round number, such as 100,000. (Other large round numbers would work, too.)

$$start = \frac{100{,}000}{100 + 1{,}200} = \frac{100{,}000}{1{,}300} = 76.923$$

$$finish = \frac{100{,}000}{1{,}600 + 1{,}200} = \frac{100{,}000}{2{,}800} = 35.714$$

At this point, we could do further calculations, but we can go ahead and estimate from here. If something goes from exactly 70 to exactly 35, that's a 50% decrease. This decreased from over 70 to slightly more than 35, so we expect that it's a bit more than 50% decrease. A decrease of 54% is the only answer choice close. Because the answer choices are so spaced out, we can make a conclusion from this alone.

Answer: **E**

Trigonometry

Sine, Cosine, and Tangent

In any right triangle with an angle θ, we can set up some basic ratios.

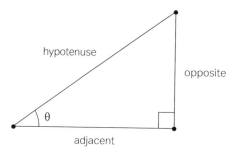

The leg that touches the angle is adjacent (adj). The other leg is opposite (opp) because it is opposite the angle. The longest side is the hypotenuse (hyp).

We can say that

$$\sin \theta = \frac{\text{opp}}{\text{hyp}}$$

$$\cos \theta = \frac{\text{adj}}{\text{hyp}}$$

$$\tan \theta = \frac{\text{opp}}{\text{adj}}$$

For many generations, students have had remember these three ratios by the mnemonic SOHCAHTOA. If you can remember that, and remember how to spell it, you can remember a great deal about right-triangle trigonometry.

These ratios mean that we can also express tangent as a ratio of sine and cosine. In the big scheme of trigonometry, we can express all the trig functions in terms of other trig functions, but let's focus on tangent for the moment:

$$\tan \theta = \frac{\sin \theta}{\cos \theta}$$

Here's a practice problem:

Practice Question

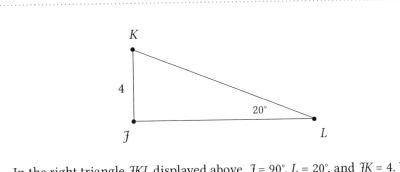

In the right triangle *JKL* displayed above, *J* = 90°, *L* = 20°, and *JK* = 4. Which of the following would be an expression for the area of triangle *JKL*?

A. $8 \sin 20°$

B. $8 \cos 20°$

C. $8 \tan 20°$

D. $\dfrac{8}{\sin 20°}$

E. $\dfrac{8}{\tan 20°}$

Answer and Explanation

We know that the area of a triangle is $A = \frac{1}{2}bh$ (we looked at this on page 156). We know $h = 4$. We know that length of $JL = b$, which we need to find. Since $JK = 4$ is the opposite and $JL = b$ is the adjacent, we need to use the tangent.

$$\tan \theta = \frac{\text{opp}}{\text{adj}}$$

$$\tan 20° = \frac{JK}{JL} = \frac{4}{b}$$

$$b \times \tan 20° = 4$$

$$b = \frac{4}{\tan 20°}$$

$$A = \frac{1}{2} \times 4 \times \frac{4}{\tan 20°} = \frac{8}{\tan 20°}$$

Answer: **E**

You may remember something from high school math class called the *Pythagorean identity* (or *identities*) in trigonometry: the ACT Math Test doesn't seem to ask about these directly, but if a right triangle appears, there is always a chance that the good old-fashioned Pythagorean theorem will come into play.

In particular, the Pythagorean triplets we discussed above on page 151 come into play here: {3, 4, 5}, {5, 12, 13}, and {8, 15, 17}. For example, if tan θ = $\frac{4}{3}$, then, if we were to sketch the 3-4-5 triangle, we can see that sin θ = $\frac{4}{5}$ and tan θ = $\frac{3}{5}$. Pythagorean triplets can be a quick shortcut in trig problems, so keep an eye out for them.

All the ratios in the two special right triangles (the 45-45-90 triangle and the 30-60-90 triangle, discussed above on page 152) can show up in trig questions as well. The ACT Math Test could also ask you about the sine, cosine, or tangent of 30°, 45°, or 60°—but if it did, it would be likely to give you a table, more values, or the opportunity to figure it out with SOHCAHTOA.

Practice Question

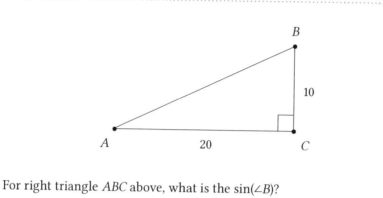

For right triangle *ABC* above, what is the sin(∠*B*)?

F. $\frac{10}{20}$

G. $\frac{20}{10}$

H. $\frac{\sqrt{500}}{10}$

J. $\frac{10}{\sqrt{500}}$

K. $\frac{20}{\sqrt{500}}$

Answer and Explanation

First, we need to find the hypotenuse, and we need to use the Pythagorean theorem to find it.

$$c^2 = a^2 + b^2 = 100 + 400 = 500$$
$$c = \sqrt{500}$$

Sine is opposite over hypotenuse. Since the angle is at *B*, the opposite side is the horizontal side here; *AC* = 20.

$$\sin(\angle B) = \frac{20}{\sqrt{500}}$$

Answer: **K**

Once again, it's very good to be on the ball with SOHCAHTOA, because the ACT Math Test always asks at least one question about it!

Unit Circle Trigonometry

Much of the trigonometry you'll need to know for the ACT Math Test goes beyond the bounds of SOHCAHTOA, that is, beyond the trigonometry of right triangles alone. One of the biggest limitations is that all the base angles in a right triangle have to be less than 90°, but there are all kinds of angles bigger than that in the real world. Your own elbow can go from a relatively small angle to 180° when extended. (But hopefully not hyperextended!) And think about a wheel on a car: if it turns once around, it turns 360°. So say that you drive your car for an hour—how many degrees does a wheel on your car turn then? Certainly a lot more than 90°!

Mathematicians use the **unit circle** to extend the idea of SOHCAHTOA to much larger angles. The unit circle has a center at the origin, (0, 0), and a radius of $r = 1$. Also, its equation is $x^2 + y^2 = 1$.

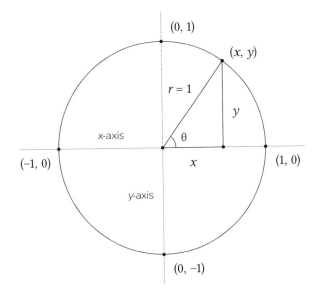

The diagram above displays the unit circle, and a radius in the first quadrant forms the hypotenuse of a little right triangle, with θ measured counterclockwise from the positive x-axis. If we call the point where the radius intersects the unit circle (x, y), notice that these coordinates give not only the lengths of the legs of this right triangle, but also, because the hypotenuse equals 1, we can say that $\cos \theta = x$ and $\sin \theta = y$.

Those last two formulas lead to an extraordinary insight. Back in SOHCAHTOA-land, we defined sine and cosine in terms of the ratios of sides in a triangle. Using those ideas, we see that we also can define both sine and cosine in terms of (x, y), the point where the radius intersects the unit circle. The beauty of this new "unit circle" definition of the trig functions is that it's perfectly consistent with everything we knew in SOHCAHTOA-land, but it allows us to wrap our angles all the way around the circle and follow what happens with the trig functions. Once we have the unit circle definitions, we can start to think about sine and cosine as official mathematical functions. Of course, since tangent is a ratio of sine and cosine, it follows that $\tan \theta = \frac{y}{x}$.

All angles in the unit circle are measured counterclockwise from the positive x-axis. Of course, in Q1, both $\sin \theta$ and $\cos \theta$ are positive, but signs change in other quadrants. In Q2, $\sin \theta$ is still positive but $\cos \theta$ is negative. In Q3, both $\sin \theta$ and $\cos \theta$ are negative. In Q4, $\sin \theta$ stays negative but $\cos \theta$ becomes positive. Notice that $\tan \theta$ is positive in Q1 and Q3, where x and y have the same sign, and it is negative in Q2 and Q4, where x and y have opposite signs. You can (but don't have to!) envision this in the following way:

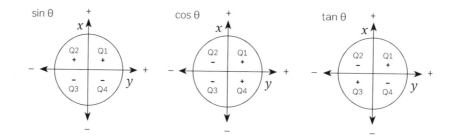

Practice Question

If $180° < \theta < 360°$ and $\tan \theta = +\frac{15}{18}$, what are all the possible values of $\cos \theta$?

A. $+\frac{8}{17}$ and $-\frac{8}{17}$

B. $-\frac{8}{17}$

C. $+\frac{15}{17}$ and $-\frac{15}{17}$

D. $-\frac{15}{17}$

E. $+\frac{8}{15}$

Answer and Explanation

The angle range is Q3 and Q4. We know that $\tan \theta$ is positive in Q3 (where both x and y are negative) and negative in Q4 (where only y is negative). Thus, since the tangent given is positive, the angle must be in Q3, where both sine and cosine are negative.

We know 8 and 15 are two legs of an {8, 15, 17} triangle. Let's ignore positive/negative signs for a moment. If opp = 15 and adj = 8, then hyp = 17, and $\cos \theta = \frac{\text{adj}}{\text{hyp}} = \frac{8}{17}$. That's the correct absolute value: now we just have to make that negative for the quadrant.

$$\cos \theta = -\frac{8}{17}$$

And it has only that one value, because we are in Q3 only.

Answer: **B**

What is the value of sin 300°?

F. $+\frac{1}{2}$

G. $-\frac{1}{2}$

H. $+\frac{\sqrt{3}}{2}$

J. $-\frac{\sqrt{3}}{2}$

K. $-\sqrt{3}$

Answer and Explanation

This angle is in Q4, just 30° below the *x*-axis, so this would be a reflection over the *x*-axis of a 30-60-90 triangle in the first quadrant.

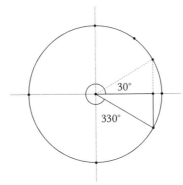

This is the unit circle, so the hypotenuses have lengths of 1. The *y*-legs of the triangles are half the hypotenuse, $+\frac{1}{2}$ for the 30° triangle and $-\frac{1}{2}$ for the 330° triangle. The *x*-leg is the same positive value for both triangles, and this has to be:

$$x = +\frac{\sqrt{3}}{2}$$

The cos(330°) equals this *x*-value.

Answer: **H**

Radians

Up until trigonometry, you probably measured all angles in degrees. But once we get to trigonometry, we start using this new angle measure, radians. Why?

Why *degrees*? In the degrees system, there are 360 units around the whole circle. This has its roots in an ancient Babylonian religion, in which 60 and 360 were considered sacred numbers. This was a long-forgotten religion based on extensive mythology and it regularly involved the wholesale slaughter of assorted barnyard animals. There aren't many people around anymore who consider the *Enuma Elish* sacred, but for some reason, we're still stuck with their system for measuring angles! You see, we're used to degrees, but they're based on something totally arbitrary from so long ago that almost no one remembers it!

Rather than pick something arbitrary as the basis for angle measure, more modern mathematicians thought it would be more valuable to use an inherent property of the circle itself. Well, the most fundamental property of any circle is its radius. How do we get an angle from that? A radian is an angle whose arc length is one radius. In other words, we measure the size of the angle in terms of the number of radii around the angle's arc. The angle measure in radians is equal to the number of radii it is around. Well, we know $c = 2\pi r$, so there are 2π radii around the whole circle. In other words, an angle of $360°$ corresponds to an angle of 2π radians. Divide each by two: an angle of $180°$ equals an angle of π radians.

This equation, $180° = \pi$ radians, is a very handy starting point. Divide this by two: we get $90° = \frac{\pi}{2}$ radians: that's a right angle in radians! Now, divide this by two: we get $45° = \frac{\pi}{4}$ radians: that's the angle in radians in an isosceles right triangle. Go back to the first equation, $180° = \pi$ radians, and divide it by 3: we get $60° = \frac{\pi}{3}$ radians. Now, divide this by two: we get $30° = \frac{\pi}{6}$ radians. It's very good to know and be able to recognize the radian measures of the angles in the two special triangles, because they show up a lot in trig. Finally, go back to that equation, $180° = \pi$ radians. We could divide by either side of the equation to get a fraction that equals one (i.e., a conversion factor) for converting between degrees and radians. Whatever term is on the bottom is the one that is going to cancel; it's the one we want to eliminate. Thus,

we multiply by $\frac{\pi}{180°}$ to change degrees to radians

we multiply by $\frac{180°}{\pi}$ to change radians to degrees

Remember, because we're in the unit circle, we can have angles much larger than $360°$ or 2π radians. If we wrap a larger angle all the way around the unit circle and land at the same place as a smaller angle, then these two angles are *coterminal*: they "stop" at the same place, even though one went all the way around more times than the other to get there. For example, $1°$ and $361°$ and $721°$ and $36{,}001°$ are all coterminal angles. Similarly, $\frac{4\pi}{3}$ and $\frac{10\pi}{3}$ and $\frac{16\pi}{3}$ and $\frac{22\pi}{3}$ are all coterminal: they all differ by $\frac{6\pi}{3} = 2\pi$, which is a full circle.

A ray centered at the origin and starting at the positive *x*-axis is rotated counterclockwise, first by an angle of $\frac{3\pi}{5}$, then by an additional right angle. The resultant ray coterminal with a ray that starts at the positive *x*-axis is rotated by what single angle?

F. 108°

G. 135°

H. 175°

J. 198°

K. 225°

Answer and Explanation

First, we have to convert the radian angle to degrees.

$$\frac{3\pi}{5} \times \frac{180°}{\pi} = 3 \times 36° = 108°$$

But wait! That's not the answer! That's simply the first angle of rotation. After this, we have to turn an additional right angle, or 90°, for a grand total of 198°.

Answer: **J**

Other Functions and Identities

The original three trig functions that we've been discussing are the sine, the cosine, and the tangent. Three additional functions can be defined as the reciprocals of these original three functions: the cotangent (cot), the secant (sec), and the cosecant (csc).

$$\cot\theta = \frac{1}{\tan\theta} = \frac{\cos\theta}{\sin\theta}$$

$$\sec\theta = \frac{1}{\cos\theta}$$

$$\csc\theta = \frac{1}{\sin\theta}$$

A common point of confusion is to think that **sec**ant goes with **s**ine, or **cos**ecant with **cos**ine (they don't!). Because of the similarities in the names, that's a tempting mistake to make. Be careful! It will help you to know that no trig function is the reciprocal of another function whose name starts with the same letter!

Often, when you have to simplify an expression involving these functions, it's helpful to put everything in terms of sine and cosine.

$$\frac{(\sin\theta)(\sec\theta)}{(\cos\theta)(\csc\theta)}$$

For all values of θ, the expression above is equivalent to which of the following?

A. 1

B. $\cot\theta$

C. $\cot^2\theta$

D. $\tan\theta$

E. $\tan^2\theta$

Answer and Explanation

$$\frac{(\sin\theta)(\sec\theta)}{(\cos\theta)(\csc\theta)} = \frac{\sin\theta\left(\frac{1}{\cos\theta}\right)}{\cos\theta\left(\frac{1}{\sin\theta}\right)} = \frac{\sin^2\theta}{\cos^2\theta} = \tan^2\theta$$

Answer: **E**

Trigonometric Equations

The ACT Math Test sometimes gives us simple equations involving trig functions, and our job is figure out what values of the angle θ solve this equation. For example, let's look at this linear equation:

For $0 < \theta < 360°$, $\tan\theta + 1 = 0$

We always begin by solving the equation for the trig function:

$\tan\theta = -1$

The tangent equals 1 when sine and cosine are equal, at 45° angles. The tangent is negative in Q2 and Q4, where x and y have opposite signs. Thus, the solutions would be the angles 45° away from the axes in Q2 and Q4. In Q2, this would be 90° + 45° = 135°. In Q4, this would be 360° − 45° = 315°. Notice that those two angles are 180° from each other.

And here's an equation involving a square:

For $0 < \theta < 360°$, $4\cos^2\theta = 3$

For this equation, we would have to isolate the cosine squared, and then take a square root, which will give us a plus or minus sign.

$4\cos^2\theta = 3$

Isolate the cosine squared by dividing each side by 4.

$$\cos^2 \theta = \frac{3}{4}$$

Finally, take the square root of both the numerator and the denominator in the fraction to get rid of the square.

$$\cos \theta = \pm\frac{\sqrt{3}}{2}$$

Let's focus on the positive Q1 angle first. When the adj = $\sqrt{3}$ and the hyp = 2, the opp = 1. This is a 30-60-90 triangle, from the vantage of the 30° angle. Thus,

$$\cos 30° = +\frac{\sqrt{3}}{2}$$

There are two angles that give the positive output, in Q1 and Q4, and two more that give the negative output, in Q2, and Q3. In a quadratic, it's not unusual to get four different angles for the solution. Here, we need the angle in each quadrant that is 30° from the x-axis. These four angles would be {30°, 150°, 210°, 330°}. That's the solution.

Practice Question

Let θ be the radian measure of angles $0 < \theta < 2\pi$ that satisfy the equation below.

$$2\cos^2 \theta + 3\cos \theta + 1 = 0$$

Which of the following is a complete set of the possible values of θ?

A. $\pi, \frac{2\pi}{3}, \frac{4\pi}{3}$

B. $\frac{3\pi}{2}, \frac{2\pi}{3}, \frac{4\pi}{3}$

C. $\pi, \frac{7\pi}{6}, \frac{11\pi}{6}$

D. $\frac{3\pi}{2}, \frac{7\pi}{6}, \frac{11\pi}{6}$

E. $\pi, \frac{7\pi}{6}, \frac{11\pi}{6}, \frac{2\pi}{3}, \frac{4\pi}{3}$

Answer and Explanation
Sometimes, in a quadratic, it can be helpful to replace the trig function with the letter *u*, because it can be simpler to do the algebra with an ordinary letter. Here, we get

$$2u^2 + 3u + 1 = 0$$

This factors into

$$(2u + 1)(u + 1) = 0$$
$$(2u + 1) = 0 \quad \text{or} \quad (u + 1) = 0$$
$$u = -\frac{1}{2} \quad \text{or} \quad u = -1$$

Now that we have individual values for u, set cosine equal to each of these values. So, first of all,

$$\cos \theta = -1$$

Remember that $\cos \theta = x$. Where on the unit circle do we get an x-value of –1? This happens all the way on the left side, where the negative x-axis intersects the unit circle at (–1, 0). The angle there is 180° or π radians. That's one value of the angle. Next, let's look at that other value of u.

$$\cos \theta = -\frac{1}{2}$$

Think about the positive value for a moment. If the cosine equals $\frac{1}{2}$, then adj = 1, hyp = 2, and opp = $\sqrt{3}$. This is a 30-60-90 triangle from the vantage of the 60° or $\frac{\pi}{3}$ angle. The cosine is negative in Q2 and Q3, where x is negative. These would be the angles that are away from the negative x-axis. These angles are $\frac{2\pi}{3}$ and $\frac{4\pi}{3}$.

Altogether, the three roots are: π, $\frac{2\pi}{3}$, and $\frac{4\pi}{3}$.

Answer: **A**

Inverse Trig Functions

Every trig function's input is an angle, and its output is a ratio in a triangle. Fundamentally, an inverse swaps the output and the input. This means that an inverse trig function always has an input that's a ratio in a triangle and its output is an angle.

It may be that in trigonometry class, you learned a great deal about the domain and range of these inverse trig functions, their graphs, etc. Fortunately, the ACT Math Test has a very limited scope in asking about them. The ACT tends to ask about an inverse trig function of a regular trig function, e.g., $\sin\left(\cos^{-1}\left(\frac{4}{5}\right)\right)$. The output of $\cos^{-1}\left(\frac{4}{5}\right)$ is an angle, and we have to take sine of this angle. Notice there is ***absolutely no reason*** to find the numerical value of the angle itself. Instead, the whole point is to think about the geometry of the triangle. Think about $\cos^{-1}\left(\frac{4}{5}\right)$: this is an angle in a right triangle with an adjacent leg of 4 and a hypotenuse of 5. In that triangle, the other leg, opposite from this angle would have a length of 3.

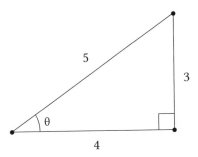

The numbers in the ratio tell us about the kind of right triangle and where the angle is in that triangle; we can use the Pythagorean theorem to find the third side. Then, we can find any trig function of that angle. Here, since $\theta = \cos^{-1}\left(\frac{4}{5}\right)$, we can say that $\sin\theta = \sin\left(\cos^{-1}\left(\frac{4}{5}\right)\right) = \frac{3}{5}$. It's all about determining the sides of the right triangle. The ACT Math Test sometimes gives us a present and prints the relevant triangle on the test to simplify things.

Practice Question

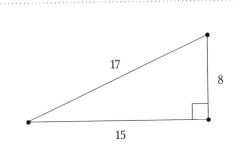

In the right triangle above, both $\tan^{-1}\left(\frac{8}{15}\right)$ and $\tan^{-1}\left(\frac{15}{18}\right)$ are angles in the triangle. What is the value of $\cos\left(\tan^{-1}\left(\frac{8}{15}\right) + \tan^{-1}\left(\frac{15}{8}\right)\right)$?

A. 0

B. 1

C. $\frac{8}{17}$

D. $\frac{15}{17}$

E. $\frac{8}{15}$

Answer and Explanation
Think about those two angles in this triangle.

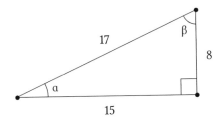

The angle $\tan^{-1}\left(\frac{8}{15}\right)$ is the angle with an opposite side of 8 and an adjacent side of 15, so this has to be α. Similarly, the angle $\tan^{-1}\left(\frac{15}{8}\right)$ is the angle with an opposite side of 15 and an adjacent side of 8, so this has to be β. These are the two acute angles in this right triangle. We are taking the cosine of the sum of those two angles. The sum of the two acute angles in a right triangle is always 90°, so we're really taking the cosine of 90°.

$$\cos\left(\tan^{-1}\left(\tfrac{8}{15}\right) + \tan^{-1}\left(\tfrac{15}{8}\right)\right) = \cos(\alpha + \beta) = \cos(90°) = 0$$

Answer: **A**

Graphs of Trig Functions

The ACT Math Test expects you to recognize the graphs of $y = \sin(x)$ and $y = \cos(x)$ and the basic transformations of those graphs. It does not expect you to know about the graphs of the other four trig functions and all their asymptotes.

Here's $y = \sin(x)$.

The sense of sight depends on light, an electromagnetic wave, which follows a sine curve. Hearing depends on sound waves whose pressure patterns also follow a sine curve. Thus, the majority of information that we receive in a day arrives to us via a mechanism dependent on a sine curve!

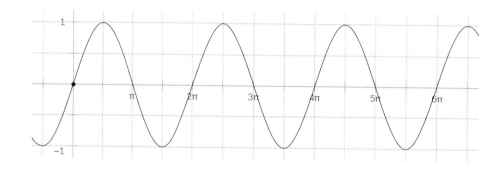

A few important things to notice are, first, that the graph peaks at $y = +1$ and hits the lowest points, the troughs, at $y = -1$. The graph passes through the origin and intersects the y-axis at multiples of π. The peaks and troughs come at the odd multiples of $\frac{\pi}{2}$. The midline of the graph is the x-axis.

Here's $y = \cos(x)$.

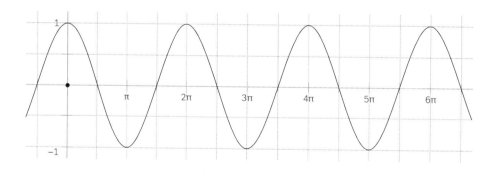

This has the exact same shape as the $y = \sin(x)$ graph: each one can be viewed as a horizontal translation of the other. Like $y = \sin(x)$, this peaks at $y = +1$ and hits its troughs at $y = -1$. The graph of $y = \cos(x)$ passes through a peak at (0, 1) and has subsequent peaks and troughs at multiples of π (where $y = \sin(x)$ intersects the x-axis).

The graph of $y = \cos(x)$ intersects the x-axis at every odd multiple of $\frac{\pi}{2}$ (where $y = \sin(x)$ has its peaks and troughs). The midline of the graph is also the x-axis.

It's good to recognize those two graphs, to be able to tell them apart, and to recognize their basic properties.

The ACT Math Test expects you to know these and it expects you to be able to transform them. We already discussed the transformation of functions above on page 234; let's repeat these general points for trig functions.

Case I: multiplication on the outside: $y = \sin(x)$ vs. $y = A \sin(x)$

All operations on the outside change the function vertically. If we multiply on the outside by a number greater than 1, the function is stretched vertically, so that the peaks get higher and the troughs go lower. This factor A has an important name: it's called the *amplitude* of the sine function, and it gives the height of the peak as measured from the midline as well as the depth of the trough as measured from the midline. Unlike some of the vocabulary we've seen so far, the ACT *does* expect you to know that word.

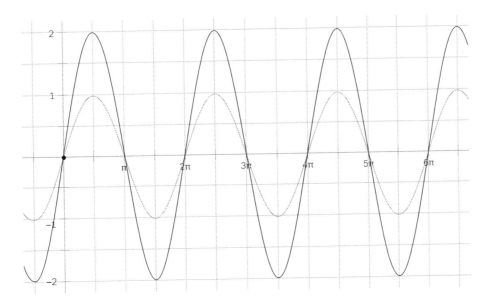

In the above graph, $y = \sin(x)$ is in gray and $y = 2 \sin(x)$ is in black. Here, the amplitude is $A = 2$.

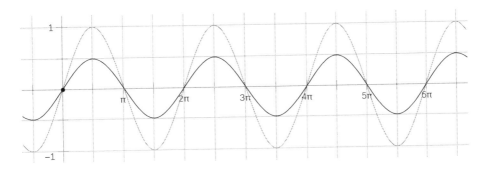

In the above graph, $y = \sin(x)$ is in gray and $y = \frac{1}{2}\sin(x)$ is in black. Here, the amplitude is $A = \frac{1}{2}$.

Case II: addition/subtraction on the outside: $y = \sin(x)$ vs. $y = \sin(x) \pm D$

Adding or subtracting on the outside produces a vertical shift. If D is a positive number, then $y = \sin(x) + D$ shifts the entire graph up, moving every point up D units vertically. If we add a negative number or subtract a positive number on the outside, $y = \sin(x) - D$, this would shift the entire graph down, moving every point down D units vertically. Unlike a vertical stretch, both peaks and troughs would move in the same direction, up together or down together.

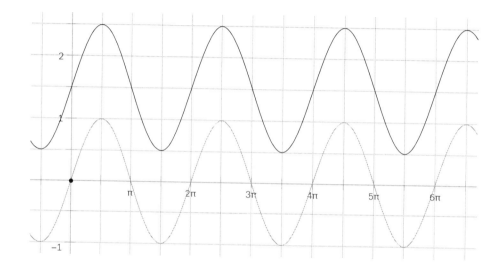

In that graph, $y = \sin(x)$ is in gray and $y = \sin(x) + 1.5$ is in black. Notice that the midline of the transformed graph is higher: that imaginary midline is at $y = 1.5$ now.

Case III: addition/subtraction on the inside: $y = \sin(x)$ vs. $y = \sin(x \pm C)$

We talked about the transformation of functions on page 234. Remember that we pointed out that all the transformations that involve some mathematical operation on the inside are anti-intuitive: they do the opposite of what one might expect. Also, all operations on the inside change the function horizontally.

If we add a positive number on the inside, paradoxically, this moves the function to the left. Similarly, if we subtract a positive number, we move the function to the right.

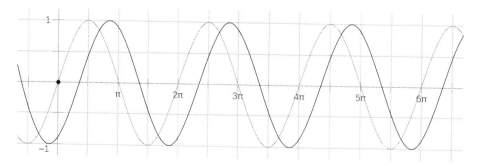

In that graph, $y = \sin(x)$ is in gray and $y = \sin\left(x - \frac{\pi}{3}\right)$ is in black. Because we subtracted a positive number, the graph moved to the right.

Case IV: multiplication on the inside: $y = \sin(x)$ vs. $y = \sin(Bx)$

As in Case III, everything we do on the inside is anti-intuitive. If we multiply by a number greater than 1, we horizontally compress the function.

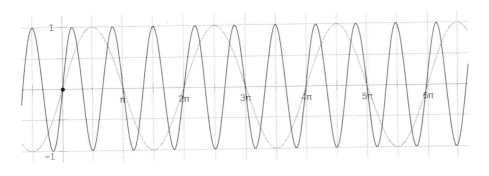

In that graph, $y = \sin(x)$ is in gray and $y = \sin(3x)$ is in black. Because we multiplied by a number greater than 1 on the inside, this "squeezed" the function horizontally. The horizontal length of a full cycle (midline to peak to midline to trough to midline) is called the *period* (and you should know this for the ACT Math Test). The period of $y = \sin(x)$ is $p = 2\pi$. If we multiply x by B, then the period gets divided by B, $p = \frac{2\pi}{B}$. The black function above has a period of $p = \frac{2\pi}{3}$.

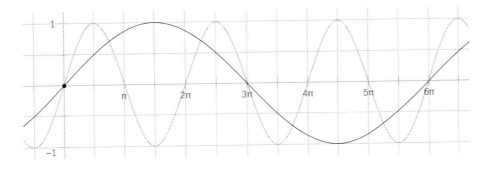

In that graph, $y = \sin(x)$ is in gray and $y = \sin\left(\frac{x}{3}\right)$ is in black. Because we divided on the inside by a number greater than 1 (or in other terms, multiplied by a fraction between zero and 1), this "stretched" the function horizontally. Here, $B = \frac{1}{3}$, so $p = \frac{2\pi}{B} = 6\pi$.

In trigonometry class, you may be responsible for a fully transformed sine curve that has experienced all four cases at once: $Y = A \sin(Bx + C) + D$. The ACT Math Test tends not to give you all four of those at once. In particular, it's very tricky when Cases III and IV are combined, but don't worry! The ACT doesn't ask about that. The ACT tends to ask about just two, maybe three, transformations at once.

Here's an ACT-level practice question.

Practice Question

The functions $y = \sin(x)$ and $y = P\sin(x + Q) + R$, for constants P, Q, and R, are graphed in the standard xy-coordinate plane below. Which of the following statements about the values of P, Q, and R is true?

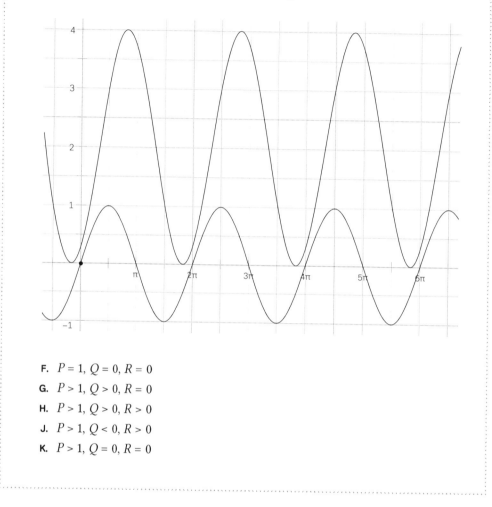

F. $P = 1$, $Q = 0$, $R = 0$
G. $P > 1$, $Q > 0$, $R = 0$
H. $P > 1$, $Q > 0$, $R > 0$
J. $P > 1$, $Q < 0$, $R > 0$
K. $P > 1$, $Q = 0$, $R = 0$

Answer and Explanation

First of all, this graph has been vertically stretched, so $P > 1$. It also has been vertically shifted up, because the midline is above the x-axis, so $R > 0$. Finally, the graph has been shifted slightly to the right: notice that the peaks of the transformed graph are slightly to the right of the peaks on the ordinary $y = \sin(x)$ graph. For a horizontal shift to the right, we need $Q < 0$.

Answer: **J**

Trigonometry in Non-Right Triangles

Finally, let's circle back to trigonometry in triangles, but this time, it's all triangles. When we were looking at only right triangles, we could use SOHCAHTOA. With non-right triangles, SOHCAHTOA is out the window, but fortunately we have some other rules we can use. In all formulas, A and B and C are the three angle measures, and a and b and c are the measures of the sides opposite these angles, respectively.

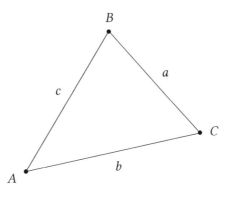

I. The Law of Sines

$$\frac{\sin(A)}{a} = \frac{\sin(B)}{b} = \frac{\sin(C)}{c}$$

If we knew the measurements of two sides and one angle of a triangle, or two angles and one side, we typically would need to set equal just two of these ratios.

II. The Law of Cosines

$$c^2 = a^2 + b^2 - 2ab \times \cos(C)$$
$$b^2 = a^2 + c^2 - 2ac \times \cos(B)$$
$$a^2 = b^2 + c^2 - 2bc \times \cos(A)$$

We show all three versions here, for clarity. We would never need more than one of these to solve any particular math problem. Notice that this is a generalized version of the Pythagorean theorem, valid for all triangles, right and non-right: when $C = 90°$ in a right triangle, $\cos(C) = 0$, and the formula reduces to the original Pythagorean theorem.

III. The General Area Formula

$$Area = \tfrac{1}{2}ab \times \sin(C)$$

$$Area = \tfrac{1}{2}ac \times \sin(B)$$

$$Area = \tfrac{1}{2}bc \times \sin(A)$$

As with the law of cosines, we're giving all three versions for clarity. We would never need more than one of these to solve any particular math problem.

You do **not** need to memorize these. Whenever the ACT Math Test asks about these, it is gracious enough to give the formulas to you: you simply need to know how to use them.

So what do these formulas look like in practice? Suppose we start with triangle ABC, in which we know that $a = 8$, $b = 5$, and $\angle B = 70°$.

What else about this triangle can we find?

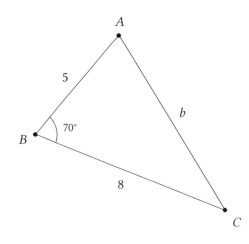

Whenever we have SAS (side-angle-side, or two sides and the angle between them), we have to use the law of cosines to find the third side.

$$b^2 = (8)^2 + (5)^2 - 2(8)(5) \times \cos 70°$$

The ACT Math Test often leaves answers in this uncalculated form for these problems. Here, we'll solve for b using a calculator to use this value to find the other two angles.

$$b = 64 + 25 - 80 \times \cos 70° = 7.851$$

We can use the law of sines to find the other two angles.

$$\sin(A) = \frac{a \times \sin(B)}{b} = \frac{8 \times \sin(70°)}{7.851} \quad \Rightarrow \quad A = 73.24°$$

$$\sin(C) = \frac{c \times \sin(B)}{b} = \frac{5 \times \sin(70°)}{7.851} \quad \Rightarrow \quad C = 36.76°$$

Now, we have all three sides and all three angles in this triangle. We also could use the original information to find the area.

$$Area = \frac{1}{2}ac \times \sin(B) = \frac{1}{2}(8)(5) \times \sin(70°) = 20 \times \sin(70°)$$

The side lengths of the triangle shown below are 4, 7, and 10. Which of the following equations, when solved for θ, gives the measure of the only obtuse angle in the triangle?

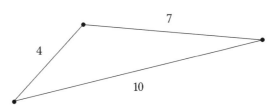

Note: For any triangle with sides of length a, b, and c that are opposite angles, *A*, *B*, and *C*, respectively, $\frac{\sin(A)}{a} = \frac{\sin(B)}{b} = \frac{\sin(C)}{c}$ and $c^2 = a^2 + b^2 - 2ab\cos(C)$.

A. $\frac{\sin\theta}{10} = \frac{1}{4}$

B. $\frac{\sin\theta}{10} = \frac{1}{7}$

C. $4^2 = 7^2 + 10^2 - 2(7)(10)\cos\theta$

D. $7^2 = 4^2 + 10^2 - 2(4)(10)\cos\theta$

E. $10^2 = 4^2 + 7^2 - 2(4)(7)\cos\theta$

Answer and Explanation

Whenever we have three sides and no angles, we cannot use the law of sines. We have to use the law of cosines instead. Notice, also, that the only obtuse angle must be the largest angle in the triangle, which must be opposite the longest side in the triangle. Thus, the obtuse angle in this triangle is opposite the side of length 10. In the law of cosines, we have to say that c = 10 and C is the angle θ that we want to find. Therefore,

$$c^2 = a^2 + b^2 - 2ab\cos(C)$$
$$10^2 = 4^2 + 7^2 - 2(4)(7)\cos\theta$$

Answer: **E**

Advanced Topics

The ACT Math Test covers many topics, from ideas you learned about on the first day of Algebra 1 to the most arcane high-level topics of the most advanced possible precalculus class, from *"just about anyone would know this"* to *"Holy Smokes! Does anyone at all know about this?"*

The ACT Math Test has a few of these advanced topics. You would see only a couple of these on the ACT Math Test, and certainly no more than one on any particular topic. Only devote time and energy to learning and studying these topics if you feel you're quite solid on all the rest of the ACT Math material; otherwise, the time-to-point trade-off just isn't big enough!

Formal Logic

The formal logic tested on the ACT Math Test revolves around if-then statements. Three big ideas here can take you a long way.

Big Idea #1: Deductions from an if-then statement

If we are told that the statement "If P, then Q" is true, and we are told that "P" is true, then we can logically deduce that "Q" is true. This is a correct deduction.

If we are told that the statement "If P, then Q" is true, and we are told that "Q" is true, we cannot make any deduction. It would be logically incorrect to deduce "P" under those circumstances.

For example, a true if-then statement is "If a person is in Berkeley, CA, then she is in the United States." If someone tells us that "Lena is in Berkeley, CA," then we can correctly deduce that Lena is in the US. On the other hand, if someone tells us that "Meghan is in the US," then we can't make any deduction: the statement certainly would not allow us to establish whether Meghan is in Berkeley; for example, Meghan could be in Portland, OR, or Piscataway, NJ—still in the US but not in Berkeley, CA.

Big Idea #2: Alternate forms of if-then statements

1. The statements "only if J happens does K happen" and "K only if J" are logically equivalent to "If K, then J."

   "Only if the car has gas in the tank does it run" is logically equivalent to "If the car runs, then it has gas in the tank."

2. The statements "every S is T" or "all S's are T" are equivalent to "if S, then T."

   "All squares are rhombuses" is logically equivalent to "If a shape is a square, then it is a rhombus."

The advantage of rewriting these statement into if-then form becomes apparent with Big Idea #3.

Big Idea #3: The contrapositive

Let's start with the generic "if P, then Q." Let's assume that this original statement is true. We'd like to make changes to this to produce another true statement from this original statement, and we come up with the following three possibilities—but they don't all work.

1. "If Q, then P" (the converse): This simply swaps the order of the two pieces.
2. "If not P, then not Q" (the inverse): This negates each piece.
3. "If not Q, then not P" (the contrapositive): This negates each piece and swaps the order.

The first two are invalid and illogical deductions, not equivalent to the original, but the third, the *contrapositive*, is 100 percent equivalent to the original. If the original statement is true, then the contrapositive is also true.

Example

original = "If the car runs, then it has gas in the tank." (true)

converse = "If the car has gas in the tank, then it runs." (not necessarily true: What if it has a dead battery? A full tank of gas won't fix that!)

inverse = "If the car does not run, then it does not have gas in the tank." (again, not true: It could be a dead battery.)

contrapositive = "If the car does not have gas in the tank, then it will not run." (true)

Notice that the contrapositive allows us to make a deduction from another statement.

Let's say the original is one we had above: "If someone is in Berkeley, CA, that person is in the US." We already saw that if we are told "Peter is in Berkeley, CA," then we can deduce that "Peter is in the US."

Well, the contrapositive equivalent of that original statement would be: "If someone is not in the US, then that person would not be in Berkeley, CA." Thus, if we are given the statement "Nick is not in the US," then we can correctly deduce that "Nick is not in Berkeley, CA." We can make deductions from the original and from the contrapositive.

Suppose the following statement is true for all students at Omega High School.

Every member of the Key Society is a member of the Psi Omega Club.

Suppose Bill and Ted are students at Omega High School, and we are told that Bill is not a member of the Key Society and Ted is not a member of the Psi Omega Club. If all these statements are true, which of the following is the complete set of necessarily true statements that follow?

A. Bill is not a member of the Psi Omega Club.
B. Ted is not a member of the Key Society.
C. Bill is not a member of the Psi Omega Club and Ted is not a member of the Key Society.
D. Neither Bill nor Ted is a member of either club.
E. Nothing can be deduced from these statements.

Answer and Explanation
Use the following symbolic representation.

P = member of the Key Society
Q = member of the Psi Omega Club

We are told "Every P is Q." This is equivalent to "If P, then Q." The equivalent contrapositive "If not Q, then not P." From these statements, we can make a valid deduction, given either "P is true" or "not Q is true."

One statement we are given is that "Bill is not P." We can draw no conclusion about whether Bill is a member of the Psi Omega Club.

The other statement we're given is that "Ted is not Q." From the contrapositive, we can make a clear deduction: it must also be true that "Ted is not P" or that Ted is not a member of the Key Society. That is the only deduction we can make from these two statements, and we know nothing else about the excellent adventure of these two students.

Answer: **B**

Logarithms

We undo addition by subtraction. We undo multiplication by division. How do we undo exponentiation? Notice that things get tricky here, because addition and multiplication are commutative ($a + b = b + a$, and $a \times b = b \times a$), but exponentiation is not commutative ($a^b \neq b^a$). Suppose we have an exponent operation, $N = b^k$: this is already solved for N. We would have to do one thing to solve for the base b and something else to solve for the exponent k. So unlike addition and multiplication, exponentiation doesn't have just one inverse operation.

If we want to solve for the base b, we can use **roots**. We talked on page 138 about square root and higher-order roots.

$$N = b^k \quad \Rightarrow \quad b = \sqrt[k]{N}$$

But to solve for the exponent, we need to dive into logarithms. The logarithmic form is the form that allows us to rewrite an exponential equation to solve for the exponent.

$$N = b^k \quad \Rightarrow \quad k = \log_b N$$

A *logarithm* is an exponent. The logarithm $\log_b N$ is **the exponent we would have to give the base b to get an output of N**. The equation on the left is called exponential form and the equation on the right is logarithmic form: it's very important to be able to switch between those two forms as needed. Here are a few examples with simple numbers, in both exponential and logarithmic forms.

$$25 = 5^2 \quad \Rightarrow \quad 2 = \log_5 25$$
$$16 = 2^4 \quad \Rightarrow \quad 4 = \log_2 16$$
$$27 = 3^3 \quad \Rightarrow \quad 3 = \log_3 27$$
$$1,000,000 = 10^6 \quad \Rightarrow \quad 6 = \log_{10} 1,000,000$$

Notice that $\log_5 25$ is the exponent we would have to give to 5 to have an output of 25, and that exponent is 2. Notice that $\log_2 16$ is the exponent we would have to give to 2 to have an output of 16, and that exponent is 4. Notice that $\log_3 27$ is the exponent we would have to give to 3 to have an output of 27, and that exponent is 3. Notice that $\log_{10} 1,000,000$ is the exponent we would have to give to 10 to have an output of a million, and that exponent is 6. **A logarithm is an exponent!**

Go back to the algebraic expressions of the exponential form $N = b^k$ and the logarithmic form $k = \log_b N$. The exponential form is to solve for the power N, so we can substitute this into the logarithmic form:

$$k = \log_b b^k$$

In a way, this is pretty meaningless: what exponent would we have to give b to get an output of b^k? Of course, we would need the exponent k! Notice that the logarithmic form is solved for the exponent k, so we can substitute this into the exponential form:

$$N = b^{\log_b N}$$

This is also meaningless: we know that, by definition, $\log_b N$ is the exponent we would have to give to b to get an output of N. Well, if we do give this exponent to b, what output do we have? We get the output of N, as promised!

These two equations are tautologies: a tautology is a statement that is so obviously true that it contains no real information, such as "*My favorite hat is a hat*" or "*My sister's cat is a mammal.*" The ACT Math Test will not expect you to know the word "tautology," but it will expect you to recognize these two forms: they allow us to do instantly what appears to be a very complex calculation. For example, the ACT might ask us to evaluate the following:

$$3^{\log_3 5} = ?$$

Well, $\log_3 5$ is the exponent we would have to give to 3 to get an output of 5. Here, we're giving this exponent to 3, so of course, we get an output of 5. Done! This expression equals 5. Absolutely no calculation is needed if you understand what's being asked.

Here's a practice problem:

Practice Question

$$N = A(1 - b^{pt})$$

Which of the following equations shows the formula above solved for t?

F. $t = \frac{1}{bp}\left(1 - \frac{N}{A}\right)$

G. $t = \frac{1}{p}\left(1 - \frac{N}{bA}\right)$

H. $t = \frac{1}{p}\log_b\left(1 - \frac{N}{A}\right)$

J. $t = \log_b\left(\left(1 - \frac{N}{A}\right)^p\right)$

K. $t = \log_b\left(\frac{1}{p} - \frac{N}{A}\right)$

Answer and Explanation
First, divide by A:

$$\frac{N}{A} = 1 - b^{pt}$$

Now, subtract N/A from both sides, and add the power to both sides.

$$b^{pt} = 1 - \frac{N}{A}$$

In this form, b is the base, pt is the exponent, and $\left(1 - \frac{N}{A}\right)$ is the power. Now, we can rewrite this exponential form into logarithmic form.

$$pt = \log_b\left(1 - \frac{N}{A}\right)$$

$$t = \frac{1}{p}\log_b\left(1 - \frac{N}{A}\right)$$

Answer: **H**

That covers much of what the ACT Math Test will ask about logarithms, but it's possible that it will ask about the laws of logarithms. Because of this, it's important to understand that **the laws of logarithms are simply the laws of exponents, restated in logarithmic form**. If you understand the laws of exponents (discussed above on page 133), then you already understand the laws of logarithms. The chart below summarizes the relationship. Everywhere in the "verbal" column where you see the word "exponent," remember that this word can be replaced by the word "logarithm," because at its very essence, a logarithm is an exponent!

Verbal Form	Exponent Form	Logarithm Form
If $b \neq 0$, then an exponent of zero produces a power of 1.	$b^0 = 1$	$\log_b 1 = 0$
The pth root of b is b with an exponent of $\frac{1}{p}$.	$b^{\frac{1}{p}} = \sqrt[p]{b}$	$\log_b(\sqrt[p]{b}) = \frac{1}{p}$
Multiplying powers means add the exponents.	$(b^n)(b^m) = b^{n+m}$	$\log_b MN = \log_b M + \log_b N$
Dividing powers means subtract the exponents.	$\frac{b^n}{b^m} = b^{n-m}$	$\log_b\left(\frac{M}{N}\right) = \log_b M - \log_b N$
Raising a power to an exponent means multiply the exponents.	$(b^n)^p = b^{np}$	$\log_b(N^p) = p \times \log_b N$

Practice Question

Which of the following is equal to the value of $\log_2(\sqrt[5]{8})$?

A. -2

B. 0.6

C. $\frac{5}{3}$

D. 15

E. $\sqrt[5]{3}$

Answer and Explanation

$$\log_2(\sqrt[5]{8}) = \log_2(8^{\frac{1}{5}}) = \frac{1}{5}\log_2 8 = \frac{1}{5}(3) = \frac{3}{5} = 0.6$$

Answer: **B**

Practice Question

> If $10^A = 3$ and $10^B = 5$ and $10^P = 750$, then which of the following is an equation that correctly relates A and B and P?
>
> F. $P = 10AB^2$
>
> G. $P = 2(A + B)$
>
> H. $P = 2(A + B) + 10$
>
> J. $P = A + 2B + 10$
>
> K. $P = A + 2B + 1$

Answer and Explanation

Rewrite the exponential equations in logarithmic form and apply the laws of logarithms.

$A = \log_{10}3$ and $B = \log_{10}5$

$P = \log_{10}750 = \log_{10}(75 \times 10) = \log_{10}(3 \times 25 \times 10)$

$P = \log_{10}3 + \log_{10}25 + \log_{10}10 = \log_{10}3 + \log_{10}5^2 + \log_{10}10$

$P = \log_{10}3 + 2\log_{10}5 + \log_{10}10 = A + 2B + 1$

Answer: **K**

Compound Interest

#lifehacks101: When you put money in the bank or invest money, that money earns interest: essentially, the bank or investment firm is paying you for doing the favor of letting them play with your money. Conversely, when you borrow money, either through a mortgage or an auto loan or credit card debt, the lending institution charges you interest on the amount borrowed: essentially, you will be paying over an extended period for the favor of getting all that money in a lump sum. Loans for tangible assets, such as a house or car, tend to have reasonable interest rates, but credit cards have notoriously high interest rates. If you buy something for $300 on a credit card and then just make the monthly minimum payment for years, you could wind up paying double or triple the price of the item overall! The ACT isn't going to ask you why credit cards aren't a great purchasing option, but hey, bonus takeaway.

In grade school, you learn about something called "simple interest," a complete fiction that is taught only to school children who don't understand exponents. In the "simple interest" model, the person deposits his principal, and in all subsequent periods, interest accrues only on that principal. Nobody in the real world cares about simple interest. Now that you understand exponents, you can understand how things in the real world really work: *compound interest*. The "compound interest" model involves *interest on interest*: on the very first occasion that interest is earned, it may look like simple interest up to that point, but once interest starts building up, each new interest payment is based on the total in the account—the principal and all the interest that has accumulated up to that point. Thus, in the compound interest scheme, used all the time in the real world, investments soar over time and debts spiral out of control.

How does this work? Let's take a simple scenario, an investment of $1,000 invested at 4% annual interest, compounding annually. The phrase "compounding annually" tells us how frequently the interest is given: in this example, it's given only once a year. After one year, the interest is added: 4% of $1,000 is $40, so now the money in the account is $1,040 (the same as we would have gotten with simple interest). After two years, interest is added again, now 4% of $1,040, which is $41.60, so the new amount in the account is $1,081.60. After the third year, interested is added yet again, now 4% of $1,081.60, which (rounded to the nearest penny) is $43.26, so the new amount in the account is $1,124.86. That's the basic pattern. Notice that, once the interest is paid (say, at the end of the first year), there's just money in the account, and it really doesn't matter which part was principal and which is interest: if, at the end of one year, you had decided to withdraw your investment, the bank would have handed you $1,040 in cash, all in dollars, with no distinction between your original money and the interest. Because that distinction doesn't matter, it makes sense for all future cycles of interest to pay interest on the total sum. That's the basic reason that compound interest is always used in the real world.

In that example, we were doing the calculations one step at a time, but we could be more efficient than that. Recall that when we discussed percentages on page 130, we said that we could represent a percent increase as multiplier. We have to put the percent in decimal form to build that multiplier, so the multiplier for a 4% increase would be 1.04: every year, every time interest is earned, the total amount in the account would be multiplied by another factor of 1.04. Thus, after Y years, the principal would have been multiplied by Y factors of 1.04, that is, by 1.04^Y. If A is the amount,

$$A = 1000 \times 1.04^Y$$

We could abstract a little further. If the principal is P, and the percent has a multiplier of M, then after Y years of compounding annually, the final amount A would be

$$A = P \times M^Y$$

If we represent that multiplier M in terms of r, the interest percent as a decimal, it would be $M = 1 + r$. Thus, we could write the formula as

$$A = P \times (1 + r)^Y$$

That's the formula for yearly interest compounding annually. In the real world, interest may compound more frequently—quarterly, monthly, or even daily—and these more frequent periods of compounding would change that formula, but the ACT Math Test doesn't tend to ask about compounding periods other than a year. Overall, compound interest is a relatively rare topic on the ACT Math Test, appearing only a few times in the last several years. Still, it's good to know and, unlike, say, the unit circle, has practical applications to your own life (start investing now)!

This will be the last example of a Problem Set, an Advanced Formula Problem Set on compound interest. We've already discussed ACT Math Test Problem Sets and seen an example of a Geometry Problem Set on page 204. Then we had a Data Problem Set on page 221 and our first Advanced Formula Problem Set on page 251. This is one more set to give you practice with this topic.

Use the following information to answer questions 1–3.

Solomon invests an initial amount of $20,000 in an account that compounds interest at a 5.7% annual rate. Assume that Solomon makes no withdrawal or additional deposits after that first one during the time discussed in the question.

Note: For an account with an initial deposit of P dollars that compounds interest at an annual rate of $r\%$, the value of the account Y years after the initial deposit is $A = P\left(1+\frac{r}{100}\right)^{Y}$.

1 Which of the following expressions gives the dollar amount that Solomon has in his account 10 years after his initial investment?

   A. $A = 20{,}000(1.057)^{10}$

   B. $A = 20{,}000(1.57)^{10}$

   C. $A = 20{,}000(1.57)$

   D. $A = 200{,}000(1.057)$

   E. $A = 200{,}000(1.57)$

2 Solomon's friend Midas deposited $20,000 into another account paying $Q\%$, and three years after the initial deposit, Midas had a total of $25,000 including interest. Which of the following gives the correct percent value Q for this account?

   F. $Q = \sqrt[3]{\frac{1}{400}}$

   G. $Q = \sqrt[3]{\frac{5}{400}} - 1$

   H. $Q = 100\left(\sqrt[3]{\frac{1}{4}}\right)$

   J. $Q = 100\left(\sqrt[3]{\frac{5}{4}} - 1\right)$

   K. $Q = \sqrt[3]{\frac{5}{4}} - 100$

3 Soon after depositing the $20,000 into his account, Solomon wants to calculate how long he would have to wait for the amount in the account to appreciate to $35,000. Which of the following gives the number of years, since the initial deposit, needed for the account to appreciate to a value of $35,000?

   A. $Y = 1.057\left(\frac{7}{4}\right)$

   B. $Y = 35{,}000 - (1.057)(20{,}000)$

   C. $Y = 35{,}000 - \sqrt[1.057]{20{,}000}$

   D. $Y = 1.057\log_{20{,}000}(35{,}000)$

   E. $Y = \log_{1.057}\left(\frac{7}{4}\right)$

Answers and Explanations

1 For this one, we simply plug into the formula given. We know $r = 5.7\%$, or 0.057 as a decimal (you'll need to change this into a decimal first to work with it), so,

$$1 + \frac{r}{100} = 1 + 0.057 = 1.057$$

This gets raised to the tenth power and then multiplied by $P = 20{,}000$.

$$A = 20{,}000(1.057)^{10}$$

Answer: **A**

2 First, plug $A = 25{,}000$, $P = 20{,}000$, and $Y = 3$ into the formula. Plug in Q for r.

$$25{,}000 = 20{,}000\left(1 + \frac{Q}{100}\right)^3$$

Then, we have to divide by 20,000 to get the power by itself.

$$\frac{25{,}000}{20{,}000} = \frac{5}{4} = \left(1 + \frac{Q}{100}\right)^3$$

Now, we undo the cube by taking a cube root of both sides.

$$\sqrt[3]{\frac{5}{4}} = 1 + \frac{Q}{100}$$

We're in the homestretch now! Subtract 1.

$$\sqrt[3]{\frac{5}{4}} - 1 = \frac{Q}{100}$$

Now, multiply both sides by 100.

$$100\left(\sqrt[3]{\frac{5}{4}} - 1\right) = Q$$

Answer: **J**

3 Now, we have $P = 20{,}000$, $A = 35{,}000$, $Q = 5.7\%$, and we want the value of Y. Start with these numbers in the formula.

$$A = P\left(1 + \frac{r}{100}\right)^Y$$

$$35{,}000 = 20{,}000\left(1 + \frac{5.7}{100}\right)^Y$$

$$35{,}000 = 20{,}000(1.057)^Y$$

$$\frac{35{,}000}{20{,}000} = \frac{7}{4} = (1.057)^Y$$

This is in exponential form, $N = b^k$, and can be rewritten in logarithmic form, $k = \log_b N$, to solve for the exponent.

$$Y = \log_{1.057}\left(\frac{7}{4}\right)$$

Answer: **E**

Complex Numbers

"Real" numbers are what we call the numbers on the number line, numbers such as 5, $-\frac{3}{7}$, $\sqrt{2}$, and π. Yes, those are the numbers that we call "real," but that name is deceptive, because it implies that numbers not on the number line are somehow less real or not as real as these number-line numbers are. The equation $x^2 + 1 = 0$ does not have any solution on the real number line but it can be solved with numbers *not* on the number line; having his doubts about such numbers, René Descartes coined the term "imaginary" for these numbers, but in retrospect, this is an even more unfortunate name. In modern mathematics, all these numbers are regarded as equally bona fide and real, even though some are called "real" and some are called "imaginary." About half the time, the ACT Math Test will have a question involving imaginary numbers.

The fundamental imaginary number is i, defined as $i = \sqrt{-1}$. The equation $x^2 = -1$ has two solutions, $x = +i$ and $x = -i$. The powers of i follow a definite pattern.

$i^1 = i = \sqrt{-1}$	$i^7 = -i$
$i^2 = -1$	$i^8 = +1$
$i^3 = (-1)i = -i$	$i^9 = i$
$i^4 = (-i)i = -(-1) = +1$	$i^{10} = -1$
$i^5 = i$	$i^{11} = -i$
$i^6 = -1$	$i^{12} = +1$

The pattern repeats every four numbers. This means that we know $i^{40} = i^{96} = i^{2,000} = +1$, so we could figure out any values near those (e.g., $i^{2,003} = -i$).

The sum of a real number and an imaginary number is called a **complex number**. If a and b are real numbers, then $z = a + bi$ is a complex number. The ACT Math Test expects you to know how to do basic arithmetic with complex numbers. Adding and subtracting is straightforward: we treat the real and imaginary parts separately.

$$(3 - 2i) + (-5 + 4i) = -2 + 2i$$
$$(3 - 2i) - (-5 + 4i) = 8 - 6i$$

(The ACT would tend to ask a slightly more complex question, so we'll get into those in just in a minute.)

With multiplication, we have to remember the FOIL process, discussed on page 299.

$$(3 - 2i) \times (-5 + 4i) = ?$$

The F term, the product of firsts, will be the product of two real numbers. Both the O and I terms, the products of two "outer" or two "inner" terms, will be real times imaginary numbers. The L terms, the products of the lasts, will be the product of two imaginary numbers, which are real.

$$(3 - 2i) \times (-5 + 4i)$$

$$= -15 + 12i + 10i - 8i^2$$
$$= -15 + 22i - 8(-1)$$
$$= -15 + 22i + 8$$
$$= -7 + 22i$$

Practice Question

Which of the following complex numbers equals $(2 + i)(2 + 4i)$?

F. $4 + 4i$

G. $8 + 6i$

H. $6i$

J. $8 + 10i$

K. $10i$

Answer and Explanation
To multiply complex numbers, we use FOIL.

$$F = (2)(2) = +4$$
$$O = (2)(4i) = 8i$$
$$I = (i)(2) = 2i$$
$$L = (i)(4i) = 4i^2 = -4$$

$$(2 + i)(2 + 4i) = 4 + 8i + 2i - 4 = 10i$$

Answer: **K**

Before we can discuss division of complex numbers, we have to discuss the idea of the *complex conjugate*. For any complex number, that number's complex conjugate is the complex number that has the same real part and the opposite sign imaginary part. The complex conjugate of $z_1 = 2 + 3i$ is $z_2 = 2 - 3i$, and the complex conjugate of $z_2 = 2 - 3i$ is $z_1 = 2 + 3i$. The complex numbers $z_1 = -5 + i$ and $z_2 = -5 - i$ are complex conjugates of each other, as are $z_1 = \sqrt{5} - \sqrt{2}i - i$ and $z_2 = \sqrt{5} + \sqrt{2}i + i$.

Think about what happens when we multiply a complex number ($z_1 = a + bi$) times its complex conjugate ($z_1 = a - bi$). Essentially, this recreates the difference of two squares patterns, discussed on page 217. Remember in that algebraic pattern, the cross terms (i.e., the O and I terms of FOIL) cancel:

$$(a + b)(a - b) = a^2 - ab + ab - b^2 = a^2 - b^2$$

Much in the same way, in the product of a complex number $z_1 = a + bi$ with its complex conjugate $z_1 = a - bi$, the cross terms (i.e., the imaginary terms) will cancel.

$$(a + bi)(a - bi) = a^2 - abi + abi - (i^2)b^2 = a^2 + b^2$$

The product of a complex number and its conjugate is always a positive real number. That's a big idea in complex numbers.

Now, suppose we have to divide two complex numbers; we could express them as a fraction. Of course, having an i in the denominator is like having a square root in the denominator, and it's considered in mathematical "bad taste" to have a square root in the denominator. You don't want an imaginary number in the denominator, either; think of it like bringing an imaginary friend to a dinner party. The easiest way to address i in the denominator is to multiply both the numerator and the denominator by the complex conjugate of the denominator (that won't do much for your imaginary friend, though).

For example,

$$\frac{8 + 2i}{1 + i} = \frac{8 + 2i}{1 + i} \times \frac{1 - i}{1 - i} = \frac{(8 + 2i)(1 - i)}{1 + 1} = \frac{(8 + 2i)(1 - i)}{2}$$

$$= (4 + i)(1 - i) = 4 - 4i + i + 1 = 5 - 3i$$

Once we multiply by the complex conjugate in the numerator and the denominator, the denominator becomes a real number, and we can simplify.

Practice Question

Which of the following expressions is equivalent to $\frac{15i}{1 + 2i}$?

A. 5

B. $1 - 2i$

C. $6 + 3i$

D. $10 + 5i$

E. $30 - 15i$

Answer and Explanation

We begin by multiplying numerator and denominator by the complex conjugate of the denominator.

$$\frac{15i}{1 + 2i} = \frac{15i}{1 + 2i} \times \frac{(1 - 2i)}{(1 - 2i)} = \frac{15i(1 - 2i)}{1 + 4} = \frac{15i(1 - 2i)}{5}$$

$$= 3i(1 - 2i) = 3i - 6(i^2) = 6 + 3i$$

Answer: **C**

We represent real numbers as dots on the number line. The standard way to represent complex numbers is as dots in a plane: the *complex plane.*

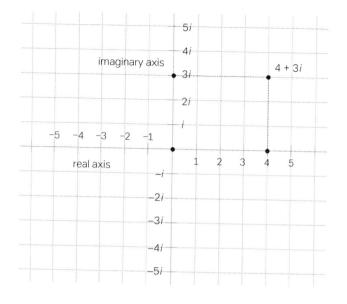

The horizontal axis is the real axis, the ordinary real number line that we always have known and loved. The vertical axis is the *imaginary axis*, with steps of i units. A complex number such as $z = 4 + 3i$ would be a point in the plane. Because both the real and imaginary parts are positive, this is in Q1 of the complex plane, and the real and imaginary numbers function as coordinates to locate the point.

For real numbers, we use the absolute value to talk about the "size" of the number, regardless of whether the number is positive or negative. The extension of the absolute value in the complex plane is the *modulus* of a complex number. The modulus is the square root of the product of a complex number with its complex conjugate.

Okay, so that's a little twisty. Let's think about that for a second.

The "complex conjugate" of a real number would just be itself. Thus, the modulus of a real number would be the square root of the product of the number with itself—in other words, the ordinary absolute value!

For the number shown above, $z = 4 + 3i$, the conjugate is $z^* = 4 - 3i$, and the modulus is

$$M = \sqrt{(4 + 3i)(4 - 3i)} = \sqrt{16 + 9} = \sqrt{25} = 5$$

Notice that the triangle formed by the lines connected to $z = 4 + 3i$ in the diagram form a 3-4-5 triangle, so 5 is the distance of the point $z = 4 + 3i$ from the origin. Recall that, on page 208, we discussed the distance interpretation of absolute value. The idea of modulus extends this: the modulus of a complex number is the distance in the complex plane from that point to the origin.

The modulus of the complex number $z = a + bi$ is given by $\sqrt{a^2 + b^2}$. How many points are there in the complex plane of the form $z = P + Qi$, where P and Q are both integers, that have a modulus equal to 5?

F. 4

G. 6

H. 8

J. 12

K. 16

Answer and Explanation

First of all, there are four points on the axes, $z = \pm 5$ and $z = \pm 5i$. Then there are the points from the 3-4-5 triangle, two in each quadrant.

Q1: $z = 3 + 4i$, $z = 4 + 3i$

Q2: $z = -3 + 4i$, $z = -4 + 3i$

Q3: $z = -3 - 4i$, $z = -4 - 3i$

Q4: $z = 3 - 4i$, $z = 4 - 3i$

That's 12 altogether.

Answer: **J**

Matrices

Perhaps the single most advanced topic that occasionally appears on the ACT Math Test involves the idea of matrices. A matrix is a rectangular array of numbers (and no Keanu Reeves. Obligatory *Matrix* joke complete). Matrices have an astonishing range of uses in science and engineering.

$$[A] = \begin{bmatrix} 5 & -2 & 3 \\ 1 & 4 & 0 \end{bmatrix}$$

This particular matrix has two rows and three columns, so it's a 2 × 3 matrix. That notation is standard for matrices: {number of rows} × {number of columns}.

This particular matrix has six numerical entries: all six can be real numbers of any kind, although on the ACT Math Test, you'll be quite likely to see only integer entries.

Here are a few more matrices.

$$[B] = \begin{bmatrix} 8 \\ 0 \\ -7 \end{bmatrix} \qquad [C] = \begin{bmatrix} 4 & 6 \\ 6 & 9 \end{bmatrix} \qquad [D] = \begin{bmatrix} 1 & 0 & 1 \\ 0 & 1 & 0 \\ 0 & 0 & 1 \end{bmatrix}$$

Notice that [B] is a 3 × 1 matrix, [C] is a 2 × 2 matrix, and [D] is a 3 × 3 matrix. Both [C] and [D] are examples of "square matrices," because the number of rows equals the number of columns.

There are a few basic mathematical operations about which the ACT Math Test could ask. The most straightforward is what mathematicians would call "scalar multiplication," which simply means multiplying a matrix by an ordinary number. This is straightforward: the multiplication simply gets distributed to every single number in the matrix. Suppose we go back to matrix [A] above and multiply that by 7.

$$7 \times [A] = 7 \times \begin{bmatrix} 5 & -2 & 3 \\ 1 & 4 & 0 \end{bmatrix} = \begin{bmatrix} 35 & -14 & 21 \\ 7 & 28 & 0 \end{bmatrix}$$

If you can distribute, then you can do scalar multiplication of matrices!

Another operation that the ACT Math Test may ask about is finding the *determinant*. The determinant is a particular number that tells us certain properties of a matrix. It's possible to find the determinant only for square matrices: matrices that are not square do not have determinants. There are complicated mathematical procedures for finding the determinant of 3 × 3 matrices and larger square matrices, procedures the ACT does not expect you to know, but there's a very simple formula for finding the determinant of a 2 × 2 matrix.

$$[M] = \begin{bmatrix} a & b \\ c & d \end{bmatrix} \quad \Rightarrow \quad \det[M] = ad - bc$$

In all likelihood, the ACT Math Test will give that formula as part of the problem. Let's use matrix [C] above.

$$[C] = \begin{bmatrix} 4 & 6 \\ 6 & 9 \end{bmatrix} \quad \Rightarrow \quad \det[C] = ad - bc = (4)(9) - (6)(6) = 36 - 36 = 0$$

As it happens, this particular matrix has a determinant of zero. While this would have important implications in higher mathematics, such as linear algebra, any implications of the numerical value of the determinant are 100 percent beyond anything the ACT expects you to know!

Practice Question

The determinant of matrix $[M] = \begin{bmatrix} a & b \\ c & d \end{bmatrix}$ equals $ad - bc$. Suppose we know, for some matrix [J], that $\det[J] = 4$. If matrix $[K] = 5 \times [J]$, which of the following would be the numerical value of $\det[K]$?

A. 0.2
B. 5
C. 20
D. 100
E. 2500

Answer and Explanation

Let's say $[J] = \begin{bmatrix} a & b \\ c & d \end{bmatrix}$, so $\det[J] = ad - bc = 4$.

We know then that $[K] = 5 \times [J] = \begin{bmatrix} 5a & 5b \\ 5c & 5d \end{bmatrix}$, so,

$$\det[K] = (5a)(5d) - (5b)(5c) = 25ad - 25bc = 25(ad - bc) = 25(4) = 100.$$

Answer: **D**

The most advanced thing that the ACT Math Test might ask about matrices is the process of matrix multiplication. There are a few rules about this we need to establish before we can talk about the process.

With numbers on the number line, we could pick *any* two numbers from the number line and it would be perfectly possible to multiply them together. Such is not the case with matrices. A very specific condition needs to be met for matrix multiplication to be possible. Suppose we have [matrix #1], a $r_1 \times c_1$ matrix, and [matrix #2], a $r_2 \times c_2$ matrix (in other words, r_1 is the number of rows in matrix #1, c_1 is the number of columns in matrix #1, and r_2 and c_2, respectively, are the numbers of rows and columns in matrix #2). The only time matrix multiplication is possible is if the number of columns in the first matrix equals the number of rows in the second matrix: only if $c_1 = r_2$ would we even be allowed to multiply [matrix #1] × [matrix #2]. For example, with the four example matrices on page 289, recall that $[A]$ was a 2×3 matrix, $[B]$ was a 3×1 matrix, $[C]$ was a 2×2 matrix, and $[D]$ was a 3×3 matrix. We would be allowed to perform only the following matrix multiplications:

$[A] \times [B]$ $[A] \times [D]$ $[C] \times [A]$

$[C] \times [C]$ $[D] \times [B]$ $[D] \times [D]$

Of all the possible combinations among these four matrices, these six combinations would be the only possible examples of valid matrix multiplication. In all six of these cases, the number of columns in the first matrix equals the number of rows in the second matrix. The other 10 combinations are cases in which matrix multiplication would be impossible:

$[A]$ with $[A]$ $[A]$ with $[C]$ $[B]$ with $[A]$

$[B]$ with $[B]$ $[B]$ with $[C]$ $[B]$ with $[D]$

$[C]$ with $[B]$ $[C]$ with $[D]$ $[D]$ with $[A]$

$[D]$ with $[C]$

Another way in which matrix multiplication is not like the ordinary multiplication of numbers is that matrix multiplication is not commutative. The ordinary multiplication of numbers is commutative, because we can flip the order and get the same result: $2 \times 7 = 7 \times 2$. This is not true at all with matrices. With these four example matrices, we just saw that $[A] \times [B]$ would be a valid instance of matrix multiplication, but $[B] \times [A]$ is not even possible (again, because the number of columns in $[B]$ doesn't equal the number of rows in $[A]$). Sometimes matrix multiplication is possible in one order and not even possible in the other order. Even if both orders are possible, in general, switching the order will produce a different result. For example, if both $[J]$ and $[K]$ are 3×3 matrices, then it's legal to compute both $[J] \times [K]$ and $[K] \times [J]$, but in general, it would not be true that $[J] \times [K] = [K] \times [J]$.

So let's go back to [matrix #1], a $r_1 \times c_1$ matrix, and [matrix #2], a $r_2 \times c_2$ matrix. We've seen that we're allowed to multiply only if $c_1 = r_2$. The product matrix must have r_1 rows and c_2 columns: it will take its number of rows from the first matrix and the number of columns from the second matrix. For example, if $[P]$ is a 5×7 matrix, and $[Q]$ is a 7×3 matrix, then $[P] \times [Q]$ would be a 5×3 matrix.

Now, how do we actually perform matrix multiplication? Let's look again at these two matrices.

$$[A] = \begin{bmatrix} 5 & -2 & 3 \\ 1 & 4 & 0 \end{bmatrix} \quad [B] = \begin{bmatrix} 8 \\ 0 \\ -7 \end{bmatrix}$$

$[A]$ is a 2×3 matrix and $[B]$ is a 3×1 matrix, so $[A] \times [B]$ will have to be a 2×1 matrix. We create each entry of the product matrix as a product of a row of the first matrix times a column of second matrix. For example, the 1st row, 1st column entry of the product matrix $[A] \times [B]$ will be the first row of $[A]$ times the first column of $[B]$. What does it mean to multiply a row times a column? Well, notice that, as part of the very condition of matrix multiplication being possible, it must be true that each row of $[A]$ has the same number of entries as each column of $[B]$. Since there are the same number of entries in the first row of $[A]$ and the first column of $[B]$, we multiply each entry in the first row of $[A]$ by its corresponding entry in the first column of $[B]$.

1st row, 1st column entry of the product = (the first row of $[A]$) × (the first column of $[B]$)

$= (5)(8) + (-2)(0) + (3)(-7) = 40 + 0 - 21 = 19$

2nd row, 1st column entry of the product = (the second row of [A]) × (the first column of [B])

= (1)(8) + (4)(0) + (0)(−7) = 8 + 0 + 0 = 8

Since [B] only had one column, we are done.

$$[A] \times [B] = \begin{bmatrix} 5 & -2 & 3 \\ 1 & 4 & 0 \end{bmatrix} \times \begin{bmatrix} 8 \\ 0 \\ -7 \end{bmatrix} = \begin{bmatrix} 19 \\ 8 \end{bmatrix}$$

Here's a slightly more elaborate example. We'll multiply these two matrices:

$$[C] = \begin{bmatrix} 4 & 6 \\ 6 & 9 \end{bmatrix} \qquad [A] = \begin{bmatrix} 5 & -2 & 3 \\ 1 & 4 & 0 \end{bmatrix}$$

[C] is a 2 × 2 matrix and [A] is a 2 × 3 matrix, so [C] × [A] will have to be a 2 × 3 matrix: it will have six entries in total, just as [A] does. Call the product matrix [P], so that [C] × [A] = [P]. For brevity, we'll introduce this notation: [P](r, c) = the entry in the rth row and cth column of [P]. Here we go!

[P](1, 1) = (the first row of [C]) × (the first column of [A])

= (4)(5) + (6)(1) = 20 + 6 = 26

[P](1, 2) = (the first row of [C]) × (the second column of [A])

= (4)(−2) + (6)(4) = −8 + 24 = 16

[P](1, 3) = (the first row of [C]) × (the third column of [A])

= (4)(3) + (6)(0) = 12 + 0 = 12

[P](2, 1) = (the second row of [C]) × (the first column of [A])

= (6)(5) + (9)(1) = 30 + 9 = 39

[P](2, 2) = (the second row of [C]) × (the second column of [A])

= (6)(−2) + (9)(4) = −12 + 36 = 24

[P](2, 3) = (the second row of [C]) × (the third column of [A])

= (6)(3) + (9)(0) = 18 + 0 = 18

Those are all six entries of [P]. We just have to put all of this together now:

$$[C] \times [A] = \begin{bmatrix} 4 & 6 \\ 6 & 9 \end{bmatrix} \times \begin{bmatrix} 5 & -2 & 3 \\ 1 & 4 & 0 \end{bmatrix} = \begin{bmatrix} 26 & 16 & 12 \\ 39 & 24 & 18 \end{bmatrix}$$

Here's a practice problem.

Practice Question

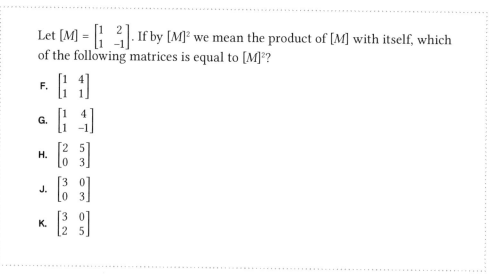

Let $[M] = \begin{bmatrix} 1 & 2 \\ 1 & -1 \end{bmatrix}$. If by $[M]^2$ we mean the product of $[M]$ with itself, which of the following matrices is equal to $[M]^2$?

F. $\begin{bmatrix} 1 & 4 \\ 1 & 1 \end{bmatrix}$

G. $\begin{bmatrix} 1 & 4 \\ 1 & -1 \end{bmatrix}$

H. $\begin{bmatrix} 2 & 5 \\ 0 & 3 \end{bmatrix}$

J. $\begin{bmatrix} 3 & 0 \\ 0 & 3 \end{bmatrix}$

K. $\begin{bmatrix} 3 & 0 \\ 2 & 5 \end{bmatrix}$

Answer and Explanation

Recall that, in matrix multiplication, we multiply the entries in each row of the first matrix with the entries in each column of the second matrix. Here, of course, both the first and second matrices are just $[M]$.

The following are the calculations for the four entries in the product matrix, $[M]^2$.

1st row, 1st column = (first row of first matrix) × (first column of second matrix)

$=(1)(1) + (2)(1) = 1 + 2 = 3$

1st row, 2nd column = (first row of first matrix) × (second column of second matrix)

$=(1)(2) + (2)(-1) = 2 - 2 = 0$

2nd row, 1st column = (first row of first matrix) × (first column of second matrix)

$=(1)(1) + (-1)(1) = 1 - 1 = 0$

2nd row, 2nd column = (second row of first matrix) × (second column of second matrix)

$=(1)(2) + (-1)(-1) = 2 + 1 = 3$

$[M]^2 = \begin{bmatrix} 3 & 0 \\ 0 & 3 \end{bmatrix}$

Answer: **J**

Summary

If you know and understand everything we've discussed in this math chapter, you're ready for your 36 on the ACT Math Test! Be careful, though: reading and saying "that makes sense" is not the same as understanding in action. Math is not a spectator sport. The only way you know you understand math is by *doing math*. We assume, as you moved through this chapter, that you completed all the practice questions that we provided. That's one level of understanding. For example, if you can solve two simultaneous equations immediately after reading a brief refresher on the topic, then that's great! The next level of understanding is to be able to handle a topic cold, out of the blue, and, with no reminder or refresher, be able to solve it from scratch. That happens only in mixed practice, with all the topics scrambled together, just as they will be on the real ACT Math Test. There's a full-length practice ACT Test at the end of this book that you may want either to use for math practice or to save for a full-length practice test. Other options for practice problems include Magoosh subscription math problems, the math sections of printed ACT practice tests, or math problems in other books. Practice, practice, practice. The more you're successful doing problems in the context of mixed practice, the more you know that you own each topic and can feel that you have the mastery you will need on test day.

ACT Math Concepts to Know

Integer Properties and Arithmetic

prime numbers: a positive integer greater than 1 that has no positive divisors other than 1 and itself

> *Important to know!* 2 is a prime number. The first 10 prime numbers are 2, 3, 5, 7, 11, 13, 17, 19, 23, and 29. Also important: 1 is NOT a prime number!

prime factor: one of the prime numbers that, when multiplied by another number, gives the original number

> *Examples:* The prime factors of 15 are 3 and 5. The prime factors of 18 are 3 and 2 because $3 \times 3 \times 2 = 18$.

multiple: the result of multiplying a certain number by an integer. Multiples can be positive OR negative.

> *Example:* When you learned your times tables, you were learning multiples. 4, 6, 8, and 10 are multiples of 2 because $2 \times 2 = 4$, $2 \times 3 = 6$, $2 \times 4 = 8$, and so on.

perfect square: a number that can be expressed as the product of two equal integers

> *Examples:* 1 (1×1), 4 (2×2), 9 (3×3), 81 (9×9), 625 (25×25)

greatest common factor (GCF): the greatest factor that divides two positive integers. To find the GCF, list the prime factors of each number, circle the pairs of factors both numbers have in common, and multiply those factors together.

> *Example:* The GCF of 12 $(2 \times 2 \times 3)$ and 30 $(2 \times 3 \times 5)$ is **6 (2×3)**. To check, make sure both 12 and 30 divide by 6.

least common multiple (LCM): the smallest positive integer that is divisible by two numbers. To find the LCM, list the prime factors of each number and multiply each factor by the greatest number of times it occurs in either number.

> *Example:* The LCM of 8 $(2 \times 2 \times 2)$ and 14 (2×7) is **56 $(2 \times 2 \times 2 \times 7)$**.

even and odd integers: Even integers can be divided evenly by two; odd integers cannot.

> *Examples:* 2, 4, 6, –2, –4, and 6 are all even. 1, 3, 5, –1, –3, and –5 are all odd.

operations of even and odd integers: It is an extremely helpful trick on the ACT to remember the following:

Addition:
even + even = **even**
odd + odd = **even**
even + odd = **odd**

Multiplication:
even × even = **even**
odd × odd = **odd**
even × odd = **even**

Subtraction:
even – even = **even**
odd – odd = **even**
even – odd = **odd**

remainder: the amount "left over" after dividing one integer by another to produce an integer quotient

> *Example:* You probably remember this from long division in elementary school:

```
      14  R1
3 | 43
  – 30
    13
  – 12
     1
```

positive and negative numbers: Positive numbers are greater than 0 and negative numbers are less than 0. 0 is neither positive nor negative!

Example: –1, –13, and –14,560 are negative numbers. 1, 13, and 14,560 are positive numbers

order of operations (PEMDAS): an acronym that helps you remember the order you must do operations in on an arithmetic problem:

1. Parentheses
2. Exponents
3. Multiplication
4. Division
5. Addition
6. Subtraction

Good to know! You may remember this better as "**P**lease **E**xcuse **M**y **D**ear **A**unt **S**ally."

rounding: a method used to make decimals shorter and simpler by leaving off some of the less significant values. For the digit you are rounding, if it is less than 5, round down, and if it is equal to or greater than 5, round up.

Examples: 23,459 rounded to the thousands place is 23,000 and rounded to the hundreds place is 23,500. 0.089 rounded to the tenths place is 0.1.

scientific notation: a method to handle very large or very small numbers without writing out all the digits. Simply count how many spaces you are moving the decimal point to the right or the left. There should always be one digit before the decimal point.

Examples: 5,340,000,000 is 5.34×10^9 and 0.0000000000425 is 4.25×10^{-11}

Fractions, Ratios, Percents, and Statistics

converting fractions to decimals: find a number you can multiply the denominator by to make it 10, 100, 1000, and so on. For example, to convert $\frac{1}{4}$ to a decimal, multiply the top and bottom by 25. This equals $\frac{25}{100}$. Take the number in the numerator and put the decimal point 2 spaces from the right, so $\frac{1}{4} = 0.25$.

Tip: It will help to memorize the decimal equivalents of common fractions.

Hint: The simplest method is to use your calculator. Simply type in the fraction and hit **Enter**: your calculator automatically will change it to a decimal.

converting decimals to fractions: Write down the decimal divided by 1, then multiply the top and bottom by 10 for every number after the decimal point. For example, to convert 0.62 to a fraction, multiply $\frac{0.62}{1}$ by $\frac{100}{100}$, which equals $\frac{62}{100}$. Now reduce: $\frac{62}{100} = \frac{31}{50}$.

Tip: It will help to memorize the decimal equivalents of common fractions.

Hint: The simplest method is to use your calculator. If you have something like a TI-83, press MATH then >FRAC.

adding and subtracting fractions: To add or subtract fractions, the denominators must be the same. Find a common denominator, convert the fractions, then add or subtract the numerators.

Example:

$$\frac{3}{4} + \frac{5}{6} = \frac{9}{12} + \frac{10}{12} = \frac{19}{12}$$

multiplying and dividing fractions:
To multiply, multiply the top numbers by each other and the bottom numbers by each other. To divide, "flip and multiply": flip the second fraction and multiply it by the first fraction.

Examples:

$$\frac{3}{4} \times \frac{5}{6} = \frac{15}{24} = \frac{5}{8} \qquad \frac{3}{4} \div \frac{5}{6} = \frac{3}{4} \times \frac{6}{5} = \frac{18}{20} = \frac{9}{10}$$

percents: A percent means parts per hundred. When expressed as a fraction, the denominator can be expressed as 100. When expressed a decimal, we simply move the decimal point two places to the left.

Examples:

$$75\% = \frac{75}{100} = \frac{3}{4}$$

$$23\% = \frac{23}{100}$$

$$75\% = 0.75$$

$$23\% = 0.23$$

percent increase and decrease: To calculate percent increase or decrease, find the difference between the two numbers you are comparing, then divide the result by the original number and multiply by 100.

$$percent\ increase = \frac{new\ number - original\ number}{original\ number} \times 100$$

$$percent\ decrease = \frac{original\ number - new\ number}{original\ number} \times 100$$

Examples:

percent increase from 24 to 36:
$$\frac{36 - 24}{24} \times 100 = 50\%$$

percent decrease from 36 to 24:
$$\frac{36 - 24}{36} \times 100 = 33.3\%$$

ratio: an expression that relates sizes of different groups or elements of a real-world situation

Example: There are 10 boys and 8 girls on the soccer team, so the ratio of boys to girls on the team is 5:4.

simple interest: The formula for simple interest, where A = the final value, P = the principal (original) amount, r = interest rate per period, and t = number of time periods, is $A = P(1 + rt)$.

Example: If Susan borrows \$4500 at a 10% annual interest rate, in 5 years, how much will she owe if she hasn't made any payments? **Answer:** $A = 4500(1 + 0.10 \times 5) = \$6750$.

compound interest: The formula for compound interest, where A = the final value, P = the principal (original) amount, r = interest rate per period, n = the number of times per year that interest is compounded, and t = number of years, is $A = P\left(1 + \frac{r}{n}\right)^{nt}$.

Example: In 3 years, how much money will \$1000 be worth if put in a savings account compounded monthly at 2% interest? **Answer:** $A = 1000\left(1 + \frac{0.02}{12}\right)^{(12)(3)} \cong \$1062$.

mean: The mean is the **average** of a set of numbers. $Mean = \frac{sum}{the\ number\ of\ things}$.

Example: What is the mean of Tony's exam scores if he scored 88, 93, 80, and 99 on his exams? **Answer:** Mean $= \frac{88 + 93 + 80 + 99}{4} = 90$.

median: The median is the middle number in a set of numbers if they were put into order.

Example: The median of −23, 29, 3, 84, and −2 is **3**. (*Hint:* If the set has an even number of items, the median is the average of the two middle numbers.)

mode: The mode is the most frequently occurring number in a set of numbers. *Note:* Not every set has a mode, and a set could have more than one mode.

Example: The mode of {3, 3, 2, 7, 6, 4, 3, 2} is **3**.

weighted average: an average resulting from multiplying each component by a factor indicating its importance

> *Example:* Many of your teachers probably use weighted averages to calculate your grades: homework might be worth 20%, participation 20%, and tests 60%, for example. If Angela has a homework grade of 98%, participation grade of 90%, and test grade of 82%, her final grade would be $(0.20)(98) + (0.20)(90) + (0.60)(82) = 86.8$.

factoring: the process of finding the factors of a number, basically splitting an expression into simpler expression

> *Example:* 2, 3, 5, 6, 10, and 15 are factors of 30 because $2 \times 15 = 30$, $3 \times 10 = 30$, and $6 \times 5 = 30$.

absolute value: the distance on the number line from a number to zero. For example, both 3 and -3 are a distance of 3 from zero, so both have an absolute value of 3. The absolute value of a positive number is simply that number, and to find the absolute value of a negative number, simply remove the negative sign in front of that number. Absolute value notation looks like this: $|-2|$.

> *Example:* The absolute value of -15, or $|-15|$, is 15.

Algebra, Exponents, and Roots

FOIL method: Foil helps us remember to how to distribute two binomials. FOIL stands for First (multiply the first terms in each), Outer (multiply the outer terms in each), Inner (multiply the inner terms in each), Last (multiply the last terms in each).

> *Example:*
>
> $$(2x + 4)(3x + 3)$$
> $$= (2x)(3x) + (2x)(3) + (4)(3x) + (4)(3)$$
> $$= 6x^2 + 6x + 12x + 12$$
> $$= 6x^2 + 18x + 12$$

inequalities: Inequalities are solved when the variable is isolated on one side of the inequality.

> *Example:*
>
> $$2x + 3 > 4x - 2$$
> $$2x + 5 > 4x$$
> $$5 > 2x$$
> $$\frac{5}{2} > x$$

inequalities with negative numbers: Remember that when multiplying or dividing by negative numbers in an inequality, you need to reverse the direction of the inequality (also known as flipping the sign)!

> *Example:*
>
> $$-2y > 3$$
> $$y < -\frac{3}{2}$$

absolute value inequalities: To solve absolute value inequalities, you need to find two solutions because the number could be either positive or negative.

> *Example:*
>
> $$|4x + 2| > 6$$
> $$-6 < 4x + 2 < 6$$

You can break it into two inequalities now:

$$-6 < 4x + 2 \qquad 4x + 2 < 6$$
$$-8 < 4x \qquad 4x < 4$$
$$-2 < x \qquad x < 1$$
$$-2 < x < 1$$

function: a special relationship where each input has a single output. Think of functions as machines that spit out certain values for each input. Functions are often written as $f(x)$ where x is the input value. *Hint:* it might be easier for you to think of $f(x)$ as a y when dealing with a basic equation.

> *Example:* If $f(x) = x + 2$, what does $f(4)$ equal? When $x = 4$, $f(4) = 4 + 2$, so $f(4) = 6$, making 6 our "output."

exponents: The exponent of a number tells how many times to use that number in a multiplication.

Example: $4^3 = 4 \times 4 \times 4 = 64$

negative exponents: A negative exponent tells us how many times to divide that number.

Example: $4^{-3} = 1 \div 4 \div 4 \div 4 = \frac{1}{64}$

adding and subtracting powers: To add or subtract exponents, the powers must be the same.

Example: $x^3 + x^3 = 2x^3$, but $x^2 + x^3$ **does not equal** x^5.

multiplying powers with the same base: To multiply exponents with the same base, add the exponents.

Example: $y^3 \times y^2 = y^5$

multiplying powers with different bases and same exponents: To multiply exponents with different bases and the same exponents, multiply the bases together and keep the exponent the same.

Examples: $y^4 \times z^4 = (yz)^4$;
$2^2 \times 3^2 = (2 \times 3)^2 = 6^2 = 36$

dividing exponents with the same base: To divide exponents with the same base, subtract the exponents.

Example: $y^5 \div y^2 = y^3$

dividing powers with different bases: To divide exponents with different bases, divide the bases and keep the exponent the same.

Examples: $y^4 \div z^4 = \left(\frac{y}{z}\right)^4$; $6^2 \div 3^2 = \left(\frac{6}{3}\right)^2 = 2^2 = 4$

square root: The square root of a number x is a number y whose square $(y \times y)$ equals x.

Example: 3 is a square root of 9 because $3 \times 3 = 9$.

cube root: The cube root of a number x is a number y whose cube $(y \times y \times y)$ equals x.

Example: 3 is a cube root of 27 because $3 \times 3 \times 3 = 27$.

rationalizing radical expressions: the process of getting rid of all the radicals that are in the denominator of a fraction. To rationalize, simplify the radicals and fractions if necessary, and then multiply both the top and bottom by a radical that will get rid of the radical in the denominator.

Example: $\frac{2}{\sqrt{6}} = \frac{2}{\sqrt{6}} \times \frac{\sqrt{6}}{\sqrt{6}} = \frac{2\sqrt{6}}{6} = \frac{\sqrt{6}}{3}$

Geometry

acute angle: an angle measuring less than 90°

obtuse angle: an angle measuring greater than 90° but less than 180°

right angle: an angle measuring 90°

area of a triangle: The formula for the area of a triangle is $\frac{1}{2}(base \times height)$. *Hint:* Remember this is because a right triangle can be considered to be half of a rectangle and the area of a rectangle is *base × height*. *Note:* Any of the three sides of a triangle can be the base, and the "height" is a line perpendicular to that base that extends from the base to the opposite vertex.

Example: Area of the shaded triangle below $= \frac{5 \times 3}{2} = 15$.

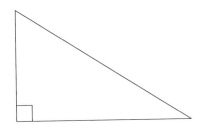

right triangle: A right triangle has one angle of 90°.

Good to know! Memorizing the common ratios of sides in a Pythagorean triple triangle can save you time on the ACT. Here are the ones to know: (3, 4, 5), (5, 12, 13), (7, 24, 25), (8, 15, 17).

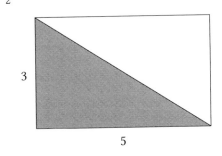

similar triangles: triangles that have corresponding (the same) angles and proportional sides. Think of them as mama and baby triangles that look alike, just one is bigger.

Important to know! You can find the missing sides of similar triangles by setting up proportions.

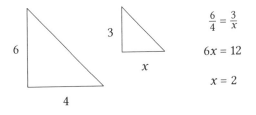

$$\frac{6}{4} = \frac{3}{x}$$
$$6x = 12$$
$$x = 2$$

special right triangles: Memorizing the side ratios of the special right triangles can save you a lot of time on the ACT. The respective sides of **30-60-90** triangles are in the ratio: $1:\sqrt{3}:2$. The respective sides of **45-45-90** triangles are in the ratio: $1:1:\sqrt{2}$.

estimating ACT figures: It's important to know that unless the figure says otherwise, ACT geometry figures are all drawn roughly to scale. You can use this knowledge to estimate side lengths and angles.

perimeter: To find the perimeter of a figure, add up all of the side lengths.

Important to know! Remember that opposite sides in a rectangle are equal to one another.

area of a parallelogram: A parallelogram is a shape with two sets of parallel sides. The area of a parallelogram is base × height.

Important to know: Remember the height may not be the length of a side!

regular polygon: A regular polygon is a multi-sided shape that has all equal angles and sides of the same length.

area of circle: $A = \pi r^2$, where A is the area and r is the radius.

circumference of a circle: $C = 2\pi r$, where C is the circumference and r is the radius.

arc: An arc is a fraction of the circumference of a circle. To find the length of an arc, you can set up a proportion of $\frac{arc\ length}{circumference}$ to $\frac{central\ angle}{360°}$.

Example: What is the length of arc ST if the radius of the circle is 3? Remember that circumference is $2\pi r$, so the circumference of the circle is 6π.

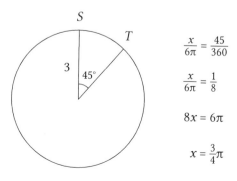

$$\frac{x}{6\pi} = \frac{45}{360}$$

$$\frac{x}{6\pi} = \frac{1}{8}$$

$$8x = 6\pi$$

$$x = \frac{3}{4}\pi$$

sector: A sector is a fraction of the area of a circle. To find the area of a sector, you can set up a proportion of $\frac{sector\ area}{entire\ area}$ to $\frac{central\ angle}{360°}$.

Example: What is the area of the sector if the radius of the circle is 3? Remember area is πr^2, so the area of the circle is 9π.

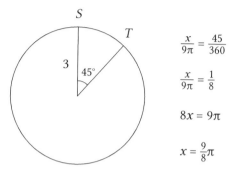

$$\frac{x}{9\pi} = \frac{45}{360}$$

$$\frac{x}{9\pi} = \frac{1}{8}$$

$$8x = 9\pi$$

$$x = \frac{9}{8}\pi$$

volume: Volume is the amount of space inside a 3D object. **Volume formulas you should know:**

Rectangular solid: $V = length × width × height$

Sphere: $V = \frac{4}{3}\pi r^3$

Right cylinder: $V = \pi r^2 h$

trapezoid: A trapezoid is a quadrilateral with exactly two parallel sides. The area of a trapezoid is

$$A = \left(\frac{b_1 + b_2}{2}\right)h$$

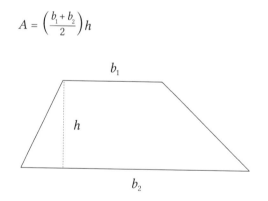

cylinder: A cylinder is a 3D shape with two identical bases that are circular.

Good to know! The volume of a right cylinder is $\pi r^2 \times height$.

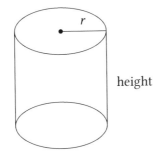

sphere: A sphere is the set of all points in 3D space that are equidistant from a fixed point, the center; the sphere is the only 3D shape whose profile or silhouette from any direction is a circle. The surface of, say, a marble or a billiard ball is a sphere.

Good to know: the volume of a sphere = $\frac{4}{3}\pi r^3$.

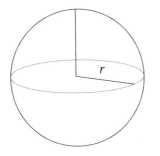

Coordinate Geometry

slope: The slope of a line tells us the direction and the steepness of a line. You are probably more familiar with it as rise over run (or change in y over change in x).

$$\text{slope} = \frac{y_2 - y_1}{x_2 - x_2}$$

slope-intercept form: The equation of a line in slope-intercept form is $y = mx + b$, where m is the slope and b is the y-intercept.

Important to know! This is the most useful form of a straight-line equation on the ACT, as it immediately gives information about the slope and y-intercept. If a line equation is not in this form, try to shift it around to this form.

standard form equation of a line: $ax + by = c$

Important to know! This is the form in which you will most often see equations of lines written on ACT questions, but it is not as useful as **slope-intercept form** or **point-slope form**.

point-slope form: The equation of a line in point-slope form is $y - y_1 = m(x - x_1)$. Point-slope form is useful because it allows you to plug in a point (x_1, y_1) and find the equation of a line.

Important to know! If you are given a point on a line in an ACT question, use point-slope form to figure out more information about that line.

x- and y-intercepts: The intercepts of a graph are where the line or curve crosses the x- or y-axis.

Important to know! To find the y-intercept, plug in 0 for x and solve for y. To find the x-intercept, plug in 0 for y and solve for x.

reflections: When you reflect a point across the x-axis, the x-coordinate remains the same, but the y-coordinate is transformed into its opposite. When you reflect a point across the x-axis, the x-coordinate remains the same, but the y-coordinate is transformed into its opposite.

Good to know! When you reflect a point, line, or curve across a line, think of the line as serving as a mirror. Where would the reflection of each point be in the mirror?

rotations: In a rotation of 90° about the origin, point $(A, B) \Rightarrow (-B, A)$. In a rotation of 180°, point $(A, B) \Rightarrow (-A, -B)$. In a rotation of 270°, point $(A, B) \Rightarrow (B, -A)$.

> *Hint:* If you have trouble visualizing what a rotated figure would look like, simply rotate your test book the number of degrees mentioned in the question.

equation of a circle: The equation of circle is $(x - h)^2 + (y - k)^2 = r^2$, where (h, k) is center of the circle and r is the radius.

graphing inequalities: To find a solution to a linear inequality on the coordinate plane, first find the equation as if it were a line. If the inequality says $y <$ that line, then shade below that line for the solution. If the inequality says $y >$ that line, then shade above that line for the solution.

> *Good to know!* If the inequality is "less than or equal to" or "greater than or equal to," then the line (and points on it) is included in the solution.

parabola: a special curve shaped like an arc; the graph of a quadratic function is a parabola. The **standard form** of a parabola is $y = ax^2 + bx + c$. The **vertex form** is $y = a(x - h)^2 + k$, where (h, k) is the vertex. If $a > 0$, then the parabola opens upwards. If $a < 0$, then it opens downward.

> *Good to know!* If the absolute value of $a < 1$, the graph of the parabola widens. If the absolute value of $a > 1$, the graph becomes narrower.

translations: A translation slides every point on a figure the same distance in a certain direction. Translations in quadratics will appear on the ACT. The basic quadratic equation is $f(x) = x^2$. Adding or subtracting values outside of the x shifts the graph up for addition and down for

subtraction. Adding or subtracting values with x shifts the graph to the left for addition and right for subtraction.

> *Examples:* $f(x) = x^2 + 2$ shifts the graph up 2 units. $f(x) = (x - 3)^2$ shifts the graph to the right 3 units.

Trigonometry

SOHCAHTOA: SOHCAHTOA is a mnemonic that helps us remember how to compute the sine, cosine, and tangent of an angle.

$$sine = \frac{opposite}{hypotenuse}$$

$$cosine = \frac{adjacent}{hypotenuse}$$

$$tangent = \frac{opposite}{adjacent}$$

reciprocal identities:

$$\text{Secant } \theta \text{ (sec)} = \frac{1}{\cos \theta}$$

$$\text{Cosecant } \theta \text{ (csc)} = \frac{1}{\sin \theta}$$

$$\text{Cotangent } \theta \text{ (cot)} = \frac{1}{\tan \theta}$$

Pythagorean identity: The Pythagorean identity is $\sin^2 \theta + \cos^2 \theta = 1$.

law of sines: The law of sines is

$$\frac{\sin(A)}{a} = \frac{\sin(B)}{b} = \frac{\sin(C)}{c}$$

law of cosines: The law of cosines is

$$c^2 = a^2 + b^2 - 2ab \times \cos(C)$$

unit circle: A unit circle is a circle with a radius of 1; the equation of the unit circle is $x^2 + y^2 = 1$. The unit circle is useful in trigonometry. Angles are measured starting from the positive x-axis in quadrant 1 and continuing counterclockwise. For the ACT, you should definitely know the radian measures of the axes and in which quadrants the trig functions are positive or negative.

Important to know! The mnemonic **A**ll **S**tudents **T**ake **C**alculus can help you remember where functions are positive: Q1: all, Q2: sine, Q3: tangent, Q4: cosine.

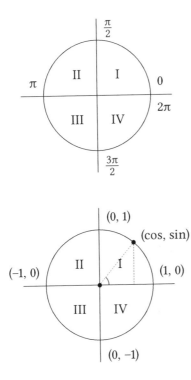

radian: an alternate system of measuring the size of angles. Unlike degrees, radians are based on inherent properties of the circle. The measure of an angle in radians equals the number of radius-lengths in the arc of the angle. For example, the angle all the way around a circle, 360°, is 2π radians, precisely because the circumference has a length of $2\pi r$.

converting degrees to radians: To convert degrees to radians, multiply by $\frac{\pi}{180}$.

Example: Convert 270° to radians. $270 \times \frac{\pi}{180} = \frac{3\pi}{2}$

converting radians to degrees: To convert radians to degrees, multiply by $\frac{180}{\pi}$.

Example: Convert $\frac{3\pi}{2}$ to degrees. $\frac{3\pi}{2} \times \frac{180}{\pi} = 270°$

inverse trig functions: Inverse trig functions are used to obtain an angle measure from any of the angle's trigonometric ratios. They are written, for example, as $\sin^{-1}\theta$ or $\arcsin\theta$.

Example: What is $\arcsin\left(\frac{1}{2}\right)$? (The ACT will give you a table of values or a diagram to solve this, or you can use your calculator.) ***Answer:*** 30°.

Advanced Topics

fundamental counting principle (FCP): The FCP is a way to figure out the total number of ways different events can occur. If there are a ways for one activity to occur and b ways for a second activity to occur, and then there are $a \times b$ ways for both to occur.

Example: Mattie has 3 pants, 4 jackets, and 6 shirts to choose from for an outfit. How many possible outfits can she make? $3 \times 4 \times 6 = 72$ possible outfits.

quadratic formula: The quadratic formula can be used to find solutions to quadratic equations ($ax^2 + bx + c = 0$). The quadratic formula is:

$$x = \frac{-b \pm \sqrt{b^2 - 4ac}}{2a}$$

Plug in the values and solve for x! (The plus-minus sign means you'll get two results).

imaginary numbers: An imaginary number is one that when squared gives a negative result. $i^2 = -1$. You can add, subtract, multiply, and divide complex numbers. To simplify an expression, you can multiply a fraction by $\frac{i}{i}$, which would create an i^2 that can then be simplified to -1.

Important to know! For the purposes of the ACT, you should remember the pattern for imaginary numbers: $i^1 = i$, $i^2 = -1$, $i^3 = -i$, $i^4 = 1$, and then the pattern continues to repeat.

complex number: the sum of a real number and an imaginary number. For example, $z = 2 + 2i$ is a complex number.

logarithms: Logarithms are the inverses of exponents; they undo exponentials. $N = b^k$ is equivalent to $\log_b N = k$.

Example: Evaluate $\log_3 9$. $\log_3 9 \Rightarrow 9 = 3^x$, $x = 2$

fundamental logarithm law #1:

$$\log_b b^k = k$$

fundamental logarithm law #2:

$$N = b^{\log_b N}$$

logarithm law for a product of powers:

$$\log_b(M \times N) = \log_b M + \log_b N$$

logarithm law for a quotient of powers:

$$\log_b\left(\frac{M}{N}\right) = \log_b M - \log_b N$$

logarithm law for an exponent:

$$\log_b N^p = p \times \log_b N$$

change of base formula: The change of base formula is $\log_b x = \dfrac{\log x}{\log b}$.

Good to know! This allows you to turn logarithmic expressions into ones you can easily plug into your calculator.

permutation: A permutation is all possible arrangements of a collection of things (order matters).

$$_n P_r = \frac{n!}{(n - r)!}$$

Example: If we have a pool of 6 students, and we select 3 to sit in row, the number of ordered arrangements of 3 of the students could be done in $_6 P_3$ ways. $_6 P_3 = \dfrac{6!}{(6 - 3)!}$, which is 120.

combination: A combination is an arrangement of things in which order does not matter.

$$_n C_r = \frac{n!}{r!(n - r)!}$$

Example: If we have a pool of 8 students, and we select 4 to be on a team, the number of possible teams is $_8 C_4 = \dfrac{8!}{4!(8 - 4)!}$, which is 70.

matrices: A matrix is a rectangular array of numbers defined by the number of rows and columns it contains, in that order (e.g., a 2 × 3 matrix has 2 rows and 3 columns).

Example of a 2 × 3 matrix:

$$\begin{bmatrix} 3 & 4 & 7 \\ 2 & 3 & 1 \end{bmatrix}$$

scalar multiplication of a matrix: Scalar multiplication is multiplying a matrix by an ordinary number. To do this, multiply each entry by that number.

Example:

$$2 \times \begin{bmatrix} 3 & 4 & 7 \\ 2 & 3 & 1 \end{bmatrix} = \begin{bmatrix} 6 & 8 & 14 \\ 4 & 6 & 2 \end{bmatrix}$$

adding matrices: In order to add matrices, the matrices need to have the exact same dimensions. If this is the case, then add or subtract the corresponding pairs of entries.

Example:

$$\begin{bmatrix} 8 & -9 \\ -4 & -5 \end{bmatrix} + \begin{bmatrix} 4 & -4 \\ 2 & 8 \end{bmatrix} = \begin{bmatrix} 12 & -13 \\ -2 & 3 \end{bmatrix}$$

Need a study break? Have fun coloring!

Your College Search

Let's take a break from all this studying to remember why you're doing all this in the first place: to pursue your college dreams.

Notice that we said "your" college dreams. Despite all the talk about a "college search," the vast majority of college applicants never truly search for a school themselves. What often happens is that students make a list of colleges that their friends, parents, and counselors like, or they simply apply to schools that they've seen on a lot of t-shirts or TV shows. That's a fairly impersonal way to create a college list!

More importantly, that's not nearly as exciting or motivating as finding a college that is the best fit for the next phase in *your* educational journey. (An added bonus is that you'll create some certainty for yourself: knowing what college you want to go to will help you figure out your ACT score goals.)

Here's a process you can use to reflect on and figure out what you want in a college:

Step 1: Take a Self-Inventory

Ask yourself these questions: What do I like and dislike about my current school? How do I learn best? Do I like to study alone or with a group? Do I like to have personal interactions with my teachers? Do I like socializing in large or small groups? Does climate have a serious impact on me? Do I need or want to be close to home? Do I like to be involved in a lot of activities? Do I need school spirit? Sports? Theater?

There are so many questions to ask and lots of resources for self-assessments out there. Taking stock of what you want and need will help you know what to look for as you research schools.

Step 2: Establish Your Must-Haves

Take a look at the following list of criteria and determine your requirements for each category. Are there any deal-breakers? Are there any you don't have particularly strong feelings about? Be careful when eliminating anything you aren't sure about at this point: If you've never seen a small liberal arts school before, how do you know you don't want to go to one? If you don't know, then take some college tours before you rule anything out.

Curriculum: Have you already decided on a major to pursue? Do you want to make sure you have options? Do you want to have a core curriculum or total freedom? Do you want to double major? Do you want to design your own major?

Location: Is it important for you to be close to/far from home? In a certain geographical region or climate?

Size: Small? Medium? Large? Mega? Don't forget to consider the size of the individual program you're looking at, not just the whole school. This has an impact on how much contact you'll have with those impressive professors you've read about on the departments' websites, particularly in your first year or two of college.

Resources: Do you need specific resources for learning needs or psychological, social, or medical concerns? Do you desire a strong cultural or ethnic group support network? Do you want robust internship or research opportunities?

Activities: What types of activities are you interested in participating in while in college, both on and off campus? What type of leadership, service, and study abroad opportunities would you like to pursue?

Cost and Financial Aid: How much can you/your family afford to pay for college? What level of financial aid do you need?

Step 3: Research, Explore, and Visit

Once you've determined what you are looking for in a college experience, you can begin exploring schools that meet your criteria. College Navigator (nces.ed.gov/collegenavigator) and College Scorecard (collegescorecard.ed.gov) are good tools to launch your college search based on the criteria you've established. You can also check out our list of the best "Free College Search Resources" on our Magoosh ACT blog (magoosh.com/hs)!

Once you've developed an exploratory list, lay out a plan for visits. If you don't have the time or means to visit colleges far away, pick a selection of different types of schools within a day's drive. Even if you definitely don't want to go to, say, the small liberal arts college half an hour away, seeing the campus can still give you an understanding of what a school of that size feels like. Plan out a handful of weekend trips to visit two to four schools each weekend (any more than that and they'll all start to run together in your mind).

For the schools you can't visit (and even for the ones you can), do research online, get on mailing lists, visit with the rep when they come to your school, talk to current students and alumni, and go to college fairs. Learn as much as you can!

Step 4: Refine Your List

Once you've done your exploration, refine your college list. The length of this list can vary. Some students have three or four schools, while others have 15. Whatever you do, make sure to cover your bases. You should have a balance of good bets (schools you have more than a 75 percent chance of getting into), targets (schools you have a 25 percent to 75 percent chance of getting into), and reaches (schools you have less than a 25 percent chance of getting into). Of course, there's no hard-and-fast formula that will give you exact odds of admission, but make an educated guess based on the data you currently have.

Step 5: Express Your Interest

Now that *you* know which schools you are interested in, make sure *they* know it, too! Take advantage of opportunities for interviews and meetings with representatives and alumni; get on their mailing lists. Even if these contacts don't seem to lead anywhere, when it comes time for your application, you'll be able to check off all sorts of boxes that show your demonstrated interest in the school. Your essays will reflect your efforts. Go to each school's website and find the admissions representative who will be reading your application (sometimes this is based on the alphabet or geography, sometimes on other criteria). This person is going to be your contact throughout the admissions process. Definitely don't pester him or her, but don't hesitate to reach out if you have important questions or if you need to follow up with information regarding your application.

Remember, this is YOUR college search! All sorts of people—from your parents to your friends to your teachers—are going to have their own thoughts about it. Listen to them, but don't be swayed by the opinions of others. If you have a better sense of who you are and what you want in a school, you'll be much less likely to fall into this trap and far more likely to fall in love with your chosen school once you get there.

Intro to Financial Aid

For high school seniors everywhere, navigating the ins and outs of financial aid can be completely confusing. So many deadlines, so many forms, so many weird acronyms that would make interesting band names (FAFSA NATION, anyone?).

In all honesty, everything can get a bit overwhelming. In this section, we'll guide you through the basics of the process step by step.

But first of all, the big question . . .

Why do I need financial aid?

College is a wallet demolisher. Costs not only include tuition but also room and board, textbooks, personal and travel expenses, and, well, you name it. It's expensive! More and more students these days are graduating with enormous amounts of debt—you can help avoid this by thinking early about how to maximize the amount of financial aid you're eligible for.

There is a nifty calculator on finaid.org for calculating how much federal financial aid you could qualify for based on your EFC (Estimated Family Contribution). Even if you don't think you will qualify for much aid, you should try anyway. You never know what you might qualify for!

Financial aid can come in the form of institution-based financial aid, given out by the school; federal aid; and separate scholarships run by private organizations. They are all potentially critical sources of aid.

Deadlines

The FAFSA, CSS, scholarship applications, Cal grants, tax return information . . . there are so many forms to send in! Most colleges have a specific deadline for aid applications, so make sure you find out what the deadlines are for your schools.

First things first: before you start this process, it's important to write down *all* of your deadlines for *all* of the schools to which you're applying.

For many colleges, these forms are due at the beginning of February. Other colleges have deadlines in March or even April or May. If you can't find deadline information on one of your colleges, call the Admissions Office! It won't hurt to check.

So . . . what are all these forms I have to submit?

The most popular and well-known form is the infamous FAFSA.

It stands for the "Free Application for Federal Student Aid." As the name says, it's completely free, and if you enter your financial info and submit your application, you can receive an estimate for how much aid the government can give you. This application is nice because you can submit the same one to all of your schools. Within a few weeks of submitting the FAFSA, a paper Student Aid Report will be mailed to you, detailing information from your FAFSA and your Expected Family Contribution. If you also provided an email address, you'll receive a link to your results after just a few days.

Overall, the FAFSA is a bit faster and easier to complete than the other major financial aid form.

CSS

Not every school requires the "College Scholarship Service"—in fact, many schools only require the FAFSA! There are about 200 colleges, however, that do require the

CSS Profile. These colleges include a lot of the top schools, like Ivy League universities. Check with your school (or potential school) to see if it requires this form. Otherwise, you might be missing out on a huge portion of financial aid.

Using information provided on the CSS, schools will compute how much institutional aid you are eligible for. If your Estimated Family Contribution is less than the college's tuition fees, you might qualify for need-based financial aid.

Institution-Specific Financial Aid Documents

Some schools have their own separate financial aid forms as well. These institution-specific forms can be difficult to find, and the best way to find out if they even exist (and then where they are) is to ask the admissions office. Make sure you know if any of your schools require this.

Other

Merit Aid

This is another type of student aid that is awarded based on your test scores and other factors, such as your academic, athletic, or musical achievements. These types of awards aren't tied to your financial situation. It's less common than need-based aid, but it's worth checking out. You may have an achievement or skill that can help fund your tuition. For example, National Merit and National Achievement scholars may sometimes qualify for merit aid at their chosen colleges.

Private Scholarships

Sometimes, you can receive an institutionally based scholarship just by sending in your application. No extra forms needed. There are tons of other scholarships out there, however, that require a little bit more initiative on your part.

Spend some time searching online for scholarships that are being offered locally, or scholarships that pertain to your demographic, career goals, major choice, high school, etc. There are tons of these out there and they can really add up. It's also worth checking with your high school counselor about scholarships other students at your school have qualified for in the past.

There's a lot more information out there, but what you'll need to do will depend on your individual circumstances. While this is just a brief glance into college financial aid options, it should help clear up the process for you!

Don't let the cost of college get you down or automatically assume it will be an obstacle to your college dreams. With the right financial aid, no school is out of reach.

Chapter 7

ACT Reading Test

Each of us has a specific kind of "reading brain," or a way we approach certain kinds of texts. For example, few of us will squeal with excitement when a 17th-century treatise on the structure of parliamentary government is dropped in our laps (even making it through that description can be tough going!). Hand us the ninth installment in a series about a famous British wizard, though, and our brains will be riveted for days.

As high school students, you've trained your brain not only to read stuff that you probably aren't very interested in (yes, we're talking about schoolwork) but also to read it in such a way that you absorb each detail, understand every word, and slowly figure out how everything comes together. After all, you'll be tested on it the next morning (and yes, procrastinators, we're referring to you).

But when it comes to ACT prep, your "reading brain" has to do something it likely isn't used to, because ACT texts are a whole different ball game. And so your brain gets confused. Throw in a ticking clock, and it can get downright discombobulated.

That's because while our English classes teach us how to *read* critically, we usually aren't taught how to *skim* critically. In other words, you're used to doing one thing (reading to absorb and retain), and now you're forced to rush through mountains of text on a totally unfamiliar topic—only to have to answer a handful of questions on whatever obscure topic it might be and then forget everything you just read about the topic, immediately moving on to the next one.

So the first thing you need to do on the ACT Reading Test—before learning question types and passage types, how to eliminate wrong answer choices, etc.—is to train your "reading brain" to read an ACT passage.

If this seems silly to you ("I like my reading brain just the way it is!"), remember that the ACT is a test for college preparedness. And guess what kind of reading brain typical college graduates—who've spent the last four to five years of their lives reading hundreds of pages a night—have? Yep, not the kind where they cram lots of details in their heads to ace the next day's quiz, but the kind where they scan a text with

Many believe that the hardest English language novel to read is *Finnegans Wake* by James Joyce. The book contains its own dialect comprised of words from languages living and dead, and a unique stream-of-consciousness narrative style: "Rot a peck of pa's malt had Jhem or Shen brewed by arclight and rory end to the regginbrow was to be seen ringsome on the aquaface."

purpose, looking at the overall structure and ideas, the location of important details (but not necessarily the details themselves!), and other text features. This will probably sound totally foreign, but don't worry: we're about to show you exactly how to train your brain to do it!

Before we get into training mode, though, let's quickly go over what the ACT Reading Test is going to assess you on.

At a Glance

What to Know

- Reading is the third section of the ACT.
- You have a 35-minute time limit.
- You will read four passages (one fiction, one social science, one humanities, and one natural science).
- You will see 40 multiple-choice questions (10 for each passage).

What to Study and Practice

- If you aren't reading regularly, start now. Read high-quality fiction and nonfiction, such as newspapers and news magazines covering a variety of topics (think: the *New York Times*, the *New Yorker*, the *Economist*, and *Scientific American*).
- Active reading. Whenever you read something new, practice:
  - Determining the main idea of the entire piece as well as individual paragraphs
  - Finding cause-effect relationships
  - Figuring out the sequence of events
  - Understanding the author's tone and purpose

  (*The ACT will test you on all of the above!*)
- Vocabulary, but *only* if it is a real weakness of yours. The ACT won't test you on very difficult words, but you'll see a few "word-in-context" vocabulary questions, and you'll need a solid high school-level vocabulary to fully understand the passages.

What Not to Study

- Subject-specific knowledge. (Although we at Magoosh are fans of knowledge in general, everything you need to answer the reading questions will be contained within the passages, whether you're familiar with the topic or not.)
- Difficult vocabulary words. (You get a break here!)

Overview

What Does the ACT Reading Test Assess?

- The ACT Reading Test assesses your ability to read through lots of text and pick up on the general ideas contained in the paragraphs, as well as the general idea of each passage.
- It does **not** test your ability to learn the information in the passages. You just have to be able to answer the questions correctly.
- Success on the ACT Reading Test requires learning how to read the passages within the time constraints while still picking up enough information from the passages to answer the questions.

Is the ACT Trying to Trick You?

- Not really! Trap answers exist on the ACT for students who skim far too quickly or are looking at the wrong passage by accident. They don't tend to be as tricky as trap answers on the SAT (if studying for both tests, it's good to develop strategies for each specific test—more on this soon).

Top Tips for the ACT Reading Test

1. Don't go to the answer choices first!
2. Go to the passage first.
3. You'll *always* find clear evidence in the passage that answers the questions (try not to "convince yourself" of the right answer; if you need convincing you're probably on the wrong track).
4. When going back to the passage, know what the question is asking (in other words, what you're looking for in the passage), where to look for that info, and (the step that most students ignore at their peril!), how to put the answer in your own words. This is where you, not the answer choices, do the thinking.
5. Don't spend your time going back and forth between answer choices. The information that answers the question will always be located somewhere in the passage. Good ACT test-takers are those who can find the information quickly and aren't duped into choosing an answer choice just because it "sounds right."

How to Read an ACT Passage

1. **Focus on the topic sentence of each paragraph.** Typically, the first sentence will tell you what the paragraph is about. The sentences following will provide details building off of the topic sentence. Sometimes, when we rush, we plow through the topic sentence without slowing down a moment to think, "so this is what the paragraph will talk about." Even if the first sentence isn't a topic sentence, there usually will be one soon after.

   Another way of looking at this is to remember that not every sentence is created equally. The first sentence of the entire passage is often very important (sometimes the most important!) as are the topic sentences of each paragraph. To understand what the passage is about, and to make more sense out of the details in the paragraph, it's a good idea to pay special attention to the first sentence of each paragraph.

2. **Understand the main point of each paragraph.** Focusing on the topic sentence doesn't mean ignoring what follows. The rest of the paragraph is important, too, but you don't want to get bogged down in the details. Again, you won't be tested on the nitty-gritty, but on the big ideas. By the end of each paragraph, you should be able to summarize what the paragraph was about.

   Let's take a look at this paragraph and put that strategy into practice:

   Edmund Burke, the British writer of political theory, believed government had been improved by every preceding generation up to his own. He saw the successive effort of early Greek democracies and Byzantine emperors and the rules set forth by the Magna Carta coalescing into a consummately effective—though far from perfect—society. In his eyes, the British parliamentary system of his day represented the realization of all of the efforts theretofore drawn together by the work of Enlightenment philosophers in the 18th century. It was the fullest expression of liberty balanced with order yet known to man. A deep sense of gratitude to his forbears reigned in every word from his lips and from his pen.

And yes, we chose a tough passage—that was intentional! After all, it's relatively easy to skim a paragraph and get the general meaning when the writing is straightforward and the paragraph is fewer than 10 lines long. The writing here is dry, the vocabulary aggressive, and the subject matter pretty obscure.

When you read this, by the time you get to the part in the middle about "coalescing into a consummately effective ...," you might already be scratching your head as to what the paragraph is about. You might read faster to get to the end, hoping that you'll "get" what the paragraph is about, or you might try to read the same sentence over and over again (don't!).

Instead, focus on the topic sentence, which we'll slightly paraphrase here: "Burke ... believed government was improved by each generation up till the present."

Now we can deduce that the long, convoluted sentence about Byzantine emperors right after the intro just gives a specific example of that idea. Do you have to understand every word to do that? No—you just have to understand the function of the sentence. (If a specific question happens to ask about this sentence, then you can return to it later and read more closely.)

On your ACT, you should shoot to get a little bit more than just the function of the sentence, when you can. A good strategy is to paraphrase, or simplify, using your own words. Let's take a look at that tough sentence:

> *He saw the successive effort of early Greek democracies and Byzantine emperors and the rules set forth by the Magna Carta coalescing into a consummately effective— though far from perfect—society.*

Here's one way to paraphrase it: "Greek government stuff and Byzantine emperors and Magna Carta all built on each other to make an effective society." Or even simpler, "different kinds of government led to the government Burke had" (notice how similar that is to the topic sentence).

The next sentence identifies his specific government: the parliamentary system, which offered the most liberty to date, as the following sentence mentions. By the time you get to the last sentence, you have the main point of the paragraph. There's no need to get tripped up by the word "forbears," or any phrase in the last sentence. You've got the main idea, which is some variant of "All governments from way back built on each other to create Burke's great free society."

3. **Take a quick "mental snapshot" of each paragraph.** Is that sentence we just came up with about governments a wonderful sentence? No, it's pretty poorly written. But that's not the point, because you're not writing all of this out in the margin, nor are you writing an AP English paper on the passage. The paraphrase is something that you should ideally be doing in your head, after you finish each paragraph.

We call it "taking a mental snapshot," and it requires pausing for a few seconds to summarize the paragraph in your own words.

You might think, "no way, that'll slow me down." But if you practice it regularly, the exact opposite happens. Because you are invested in the passage and thinking about what you've read, you aren't rereading certain parts or getting to the middle of the passage only to realize you aren't sure what you are reading.

Additionally, when you're doing the question and it's time to go back to the passage, you'll have a far better idea of where to look for information.

4. **Watch out for "rough patches."** It's tempting to reread the difficult parts or slow down when you come across them. But you'll notice something about these "rough patches": they usually come at the middle or the end of the passage. Remember that the most important part is the topic sentence, which often summarizes the main point of the paragraph.

So why not just read the topic sentence of each paragraph? Well, you might actually want to do that if you are running out of time. But we don't suggest that as a general approach, mostly because you'll lose the connections between ideas and the way paragraphs flow together. You can walk away from the passage with a disjointed sense of the meaning. If every other sentence in the paragraph were difficult, it might still make sense as a strategy. But there's usually just one rough patch in a paragraph, and some paragraphs don't contain any rough patches at all!

5. **Don't read parts over and over.** Remember this sentence? Yes, we know, it'll probably end up giving you nightmares:

> *He saw the successive effort of early Greek democracies and Byzantine emperors and the rules set forth by the Magna Carta coalescing into a consummately effective—though far from perfect—society.*

The first time you encounter them, sentences like that one will probably be difficult to paraphrase. You might not even get to the end of them before throwing up your hands and muttering something that doesn't bear repeating.

Unfortunately, the temptation is to go back and reread and then re-reread such a sentence, your face turning tomato red. But we're telling you to skip that! Your comprehension of the passage will not fall apart because of this sentence. On the other hand, by rereading this sentence several times and taking yourself "out" of the passage, your general comprehension will likely suffer. Besides that, you'll be totally flustered, and that doesn't bode well for the three sections of the test that you have yet to get to.

Just to show you how unimportant many of these rough patches are, we're going to remove the sentence from the paragraph:

> *Edmund Burke, the British writer of political theory, believed government had been improved by every preceding generation up to his own. In his eyes, the British parliamentary system of his day represented the realization of all of the efforts theretofore drawn together by the work of Enlightenment philosophers in the 18th century. It was the fullest expression of liberty balanced with order yet known to man. A deep sense of gratitude to his forbears reigned in every word from his lips and from his pen.*

Nothing has really changed. The point is still that his society resulted from the work of previous people and that it was a great improvement ("fullest expression of liberty").

So the next time you're reading a tough passage (and we recommend applying these techniques ASAP), force yourself to a) take mental snapshots and b) not reread any sentence (unless it's a topic sentence, which will be relatively straightforward anyhow).

And we promise that there won't be any quiz on that one sentence you just happened to skip, nor will there likely be a test question about it.

6. **Simplify difficult-to-read proper nouns, names, people, etc.** When you're skimming for meaning, as we've been discussing in this section, you don't want to string words together, giving each equal weight—just as you don't want to give

equal weight to sentences within the paragraph. A tough vocabulary word might demand your attention, but as we showed in the previous point, glossing over something that might slow you down doesn't necessarily hurt your understanding of the paragraph.

One kind of word that you might be tempted to latch onto, or at least pronounce syllable by syllable, is a name. Edmund Burke (from the example above) is a relatively tame affair. But when the name is something like Mihaly Csikszentmihalyi, the last thing you want to try to do is sound that one out. (And yes, that is a real name of an actual scholar.) One way is to use initials in your head. So if you see Mihaly Csikszentmihalyi, just think, "M. C."

You can also gloss over descriptors. For instance, if a passage says "Neville Fustlebottoms, a prominent neurolinguistics professor at the Fullman Institute of Health, at [Insert prominent university here]," you should just think, "N. F., big professor."

Applying this to the passage on Edmund Burke, we're going to put a strikethrough line through the unimportant parts. That's not saying that you should ignore them completely (it's somewhat important that Burke is British), but you should give them less weight.

> [Burke], the ~~British~~ writer of political theory, believed government had been improved by every preceding generation ~~up to his own~~. He saw the successive effort of early ~~Greek~~ democracies and ~~Byzantine~~ emperors and the rules set forth by the Magna Carta coalescing into a consummately effective—though far from perfect—society. In his eyes, the British parliamentary system of his day represented the realization of all of the efforts theretofore drawn together by the work of ~~Enlightenment~~ philosophers in the 18th century. It was the fullest expression of liberty balanced with order yet known to man. A deep sense of gratitude to his forbears reigned in every word from his lips and from his pen.

While this might not seem like a lot, success on the ACT Reading Test has a lot to do with pacing. And given there's lot of reading (more than 3,000 words), this strategy can add up to big time savings.

7. **Walk away with the main idea.** By creating a series of mental snapshots, you'll have a pretty good idea what the main idea of the passage is. Still, you should pause for five seconds and summarize in your own words what the passage as a whole was about. And that's definitely not time wasted, because there's almost always a question that asks you either what the main idea or the primary purpose of the passage is.

If you're stumped or if you're running out of time and couldn't read the entire passage, a good strategy is to read the first and last paragraphs. Focus especially on the first sentence of the first paragraph and the last sentence of the passage.

8. **Get excited!** We're finally here, at the end of the tips section. And the last tip is actually something to do before you even begin the passage. It may seem simple,

The Sorbonne is one of the oldest universities in the world. It was incorporated around 1150—that's essentially half a millennium before the founding of Harvard, the oldest college in North America!

but it's super-important and often separates those who nod off halfway into the passage from those that blaze through the questions: Get excited!

That's right. Treat the paragraph on Edmund Burke as though it's the most interesting thing ever. "Wow, each successive government from the ancient Greeks onward built upon each other to result in the awesome society Burke lived in! How optimistic!"

Mustering this kind of excitement comes down to both the ability to trick yourself and—more importantly—practice. The more often you can convince yourself to get excited about the passage, the easier it'll become.

Wait a second. What about active reading?

Throughout this section, we've been teaching some of the tenets of a system called "active reading," but we've yet to call it that. Why? Well, we feel it's become a buzzword, and as a student, you've likely heard the phrase many times already. You might have a loose sense of what it means, so if we'd begun this section saying, "let's talk about active reading," you might have tuned out. But there are important points here that we didn't want you to skip!

If you haven't heard of active reading, it's the idea that you make intelligent connections between the ideas you're reading, even anticipating what's coming next. You should be aware of major transitions, both within paragraphs and between paragraphs. Some of your teachers might have even have come up with their own systems, including things like underlining topic sentences or writing "insights" in the margins.

The problem is that people have slightly different definitions of active reading. The active reading that might help you get an A in your AP English class is likely not the same kind of reading that we've talked about here—reading that is designed specifically to help you be successful on the ACT.

Are these general tips applicable to, say, a fiction passage?

We're happy you asked. The truth is some of these tips might work better for certain kinds of passages than for others. And yes, it's true that fiction passages aren't laid out or developed the same way nonfiction writing tends to be.

So below, we're going to introduce the four different kinds of passages you'll see on the ACT and which techniques work well for each one.

ACT Passage Types

The Four Types of ACT Reading Test Passages

You'll see the following passage types on test day:

- Fiction
- Social Sciences
- Humanities
- Natural Sciences

... and you'll always see them in that order!

There are four types of passages on the ACT Reading Test, and they're always laid out in the same order. This is good to know if you struggle with social sciences, which comes second. Why? If you've found you do better on natural sciences, which comes last of the four passages in the Reading section, doing that passage second, instead of the social sciences passage, might be a good idea, for example.

Below are discussions of the four passage types, in the order in which they appear in the ACT Reading Test.

Fiction Passage

These passages tend to come from 20th- and 21st-century novels or short stories. The passages aren't too dense or full of difficult vocabulary, and they aren't taken from 19th-century British novels full of odd turns of phrases (this kind of passage is common on the SAT, though).

How to approach the ACT fiction passage

In the previous section, we spent a lot of time talking about how to approach passages and particularly how to break down and process the information they contain. The fiction passage is not quite the same as the nonfiction prose passage. In the first place, you're thrown into the middle of a story. Focusing on the first sentence of each paragraph could get you lost quickly, especially if the passage is full of dialogue or is only two long paragraphs. In the latter case, you'd essentially miss the entire story. And because you're already on, say, page 182 of a coming-of-age novel about a protagonist from Mumbai, the most important thing to do is get your bearings.

Luckily, each work of fiction contains a "blurb," or italicized introduction, that will give you some background information on what you're reading. Once you have that, it's easier to make sense of the story.

Here are two examples of blurbs that you could see on the ACT:

The following describes the author's life growing up on a farm in rural Kansas. He spent most of his life on a farm, where the following takes place.

The narrator decides how to proceed now that those whom he trusted have abandoned him.

When reading, you'll want to keep an eye out for big ideas in the passage. Does the character come to any realizations or understandings? How does he or she feel about another character? Why does he or she feel this way? Does another character teach or show him or her a skill or a lesson? What does the character learn about him- or herself?

What you don't want to do is get bogged down in the setting (unless it captures the character's mood, which strongly suggests the author is making a connection or a metaphor or the like). Other details, like what the characters were wearing, typically aren't important, either. There are a few exceptions to this: for example, if the character's social standing is important and they're wearing something that reveals this.

By the end of the passage—and yes, you should try to read every word, though it's a good idea to pick up the pace when you come to details—you should be able to answer the question: What was the big idea that the author was trying to communicate? This isn't what the passage was about—say, dinosaur extinction—but rather the main point of the passage: for example, there's a new theory about why the dinosaurs went extinct, but it lacks sufficient evidence to be credible.

Extra Tips for the ACT Fiction Passage

Make sure not to read too much into the passages and make connections that aren't there. The reason we say this is in English class, you might indeed be rewarded for making these "leaps of insight." But on the ACT passages, you should stick as closely as possible to what the text is saying—or, at least, what it's implying, using concrete and specific details.

For instance, let's say the main character discusses feeling unhappy that his father has asked him to paint the house, and you encounter a question about his attitude. If one of the answers is something like "the character has long had a deep resentment toward his father," don't choose this on the grounds that it *kind of* seems that he's not happy that his father is having him do something he doesn't like and *probably*, maybe, has done that before. From there, you might start to justify the idea that over the years, the boy has *probably* come to dislike his dad.

There are a whole lot of "maybes," "kind ofs," and "probablys" there. That's the kind of thinking that, though it might seem sensible and even get a smile from your English teacher, will lead you to the wrong answer on the ACT fiction passage. The correct answer is going to be something that doesn't rely on a string of *maybes*.

The Three Nonfiction Passages

Social Science passages present information gathered by research. As you're reading, focus on names, dates, and concepts. You should pay close attention to which name goes with which concept in a discussion and keep track of who said what. You should also particularly watch for cause-effect relationships, comparisons, and sequences of events.

Otherwise, focus on the topic sentences and consider how they determine which details are mentioned in the paragraph to get a quick sense of where important information is in the passage.

Humanities passages describe or analyze ideas or works of art. Some humanities passages that are from memoirs or personal essays may seem a bit like fiction passages, but the ACT treats them as fact here. You should pay close attention to the author and particularly to the author's point of view. Sometimes a question will ask you to predict the author's likely response to a hypothetical argument or situation. Otherwise, in these passages, the kinds of relationships you're asked to infer or identify are those between events, ideas, people, trends, or modes of thought.

Natural Science passages usually present a science topic and an explanation of the topic's significance. In a natural sciences passage, the author is typically concerned with the relationships between natural phenomena. As with social science passages, you should pay special attention to cause-effect relationships, comparisons, and sequences of events. You always need to keep track of any specific laws, rules, and theories—so underline them as you go!

Question Types on the ACT Reading Test

Out of all the sections on the ACT, the Reading Test is the one students tend to approach with the least rhyme or reason: read the passage, answer the questions; there's not much more to it than that, right?

Wrong.

In addition to learning how to read strategically, getting familiar with the question types on the ACT Reading Test can help you learn how to approach certain questions, which questions you might want to skip or save for last, and which questions have certain tricks or traps. By understanding how the test works, you'll be able to get more questions right.

Convinced? Good! Now, let's break it down.

There are eight basic question types on the ACT Reading Test:

- Detail
- Main Idea
- Comparative Relationships
- Cause-Effect Relationships and Sequence of Events
- Inferences/Generalizations
- Meaning of Words
- Author's Voice
- Author's Method/Purpose

Here's what you need to know about each of them:

Detail Questions

Detail questions ask you to find details in the passage (go figure, right?). Most of the time, they involve nothing more than simply locating a word or phrase in the text. Most students find that these are the easiest questions of the bunch. The trick, though, is that ACT Reading Test passages are long, and detail questions often don't give line numbers or paragraph references, so don't get caught up in a three-minute long fruitless search of the passage as you attempt to find out whether the girl's coat is yellow or blue. If you can't find the answer within 30 seconds or so, make a guess and move on to the other questions. You might actually find the answer you're seeking as you search the passage for other answers.

> The passage states that, on average, students in 2015 applied to how many more colleges than students in 2005?

We won't excerpt an entire passage to illustrate this. Just remember that the key is finding the information buried in the passage.

Main Idea Questions

Main idea questions ask you to determine the primary message of a paragraph, section, or an entire passage. You'll see a main idea question on just about every single ACT Reading passage, so you should always be prepared to answer one. How can you do this? After you finish reading the passage, summarize the main idea of the passage so you have it straight in your mind and won't be tempted by distracting answer choices that misstate what the passage says or pick up on only one part of the passage. For questions that ask you about a specific paragraph or section, remember that the first and last sentences of paragraphs are often key.

Our Russian family was no challenge for our head chef, Monsieur Cubat—with the exception, perhaps, of my mother. My father preferred simple foods: borscht, fish, suckling pig. Mama was even stranger, having grown up in England. If you asked what her favorite foods were, she'd think for a moment and then say something vague about eggs or beef or rice pudding. She hadn't eaten any meat since the war began, though I don't know why. Instead, as we ate the first course of plaice, she had poached eggs; as we ate roast beef with horseradish, she ate a pair of baked apples.

The main purpose of the third paragraph is to demonstrate how the mother is:

A. an outsider.
B. special.
C. bizarre.
D. reticent.

With this paragraph, we can start to gather the main idea by looking at the first sentence: we already know that the mother is the exception to the rule in this family. The last sentence helps to confirm this, as it shows how she eats food that is different from the rest of the family. We don't have enough information to interpret this as "bizarre" or "special," but we do have enough information to know that she's "an outsider," which the information about having grown up in England confirms. So, the answer is **A**!

When you're looking at an entire passage and summarizing the main idea of a paragraph, a good strategy is to read the paragraph the question references and then answer the question in your own words. Because that's difficult to do with an entire passage, we recommend always formulating a main idea as soon as you have finished reading the passage.

Comparative Relationships

Comparative relationship questions ask you to evaluate how two or more people, viewpoints, events, theories, or so on compare. They are certainly higher-level than detail questions, but they aren't too scary. To get these questions right, you just need to understand the gist of the two things the test is asking you to compare.

He couldn't see it. I mean literally. He was in every scene, the spotlight always on him. The director, on the other hand, had time to interact with the other minor actors. In fact, he actually knew them by name, knew the chemistry they had. So when it came time to use a new group of actors in the scene, the director was surprised that the leading star spoke the most vehemently on the issue.

According to the author, the significant difference between the director's opinion and the star actor's opinion was:

A. the director was more informed.
B. the actor had studied the issue more deeply.
C. the actor was less emotional.
D. the director had less rapport with the other actors.

These questions test high-level comprehension and typically don't go too far beyond what the text literally states. In this case, the answer is **A**.

Cause-Effect Relationships and Sequence of Events

The ACT categorizes cause-effect and sequence-of-event questions separately, but we're grouping them together because they're fairly similar. Basically, they both require you to understand what happened before something else or what happened to cause something else. These questions are like detail questions in that the answer will be directly stated in the passage. However, you will need to be careful about realizing that the order events are discussed in the passage is not necessarily the order in which they happened.

I did not make any major mistakes that I could remember. I guess it was the little things: the cash registers not having the exact change, customers getting fries when they'd asked for a shake, the ketchup dispenser being filled with mustard. But one day Mr. Franklin told me that he'd found someone else to take my shift. And that was it. I resolved after that day to stop daydreaming, to pay more attention to the here and now, and not some future time when everything might be better.

The narrator conveys that her dismissal from her first job directly resulted in:

A. a new job with more responsibilities.
B. making small mistakes at her job.
C. a decision to change how she approached her life.
D. a major change in her career plans.

As long as you carefully read the question and the entire passage, which ends with the effect the narrator's dismissal had on her, you should arrive at **C**. If you misread the question or only read the first part of the excerpt, you might end up with B.

Inferences/Generalizations

Students tend to find that inference and generalization questions are typically the hardest on the ACT Reading Test, because the answers won't be directly stated in the passage but will require you to take a lot of information and boil it down. The most important thing to remember with these question types is never to infer TOO much. You will only ever have to make a teeny, tiny leap beyond what the passage states. This means that if you find yourself rationalizing how an answer choice *could* be true, STOP! You're going too far.

> With her trademark hello, a theatrical wave starting at her waist and culminating above her head, his mother burst into the room. "Roland, do I have news for you."
>
> He had gotten her message last night, about how she had big plans for his high school graduation, despite two years and not one phone call. But whenever she did call, saying she had a plan, his mother was usually at his father's doorstep the next day.
>
> It would be reasonable to infer that the boy was not surprised by the arrival of his mother because:
>
> **A.** she really did want to see him despite their distance.
> **B.** her behavior tended to follow a predictable pattern.
> **C.** she consistently attended events pertaining to his life.
> **D.** she was deeply devoted to her son.

It is easy to rationalize A—the wrong answer—by thinking that his mother *seems* like she wants to see him because when she calls, she does show up. So it *could* be that she wants to see him.

B, on the other hand, sticks very close to the text, specifically, "But whenever she did call ... father's doorstep the next day." This is clearly an example of behavior following a predictable pattern. There's no need for us to justify it by bringing our own interpretation into the way that we might with A: "a mother typically wants to see her children, and whenever she calls she wants to see him. So A *kind of* works." No! A doesn't work at all. *Kind of* actually never works for the ACT—when in doubt, stick to the text! **B** works better.

Meaning of Words

Meaning-of-words questions are also known as word-in-context questions. Typically, they don't quiz you on difficult vocabulary here. Most of the time, the passage will pick a word that might have multiple meanings depending on the context and ask you to pick out the right one. There are two main strategies to approach these types of questions. The first is to put a blank where the word is in the passage and then fill it in with your own word. Then, go to the answer choices and see which one best matches up with what you chose. The other strategy is to read each of the answer choices back into the passage and see which one makes the most sense in the context of the passage (even if it doesn't grammatically make sense).

Scientists have combed through the fossil record, looking for signs that birds might have, at some point, diverged from dinosaurs. And what they have found has not only surprised them but also threatens to overturn some established theories.

As it is used in line 58, *combed through* most nearly means:

A. moved their fingers through.
B. disturbed.
C. set straight.
D. closely examined.

Notice how A and C both play on common definitions of the word "combed." Only by going back to the passage and plugging in our own word or words can we arrive at **D**. The golden rule for these types of questions is always: refer back to the passage.

Author's Voice

Author's voice questions ask you to draw a conclusion about how an author (or narrator) feels about his or her subject. These can be difficult questions, but about half of ACT Reading passages are going to ask you a question like this, so you should prepare for them as you read the passages on test day. Going back to determine tone without rereading (which you likely don't have time for) is even trickier, and it's a complication you don't need. As you read, look for clues that indicate how an author or narrator feels about the subject: often, there are hints in the author's use of strong choices in adjectives, adverbs, or verbs. Tone or voice questions are often particularly important on the fiction passage.

> The winter months did not come gently. There was the constant threat of snow storms, frost-bitten hunters returning to camp, their dogs gaunt from eating whatever stale meat remained. But what was perhaps worse were the nights. They seemed to have no end. Once darkness closed around you, it lasted for months, the hour or so of daylight providing little relief.

> The narrator recalls her childhood in a remote area of Canada with a feeling of:
>
> A. nostalgia.
> B. sadness.
> C. dread.
> D. curiosity.

There's a negative feeling permeating these few sentences, which can help us narrow the answer choices to B and C. Yet there's an important difference between B and C. Sure, the narrator might have been sad because of the long, cold winter nights. But the paragraph *more directly* conveys dread ("seemed to have no end," "darkness closed around you," and "little relief"). **C** is the correct answer.

Author's Method/Purpose

Author's method or author's purpose questions ask you to draw conclusions about what an author is trying to achieve with a passage or why he or she developed the passage in a certain way. These are not incredibly common questions, but you should still be prepared for them. The best way to prepare for these question types is to pay close attention to the structure of the passage as you read and think about how each paragraph builds on the previous one.

> In the context of the whole passage, the author most likely chose to include the examples of the extinction of certain bird species in order to:

We won't excerpt an entire passage just for this one question. But here's a good tip: after reading the passage, you should try to answer the question yourself. That way, you think about it first before diving into the answer choices.

Comparison Passages

Comparison passages (or dual passages) are relatively new on the ACT Reading Test—they've only popped up in the last couple of years. But they're now customary, and you can expect to see one in one of the four sections on the ACT Reading Test. These passages tend to intimidate students, but they aren't nearly as scary as you might think they are. Most of the questions you'll encounter will only apply to one of the two passages in the set, and you'll only see two to four questions that have to do with both.

> Compared to the author of passage B, the author of passage A would be more likely to support:

Again, we won't excerpt an entire passage just to make our point. Instead, here's how to strategically tackle these comparison passages:

1. **Know in advance that there are going to be certain ways in which these two passages compare or contrast.** This is why they were chosen, after all! So read the first passage as you would any other passage—looking for the main idea and key points. Then, when you read the second passage, look specifically for the ways in which it is similar to and different from the first one in terms of how it approaches its topic. Note these similarities and differences; we guarantee the questions will ask about them.

2. **Read the first passage and then answer the questions about it, then read the second passage and answer the questions about it, and then answer the questions about both.** The upside to the dual-passage section is that you can break up your reading into smaller chunks. There will be a clear series of questions that pertain only to the first passage, so you'll have all the information you need to answer those questions after you've read the first one. So take a break at this point and do those first. This also helps you avoid any distractor answer choices that appear in the second passage because you won't even have read it yet.

    Follow the same procedure for the second passage, and then answer the questions that are about both passages.

3. **Know that almost all of the questions about both passages will have to do with big ideas—namely, main idea, tone, and purpose.** You might see a few questions that compare details, but most of the questions about both passages have to do with big ideas. So you want to be extra sure on these passages that you have the main idea, tone/attitude, and purpose of each passage straight. Jot them down after you finish reading. For example, on a natural sciences passage examining the connections between meditation and heart rate, you might jot down something like "New studies show meditation increases heart rate (main idea); skeptical (tone); to inform (purpose)." Do this for both passages, and it will become MUCH easier to answer those questions about both passages. Promise.

4. **If timing is an issue for you, or comparison passages are not your thing, leave this passage set for last and strategically use the time you have left.** If you're prone to running out of time on the ACT Reading Test, the dual passage is a great

one to leave for last. Check the list of questions before you begin to see which passage has the most questions about it, and do that passage first (they might have the same number, in which case, read the shorter passage first). Then, do the other passage and questions. This will help you make the most of the precious dwindling minutes at the end of the test.

Common Mistakes on the ACT Reading Test

Inferring too much. The ACT is very literal. Most of the answers will be directly stated in the passage. If they aren't, then the ACT only wants you to make teeny tiny inferences that directly and logically connect to what is stated in the passage, not grand leaps in thinking. If you find yourself rationalizing how an answer *could* be true, STOP. You're going down the wrong path!

Not noticing transitions. If there's a change in perspective or the author introduces a new counterargument or direction, the ACT will almost always ask you about it. Take note of those transition words and phrases.

Still Struggling?

If you're still struggling with ACT Reading Test questions, a few things could be going on:

- You're initially reading too fast.
- You're reading the passage but you aren't retaining the information (the passage is "a blur").
- You aren't looking at the right part of the passage when you get to the questions.
- You don't have enough time to apply the right approach to the questions.
- You're misinterpreting the passage.
- You struggle with the words or turns of phrases the author uses and therefore struggle to understand the general idea(s).
- Or a combination of these.

You can overcome any of these obstacles with time and work. The takeaway is to figure out where you are struggling. That way, you can focus on these areas. Below, we'll give you some approaches for dealing with these issues.

Core Causes of ACT Issues

Not enough outside reading

Some of us struggle with one kind of passage more than others. If this describes you, you might want to work more on that kind of reading if you have at least a few weeks before the test.

One way to become better at a specific type of reading is to do more of that kind of reading. For instance, let's say you dread ACT science passages. To become more at ease with this kind of writing, open up an issue of *Scientific American* or *Discover*, just to name two of the most prominent science magazines (incidentally, both the SAT and ACT adapt passages from these sources).

Read the relatively long articles, which usually clock in at around three pages. You should read these articles the way you would an ACT passage (see the section on "How to Read an ACT Passage"). You should be focusing on topic sentences, taking mental snapshots. On the other hand, if you read an article just for entertainment, you're not doing yourself any favors. The point is to train your "reading brain" to read a certain way—the way you read an ACT passage. The more automatic this process becomes—and the more you use it on subject material you struggle with—the easier test day will be.

Tricky answers

Sometimes, you can be a strong reader and still not get every ACT Reading Test question right. In this case, outside reading isn't going to help you much. Rather, it's your performance on the ACT itself that needs a boost. If that sounds like what's happening for you, then you should focus on making sure you're reading the questions carefully and not getting tricked by trap answers, etc. (See the section below on "Wrong Answer Types.")

Pacing

If you don't have much time at the end of the ACT Reading Test (or even if you do!), a good strategy is to skip the passages you struggle with. Then, at the end of the test, go back to them. It's better to feel in control psychologically than to feel frustrated at the beginning of the reading section because you struggled (and burned up a lot of time) getting through a tough passage.

ACT Reading vs. SAT Reading

Many students tend to study for the ACT and the SAT within the same year, or even (in quite a few cases) within the same month. While the reading sections are pretty similar on the surface, it's important to know the differences between the tests.

The ACT passages are longer than SAT passages (800 vs. 600 words). ACT passages tend to be a little easier; or at least, the difference between the easiest-to-read passage and the hardest-to-read passage is not as large as it is on the SAT.

What that means is that you don't need to pick up a copy of Mary Shelley's *Frankenstein*, or whatever 19th-century British novel is least painful to you, as we advise students to do when prepping for the SAT.

But your "reading brain" should be used to sifting through lots of text to get the main meaning for ACT Reading. To this end, we encourage outside reading.

Also, don't feel you need to brush up on your vocabulary when prepping for the ACT the way you have to do with the new SAT. On SAT Reading passages, you need to be familiar with a certain level of vocabulary; having a weak vocabulary can hurt you more on the SAT than on the ACT.

Finally, and perhaps most importantly, is the level of trickiness. Simply put, the ACT rewards you for understanding the passage. Eight times out of 10, if you understand the passage, and you carefully read the answer choices/aren't rushing to finish, you'll get the question right. The SAT answer choices are more deceptive and filled with traps. Even if you understand the passage, you can miss half the questions if you're not careful.

What this means is that if you've just finished prepping for the SAT, you've practiced being very careful when choosing an answer. This same level of caution is typically unnecessary on the ACT and will only slow you down.

This brings us to the last important difference between the two tests: time. The ACT Reading Test has less time per question, though the total amount of text you'll read overall is nearly the same amount as on the SAT. Luckily, the passages tend not to be as difficult. But your "reading brain" might have to adjust by reading the passage slightly faster than it would on the SAT.

The catch is that speeding up can lead you to miss a question. So what's the right balance between time reading the passage and time answering the questions? A good approach is to pay attention to how you're currently approaching passages and trying to figure out where the weakest link is: understanding the passages, answering the questions, reading speed, or some mixture of the three. We'll talk more about how to do this in the pacing section.

Wrong Answer Types

In the previous section, we talked about how the ACT is not as tricky as the SAT in terms of the wrong answer traps. While this is true, it doesn't mean that the ACT is without trap answers. In fact, for every passage, there are at least two questions that have two answer choices that seem very similar, though only one is correct.

How do you know which one to choose? Well, before we discuss a few strategies you can employ, it's good to understand the different types of answer choices. They fall into one of several "buckets."

The Exact Opposite

We've mentioned throughout this section how important pacing is—and how little time the ACT gives you. So it's easy to see how many students end up picking this wrong answer choice; they aren't reading it carefully, often because of time pressure. Basically, what this answer choice does is state the answer perfectly but then drop the word "no" or "not" that makes it the exact opposite of the correct answer.

"The Rotten Spot"

This is a variant of the "exact opposite" but is a little subtler. Often an answer choice is correct, but then it adds a little something—a qualifier, new information—that makes it wrong. That something doesn't have to be a flat out "no" or "not," but it can be something that's slightly off.

The thing is, our natural tendency is to read the part of the answer choice that sounds good, and not really pay attention to the part that's somewhat wrong. For instance, if a passage discusses the main character's experience learning that he can't always trust his friend because his friend oftentimes unintentionally misinterprets what he says, a wrong answer choice might be phrased like this:

"The main character realizes that his friend is unreliable because he has a poor memory."

Right away our brains latch onto the word "unreliable" and we don't really take in the "poor memory" part. But the passage mentions that the friend misinterprets what the main character says, not that the friend has a poor memory. Again, this is a mistake that students tend to make because they're rushing.

So why call this "The Rotten Spot"? Well, think about picking up a piece of fruit at the supermarket. What's the first thing you do? You turn it over in your hand, looking for the rotten spot. You're not looking at one side of the orange, thinking, "hey, this is nice and shiny!" You're looking to see if any part of the orange is bad. That's the same attitude you need to evaluate an ACT answer choice. Read the entire thing to see if any part of it is off/incorrect.

The Word Salad

Sometimes the test writers will take information that's mentioned in the passage—the keywords, the big ideas—and they'll throw them together in an answer choice that claims something that the passage wasn't saying. Unlike the first two kinds of wrong answer choices, this answer choice doesn't hinge on one word. You'll have to read the entire answer choice and make sense of it as a whole before determining whether it is right or wrong.

Too Extreme

Sometimes an answer choice is somewhat correct but will use extreme language. For instance, "the friend was completely outraged" is a highly unlikely answer on an ACT Reading Test question. Instead, the correct answer will be something like, "the friend is somewhat upset." That's not to say that all extreme answer choices are wrong, but if you choose an answer choice with extreme language, it has to be clearly backed up by the passage.

Never Said That

A common wrong answer choice mentions something that wasn't even in the passage or completely misinterprets the passage. This kind of answer choice tends to be the least tempting. Students usually pick these if they a) really don't understand the passage or b) are running out of time. It's good to be aware of these kinds of answer choices because you'll see a lot of them, but they're easier to eliminate than other wrong answer choice types.

Pacing Tips

Procrastination—we've all been there. Whether we get easily distracted, put off work we find too overwhelming or intimidating, or, hey, we just have better things to do, sometimes we start a task behind schedule—and then it's too late.

As much as we can all relate to this, it's a risky game to play when you're taking the official ACT, and sometimes test-takers don't even know they're doing it. Even with the best of intentions, it's difficult to give the maximum number of questions the maximum amount of attention to get that maximum number of points.

What's that mean for you as a test-taker? It's time to come up with a game plan. These strategies will keep you moving through ruts and progressing at the right pace so that time will be on your side on ACT Reading:

1. **Once you start a passage, commit to it.** Going through the passages in the order the test presents them may not be so important, but not wasting time jumping back and forth is. You'll lose valuable time confusing yourself, and even those precious page-turning seconds should not be wasted.

2. **Don't pore over the passage.** Since ACT writers only include questions that require just a few minutes of reading, spending that extra time won't help you answer the questions. Be attentive but also quick: you don't want to do all that careful reading with nothing to show for it.

3. **Take the guesswork out of guessing.** There is no penalty for guessing on the ACT! If you have only a matter of seconds to finish a question without even taking the time to read it, you should guess—and your chances of getting the question right expand greatly with each answer choice you're able to eliminate. Unless you are aiming for a 30+, some guesswork won't kill your score. Of course, with effective time management, you should only need to resort to guessing on a handful of the more challenging questions.

Why You Might Need to Skip a Passage to Get a Higher Score

In an ideal world, all 40 questions on the ACT Reading Test would be easy to answer in 35 minutes. But in reality, many students find that they're either rushing through the questions with low accuracy or only able to make it through two or three passages in the given time.

One of the things we hear a lot from frustrated students is that there isn't enough time on the test to take notes or follow the recommended ACT Reading strategies. Let's look at two students and their scores and see how slowing down and taking notes, even at the expense of leaving an entire passage blank, can actually increase your score on the ACT Reading Test!

Student 1: Marion

Let's say Marion doesn't take any notes. She skims the passage and reads the questions quickly, then scans the passage again, hoping to locate the correct answer. Her goal is to try to complete all 40 questions, which she's able to do by spending approximately eight to nine minutes on each passage. But because she rushed through the questions without really understanding any of the passages, she only gets 5/10 questions correct on each Reading passage, or 20 correct answers total.

Final Scaled Score: 20

Student 2: Steven

Now, let's look at another student. Steven reads each passage, carefully taking notes and breaking the passage down. He practices active reading and asks himself questions about the author's main idea and point of view as he reads. This means that he only has time to do three out of four passages. For the last passage, he quickly guesses on the 10 questions because he knows there is no wrong answer penalty on the ACT. He spent about 11–12 minutes on each of the first three passages.

Because Steven really understood the passages, he gets 8/10 questions right on the first three passages he completed. His accuracy is much higher than Marion's because of the time he spent thinking critically and analyzing the passage. For the last passage, he gets two questions correct out of the 10 guessed questions. This makes his total correct answers 26.

Final Scaled Score: 26

The outcome

It's pretty amazing how Steven took three more minutes on each passage, got only three more questions correct on each of the first three passages, did not even read the fourth passage, and yet received a scaled score that was a full five points higher than Marion's!

Takeaway: If you're struggling with pacing and accuracy on the ACT Reading Test, try the "three out of four" method that Steven used!

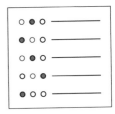

ACT Reading Practice Questions

Note: The following is not meant to serve as a full practice section and so does not include a fiction passage.

The three following practice passages are accompanied by several questions. Read each passage, and then select the best answer to each question. You may go back to the passages as often as you need.

The next 10 questions relate to the following passage.

PASSAGE I

1   Over the last three decades, private college and university enrollment has rapidly grown in response to needs that are unmet by public schools. Whether it
5   is the difficulty of obtaining admission to certain higher education institutions or the desire to go to a religious school, the needs of the world's high school graduates have created a global
10 demand for private higher education. In particular, the limited number of student slots available in public higher education and the increasing number of college-ready citizens create a demand more
15 easily met by private schools than public.

   While almost every country has seen growth in private colleges and universities in the last century, the purpose of private higher education
20 varies by context. Most countries' elite universities are public, and private schools exist to offer alternative opportunities. (The United States, Japan, and Korea's elite private schools are
25 unusual in this regard.) Furthermore, even in countries with elite private universities, the recent enrollment growth in private higher education has not taken place in the elite schools,
30 such as Harvard or Vanderbilt, but in for-profit colleges and universities, such as Phoenix. These for-profit schools do

not have the tax-exempt status of public schools and nonprofit schools but are
35 run as businesses. While many nonprofit private schools have a long history of providing excellent education, many of their for-profit counterparts have raised some eyebrows.

40   As more people pursue higher education, minorities and women are enrolling in private schools in greater numbers, particularly for-profit institutions. By opening college
45 education to more citizens, the for-profit private schools have the potential to promote equality. This is the major benefit higher education experts hope these schools will provide one day.
50 In America, for-profit schools have managed to compete with public schools in several ways. Compared with public schools, for-profit schools are more efficient and more stable in their funding
55 in times of crisis.

   When jobs become scarce, people who have been laid off look for ways into available employment. Jobs that remain available during economic recessions
60 usually require higher education. This can mean a huge increase in college enrollment immediately following an economic crisis. Due to their efficiency, for-profit schools are capable of rapidly

increasing the number of students they can teach at a given time. For public schools, economic hardship tends to decrease enrollment because the government lacks extra funds for professors, administrators, and building maintenance.

The for-profit private sector's lack of government funding can be both benefit and burden for the school. On the one hand, a for-profit private institution must generate more of its budget than a public one. On the other hand, for-profit schools' freedom from certain government regulations allow them to respond to market forces more quickly to meet student demand. The flexibility has the potential to produce excellent results, presenting one of the major advantages of for-profit schools.

At this time, this flexibility comes with a cost beyond the financial burden. The sensitivity to market forces resulting from limited government funding provides a threat to quality. For instance, the number of Latin American students who enrolled in college increased rapidly in the last few decades. Much of the enrollment occurred in for-profit schools. When these institutions opened doors to massive numbers of new students, finding enough qualified teachers became impossible. As a result, unqualified teachers were hired. Latin America now faces a generation of college graduates who struggle to perform in the workplace due to no fault of their own but rather the poor quality of their instruction.

At the same time, for-profit schools do serve a purpose. They see great success in fields that lead directly into the workforce, such as cosmetology and automotive repair. When it comes to vocational training, for-profit education has the potential to increase opportunity by enrolling students of varied academic backgrounds and teaching them job-specific skills. However, many for-profit schools do not limit themselves to vocational training, often awarding degrees in psychology, literature, math, and other fields.

Although for-profit institutions have had some success, there is much room for improvement in their policies. While these schools may increase access to higher education for nontraditional and underserved populations, their tuition costs (which average five times those of a community college) can burden students with considerable debt without necessarily leading them to new employment. The high cost of these schools also indirectly harms taxpayers; for-profit institutions consume almost a quarter of government aid for low-income scholars and billions of dollars in student loans in the United States alone.

Taking all of the evidence into account, it is clear that following the overwhelming call of the almighty dollar does not necessarily lead to good education. And giving students equal access to bad education does not lead to equality, either. Markets do a better job of ensuring efficiency than effectiveness. Whatever drawbacks public funding may have, the more regulated processes of the government at least ensure that institutions do not hire underqualified teachers. There may be a day when for-profit private schools learn how to balance their priorities and contribute positively to the lives of students. However, much work stands in their way.

1 According to the passage, what major benefit do for-profit schools offer?

   A. Equality
   B. Job-specific training
   C. Quality teachers
   D. Government funding

2 Paragraph 2 ("While almost every country … raised some eyebrows") implies that a major purpose of private schools in countries other than the United States, Korea, and Japan is:

   F. enrolling students who are not accepted by elite schools.
   G. providing elite educational opportunities.
   H. extending government funds to low-income students.
   J. swindling students out of money.

3 For the passage's author, the last sentence in paragraph 8 ("The high cost of these schools … in the United States, alone") primarily serves to support the point that for-profit schools:

  A. have the advantage of not relying on government funds.
  B. sometimes fail to hire qualified teachers.
  C. come with large financial burdens.
  D. offer effective vocational training.

4 In the passage, each of the following is given as a weakness of some for-profit schools EXCEPT:

  F. expensive tuition.
  G. low quality of instruction.
  H. training in automotive repair.
  J. meeting the enrollment needs of students.

5 The passage tells us that for-profit schools in Latin America created a decrease in:

  A. options for majors and minors.
  B. student enrollment.
  C. effective funding practices.
  D. quality of teachers.

6 As it is used in paragraph 7 ("At the same time … and other fields"), the word *vocational* most nearly means:

  F. spoken aloud.
  G. job-oriented.
  H. purposeless.
  J. superfluous.

7 According to the author of this passage, what real or potential advantages do for-profit private schools have over public schools?

  I. Flexibility for changes
  II. Capacity for student enrollment
  III. Affordability for students

  A. I and II
  B. II and III
  C. II only
  D. I and III

8 The author's attitude toward for-profit private institutions is:

  F. hopeful.
  G. positive.
  H. spiteful.
  J. cautious.

9 Which of the following is used in the passage as an example of a for-profit school?

  A. Harvard
  B. Phoenix
  C. Vanderbilt
  D. Walden

10 Which of the following changes to for-profit schools would the author probably recommend?

  F. More access to government funds
  G. Increased accountability in teacher selection
  H. Extended opportunities for student enrollment
  J. Reduced international trade

The next 10 questions relate to the following passage.

PASSAGE II

1 After cramming the first 13 years of his life with every dinosaur book and mythical illustration that he could lay eyes on, Ray Harryhausen went to see *King Kong* with his aunt and parents. Upon
5 witnessing the cutting edge special effects, the boy flew into a new obsession full-force, tracking down everything he could find that would solve the mystery, "How did they make it move like that?" Once he discovered the answer in stop-motion
10 animation, he dedicated himself to the hobby.

At the age of 18, he could be seen daily in his mother's garden, forcing a video camera to film stop-motion animation of a wood-framed stegosaurus, a brontosaurus, and a bear he had
15 fashioned from clay and fabric. This experiment took months to complete. When finally he got to see his little movie, he found that the film was an utter failure. After hours of painstaking, meticulous work, Harryhausen's results were a
20 spotty, jerking animation with shadows flitting in every direction as the sun moved.

More than any other moment in his life, Harryhausen's response to this failure revealed his work ethic. When an artist has racked
25 up a certain amount of success, the man can frequently recover from a failure. By then, he has plenty of evidence to prove to himself that he is good at his work. But when a beginner's first arduous step proves only that he is an artist of
30 disaster, the ability to move forward is more than perseverance. It is heroism.

When Harryhausen watched the terrible film, he made the hero's decision. He tried again. This time, he moved his "studio" inside the garage so
35 that the sun's movement would not change the lighting. This time, he used a camera that had a one-frame shot feature. This time, the results were much improved. The only drawback was that his father had to park in the driveway for

40 months while Harryhausen filmed. Without a studio to back his project financially or even an audience outside of his supportive mother and father, Harryhausen labored long hours over an ambitious project called *Evolution of the World*.

45 During work on the amateur project, Harryhausen met Willis O'Brien, the mastermind behind *King Kong*. The young man brought a hand-made model of a brontosaurus to the meeting. The sculpture had won him a prize less than a year
50 before. But, for O'Brien, it was inadequate. After comparing the legs of the sculpture to overcooked sausages, he told Harryhausen to study anatomy. Surprisingly, Harryhausen was less insulted than grateful. In the following months, Harryhausen
55 could be found whiling away hours at the zoo. The elephant's knees, the giraffe's stride, the kangaroo's leap taught Harryhausen the subtleties of natural movement. He brought his old question with him: How did they move?

60 Not long after his visit with O'Brien, Harryhausen got his first professional job in cinema: puppetry. The project gave him the opportunity to animate using stop-motion in a professional setting, but the rigidity of the
65 puppet's motions left him uninspired. After dedicating years to understanding realistic movement, Harryhausen had a sense of taking a few steps backward as an artist. After a few years of puppetry, he decided to move on. He joined the
70 Army in the Special Services division to create films for military orientation.

After this, Harryhausen had a moderately impressive resume that created inroads into artistically interesting films. O'Brien offered him
75 a position as an assistant on his new film, *Mighty Joe Young*, giving Harryhausen the chance to see firsthand the answer to his old question, "How do they make it move like that?" Over the course of this movie and the next, Harryhausen
80 began experimenting with ways of separating the background and foreground of the film in live action animated sequences in order to incorporate stop-motion animated models more realistically. The results stunned audiences.

Throughout a dozen films between 1940 and 1957, Harryhausen's constantly improving special effects brought dinosaurs and giants and even a cyclops into realistic interactions with live actors. At the height of complexity, *Jason and the Argonauts* featured a band of seven skeletons in an elaborately choreographed sword fight with three living men. The sequence took months to complete. It remains one of the most lauded accomplishments in special effects history, analyzed by college film students even today. It was his greatest achievement.

Harryhausen's popularity waxed and waned over the course of his career, but his abilities did not. As long as he contributed to films, he continued striving to improve upon his previous techniques, moving flawlessly from black-and-white films to color, from ancient monsters to futuristic aliens. Upon Harryhausen's death in 2013, modern film directors and special effects designers like Peter Jackson and Steven Spielberg flooded the news with statements of admiration toward the man who inspired their imaginations so much, simply by pursuing the question, "How did they make it move?"

11 It is reasonable to infer from the passage that Harryhausen considered O'Brien to be:

   A. an artist worthy of imitation.

   B. unkind and demanding.

   C. his primary competitor.

   D. a fraud and a trickster.

12 The main purpose of this passage is to:

   F. describe Harryhausen's work on *Jason and the Argonauts*.

   G. present the ideal path toward a career in cinema.

   H. discuss the merits and drawbacks of Harryhausen's special effects.

   J. summarize Harryhausen's development as an artist.

13 The passage suggests that Harryhausen's interest in special effects was caused by:

   A. his experience creating motion pictures for the military.

   B. watching a movie as a child.

   C. his work as a puppeteer.

   D. seeing animals at the zoo.

14 According to the passage, the stop-motion project Harryhausen attempted as an 18-year-old was hampered by all of the following EXCEPT:

   F. the sun's motion.

   G. the kind of camera.

   H. his parents.

   J. shadows.

15 The main idea of paragraph 3 ("More than any … It is heroism") is that:

   A. although Harryhausen tried very hard, he did not have the skills or character traits to accomplish his goals.

   B. Harryhausen's willingness to continue trying despite his early failures was praiseworthy.

   C. when Harryhausen watched his first film, he did not understand the gravity of his failure.

   D. artists must be experienced in order to recover from failure.

16 According to the passage, Harryhausen's greatest film was:

   F. *King Kong.*

   G. *Evolution of the World.*

   H. *Mighty Joe Young.*

   J. *Jason and the Argonauts.*

17 The author makes it clear that Harryhausen's parents were:

   A. annoyed by his preoccupations.
   B. supportive of his dreams.
   C. indifferent to his interests.
   D. upset by his goals.

18 The author probably repeats the question, "How did they make it move?" in order to highlight:

   F. Harryhausen's intricate understanding of animal anatomy.
   G. Harryhausen's lifelong curiosity and eagerness.
   H. Harryhausen's obsessive-compulsive personality.
   J. Harryhausen's waxing and waning popularity.

19 According to the passage, Harryhausen's enlistment in the Army followed immediately after:

   A. Harryhausen learned to separate background from foreground.
   B. helping with *Mighty Joe Young*.
   C. Harryhausen's work as a puppeteer.
   D. the failure of *Evolution of the World*.

20 In paragraph 2 ("At the age … the sun moved"), the word *fashioned* most nearly means:

   F. created.
   G. emerged.
   H. uncovered.
   J. expanded.

The next 10 questions relate to the following passage.

PASSAGE III

1 Most of today's scientists conceptualize the human memory in terms of a dual-system structure, divided into a short-term memory and a long-term memory. Both members of this system perform
5 unique and complementary functions that make both activity and memory possible.

   One part of the brain (the highly developed frontal lobe) performs short-term memory functions by interacting with memories that
10 are rapidly created by the sense receptors. Information can remain in the short-term memory for 15–20 seconds before it is either repeated, forgotten, or transferred to long-term memory. In addition to this time limit, research
15 suggests that the short-term memory has a quantity limit, retaining only approximately seven discrete items at a given time. However, this quantity does come with a degree of flexibility; while many people's short-term
20 memories would struggle to contain the eight distinct items in the number 19891031, people that group these items into a year, month, and day (i.e., 1989, October 31) will have no trouble containing these three items of information in
25 their short-term memories. Research suggests that such grouping strategies usually lie at the heart of certain individuals having "good" memories.

   As suggested by its name, the long-term memory can contain information for a greater
30 period of time than the short-term memory. It also lacks the short-term memory's quantity restrictions. The processes of the long-term memory primarily occur in the brain's hippocampus. A specific instance stored in
35 the long-term memory may remain intact for a person's entire lifetime, and the quantitative limits of the long-term memory have not been reached. Once a long-term memory has been formed, the short-term memory may

theoretically access it whenever needed. In an astonishing feat of consciousness, when the short-term memory is presented with a specific set of numbers in a long division problem never before seen, it can plug these new numbers into 45 the long division formula retrieved from the long-term memory.

This ability to draw formulas illustrates the cyclical relationship between long-term and short-term memory. Not only does the short-term 50 memory draw from the long-term memory, but the reverse is true as well: in order for information to enter the long-term memory, it must first pass through the short-term memory. Most scientists agree that the amount of time 55 information spends in the short-term memory is the determining factor in whether or not it will be organized into the long-term memory. Since the short-term memory naturally loses information after about 20 seconds, holding 60 information in this part of the memory requires a degree of focus, repetition, and conscious choice. Once enough time has been spent reviewing the information in the short-term memory, the brain organizes it into the long-term memory.

65 However, there are times when long-term memories prove inaccessible due to either retrieval failure or forgetting. Retrieval failure occurs when an individual has information in his or her long-term memory but cannot access it at a 70 given moment. This is commonly referred to as having something "on the tip of your tongue." The information is not lost but temporarily inaccessible.

On the other hand, information is sometimes truly lost from the memory in a process familiar 75 to all human beings: forgetting. If information is not reviewed occasionally, it will decay. To avoid decay in the short-term memory, information must be reviewed at intervals of no more than 20 seconds. In the long-term memory, the science 80 is far less precise, largely because people forget items from long-term memory for a variety of reasons. The information may become irrelevant to them, such as the day-to-day procedures of a former job. The memories may be so upsetting

85 that the person willfully forgets them, such as those of a violent mugging. The person may incur brain damage that results in certain memories becoming either erased or irrevocably inaccessible. The reasons information leaves the long-term 90 memory are both numerous and complex; however, most of these memories are simply lost because they are not reviewed frequently.

Perhaps ironically, scientists primarily research forgetting in order to improve our 95 understanding of remembering. Through continued research into the means by which we forget, scientists stand to improve the conditions of patients with Alzheimer's disease and people suffering from head injuries.

100 The dual-system structure of memory utilized by today's scientists provides a useful framework for understanding human cognition. Other frameworks have been accepted in the past, and further frameworks will be created in the future, 105 with the slowly unraveling truth of the human memory always as their model.

21 The primary purpose of the passage is to:

A. describe the dual-system structure used by today's scientists to explain human memory.

B. analyze the various reasons for memory loss and forgetfulness.

C. explain the functions of parts of the brain in memory formation.

D. compare today's framework for understanding memory to the frameworks of past ages.

22 Overall, the author's attitude toward the study of human memory can best be described as:

F. ridiculing and pessimistic.

G. jovial and excited.

H. positive and professional.

J. critical and derisive.

23 As it is used in paragraph 4 ("The ability to … long-term memory"), the word *draw* most nearly means:

    A. produce.

    B. sketch.

    C. lower.

    D. pull.

24 According to the passage, how long can information remain in the short-term memory?

    F. Indefinitely

    G. 15–20 seconds

    H. About 7 seconds

    J. 31 seconds

25 According to the passage, the short-term memory has what advantage over the long-term memory?

    A. The short-term memory can hold a greater quantity of information at a given time than the long-term memory.

    B. The short-term memory does not have the narrow time restrictions of the long-term memory.

    C. The short-term memory can gain information directly through the senses.

    D. The short-term memory is less sensitive to brain damage than the long-term memory.

26 The author states that the reason scientists study forgetting is:

    F. to improve memory.

    G. to produce medication.

    H. to enhance short-term memory use.

    J. to avoid the "tip of the tongue" problem.

27 As it is used in paragraph 2 ("One part of … having 'good' memories"), the word *discrete* most nearly means:

    A. individual.

    B. secretive.

    C. conclusive.

    D. modest.

28 In the passage, all of these are given as reasons for long-term memory loss EXCEPT:

    F. brain damage.

    G. willful forgetting.

    H. lack of review.

    J. misunderstanding.

29 According to paragraph 4 ("This ability … long-term memory"), what do most scientists believe is the factor that determines whether information will enter the long-term memory?

    A. Quantity of information in the short-term memory

    B. Amount of time spent in the short-term memory

    C. The information already in the long-term memory

    D. The person's desire to remember the information

30 Based on the passage, the author understands the dual-system structure of memory as:

    F. biological fact.

    G. a good way of thinking about memory.

    H. the perfect model for understanding memory.

    J. the result of research into forgetfulness.

STOP During the test, you will need to wait until instructed to turn the page.

ACT Reading Answers and Explanations

1 The seventh paragraph explains that for-profit schools effectively train students in fields that lead directly into the workforce. Therefore, the answer is **B**. While the author states that A is something experts hope will be accomplished, it is immediately followed by "one day," suggesting it hasn't happened yet. Additionally, the author later states, "giving students equal access to bad education does not lead to equality." Neither C nor D are suggested as qualities of for-profit schools.

Answer: **B**

2 Since the public schools in most countries are elite, the "alternative opportunities" offered by private schools most likely refers to enrolling students who could not gain admission to these schools. Therefore, the answer is **F**. G is incorrect because paragraph 2 states that most countries have elite public schools, not elite private ones. Neither H nor J are mentioned in paragraph 2.

Answer: **F**

3 This paragraph focuses on the cost of for-profit schools, and this sentence extends the reader's understanding of that cost to include people besides the student. Therefore, the answer is **C**. The sentence contradicts A since it shows that government funding does come to these schools through scholarships. Neither B nor D are mentioned in this paragraph or have to do with the sentence.

Answer: **C**

4 Training in automotive repair is something the passage identifies as a strength of current nonprofit school practices. Therefore, the answer is **H**. F is mentioned as a weakness of for-profit schools in paragraph 8, G comes in the Latin America example in paragraph 6, and the final paragraph argues that following market trends, J, does not lead to good education.

Answer: **H**

5 Paragraph 5 explains that Latin American schools increased enrollment rapidly and could not hire enough qualified teachers. Therefore, the answer is **D**. The text contradicts B, since the schools enrolled the students. A and C are not mentioned.

Answer: **D**

6 The sentence before the word *vocational* states, "They see great success in fields that lead directly into the workforce." From the context, it is clear that vocational has something to do with this, so **G** is the best choice. F is a distractor, since vocational and "vocal" sound and look similar, but it does not fit the context of the sentence. H is too negative for such a positive sentence. J has nothing to do with the sentence and is only present to intimidate the student with a more difficult vocabulary word.

Answer: **G**

7 Paragraph 5 states that one of the major advantages of for-profit schools is their flexibility (I). Paragraphs 2, 3, and 4 all discuss the for-profit schools' ability to increase student enrollment easily (II). Therefore, the answer is **A**. However, paragraph 8 states that these schools cost a lot of money, ruling out (III), which eliminates B and D.

Answer: **A**

Answer: J

8 The author is cautioning the reader about some of the practices of for-profit schools. Therefore, the answer is **J**. Due to the author's reliance on evidence and the willingness to hope for future improvement in for-profit schools, H is too strongly negative. Similarly, the tone is also too negative for F or G to be true.

Answer: B

9 In paragraph 2, the author writes, "the recent enrollment growth in private higher education has not taken place in the elite schools, such as Harvard or Vanderbilt, but in for-profit colleges and universities, such as Phoenix."

Answer: G

10 The author of the passage is very concerned about the lack of quality education in these schools. If the schools were more accountable for selecting good teachers, this would help improve the quality of education. The other answer choices don't have to do with educational quality.

Answer: A

11 Harryhausen's interactions with O'Brien are all portrayed positively in the passage. When Harryhausen receives criticism from O'Brien, he is grateful and takes the advice. Therefore, the answer is **A**. This is not the attitude someone has toward someone who is unkind and demanding B or a fraud and a trickster D. Additionally, since Harryhausen willingly worked with O'Brien, it is unlikely that he saw the man as a competitor C.

Answer: J

12 The passage does much more than describe the work on *Jason and the Argonauts*, making answer choice F too narrow. Both G and H lie outside the scope of the passage, which does not address them at all. However, from the beginning of the passage to the end, the piece focuses on Harryhausen's artistic development. Therefore, the answer is **J**.

Answer: B

13 All of the other answer choices take place after Harryhausen's efforts to create special effects sequences at home. It is only after seeing *King Kong* at the beginning of the passage that he begins to be interested in special effects. Therefore, the answer is **B**.

Answer: H

14 Paragraphs 2–4 suggest that the sun's movement F created problems with shadows J and that the camera was not appropriate for stop-motion G. However, his parents do not factor into the description. Therefore, the answer is **H**.

Answer: B

15 The author believes that Harryhausen at least had the right character traits to achieve his goals, so A cannot be true. The author seems to believe that the first failure was not very grave but was simply part of the learning process, so C is unlikely. Although experience is presented as helpful for an artist recovering from failure, it is not presented as necessary in D. However, the author seems to have included this paragraph in order to point out the praiseworthy perseverance Harryhausen displayed. Therefore, the answer is **B**.

16 The eighth paragraph ends a description of *Jason and the Argonauts* with the sentence "It was his greatest achievement."

Answer: **J**

17 The parents are mentioned three times: once when they went to see *King Kong* with Harryhausen, another time when Harryhausen's father agreed to park his car in the driveway while his son filmed in the garage, and another time when they are presented as the one willing audience young Harryhausen had. This evidence suggests that they responded positively toward his dreams. Therefore, the answer is **B**.

Answer: **B**

18 Harryhausen begins thinking about this question before learning about animal anatomy, so F is incorrect. Although Harryhausen is presented as a driven personality, the author makes no suggestion that he was unhealthy in his pursuit of his interests, so H can't be right. The question is unrelated to how popular Harryhausen's films were, so J is incorrect. The only thing it addresses is how curious and eager to learn he was, as shown by his willingness to study animals at the zoo and spend his teenage years researching stop-motion. Therefore, the answer is **G**.

Answer: **G**

19 Answer choices A and B represent events that occurred after he joined the Army. D happened before he joined the Army but not immediately before. Also, since it was a personal project, there is no indication that *Evolution of the World* was a failure. Harryhausen went directly from working on puppetry to his work for the Army. Therefore, the answer is **C**.

Answer: **C**

20 In the passage, *fashion* is clearly something that he did to the stegosaurus and bear, using cloth and metal framework. The only answer choice that fits the context is F, "created." It is not possible to "emerge" creatures from cloth and metal framework, so G is incorrect. "Uncovered" suggests that the creatures were already in the cloth and metal and Harryhausen found them there, which is unlikely, eliminating H. The word "expanded" indicates growth, rather than creation, so you can eliminate J.

Answer: **F**

21 The passage explains the short-term and long-term structure used by today's scientists to explain memory. Therefore, the answer is **A**. While B and C represent information presented in the passage, the scope of the passage is much broader than these two specific points. On the other hand, the scope of the passage is too narrow for D since the passage only explains today's framework for understanding memory.

Answer: **A**

22 The author explains the human memory with only a few examples of editorializing (comments such as "in an astonishing feat ..." are very positive). Apart from these moments of excitement, the passage is primarily professional. Therefore, the answer is **H**. The positivity is not pronounced enough to merit a description such as "jovial and excited" as offered in G, while F and J are too negative to describe the passage at all.

Answer: **H**

Answer: D   **23** The passage states, "Not only does the short-term memory draw from the long-term memory, but the reverse is true as well." Since the author has just stated that the short-term memory accesses formulae in the long-term memory, *draw* must mean something like "access" or "get." The closest word to this is "pull." Therefore, the answer is **D**. While sketch B is a common meaning of the word "draw," it does not fit the context, and neither do "produce" A nor "lower" C.

Answer: G   **24** Paragraph 2 states that short-term memory can store information for 15–20 seconds. Therefore, the answer is **G**. Seven in answer H represents the number of items it can store, not the amount of time it can store them.

Answer: C   **25** While the short-term memory has a tight time restriction and quantity limit (disproving A and B), it is able to obtain information directly from the senses. The long-term memory can only gain access to information that has spent enough time in the short-term memory. Therefore, the answer is **C**. The passage does not say anything about parts of the memory being more or less sensitive to brain damage, so D is incorrect.

Answer: F   **26** In paragraph 7, the passage states, "scientists primarily research forgetting in order to improve our understanding of remembering." The answer most similar to "improve our understanding of remembering" is **F**, "to improve memory."

Answer: A   **27** Although "secretive" from B and "modest" from D can be meanings of *discrete*, only "individual" from **A** fits the context of the sentence. "Conclusive" from C indicates certainty, which does not fit the meaning of the sentence.

Answer: J   **28** Paragraph 6 states that people may lose memories due to brain damage (answer F), choosing to forget an unpleasant experience (answer G), or not reviewing the information frequently enough (answer H). However, it does not state that misunderstanding information can lead to forgetfulness. Therefore, the answer is **J**.

Answer: B   **29** The passage states, "Most scientists agree that the amount of time information spends in the short-term memory is the determining factor in whether or not it will be organized into the long-term memory." Therefore, the answer is **B**. Although it is reasonable to think that A, C, or D might have an effect on long-term memory formation, there is nothing in the passage to indicate that this is true.

Answer: G   **30** In the first and last paragraphs, the author explains that this is one way of thinking about the human memory. Therefore, the answer is **G**. It is presented as a good model but not a biological fact as in choice F. Since the author states that the model will be improved upon, the author does not present it as a perfect model, so H is incorrect. The author makes no connection between this model of understanding memory and research into forgetfulness, so J doesn't work, either.

Chapter 8

ACT Science Test

Introduction to the ACT Science Test

Most of us haven't taken a class just called "Science" since middle school, so facing an ACT-level science test can be a little scary. After all, what class has directly prepared us for something like this? But don't worry. Just like all the other sections on the ACT, the ACT Science Test is very predictable once you get used it. So let's make friends with the monster!

You can learn how to get better at this test by practicing techniques that have been designed specifically for the ACT Science Test: strategies you'll find right here in this chapter. You see, despite its name, the ACT Science Test doesn't really test much of your scientific knowledge. Instead, most questions are going to test how well you interpret scientific charts, graphs, figures, and tables of data; your ability to visualize scientific experimental setups; and your understanding of scientific hypotheses and supporting evidence.

Now, while it's true you that don't need to know a *lot* of scientific facts to do well on the ACT Science Test, you will see a small handful of questions that require you to bring in outside knowledge from chemistry, biology, physics, or earth and space science. Generally speaking, these questions will be on topics you likely covered in your introductory high school science classes or even in your middle school classes. But if you're concerned about getting a top score, it's worth refreshing your basic knowledge in all of these disciplines so that you can correctly answer questions that do require outside knowledge. (Later in this chapter, we have a list of concepts to know with important scientific terms and their meanings to get you started!)

To get a high score on the ACT Science Test, it also helps if you know how to work quickly. Although this may not sound like a skill you can learn, it actually is—no one is born knowing how to work both accurately and speedily. The more you practice, the more you'll learn how to make good decisions about which questions or passages you should work on, and which you should skip and take a guess on. Our section in this chapter on ACT Science Test pacing (page 388) is a good place to start prepping yourself to develop these skills.

If you consider yourself to be a "science person," you may feel a little more comfortable with the material you'll be presented with in this section of the test, but trust us: being a science wiz is not a requirement. No matter what score you're aiming for, with the right mindset and the right strategies, we promise you that the ACT Science Test can be mastered.

At a Glance

What to Know

- Science is the last multiple-choice test on the ACT.
- You have a 35-minute time limit.
- You'll most likely face six or seven passages (two or three Data Representation passages, two or three Research Summaries, and one Conflicting Viewpoints passage).
- You'll see 40 multiple-choice questions.
- You'll encounter a few, but not many, questions that will ask you to use some outside science knowledge.

What to Study

- How to read scientific charts and graphs (your high school science textbooks and the practice passages in *The Official ACT Prep Guide* and on act.org are good sources)
- How to work fast! ACT Science is a notoriously time-pressured test that overwhelms students with information. Doing practice tests under timed conditions can help you learn to find the information you need and tune out the rest.
- Basic scientific concepts
- For the super-motivated student: practice reading science articles geared toward the general population, such as those from *Popular Science*, so that you can get more comfortable with ACT Science Test topics. If you're really motivated, check out the academic science articles from the Public Library of Science at www.plos.org. (Note that this is a long-term prep strategy! It's unlikely to help you move your score up in the short term, but it can help you get much more comfortable with scientific writing and experimental setups.)

What Not to Study

- Science! (Well, for the most part. As we mentioned, only a few questions will ask students to use outside science knowledge, and you'll likely already have learned most of the concepts tested in your science classes at school. If you're aiming for a top score and feeling shaky on your protons and neutrons, check out the science terms at the end of this chapter.)

Top Four Tips to Improve Your ACT Science Test Score

ACT Science Tests are a little like olives; you either love them or you hate them. The nice thing, though, is that no matter where you fall on this love/hate spectrum, you can learn to at least *like* the ACT Science Test; you just have to get used to it. This comes with practice.

So here are some of the top strategies that will help you get cozier with the ACT Science Test (and be fully prepared for it).

1. **Take practice ACT Science Tests.** The ACT Science Test is unique. Unlike the ACT English Test or ACT Math Test, you can't effectively prepare for it by studying grammar rules or geometry formulas. Heck, you can't even prepare for it by studying *science*. It's rather ironic, but it's true. The ACT Science Test is more a test of scientific reasoning and data analysis than a test of science content.

   The most effective way to prepare for this test is to do a lot of ACT Science Test practice questions. Where can you find these questions? Well, this book is a good start. We also have practice passages in Magoosh's online ACT prep. You can find full-length tests in the *Official ACT Prep Guide*, plus free official practice passages and a full-length test on the ACT Student website (this test is in a guide called "Preparing for the ACT" and a version is released every year).

2. **Take timed practice tests.** Once you get familiar with the ACT Science Test, it's crucial that you practice taking tests under timed conditions. There are six to seven passages on the ACT Science Test and a 35-minute time limit, meaning you have about five to six minutes per passage. Some passages will take you more time than others, but practice timing yourself to see if you're able to work at this approximate pace. If you're not able to achieve this pace right now, don't get discouraged! The best strategy for you might be to focus on completing fewer passages in order to get your best score (it is okay to plan to skip one or even two passages). But it's really important that you figure this out in practice and not during the real exam.

3. **Read scientific writing.** The more you read about science, the more comfortable you will be with the lingo, terminology, and strange units on the ACT Science Test. Devote a little more attention to your school's science textbooks and lab experiments. Focus particularly on understanding the hypothesis, the control, the variables, and the results of the experiments you encounter.

4. **Review fundamental scientific concepts.** Every ACT Science Test will have a few questions that require you to bring in outside science knowledge. There won't be many of these, and any outside knowledge required will be on a pretty basic level. The ACT doesn't provide a list of what could be tested, but we've combed through previous exams and official materials and have a pretty good idea what the ACT considers fair game: you can find our list of must-know science concepts at the end of this chapter. Study these and you should be in pretty good shape for whatever the ACT throws at you!

ACT Science Basics: The Scientific Method

While early scientists like Aristotle and Roger Bacon made important contributions to the scientific method, these procedures were not widely practiced until the Renaissance, when Sir Francis Bacon and Galileo Galilei wrote more explicitly about how science was conducted in practice.

Although there's very little actual science knowledge tested on the ACT Science Test, one foundational process you definitely should be familiar with is the scientific method. Let's do a little refresher on Science 101.

At its core, the scientific method is an organized, systematic way of figuring out a phenomenon. So that covers everything from finding the best method for removing ice from frozen streets to an explanation of the formation of the universe.

We don't have enough space here to address the beginning of time, so let's imagine that we're interested in removing ice from streets.

Step one of the scientific method is to **ask a question**. In this case, the question would be: what's the best way to melt ice when temperatures outside are below freezing?

Step two is to **do background research** on the issue. What materials or chemicals are currently being used to melt ice? What are the chemical properties that assist in melting ice in certain environments or at certain temperatures?

Step three is to **construct a hypothesis**, which is an explanation of a phenomenon based on initial evidence, which may be very limited. It's a starting point for further scientific exploration, in which we determine whether or not this hypothesis appears to be true.

In our example, our hypothesis might be that calcium chloride would work best in our environment to melt ice.

We then move to …

Step four, which is to **conduct experiments to test this hypothesis**. Was our guess right?

In order to obtain some proof to back up this guess, we would want to test different chemicals on patches of ice while making sure all the other variables in the environment are as identical as possible.

Step five is to **analyze results**. Which chemical melted the most ice in the same time period?

Step six is to **draw a conclusion**: did your experimental results provide evidence that calcium chloride was the best de-icing agent?

To recap, the stages of the scientific method are:

1. ask a question.
2. do background research.
3. construct a hypothesis.

4. conduct experiments to test the hypothesis.
5. <u>analyze results</u>.
6. <u>draw a conclusion</u>.

We've underlined the last two steps in the list because they're the most important to consider for the ACT. In the passages on the ACT Science Test, you'll find hypotheses and descriptions of experiments that have been conducted, as well as the results and data from these experiments. But what you won't see directly stated is what we've underlined above: the analysis and the conclusions of these experiments.

Why doesn't the ACT provide you with an experiment's analysis or conclusion? The reason is simple: they are precisely what the ACT is going to ask *you* to address in your answers to the questions. The ACT may also ask you a handful of questions directly about the scientific method itself. We're going to walk through a couple of examples of these types of questions shortly. But first, let's take a look at some terms we need to know.

Scientific Method Terminology

Every experiment has what's called an *independent variable* and a *dependent variable*.

The **independent variable** is what is changed or manipulated by the researchers.

In the case of our de-icing experiment, the students are changing the chemical they're using to melt the ice, so the chemical is our independent variable. In order to ensure that any outcomes are a result of changes in the independent variable, a good science experiment eliminates all other possible differences. The students in our experiment would want to test the chemicals on equivalent amounts of ice for the same time period and in the same location to help ensure that the independent variable is the only measurable change.

The **dependent variable** is the response measured based on the change in the independent variable.

In other words, the dependent variable *depends* on the independent variable. In our example, the dependent variable is the amount of ice that each chemical melts (measured in some scientific unit; let's say millimeters).

In many experiments, we also have what is called a *control*, and the control group's job is to make sure that there's nothing else interfering with our experimental results. So, in the case of this hypothetical experiment, we'd want to place an *untreated* tray of ice in the same location and measure the melting of the experimental groups against the melting of the untreated plate of ice. We can't just assume that any ice melting is entirely a result of the chemicals; the control, the untreated plate of ice, helps us to be more confident in our results.

It's important to understand the scientific method on the ACT for two reasons.

The first is that all (yes, *all!*) of the questions on the ACT Science Test will pertain to experiments in some way, most explicitly in the Research Summaries passages. It'll be impossible for you to get inside the heads of the test-makers if you don't understand how scientific experiments are conducted.

The second is that there will be also a handful of questions that *directly* test you on the scientific method. You can find a couple of examples of these types of questions in the "Question Types" section of this chapter.

ACT Science Basics: Understanding Tables, Graphs, and Figures

If there's one thing you need to be comfortable with on the ACT, it's how to read tables, figures, and graphs. Here's a review of the basics, along with some specific tips on what to know about these visual aids on the ACT Science Test.

Tables

Tables organize information into columns and rows. They allow us to link attributes and see their relationships. For example, here's a simple chart of the number of students from different schools who are taking the ACT and SAT:

	ACT	SAT
Marlborough	180	112
Tamarindo	134	154
Glover	90	110
Hass	168	182

If you wanted to know how many students at Glover High School were taking the ACT, well, you would find the column for "ACT" and the row for "Glover" and see what the value is in the cell where they intersect.

You can also combine information. For example, if you wanted to know how many students total at all four schools were taking the ACT, you would just add up all the numbers in the column for ACT (the answer is 572). If you wanted to know how many tests (ACT or SAT) were taken at Tamarindo High, you would add together all the values in the row for Tamarindo (the answer is 288).

Let's look at some more ACT-like tables:

Table 1

Response Measure	P. falciparum			P. vivax		
	Drug Combo C	Drug Combo D	Drug Combo E	Drug Combo C	Drug Combo D	Drug Combo E
	% patients free of parasites					
Day 1	0	25	90	62	87	55
Day 2	30	49	95	85	90	58
Day 7	75	51	100	99	97	76
Day 14	100	51	100	100	100	99
Day 42	100	52	100	20	100	89

Table 1 adapted from Laman, Moore, et al., "Artemisinin-Naphthoquine versus Artemether-Lumefantrine for Uncomplicated Malaria in Papua New Guinean Children: An Open-Label Randomized Trial," *PLOS Medicine* 11, no. 12 (2014), doi.org/10.1371/journal.pmed.1001773.

Table 2

Trial #	Battery Voltage (V)	Resistance (Ω)	Current (A)
1	6	3	2.000
2	9	3	3.000
3	12	3	4.000
4	6	6	1.000
5	9	6	1.500
6	12	6	2.000
7	6	9	0.667
8	9	9	1.000
9	12	9	1.333

There's a lot of random information here, but we're going to focus on the format of what you'll see in ACT tables. The first thing to note about tables or graphs on the ACT is how important the labels are. You should get used to matching the labels with key words and phrases in the question and answer choices. Look on the top, bottom, left, and right sides of graphs and diagrams as well as within the graphs and figures to familiarize yourself with all of the data labels.

For example, in Table 2, do a quick scan and note the terms *voltage*, *resistance*, and *current* appearing at the top and the different trial numbers down the left side. When you're looking at a test page covered with information, it can get overwhelming pretty quickly, so practice focusing on just the labels before anything else.

Tables, as opposed to graphs, make it easy to see the exact numbers in the data.

In Table 1, we can see that each column is tracking the percentage of patients on each particular drug combination who were free of parasites on each day of the trial. If a question was about Drug Combination C and what happened on Day 14, we would want to mark the cells where the first column labeled Drug Combination C intersects with the row for Day 14 and where the second column labeled Drug Combination C intersects with the row for Day 14.

Graphs

Graphs show the relationship between two things with lines, curves, bars, or other indicators. The same information can usually be conveyed in a table or graph, but graphs make it a little easier to see trends in data and compare data visually, which is why data tables are often turned into graphs.

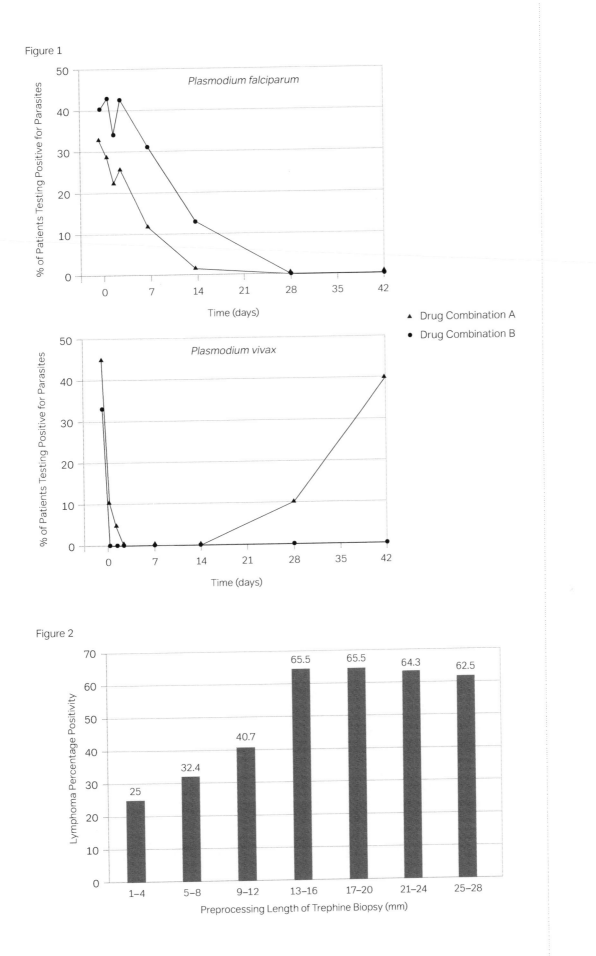

Figure 1

Plasmodium falciparum

▲ Drug Combination A
● Drug Combination B

Plasmodium vivax

Figure 2

Figure 1 adapted from Laman, Moore, et al., "Artemisinin-Naphthoquine versus Artemether-Lumefantrine for Uncomplicated Malaria in Papua New Guinean Children: An Open-Label Randomized Trial," *PLOS Medicine* 11, no. 12 (2014), doi.org/10.1371/journal.pmed.1001773.

Figure 2 adapted from Surbhi Goyal, Usha Rani Singh, and Usha Rusia, "Comparative Evaluation of Bone Marrow Aspirate with Trephine Biopsy in Hematological Disorders and Determination of Optimum Trephine Length in Lymphoma Infiltration," *Mediterranean Journal of Hematology and Infectious Diseases* 6, no. 1 (January 2014), 10.4084/MJHID.2014.002.

Above are a couple of examples of the most common type of graphs you'll see on the ACT: Figure 1 is a line graph and Figure 2 is a bar graph.

There are a few things important to note about graphs like these.

Typically, the *independent variable* is graphed along the horizontal axis and the *dependent variable* is tracked along the vertical axis (check on the section above on the scientific method if the meaning of these terms has slipped your mind!).

In layman's terms, what's *changing* in the experiment is tracked along the bottom and the resulting *effect of that change* is tracked along the side of the graph.

So, for example, in Figure 2, we have a chart showing the correlation between the length of a biopsy and a positive test for lymphoma. The independent variable—what the researchers are manipulating—is the length of the biopsy, which is tracked along the horizontal axis. What's dependent on this is the percentage of biopsies testing positive for lymphoma, which is noted along the vertical axis.

Figure 3

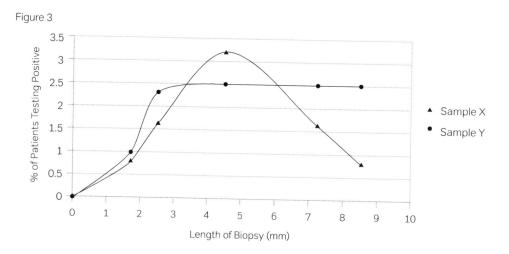

Something to notice on graphs are the points where something interesting happens in the data. So, for example:

- Where does the line spike up or dip down?
- Where does a line (or a series of bars) level out after some variability? Or does it trend upward to infinity or downward to zero?

Often, questions on the ACT will target these key points in some way, so noticing them in advance will help you make sense of the data and be prepared for questions that might hint at where something special happens in the data.

Explanatory Tables and Figures

Data tables and graphs aren't the only visuals you'll see on the ACT Science Test, though. Sometimes, you'll come across explanatory tables and figures, which provide vital (and usually pretty complex) information in a visual way. These tables and figures can take on a variety of forms, but here are a few possibilities.

Table 1: Pollutant Standards

Pollutant	Sources	National Standard
Ozone (O_3)	Produced by reaction of volatile organic compounds (VOCs) and NOx in the presence of sunlight	0.075 ppm
Particulate Matter (PM)	Fuel combustion, industrial processes, agriculture, and unpaved roads. Produced by chemical reactions involving sulfur dioxide.	PM2.5: 12 $\mu g/m^3$ PM10: 150 $\mu g/m^3$
Lead (Pb)	Smelters and other metal industries, combustion of leaded gasoline by aircraft, waste incinerators, battery manufacturing	0.15 $\mu g/m^3$

Table 1 adapted from information in *Our Nation's Air: Status and Trends Through 2010* (Research Triangle Park, NC: US Environmental Protection Agency, 2012).

Figure 4: DNA Replication Models

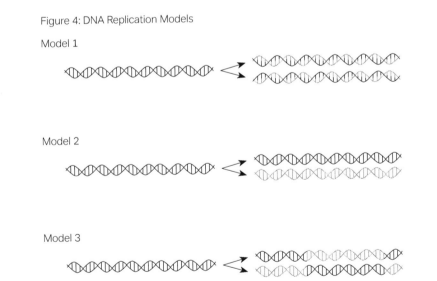

Model 1

Model 2

Model 3

Figure 4 adapted from Mike Jones, "An overview of three postulated types of DNA replication," *Wikimedia Commons*, September 15, 2005, commons.wikimedia.org/wiki/File:DNAreplicationModes.png.

While the ACT won't test you on all of the information in a passage (and sometimes it won't test you on very much of it at all!), if you see an explanatory chart or diagram in the passage like the ones above, *pay attention to it.*

The appearance of an explanatory diagram or chart usually means that the ACT test-makers thought that something was sufficiently complex that it would be better presented in a visual format rather than in text. And often this also means that you'll be using it in some capacity—so heads up!

Strange Figures

You should know that the ACT does like to throw some strange figures or illustrations at you; these figures may not look like anything you've ever seen in a science class, either. This isn't because you are expected to understand really complex scientific situations, but rather because the test-makers want to make sure that you understand the fundamentals of how scientific data can be presented and know how to apply those principles to lots of different figures and graphs.

If you see a really complex table or graph, don't panic. Instead, focus on the labels and finding the points where the labels listed in the question "meet up," just as you would on a regular table or a bar or line graph.

If you're not completely comfortable with all of these figures, don't worry. The ACT Science Test Strategy section of this chapter (page 375) goes into more detail about how you'll be expected to use tables, graphs, and figures on the ACT.

ACT Science Format

Passage Types

There are three distinct passage types on the ACT Science Test: Data Representation, Research Summaries, and Conflicting Viewpoints. Here's how the format breaks down on most tests.

Passage Type	Number on Test
Data Representation	2 or 3
Research Summaries	2 or 3
Conflicting Viewpoints	1

Although the ACT could make changes to this format at any time, the most likely grouping that you'll face at the moment will include two Data Representation passages, three Research Summaries passages, and one Conflicting Viewpoint passage (six passages total).

We say "most likely" because this is what we've seen on the majority of recent ACT Science Tests. But because the ACT test-maker hasn't confirmed this order, you should be prepared for a different mixture of passage types, and you might even see seven passages (the practice test in this book has seven). Rest assured that the total number of questions on an ACT Science Test is always 40.

Here's what you're going to face on each passage type:

Data Representation Passages

Data Representation passages are typically the most straightforward of the three ACT Science passage types. These passages present students with a few figures, graphs, or charts, without the complexity of the experimental setups or scientific hypotheses you'll face on Research Summaries or Conflicting Viewpoints passages.

This doesn't mean that Data Representation passages are easy, but most students find them to be the easiest out of the three types because they rarely ask students to do the kind of higher-level scientific reasoning that the two other passage types require. As a result, students who are uncomfortable with the Science section often like to concentrate on these passages first. *(Tip: This could be a good pacing strategy for you. Learn to recognize Data Representation passages and get them out of the way first!)*

How to recognize a Data Representation passage

These passages won't have headers such as "Experiment 1," "Study 2," or "Scientist 1," and they often have a lot less text than the other passage types.

Research Summaries

Research Summaries provide descriptions of one or more related experiments or studies conducted by hypothetical scientists or science students. These passages generally have more text than Data Representation passages because they describe the design and procedures of a particular study in addition to presenting its results on tables or graphs. The questions with these passages ask students to understand, evaluate, and interpret the design and procedures of the experiments, and then analyze the results.

How to recognize a Research Summaries passage

These passages typically include one or more experiments or studies with headers such as "Experiment 1," "Trial 2," or "Study 3."

Conflicting Viewpoints

There is generally only one Conflicting Viewpoints passage on each ACT Science Test. This passage type typically presents two (sometimes three) alternative viewpoints, hypotheses, or theories on a specific scientific phenomenon. Some students refer to these passages as "Fighting Scientists" passages because these different viewpoints always fundamentally disagree with one another—even though they may, and actually often will, agree on some points. Your job is to notice all the similarities and differences between the viewpoints and answer the questions that follow. These questions might ask you to determine which scientists or theories would agree with a certain point, or how new information might strengthen or weaken the different hypotheses.

How to recognize a Conflicting Viewpoints passage

These passages typically have no figures or diagrams, or only one or two simple diagrams, and a lot of text. Because you have to read these passages in full and because the questions often involve a lot more critical thinking than other passage types, many students like to save this passage type for last.

Remember that you can do the passages in any order that you want! As you practice, notice whether you struggle with one passage type more than the others; start with the ones you find easier to get your feet wet and pick up as many points as you can in case you run out of time. If any passage seems too complicated or intimidating, remember that you can skip it and come back to it at the end!

Question Types

Knowledge is power, and becoming familiar with the question types on the ACT Science Test can do wonders for your score. Learning these question types will make an unfamiliar test seem like an old friend (well, maybe an acquaintance) and can help you identify your plan of attack for different questions more easily. You won't find these question types labeled as such on the ACT, but trust us: they are there, and they are worth knowing.

The Five Major ACT Science Test Question Types

Note: These are not official categories or titles, and other ACT prep resources might use different names. However, these are the categories we use at Magoosh, and the ones that have been most helpful to our students:

1. Detail questions
2. Pattern questions
3. Inference questions
4. Scientific method questions
5. Compare and contrast questions

Let's break them down a little more:

Detail questions

Detail questions ask you to locate and report back on a specific data point from a graph, a chart, a table, a diagram, or sometimes text in a passage. For the most part, they're pretty straightforward.

These questions are all about finding the right information. If there's any trick to them, it's making sure that you're looking in the right place. Often, the ACT will give you multiple figures or graphs with the same labels on the horizontal and vertical axes or with similar numbers in the data. When we see students miss these detail questions, the most common reason is because they mixed up which chart or graph they were supposed to be looking at, or which axis.

Here's an example of a detail question:

Plants	Height (inches)		
	30 days	60 days	90 days
Plant 1	4.7	5.8	7.2
Plant 2	6.2	6.8	8.1
Plant 3	8.2	10.1	12.3

What was the approximate growth of Plant 3 between 60 days and 90 days?

Most of what you see on the ACT is going to look a little bit more complex than what you see above, but this question works for illustrative purposes. For a question like this one, you need to find the height at 60 days (10.1 inches) and the height at 90 days (12.3 inches) and subtract the 60-day height from the 90-day height.

This tells us that the change in height is 2.2 inches. The key here is to make sure we're looking at the values for Plant 3—not Plant 1 or 2.

Here are two other detail question stems, just to give you a couple more examples:

The highest monthly average air temperature recorded during the first 6 months of the study was:

According to Scientist 1, compared to burning biomass, burning coal creates less of which of the following?

Again, all you need to do is look up this information in the passage and sometimes make basic calculations with it; you don't need to infer anything.

Pattern questions

Pattern questions ask you to do a bit more than just find a data point or a detail in the passage. They ask you to *predict* a trend or a relationship among the given data points.

You generally solve these problems by *interpolating*, which is finding a point between existing data points, or *extrapolating*, which is following a trend beyond the existing data. But you don't need to know these terms (although, hey, bonus vocabulary!), and the process is easier than it sounds. Let's look at an example.

Here is a sample line graph of the same data as in the previous problem.

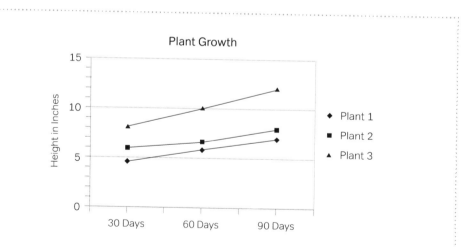

1 Given constant growth, approximately how tall would Plant 2 be at 45 days?

   A. 5 inches

   B. 6.5 inches

   C. 9 inches

   D. 12 inches

To answer this question, we need to interpolate and find the data point for Plant 2 that's halfway between 30 days and 60 days. Use your finger or pencil to trace the chart to that point and mark it with your pencil. As with a lot of ACT Science Test questions, you may not be able to get an exact answer based on the given graph, but a ballpark answer will be sufficient. The ACT will never give you two values so close together that they could both be correct.

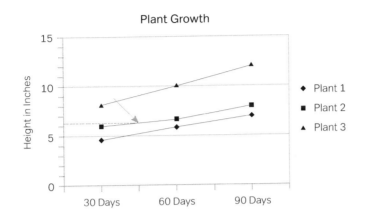

It looks like the height of Plant 2 at 45 days would be between 6 and 7 inches, so the best answer is **B**.

---

2 How tall would Plant 3 be after 120 days, given constant growth?

  F. 9 inches
  G. 11 inches
  H. 14 inches
  J. 20 inches

Use your pencil to extend the line out to where 120 days would be (or if you want to use the fancy term, "extrapolate" from the pattern where the line would be at 120 days), and then refer to the vertical axis to estimate what the height of Plant 3 would be at that point. We could make an informed guess it might be somewhere around 14 inches tall, assuming growth was constant, so our answer is **H**.

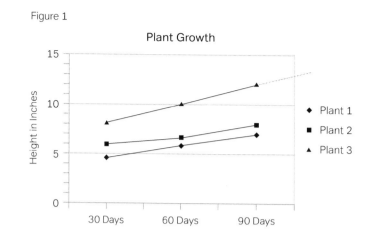

Figure 1

To recap, the answers to pattern questions are almost always found by finding additional data points between existing ones or extending a pattern of data beyond what's presented to you.

Inference questions

Now things start to get a bit more complicated.

Inference questions ask you to draw conclusions from the data and any additional information provided. Sometimes you'll have to take information from a couple of different experiments or studies, and sometimes you'll have to determine how new information would affect the given experiment.

For example, you might be asked to figure out what would happen if students conducting an experiment decided to alter one of the variables in an experiment. Let's say you and your friend Joe are testing friction in physics class by sliding a brick across the table. An inference question might ask, What would happen if you changed the texture of the surface of the table?

Don't panic yet.

In most cases, all the information you need to solve this problem will be provided for you, but there isn't going to be any *one* piece of data that you can point to for the answer. You're going to have to look at multiple pieces of data and draw some inferences.

Here is another example of what an inference question might look like on the test:

> How would the results of Experiment 1 be affected, if at all, if the syringe contents were adjusted to decrease the concentration of magnesium hydroxide?

For an inference question, we're going to be *applying* data and information from the passage. And that's what can make these questions more difficult than detail and pattern questions.

Since inference questions can be a bit more challenging, we're giving you a question below that's harder than the examples above! Are you up for the challenge?

Blood typing is a way of classifying blood based on which antigens are present on the surface of red blood cells (RBCs). Antigens are molecules that can produce a response by the immune system. The immune system, in turn, produces antibodies that bond tightly to their specific antigen.

ABO blood type in most cases is determined by the two alleles (gene variants) of the ABO gene an individual carries. This gene encodes a glycosyltransferase—an enzyme responsible for producing antigens on the surface of the red blood cell. People with an IA allele for this gene produce type A antigens, while people with an IB allele produce B antigens. The third possible allele, IO, results in the production of a nonfunctional glycosyltransferase. The combination of alleles, also known as genotype, determines a person's blood type.

Blood transfusions can only be performed safely if the recipient does not produce antibodies to any of the antigens found on the donor RBCs. Type O individuals, for example, cannot receive A or B blood because they produce antibodies to A and B antigens. Individuals who produce A and B antibodies can, however, safely receive Type O blood.

The relationship between an individual's genotype for the ABO gene, ABO type, and ABO antibodies produced is illustrated in Table 2.

Table 1: ABO Genotypes

Genotype	Blood Type	Antibodies Produced
$I^A I^A$ or $I^A I^O$	A	B
$I^O I^B$ or $I^B I^B$	B	A
$I^A I^B$	AB	—
$I^O I^O$	O	A + B

In 1952, an additional gene was found that affects blood type. This gene, FUT1, codes for fucosyltransferase, an enzyme that is responsible for an earlier step in the production of RBC antigens. In patients with type A, B, or AB blood, the H antigen is modified to produce A and/or B antigens, while in type O individuals, the H antigen remains unchanged, as shown in Figure 1. The H antigen remains present in modified or unmodified form in A, B, AB, and O blood types.

Continued on next page

Dr. Charles Drew was an American scientist who figured out how to separate the plasma from blood to create a more effective system of blood storage. This innovation allowed for the massive blood banks used during World War II and continues to save the lives of trauma victims today.

There is a rare allele of the fucosyltransferase gene that produces a non-functional enzyme. Individuals with this allele are said to have the rare Bombay blood type, and they are the only individuals who produce antibodies to the H antigen.

Figure 1: Production of RBC antigens

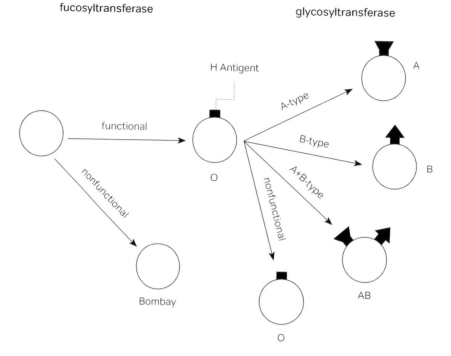

Table 2 shows the relationship between FUT1 genotype and the presence or absence of functional fucosyltransferase.

Table 2

Genotypes	Fucosyltransferase
HH	functional
Hh	functional
hh	nonfunctional

Based on the passage, individuals of the Bombay blood type can receive blood from individuals with which of the following blood types?

A. Only Bombay blood type
B. Only O blood type
C. Only non-Bombay blood types
D. All blood types

The answer is **A**, "Only Bombay blood type." The passage tells us that blood transfusions can only be performed safely if the recipient does not produce antibodies to any of the antigens found on the donor RBCs. The passage also tells us that the H antigen is present in A, B, AB, and O blood types, and that individuals with the rare Bombay blood type are the only individuals who produce antibodies to the H antigen. Therefore, those with the Bombay blood type cannot receive blood from any of the other blood types except Bombay.

Scientific method questions

Every ACT Science Test includes a few scientific method questions. Practice recognizing them to grab some easy points!

Scientific method questions ask you to consider how experiments are designed or set up, how experimenters interpret data, or how hypotheses are tested. Basically, they ask about anything involved in conducting good scientific experiments.

Here are some examples:

Which of the following is an independent variable in Experiment 1?

Which of the following variables was kept constant in Study 2?

Which of the following statements best explains why, in Experiment 2, the experimenter waited five minutes before testing the temperature of the water?

You can see that to answer these questions, you need to know a little bit of information about how science experiments are conducted, such as knowing what independent and dependent variables are. (*Hint:* Check out the "Scientific Method" section of this chapter!) Yet most of what you're going to be using to answer these types of questions is just good common sense.

Practice Questions

In Experiment 1, students filled equal-sized trays with 1 L of water, froze them, and then sprayed each tray with 100 mL of a different chemical de-icer and placed them in a freezer set at 30°F.

In Experiment 2, students replicated the treated trays from Experiment 1 and placed them on the sidewalk outside at 9 a.m. when the temperature was 28°F. They left the trays for three hours and then measured the ice melted in each tray after each hour.

1 Which of the following factors was NOT directly controlled by the students in Experiment 2?

  A. The size of the trays
  B. The temperature of the outdoor environment
  C. The amount of chemicals sprayed on each tray
  D. The initial amount of ice in each tray

2 A student, after examining the trays in Experiment 2, was concerned that patchy sunlight might be interfering with the results of the experiment. Which of the following procedures would best help the student investigate the impact of sunlight on the ice?

  F. Moving the trays indoors to an air-conditioned classroom
  G. Moving the trays to a completely shaded location
  H. Creating identical pairs of trays with each chemical and placing one set in the same location as Experiment 2 and one set next to the first under a shade that completely blocks sunrays
  J. Creating identical pairs of trays with each chemical and placing one set in in the same location as Experiment 2 and one in a nearby location shaded by a tree

Answers and Explanations

1 Remember, anything that changes or varies in an experiment is *not* controlled for. The information for Experiment 2 tells us that the trays were set up in the same fashion as Experiment 1. We know that all the trays were the same size, so we can rule out answer choice A. We also know that the trays were sprayed with 100 mL of de-icer, so we can rule out answer choice C (this, by the way, is our independent variable), and we also know that they were all filled with the same amount of water, so we can rule out answer choice D. But answer choice **B**, "The temperature of the outdoor environment," stands out. Initially it might seem like there's a constant temperature the trays are being exposed to: 28°. But the outdoors is not nearly as controllable as the freezer, and since the trays were left outside for three hours, it stands to reason that the temperature might vary a bit. Regardless, the students aren't doing anything to control the temperature, so it could potentially change throughout the course of the experiment. Our answer is **B**.

2 We can rule out answer choice F, because if we move all the trays indoors, then we wouldn't really know if the sunlight was causing a difference. Same thing with choice G: moving all the trays to a shaded location wouldn't help us know if the sunlight is making a difference. But answer choices **H** and J offer us that all-important *control*: a set of trays that is in the same location where the student thinks there might be an interference and an identical set in another location not affected by the sun. But because the question is asking us what would BEST help the student investigate the problem, J is not the best answer; if the student were to place the trays in another shaded location, there might be other variables that could interfere (such as the surface temperature of the ground), so **H** offers us the best option, giving us a control.

Compare and contrast questions

Compare and contrast questions appear only with the Conflicting Viewpoints passage (the passage type that asks you to compare and contrast two or more different scientific opinions on a situation).

These questions ask you to compare various aspects of opposing arguments, such as how one scientist might respond to another scientist's argument. Or, it might introduce additional variables and ask how they would affect the arguments presented.

Here are some examples of what compare and contrast question stems look like:

Scientist 2's views differ from Scientist 1's views in that only Scientist 2 believes that solar energy can be more effectively harnessed by:

Both scientists would most likely agree that the increase in radiation levels was due to:

If it was determined that the asteroid broke apart prior to entering the planet's atmosphere, how would this affect the arguments of both scientists?

Like inference questions, these questions require us to make some logical leaps, so they often tend to be on the harder side. To practice compare and contrast questions, see the practice questions at the end of the chapter for some example passages.

Okay! Now that you've learned the five major ACT Science Test question types, let's talk about why all of this matters:

- Knowing the ACT Science Test question types can help you save some time and some mental energy on a very fast-paced test because you'll have a better idea of what your process should be when approaching these questions.

- If you see a pattern question, for instance, you might know immediately that you need to trace a line graph beyond the existing graph or determine in which direction numbers are increasing on a chart. Recognizing an inference question might clue you into the fact that you need to read some background information in the passage in order to draw some appropriate conclusions.

- If the ACT Science Test is a weak section for you, or if you're running out of time, knowing how to identify the typically easier question types (detail and pattern questions) can help you pick up points more easily and quickly.

- Simply knowing what to expect and realizing that there is some method to the ACT Science Test madness can help make this test seem a lot less intimidating.

ACT Science Strategy

Using Key Terms

One of the most fundamental strategies for doing well on the ACT Science Test is knowing how to identify the key terms in the question and find them in the passage. Since there's intense time pressure on the ACT Science Test, it's essential to be able to quickly pull out the key pieces of data and use them. This means training your brain to hone in on what we call *key terms* rather than trying to understand everything in the passage in detail. Tuning out the noise will allow you to increase the number of questions you can confidently get right, but this strategy does take some getting used to.

What are "key terms"?
Key terms are the words, phrases, units, or numbers that are essential to answering that question and that appear in the tables, graphs, figures, or passage.

Key terms always include:
- the name and number of the figure, table, or experiment to which the question refers;
- specific names of substances, objects, and categories;
- any numbers or percentages that appear in the question;
- any trial or group numbers that appear in the question;
- anything that is capitalized or has a numerical value; and
- what the question is actually asking you to find.

For every single question on the ACT Science Test, underline the key terms. This helps keep you engaged and focused on what is important.

Here's an example question:

> Based on the results in Figure 1, which of the following could be the absorbance values for samples containing 4 ppm of chromium and copper, respectively?

And here it is again with the key terms underlined:

> Based on the results in <u>Figure 1</u>, which of the following could be the <u>absorbance values</u> for samples containing <u>4 ppm</u> of <u>chromium</u> and <u>copper</u>, respectively?

Now, let's try to answer it. We'll even obscure the other words in the question so that you can practice tuning out the noise and focusing only on the key terms:

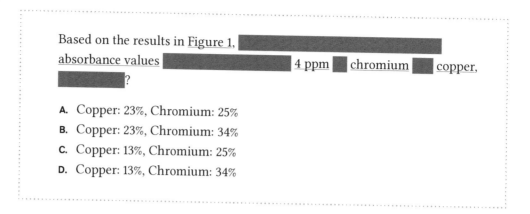

Based on the results in <u>Figure 1</u>, ▓▓▓▓▓▓▓▓▓▓▓▓
<u>absorbance values</u> ▓▓▓▓▓▓▓▓ 4 ppm ▓ <u>chromium</u> ▓ <u>copper</u>,
▓▓▓▓▓?

   A. Copper: 23%, Chromium: 25%
   B. Copper: 23%, Chromium: 34%
   C. Copper: 13%, Chromium: 25%
   D. Copper: 13%, Chromium: 34%

Now, focus on ONLY those key terms and find them in the figure below.

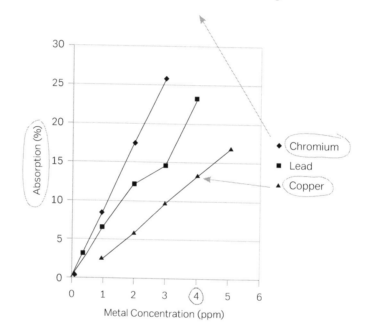

We've circled the key terms for you, but to avoid making mistakes, you should do this as well when you are annotating the ACT Science Test!

See how the key terms seem to automatically point us to the correct percentages in the answer? Copper at 4 ppm is at about 13%. Chromium is off the chart, but if the line continued (to where the arrow we drew in is pointing), we could estimate that it would be at about 34% ppm, so our answer is **D**.

It takes self-discipline to underline or circle the key terms on every single question, but it will greatly reduce the number of errors you make on the ACT Science Test. These notations help your brain hone in on what's important and tune out the rest—this makes the effort well worth it!

Dealing with Unfamiliar Terms

As we've already mentioned, the ACT Science Test is all about getting comfortable with uncomfortable situations. In a lot of cases, the unfamiliar terms that you'll encounter on the ACT Science Test are one of the factors that lead to discomfort.

Let's look at an example. This is an ACT question in which we've replaced all the actual terms with fake, science-y sounding words, so the playing field is completely leveled here. Regardless of how much science you know, no one will be able to figure this out based on background knowledge.

Agrusulator 1	Agrusulator 2	Interepulse (Ψ_1)	Valcoplitude (Ψ_2)
Glommtom	Hydruticle	25	18
Glommtom	Hydruticle	45	32
Glommtom	Hydruticle	80	48
Glommtom	Geoitum	25	24.99
Glommtom	Aerosulator	25	16
Glommtom	Helievice	25	10
Hydruticle	Glommtom	25	34
Hydruticle	Glommtom	35	50
Hydruticle	Glommtom	45	70
Hydruticle	Glommtom	25	39

Based on the data in Table 1, which of the following could possibly be the valcoplitude when the first agrusulator is glommtom and the second agrusulator is hydruticle, given an interepulse of 28?

A. 15 ψ

B. 20 ψ

C. 31 ψ

D. 36 ψ

Okay, what?

Without knowing what any of this means, we promise you that you can still answer the question.

Let's look at the table and see what we can figure out. If our first agrusulator is glommtom and the second one is hydruticle, that means we want to be looking at the first three rows of the chart, where glommtom is listed first and hydruticle is listed second. The question tells us our interepulse is 28, which would fall between rows 1 and 2 of the chart (row 1 has an interepulse of 25 and row 2 has an interepulse of 45). Further examining the rows 1 and 2, we can see that valcoplitude for an interepulse of 28 would likely be between 18 ψ and 32 ψ. This lets us eliminate answer choices A and D. Now, to decide between 20 and 31, we need to look at whether a 28 interepulse is closer to 25 or 45. We know that 28 is a lot closer to 25 than it is to 45. We can infer that the valcoplitude would likely be closer to 18 than it is to 32 (since the valcoplitude for an interrepulse of 25 is 18). So our answer would be **B**, 20 ψ.

Bonus tip: You'll likely encounter several long and unfamiliar words on the ACT Science Test (or on other tests). When reading them or jotting down notes, use abbreviations. For instance, "agrusulator" could become "AG" and "valcoplitude" could become V. That keeps things much simpler.

For many of the questions you see on the ACT Science Test, you don't need to completely understand the terms and units in order to answer the question—you just need to be able to recognize them and find them in the passage. Time to breathe a sigh of relief!

Finding Trends and Patterns

As we've seen, one of the most important skills you need to master in order to succeed on the ACT Science Test is quickly and accurately determining trends and patterns in figures and tables. Let's talk a little bit more about what that means.

Imagine you see the following figures on a Science passage (don't worry about understanding what the terms mean right now; you don't need to):

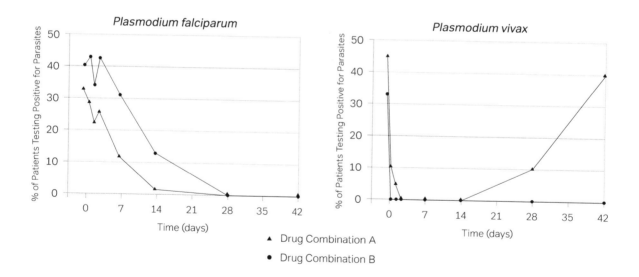

Figures adapted from Laman, Moore, et al., "Artemisinin-Naphthoquine versus Artemether-Lumefantrine for Uncomplicated Malaria in Papua New Guinean Children: An Open-Label Randomized Trial," *PLOS Medicine* 11, no. 12 (2014), doi.org/10.1371/journal.pmed.1001773.

Now, imagine you see a question like this:

Between days 14 and 42, the percentage of patients testing positive for *Plasmodium vivax* after being treated with Drug Combination A:

A. increased only.

B. decreased only.

C. increased then decreased.

D. decreased then increased.

What do you need to know?

To begin with, you need to know what it means when lines slope downward or upward on a graph. We can figure this out by looking at our *x*-axis and *y*-axis. The *x*-axis (the horizontal axis) shows days of the study increasing from left to right, so the study is progressing in time from left to right. The *y*-axis (the vertical axis) shows that the percentage of patients testing positive for parasites increases from bottom to top.

This means that if a line is trending upward as the days go on, then the percentage of patients testing positive for parasites is increasing over time. If it is trending downward, then the percentage of patients testing positive is decreasing over time.

Note that if we look at the Drug Combination A line for Plasmodium vivax (the one with the triangles) over the course of all of the days, the line goes down, then levels out at the bottom, then shoots up again. This is why you might see answer choices like C and D, in the question above, which describe some variability in the line on a graph. In this case, though, note that the question limits us to only what happens between days 14 and 42, which is different than the whole length of the study.

Second of all, on these pattern questions, you always need to make sure you're looking at the right figure. This is a common mistake students make on the ACT Science Test. If you neglected the reference to *Plasmodium vivax* in the question and accidentally looked at the first figure for *Plasmodium falciparum*, you might select B, decreased only, as your answer. But the question is asking us about Plasmodium vivax, so we need to look at the second figure. Now, if you chose the correct figure, but neglected to note that the question asks about days 14 to 42, you might incorrectly select D, decreased then increased, because the line for Drug Combination A does seem to do that over the course of the study. But if we limit our scope to between days 14 and 22, we see that the percentage of patients infected <u>increases only</u>, so the answer is **A**.

Trends and patterns questions might also refer to tables of data. In this case, you don't have lines to help you see the direction data is moving in, so you need to look at the values in the table to help you figure out the trend.

Imagine you see this table:

Response Measure	P. falciparum			P. vivax		
	Drug C	Drug D	Drug E	Drug C	Drug D	Drug E
	% patients free of parasites					
Day 1	0	25	90	62	87	55
Day 2	30	49	95	85	90	58
Day 7	75	51	100	99	97	76
Day 14	100	51	100	100	100	99
Day 42	100	52	100	20	100	89

Table adapted from Laman, Moore, et al., "Artemisinin-Naphthoquine versus Artemether-Lumefantrine for Uncomplicated Malaria in Papua New Guinean Children: An Open-Label Randomized Trial," *PLOS Medicine* 11, no. 12 (2014), doi.org/10.1371/journal.pmed.1001773.

And this question:

As the percentage of patients infected with *P. falciparum* and treated with Drug Combination C decreased, the percentage of patients infected with *P. vivax* and treated with the same drug combination:

A. increased only.

B. decreased only.

C. increased then decreased.

D. decreased then increased.

This one might trip you up if you don't note one important detail: the chart shows "percent of patients free of parasites," NOT "percent of patients infected." This is a common way that the ACT Science Test complicates questions. If we look down the column for patients infected with *P. falciparum* and treated with Drug Combination C, we see that the number of patients *free* of the parasite increases as we go down the column (this logically means that the number of patients *infected* decreases as we go down the column). In other words, we're reading the trend going down the column, not going up the column.

We'd suggest drawing an arrow on the table in the correct direction to keep this fact straight in your head:

Response Measure	P. falciparum			P. vivax		
	Drug C	Drug D	Drug E	Drug C	Drug D	Drug E
	% patients free of parasites					
Day 1	0	25	90	62	87	55
Day 2	30	49	95	85	90	58
Day 7	75	51	100	99	97	76
Day 14	100	51	100	100	100	99
Day 42	100	52	100	20	100	89

Now, we need to look at what happens to the numbers in the Drug Combination C column under *P. vivax* as we follow the column in this same downward direction. We can see that the percent of patients *free* of parasites increases from 62 to 100, then decreases from 100 to 20. This means that the number of patients *infected* decreases then increases, so our answer is **D**. Though this kind of table-reading can be confusing at first, it's a good thing to get used to, as this will pop up all the time on the test.

Sometimes There Is No Trend!

On some ACT Science Test questions, you'll see that one of the answer choices states something along the lines of "there is no trend," or "neither increasing nor decreasing." Sometimes the data has no apparent pattern or trend to it: this can be true in real-life scientific situations, as well. Don't worry if you can't find a trend; if one of your answer choices gives you the option to select that there is no pattern to the data, this very well might be the case.

Learning how to find patterns and trends on ACT Science Test tables and figures (and making sure you're following them in the right direction) is an important skill to master if you want to get a higher ACT Science Test score. Practice reading tables and figures in order to determine when values are increasing or decreasing. Most importantly, make sure you are looking at the right table/line/column/data point!

Linking Tables, Graphs, Figures, and Information

While many questions on the ACT only require you to look at one figure or table, there are also those that require you to combine information gleaned from multiple figures, tables, or even different sections of the written passage. This is not as intimidating as it might initially seem—as long as you follow one key process. We call this *finding the link* (a really creative title, we know).

If a question asks you to look at multiple sources, you want to find the key terms that appear in both sources. These are your "links" that help you connect the dots between the data.

Let's look at an example question:

> Considering the data in Figure 1 and Table 1, which of the following could have been the absorption level measured for lead in Sample 5?
>
> **A.** 5%
> **B.** 7%
> **C.** 13%
> **D.** 17%

Here are the related figures:

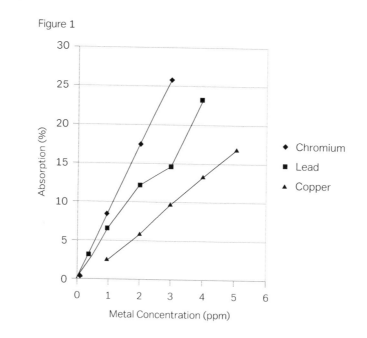

Figure 1

Table 1

Sample #	Site #	Lead in 100 mL (ppm)	Chromium in 100 mL (ppm)	Copper in 100 mL (ppm)
1	1	0.5	1.1	2.1
2	1	0.8	0.9	1.9
3	1	1.2	2.8	2.2
4	2	2.2	0.1	3.3
5	2	2.3	0.1	3.9
6	2	4.8	0.2	6.2

The fact that there are two different sources (Figure 1 and Table 1) referenced in the question clues us into the fact that we should be looking to apply this strategy of "finding the link."

We can see that Figure 1 contains several of the key terms from the question—"lead" and "absorption"—but not "Sample 5." On Table 1, we find "lead" and "Sample 5," but not "absorption." In this case, "lead" is a link, because it appears on both figures. Knowing this, we still need a little more help to actually connect the dots for this question. Let's look to see what else appears in both Figure 1 and Table 1. The answer is "ppm." And this is our key link.

Notice that on the horizontal axis of Figure 1, we have ppm listed across the bottom, and along the top of the Table 1, we see ppm as well (ppm, if you are curious, stands for "parts per million"). Let's start with Table 1. Find the value that's in the row for Sample 5 and in the column for "Lead in 100 mL (ppm)." It's 2.3 ppm. We circled it below, as you should on your test.

Table 1

Sample #	Site #	Lead in 100 mL (ppm)	Chromium in 100 mL (ppm)	Copper in 100 mL (ppm)
1	1	0.5	1.1	2.1
2	1	0.8	0.9	1.9
3	1	1.2	2.8	2.2
4	2	2.2	0.1	3.3
5	2	2.3	0.1	3.9
6	2	4.8	0.2	6.2

Now, we can link this to Figure 1, because we know that *ppm* appears on both. Find where 2.3 ppm would fall along the horizontal axis of Figure 1 and follow the "lead" line (our other link) to see what the absorption for the lead line is at 2.3 ppm (again, we've marked it below as you should on your test).

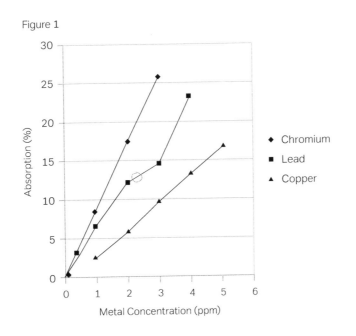

Figure 1

Looks like the absorption percentage (on the vertical axis) is closest to 13%, and so our answer is **C**.

To recap, the basic process for linking charts and graphs is to find the key terms in your question, figure out which terms appear in both places referenced in the question, and use these key terms to connect the dots. This takes a little practice, but once you get used to it, you'll be surprised how quickly you can answer some questions without even needing to fully understand what the question is asking!

Math Problems on the ACT Science Test

The ACT Science Test is also going to involve a bit of math, so you don't want to be surprised by it. The math won't be very complex, but you will face about one to five problems per test that will require you to do basic calculations.

What kind of math problems are on the ACT Science Test?

We wish that we could give you a more specific answer. But the honest answer is that there is no one type of math problem that might appear. No matter what, though, know that the math won't be too complicated (no calculators allowed!). Also, you generally only need to obtain a "close enough" result to select the correct answer.

Here are a couple examples:

- A passage might let you know that there are 40 mL of chlorine in a 100 mL solution, but will ask you to give your answer as a percent: "What percent of the solution is chlorine?" (The answer would be 40/100, or 40%.)

- A passage might show you a diagram of cannonballs being launched from a cannon, and the problem will ask you to determine the ground distance covered, in which case you would need to subtract the starting position from the landing position.

Scientific Notation

One famous number that always appears in scientific notation is Avogadro's constant. Amadeo Avogadro correctly proposed that a specific volume of gas (at a fixed temperature and pressure) would have the same number of molecules regardless of what the gas was. The value of Avogadro's constant is approximately $N_A = 6.02 \times 10^{23}$.

Although the ACT Science Test could test you on a variety of arithmetic or basic algebra-style problems, there is one specific nugget of math knowledge that you should definitely be familiar with: scientific notation. On past exams, there have been a few questions that have asked students to convert a value to scientific notation, but even if you don't stumble upon one of these, you'll often see values in the passages or in answer choices that are written in scientific notation, so you should have a basic idea of what this means.

Let's review!

Scientific notation is a way of making very large numbers or very small numbers less unwieldy. Scientific notation is always written as a number times a power of 10. The exponent of the 10 helps account for all of those zeros.

So, for example:

$$10,000 = 1 \times 10^4$$
$$0.0001 = 1 \times 10^{-4}$$

For numbers that are greater than 10, we move the decimal point to the left, and the power of 10 is positive. For example, if our number is 36,000, we move the decimal point four spaces to the right, giving us 3.6×10^4.

If we have a number that is less than zero, we are going to move the decimal to the right, and the power of 10 is going to be negative. For example, if the number is 0.000036, we are going to move the decimal five places to the right and we end up with 3.6×10^{-5}.

The number of places we move the decimal point tells us what the value of our exponent should be; the direction we move it tells us whether it should be positive or negative (move it to the left and the exponent will be positive; move it to right and it will be negative).

All right. Now, let's take a look at two examples of math-y problems on the ACT Science Test, so you can see what they look like:

Practice Questions

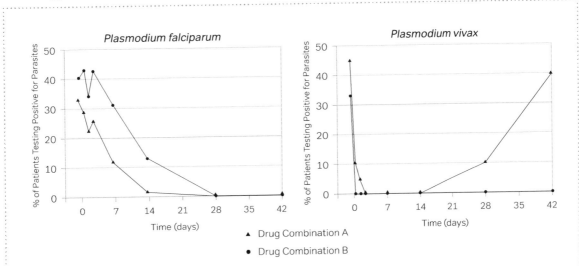

Source: Figures adapted from Laman, Moore, et al., "Artemisinin-Naphthoquine versus Artemether-Lumefantrine for Uncomplicated Malaria in Papua New Guinean Children: An Open-Label Randomized Trial," *PLOS Medicine* 11, no 12 (2014), doi.org/10.1371/journal.pmed.1001773.

1 If 1,000 patients in the P. falciparum group were treated with Drug Combination B in Experiment 1, approximately how many of those patients remained infected on Day 14?

A. 0

B. 10

C. 100

D. 200

2 The maximum speed of light, often represented as *c*, is approximately 3.0×10^8 meters per second. However, light only travels at this speed in a vacuum: when light travels through other materials, or optical media, it moves more slowly. The degree of slowing is determined by the optical density of the medium: the denser the medium, the slower the speed.

The index of refraction, *n*, of a given optical medium tells us how much slowing occurs in that medium.

The index of refraction can be calculated using the following equation (where *v* represents the speed of light in a given medium): $n = \frac{c}{v}$

Given the data in the passage, the speed of light through a hypothetical material with an index of refraction of 2 would be approximately:

F. 6×10^8 meters per second.

G. 3×10^8 meters per second.

H. 1.5×10^8 meters per second.

J. 1.5×10^4 meters per second.

1 We need to look at the Plasmodium falciparum line at day 14, and we're interested in Drug Combination B, the dashed line. At day 14, Drug Combination B shows that around 10% of patients remain affected. So in order to answer this question, what we need to do is find 10% of the 1,000 patients who were treated. 0.10(1000) = 100, so our answer is **C**.

2 The passage tells us that n is the index of refraction, c is the speed of light in a vacuum, and v is the speed of light in a given medium. In our problem n is 2, and c is always approximately 3.0×10^8 *m/s*. (*Note:* As long as the exponents are the same, we can treat the numbers in front of the rest of the scientific notation as regular numbers.) So we can plug these values into our equation: $2 = 3.0 \times \frac{10^8}{v}$. If we solve the equation for v, we get 1.5×10^8 *m/s*, and our answer is **H**.

There you have it. Don't be caught off guard when math questions pop up on the ACT Science Test!

Strategies for the Conflicting Viewpoints Passage

Let's take a few minutes to highlight specific strategies for the Conflicting Viewpoints passage, since it does require strategies different from the other passage types on the ACT Science Test.

As you may recall, the first few paragraphs of a Conflicting Viewpoints passage will describe a phenomenon, and the remaining paragraphs will outline each student's or scientist's viewpoint. These passages typically contain more words than Research Summaries or Data Interpretation passages, so your reading skills will definitely be useful here! You do actually have to read these passages in order to answer the questions effectively, **so advice about going to the questions first doesn't apply to this section of the ACT Science Test!** However, you could potentially read the passages in parts if that's easier for you or if you're running out of time (more on that in the section on ACT Science Test Pacing).

Let's look at some of our top tips for handling Conflicting Viewpoints passages.

1. **Identify what's being studied.** This background information is usually located in the very first paragraph. What's the main subject the students or scientists are studying? This paragraph will often include unfamiliar scientific terminology, but don't panic! The passage will likely define any new vocabulary. Locate and underline the phenomenon being studied before you move on to the viewpoints. This will help you orient yourself and better understand the perspectives.

2. **Figure out the opinions.** Each student or scientist will have a basic theory regarding the phenomenon. This opinion usually appears in the first sentence underneath the person's name. Try to put yourself in each scientist's shoes. Ask yourself: how are the basic theories different? How are they similar (if at all)?

Underline this information so you can easily reference it later. You might even jot down a quick summary of each scientist's viewpoint in the margins so you don't forget it.

3. **Circle any relevant data.** Once you've located and underlined the scientists' basic theories, identify what data they're using to support these theories. Are there any graphs or figures involved? Make sure to mark on the figure exactly what each theory describes and label it "Student 1," "Student 2," etc.

Consider whether any of the supporting data is contradictory. For example, if Student 2's theory is correct, does that make Student 3's theory incorrect? If no support is provided for a theory, make sure to write "No Support" next to the relevant section in the margins.

The main goal of the Conflicting Viewpoints passages is for you to understand what the argument or conflict is about, and for you to determine what is different about each point of view. As you carefully read and try to understand the phenomenon, basic theories, and support presented by each viewpoint, it's also helpful to consider the strengths and weaknesses of each argument. What needs to be true in order for each theory to be correct? What assumptions are the scientists or students making?

You may find yourself taking a little more time with these passages than you do on the other passage types to understand all of the viewpoints and answer the questions. Make sure you get plenty of practice with Conflicting Viewpoints passages before your test so you're comfortable and confident with the format.

You may feel more pressure on the Science Test in terms of timing than on other ACT Tests, but *don't skim the Conflicting Viewpoints passages*—you'll need to truly understand each viewpoint to correctly answer the questions. Otherwise, you'll waste more time rereading later as you answer the questions.

Tip: If you're not sure what a Conflicting Viewpoints passage looks like, see Passages V and VI in the ACT Practice Passage section at the end of this chapter!

ACT Science Test Pacing

Pacing is, without a doubt, the biggest challenge most students face on the ACT Science Test. You're likely already fatigued after hours of English, math, and reading. The passages are full of words and data you'll never need to answer the questions. Scientific jargon abounds. And you have to work at a lightning pace of 30–40 seconds per question in order to give yourself some buffer time to read any part of the passages you need to.

So how do you do it all and get your best score?

Here are our top tips for great pacing on the ACT Science Test:

1. **Pace yourself per passage.** Do a brief scan of the section when the proctor announces, "Begin." If you see six passages, plan for a general pace of six minutes per passage. If you see seven, plan for about five minutes per passage. Most students will do best when they leave the Conflicting Viewpoints passage for last, because it takes the longest.

    Some passages are longer or shorter, easier or harder, so don't freak out if you get off pace a little bit; just check your watch after each passage to see where you are and try to make up ground if possible.

2. **Start with the Data Representation passages.** Remember, you can do the passages in any order you want; don't just plod through the ACT Science Test in the order the passages are presented to you. This is not a test where questions are ordered from easy to hard. In fact, the very first passage you see could potentially be the hardest of the bunch (which would be a pretty rude awakening!).

    Instead, scan through the test and start with the Data Representation passages. These are the ones that will have the least amount of text and the greatest number of (generally easier) detail and pattern questions. If you've been practicing, you'll be able to recognize these at once, and you'll gain confidence as you knock off these quicker questions. If you already know that you won't have time to finish the Science section, you should still start with these passages, so that you can get to as many passages and pick up as many points as you can.

    If you don't want to worry about which passage types are which, you can start with the passages that look easiest and most straightforward to YOU. As you practice, you'll get a better sense for this. We've mentioned that many students find the Conflicting Viewpoints passage to be the hardest, but we also know students who think it's the easiest! But don't overthink this initial evaluation process. Get started on a passage as soon as you can; the clock is ticking!

3. **Only read the passage when warranted.** You won't need the bulk of information presented in Science passages to answer the questions. Be smart and don't waste your time here. Most of the questions are going to point you directly to the charts, graphs, and figures you see embedded in the passage.

    Instead of reading the passage first, do only the briefest of scans to get an overall sense of what the passage is about, and then proceed directly to the questions. Be smart and ONLY read the passage when warranted. After you read a question and you're ready to find the answer, look for the answer on the tables and figures first. If you can't find it there, see if you can find it in the explanatory information around the tables and figures. If it's not there, THEN look for it in the passage. In other words, start with the data and move outward, and you'll generally find your answers more quickly.

The one important exception to this rule is the Conflicting Viewpoints passage. This passage you do have to read, although you don't necessarily have to read it all at once before answering questions: see the next tip.

4. **Read the Conflicting Viewpoints passage in parts.** The questions on the Conflicting Viewpoints passage will always tell you whether they pertain to, for example, Scientist 1's hypothesis, Scientist 2's hypothesis, or both, or they might tell you they pertain to the information in the passage, in which case the answer is typically found in the information preceding the hypotheses. This means you can choose to read just the first hypothesis and then answer questions on that hypothesis, then read the second hypothesis, and answer questions on that hypothesis, and *then* answer questions pertaining to both of the hypotheses. This could help spare you from information overload or confusing the hypotheses. It can also be helpful if you're running out of time. If you don't have time to read all of the Conflicting Viewpoints passage, scan the questions to see which hypothesis has the most questions associated with it and just read that section and answer the corresponding questions. You don't want to spend the last five minutes of the test just reading everything and not getting to any questions!

5. **Don't hesitate to skip (and take a guess) on questions.** This rule applies across the board on the ACT, but is particularly relevant to the ACT Science Test, where timing is such a challenge. If you're confused by a question, see if you can eliminate any answer choices that seem completely off-base and take a quick guess from the remaining choices. You may find that a later question in the set helps clarify information for you that will help you answer the question that initially gave you trouble.

Remember, there's no penalty for wrong answers on the ACT, so don't waste this opportunity for a few blind, lucky guesses to pan out in your favor.

6. **Practice taking timed sections.** Because proper pacing is so critical to success on the ACT Science Test, it's important that you take practice tests under timed conditions. You don't have to start this way, but make sure you eventually start setting a timer as part of your prep.

7. **Determine in advance whether or not you are going to attempt all of the passages.** If you find that you're really struggling with time, you may need to make a decision during your test prep to concentrate on only five, or maybe even four, passages of the ACT Science Test, and guess on the rest. This way, you won't rush and make silly mistakes, and you might actually find you can get a higher score by doing fewer passages than rushing through and only half-doing all the questions.

Common Mistakes on the ACT Science Test

Mixing up labels and data. The ACT Science Test will often give you multiple charts, diagrams, and figures that include the same or similar types of information. Always make sure you're looking at the correct table or the correct line on a line graph.

Ignoring NOT and EXCEPT in the questions. Sometimes it seems like putting words in all caps is a signal for your brain to ignore them rather than notice them. When you see "NOT" or "EXCEPT" in a question, circle it, draw arrows to it, do whatever it takes for you to remember you are looking for what *doesn't* fit, not what does.

ACT Science Test Practice Passages

Data Representation

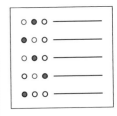

PASSAGE I

A *water mass* is a volume of seawater with distinct properties based on where it originates. The density of a water mass varies as a function of both salinity (in parts per thousand: ‰) and temperature (℃). The amount of salt dissolved in water increases its density. Water masses of lower temperature are also of higher density. Oceanographers use these properties to identify and trace water masses in the ocean. Figure 1 shows variations in the density (D) of water masses in g/cm³ relative to temperature (℃) and salinity (‰) at atmospheric pressure. Contour lines on the graph indicate constant density.

Figure 1

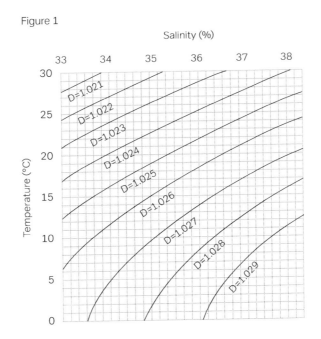

Figure 1 adapted from "ES2202: A Graph to Determine Density," *McDougal Littell Classzone*, accessed March 14, 2018, www.classzone.com/books/earth_science/terc/content/investigations/es2202/es2202page03.cfm.

1 Water masses of the same density mix easily, while water masses of differing densities do not. Will a water mass that is 12℃ and 34‰ salinity mix easily with a water mass that is 12℃ and 38‰ salinity?

A. Yes, because the water masses have the same temperature.

B. Yes, because the water masses share a common density.

C. No, because the water masses have different densities.

D. No, because the water masses differ in salinity.

2 Based on the information in Figure 1, for a water mass at a given temperature °C, as the salinity increases, the density:

   F. increases only.

   G. decreases only.

   H. increases then decreases.

   J. decreases then increases.

3 The ocean's densest water mass is the Antarctic Deep Water mass, which has a temperature of –1.9°C and a salinity of 34.4‰. Based on the information provided in Figure 1, the density of the Antarctic Deep Water mass would most likely be:

   A. less than 1.027 g/cm³.

   B. between 1.027 g/cm³ and 1.028 g/cm³.

   C. between 1.028 g/cm³ and 1.029 g/cm³.

   D. greater than 1.029 g/cm³.

4 According to Figure 1, a water mass with 34‰ salinity at a temperature of 16°C will have a density of:

   F. 1.023 g/cm³.

   G. 1.024 g/cm³.

   H. 1.025 g/cm³.

   J. 1.026 g/cm³.

5 The average temperature and salinity of the Atlantic Ocean are 3.7°C and 34.8‰. Based on the information provided in Figure 1, seawater at 12.0°C and 37.2‰ salinity flowing from the Mediterranean Sea into the Atlantic would most likely:

   A. rise because its density is lower than that of the Atlantic Ocean.

   B. mix because its density is the same as that of the Atlantic Ocean.

   C. rise because its temperature is higher than that of the Atlantic Ocean.

   D. sink because its density is higher than that of the Atlantic Ocean.

6 According to Figure 1, a water mass with a density of 1.023 g/cm³ at a temperature of 25°C will have a salinity of:

   F. less than 34‰.

   G. between 34‰ and 35‰.

   H. between 35‰ and 36‰.

   J. greater than 36‰.

7 When water masses of the same density but different temperature and salinity mix, the properties of the resulting seawater mixture fall at some point on a straight line joining their original locations on the graph. Based on Figure 1, mixing a water mass of 3°C and 33.8‰ salinity with a water mass of 18°C and 37.4‰ salinity will produce a mixture with a density of:

   A. between 1.026 and 1.027 g/cm³.

   B. 1.027 g/cm³.

   C. between 1.027 g/cm³ and 1.028 g/cm³.

   D. greater than 1.028 g/cm³.

PASSAGE II

The maximum speed of light, often represented as c, is approximately 3.0×10^8 meters per second. However, light only travels at this speed in a vacuum: when light travels through other materials, or optical media, it moves more slowly. The degree of slowing is determined by the optical density of the medium; the denser the medium, the slower the speed.

How much slowing occurs in an optical medium can be represented by the index of refraction, n, of that medium. Less optically dense materials have lower indices of refraction. For example, the refractive index of glass is 1.5, which means that light travels 1.5 times faster in a vacuum than it does in glass.

The index of refraction can be calculated using the following equation (where v represents the speed of light in a given medium):

$$n = \frac{c}{v}$$

Table 1 lists the refractive indices of various transparent materials.

Table 1

Material	Index of Refraction
Vacuum	1
Air	1.0003
Water	1.333
Glycerin	1.47
Glass	1.5
Diamond	2.417

One consequence of differences in light speed in different media is a phenomenon known as refraction. Light is refracted when it changes direction due to a change in media. The amount of direction change that occurs when light passes between two media can be quantified by measuring the angle of refraction ($\theta 2$) versus the angle of incidence ($\theta 1$), as shown in Figure 1. These angles are measured from the normal,

which is a line perpendicular to the interface between the two materials.

Figure 1

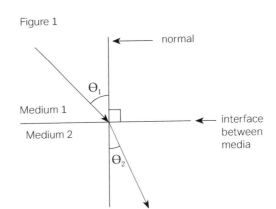

Table 2 provides some examples of corresponding angles of incidence and angles of refraction for various media pairings.

Table 2

Medium 1	Medium 2	Angle of Incidence (θ_1)	Angle of Refraction (θ_2)
Vacuum	Water	25	18
Vacuum	Water	45	32
Vacuum	Water	80	48
Vacuum	Air	25	24.99
Vacuum	Glass	25	16
Vacuum	Diamond	25	10
Water	Vacuum	25	34
Water	Vacuum	35	50
Water	Vacuum	45	70
Glass	Vacuum	25	39

8 According to Table 2, when Medium 1 is a vacuum and Medium 2 is water, as the angle of incidence increases, the angle of refraction:

F. increases only.

G. decreases only.

H. increases until 45° then decreases.

J. stays the same.

9 Based on the information in Table 1, which of the following lists the materials in increasing order of optical density?

  A. Air, glass, water, diamond
  B. Diamond, glass, air, water
  C. Diamond, glass, water, air
  D. Air, water, glass, diamond

10 Based on the data in Table 2, which of the following could possibly be the index of refraction of light moving from a vacuum into water, given an angle of incidence of 28°?

  F. 15°
  G. 20°
  H. 31°
  J. 36°

11 Given the data in the passage, the speed of light through a hypothetical material with an index of refraction of 2° would be approximately:

  A. 6×10^8 meters per second.
  B. 3×10^8 meters per second.
  C. 1.5×10^8 meters per second.
  D. 1.5×10^4 meters per second.

12 According to the data in Table 1 and Table 2, which of the following best represents the relationship between the change in direction of light as it passes between two different media and the indices of refraction for those media?

	n of Medium 1 > *n* of Medium 2	*n* of Medium 1 < *n* of Medium 2
a.	$\theta_1 > \theta_2$	$\theta_1 < \theta_2$
b.	$\theta_1 < \theta_2$	$\theta_1 > \theta_2$
c.	$\theta_1 > \theta_2$	$\theta_1 > \theta_2$
d.	$\theta_1 < \theta_2$	$\theta_1 < \theta_2$

  F. a
  G. b
  H. c
  J. d

Research Summaries

PASSAGE III

Guppies (*Poecilia reticulata*) display a bright and complex pattern of colored spots that can change from generation to generation. Colored spot patterns in male guppies are essential to attracting female mates, but these displays must be balanced with the need for camouflage from predators.

Scientists performed two experiments to study the effects of predation on the number, color, and size of spots displayed by male guppies.

Experiment 1
Scientists constructed 3 ponds to mimic native guppy habitat, each with fine gravel at the bottom. A founding population of 200 guppies was placed into each pond. After 6 months, the dangerous guppy predator pike cichlada (*Crenicichla alta*) was introduced into pond 1. In pond 2, giant rivulus (*Rivulus hartii*), a species that rarely preys on guppies, was introduced. Pond 3 was kept free of predators.

Figure 1 shows the change in the total number of spots per male fish over the course of the experiment. The average number of spots in the foundation population was recorded (Census F). 6 months later the number of spots was recorded for the guppies in each pond (Census S). *C. alta* and *R. hartii* were added to ponds 1 and 2 at this time. 5 months after the start of predation, a census was taken of the guppies in each pond and the number of spots recorded (Census I). A second census was taken 9 months later (Census II). Figure 2 presents the average number of spots of each color, as well as the average total number of spots per guppy, recorded at Census II.

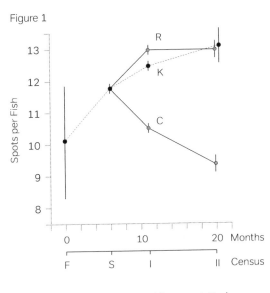

Figure 1

R = Pond with *R. hartii* (low predation)

C = Pond with *C. alta* (high predation)

K = Control pond (no predation)

Figure 2

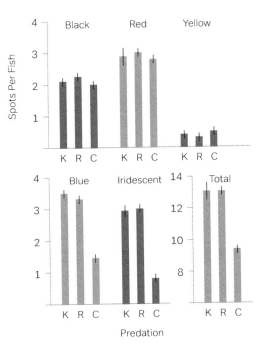

R = Pond with *R. hartii* (low predation)

C = Pond with *C. alta* (high predation)

K = Control pond (no predation)

Figures 1–3 adapted from John A. Endler, "Natural Selection on Color Patterns in *Poecilia reticulata*," Evolution 34, no. 1 (January 1980): 76–91.

Experiment 2

Scientists constructed 6 ponds to mimic native guppy habitat. Ponds F1–F3 contained fine gravel, with a grain size of 2–3 mm, while Ponds C4–C6 contained coarse gravel, with a grain size of 7–15 mm. Experiment 1 was repeated for each set of 3 ponds. A founding population was introduced to each set of ponds. 6 months later the guppy predator *C. alta* was added to ponds F1 and C1, and *R. hartii* was added to ponds F2 and C2. 20 months after the start of the experiment, a census was taken of the guppies in each pond and the relative spot size* was recorded. Results are presented in Figure 3.

relative spot size = ratio of spot size to body size

Figure 3

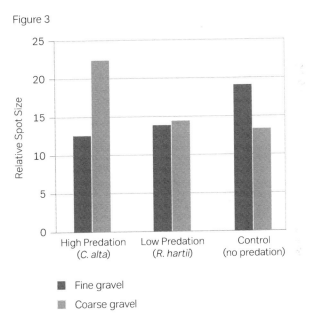

13 Suppose Experiment 1 was carried on for a total of 30 months. Based on Figure 1, which of the following gives the most likely average number of spots among guppies in the pond containing *C. alta* at the end of the experiment? The average would most likely be:

A. fewer than 9 spots.

B. from 9 to 10 spots.

C. from 11 to 13 spots.

D. more than 13 spots.

14 The scientists hypothesized that in the absence of predation, guppies with spots that contrasted with the background would have more success finding mates than guppies with less visible spots. Do the results of Experiment 2 support this hypothesis?

- **F.** Yes, because in the control ponds, spot size was smaller in ponds with fine gravel and larger in ponds with coarse gravel.
- **G.** Yes, because in the control ponds, spot size was larger in ponds with fine gravel and smaller in ponds with coarse gravel.
- **H.** No, because in the control ponds, spot size was smaller in ponds with fine gravel and larger in ponds with coarse gravel.
- **J.** No, because in the control ponds, spot size was larger in ponds with fine gravel and smaller in ponds with coarse gravel.

15 According to Figure 2, which of the following spot colors was most affected by the introduction of the guppy predator *C. alta*?

- **A.** Black
- **B.** Red
- **C.** Yellow
- **D.** Blue

16 Over the 20 months of Experiment 1, for the control pond with no predation, the total number of spots per guppy:

- **F.** increased then remained constant.
- **G.** decreased then remained constant.
- **H.** increased only.
- **J.** decreased only.

17 Based on the results of Experiments 1 and 2, which of the following statements best describes the effects of introducing a population of *R. hartii* into a population of guppies? On average, after 20 months the generation of guppies will have:

- **A.** fewer spots than they would if *R. hartii* had not been introduced.
- **B.** more colorful spots than they would if *R. hartii* had not been introduced.
- **C.** larger spots than they would if *R. hartii* had not been introduced.
- **D.** little discernible difference from their appearance if *R. hartii* had not been introduced.

18 18 months after the start of Experiment 2, a guppy was selected at random from Pond F1 and its spots were measured and counted. In comparison with a guppy taken at random from month 5, the guppy would most likely have:

- **F.** a greater number of larger sized spots.
- **G.** a greater number of smaller sized spots.
- **H.** a smaller number of larger sized spots.
- **J.** a smaller number of smaller sized spots.

PASSAGE IV

Bioremediation is one method of cleaning up water contaminated with crude oil waste by using bacteria to metabolize petroleum hydrocarbons. A researcher conducted 2 studies to examine the effect of incubating 139SI, a peculiar strain of the bacterium *B. salamaya*, in media contaminated with crude oil to determine the bacteria's usefulness for bioremediation.

Study 1

Flasks containing a bacterial growth medium were incubated for 7 weeks (42 days) at 35°C in media contaminated with 2% and 1% of crude oil waste, respectively. An inoculum with 139SI was added to each flask. Flasks containing crude oil waste, but none of the inoculated strain, were used as controls. Every 7 days, 4 flasks prepared as described were removed from the incubator. The percentage of total petroleum hydrocarbons (TPH) consumed was calculated, and the percentage of TPH remaining from the initial level is plotted in Figure 1.

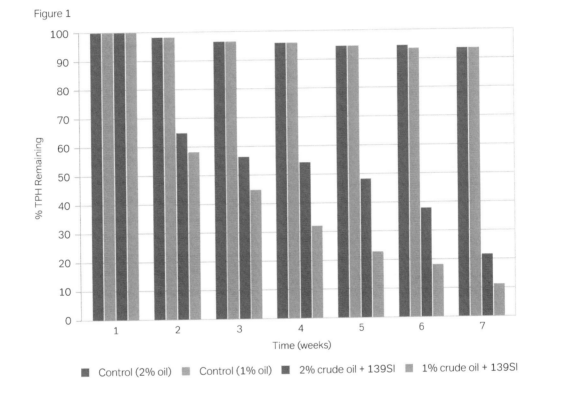

Figure 1

Study 2

To test the microbe's ability to utilize petroleum hydrocarbons as a source of energy, total biomass concentrations were measured after each week. The results are presented in Figure 2. The number of colony forming units of the bacteria (CFU/mL) was also measured to determine the increase in microbial population during the remediation process. Results of the microbial population counts for the inoculated flasks contaminated with 1% oil are presented in Figure 3.

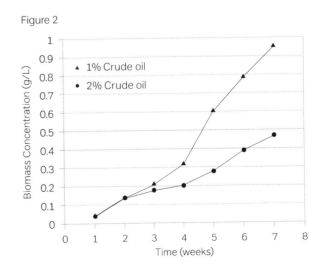

Figure 2

Figure 3

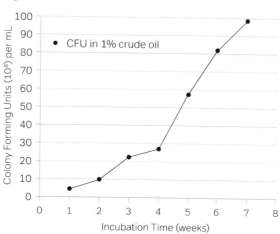

Data adapted from Salmah Ismail and Arezoo Dadrasnia, "Biotechnological Potential of *Bacillus salmalaya* 139SI: A Novel Strain for Remediating Water Polluted with Crude Oil Waste," *PLOS Medicine* 10, no. 4 (13 April 2015), doi.org/10.1371/journal.pone.0120931.

19 If Study 1 were repeated with a growth medium contaminated with 1.5% crude oil, the % TPH remaining after 6 weeks incubation would most likely be:

- **A.** less than 10.
- **B.** between 11 and 18.
- **C.** between 19 and 37.
- **D.** greater than 38.

20 Based on the results of Studies 1 and 2, what was the relationship between the level of crude oil contamination and 139SI's effectiveness at bioremediation?

- **F.** 139SI was most effective at the highest level of crude oil contamination tested.
- **G.** 139SI was most effective at the lowest level of crude oil contamination tested.
- **H.** 139SI was most effective at the lowest level of biomass concentration measured.
- **J.** There is no relationship between the level of crude oil contamination and 139SI's effectiveness at bioremediation.

21 What percentage of the degradation of TPH in the 1% crude oil contaminated samples can be attributed to the metabolic activity of 139SI bacterial strain over the course of the 7-week trial in Study 1?

- **A.** 12%
- **B.** 22%
- **C.** 72%
- **D.** 82%

22 Which of the following statements best describes the relationship between the number of colony forming units and total biomass concentration in the 1% crude oil contaminated samples, as shown in Study 2?

- **F.** As the number of colony forming units increases, the biomass concentration increases.
- **G.** As the number of colony forming units increases, the biomass concentration decreases.
- **H.** As the number of colony forming units decreases, the biomass concentration remains constant.
- **J.** As the number of colony forming units decreases, the biomass concentration increases.

23 Based on the results given, which of the following graphs best shows the relationship between % TPH remaining and biomass concentration?

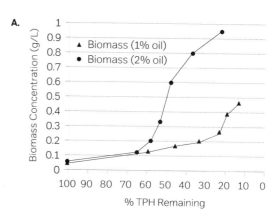

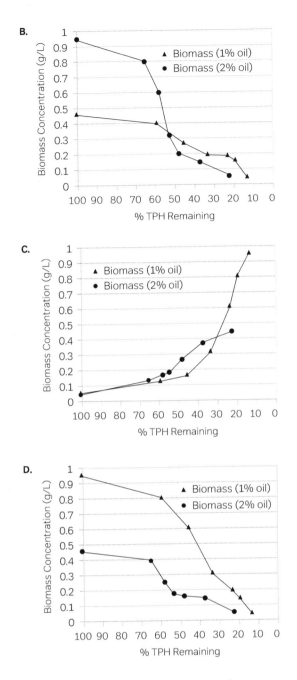

B.

Biomass Concentration (g/L) vs % TPH Remaining
- ▲ Biomass (1% oil)
- ● Biomass (2% oil)

C.

Biomass Concentration (g/L) vs % TPH Remaining
- ▲ Biomass (1% oil)
- ● Biomass (2% oil)

D.

Biomass Concentration (g/L) vs % TPH Remaining
- ▲ Biomass (1% oil)
- ● Biomass (2% oil)

24 According to the results of Study 1, the percentage of initial hydrocarbons consumed by the bacteria over the course of the 7-week study:

- **F.** decreased in the 1% crude oil flasks but increased in the 2% crude oil flasks.
- **G.** increased in the 1% crude oil flasks but decreased in the 2% crude oil flasks.
- **H.** decreased in both the 1% crude oil flasks and the 2% crude oil flasks.
- **J.** increased in both the 1% crude oil flasks and the 2% crude oil flasks.

PASSAGE V

The organic molecules associated with life are *chiral*, that is, they exist exclusively as one of two symmetrical mirror-image forms. Amino acids and proteins are composed entirely of left-handed forms, while nucleic acids, including RNA and DNA, are composed entirely of right-handed forms. Because biomolecules in living cells exist exclusively in one chiral form, they are referred to as being "homochiral." Two scientists discuss the origins of homochirality.

Scientist 1

Homochirality of biomolecules originated after biological life emerged. Chemical reactions show little preference for right- or left-handedness in their products, and precursors to biomolecules synthesized in the laboratory produce both left- and right-handed molecules in roughly equivalent numbers. Therefore, it is reasonable to conclude that life emerged from a prebiotic milieu containing a roughly equal mixture of right- and left-handed molecules.

During the primordial period, primitive organisms utilizing competing left- and right-handed biomolecular machinery arose, but chance events eliminated one of the species. Organisms that utilized left-handed amino acids and right-handed nucleic acids developed D-peptidase, an enzyme toxic to those that utilized the reverse system. This surviving population became the ancestors for all organisms that subsequently evolved on Earth.

Scientist 2

The homochirality of biomolecules must have originated before biological life. The self-replicating molecules essential for living organisms would be impossible without it. DNA and RNA are incapable of complementary pair bonding in the absence of right-handed nucleotides. DNA cannot form a helix if even a small proportion of the left-handed form is present. The presence of even a tiny fraction of left-handed nucleotides interferes with RNA replication, and a single right-handed amino acid will disrupt the stability of protein structures.

Crystalline surfaces of common rock-forming minerals are likely to have played a role in the origin of the "handedness" of biomolecules. Surfaces of common rock-forming oxides, silicates, and carbonates select and concentrate specific amino acids, and the chiral surfaces of these minerals have been shown to separate left- and right-handed molecules. Thus, mineral surfaces may have contributed to the transition from a heterochiral prebiotic "soup" to the homochiral molecules essential to the origin of life on Earth.

Sources: 1) W. A. Bonner, "The Origin and Amplification of Biomolecular Chirality," *Origins of Life and Evolution of the Biosphere* 21, no. 2 (1991): 59–111. 2) M. H. Engel and S. A. Macko, "Isotopic Evidence for Extraterrestrial Non-Racemic Amino Acids in the Murchison Meteorite," *Nature: International Journal of Science* 389 (18 September 1997): 265–68, www.nature.com/nature/journal/v389/n6648/abs/389265a0.html. 3) "Chirality," *All About Science*, accessed March 15, 2018, www.allaboutscience.org/chirality.htm. 4) R. M. Hazen and D. A. Sverjensky, "Mineral Surfaces, Geochemical Complexities, and the Origins of Life," *Cold Spring Harbor Perspectives in Biology* 2, no. 5 (May 2010), www.ncbi.nlm.nih.gov/pubmed/20452963.

25 Despite numerous attempts, scientists have failed to come up with a chemical mechanism capable of producing chirally pure biomolecules of a single "handedness." That is, every proposed mechanism produces a mixture of both left- and right-handed molecules. How do these results affect the scientists' viewpoints, if at all?

A. They weaken Scientist 1's viewpoint only.

B. They weaken Scientist 2's viewpoint only.

C. They strengthen both scientists' viewpoints.

D. They have no effect on either scientist's viewpoint.

26 Based on the information in the passage and Scientist 2's discussion, the self-replication of DNA and RNA molecules depends on the presence of:

F. left-handed nucleotides only.

G. right-handed nucleotides only.

H. an equal mixture of both left- and right-handed nucleotides.

J. mineral surfaces that separate left- and right-handed molecules.

27 Which scientist indicates that the homochirality of biomolecules developed through natural selection?

A. Scientist 1, because that scientist states homochirality was selected and concentrated by mineral surfaces.

B. Scientist 1, because that scientist states homochirality descended from a surviving population of primordial organisms.

C. Scientist 2, because that scientist states homochirality was selected and concentrated by mineral surfaces.

D. Scientist 2, because that scientist states homochirality descended from a surviving population of primordial organisms.

28 Which of the following generalizations about the origins of homochirality is most consistent with Scientist 2's viewpoint?

F. The emergence of homochirality preceded the emergence of living organisms.

G. The emergence of living organisms preceded the emergence of homochirality.

H. The emergence of homochirality and the emergence of life occurred simultaneously.

J. The emergence of living organisms and the emergence of homochirality are unrelated.

29 Organic molecules on the early Earth may have come from comet and meteorite impacts. Laboratory analyses of meteorites have indicated a predominance of left-handed amino acids, suggesting they might provide an origin for homochirality. Is this information consistent with the viewpoint of Scientist 1?

   A. Yes, because Scientist 1 indicates that life emerged from organic molecules of extraterrestrial origin.

   B. Yes, because Scientist 1 indicates that a predominance of left-handed amino acids was essential for life to emerge.

   C. No, because Scientist 1 indicates that a mixture of left- and right-handed organic molecules was present when life emerged.

   D. No, because Scientist 1 indicates that extraterrestrial origins of organic molecules are impossible.

30 According to Scientist 2, which of the following molecular forms is NOT compatible with existing self-replicating biological mechanisms found in living organisms?

   F. Right-handed RNA nucleotides

   G. Right-handed DNA nucleotides

   H. Right-handed amino acids

   J. Left-handed amino acids

31 With which of the following statements about living organisms would both scientists agree? Living organisms:

   A. emerged simultaneously with homochiral molecules.

   B. originated from a mixture of right- and left-handed molecules.

   C. emerged after homochiral molecules.

   D. originated from nonliving molecules.

PASSAGE VI

Deoxyribonucleic acid, or DNA, is the molecule within living organisms that encodes the genetic code that informs an organism's development and functioning. This molecule consists of two long strands, each of which is made up of subunits called nucleotides. These two strands wind around one another, forming the characteristic double helix shape of DNA.

There are four nucleotides used in the production of DNA—guanine, adenine, cytosine, and thymine—that are often referred to as G, A, C, and T, respectively.

Nucleotides pair up in a predictable way as illustrated in the figure: for every "G" on the first strand, there is a "C" on the opposite strand, and for every "A" on the first strand, there is a "T" on the opposite strand. A set of two paired nucleotides is typically referred to as a base pair, and the nucleotides within each pair are held together with hydrogen bonds. Because of the consistency of these pairings, the two individual paired strands can be said to be complementary: the sequence of nucleotides on one strand can be entirely determined if the sequence of bases on the opposite strand is known.

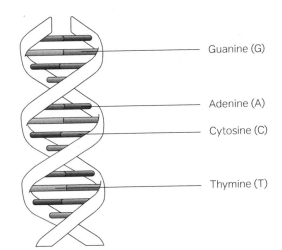

During the process of DNA replication, two identical DNA molecules are produced from a single original piece of DNA through the action of an enzyme known as DNA polymerase. Shortly after James Watson and Francis

Crick determined DNA's structure, there was substantial debate in the scientific community regarding how this process occurs. Two of the prevailing viewpoints in this discussion are given below.

Scientist A

When DNA is not in the process of being replicated, it is found tightly coiled and bound to proteins. Prior to replication, the coiling is loosened and some of the proteins are removed, allowing the two strands of the DNA molecule to be separated. DNA polymerase then acts on each of these individual strands separately, adding new nucleotides by matching them to complementary nucleotides on the original strand. Proteins bind to both new DNA molecules following the completion of replication, facilitating the re-coiling of the DNA.

Scientist B

It is known that intact DNA is typically found bound to proteins known as histones. During DNA replication, the histones remain attached to the DNA molecule, but serve to slightly alter the shape of the double helix, allowing DNA polymerase to access and "read" the base pairs while leaving the overall structure intact. DNA polymerase slides along the length of the DNA-histone molecular complex, producing an entirely new double-stranded DNA molecule bound to new histones as it is synthesized.

32 Scientists A and B would likely agree that:

F. enzymes are not required for the process of DNA replication.

G. histones are required for the process of DNA replication.

H. histones are not required for the process of DNA replication.

J. DNA polymerase "reading" the sequence of base pairs on the original DNA molecule is required for the process of DNA replication.

33 Based on the description of DNA given in the passage, which of the following could be the nucleotide composition of a DNA double helix?

A. 20% adenine, 20% guanine, 30% thymine, 30% cytosine

B. 60% adenine, 20% thymine, 10% guanine, 10% cytosine

C. 20% adenine, 20% thymine, 30% guanine, 30% cytosine

D. 60% adenine, 20% guanine, 10% thymine, 10% cytosine

34 Consider the following diagrams showing possible mechanisms of DNA replication. Which of the following best describes how the diagrams relate to the hypotheses of Scientists A and B?

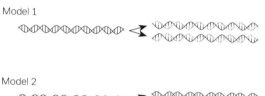

Model 1

Model 2

Model 3

Adapted from Mike Jones, "An overview of three postulated types of DNA replication," *Wikimedia Commons*, September 15, 2005, commons.wikimedia. org/wiki/File:DNAreplicationModes.png.

F. Scientist A = Model 1, Scientist B = Model 2

G. Scientist A = Model 2, Scientist B = Model 1

H. Scientist A = Model 3, Scientist B = Model 2

J. Scientist A = Model 2, Scientist B = Model 3

35 Another Scientist, Scientist X, writes a paper arguing that it is very unlikely that histones separate from the original DNA molecule during replication. Scientist B would most likely:

A. agree with Scientist X because Scientist B believes histones and DNA are chemically impossible to separate.

B. agree with Scientist X because Scientist B believes histones must stay attached to the original DNA molecule for replication to proceed.

C. disagree with Scientist X because Scientist B believes histones and DNA are chemically impossible to separate.

D. disagree with Scientist X because Scientist B believes histones must stay attached to the original DNA molecule for replication to proceed.

36 According to Scientist A, proteins attached to the DNA molecule:

F. separate from the DNA prior to replication.

G. separate from the DNA following replication.

H. separate from the DNA during replication.

J. remain attached to DNA permanently.

37 A new enzyme is discovered to be required for the process of DNA replication. This enzyme is shown to slide along the length of the DNA double helix, "unzipping" the two strands from one another as it goes. The existence of this enzyme provides support for which of the scientist's positions?

A. Scientist A only

B. Scientist B only

C. Both Scientist A and Scientist B

D. Neither Scientist A nor Scientist B

38 According to the passage, if one strand of a DNA molecule contains the sequence "GGCTTAC," which of the following sequences must the complementary strand include?

F. AATCCGT

G. AAGTTCA

H. CCGAATG

J. CCTGGTA

ACT Science Answers and Explanations

PASSAGE I

Answer: C

1 Looking up the density for a water mass that is 12°C and 34‰ salinity, we find that it is 1.026 g/cm³. Doing the same for a water mass that is 12°C and 38‰ salinity, we find a density of 1.029 g/cm³. The water masses are of different densities, so they should not mix easily, according to the information provided in the question. The answer is **C**.

Answer: F

2 Pick a temperature value along the y-axis (a given temperature). Note that salinity increases along the x-axis; move your finger along the x-axis at the point you chose on the y-axis. Notice that you cross the marked density contour lines as you go. The values of the density contour lines increase as the salinity increases. The answer is **F**.

Answer: B

3 The temperature data provided in the chart starts at 0°C. However, we can extrapolate the contour line beyond the edge of the graph. Extend the vertical line from 34.4‰ salinity down 1.9 units below the x-axis. Mark that spot. Then, extend the D = 1.028 g/cm³ contour line along its current trend. You'll find that it passes below that point. Thus, we can conclude that the Antarctic Deep Water mass has a density of between 1.027 g/cm³ and 1.028 g/cm³. The answer is **B**.

Answer: H

4 If we go to Figure 1 and look up the salinity value on the x-axis and temperature value on the y-axis, we find that they intersect at the contour labeled D = 1.025. The answer is **H**.

Answer: D

5 Looking up the density for a water mass from the Atlantic Ocean at 3.7°C and 34.8‰, we find a density of between 1.027 g/cm³ and 1.028 g/cm³. Doing the same for a water mass from the Mediterranean at 12.0°C and 37.2‰, we find a density of between 1.028 g/cm³ and 1.029 g/cm³. Because seawater coming in from the Mediterranean is denser than that of the Atlantic, we could expect the Mediterranean seawater to sink. The answer is **D**.

Answer: G

6 Go to Figure 1 and look up 25°C along the y-axis. Trace a straight, horizontal line from that point along a line of constant temperature until you hit the contour line at 1.023 g/cm³. Looking up at the corresponding salinity value from that point of intersection (along the horizontal/x-axis) gives us a salinity of 34.6‰, which is between 34‰ and 35‰. The answer is **G**.

7 Looking up the density for a water mass of 3℃ and 33.8‰ salinity, we find that the density is 1.027 g/cm³. Looking up a water mass of 18℃ and 37.4‰ salinity, we find that it lies on the same line contour line (1.027 g/cm³). A straight line connecting these two points falls into the region between 1.027 and 1.028 g/cm³. The answer is **C**.

Answer: **C**

PASSAGE II

8 Examining the first three lines of the table (the rows in which Medium 1 is a vacuum and Medium 2 is water) shows us that the angle of incidence is always higher than the angle of refraction. You can also note that for any given pairing, increasing the angle of incidence increases the angle of refraction. The answer is **F**.

Answer: **F**

9 The passage states that the denser a particular medium is, the more slowly light travels through it. The passage also states that the degree of slowing in an optical medium can be represented by the index of refraction. The refractive index of glass, for example, means that light travels 1.5 times faster in a vacuum than in glass. This means that a higher refractive index means a lower speed of light through the medium. Therefore, materials with higher indices of refraction will have higher optical densities. Table 1 shows us that, in increasing order, the refractive index of air is 1.0003, water is 1.333, glass is 1.5, and diamond is 2.417, so our answer is **D**.

Answer: **D**

10 To solve this problem, we need to predict a data point between existing data points (also known as *interpolating* data). An angle of incidence of 28° would fall between 25 and 45 on the table, so we know that the index of refraction needs to be between 18 and 32.

Vacuum	Water	25	18
Vacuum	Water	45	32

Only answer choices G and H meet these criteria. However, 28 is far closer to 25 than to 45, which means the angle of refraction should be closer to 18 than 32, so our answer must be **G**.

Answer: **G**

11 We know from the passage that the refractive index of a material relates directly to the speed of light through the medium (as the passage states, the refractive index of glass is 1.5, which means that light travels 1.5 times faster in a vacuum than it does in glass). A refractive index of 2 would mean that light moves twice as fast through a vacuum as through that material. Therefore, to find the speed of light in this material, you would divide the speed of light in a vacuum (3.0×10^8 m/s) by 2. Our answer is **C**.

Answer: **C**

12 When the *n* of Medium 1 is greater than the *n* of Medium 2, the angle of incidence (θ_1) is greater than the angle of refraction (θ_2). When the *n* of Medium 1 is less than the *n* of Medium 2, the angle of refraction is greater than the angle of incidence.

Answer: **G**

This is a more complex problem because it requires keeping track of several different pieces of data at once. To solve it, we can pick the examples of "water" and "vacuum" from Table 2 because we have numerous example pairings for these two materials. First, let's look at when water is Medium 1 and the vacuum is Medium 2. In each of the incidences for this pairing in Table 2, the angle of incidence is less than the angle of refraction, so we can eliminate answer choices F and H. Now we need to look at an example where Medium 1 has a lower refractive index than Medium 2, so we can again use a vacuum and water as our examples, but we need to look at the lines on the chart where a vacuum is listed as Medium 1 and water is listed as Medium 2. These would be the first three lines of our chart. In each of these incidences, the angle of incidence is higher than the angle of refraction, so we can eliminate answer choice J and know that our answer is **G**.

PASSAGE III

13 According to Figure 1, in the pond that contains the predatory fish *C. alta*, the number of spots per guppy declines in each generation. After 20 months, the number of spots per fish is between 9 and 10, with a downward slope. Based on that, we can expect that after an added 10 months, the average number of spots per fish will probably be even fewer than 9. The answer is **A**.

14 If the hypothesis is correct, in a pond without predators, we'd expect to see a contrast between spot size and the size of gravel in the ponds. In other words, spots would be larger on fish living with fine gravel and smaller on fish living with coarse gravel in the control ponds. (Remember that the control ponds are the ones without any predatory fish.) Figure 3 shows a relative spot size of 19 in the fine gravel ponds and 13.5 in the course gravel ponds. Since the relative spot size is larger in the fine gravel ponds, the hypothesis is supported. Our answer is **G**.

15 According to Figure 2, there was very little difference in the number of black, red, or yellow spots between the control populations and the guppy populations that were in ponds with *C. alta*. On the other hand, the number of blue and iridescent spots decreases from roughly three spots per fish to one spot per fish when there are *C. alta* predators. So our answer is **D**.

16 In Figure 1, the control pond with no predators (K) shows a steady increase in the number of spots per fish from the foundation (F) at 0 months to the last census (Census II) at 20 months, even though it does slow slightly in the final months. But slowing is not the same as remaining constant! Also, be careful not to confuse the control pond (K) with the pond with *R. hartii* (R), in which the total number of spots per guppy appears to increase until Census I and then remains constant. The answer is **H**.

17 Based on Figure 1, the introduction of *R. hartii* has little effect on the number of spots per fish compared to the same number in the control group. After 20 weeks, the number in the two groups is basically the same. And Figure 2 tells the same story: the introduction of *R. hartii* has little effect on the number of spots of any one color. Meanwhile, based on Figure 3, the introduction of *R. hartii* has little effect on relative spot size. The spot size for the guppies is the same as the control in both the pond with fine gravel and the pond with coarse gravel when *R. hartii is present*. Taken together, we can say that the introduction of *R. hartii* has little effect on the number, color, or size of spots presented by guppies. In other words, there should be no real difference between the spots presented by guppies 20 months after the introduction of *R. hartii* and spots of guppies without that predator around. So our answer is **D**.

Answer: **D**

18 According to the introduction to Experiment 2, Pond F1 contained fine gravel. The guppy predator *C. alta* was introduced after 6 months. So at 5 months in a fine gravel environment, a guppy taken from this generation hasn't had any predators around. The results of Experiment, which also used fine gravel, suggest that this guppy would have between 11 and 12 spots (Figure 1). The results of Experiment 2 suggest that this guppy wouldn't need camouflage. But those conditions radically change after the introduction of *C. alta* to Pond F1. The results of Experiment 1 indicate that, after 18 months, the total number of spots per fish should decline in the presence of *C. alta*. The results of Experiment 2 indicate that, in a tank containing fine gravel, the relative spot size will be smaller in the presence of *C. alta* than it would be for a control population. Taken together, these two points say that a guppy taken at random from Pond F1 after 18 months would most likely have *fewer* spots than a guppy taken at random after 5 months and that these spots should be *smaller*. The answer is **J**.

Answer: **J**

PASSAGE IV

19 Answering this question requires interpolation from the data given in Figure 1. If we look up the % TPH remaining after week 6 in Figure 1, we find 18% TPH for the 1% crude oil contaminated flasks, and 38% for the 2% crude oil flasks. We would expect a flask contaminated with 1.5% crude oil to fall about halfway between these two numbers. Answer choice **C** gives the inner bounds of the difference between the values after week 6 and is the best answer choice.

Answer: **C**

20 The results of Study 1 indicate that 139SI removed a greater percentage of initial TPH at a crude oil contamination level of 1% than of 2%, while the results of Study 2 indicate that the bacterial strain produced more biomass in the 1% crude oil contaminated samples. We can't make a conclusion about the number of colony forming units, because results were presented only for the 1% crude oil contaminated samples. The best conclusion that can be drawn from these results is that 139SI was most effective at the lowest level of crude oil contamination tested (1%). Our answer is **G**.

Answer: **G**

21 To answer this question correctly, take note of the role of the control in Study 1. The data in Figure 1 show that only 94% of the initial TPH remained in the control flasks containing the 1% crude oil contaminated samples that weren't inoculated with the 139SI bacterium. Therefore, not all of the degradation of TPH can be attributed to the metabolic activity of 139SI. To arrive at the percentage of degradation of TPH that can be attributed to the metabolic activity of 139SI, subtract the 12% remaining at the end of the 7-week trial for the 1% crude oil contaminated samples from the 94% remaining in the control samples: 94% – 12% = 82%. A and B are incorrect because they merely give the remaining % TPH after the 7-week trial for the 1% and 2% crude oil contaminated samples respectively. C is incorrect because it gives the percentage of degradation of TPH attributable to the metabolic activity of 139SI in the 2% crude oil contaminated samples. The correct answer is **D**.

22 Figure 2 shows the biomass concentration (g/L) for the 1% crude oil samples increasing only. Figure 3 shows the colony forming units (10^8 per mL) increasing only. Therefore, we can conclude that as the number of colony forming units increases, the biomass concentration also increases. The answer is **F**.

23 The most efficient way to answer this question is to first notice the trend and then eliminate the answer choices that don't reflect the overall trend. For this question, figure out how biomass varies with % TPH. Notice that for each of the scatterplots, % TPH remaining decreases along the *x*-axis from 100% to 0%. This is consistent with the data presented in Figure 1, in which % TPH remaining decreases every week over the course of the study for both the 1% and 2% crude oil contaminated samples.

Now examine the biomass concentration values over the same period, as presented in Figure 2. As the weeks in the study go by, the biomass concentration increases every week. So, we're looking for the charts that display an *increase* in biomass as the % TPH *decreases*. Only answer choices A and C display such a relationship, so we can eliminate answers B and D. Note that the total increase in biomass for the 1% crude oil flasks is roughly double that of the 2% crude oil flasks. Only answer choice **C** displays such a relationship, so eliminate A and choose **C**.

To confirm this choice, simply pick a pair of values for the 1% and 2% crude oil contaminated samples, respectively. For the 1% contaminated samples, Figure 1 shows that the % TPH remaining at week 7 was 12%, and Figure 2 shows that the biomass concentration at week 7 was roughly 0.95 g/L. Note that the point (12%, 0.95 g/L) appears on the chart in **C**. For the 2% contaminated samples, Figure 1 shows that the % TPH remaining at week 7 was about 21%, and the biomass concentration was about 0.47 g/L. The point (21%, 0.47 g/L) also appears on the chart in **C**. Every other plotted point on the chart in **C** could be confirmed in the same manner. None of the other answer choices correctly plot these points, which means we can confirm that our answer is **C**.

24 Be careful when reading this question! The question stem asks about "the percentage of initial hydrocarbons *consumed by* the bacteria." In Figure 1, the percentage of initial hydrocarbons decreases each week for both the flasks contaminated by 1% and 2% crude oil, but in order for this to be true, the percentage of initial hydrocarbons *consumed by* the bacteria must *increase* over the time period. Thus, answer choice H is incorrect, and answer choice **J** is the correct one. Answer choices F and G are both incorrect because the % TPH continually drops for both the 1% and 2% contaminated flasks.

PASSAGE V

25 Scientists' inability to come up with an experimental mechanism capable of producing chirally pure molecules of a single "handedness" (that is, a homochiral situation) does not weaken Scientist 1's viewpoint, because Scientist 1 states that "that life emerged from a prebiotic milieu containing a roughly equal mixture of right- and left-handed molecules."

Scientist 2, however, states that "the homochirality of biomolecules must have originated before biological life," while insisting that a homochiral environment was necessary for the emergence of life. The inability of scientists to come up with an experimental mechanism capable of producing molecules of a single handedness weakens this argument, because, according to Scientist 2, such a mechanism is required for homochiral conditions to be present for the emergence of life. The answer is **B**.

26 According to Scientist 2, "the self-replicating nature of the biological molecules essential for life is impossible without" homochirality, and "DNA and RNA are incapable of complementary pair bonding in the absence of right-handed nucleotides." The next sentences states that "DNA cannot form a helix if even a small proportion of the left-handed form is present," and "A tiny fraction of left-handed nucleotides terminates RNA replication." This information eliminates answer choice F (left-handed nucleotides only). Answer choice **G** is the correct answer: right-handed nucleotides only. This is further supported by the introduction to the passage, which states that "nucleic acids are composed entirely of right-handed forms."

27 This answer choice depends on outside scientific knowledge regarding the definition of natural selection. The key principle of Darwinian evolution is natural selection, which is the principal mechanism for evolution: descent with modifications. Only Scientist 1 presents an argument for the origins of homochirality that depends on natural selection. The entire second paragraph of Scientist 1's viewpoint is dedicated to an argument based on natural selection: "primitive organisms utilizing competing left- and right-handed biomolecular machinery arose, but chance events eliminated one of the species ... [The] surviving population became the ancestors for all organisms that subsequently evolved on Earth." The correct answer is **B**.

Answer: F

28 Scientist 2 insists that "the homochirality of biomolecules must have originated before biological life," and then states numerous reasons why it was imperative for biomolecules to be homochiral prior to the emergence of living organisms. Answer choice G is incorrect because it characterizes Scientist 1's viewpoint, rather than Scientist 2's. Answer choice H is incorrect because Scientist 2 insists that homochirality occurred before the emergence of life, not simultaneously with it. Answer choice J is incorrect because all of the statements in the first paragraph of Scientist 2's viewpoint argue that the emergence of life was dependent upon the prior existence of homochirality in biomolecules. The correct answer is **F**.

Answer: C

29 Scientist 1 writes, "it is reasonable to conclude that life emerged from a prebiotic milieu containing a roughly equal mixture of right- and left-handed molecules." This statement is inconsistent with the hypothesis provided by the question stem, which indicates that early organic molecules provided by meteorites and comets show a predominance of left-handed amino acids. The answer is **C**.

Answer: H

30 Scientist 2 states, "a single right-handed amino acid will disrupt the stability of protein structures." From this statement, we can infer that amino acids are left-handed, eliminating answer choice J. Scientist 2 also states, "DNA and RNA are incapable of complementary pair bonding in the absence of right-handed nucleotides. DNA cannot form a helix if even a small proportion of the left-handed form is present. The presence of even a tiny fraction of left-handed nucleotides terminates RNA replication …" This eliminates answer choices F and G because both RNA and DNA require right-handed nucleotides. This leaves answer choice **H** as the correct answer.

Answer: D

31 Scientist 1 states, "life emerged from a prebiotic milieu containing a roughly equal mixture of right- and left-handed molecules," and Scientist 2 states, "Crystalline surfaces … played a role in the origin of the 'handedness' of biomolecules," and "may have contributed to the transition from a heterochiral prebiotic 'soup' to the homochiral molecules essential to the origin of life on Earth." Thus, both authors agree that living organisms emerged from an environment composed of nonliving molecules. Answer choice A is incorrect because neither Scientist 2 nor Scientist 1 would agree with the statement. Scientist 1 states that "life emerged from a prebiotic milieu containing a roughly equal mixture of right- and left-handed molecules," while scientist 2 states, "the homochirality of biomolecules must have originated before biological life." Answer choice B is incorrect because only Scientist 1 would agree with the statement. Answer choice C is incorrect because only Scientist 2 would agree with the statement. The correct answer is **D**.

32 In the models of both Scientist A and B, DNA polymerase uses the base pairs of the existing DNA molecule as a template for the new DNA molecule, so our answer is **J**. The passage tells us that DNA polymerase is an enzyme, so F is incorrect. Scientist A does not discuss histones, so G is incorrect, and Scientist B discusses the importance of histones in replication, making H incorrect and leaving us with **J**.

Answer: **J**

33 As explained in the passage, for every A on one strand, there is a T on the opposite strand, while for every G, there is a C. Therefore, any given molecule of double-stranded DNA must have equal amounts of A and T nucleotides and equal amounts of G and C nucleotides. The only answer choice that fits these criteria is **C**.

Answer: **C**

34 Our answer is **F**. Scientist A describes the two original strands as splitting apart, with each one incorporated into a new DNA double helix, which fits the diagram in Model 1. Scientist B describes the original DNA molecule staying intact, and an entirely new one being formed, which fits the diagram in Model 2. Model 3 is a different model entirely than those described in the passage: in this third model, the original double helix is broken into segments that act as templates for the creation of new DNA molecules.

Answer: **F**

35 Scientist B believes that histones play a key role in the replication process (they change the shape of the helix so that DNA polymerase can "read" the base pairs). Scientist B also states that DNA is bound to histones and at no point does the histone separate from the original molecule during replication (although Scientist B does state that the new DNA molecule is bound to new histones). Therefore, we know that Scientist B agrees with Scientist X. Answer choice **B** makes the most sense, because at no point is there a discussion of whether or not histones and DNA are chemically impossible to separate.

Answer: **B**

36 Answer choice **F**—that the proteins attached to the DNA molecule "separate from the DNA prior to replication"—is stated directly in Scientist A's hypothesis in the second sentence.

Answer: **F**

37 The answer is **A**. Only Scientist A's model of DNA replication requires the separation of the two DNA strands. Scientist B's model involves the reading and replication of the DNA double helix while leaving the overall structure intact.

Answer: **A**

38 According to the information in the passage, answer choice **H** is the only option that follows the base pairing rules: guanine (G) always pairs with cytosine (C) and thymine (T) always pairs with adenine (A) on the complementary strand, so our answer is **H**.

Answer: **H**

ACT Science Test Concepts to Know

Remember when we told you that your priorities should be learning how to read charts and graphs, practicing pacing, and getting comfortable with the format of the ACT Science Test? Yep, that's still true!

However, that does leave the pesky handful of questions that will require you to bring in outside knowledge in order to answer them. If you're aiming for a top ACT Science Test score, it's imperative that you review some fundamental scientific concepts.

Having a good grasp on the foundational concepts of the scientific method, biology, physics, chemistry, and earth science will also help you move more quickly through the ACT Science Test, even if you aren't aiming for a near-perfect score. Knowing these concepts will make the experiments and studies presented far less overwhelming.

There's no definitive list of concepts tested on the ACT test—everything generally taught in middle school or high school science classes *could* make an appearance on the exam. However, there are some concepts that come up again and again, so we've whipped up the following list of important concepts for you to study. If you learn these, you'll be in good shape.

We recommend using a sheet of paper to cover the definition while you quiz yourself. Then, as you start to get good at these concepts, make flashcards for the terms that you need extra help remembering. Just be sure to remove any obvious clues from the definition side of the card!

The variable in a science experiment that's changed by the scientist

Example: In an experiment testing which fertilizer works best for daffodil growth, the independent variable would be the fertilizers tested.

---

independent variable
SCIENTIFIC METHOD

The variable in a science experiment that depends on the independent variable. It's the variable scientists watch to see how it responds to changes made with the independent variable.

Example: In an experiment testing which fertilizer works best for daffodil growth, the dependent variable would be the respective heights of the plants treated with different fertilizers.

---

dependent variable
SCIENTIFIC METHOD

The group that is treated in the same way as the experimental group, except that it does not receive the treatment of the independent variable. It "controls" for all other variables that might affect an experiment other than the independent variable.

Example: In an experiment testing which fertilizer works best for daffodil growth, the control would be the plants that were not treated with any fertilizer at all.

---

control
SCIENTIFIC METHOD

The claim that is tested in a study or experiment

Example: If the question is "Does UV radiation cause skin cancer?", a hypothesis might be: UV radiation causes skin cancer because it damages the DNA in your skin cells, which causes cells to grow out of control. (Then a scientist would test this to see if it's true!)

---

hypothesis
SCIENTIFIC METHOD

The substance that composes all observable physical objects and gives them mass. Observable matter can exist in four states: solid, liquid, gas, and plasma.

Good to know! A vacuum is the absence of matter.

---

matter
EARTH AND SPACE SCIENCE

The amount of matter in an object. *Gravitational mass* is a measurement of how much gravity an object exerts on other objects.

Good to know! Mass differs from weight in that the mass of an object never changes, but weight changes based on the force of gravity. On Earth, weight = mass × the force of Earth's gravity ($9.8 \ m/s^2$).

---

mass
EARTH AND SPACE SCIENCE

The change of minerals or texture in rocks, usually due to heat, pressure, or chemicals

Example: Marble is metamorphosed limestone; it is limestone that has been recrystallized, resulting in a change in color and texture.

---

metamorphism
EARTH AND SPACE SCIENCE

Chemically, the Earth can be divided into three layers: the *crust* (which is solid), the *mantle* (which can be divided into the upper and lower mantle and is solid/plastic), and the *core* (which can be divided into the outer core, which is liquid, and the inner core, which is solid).

Did you know? Scientists determine the composition of the Earth through seismic monitoring (measuring earthquake waves) as well as measurements of gravitational and magnetic fields of the Earth.

---

three primary layers of the Earth
EARTH AND SPACE SCIENCE

The breakdown of soil, rock, or other surface material due to processes such as water flow or wind that move material from one location to another

Example: The Grand Canyon in the US was formed by water flowing through it and eroding the rocks.

---

erosion
EARTH AND SPACE SCIENCE

From lowest to highest, they are the *troposphere* (where most of the clouds are), *stratosphere* (where the ozone layer is), *mesosphere*, *thermosphere*, and *exosphere*.

Did you know? A sixth layer, the ionosphere, overlaps other atmospheric layers. The air is ionized by the sun's ultraviolet rays, which affects the transmission of radio waves.

five primary layers of the atmosphere

EARTH AND SPACE SCIENCE

The height of an object or point in relation to either sea level or ground level

Example: The altitude of Mount Everest is 8,848 meters above sea level.

altitude

EARTH AND SPACE SCIENCE

The frictional force air exerts against a moving object, also called "drag"

Example: when you're trying to run into a headwind and it feels so much harder to get anywhere

air resistance

EARTH AND SPACE SCIENCE

The gravitationally curved path of an object around a point in space. Orbits typically refer to planets moving around a star, or moons going around planets, in an elliptical shape.

Example: The Earth chugs around its orbit around the sun approximately once every 365 days.

orbit

EARTH AND SPACE SCIENCE

A planet that has a solid surface and other "Earth-like" features

Examples: Mercury, Venus, Earth, Mars

terrestrial planet

EARTH AND SPACE SCIENCE

A giant planet composed mainly of hydrogen and helium

Examples: Jupiter, Saturn, Uranus, and Neptune

gas giants

EARTH AND SPACE SCIENCE

The network of organs and vessels responsible for the flow of blood, nutrients, hormones, oxygen, and other gases to and from cells in the body. Also goes by the name "cardiovascular system."

Starring components: the heart, the arteries, veins, and blood

circulatory system

BIOLOGY

The organs and glands in the body that are responsible for the ingestion, digestion, and absorption of food

Starring organs: mouth, esophagus, stomach, intestines, liver, gallbladder, pancreas, rectum, anus

digestive system

BIOLOGY

The organs that allow the body to breathe and exchange oxygen and carbon dioxide throughout the body

Starring organs: nose, mouth, trachea, lungs, bronchi

respiratory system

BIOLOGY

The process used by plants and other organisms to convert light energy (generally from the sun) into sugars that can be converted into fuel for living things. Chlorophyll (the green pigment in plants) is essential for photosynthesis.

Hint: "photo" means light and "synthesis" means putting together.

photosynthesis
BIOLOGY

The transfer of pollen from the stamen (male reproductive organ) to the pistil (female reproductive organ) in plants to start the production of seeds

Hint: This is why your parents told you about the "birds and the bees": these creatures often accidentally move pollen from one part of the flower to another.

pollination
BIOLOGY

A state change. In an insect or amphibian, metamorphosis is the process of transformation from an immature form to a mature form.

Example: Caterpillars become butterflies through metamorphosis.

metamorphosis
BIOLOGY

A form of a gene. Some genes have a variety of different forms. Humans have two alleles at each genetic locus, with one allele inherited from each parent.

Example: Your hair color is determined by whichever alleles of a gene you inherit.

allele
BIOLOGY

Region of DNA that act as instructions to make proteins. They are important because they determine hereditary traits: each person has two copies of each gene, one from each parent.

Examples: Humans have genes that determine blood type, eye color, certain genetic disorders, and body type.

genes
BIOLOGY

Structures located inside the nucleus of animal and plant cells. Chromosomes contain most of the DNA of an organism.

Important to know! Females have two of the same sex chromosomes (XX); males have two distinct ones (XY). The presence or absence of the Y chromosome determines the sex of mammals and many other animals.

chromosomes
BIOLOGY

Large molecules consisting of chains of amino acids. They do most of the work in a cell and are required for the function of the body's tissues and organs.

Did you know? The body does not store protein; that's why we must ingest it to build our muscular beach bodies.

proteins
BIOLOGY

Deoxyribonucleic acid stores hereditary biological information. DNA molecules carry the instructions for the development, functioning, and reproduction of all known living organisms and many viruses.

Important to know! The structure of DNA is a "double helix": two strands coiled around each other made up of nucleotides.

DNA
BIOLOGY

The building blocks for the double helix of DNA and RNA

Important to know! In DNA, cytosine (C) always pairs with guanine (G), and thymine (T) always pairs with adenine (A).

nucleobases
BIOLOGY

A molecule made up nucleotides that acts as a messenger between DNA and ribosomes to make proteins

Good to know! Like DNA, RNA carries hereditary genetic information. Unlike DNA, which is double-stranded, RNA exists in a single-stranded form.

RNA
BIOLOGY

A complex machine found in all living cells that serves as the site where proteins are made

A helpful image: DNA and RNA are the planning managers of a cell and the ribosome is its factory, manufacturing the proteins essential to life.

ribosome
BIOLOGY

An organelle found in most cells, where respiration and energy production occur

Good to know! Mitochondria generate ATP, which is used as a source of chemical energy.

mitochondrion
BIOLOGY

An individual's collection of genes. Genotype can also mean the two alleles inherited for a particular gene.

Examples: You might remember genotypes from Mendel's pea plant experiments: genotype determines flower color, pod shape, seed shape, pod color, etc.

genotype
BIOLOGY

The movement of molecules through a semipermeable membrane from a less concentrated solution into a more concentrated one to cause equilibrium

Did you know? Pruned fingers after sitting in a bathtub are an example of osmosis: your fingers aren't shrinking; they're swelling because the water is trying to get into your body to cause equilibrium.

osmosis
BIOLOGY

An individual's observable traits, such as height, eye color, or hair color

Did you know? Lots of people get genotype and phenotype confused. Genotype is the genetic code that influences many of an organism's traits but is not wholly responsible. Phenotype is the visible or expressed trait; it depends on the genotype but can be influenced by environment.

phenotype
BIOLOGY

The terms *dominant* and *recessive* describe the inheritance patterns of certain traits, meaning how likely it is that a certain phenotype gets passed on to offspring. Dominant traits are more likely to be inherited.

Important to know! Individuals who have one dominant and one recessive allele will typically have the dominant phenotype, but they are carriers of the recessive allele and can pass it on.

dominant and recessive traits
BIOLOGY

The part of the cell division cycle in which the chromosomes in a cell's nucleus are separated into two identical sets of chromosomes, and each set ends up in its own nucleus

Important to know! There are four stages to mitosis: prophase, metaphase, anaphase, and telophase.

mitosis
BIOLOGY

A type of cell division that results in four daughter cells, each with half the number of chromosomes of the parent cell

Important to know! Mitosis and meiosis are different. Mitosis has one division and meiosis has two divisions.

meiosis
BIOLOGY

During interphase, the cell grows and makes a copy of its DNA. During the mitotic phase, the cell separates its DNA into two sets and divides its cytoplasm, forming two new cells. The mitotic phase is further divided into mitosis (the division of chromosomes in the nucleus) and cytokinesis (the division of the cytoplasm).

stages of cellular division
BIOLOGY

An organism with a complex cell or cells. Unlike a prokaryotic organism, a eukaryotic organism has a nucleus.

Team Eukaryote: humans, cats, palm trees, mushrooms, yeast, and pretty much anything that's not bacteria or archaea

eukaryotic organism
BIOLOGY

A single-celled organism that lacks a nucleus

Team Prokaryote: bacteria (such as E. coli and streptococcus, which causes strep throat) and archaea

prokaryotic organism
BIOLOGY

When a system absorbs energy from its surroundings, usually in the form of heat

Examples of endothermic processes: baking cookies, melting ice, photosynthesis

endothermic
CHEMISTRY

When a system releases energy, usually in the form of heat, but also in the form of light, electricity, or sound

Examples of exothermic processes: starting a fire, nuclear fission, rusting iron

exothermic
CHEMISTRY

The smallest unit in a chemical element. Each atom consists of a nucleus, which consists of protons and neutrons, and a set of electrons that move about the nucleus.

atom
CHEMISTRY

The positively charged central core of an atom, consisting of protons and neutrons

nucleus
CHEMISTRY

An electrically charged atom (or group of atoms) formed by the loss or gain of one or more electrons

ion
CHEMISTRY

A group of two or more atoms linked together by sharing electrons in a chemical bond

Good to know! Molecules are the smallest part of a compound that can participate in a chemical reaction.

molecule
CHEMISTRY

A substance that dissolves a solute (a chemically different liquid, solid, or gas, resulting in a solution)

Example: If you mix a spoonful of salt in a glass of water, the water is the solvent.

solvent
CHEMISTRY

Substances participating in a chemical reaction that are consumed during the reaction to make the products

reactant
CHEMISTRY

The substance that results from the combination of the reactants in a chemical reaction

product
CHEMISTRY

The measurement of the size of an atom. You can closely approximate atomic mass by adding the number of protons and neutrons. Measured in atomic units (u).

atomic mass
CHEMISTRY

A numeric scale used to specify the acidity or alkalinity (basicity) of an aqueous solution. Solutions with a pH less than 7 are acidic, and solutions with a pH greater than 7 are alkaline or basic.

Did you know? Pure water is neutral, neither an acid nor a base.

pH
CHEMISTRY

Acids have various defining characteristics that distinguish them from bases, including having a pH of less than 7, tasting sour, and producing a piercing pain in a wound.

Examples: lemons, vinegar, sulfuric acid

acid
CHEMISTRY

Bases have various defining characteristics that distinguish them from acids, including a pH greater than 7, a bitter taste, and a slippery feel.

Examples: baking soda, Tums, ammonia

base
CHEMISTRY

The extent to which a fluid resists the tendency to flow

Examples: Molasses and toothpaste have a high viscosity; milk and oil have a low viscosity.

viscosity
CHEMISTRY

The change of a gas or vapor to a liquid, either by cooling or by being subjected to increased pressure

condensation
CHEMISTRY

The change of a liquid to a gaseous state due to an increase in temperature and/or pressure

---

evaporation
CHEMISTRY

A negatively charged subatomic particle found in a "cloud" around the nucleus of an atom. Electrons are extremely small compared to the other parts of an atom and can be gained or lost.

---

electron
CHEMISTRY

A positively charged subatomic particle in the nucleus of an atom

---

proton
CHEMISTRY

A subatomic particle in the nucleus of an atom with about the same mass as a proton but without an electric charge

---

neutrons
CHEMISTRY

The number of protons in the nucleus of an atom. The higher the atomic number, the heavier the atom is.

Important to know! Atomic number is crucial because it determines the chemical properties of an element and its place on the periodic table. Elements are ordered according to their atomic numbers.

Also important to know! Atomic mass is approximately equivalent to the number of protons and neutrons in the atom (the mass number).

---

atomic number
CHEMISTRY

---

molar mass: also known as molecular weight, molar mass = **grams/mole**. It is the sum of the total mass in grams of all the atoms that make up a mole of a particular molecule.

Good to know! You don't need to memorize this for the ACT, but a mole is approximately equal to 6.02×10^{23} atoms. Celebrate Mole Day on October 23 (10/23)!

---

molar mass
CHEMISTRY

A form of the same element that contains an equal number of protons as the primary form of the element but a different number of neutrons

Example: Hydrogen-3 (tritium) is a radioactive isotope of hydrogen. Its nucleus has one proton and two neutrons, resulting in triple the mass of ordinary hydrogen.

---

isotope
CHEMISTRY

The temperature at which the solid phase of a substance begins to change to a liquid

Important to know! The melting point is virtually the same as the freezing point. For example, think about water. The temperature at which ice begins to melt is the same at which water begins to freeze into ice.

---

melting point
CHEMISTRY

The point at which a liquid phase of a substance begins to change into a gas or vapor

Example: Think about a boiling pot of water and the water turning into the water vapor steaming from the pot.

---

boiling point
CHEMISTRY

The temperature at which a liquid phase of a substance begins to turn into a solid

Important to know! The freezing point is virtually the same as the melting point. For example, think about water. The temperature at which ice begins to melt is the same at which water begins to freeze into ice.

---

freezing point

CHEMISTRY

A homogeneous mixture composed of two or more substances. In a solution, a solute is the substance dissolved in another substance, known as the solvent.

Example: mixing salt into water to create a solution of salt water (gargle it for a sore throat!)

---

solution

CHEMISTRY

A substance that is dissolved in another substance (the solvent), usually the component of the solution present in the lesser amount

Example: If you mix a spoonful of salt in a glass of water, the salt is the solute.

---

solute

CHEMISTRY

The rate at which an object changes its velocity with regard to time

Good to know! Acceleration is a vector quantity, meaning that it has to do with position. Any change in the velocity, whether increasing speed, decreasing speed, or changing direction, results in an acceleration. It doesn't just mean speeding up!

---

acceleration

PHYSICS

An attribute with two possible values. In physics, it's mainly used to describe electric charges (positive and negative) and magnets (north and south).

Good to know! On the ACT, you'll see this most often on electric circuit setups: electrons flow in the same circuit by starting at the negative (–) terminal and flowing through to the positive (+) terminal.

---

polarity

PHYSICS

The upward force on an object produced by the surrounding liquid or gas in which it is immersed, due to the pressure difference of the fluid between the top and bottom of the object

Example: It's easier for you to stay afloat in salt water than in fresh water because salt water is denser and thus provides more buoyant force.

---

buoyancy

PHYSICS

An oscillation, or disturbance, that travels through space or mass and is accompanied by a transfer of energy

Good to know! There are two main categories of waves: mechanical waves that require a medium to transmit energy (such as ocean waves, sound waves, and slinky waves) and electromagnetic waves that can transmit energy through a vacuum (such as radio waves, microwaves, UV rays, and gamma rays).

---

waves

PHYSICS

The "height" of a wave measured from its equilibrium position; the maximum displacement or distance moved by a point on a wave

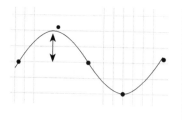

---

amplitude

PHYSICS

How often the particles of the medium vibrate when a wave passes through the medium

Good to know! A typical unit of frequency is the Hertz (Hz) where 1 Hz equals 1 cycle/second.

---

frequency

PHYSICS

The distance from a particular height on a wave to the next spot on the wave where it is the same height and going in the same direction

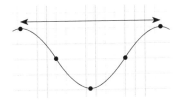

wavelength
PHYSICS

A characteristic of a unit of matter that expresses the extent to which it has fewer or more electrons than protons. A negatively charged atom has more electrons than protons; a positively charged atom has more protons than electrons.

Important to know! Like charges repel each other; opposite charges attract.

charge
PHYSICS

A wired path between two or more points across which an electrical current can be carried. A simple circuit has a source of voltage (often a battery), a conductive path that allows for the movement of charges (typically wire), and a resistor (possibly a light bulb, a motor, a speaker, etc.).

Ohm's Law is the most frequently tested concept on electrical circuits on the ACT. It will be provided for you, but just so you know, it is V = I × R (where V is the voltage measured across the conductor in volts, R is the resistance in ohms, and I is the current measured in amperes).

electrical circuit
PHYSICS

An electrical device, consisting of one or more pairs of conductors separated by an insulator, used to store electric charge when a voltage is applied

Important to know! Current only flows when a capacitor is charging or discharging, not when it's fully charged.

capacitor
PHYSICS

An electrical component that consumes electrical energy when current flows through it

Important to know! Resistance is measured in ohms (Ω).

resistor
PHYSICS

The flow of electrically charged particles. In electric circuits, this charge is typically carried by electrons in a wire.

electrical current
PHYSICS

Often shortened to *amp*, it is the unit of electric current.

ampere
PHYSICS

A unit of both voltage and electric potential. It refers to the energy that could be released if electrical current is allowed to flow.

the height of an object or volt
PHYSICS

Heat transfer by mass motion of a fluid such as air or water when the heated fluid is moved away from the source of heat, carrying the energy with it. There are three primary means of heat transfer: conduction, convection, and radiation.

Example: A convection oven is an oven that has fans to circulate air around food, which allows more heat to be transferred to the food.

the height of an object or convection
PHYSICS

Heat transfer through collisions between neighboring molecules. There are three primary means of heat transfer: conduction, convection, and radiation.

Example: A pot getting heated by sitting on a hot burner is an example of conduction.

conduction

PHYSICS

Transmission of energy in the form of waves or particles through space. There are three primary means of heat transfer: conduction, convection, and radiation.

Example: warming your toes by a campfire

radiation

PHYSICS

The energy possessed by an object due to its motion

Example: A downhill skier headed down the mountain has a lot of kinetic energy (enough energy to knock down some unsuspecting bystanders if he or she isn't a good skier).

kinetic energy

PHYSICS

The stored energy possessed by an object due to its position

Important to know! Gravitational potential energy is the energy stored in an object as a result of its height.

potential energy

PHYSICS

The sum of potential energy and kinetic energy, which means the energy an object has due to its position and/ or motion

Example: Think about dropping a brick off a tall building (but don't do it! It's dangerous!). The potential energy of the brick's height becomes kinetic energy as it falls. The total mechanical energy remains constant from top to bottom.

mechanical energy

PHYSICS

When a force is applied to an object resulting in a displacement of the object in the direction of a force

Example: When a brick is dropped from a building, the work done on the brick as it falls is equal to the weight of the brick multiplied by the distance it falls (the displacement).

work

PHYSICS

The compactness of an object, measured in mass per unit volume—in other words, density = mass/volume

Important to know! If an object weighs more than an equal volume of water, it will sink; if it weighs less, it will float.

density

PHYSICS

The states of matter observable in everyday life are solids, liquids, gases, and plasma. Solids have a stable shape and definite volume. Liquids take the shape of their container and have a definite volume if temperature and pressure are constant. Gases and plasmas have no definite shape or volume.

four states of matter

PHYSICS

The rate at which the position of an object changes in a certain direction

Good to know! Velocity is a vector quantity (it has to do with position) and speed is a scalar quantity. Speed refers to how fast an object is moving. Vector has to do with a position: if a person took one step forward and one step back to the original position, velocity would be zero.

velocity

PHYSICS

Chapter 9

ACT Writing Test

The ACT Enhanced Writing Test (a.k.a. the ACT essay) measures your ability to evaluate different perspectives on a debatable topic and write an essay (within a time limit!) that presents your own argument on the issue and supports it with specific details and examples. Technically, it's an optional component of the ACT. However, there are many colleges and universities that require or recommend it for admissions, so start flexing those handwriting muscles if that applies to you!

At a Glance

What to Know

- The ACT Writing Test is the last section of the ACT (meaning you have to push through and keep going after your non-Writing-Test friends scamper off to freedom).
- You have 40 minutes in which to plan and write your essay.
- The ACT will give you one essay prompt that will present you with a debatable topic and three different perspectives on it. The prompt will ask you to evaluate the different perspectives, present your own perspective (which may agree in part or in full with any of the provided viewpoints), and explain the relationship between your viewpoint and the provided ones.
- Your essay will get five scores: a subject-level writing score (this is your "overall" essay score) and four domain scores: Ideas and Analysis, Development and Support, Organization, and Language Use and Conventions. The subject-level score is a rounded average of the four domain scores.
- All five scores are on a scale from 2 to 12.
- The essay is scored by two graders, each of whom will assign you a score of 1 to 6 in the four different writing domains. Your total domain scores will be the sum of the two graders' scores. (But don't worry—if they disagree by more than one point, a third reader will be brought in to read your essay and settle the dispute, deciding in favor of one grader or the other.)

What to Study

- Practice planning and writing essays on sample ACT essay prompts. Although writing full-length essays is the best practice, 10-minute outlining sessions in which you plan out your essay (like you'll do on the test) can go a long way in helping you learn how to quickly generate and organize your ideas, even if you don't always write the full essay.
- Share your writing with the strong writers you know and get feedback from them. Have them score your practice essays using the ACT rubric, which you can access on the ACT website (https://www.act.org/content/dam/act/unsecured/documents /Writing-Test-Scoring-Rubric.pdf).
- Review the sample essays on the official ACT website (www.act.org/content/act /en/products-and-services/the-act/test-preparation/writing-sample-essays.html) so that you can get a sense of which kinds of essays get which scores. This can be incredibly helpful. We also have a range of sample student essays for you to peruse later in this chapter ... stay tuned!
- Learn about current events and form your own opinions on them. Engage in lively debates with your friends and family so that you can practice supporting your opinions and anticipating opposing arguments.

What Not to Study

- You don't need to memorize specific prompts. Focus instead on collecting pieces of evidence that can be applied to various essay prompts and themes.

Top Tips for the ACT Writing Test

To give you a page to come back to easily, here are our top tips for the ACT Writing Test (and our top tips for students who want to get the highest scores). Keep these handy as you practice!

1. Choose to agree with one of the three perspectives rather than presenting your own. You can get a perfect score by agreeing with one of the perspectives; with such a limited amount of time to write, why make your life harder (and risk going off topic) by developing a fourth perspective? (If you are a VERY strong writer, you may be able to score a slam dunk by modifying one of the perspectives or narrowing its focus slightly—but avoid the temptation to do something completely different. It's too easy to get offtrack.)

2. Never, ever, ever be wishy-washy. Pick a side. You have three perspectives to evaluate, but this definitely doesn't mean that you should agree with all of them. At least two of these perspectives will be in conflict with one another, and the essay asks you to develop and support *one* argument. And you can't possibly do that if you try to agree with all the perspectives. Decide what your stance is on the debatable issue and then agree with the perspectives that help support your argument. Challenge the ones that don't.

3. On that note, when you pick your perspective, pick the one that you can more easily think of concrete, specific examples for, even if you don't necessarily agree with it.

4. Use a five-paragraph essay structure: an introduction with a clear thesis; one body paragraph on each of the perspectives (ending with the one that fits in best with your perspective), including a concrete piece of evidence; and a conclusion that ties everything together.

5. Where appropriate, consider including counterarguments and examples regarding the perspectives you don't agree with. (But make sure that it's a criticism someone might actually use. Making a weak counterargument only makes your essay look weak!)

6. Try to vary your types of evidence among historical circumstances, personal examples (to be used sparingly, as mentioned above), common knowledge, and objective reasoning; this makes your argument much more persuasive, which leads to a higher score!

7. Remember to keep your handwriting legible. An essay the graders can't read will be given a zero, no matter how great the content is.

8. Resist the urge to edit too much as you go. Changing a word here or there is fine, but don't worry about perfection in a 40-minute essay. The graders know you don't have a lot of time.

9. Finally, keep an eye on the time. Devote about 10–15 minutes to prewriting, 20–25 minutes to writing, and two to three minutes to proofreading. Wear a watch so you know for a fact how much time you have left. Your proctor may not be the greatest at reminding you how much time has passed, and on the essay, every minute really counts. (And no, you won't be able to use your phone, even to keep time!)

Common Mistakes on the ACT Writing Test

Forgetting to address your perspective and AT LEAST one other perspective. If you find that you always run out of time on the essay, then start by addressing one perspective and then introduce your own perspective. You can't be penalized for following the instructions, and the ACT only requires that you address two perspectives in your essay.

Wasting time coming up with a brand-new argument for your perspective. Why not make your life easier? If you choose one of the given three perspectives to agree with (at least mostly), then you don't have to come up with an entirely new option to present as your own. This will save you time during the planning process.

ACT Essay Basics

There are a few things that you definitely need to know about the ACT Writing Test, even if you're taking the exam tomorrow. First of all, it's the last section on the ACT. This means that after you show off your skills reading and interpreting passages, calculating the square root of *x*, correcting dangling modifiers, and comparing experiments, you're going to sit down and write an essay, just to cap it all off.

The ACT essay is not required; however, it's a good idea to take it, because many colleges and universities prefer or even require ACT Writing Test scores. It's important to realize this in any case, because you'll need to register for the ACT *with* Writing to make sure you have the chance to take it on the official exam.

What can you expect on the ACT essay? You'll open your test booklet to see one prompt, which you'll respond to in No. 2 pencil (not mechanical!) on the provided answer sheet.

The essay is an exercise in both persuasion and analysis. You'll get three perspectives on an issue and be asked to "evaluate and analyze" the three perspectives, "state and develop" your own perspective, and "explain the relationship" between your perspective and the given perspectives. You can choose to agree with one of the provided viewpoints or come up with your own.

That can sound a little abstract, so let's take a look at a sample prompt.

Sample ACT Essay Prompt

Censorship

Almost since human beings began sharing ideas, the issue of censorship (officially suppressing ideas or writing) has been debated. Proponents of censorship argue, for example, that offensive material might morally corrupt children or that governments have the right to protect their national secrets. Opponents argue that censorship infringes on individual freedoms and hampers progress. Censorship has long been an issue regarding books and newspapers; now, it has become a critical issue concerning the great amount of information on the internet. Given the continued impact of censorship on various aspects of our lives, it is an issue worth examining.

Read and carefully consider these perspectives. Each suggests a particular way of thinking about the impact of censorship.

Perspective 1	Perspective 2	Perspective 3
Selective censorship prevents children from being exposed to offensive material. It allows parents and caretakers to determine what material children are ready for and when they are ready based on their maturity level.	Censorship intrudes upon freedom of the press and freedom of speech. Individuals have the right to learn about their world, both its positive and negative aspects, and express their ideas on it.	Censorship should not be condoned because it places too much power in the hands of a few: no government or leadership system should be allowed to decide what information should reach the public.

Continued on next page

427

As you can see, there's quite a lot of text here! We're going to go ahead and break it down in more detail, but we wanted you to get a visual of what it looks like on the page as we talk about the different parts.

The first part is the introductory discussion of an issue. That's this part:

Censorship

Almost since human beings began sharing ideas, the issue of censorship (officially suppressing ideas or writing) has been debated. Proponents of censorship argue, for example, that offensive material might morally corrupt children or that governments have the right to protect their national secrets. Opponents argue that censorship infringes on individual freedoms and hampers progress. Censorship has long been an issue regarding books and newspapers; now, it has become a critical issue concerning the great amount of information on the internet. Given the continued impact of censorship on various aspects of our lives, it is an issue worth examining.

So, this first part sets the issue up for us. It defines censorship and gives us examples. It tells us about some of the debate surrounding censorship. It asks questions; it gives us a little food for thought.

This is really important to read because you can use the examples from the introductory material in your essay (although you should definitely think up your own examples too). In short, it gives you some things to start working with and to start developing your own perspective on the issue, but you do NOT need to necessarily include in your essay information that appears here, although you could.

The next part gives you three perspectives on this issue in three boxes. That's this part of our sample prompt:

An example of attempted censorship concerns the destruction of the Temple of Artemis at Ephesus, one of the Seven Wonders of the World, in 356 BCE. Herostratus burned the temple in an attempt to get his name remembered in history. The outraged Ephesians put him to death and forbade the mentioning of his name in an attempt to deprive him of the fame he sought.

Perspective 1	Perspective 2	Perspective 3
Selective censorship prevents children from being exposed to offensive material. It allows parents and caretakers to determine what material children are ready for and when they are ready based on their maturity level.	Censorship intrudes upon freedom of the press and freedom of speech. Individuals have the right to learn about their world, both its positive and negative aspects, and express their ideas on it.	Censorship should not be condoned because it places too much power in the hands of a few: no government or leadership system should be allowed to decide what information should reach the public.

Each perspective may be in favor of the topic, against it, partially supporting it, or providing some type of special perspective on that issue. **This is the most important part of the essay prompt to pay attention to** because the third part, the essay task, is going to ask you to evaluate these perspectives.

Finally, you'll see the essay task:

Essay Task
Write a unified, coherent essay in which you evaluate multiple perspectives on censorship. In your essay, be sure to:

- *clearly state your own perspective on the issue and analyze the relationship between your perspective and at least one other perspective;*
- *develop and support your ideas with reasoning and examples;*
- *organize your ideas clearly and logically; and*
- *communicate your ideas effectively in standard written English.*

Your perspective may be in full agreement with any of those given, in partial agreement, or completely different.

The essay task is going to be worded basically the same way on every test. (This means that if you get familiar with it today, you won't have to spend time rereading it on test day!) You have three things to accomplish as part of your essay task:

1. You have to analyze and evaluate the perspectives that are given.
2. You have to present your own perspective on it.
3. You have to explain the relationship between your perspective and the others.

In order to get a good score, you need to do all three of these tasks.

Let's talk about how the essay is scored. We're going to work backward a little bit and start with what you see on your test report.

Scoring the ACT Essay

Unlike other sections on the ACT, the essay is scored between 2 and 12, rather than between 1 and 36. Two graders will individually score students from 1 to 6 on the four domains: Ideas and Analysis, Development and Support, Organization, and Language Use and Conventions. These scores will be added together between the two graders, and **the final ACT Writing Test score from 2 to 12 is an AVERAGE of all the domain scores**.

Your score report will reveal each of your domain scores, so you'll get to see how much of an impact your grammar had on your composite score versus your ideas. You're going to get a fair amount of feedback on why your essay received the score it did.

You'll will also receive an ELA score, which combines the essay score with your score on the ACT English Test and the ACT Reading Test multiple-choice sections (although this score is not widely used, except sometimes to compare ACT to SAT scores).

Knowing how the ACT essay is scored will help you to write stronger essays. How? Take a look at what the exam's looking for in these areas and see how you can improve your writing in different domains.

What Exactly Are the Domain Scores Measuring?

Ideas and Analysis means that the graders are looking for you to demonstrate critical thinking at a reasonably high level. Rather than just being able to understand a series of opinions, the ACT Writing Test wants you to interpret them and come up with your own argument or synthesis.

The **Development and Support** domain tells us that the ACT essay is evaluating your ability to craft a whole argument rather than just a thesis statement. Again, it's testing your critical reasoning skills: can you determine, in a limited timeframe, what makes for convincing evidence for your argument?

The **Organization** category indicates that the ACT is also testing how *clearly* you can present this information in a short essay, in a way that makes sense not just to you but also to the reader.

Finally, you can look at **Language Use and Conventions** as ACT English in practice. How're your vocabulary and grammar? Can you write in an efficient and readable way? How eloquent (to an extent) can you be?

Or, in other words, your ACT essay has four major goals:

- **Make judgments:** The graders evaluate how well you understand the perspectives and their implications, values, and assumptions. Did you understand the question they presented to you? Did you pick a side? Did you understand the strengths and weaknesses of different perspectives on an issue?

- **Develop a position:** The graders evaluate how well you support the argument you make in your essay. Do you give clear facts and relevant details that really help your argument be more persuasive? Do you vary the types of evidence you use? Do you show the graders that you know the difference between assertion (just saying something) and evidence (showing *why* that assertion is true)? The more specific you can be, the more you show the graders how well you understood the topic and its controversy. This goes hand in hand with your ability to make judgments.

- **Organization and focus:** The graders evaluate how logically you present your ideas. Do you have a clear introduction, body, and conclusion? Are your body paragraphs ordered in a way that makes sense? Can the graders follow your train of thought clearly from beginning to end? Do you use transitions between and among your paragraphs to show the readers how they all link together? Do you stay on topic?

- **Communicate clearly:** The graders also look at how well you express yourself, in accordance with the rules of Standard Written English (a.k.a. "School, Work, and Business English," as far as we're concerned). Do you vary your sentence structure so that some sentences are short and others are long? Is your word choice effective? How's your grammar? If there are errors, are they particularly distracting? Can the readers still get your point, or can they not understand what you're saying?

Now that we've seen both what your task will be and what the ACT essay graders are looking for, let's go ahead and make a plan of attack!

Timing Your Essay

It's time to talk about everybody's favorite topic: time management!

Time management is key to getting a great score on the ACT essay. Since you've already seen the many components of the ACT essay prompt, this probably doesn't come as a big surprise to you. On test day, you'll think through a complicated and debatable topic, state your position on it, come up with supporting examples … and then actually write it! Even then, you're not done: you should take a few minutes to proofread at the very end.

And did we mention you only have 40 minutes in which to do this?

It sounds scary, but there's good news: you're about to learn a process that will make those 40 minutes work *for* you rather than *against* you. What's more, instead of thinking about *all those things* the ACT essay makes you do, you're going to focus on just four:

1. Planning
2. Outlining
3. Writing
4. Proofreading

That's it! Four things? Now, *that* is manageable in 40 minutes. So let's talk about what each step entails, as well as the time you'll spend on it, before taking a deeper dive later on.

Planning: 7 Minutes

You read that right! Seven minutes is about the time you should spend planning your essay.

Why? It might seem counterintuitive, but **it's much better to spend more time planning and less time writing** than the other way around. The highest-scoring essays aren't always that long, but they do always use great examples—and it's really hard to come up with those once you're in the middle of writing.

We'll get more into what effective planning entails a little later, but for the moment, know that you should spend it doing the following things:

- **Minute 1:** Read the prompt and perspectives.
- **Minutes 2–7:** Brainstorm examples, arguments, and counterarguments.

Outlining and Organizing: 8 Minutes

Eight minutes may sound like a lot of time to outline an essay—particularly one that will probably be around five paragraphs long! But notice that we didn't just say "outlining." We also said "organizing."

During this time, you'll sketch out your examples, choose your perspective, develop your thesis, and create a rough (very rough) outline. Going along with the schedule so far, that looks something like this:

- **Minutes 8–15:** Choose your perspective, develop your thesis, and sketch a brief outline.

Writing: 20–25 Minutes

You know all that time you just spent planning and organizing your essay? *This* is where it pays off. We'll take a really close look at what each part of your essay should do in a few sections below, but for the moment, keep the following time frame in mind:

- **Minutes 16–19:** Write your intro paragraph.
- **Minutes 20–37:** Write your body paragraphs.
  If you're writing two body paragraphs:
  - Minutes 20–27: Paragraph 1
  - Minutes 28–37: Paragraph 2

  If you're writing three body paragraphs:
  - Minutes 20–25: Paragraph 1
  - Minutes 25–30: Paragraph 2
  - Minutes 30–37: Paragraph 3

  If you're writing four body paragraphs:
  - Minutes 20–24: Paragraph 1
  - Minutes 25–29: Paragraph 2
  - Minutes 30–34: Paragraph 3
  - Minutes 35–37: Paragraph 4
- **Minute 38:** Write a brief conclusion.

With enough practice, this schedule will become second nature by test day. For the moment, the most important thing to note is relative time distribution. Where should you allocate the most time? To your body paragraphs! No fancy intro and definitely no fancy conclusion.

Proofreading: 2–3 Minutes

It's vital to go through what you've written and scan for grammatical or spelling errors (now's not the time to change your mind on what you want your third body paragraph to be about).

With that said, there is one scenario in which you should forego proofreading, and that's if the choice is between finishing your last body paragraph or proofreading. Not finishing the last body paragraph will knock serious points off of your score, so it's better to risk spelling and grammar errors than not finish your essay.

On the other hand, if it comes down to not finishing your *conclusion* and not proofreading, write one sentence in which you restate your thesis in different words and then proofread your heart out. Conclusions do not have the same importance on the ACT essay as body paragraphs!

Timing Recap

When you put it all together, here's what an approximate breakdown of your 40 minutes now looks like:

- **Minute 1:** Read the prompt and perspectives.
- **Minutes 2–7:** Brainstorm examples, arguments, and counterarguments.
- **Minutes 8–15:** Choose your perspective, develop your thesis, and sketch a brief outline.
- **Minutes 16–19:** Write your intro paragraph.
- **Minutes 20–37:** Write your body paragraphs.
- **Minute 38:** Write a brief conclusion.
- **Minutes 39–40:** Proofread.

Remember, though, that constantly checking the clock takes time, too! Make sure you get in enough practice before the official exam that you have a rough idea of how long each task takes you so that you don't end up clock-watching during your test.

You've seen the components of the ACT essay. You've seen the criteria on which the graders will score you. You've seen how to best use your time writing the essay: planning, organizing, writing, and proofreading.

With all that in mind, it's time to look a little closer at each one of those tasks so you can master it on test day! First things first: you'll need a good plan.

Planning Your Essay

Back in the olden days (i.e., pre-2015), the ACT only gave students 30 minutes to write the essay. While the additional 10 minutes you now have may seem like a luxury, they're there for a reason because the new ACT essay task is a demanding one. If you don't devote some time to figuring out how you are going to strategically tackle it, it's unlikely you'll get the score you want.

How Not to Use the First 10 Minutes

If you've chatted with friends or read other test prep books or had a tutor, you may have heard that the first thing you should do on the ACT essay is pick a side. Not so! In fact, you won't choose your own perspective until … oh, about eight minutes into the essay section.

The reason for this is that the most important factor in choosing your perspective is not what you actually believe. In an ideal world, that would be the case. However, if you can't think of good examples to support what you believe, it's better to argue for the side you can think of the best examples for. In other words, the most important factor is actually choosing the perspective for which you can find the best examples. And so, before you do anything else … you're going to brainstorm examples for multiple perspectives!

"Isn't this a waste of time?" Nope. Not only do you need to know which perspective you can write the best essay on, but you also need to have some counterarguments in hand for addressing the other perspectives, should you choose to do so (see "How many perspectives do I have to write about?" in the next section).

What You SHOULD Do in the First 10 Minutes

We know that the ACT essay muse isn't always there when you need her, and it's pretty easy to spend your "extra" 10 minutes staring at the essay prompt. The worst of all possible worlds! To avoid this scenario, let's break down what you should do (besides writing a thesis statement!) during this time. That way, you won't end up getting stuck with weak examples, rambling organization, or hallucinations caused by staring at blank paper for too long.

In the first minute, read the prompt and perspectives. Don't do anything else yet; just remember what your task is. You're going to analyze and evaluate these perspectives before anything else, including coming up with your own perspective. So spend this minute thinking about what each one is actually saying: underline key words, jot down notes in the margins, circle phrases, and make sure you understand the gist of each argument.

Brainstorming examples

For a lot of students, one of the biggest sources of anxiety around the ACT essay is the fear that they will panic and won't be able to think of any good examples on test day. Now, of course, it's impossible to come up with *exact* examples in advance (after all, you won't know your topic until the day of the test!). On the other hand, you can absolutely prepare yourself to come up with great examples.

How? Don't think in terms of examples per se. Instead, think about categories of examples. You can have a ready-made list of categories: in other words, a list of the *kinds* of examples you'll come up with. More specifically, you might think about ...

- Current Events
- Sports
- History
- Art
- Literature

- Science/Technology
- Politics
- Entertainment
- Business
- Personal Experience

This way, you might not be able to work in your favorite anecdote about Claude Monet—but you may be able to make a point about the impressionists that's more germane to your argument. Your example of the American Dream in *The Great Gatsby* might not come into play, but you may be able to use what you know about the Lost Generation to make a strong point. By thinking about the kinds of examples you want to use on the exam, rather than the actual examples themselves, you'll be setting yourself up for greater success.

Personal Experience Examples

Personal experience should always be one of your go-to categories. If nothing else, it's comforting to know that you won't draw a complete blank on an essay topic: you have your whole life to pick examples from!

With that said, we've seen that events from history or current events tend to make better examples and to get higher scores. These examples show that you're knowledgeable and educated; they show that you know about your world; they show that you read and remember information. They also create a connection between you and your reader—after all, graders can relate to current events far better than they can relate to an issue that only affected your school board. That's just human nature, and strong writers will use that connection with the reader to their advantage.

This doesn't mean you can't use personal examples *if that's all you can come up with*. Specific, personal examples are better than having vague or no examples. But for a higher score, try using at least one example in your essay that pertains to issues beyond your own life experience.

Takeaway: Have some personal experience examples ready to use just in case, but it's better to use examples from other categories.

You definitely don't need to have all of these categories in your head! Maybe you have three go-to categories that you know a lot about. If you can use those three categories to find examples that work well to support your points, that's all you'll need!

Making Up Examples

Can you make up examples for the ACT essay? Sure. Should you? No.

Now, we know that's a controversial statement. And it's true that you might not get caught, but there are still reasons to avoid doing this.

Essay graders are pretty good at knowing when you're full of it. They read a lot of these essays. They will know when you are miraculously able to repeat the perfect quotation from FDR, word for word, to support your argument on this topic you didn't know ahead of time.

It may be more tempting to make up a personal experience example. E.g., "When I was in middle school, the Parent-Teacher Association voted to ban *The Adventures of Huckleberry Finn*. Okay, so no grader's going to know whether or not this happened at your school. But here's the thing: personal experiences are not the best examples to use on the ACT essay *anyway*. For why, see the previous box!

Takeaway: It's better to use real examples than to make them up.

Of course, we recommend jotting down the ideas you have for examples. Because you'll be evaluating so many facets of the debate, making a chart can be incredibly helpful here. It doesn't have to be fancy—something like what is below works really well:

Perspective	Support (For)	Challenge (Against)
1		
2		
3		

In the first column, you'll list the three perspectives. In the second column, list supporting arguments and examples. In the third column, list challenges, or examples arguing against the perspectives.

You may struggle with thinking of material to fill out all of the rows and columns in your chart, but do the best job you can to get something down for each cell.

Think back to the censorship prompt we looked at in detail earlier. Here's an example of a chart that's somewhat filled in, based on what one hypothetical student might achieve in a few minutes of planning on the test.

Perspective	Support (For)	Challenge (Against)
1 Shelter Children	FCC regulates television based on time of day. *Indecency* must be scheduled for late night hours so children don't accidentally tune in.	Exposure to good and bad helps students learn to make decisions.
2 Intrudes on Freedoms	• Internet censorship during Arab Spring shut down dissent against government. • Ed Snowden revealing NSA documents, demonstrated widespread gov't surveillance (too controversial?)	If government secrets get out, can put country at risk. Example?
3 Too Much Power for a Few	Comedy Central has censored certain shows and videos and not others—pressured by certain parent groups.	How else could their decisions be made? Impossible to have everyone involved.

A few things to notice here: some examples are stronger than others. Some you might not want to write about at all. It's okay to make "notes to self," such as the fact that Snowden's NSA document leak might be too controversial for some readers. It's your chart; make the notes that are most helpful for you.

Then go on to evaluate your examples. Let's say that you just studied the Arab Spring in history class, so the details are fresh in your mind and you know you could write an awesome paragraph about it. Or maybe Trevor Noah just made some joke about *The Daily Show*'s network, Comedy Central, and you ended up doing some research and reading some articles about the controversy surrounding the network and activist groups, which were pretty memorable. You know a handful of relevant facts about each example, which makes it strong enough to write about in your essay.

Look at that—all those examples, and you're only about seven minutes into the essay! It's time to start getting picky.

Vague Examples

The best examples are not vague hypotheticals. It can be tricky to figure out whether your examples are specific enough, but one thing you *can* do is look at the above table of examples, then compare them to the below examples, which are not specific enough for a high-scoring essay. You'd also find it difficult to write a full body paragraph on any of these!

- "No one likes when he or she isn't allowed to do things he or she wants to do." Not very specific, is it? Also—who is going to argue against this?
- "People often claim they want freedom of speech until they are offended by speech they don't like." Pretty vague, huh? If you find that you're using phrases like "no one likes this," or "people often do this," you may be in danger of falling into the vagueness trap.
- "Machines can help us do things we want to do. If people lose their jobs to machines, then they may lose their homes." Well, this one's a little bit more specific, although not much. Yes, we're talking about specific things—homes and jobs. But while this *might* happen, we're still talking in hypotheticals.

Takeaway: Concrete, real-world examples work best on the ACT essay.

Setting up your thesis

Remember, you're not looking for the perspective that you agree with most, and you're definitely not looking for the "right" perspective. There is no right perspective; graders will read essays defending all three and won't penalize any essay for which perspective it supports. Note, though, that if you go way offtrack and your thesis has nothing to do with the issue at hand (or is peripheral to it), then your score will drop—potentially pretty low.

That's what you're *not* looking for. But what are you looking for in your thesis?

You're looking for a thesis that you can support with awesome examples. Here's what to do: choose your two to four best examples. As you do so, consider some very particular criteria:

1. What examples can you use to support the same thesis?
2. What examples can you provide the most specific details about?
3. Which examples do you know the best?
4. Which examples are not too controversial?*

Beware of examples that people have really, really strong feelings about. There's no need to ruffle any feathers; you can write a high-scoring essay that's not offensive to any potential reader.

So let's return to the previous example, the censorship prompt, and imagine that you've already created the brainstorming chart above with your examples. At this point, you have two strong examples supporting the perspective that censorship places too much power in the hands of a few: the Arab Spring and Comedy Central. This could definitely work as a thesis.

On the other hand, you might also consider writing about that first perspective: the idea that censorship protects children. You could *also* use the Comedy Central issue as an example of how we don't need censorship to protect children. If you chose to do that, it would work best as an example of parent groups controlling network programming for no reason; if certain programs are scheduled to air late at night, then we may not need outright censorship, just some restrictions.

There's no right or wrong answer to this prompt. We can't stress that enough. For the moment, let's move forward with the assumption that you've decided to take the perspective that censorship places too much power in the hands of a few. The examples for that perspective are strong; they hold up pretty well to scrutiny.

Seven to eight minutes in and you already have a perspective and examples! You're well on your way to a great score. Now, the next big question: what are you going to do with them?

Outlining/Organizing

Believe it or not, at this point (seven to eight minutes in) you should still be prewriting!
Yes, you have your perspective and your examples; now, it's time to develop your
thesis more and briefly outline the structure of your essay (don't worry, we'll make it
easy for you—there are two simple formats you can use that work really well).

How to Make Sure You Do Everything the ACT Essay Asks You to Do

It's time to dig in and start thinking about the essay as a whole. Before we get into the actual writing,
let's recap what your essay needs to do:

1. **Analyze and evaluate the perspectives given.** You're required to analyze at least one of them
   (as well as your own), but you'll often find that your job is easier if you address two or all three.
   Why? Because it gives you more to talk about.

   To get a good score on this domain, you need to go beyond just repeating, or paraphrasing, what
   the perspectives say. You need to elaborate on them with your own examples and analysis. Do you
   think they're true or not true? Do you agree with them or not? Don't be afraid to disagree with
   them, by the way.

   Essay graders will reward you for challenging some of the perspectives. Being able to see
   multiple sides of an issue and being able to critique perspectives is a really important skill that
   they like to see in high school students. So don't just agree with all of them or just repeat what all
   of them say. If you don't agree with one or more of the perspectives, make sure to say so and then
   support your opinion with examples.

2. **State and develop your own perspective on the issue.** But wait! Notice this part of the
   prompt, which says your perspective *may be in full agreement, partial agreement, or wholly different
   from any of the others.* This means that you don't need to necessarily come up with an entirely
   new perspective that no one's ever thought of in order to get a great score. You can take one of the
   viewpoints that's already been provided to you.

   Be very wary of the option to choose a "wholly different" perspective.

   First of all, if you do that, it creates a lot more work for you! You have to analyze something
   entirely new along with the given perspectives.

   Second of all, going for the "wholly different" angle means you run the risk of going off topic.
   If it's only loosely tied to the prompt, you might have trouble tying it into the original prompt and
   perspectives. And then can you end up with a much worse grade.

   In short, if you don't stick close to the task, bad things will happen (to your score, that is). As
   a general rule of thumb, we suggest that you choose the option to agree in full or in part with at
   least one of the perspectives. Now, some superstar writers out there may be able to impress graders
   with your out-of-the-box thinking. But, trust us, you can get a perfect score by sticking to one of
   the given topics, so you really need to think about whether or not it is worth the risk to propose
   something totally new.

3. **Explain the relationship between your perspective and those given.** This is not worth
   devoting explicit attention to in your essay. It should really just happen naturally as you transition
   from evaluating the perspectives to explaining your own.

   It's also something you can tick off in the conclusion by writing a quick sentence that compares
   your perspective to the others. Don't get overwhelmed by all of these things that you have to do!
   Focus on the first two points above and you're going to be golden.

You've already selected your perspective and thought of some examples … now, you'll need to develop them.

Developing Your Thesis

At this point, it's important to make a distinction between your *perspective* and your *thesis*. These are two different things—however slight the difference may seem!

A high-scoring essay usually won't begin with a statement like "I agree with perspective three." Nor, however, will it begin with a simple restatement of the perspective itself. Put yourself in the graders' shoes: can you imagine how many of these things they've read? You don't need to repeat the perspective; they definitely know what they are by now.

Here's the perspective that the sample essay in the previous section chose to support:

Perspective 3: *Censorship should not be condoned because it places too much power in the hands of a few: no government or leadership system should be allowed to decide what information should reach the public.*

However, you might decide when you're looking over your examples that you also have good arguments to support Perspective 2. That's great! You can add elements of that into your thesis as well.

Perspective 2: *Censorship intrudes upon freedom of the press and freedom of speech. Individuals have the right to learn about their world, both its positive and negative aspects, and express their ideas on it.*

Repeating both of those would take up valuable time at the beginning of your essay. Besides, it's better to condense them into a single statement. Note that you don't have to reinvent the wheel when writing your thesis. You can borrow some of the language from the perspective you're going to support—just don't borrow all of it! For instance, an example of a thesis you might come up with could be:

Censorship should not be condoned because it allows small groups of individuals to possess an excessive level of control over fundamental human rights.

That's as complicated as it needs to get. It spells out which position you're supporting by echoing *some* of the language ("censorship should not be condoned …") from the third perspective. On the other hand, it's also perfectly tailored to allow you to write about the two examples—the Arab Spring and Comedy Central—that you've decided you can best support.

Ordering Your Examples

Once you've refined your perspective into a thesis statement, it's time to put the perspectives in order. You'll want to discuss more than just your own perspective—in fact, the prompt requires that you compare it with at least one other. Ideally, you'll address all three perspectives, writing a bit more about the one you've chosen to support, but a lot will depend on the topic and how quickly you write (we'll get into full-essay organization in the next section).

At this point in the essay-writing process, you'll need to decide which perspective (and example) you want to discuss first; which one (and its example) you want to discuss second; and which perspective and example you want to conclude with.

Notice that **you do not need to talk about the perspectives in the order the prompt presents them**! Forget about that order. What you'll need to do is put them in the order that works best for your argument.

Using the example above, you'd start out with your thesis. Let's say that you're worried about time, so you've decided to put one of your perspectives first to make sure that you can elaborate on it enough. At this point, your notes might look something like this:

1. <u>Thesis</u>: Censorship should not be condoned because it allows small groups of individuals to possess an excessive level of control over fundamental human rights.

2. <u>P3 (power in hands of a few)</u>: One person or one small group who finds something offensive (and has money and influence) can easily cause it to be censored for everyone.
   - Parent groups that censor books at a school or object to TV show (Comedy Central example)

In this example, Perspective 3 is first, and this leads really nicely off of the thesis statement. Then, because your thesis is a combination of Perspectives 2 and 3 (and your Arab Spring example is also pretty strong), you decide to add the following to your outline:

1. <u>Thesis</u>: Censorship should not be condoned because it allows small groups of individuals to possess an excessive level of control over fundamental human rights.

2. <u>P3 (power in hands of a few)</u>: One person or one small group who finds something offensive (and has money and influence) can easily cause it to be censored for everyone.
   - Parent groups that censor books at a school or object to TV show (Comedy Central example)

3. <u>P2 (intrudes on freedoms)</u>: Total censorship of internet in Egypt during Arab Spring showed just how much power governments can have to suppress those who disagree. This infringes on basic human rights. A government is a small group of individuals not always representing the interests of all the people.

Notice that by using this structure, you've covered three important components of the essay in your first three paragraphs. You have a strong thesis statement, you've discussed two of the perspectives, and you've done so with two strong examples.

Now is a great time to discuss the remaining perspective, Perspective 1, about protecting children. Remember, in this example, you're arguing that this is not a valid perspective (though the opposite could certainly be argued, as well!). Keep adding to the outline:

1. <u>Thesis</u>: Censorship should not be condoned because it allows small groups of individuals to possess an excessive level of control over fundamental human rights.

2. <u>P3 (power in hands of a few)</u>: One person or one small group who finds something offensive (and has money and influence) can easily cause it to be censored for everyone.
   ○ Parent groups that censor books at a school or object to TV show (Comedy Central example)

3. <u>P2 (intrudes on freedoms)</u>: Total censorship of internet in Egypt during Arab Spring showed just how much power governments can have to suppress those who disagree. This infringes on basic human rights. A government is a small group of individuals not always representing the interests of all the people.

4. <u>P1 (shelter children)</u>: It's true that children should not be exposed to everything, but there are ways to regulate without outright censorship.
   ○ FCC indecency laws
   ○ Parental controls on remote
   ○ Dismiss argument > don't need censorship to protect children

In keeping with the thesis, you've argued that Perspectives 3 and 2 are both correct in some way. Now, you're rebutting Perspective 1, which says that we need censorship to shelter children. As outlined, this essay will state that it's true that children shouldn't be exposed to everything, but there are already ways in which content is regulated (using the examples of FCC indecency laws and parental controls on remotes).

This leaves you an awesome opportunity to segue into a conclusion. This doesn't have to be fancy; you can simply state that censorship is bad because it allows small groups of people to control information; it's more often used to control than to protect; and we don't need more protection, anyway.

What if you wanted to use a different structure for this essay, though? For example, you might want to discuss the perspective you agree with *least* (here, P1) before building up to the perspectives with which you agree more. The best structure for you will depend on how many perspectives you choose to engage with, as well as how quickly you write. You only *need* to engage with one other perspective, although we recommend that you engage with more if you have the time (more on this in a moment!). Not to worry! Here are a couple organizational models to help you out.

Structuring Your Essay

In this section, we'll look at three possible structures, which you can learn and apply to any topic you encounter on the official exam.

No matter *what* the topic is, keep in mind that the ideal length for an ACT essay is between four and six paragraphs. If it's fewer than four paragraphs, you most likely haven't explained your perspective in enough depth or used enough examples. If it's longer than six paragraphs, you probably haven't gone into enough depth with your examples, and you may be rambling off topic.

But don't worry! You want to be flexible on test day, but there are three different essay structures you can use and shape as you need to—and you can learn about them (and practice with them!) in advance.

The first two structures have some basic similarities. Your first paragraph should always be an introduction, even if it's brief. The next paragraphs evaluate the three perspectives, in whatever order naturally leads to your argument. Then, you should argue for your perspective—spend the most time and space on this section! If you have time left over, write a brief conclusion; if not, restate your thesis to conclude.

Let's take a look at the first two options, then discuss the benefits of each.

Option 1	Option 2
1 Introduction	**1** Introduction
2 First perspective (support or challenge)	**2** First perspective (support or challenge)
3 Second perspective (support or challenge)	**3** Second perspective (support or challenge)
4 Third perspective (support)	**4** Third perspective (challenge)
5 Your perspective	**5** Your perspective
6 Conclusion	**6** Conclusion

You may have noticed that these options are very similar. In fact, the biggest difference in these is in the third perspective: are you going to lead into your own perspective by challenging another perspective or supporting a similar perspective?

So when should you use Option 1? Use Option 1 when you have great examples that support the third perspective you're discussing. On the other hand, use Option 2 if your best examples are actually counterexamples (or challenges to the third perspective you're discussing). You could think of these as Option A (*actually* supporting the third perspective) and Option C (using *counterexamples* to *challenge* the third perspective), if it helps!

It's as simple as that!

Keep in mind that you can always combine the first two perspectives or the third perspective and your own perspective into the same paragraph if you're running short on time—don't feel as though you need to stick exactly to these structures!

But if the prospect of 5–6 paragraphs is overwhelming and you know you won't write that quickly on test day, don't despair! Option 3 is perfect for you:

Option 3
1 Introduction
2 One other perspective (support or challenge)
3 Your perspective
4 Conclusion

If you have trouble writing about all the perspectives within the given time limit, know that this is *not* a requirement! You can still get a strong score writing primarily about your own perspective, as long as you compare it with at least one other. (By the way, you can think of Option 3 as Option E (*evading* the third perspective), for the acronym ACE, to remember these options!)

Speaking of which …

How many perspectives do I have to write about?

If you're confused on this point, we don't blame you! Previous and recent versions of the ACT Writing Test required you to address all three perspectives to get a high score.

Is that still true? Take a look at the current version of the essay task:

> *Write a unified, coherent essay in which you evaluate multiple perspectives on censorship. In your essay, be sure to:*
>
> - *clearly state your own perspective on the issue and analyze the relationship between your perspective and at least one other perspective;*
> - *develop and support your ideas with reasoning and examples;*
> - *organize your ideas clearly and logically; and*
> - *communicate your ideas effectively in standard written English.*
>
> *Your perspective may be in full agreement with any of those given, in partial agreement, or completely different.*

Nowhere does this prompt say that you need to discuss more than two perspectives (your own and at least one other). If you struggle for time on the essay, this can be a big relief!

With that said, the highest-scoring essays (10+) are still those that engage with all three perspectives. The reasons for this are that it better fulfills the "multiple perspective" aspect of the prompt; it shows that you've thought critically about all perspectives presented; and, most importantly, it gives you more to write about!

Prewriting Notes

On the ACT, you'll have significant blank space in the test booklet to plan your essay. This is where you are going to be writing down all your thoughts: developing an outline, putting down your examples, doing some brainstorming, coming up with a thesis statement.

But remember that none of this is going to be graded. This is in your test booklet. It's not on the answer booklet where you'll write your essay, so make sure that you don't write things here that you want the graders to see.

You don't need to waste time making your planning pretty and perfect. No grader's going to see it. But it's really important that you use your space to plan your essay so that when you're writing your essay, it's not all just one big nonsensical blob (which would be really, really bad). Let's take a closer look at the writing portion of the essay task.

Writing

After brainstorming, evaluating perspectives, and coming up with your own thesis and examples, you'll still have around 20–25 minutes left to write your essay—plenty of time to get a great score. But if you're like a lot of students, you may still look at that blank paper and wonder: where do I start?

Elements of Your Essay

The introduction

One easy way to begin is to skip a line or two and just start with your thesis. You've already written that! If you have time later, you can come back and add in a bit more information. (This is a great place to use that introductory information from the prompt, by the way—just make sure to rephrase it in your own words!)

Starting to write your essay can be stressful, but remember that your introduction doesn't have to be fancy. In fact, it *shouldn't* be fancy: your time will be better spent elaborating your own position on the topic. Think short and sweet: two to three sentences will absolutely suffice—four if you're a fast writer. Don't waste time trying to remember the perfect quote: it'll stress you out, and it's not the best way to open your essay, anyway!

Spend three minutes *max* writing your introduction. We know that doesn't sound like a lot! However, if you go in with a plan, it's completely workable.

You don't have a plan, you say?

Sentence 1: Introduce the topic.
Sentence 2: Transition to your thesis.
Sentence 3: State your thesis.

That's all you need!

And remember: if you have writer's block, just write down your thesis (leaving some room for two earlier sentences so you can come back if there's time) and jump into your body paragraphs.

Body paragraphs

In the sandwich of your ACT essay, the body paragraphs are the meat (okay, we might be hungry right now—but the metaphor still stands). This is where you want to spend most of your time. Around four minutes per paragraph is a good average, with slightly more time spent on the paragraph about your perspective and slightly less on the others.

Just as with other elements of the ACT essay, you can absolutely prepare for the body paragraphs without knowing what your topic is. This is the general format for a great body paragraph:

1. [Transition: use in every paragraph except the first]
2. Statement of opinion on a given perspective
3. Example
4. Analysis
5. [Elaborate on your own perspective: use only in the paragraph about your perspective]

Breaking this down a little further, transitions are key to getting a high score on the ACT essay. They provide you with a chance to show off your critical thinking skills, your language skills, and your comparison skills. Just like with the introduction, though, it can be a little intimidating to write that first sentence of a new body paragraph.

The answer here is to come prepared! You'll have already thought about the relationship between and among the perspectives in your prewriting phase, so just make sure you have the language skills to properly phrase the transition.

There are only a few basic transitions. You can add to the previous thought ("Just as … so too …"), compare ("In a similar vein …"), or contrast ("While this may be true in some cases …"). There are so many transition words and phrases that we won't get into them all here: practice using as many as you can in context as you write sample essays!

After you've made a transition from the previous paragraph (for all but the first body paragraph, which doesn't need a transition from the introduction), state your opinion on the given perspective. You've already set this up in your prewriting, so just jot it down. The same goes for the example that follows: present the example, then provide a sentence or two in which you analyze it. If you're aiming for a top score, it's a good idea to set up your transition to the following paragraph in the final sentence (e.g., "… however, not everybody shares this opinion"), but it's not mandatory.

In most cases, you'll wrap up the body paragraph there. The only place where this isn't true is in the paragraph in which you explain your own perspective. There, you'll want to make sure that you present your examples thoroughly and analyze them carefully, with more elaboration than you used in the previous body paragraphs. This paragraph should end up being at least slightly longer than the others; aim to spend about a minute more writing it than each of the others.

Conclusion

It's nice to have a conclusion. It's not 100 percent necessary, but it is nice.

Don't get us wrong: you should, at the very least, restate your thesis in order to close out the essay and demonstrate to the graders that you know standard essay conventions. On the other hand, don't belabor your conclusion. Two to three sentences is the perfect length.

Running out of time?

You can omit the conclusion if you're running out of time for proofreading; just do a quick, one-sentence recap of your thesis and move on.

Writing Considerations

The content and organization of your essay are by far the most important elements of your score. However, language use is still something graders will look at. So how should you take this into consideration?

First of all, do *not* get caught up in editing as you go. A few spelling mistakes here and there will hurt your score far less (if they hurt it at all) than not finishing the paragraph about your own perspective.

Don't try to use enormous vocabulary words; if you can state your thought more simply, do it. It'll make things way easier on your graders, and happy graders mean better scores!

Finally, leave two to three minutes at the end for proofreading. Even if you don't end up getting the chance to use it (see the section on timing above for exceptions), intending to proofread at the end will keep your focus where it should be during the majority of your writing time: on writing the essay!

Sample Essays

Ready to take a look at some possible answers to the prompt we've been working through? You got it!

Remember that the ACT grades your essay on four domains. The scores you receive on each domain from two different graders are added together, and the overall score is created by averaging these combined domain scores together. Therefore, when you see an essay received a score of 5/5/4/5, this means it received a score of 5 on Ideas and Analysis, 5 on Development and Support, 4 on Organization, and 5 on Language Use from one grader. Assuming a second grader scored this essay with a score of 5/4/4/5, the overall score would be calculated as:

Ideas and Analysis: 5 + 5 = 10
Development and Support: 5 + 4 = 9
Organization: 4 + 4 = 8
Language Use: 5 + 5 = 10

The average (10 + 9 + 8 + 10) is 9.25, which would round to an **overall score of 9** out of a total possible 12.

You can find the ACT's complete scoring rubric on the ACT's official website.

Sample Student Essay #1

Although we live in an age with a drastic increase in access to information, this does not mean that we need to embrace censorship any more than we have in the past. Censorship should not be condoned because it allows small groups of individuals to possess an excessive level of control over fundamental human rights.

Historically, the right to control information, when given, has always found its way into the hands of a single individual or small group. These "influencers" may have money, influence, political power, or all three, and through these means, they can cause something they find offensive to be censored for everyone. One recent example of this is a series of shows on the TV channel Comedy Central. The channel has come under attack from religious groups, parent groups, and other interest groups who want the channel to remove certain content from the airwaves. But these are the voices of the few: what about the interest of the many?

Censorship intrudes on the rights of the public, particularly the freedom of speech. In many historical instances, governments have abused the power of censorship to suppress the ideas of their detractors. This occurred recently when officials in Egypt shut down the internet during the Arab Spring protests to prevent protesters from organizing and sharing news of the uprising on social media. In Saudi Arabia and Barain, bloggers were arrested and punished for speaking out against authorities. Examples such as these demonstrate that censorship is a tool that can, and will, be used by groups in power to prevent the public from learning about alternative viewpoints.

Despite the evidence that censorship is a power that can easily be abused, some individuals still maintain that it is necessary to protect children from obscene material. However, there can be measures in place to help safeguard children that do not require outright censorship. The FCC, for example, has indecency and profanity regulations that ensure that television shows containing objectionable material are only aired late at night. This protects the youth without preventing the general public from being able to see certain shows. Censorship is not necessary to safeguard the public; we can achieve this without resorting to extremes.

The fundamental problem with censorship comes down to this: who decides what the public should see? If censorship is condoned, it will always end up in the hands of the few to decide what the many are exposed to, which is unnecessary when there are ways to regulate information without resorting to outright censorship.

Sample student essay #1 score: 6/6/6/6

Ideas and Analysis (6): The writer presents an argument that critically engages with multiple perspectives on the issue, with analysis that clearly and consistently examines underlying complexities and assumptions. For example, the author picks apart the idea that censorship is the only way to safeguard against children accessing inappropriate information. The essay also presents insightful and compelling analysis on the role of censorship during the Arab Spring protests.

Throughout the essay, the writer develops support for the rhetorical question posed in the concluding paragraph ("who decides what the public should see?"), leading the essay to a satisfactory conclusion.

Development and Support (6): There's great critical analysis of the issues that deepen insight and broaden context. The idea of "influencers" who have too much power is woven through several distinct examples: television programming and political conflict. This idea is also explored in the third body paragraph, which presents a counterargument to Perspective 1.

Organization (6): This essay has strong organization, and there is a logical progression of ideas. The transitions within paragraphs are superb, and there are clarifying introductory and concluding sentences to each body paragraph. The writer addresses all three perspectives in the prompt and does so in a way that is not disjointed but productively integrated into a strategic essay that develops the writer's point of view.

Language Use (6): The use of language in this essay is clear. Word choice is skillful and precise and there are strategic stylistic choices, evident in phrases such as "familiar with its abuses" and "history has shown that it is far more often used to control the public than to protect it." There are very few errors, such as the misspelling of "Bahrain," but these are easily forgiven in a timed essay and do not impede meaning.

Sample Student Essay #2

Should we censor content to keep children from being exposed to offensive material and to protect the public interest? Or is it better to have unlimited freedom of press and freedom of speech? Who should decide what the public sees or doesn't see? Generally, it is better to respect freedom of press and freedom of speech, with only a few exceptions for public safety, so that individuals can make better decisions for themselves.

There are numerous cases in which parental groups have banned classic works of great literature from public schools. For example, *The Adventures of Huckleberry Finn* has been banned from both schools and libraries for its inclusion of offensive language and depiction of slavery. However, letting students read such an important work of literature, which some have argued actually critiques slavery, is more important than any possible offense it might give. Another example of a more recent book that some groups tried to ban is *Harry Potter*, a book that these groups believed promoted black magic. My English class, however, was able to have a productive debate on this book that opened our eyes to all sides of the issues. If we respect individuals' rights to have access to any type of literature, then they will be better equipped to make their own judgments and decisions.

It is true that society should take some steps to protect people from exposure to potentially harmful information. However, there are many ways for do this outside of the complete government censorship, including parental controls on the TV and Internet, and ratings of R and NC-17 for movies. Just as we limit children's rights for the public good, so too should we place conditional and judicious limits on other content. The freedom of the press is limited when it comes to exposing military maneuvers, just as freedom of speech is limited in cases where it affects the public good (such as the lack of the right to shout "fire!" in a crowded movie theater when there is no fire).

Censorship intrudes too much on the freedom of speech and freedom of the press and would place too much power in a hands of the few. It's best to respect access to information, with only a few exceptions for the public good.

Sample student essay #2 score: 5/5/4/5

Ideas and Analysis (5): The intro is adequate, although it would be stronger if it didn't simply rephrase the perspectives as rhetorical questions. That said, the thesis is clearly expressed at the end of the introduction, though itself is not very nuanced.

That said, the essay gets stronger in its body paragraphs. The writer produces an argument that productively engages with multiple perspectives on the issue and has precision in thought and purpose. The first body paragraph offers some support for providing access to information, although the analysis could be stronger. The writer notes that if "we respected individuals' rights to have access to any type of literature, then they will be better equipped to make their own judgments and decisions." However, he or she does not provide examples of this better decision-making, beyond a general reference to the student's debate in English class. The second body paragraph has some good support for the existing limitations on free speech that protect citizens from truly dangerous situations.

Development and Support (5): The development of ideas and claims in this essay, for the most part, deepens understanding and emphasizes the significance of the situation. Rather than viewing the issue as black and white, the author takes a stance that mostly agrees with Perspective 2 but acknowledges that some limitations on total freedom are necessary. This creates a more nuanced argument. There are several examples, from banned books to parental controls and movie ratings, that clearly support the claims.

Organization (4): Overall, the essay has a productive organizational strategy with a first body paragraph that lays out the primary argument and a second body paragraph that furthers it but qualifies it as well. However, the essay score here could be improved by more consistent and clear use of transitions between thoughts.

Language Use (5): The use of language largely supports the argument. There is variety in sentence structure and word choice, and minor errors do not impede meaning. Some sentences, such as "If we respect individuals' rights to have access to any type of literature, then they will be better equipped to make their own judgments and decisions," clearly and almost powerfully reinforce the argument of the essay.

Sample Student Essay #3

Censorship is present in all of our lives, whether we like it or not. Censorship has kept children from seeing material that is too mature for them, and it can also help governments keep their countries safe. Censorship is a helpful tool when used properly.

Censorship is important to protecting children. Not everybody has responsible parents who can be trusted to decide what is best for their children, or parents who can monitor their activity at any time of day. For example, a parent might not pay attention to what a young child watches on TV, and their child might end up watching a horror movie that gives her nightmares or overtly violent shows, and not know how to interpret the morality of these shows. We can't expect all parents to oversee what their children watch all the time, so in this sense, censorship can help us protect children.

In government, censorship has kept information from the public. It keeps newspapers from revealing where battles are taking place until they are over, or where spies are positioned. This protects government operations. For example, during World War II, the US had an official office of censorship to make sure that military secrets were not revealed in the press. Even the Supreme Court found that this type of censorship did not violate the Constitution.

The pros and cons, however, of censorship are complicated by the fact that we can't always control who the censors are. What if a censor wanted to eliminate every TV show containing ducks? This is a ridiculous example, but it shows that personal taste and interests will always affect the material that is censored. There is no such thing as a perfect censor, and that dilemma is also something important to consider.

In conclusion, censorship touches many aspects of our lives in the world today. We all need to think about the ways in which it comes into play in our own lives. But overall, it's a helpful tool when used properly because it can protect both children and nations from threats.

Sample student essay #3 score: 4/4/3/4

Ideas and Analysis (4): This essay engages with multiple perspectives on the issue, and there's clarity in thought and purpose with some recognition of underlying implications and complexities, such as acknowledging that "there is no such thing as a perfect censor."

This essay could be improved if the author emphasized more of his or her own reasoning. For example, the intro paragraph largely repeats ideas from the introductory material of the essay prompt, and the conclusion paragraph weakens the overall persuasive strength of the essay by making vague statements such as "censorship touches many aspects of our lives" and "we all need to think about the way in which it comes into play."

Development and Support (4): The development of support in this essay has clear meaning and purpose and qualifications extend the ideas and analysis. There are two reasonable examples provided: children watching inappropriate shows and censorship during wartime. The example about wartime censorship is made more compelling because it draws on external evidence from the U.S. Supreme Court to support its case.

The third body paragraph adds nuance and complexity by noting that censorship can be subjective; however, it is not clearly tied into the overall argument.

Organization (3): There is a basic organizational structure here, with ideas logically grouped, although it lacks clear transitions.

Improved organization likely would have improved this essay's score on other domains as well. The third body paragraph, which begins "the pros and cons of censorship" is particularly problematic because the reader is not sure what to do with this information. Is it weakening the writer's argument? Or is it a concession to the other side, but one that does not overturn the author's overall argument?

Language Use (4): Overall, the use of language is clear, with adequate word choice that is sometimes precise (for example, "personal tastes and interests"). While there are a few errors in grammar, usage, and mechanics, they rarely impede meaning.

Sample Student Essay #4

When we think about censorship, we often think about where it goes wrong. But there are places where censorship can work, too. It's important to consider the morales of our children when we think about censorship; when we do, you have to agree that censorship is necessary.

Children who grow up watching movies and television shows with adult content have been found to have more violent tendencies as adults. This is equally true for those who listen to music with violent lyrics, play violent video games, and read violent books. As a congressman said, "We have to keep this material out of the hands of our most vulnerable citizens."

Also, keeping national secrets is also important. How can we expect children to know what information they should or shouldn't tell other people if we disclose everything about our national agenda on television, where anyone could see it? During wartime, this could prove to be dangerous if people started talking with someone who turned out to work for the enemy.

So censorship is really a good thing. At the end of the day, it truly does protect our most risky citizens and the rest of us, too.

Sample student essay #4 score: 3/3/3/3

Ideas and Analysis (3): The writer here has a thesis that is consistent throughout the essay: censorship protects people. But the argument only provides limited context for this argument. It clearly addresses Perspective 1 about censorship protecting children, but only loosely addresses Perspective 2. This essay could be made stronger if it responded with counterarguments to some of the perspectives it takes issue with.

Development and Support (3): The development of ideas in this essay are mostly relevant, but they are overly general and imprecise. For example, the student categorically states that children who watch violent programming grow up to be more violent but does not offer any support for this. He or she quotes a "congressman" but does not state who. It makes the grader wonder if the student was trying to invent a quote because he or she thought it would help support the argument.

The use of "children" in the second body paragraph about national secrets is also confusing; it's unclear why this example would apply only to children.

Organization (3): This essay has a basic organizational structure and ideas are logically grouped together with topic sentences introducing each body paragraph. However, transitions between ideas are rudimentary ("Also" and "So"), and the body paragraphs lack conclusions.

Language Use (3): Overall, the use of language does not impede understanding, but word choice is general and occasionally imprecise (for example, "risky" citizens, when the author meant "at-risk").

President Johnson chose to keep certain aspects of the unpopular Vietnam War secret, partly because releasing these details would have fanned the fires of anti-war protests. Daniel Ellsberg later leaked the information to the *New York Times*, making all these secrets known to the American public in what are now known as the "Pentagon Papers."

Sample Student Essay #5

Some people say that we should censor. Other people do not think that censorship should be allowed. There are points both for and against censorship so let's look at a few of these.

Should we allow censorship? well, some people say yes. Censorship can help children. It can keep them from seeing things that they should not. If we don't protect children, who will? Children should not be allowed to see movies or read books like 50 Shades of Grey that are just too old for them it can corupt them and have a bad influence. Or what about slavery?

Some people say that it gives the goverment too much power. We can see that this has happened throughout history so maybe this is true. For example, if people arguing against slavery had been censored, it might never have gone away. We certainly don't want it today. Can you imagine our lives if that had hapened.

There are many different ideas about censorship, everyone should decide for themselves what they believe.

Sample student essay #5 score: 2/2/2/2

Ideas and Analysis (2): This essay lacks a clear thesis. It doesn't take a particular viewpoint on the issue. Instead, the writer presents some evidence for various perspectives, without clarifying which side he or she would support. The ACT graders would view this essay as having "little clarity in thought and purpose." In order to get a higher score, it's crucial to argue for a particular opinion on the issue!

Development and Support (2): The development here is very weak. It does reference Perspective 1 and Perspective 3 and introduces a couple of examples to support them, *50 Shades of Grey* and slavery, but the essay doesn't develop them with much detail. It asks some vague questions, such as "Can you imagine our lives if that had hapened [sic]," but doesn't explain what would have happened and why it would have been bad. The example of slavery is also a weak one because it oversimplifies a complicated historical situation that censorship, or the lack thereof, was not solely responsible for.

Organization (2): There is a rudimentary structure here with an introduction, two body paragraphs, and a conclusion. However, transitions are weak between paragraphs. Some of the ideas are poorly grouped together, such as the introduction of slavery in the second paragraph, before any context is provided.

Language Use and Conventions (2): There are quite a few errors in sentence structure in this essay, including run-on sentences and comma splices, as well as numerous punctuation mistakes. The word choice is often imprecise and unclear, and it's difficult to identify any purposeful stylistic choices. Vague pronouns such as "it" in the first sentence of the second body paragraph make the reader work harder in order to follow the student's meaning.

Tips for Top Scorers

You may be thinking to yourself, "Yeah, yeah, I get it, but I want a 10 (or an 11, or, heck, even a 12 on the ACT Writing Test)!" Well, if that sounds like you, you'll want to check out the tips below for ADVANCED students who want to achieve the highest score possible on the ACT essay.

Here are our top tips for an essay that's going to knock the socks off the graders. In order to do this, you need to remember that your graders are human beings. They are reading lots and lots of essays. And a lot of them start to sound alike. Now, the graders are pretty fair, so if you're shooting for a good score on the essay, all you really need to do is to write a clear, argumentative thesis, address all three of the perspectives, include good examples, and have a coherent structure.

But if you want a *great* score, you need to stand out from the crowd.

Here's how you can do it:

1. **Use less obvious examples.** On the first new essay on the September 2015 ACT, a whole lot of students wrote about the civil rights movement. It was an obvious example that a lot of students had studied, and it was certainly the first thing that jumped out at us as well. Now, technically, graders are not supposed to be punishing you for an unoriginal example as long as you do it well. But remember the golden rule: they're only human! If a grader reads 50 essays in a row about the civil rights movement, and then they get to yours and you're writing about the same thing, it's possible that others will have done a better job. So try not to open yourself to these comparisons. Be original!

   If your essay is different, the graders are going to sit up and pay attention. Not only that, but it will be difficult for them to compare your essay to others. If you write about the same topic as everyone else, it is likely that some people won't do it as well as you; it's equally likely that some people will do it better. That doesn't mean that you can't write about a common topic, but if you are going to do it, make sure you pick very specific examples within that topic to demonstrate your knowledge. But if you can think of something that would be less obvious—well, we would go that route.

2. **Choose the option to provide your own perspective on the ACT essay, but only switch it up slightly.** Now, this is tricky. You can get a perfect score simply by agreeing with one of the three presented perspectives. **For the vast majority of students, this is the best course of action** to make sure you don't go completely offtrack and end up hurting your score. However, if you consider yourself to be a very strong writer (and other people seem to think this of you as well), you might be able to truly impress by adding your own twist on the prompt. In most cases, the easiest way to do this is to narrow the scope of one of the perspectives.

   For example, if you look at the feedback for Sample Essay 5 on the "Intelligent Machines" prompt on the ACT website, you'll see that the graders applauded the student for evaluating the perspectives through the "lens of a particular ideology": capitalism. The prompt is about a larger issue—the positive or negative impact of "intelligent machines" in our society—but this student narrowed the scope and, in doing so, was able to provide a specific compelling argument that didn't try to address all of life in a five-paragraph essay.

3. **Spend time working on your language use** *before* **test day.**
   The highest-scoring essays on the ACT are those written by students who have some facility with language already. But if you don't get straight As in English, don't despair—just know that you'll need to think about how you use language (and how you can use it better) before test day.

   You know all the studying you're doing for the ACT English Test? Carry it on over to your practice essays. After time's up, go back and correct the grammar and style of what you've written according to the principles of grammar and usage you've just studied. Do this for every practice essay, and you'll soon know exactly what patterns of error you tend to fall into.

   And you know the studying you're doing for the ACT Reading Test? Carry that on over, too. Study vocabulary you don't know when you encounter it in practice passages. Incorporate those words into your essays, asking a teacher or trusted friend to review your usage. Read good literature out loud, listening to its rhythms. Notice that it usually uses varied sentence structures; not all sentences will simply begin "subject-verb."

   Progress may be hard to spot, but incremental improvements to your writing will pay off big—and not just on test day!

   So, for you ACT Writing Test superstars who are looking for a score in the 10–12 range, take these key tips to heart and start practicing with ACT Writing Test prompts. The ACT essay prompt is tough, but practicing with sample prompts and coming up with arguments on the fly will help you improve!

Practice

Now that you've seen some sample responses to the "Censorship" prompt (as well as detailed information about how you could approach the same prompt), let's take it a step farther: here is one more ACT essay prompt for you to practice with. We've provided worksheets for this prompt. You won't see these on test day, but if you use them now to practice an effective essay planning process, you won't need them by test day!

Ready? Let's take a look at the prompt . . .

Open Content

"Open content" works are creative works that can be freely used, copied, or modified by others, typically on the internet. One popular example of an open content website is Wikipedia, an online encyclopedia that is written collaboratively by the people who use it. Anyone can add content to the website, and it can be edited by others. Open content resources have been growing in popularity in other contexts as well: individuals can take courses taught by their peers at free online "universities" or download photographs and artwork for free on open content websites. But because there is little oversight of open content resources, many argue that these sources lack the quality of more authoritative resources and can easily spread incorrect information. Nevertheless, for many students, teachers, and members of the general public, open content materials have become go-to sources for obtaining knowledge. But should they?

Read and carefully consider these perspectives. Each suggests a particular way of thinking about the impact of open content resources.

Perspective 1	Perspective 2	Perspective 3
Open content devalues knowledge. It allows individuals who are not experts on a topic to spread inaccurate or biased information on the internet. Because it is not overseen by careful editing or established publishers or educational institutions, there is no way to ensure its quality.	Open content encourages a democratic approach to sharing information. It removes barriers to publishing and creates opportunities for all individuals to share their ideas with others.	Because open content is almost exclusively delivered via the internet, it puts at a disadvantage individuals who do not have access to the internet. Open content does not necessarily mean "free" if individuals have to pay for internet service or computer equipment to access it.

Essay Task

Write a unified, coherent essay in which you evaluate multiple perspectives on open content resources. In your essay, be sure to:

- *clearly state your own perspective on the issue and analyze the relationship between your perspective and at least one other perspective;*
- *develop and support your ideas with reasoning and examples;*
- *organize your ideas clearly and logically; and*
- *communicate your ideas effectively in standard written English.*

Your perspective may be in full agreement with any of those given, in partial agreement, or completely different.

Perspective	Support (For)	Challenge (Against)
1		

Perspective	Support (For)	Challenge (Against)
2		
3		

Thesis statement

_____

_____

_____

_____

_____

_____

_____

_____

_____

Outline

1. **Thesis:**

   _____

   _____

   _____

   _____

   _____

2. **Perspective (   ):**

   _____

   _____

   _____

   _____

   _____

   ⇦ *Add example(s) for each!*

3. **Perspective (   ):**   (Optional)

   _____

   _____

   _____

   _____

4. **Perspective (   ):**   (Optional)

   _____

   _____

   _____

   _____

   _____

5. **Your Perspective (   ):**

   _____

   _____

   _____

   _____

   ⇨ **Conclusion:**

   _____

   _____

   _____

   _____

   _____

   _____

   _____

Draft

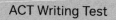

Grading Your ACT Essay

So you've done it! You've finished a practice ACT essay. Congratulations!

What now?

First, take a look at the ACT's official scoring rubric for the Writing Test (www.act.org/content/dam/act/unsecured/documents/Writing-Test-Scoring-Rubric.pdf). Notice that you'll be graded in four domains:

1. **Ideas and Analysis**
2. **Development and Support**
3. **Organization**
4. **Language Use**

It can be hard to evaluate our own writing, so you may want to let the essay sit for a few days and then come back to it with fresh eyes.

In each of the four categories, assign yourself to one of the following "scorepoints":

- **Score 6:** Responses at this scorepoint demonstrate effective skill in writing an argumentative essay.
- **Score 5:** Responses at this scorepoint demonstrate well-developed skill in writing an argumentative essay.
- **Score 4:** Responses at this scorepoint demonstrate adequate skill in writing an argumentative essay.
- **Score 3:** Responses at this scorepoint demonstrate some developing skill in writing an argumentative essay.
- **Score 2:** Responses at this scorepoint demonstrate weak or inconsistent skill in writing an argumentative essay.
- **Score 1:** Responses at this scorepoint demonstrate little or no skill in writing an argumentative essay.

Ideas and Analysis: _____
Development and Support: _____
Organization: _____
Language Use: _____

Next, because you'll have two graders on your actual essay, find a trusted friend, a parent, or a teacher, and ask them if they would grade your essay. Give them the rubric to help them accurately score your essay (and a reciprocal favor, like grading your friend's essays, probably wouldn't go unappreciated, either). Either they or you can average the scores at the end, though it will be helpful for you to know how they scored you in each of the four categories.

Ideas and Analysis: _____
Development and Support: _____
Organization: _____
Language Use: _____

Add your second grader's score to the score you gave yourself on each domain, add them together, then divide by four.

Ideas and Analysis: _____

Development and Support: _____

Organization: _____

Language Use: _____

Added Total: _____

Divided by 4: _____ ⇦ Your overall ACT Writing score

We don't blame you if you've read all that and are thinking, *Hey! You said the math section was over!* You can also check out the Magoosh ACT Essay Grader quiz to give you your scores (magoosh.com/hs/act/about-the-act/2016/what-is-a-good-act-writing-score).

Time for a break? Give these healthy and productive study break options a try!

Short Study Break (10–15 minutes)

You know that feeling when you've been studying for a while and you realize that the last several sentences you read didn't even register in your brain? Despite our best efforts, we humans can only focus for so long before we start to feel drained.

The solution? Take short 10–15-minute breaks every hour or so during your prep. You'll return to your studies feeling energized and ready to soak up even more knowledge. Just be careful to avoid breaking for too long, as that can be counterproductive and make coming back to studying even harder!

Here's what to do (and what not to do!) during these quick study breaks:

1. **Instead of sitting still, get moving!** Studying requires a lot of sitting in the same position, so wake yourself up by doing the opposite. Getting your body up out of your chair will make you feel re-energized, and the endorphins will help melt away your stress. Not sure what to do after you stand up? Try

   ○ *Stretching:* There are a lot of quick yoga videos online that require nothing more than comfy clothes and a little bit of space. Since people tend to hunch over while studying, consider finding a video that focuses on opening up your neck and shoulders.

   ○ *Cardio:* Jog around the block, alternate one minute of jumping jacks with one minute of burpees, dance to your favorite song—whatever floats your boat and gets your heart pumping!

2. **Instead of napping, breathe!** You might be feeling the urge to lay your head on your desk and fall asleep. But, as tired as you may feel, sleeping now will only make you groggier and less motivated. Don't give in just yet! Instead, try

   ○ *Relaxing breathing techniques:* Close your eyes and try breathing in through your nose for a count of four, then out through your nose for a count of four. This will signal to your brain that you are safe and help you relax. (Side note: This also works *during* the ACT!)

   ○ *Meditation:* Find a guided meditation video online, or just sit in a comfortable position with your eyes closed as you acknowledge (but don't engage with) your thoughts as they move through your mind.

3. **Instead of feeding your cravings, fuel your body!** Feeling hungry? As tempting as it is to reach for fatty, sugary processed foods right now, your body (and brain!) will appreciate some healthier options. Try fueling yourself right with whole foods like fruits and nuts. Not feeling those? Try some string cheese or hummus. Chances are you're probably in need of a good old-fashioned glass of water, too. It never hurts.

4. **Instead of checking social media, organize your workspace!** Social media has a way of breaking you out of the zone in a manner that is more distracting than productive. The updates on your phone aren't going anywhere, so if you're looking for a mindless activity to keep yourself occupied, try organizing your space instead. Make sure that your desk is tidy and uncluttered. Move distracting objects out of reach (and out of sight!). Sharpen your pencil, remember to write the date on your notes, or put away the pile of clothes on the floor. You'll be happy you did!

5. **Instead of dreading your remaining prep, plan your reward!** Staying motivated can be challenging, especially when you're in the middle of a long study session. Rather than thinking of all the work on your plate, think of what you'll do to celebrate when you're done with today's study session. You might try to

   - Catch up on all the social media notifications you've been ignoring.
   - Spend some time with your friends or family.
   - Watch your current favorite show.
   - Listen to music or a podcast.
   - Cook a nice meal or bake something delicious.
   - Read a book that has nothing to do with school.
   - SLEEP.

Chapter 10

Full-Length ACT Practice Test

How to Take an ACT Practice Test

If you're going to devote over three hours of your free time to taking an ACT practice test (and you 100 percent, absolutely, positively should!), then you're going to want to do it in the most efficient and effective way possible.

But if you're just beginning your prep, or you've already fallen into bad study habits, how do you learn the best way to take a practice test? With the help of this book, of course! Read on for all you need to know about taking an ACT practice test.

Which Practice Test Should You Take?

The first practice test you take should be as similar to a real, official ACT test as possible. The one in this book is a great place to start, as are any of the tests you'll find in *The Official ACT Prep Guide* (that's the book published by the makers of the ACT exam).

Why these practice tests?

Well, official practice tests from the test-maker are actually retired versions of the exam that real students took once upon a time. You don't get much closer to the real thing than that! *The Official ACT Prep Guide* offers three tests with answers and explanations, as well as a fair amount of other helpful prep materials.

The Magoosh ACT practice test was carefully crafted by our Magoosh experts to mirror a bona fide ACT, but it also has the added bonus of thoughtful answers and explanations—most of which are also available in video format on our website! These materials will be really important during the review stage of your practice test experience, which we'll talk more about later in this chapter.

How Many Practice Tests Should You Take?

Based on what you just read, it might sound like we're suggesting that you take a mountain of practice tests! Don't worry—that's not the case. The resources we list in this book are here to give you options and to help those of you who are starting your prep super early.

Okay, so … how many practice tests should you take? The honest answer is that it depends on how long you're studying; one a week is ideal. In fact, if you follow our One-Month ACT Study Schedule (chapter 4), you'll see that we recommend you take a full-length practice test each Saturday that you're following the guide.

If you're really gung ho about this whole practice test thing, you may wonder why we suggest only one a week. Just wait … you'll understand when we talk about the ways in which you're going to review your tests.

Where Should You Take Your Practice Test?

Let's start with some times and places where you should *not* take your practice test:

- While babysitting (unless the kids are asleep and you have three uninterrupted hours … but probably not even then)
- In a shared bedroom, or anywhere at home where you might be interrupted
- Any place where you won't have a chance to finish the exam in one sitting (on the go, in the doctor's office, in calculus class … even in study hall!)
- Loud places

That should give you a good idea of where you *should* take your ACT practice tests: in a quiet area, where you can be alone and uninterrupted for at least three hours.

Public libraries are good (if you get there at least three hours before closing!), as are university libraries. You may find your school library too distracting if lots of your classmates are around. And your school library may not even be open if you take our suggestions for …

When Should You Take Your ACT Practice Test?

When to take your test will depend, to some extent, on how far in advance you start preparing, but we suggest taking your full-length practice exam on a Saturday morning.

Why? Because all the official ACT exams are given on Saturday mornings.

Performing well that early on a weekend can be difficult, especially if you're used to doing something else at that time (like sleeping). Practicing at this time will help you build up stamina for the marathon that is the ACT. Sunday mornings also work, but we'd suggest leaving Sundays for test review. Not only will you need a fair amount of time to review your work, but completing a three-hour test after a day of rest and relaxation (or sports, work, and other non-school activities) is very different from completing it after a full week at school. (We get that you might be taking the test during a vacation, in which case Saturday practice is *slightly* less important—but most of you will be taking it during the school year!)

How to Take a Practice Test

The most important aspects of your practice test environment are the two we've already looked at: silence and continuity. But there's a lot more you can do to emulate test day conditions:

- Don't allow yourself to eat, drink, or leave the practice test for any reason, except for 10 minutes between the math and reading tests and five minutes before the Writing Test (if you are planning to take the essay). It's tough! But getting used to the conditions now will help you succeed later.
- Don't let yourself skip ahead to the next section if you finish before the time is up. Pretend it's test day, and make the most of the remaining time by double-checking your work.
- Don't let yourself go back to a previous section at any point during the exam!
- Do use an authorized calculator, No. 2 pencils, and bubble sheets for your answers.

When you've finished with the exam, reflect on your personal responses to the testing conditions. Did you wish you'd had some water during the first break? Were your legs cramping and begging for a stretch that you should have done before the exam started? Once you've completed a few practice tests, you can compile these reactions into your test-day survival guide—just another benefit of practicing under exam-like conditions.

Scoring Your ACT Practice Test

If you're like most students, you'll have one of two responses to scoring your exam:

1. You want your results as soon as possible.
2. You want to forget you ever took the test and go take a nap.

You may even be feeling both simultaneously. That's cool.

But, feelings aside, you should grade your test the day you take it (if not the second you finish it!) or the following day. The best time to review your results is when you have the questions still fresh in your mind. And they don't get any fresher than right after the test!

How do you score your practice test? Use our handy guide ...

ACT Practice Test Grading Guide

Remember back in chapter 2 when we discussed the ins and outs of ACT scoring? If you skipped that section, now's probably a good time to flip back for a refresher. Either way, let's begin with some important ACT scoring vocabulary review:

- **Raw Score:** The number of questions you answered correctly in the section.
  - *Example:* If you answer 55 questions correctly on the ACT English Test, then your raw score for ACT English is 55. Pretty straightforward so far.
- **Scaled Score:** The score that you get on each section of the ACT after your raw score is scaled. Your scaled score ranges from 1–36, with 36 being the highest possible score on a section.
  - *Example:* If you answer 55 questions correctly on the ACT English Test, then your scaled score for ACT English is 23.
- **Composite Score:** The average of your four scaled scores (English, Math, Reading, and Science). Think of this as your total ACT score, or the score you'll tell your parents when they ask, "How'd you do on the ACT?" The highest possible composite score is 36.

Now, if you'd like to grade your practice test by hand, here's what you'll need to do:

1. Find your raw scores by counting the number of questions you answered correctly on each test.
2. Convert your raw scores to scaled scores using the Raw ACT Scores and Scaled ACT Scores chart on page 21 of chapter 2.
3. Calculate your composite score by averaging your four scaled scores using the following formula:

$$\frac{English + Math + Reading + Science}{4} = ACT \text{ Composite Score}$$

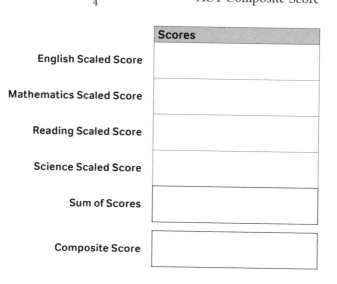

	Scores
English Scaled Score	
Mathematics Scaled Score	
Reading Scaled Score	
Science Scaled Score	
Sum of Scores	
Composite Score	

Scoring Your Writing Test (Essay)

Now that you have your multiple-choice ACT scores in hand, what are you going to do about that essay?

First, jump back to page 15 of chapter 2, where we talked about scoring the ACT Writing Test.

Next, let's talk about the ACT's official scoring rubric for the Writing Test.

The ACT will grade your essay in four categories:

1. Ideas and Analysis
2. Development and Support
3. Organization
4. Language Use

It can be difficult to evaluate your own writing, so you may want to let your practice essay sit for a few days and then come back to it with fresh eyes. This is the one exception to the "grade it soon" rule!

In each of the four categories, assign yourself to one of the following "scorepoints":

- **Score 6:** Responses at this scorepoint demonstrate effective skill in writing an argumentative essay.
- **Score 5:** Responses at this scorepoint demonstrate well-developed skill in writing an argumentative essay.
- **Score 4:** Responses at this scorepoint demonstrate adequate skill in writing an argumentative essay.
- **Score 3:** Responses at this scorepoint demonstrate some developing skill in writing an argumentative essay.
- **Score 2:** Responses at this scorepoint demonstrate weak or inconsistent skill in writing an argumentative essay.
- **Score 1:** responses at this scorepoint demonstrate little or no skill in writing an argumentative essay.

Average your four category scorepoints; that's the equivalent of one grader's writing score.

Remember that your actual ACT essay will be graded by two graders. So, to mimic the two-grader scenario, find a trusted friend, a parent, or a teacher, and ask them if they would grade your essay. Give them the rubric to help them accurately score your essay (and be sure to pay it forward!). Either you or your grader can average the scores at the end, though it will be helpful for you to know how they scored you in each of the four categories.

Add your second grader's average score to the average score you gave yourself, then divide by two. That's your practice Writing Test score.

Reviewing Your Practice Test Results

Now you have your practice ACT scores! Most students stop here, but don't celebrate just yet. Going over your practice test in detail will provide you with a treasure trove of information you can't get from practice sets and problems alone. So, where do you go from here?

The next step is to go back to the test itself with your (scored) answer sheet, any notes you took during the test, and a blank notebook. You'll need to find your wrong answers and start your "error log."

Making an Error Log

What's an error log? It's a list or table of notes containing the following:

- The practice test questions you answered incorrectly
- The correct answers to those questions
- An explanation of how you can get those questions right in the future (and good explanations on practice tests are essential!)

Be sure to date your entries and note which practice test you were reviewing, or you may get confused later when trying to measure your progress.

Once you've finished recording your missed questions and their solutions, do some analysis in the margins. Which question types did you miss more than others? Where did you get your best score? Your worst score?

As you take more practice tests, look back over your error log and review your notes from past exams. On which question types were you hoping to improve? Did you reach your goals? If not, what kinds of mistakes are you still making? Are they content mistakes, math errors, or just errors bubbling in the correct answer? Take note of this information as well.

After you've reviewed your wrong answers, go ahead and review the questions you answered correctly. (This is where a lot of people balk, but trust us on this one!) You don't need to make a "correct answer log," but do evaluate *how* you got the right answer. Were you guessing? Did you get the right answer by accident? Was this a concept you recently mastered?

All of this analysis is important for the next step, which involves making a game plan for next time and continuing to improve your practice test scores.

Final ACT Practice Test Tips: Where to Go from Here?

No matter how much time you have left before your official exam, use a study schedule that works in your time frame.

When you look at the Magoosh study schedules in chapter 4 (page 35) you'll notice that, while there are certain standard assignments, a lot of what we recommend doing is based entirely on where you are in your prep—the types of math problems that are giving you the most trouble, the English concepts you still need to perfect, and so on. That's where your error log comes in handy!

It'll continue to come in handy in the weeks and (maybe) months to come. Keep filling it out, keep practicing, and keep evaluating. That's how you'll get your big score increase.

Finally, no matter how your practice test went, please take a moment to congratulate yourself, take a deep breath, and do something fun. You've taken a hugely important step in the college application process just by spending these three-plus hours practicing. Be proud!

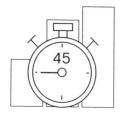

ACT Practice Test Questions

ACT English Test

45 Minutes | 75 Questions

In the following five passages, you'll find portions that have been underlined and numbered. The questions in the right-hand column will present alternatives for the underlined words and phrases. Some questions will ask you to select the answer choice that best expresses the idea, makes the statement appropriate for standard written English, or makes the wording more consistent with the passage's style and tone. If you think the original wording of the statement is the best option, select "NO CHANGE." In other cases, you'll be asked a question about the underlined text. You will need to choose the best answer to the question.

In addition, you will be asked questions about a portion of the passage or about the entire passage. In these cases, the questions do not refer to an underlined section of the passage. Instead, they are identified by a number in a box. Choose the answer that you consider best and mark that on your answer sheet. ACT recommends reading each passage through one time before answering any questions. Many of the questions will require you to read a few sentences ahead to find the answer. Make sure that you read far enough ahead before answering each question.

PASSAGE I

The Lancashire Witches

About 400 years ago, in 1612, Northwest England was the scene of England's largest peacetime <u>witch trial:</u> the trial of the Lancashire witches. Twenty people, mostly from the Pendle area of Lancashire, <u>were imprisoned</u> in the castle as witches. In the end, 10 were hanged, one died in jail, one was sentenced to the stockades, and eight were acquitted. [A] How did this witch trial come about, and what accounts for its <u>static</u> fame?

1 A. NO CHANGE
   B. witch trial and
   C. witch trial
   D. witch trial;

2 F. NO CHANGE
   G. had been imprisoned
   H. have been imprisoned
   J. were being imprisoned

3 A. NO CHANGE
   B. robust
   C. enduring
   D. vigorous

We know so much about the Lancashire witches because the trial was recorded in unique detail by the clerk of the court Thomas Potts who published his account soon afterwards. Robert Poole recently published a modern-English edition of their book, together with an essay piecing together what we know of the events of 1612. [B] It reveals how Potts carefully edited the evidence, and also how the case against the "witches" were constructed and manipulated to bring about a spectacular show trial.

It all began in mid-March when a peddler from Halifax named John Law had a frightening encounter with a poor young woman, Alizon Device in a field, near the town of Colne. He refused her request for pins, and there was a brief argument during which he was seized by a fit that left him with "his head drawn awry, his eyes and face deformed, his speech not well to be understood, his thighs and legs stark lame." We can now recognize this as a stroke, perhaps triggered by the stressful encounter. [C] Alizon Device was sent for and surprised all by confessing to the bewitching of John Law, and then begged for forgiveness. [D] 10

When Alizon Device was unable to cure the peddler the local magistrate, Roger Nowell, was called in. "With weeping tears," Alizon explained to Nowell that she had been led astray by her grandmother, "old Demdike," well-known in the district for her knowledge of old prayers, charms,

4 F. NO CHANGE
   G. court, Thomas Potts, who published
   H. court, Thomas Potts, who published,
   J. court Thomas Potts who published,

5 A. NO CHANGE
   B. its
   C. it's
   D. his

6 F. NO CHANGE
   G. evidence, but also
   H. evidence and additionally
   J. evidence and

7 A. NO CHANGE
   B. was constructed
   C. was being constructed
   D. was constructing

8 F. NO CHANGE
   G. young woman, Alizon Device, in a field near
   H. young woman, Alizon Device in a field near
   J. young woman Alizon Device, in a field, near

9 A. NO CHANGE
   B. John Law and she then begged
   C. John Law and begging
   D. John Law and begged

10 The quotation marks used in the preceding paragraph most likely indicate:

   F. direct quotes from Alizon Device.
   G. direct quotes from John Law.
   H. words quoted from a published source.
   J. an ironic tone of the author.

11 A. NO CHANGE
   B. peddler, the
   C. peddler; the
   D. peddler: the

cures, and curses. 12 Nowell quickly interviewed Alizon's grandmother and mother, as well as Demdike's supposed rival, "old Chattox." Their panicky attempts to explain themselves and shift the blame to others eventually only ended up incriminating them, and the four were sent to Lancashire prison in early April to await trial at the summer courts. 13 14 15

Adapted from Robert Poole, "The Lancashire Witches 1612–2012," *The Public Domain Review*, August 22, 2012, publicdomainreview.org/2012/08/22/the-lancashire-witches-1612-2012.

12 At this point, the writer wishes to add the following sentence:

"Old Demdike" had lived in the town for decades.

Should the writer make this addition here?

- **F.** Yes, because it helps the reader understand that old Demdike was an established member of the Lancashire community.
- **G.** Yes, because it explains why Demdike and "old Chattox" were rivals.
- **H.** No, because it interrupts the discussion at this point in the paragraph.
- **J.** No, because it doesn't explain why old Demdike was accused of practicing witchcraft.

Questions 13–15 ask about the preceding passage as a whole.

13 Given that all of the choices are true, which one most effectively concludes the essay?

- **A.** The trials of the four women were soon followed by the court appearances of 16 other accused witches, setting the stage for numerous other witch trials of the 17th century.
- **B.** While the women were in prison, they reportedly still practiced witchcraft with the other eight women imprisoned after them.
- **C.** Despite the women's ill-gotten fate, early 17th-century England was continually plagued with witchcraft well into the 18th century.
- **D.** These four women, however, would set the standard for fair trials for those accused of witchcraft in the rest of the 17th century.

14 The writer is considering deleting the word "panicky" in the final sentence of the last paragraph. Should the word be kept or deleted?

- **F.** Kept, because it helps indicate why the women's defense of themselves lacked strength.
- **G.** Kept, because it provides evidence that the women were guilty of their accused crimes.
- **H.** Deleted, because it reiterates information already stated in the previous sentence.
- **J.** Deleted, because the word provides unnecessary descriptive details.

15 The writer is considering adding the following sentence to the essay:

Before modern medicine, however, such an occurrence was often interpreted as magic or witchcraft.

If the sentence were added, it would most logically be placed at Point:

- **A.** [A]
- **B.** [B]
- **C.** [C]
- **D.** [D]

A New Runner

[1]

I watched in admiration as my father would rouse himself from bed as early as 5 a.m. to go for a run as a child. I could understand the desire in the summer, when it was already light but still cool because the sun had not yet fully risen. However, getting up in the dark cold of winter seemed totally crazy to me. Was he possessed by some kind of running demon? I knew that my dad valued his time "pounding the pavement," as he would say. [18]

16 F. NO CHANGE
G. I watched in admiration as my father would rouse himself from bed as a child as early as 5 a.m. to go for a run.
H. As a child, I watched in admiration as my father would rouse himself from bed as early as 5 a.m. to go for a run.
J. I watched in admiration as my father would rouse himself from bed as early as 5 a.m. as a child to go for a run.

17 A. NO CHANGE
B. in the cold, dark winter
C. in the dark winter cold
D. in dark winter, the cold

18 Which sentence would provide the most appropriate conclusion to Paragraph 1?

F. Still, his actions seemed a bit extreme to me.
G. I was only a child, though, and I didn't really care.
H. Sometimes, I would wonder why he did it.
J. His confusing actions passed right over my head.

[2]

[19] I'm not sure I would have started running if my little sister hadn't been so good at tennis. That might sound like a strange reason to start running, but we began taking lessons at the same time. She was amazing, hitting balls back across the net in her first five minutes on court. In fact, I made it through a week of tennis camp without ever having managed to even make contact between the ball and my racket. I simply didn't have the coordination to make them happen.

[3]

I came home from camp that Friday dejected, only to find a pair of New Balance shoes, smaller versions of my father's, in a box on my bed. My dad appeared at the door.

[4]

"You know," he said, "I have a feeling you'd make a great runner."

19 Which sentence would be most appropriate in the context of this paragraph?

- A. My dad had always wanted me to become an amazing runner, but I'd always ignored him.
- B. I had no idea how much my father's running would influence my life the summer I turned ten.
- C. My sister was never a very good runner, although she had other talents of which I was jealous.
- D. I wished I could be more like him, but I wasn't; nevertheless, I tried my best.

20 The writer is considering deleting this phrase from the sentence, adjusting capitalization as necessary. Should the writer make this change?

- F. Yes, because it makes the reader question the veracity of the essay.
- G. Yes, because it contradicts previously provided information.
- H. No, because it is important to understanding the rest of the essay.
- J. No, because it shows tension between two important characters.

21 A. NO CHANGE
- B. scoring points within the first five minutes.
- C. learning how to hit the ball as soon as possible.
- D. returning a serve on the court within her first five minutes.

22 F. NO CHANGE
- G. Nevertheless,
- H. On the other hand,
- J. Furthermore,

23 A. NO CHANGE
- B. that
- C. those
- D. this

[5]

That day, I seriously doubted him. After putting on my new shoes and bouncing up and down, <u>we go for a jog together</u>, and I couldn't even make it to the end of the street before bending over, gasping for breath. My father grinned, though, and just patted me on the back. [A]

[6]

[B] <u>Cheerfully, "Rise and shine," he said.</u> <u>I woke up at 5 a.m. the next day to find my dad dangling my new shoes over me.</u> "Today, we go around the block." [C]

[7]

[D] I did not think <u>I will be able</u> to do it, but I did, and that was how <u>we progressed. Slow but steady,</u> adding a block or two at a time. A few weeks ago, my father and I completed our annual marathon <u>that we do together every year.</u> <u>He beat me by two minutes; what can I expect?</u> The man's a running demon.

24 F. NO CHANGE
  G. we would go together for a jog
  H. we went for a jog together
  J. together, we jogged

25 A. NO CHANGE
  B. "Rise and shine," cheerfully he said
  C. "Rise and shine," he, cheerful, said
  D. "Rise and shine," he said cheerfully

26 Which placement for the underlined portion is both logical and also makes it clear that the author's father is speaking to her early in the morning?

  F. [A]
  G. [B]
  H. [C]
  J. [D]

27 A. NO CHANGE
  B. I could be able to do it
  C. I would be able to do it
  D. I am able to do it

28 F. NO CHANGE
  G. we progressed: slowly but steadily
  H. we progressed, slow, but steady
  J. we progressed; slowly but steadily

29 A. NO CHANGE
  B. that every year we do together
  C. every year that we do together
  D. OMIT this phrase, ending the sentence with a period.

30 F. NO CHANGE
  G. But what can I expect? He beat me by two minutes.
  H. He beat me by two minutes, what can I expect?
  J. He beat me by two minutes; why can I expect this?

Creating a Monster

[1]

[31] Most people today think Frankenstein is
the green monster that movies and plays put
into our minds. Although, those who have read
Mary Shelley's original novel know that this
is an erroneous name: it is not the name of the
monster but rather the name of the doctor who
created him, Dr. Frankenstein. In the novel, the
monster referencing the first man as recounted
by the Bible, is only identified as "demon," "fiend,"
or "creature," although he later refers to himself
as Adam.

31 Which placement for this paragraph is both
logical and also makes the chronology of the
passage clearer?

   A. NO CHANGE

   B. After Paragraph 2.

   C. After Paragraph 3.

   D. After Paragraph 4.

32 F. NO CHANGE

   G. from popular culture.

   H. we think of from the movies.

   J. that we have all learned about.

33 A. NO CHANGE

   B. In fact,

   C. For example,

   D. However,

34 F. NO CHANGE

   G. Frankenstein.

   H. the doctor named Frankenstein.

   J. OMIT the underlined portion, deleting the
comma and ending the sentence with a period.

35 A. NO CHANGE

   B. is only identified as "demon," "fiend,"
or "creature," although he later refers to
himself as Adam, referencing the first man
as recounted by the Bible.

   C. is only identified as "demon," "fiend,"
or "creature," referencing the first man as
recounted by the Bible, he later refers to
himself as Adam.

   D. he later refers to himself as Adam, and is
only identified as "demon," "fiend,"
or "creature," referencing the first man as
recounted by the Bible.

Mary Shelley's most famous book stemmed from a dream she had while traveling through Germany in the 1810s. On her journey, <u>she passed by an old building called Frankenstein Castle, the castle had once been the home of an experimenting alchemist</u>. She found the name of the castle intriguing. Her inspiration for the novel was further developed when she met with a group of friends and writers, including Percy Shelley and Lord Byron, in Switzerland, where she would set much of the story, and they discussed occult subjects. These discussions may have been the impetus for Dr. Frankenstein and his monster. Lord Byron was <u>the more famous writer</u> in the group and perhaps influenced the book's eventual publication.

At the time of its publication, *Frankenstein* was almost universally reviled by critics. <u>Audiences however loved it</u>, ensuring its continuous publication and widespread cultural importance. <u>Today, *Frankenstein* is considered one of the first science fiction novels, although it borrows many elements from earlier traditions, such as the Gothic and the Romantic.</u>

36 F. NO CHANGE

   G. she passed by an old home of an experimenting alchemist called Frankenstein Castle

   H. she passed by an old building called Frankenstein Castle, which had once been the home of an experimenting alchemist.

   J. she passed by Frankenstein Castle, an old building home where an experimenting alchemist had once lived.

37 A. NO CHANGE

   B. the most famous writer

   C. the famousest writer

   D. the famous writer

38 F. NO CHANGE

   G. Audiences, however loved it

   H. Audiences, however, loved it

   J. Audiences however, loved it

39 At this point, the writer is considering revising this sentence as follows:

> Today, Frankenstein *is considered one of the first science fiction novels. It borrows many elements from earlier traditions, such as the Gothic and the Romantic.*

Should the writer make this change?

   A. Yes, because it would make the separate ideas contained in the sentence easier to understand.

   B. Yes, because it would make the Gothic and the Romantic literary periods appear more distinct.

   C. No, because it would obscure the overlapping characteristics of the science fiction, Gothic, and Romantic genres.

   D. No, because it would weaken the juxtaposition of the old and new literary traditions present in the novel.

However, the story seems to have taken on a life of its own: few people can accurately identify the novel's characters. [40]

[4]

Nevertheless, the debate over the monster's proper name showed how impassioned the public still is about Shelleys work, which speak to larger issues of life and the power of creation most frightening than other similar books. Children should stay away. Whether the monster is known as Frankenstein or Adam, he still has the power to terrify kids.

40 **F.** NO CHANGE

   G. However, the story seems to have taken on a life of its own, few people can accurately identify the novel's characters.

   H. However, the story seems to have taken on a life of its own, but few people can accurately identify the novel's characters.

   J. However, the story seems to have taken on a life of its own, so few people can accurately identify the novel's characters.

41 **A.** NO CHANGE

   B. shows

   C. would show

   D. will show

42 **F.** NO CHANGE

   G. Shelleys'

   H. Shelleyes

   J. Shelley's

43 **A.** NO CHANGE

   B. which speaks

   C. that speaks

   D. that speak

44 **F.** NO CHANGE

   G. more frightening

   H. frighteningest

   J. frightening more

45 The writer is considering deleting the underlined sentences from the passage, adjusting the punctuation as needed. If the writer were to make this deletion, the passage would primarily lose:

   A. additional commentary that does not contribute to the essay's overall goal.

   B. a helpful clarification of the meaning of the first paragraph.

   C. contradictory ideas that do not explain the paradox they present.

   D. a reinforcement of a popular conception that the passage has proved to be false.

A Trip Around the World

On the morning of November 14, 1889, John Brisben Walker, the wealthy publisher of, The Cosmopolitan, boarded a New Jersey ferry bound for New York City. [A] Like many other New Yorker's, he was carrying a copy of The World, the most widely read and influential newspaper of our time. A front-page story announced that Nellie Bly, The World's star investigative reporter, was about to undertake the most sensational adventure of her career, which was an attempt to go around the world faster than anyone ever had before. [B] Sixteen years earlier, in his popular novel, Around the World in Eighty Days, Jules Verne had imagined that such a trip could be accomplished in the time stated in the title. [50] Nellie Bly hoped to do the trip in 75 days.

Immediately Walker recognized the publicity value of such a scheme, and at once an idea suggested itself:

46 F. NO CHANGE
   G. publisher of The Cosmopolitan boarded
   H. publisher, of The Cosmopolitan, boarded
   J. publisher of The Cosmopolitan, boarded

47 A. NO CHANGE
   B. Similar as many other New Yorkers,
   C. As many other New Yorker's,
   D. In the same manner as other New Yorkers,

48 F. NO CHANGE
   G. their
   H. its
   J. a

49 A. NO CHANGE
   B. career which was
   C. career: an attempt
   D. career, and

50 If the writer were to delete the preceding sentence, the paragraph would primarily lose:

   F. important context for understanding information presented later in the paragraph.
   G. an unrelated detail describing literature of the late 19th century.
   H. scientific data explaining the minimum length of a trip around the world.
   J. an indication that a trip around the world in less than 80 days could only occur in fiction, not reality.

51 Which of the following alternatives to the underlined portion would NOT be acceptable?

   A. Right away
   B. Instantly
   C. Without delay
   D. As soon as

The Cosmopolitan would sponsor their own competitor in the around-the-world race, traveling in the opposite direction. Of course, the magazine's circumnavigator would have to leave immediately, and would have to be, like Bly, a young woman. The public at that time, after all, would never warm to the idea of a man racing against a woman. [C] That morning, he met with Elizabeth Bisland, the magazine's literary editor, whom agreed to become Blys competitor. [D] In the end, Elizabeth Bisland succeeded in beating Jules Verne's 80-day mark, completing the trip in 76 days—which would have been the fastest trip ever made around the world but for the fact that Nellie Bly had arrived four days earlier.

Although she ultimately lost the race, Bisland later became friends with Nellie Bly. Prior to her trip, she had never been out of the country before, and during her competition she discovered a love of travel that would stay with her the rest of her life.

52 F. NO CHANGE
G. its own competitor
H. their competitor
J. it's own competitor

53 A. NO CHANGE
B. immediately and would be,
C. immediately and would have to be,
D. immediately, and had to be,

54 F. NO CHANGE
G. to who
H. of whom
J. who

55 A. NO CHANGE
B. Bly's competitor.
C. a competitor.
D. an opponent.

56 Which of the following alternatives to the underlined portion best introduces the topics presented in this paragraph?

F. NO CHANGE
G. Bisland was profoundly affected by the experience.
H. Bisland never forgave Walker for nominating her.
J. Bly's competitor, understandably, never went back to America.

57 A. NO CHANGE
B. prior
C. until then
D. DELETE the underlined portion.

That was what the trip had given her, <u>however, as</u> she would reflect later: the vividness of a new world, where one was for the first time, as Tennyson had written, "Lord of the senses five." "It was well," she told herself when it was all over, "to have thus once really lived." [59] [60]

Adapted from Matthew Goodman, "Elizabeth Bisland's Race Around the World," *The Public Domain Review*, October 16, 2013, publicdomainreview.org/2013/10/16/elizabeth -bislands-race-around-the-world.

58 **F.** NO CHANGE
 G. though, as
 H. therefore, as
 J. as

Questions 59 and 60 ask about the preceding passage as a whole.

59 The writer is considering adding the following sentence to the essay:

Walker had a difficult choice ahead of him.

If the writer were to make this addition, it would most logically be placed at Point:

 A. A in Paragraph 1.
 B. B in Paragraph 1.
 C. C in Paragraph 2.
 D. D in Paragraph 2.

60 Suppose the writer had intended to write a historical essay about early races around the world. Would the essay fulfill that goal?

 F. Yes, because it discusses the effect the race had on Bisland when she returned to America.
 G. Yes, because it focuses on how two women competed in a race around the world.
 H. No, because the essay primarily focuses on one race around the world.
 J. No, because the essay discusses how Bly defeated Bisland in the competition.

History of the ATM

In most busy cities and towns today, you can find automated teller machines, or ATMs, on practically every block. An ATM is an electronic communications device that allows bank customers to perform financial transactions without needing to talk to a human bank clerk. However, some people can conduct their banking business entirely using ATMs.

As with many complicated pieces of technology, it is difficult to pinpoint exactly when the first ATM was developed. In 1939, an American inventor named Luther Simjian patented an early version of an ATM that were not having much success. [65]

61 A. NO CHANGE
   B. busy cities and towns, you can find automated teller machines, or ATMs today, on practically every block.
   C. busy cities and towns on practically every block today you can find automated teller machines, or ATMs.
   D. busy cities and towns, automated teller machines, also called ATMs, can be found on every block today, practically.

62 F. NO CHANGE
   G. In fact,
   H. Additionally,
   J. For example,

63 A. NO CHANGE
   B. when developing the first ATM.
   C. when the first ATM was invented and developed.
   D. the invention and development of the first ATM.

64 F. NO CHANGE
   G. was not having
   H. did not have
   J. will not have

65 At this point, the author is considering adding the following true statement:

> *Simjian, however, is more famous for some of his other interesting inventions, such as an army flight simulator, a color x-ray machine, an exercise bicycle, and a self-posing camera.*

Should the writer make this addition here?

   A. Yes, because it adds a colorful description of Simjian's eclectic talents.
   B. Yes, because it explains why Simjian would have invented an automated banking machine.
   C. No, because it detracts from the focus of the essay by introducing unrelated details.
   D. No, because it doesn't indicate the effect these inventions had on society.

GO >

Simjian called his invention the Bankograph. The Bankograph could accept cash or check deposits at any time of day or night but not dispense money. To assuage customers' fears that they might never see their money again, there was a camera inside the Bankograph that took a picture of every deposit and provided a photo receipt to the customer. However, the Bankograph did not catch on.

[1] It was not until the late 1970s and early 1980s, however, when more of the population had became comfortable with the idea of automated technologies, that automated banking machines became more popular. [2] The first modern automated banking machine was developed in 1969, by a Dallas engineer named Donald Wetzel. [3] Wetzel's machine used plastic cards like the ones we use today. [4] Some say that it took a good old-fashioned New York blizzard to truly make ATMs a permanent institution in American life. [5] In 1977, the chairman of Citibank spent over $100 million dollars to install ATMs all over New York City, hoping they would be a success. [6] The following winter, a blizzard shut down banks in the city for days, and ATM usage suddenly increased by 20 percent. [7] This blizzard also launched Citibank's long-running "The Citi Never Sleeps" campaign, with posters and billboards showing customers trudging through snow drifts to get to Citibank ATMs. 72

66 F. NO CHANGE
   G. night, but not
   H. night and not
   J. night, and not

67 A. NO CHANGE
   B. had been becoming
   C. have become
   D. became

68 F. NO CHANGE
   G. automated technologies that automated banking
   H. automated technologies, automated banking
   J. automated technologies; automated banking

69 A. NO CHANGE
   B. 1969;
   C. 1969:
   D. 1969

70 Which of the following is NOT an acceptable alternative for the underlined phrase?

   F. all throughout
   G. throughout
   H. in
   J. across

71 If the writer were to delete the underlined portion, deleting the comma and ending the sentence with a period, the paragraph would primarily lose:

   A. an explanation of why so many people used ATMs during the blizzard.
   B. descriptive detail about the imagery of the advertising campaign.
   C. a restatement of an idea expressed earlier in the paragraph.
   D. an explanation of why ATMs became necessary in the late 1970s.

Now, there are around 2 million ATMs in the world. Even some of the most remote areas of the world are connected by ATMs; there are even two machines in Antarctica. But the ATM may have already reached its peak of popularity. Since so many people today use <u>there</u> credit and debit cards for most purchases, cash from ATMs <u>is</u> less in demand. 75

72 For the sake of logic and coherence, Sentence 1 should be placed:

F. where it is now.

G. after Sentence 2.

H. after Sentence 3.

J. after Sentence 7.

73 A. NO CHANGE

B. their

C. his or her

D. our

74 F. NO CHANGE

G. are

H. were

J. had been

75 Suppose the writer's purpose had been to write an essay about the development of automated technologies throughout the 20th century to the present day. Would the essay accomplish this purpose?

A. Yes, because it explains how ATMs developed between the 1930s and the present.

B. Yes, because it includes several examples of automated banking machines from the Bankograph to the ATM.

C. No, because it doesn't describe how the ATM developed in the early 20th century.

D. No, because it focuses only on the development of the ATM.

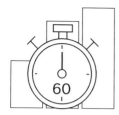

2

ACT Mathematics Test

60 Minutes | 60 Questions

Solve each problem, choose the correct answer, and then note your answer choice on your answer sheet. Be careful not to spend too much time on specific problems. Solve all the problems you can, and then come back to the ones you skipped in the time you have left.

You CAN use a calculator on this test. You are permitted to use your calculator on any problem, but some problems are better done without a calculator.

NOTE: Unless otherwise noted, all of the following assumptions are true:

1. Illustrated figures are NOT necessarily drawn to scale.
2. Geometric figures lie in a plane.
3. The word "line" means a straight line.
4. The word "average" indicates arithmetic mean.

1 Which of the following numbers is between $\frac{3}{5}$ and $\frac{5}{7}$?

A. $\frac{1}{2}$

B. $\frac{3}{7}$

C. $\frac{8}{9}$

D. $\frac{19}{35}$

E. $\frac{47}{70}$

2 $x + 2y = 5$
$2x + y = 16$

What does $x + y$ equal?

F. −4

G. −2

H. 4

J. 7

K. 9

3 To reach her destination, Jeanette must drive 90 miles. If she drives 5 miles every 7 minutes, how long will it take her to reach her destination?

A. 2 hours and 2 minutes

B. 2 hours and 6 minutes

C. 2 hours and 10 minutes

D. 2 hours and 12 minutes

E. 2 hours and 15 minutes

4 Walking at a constant rate of 8 kilometers per hour, Juan can cross a bridge in 6 minutes. What is the length of the bridge in meters? (1 kilometer = 1000 meters)

F. 480

G. 600

H. 720

J. 750

K. 800

5 After receiving a 25% discount, Sue paid $180 for a lawnmower. What is the original price of the lawnmower before the discount?

   A. $215
   B. $220
   C. $225
   D. $240
   E. $245

6 In the figure below, if f = 6 and g = 8, what does h equal?

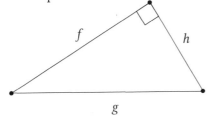

   F. $2\sqrt{7}$
   G. $3\sqrt{5}$
   H. 4
   J. 10
   K. 14

7 If $J \div 24 = K$, then $J \div 6$ =

   A. $4K$
   B. $2K$
   C. K
   D. $\frac{K}{2}$
   E. $\frac{K}{4}$

8 In order to qualify for the year-end tennis tournament, Sam must win at least 60% of his matches this year. To date, Sam has won 14 of his 18 matches. Of Sam's 13 matches remaining in the year, what is the least number that he must win in order to qualify for the year-end tournament?

   F. 4
   G. 5
   H. 6
   J. 7
   K. 8

9 Five years from now, Tatiana will be two years older than Frederico is now. If Frederico is currently 13, how old is Tatiana now?

   A. 8
   B. 10
   C. 13
   D. 15
   E. 18

10 In the Antares Corporation, $\frac{3}{7}$ of the managers are female. If there are 42 female managers, how many managers in total are there?

   F. 18
   G. 24
   H. 60
   J. 66
   K. 98

11 A company has 40 executives and 120 customer service representatives. If these are the only employees, what percentage of the employees are executives?

   A. 20%
   B. 25%
   C. 33%
   D. 40%
   E. 80%

12 If $R = 10b^2$ and b = 5, then R =

   F. 25
   G. 50
   H. 100
   J. 250
   K. 500

13 A prism with dimensions given in centimeters is shown below. If the volume of a prism is the area of a triangular base times the length of a rectangular base, what is the volume of this prism, in cubic centimeters?

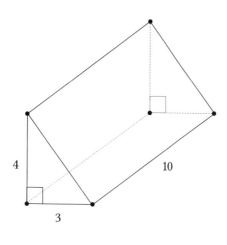

- A. 30
- B. 40
- C. 50
- D. 60
- E. 120

14 On a certain high school athletic team, the ratio of freshmen to sophomores to juniors to seniors is 1:3:4:6. If there are 60 juniors on the team, how many students in total are on the team?

- F. 90
- G. 140
- H. 150
- J. 180
- K. 210

15 A group of employees and their spouses are dining out at a fancy restaurant. When the bill for the meal comes, they initially decide to split it equally among the 8 employees of the same company. Then, a spouse insists on paying a share, so they split the bill equally among 9 people: this reduces the per-person share by $5. What was the total price of the bill?

- A. $135
- B. $180
- C. $360
- D. $450
- E. $720

16 In trapezoid $ABCD$, $BC = EF = 6$, $AF = DE = 3$, and $AB = CD = 5$. If the area of a trapezoid is given by $A = \left(\dfrac{b_1 + b_2}{2}\right)h$, then which of the following is the area of trapezoid $ABCD$?

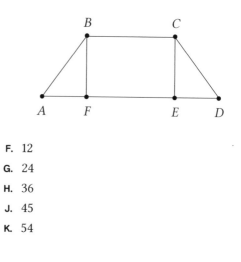

- F. 12
- G. 24
- H. 36
- J. 45
- K. 54

17 The top of a student's desk is in the shape shown below; all distances are given in inches. What is the area of this desktop in square inches?

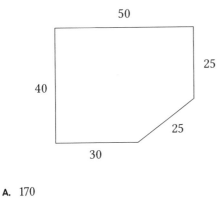

A. 170
B. 1500
C. 1700
D. 1850
E. 2000

18 If 3 apples and 4 bananas cost $1.37 total, and 5 apples and 7 bananas cost $2.36 total, what is the total cost of 1 apple and 1 banana?

F. $0.38
G. $0.39
H. $0.40
J. $0.41
K. $0.42

19 In 2004, Cindy had $4000 in a mutual fund account. In 2005, the amount in the same account was $5000. If the percent increase from 2004 to 2005 was the same as the percent increase from 2005 to 2006, how much did Cindy have in this account in 2006?

A. $5800
B. $6000
C. $6250
D. $7500
E. $9000

20 Which of the following inequalities is equivalent to $12 - 3x < -18$?

F. $x > 10$
G. $x < 10$
H. $x > -10$
J. $x < -10$
K. $x > 2$

21 Which of the following equations expresses the relationship between x and y in the table below?

x	y
4	41
7	32
11	20
13	14
16	5

A. $y = 10x + 1$
B. $y = 2x - 1$
C. $y = -x + 45$
D. $y = -3x + 53$
E. $y = -7x + 81$

22 The total cost to rent a tour bus for a day is the same for any party over 15 riders. If the cost is $720 for a group of 16 people, how much less would a group of 24 riders have to pay per person than a group of 16?

F. $10.50
G. $15
H. $25
J. $30
K. $45

23 If $f(x) = x^2 + 4$ and $f(2k) = 36$, then which of the following is one possible value of k?

A. $\sqrt{2}$
B. 2
C. 4
D. $2\sqrt{2}$
E. $\sqrt{14}$

24 A municipal water tank is a large cylinder with a radius of 20 feet and a height of 30 feet. Assuming that the tank is filled with water, what is the approximate volume of the water in cubic feet?

    F. 6,000

    G. 12,000

    H. 18,000

    J. 36,000

    K. 54,000

25 The average of x and t is y. If $s = 2y$, what is the average of s, x, and t in terms of y?

    A. $3y$

    B. $2y$

    C. $\dfrac{5y}{3}$

    D. $\dfrac{4y}{3}$

    E. y

26 If $f(x) = x^3 - 5$ and $f(k) = 3$ then $k =$

    F. -22

    G. 2

    H. 4

    J. 6

    K. 22

27 If the average (arithmetic mean) of 24 consecutive odd integers is 48, what is the median of the 24 numbers?

    A. 36

    B. 47

    C. 48

    D. 49

    E. 72

28 Suppose that 10 US dollars is equivalent to 9 euros. How do you convert from euros to US dollars?

    F. Add 1

    G. Multiply by 9

    H. Multiply by 10

    J. Multiply by $\dfrac{9}{10}$

    K. Multiply by $\dfrac{10}{9}$

29 The square base of a regular pyramid has a side length of 6 inches. Each of the other 4 faces of the pyramid is a triangle with a base of 6 inches and a height of 8 inches. The pyramid has a total surface area of 132 inches. A second regular pyramid has a square base that is 6 inches by 6 inches, but its total surface area is double that of the first pyramid. What is the height, in inches, of each of the triangular faces of the second pyramid?

    A. 11

    B. 16

    C. 19

    D. 22

    E. 44

30 $(3 \times 10^{20})(8 \times 10^{30}) =$

    F. 2.4×10^{50}

    G. 2.4×10^{51}

    H. 2.4×10^{60}

    J. 2.4×10^{61}

    K. 2.4×10^{301}

31 The figure shown below in the standard xy-coordinate plane is to be rotated 180° about the origin. One of the following graphs is the result of this rotation. Which one is it?

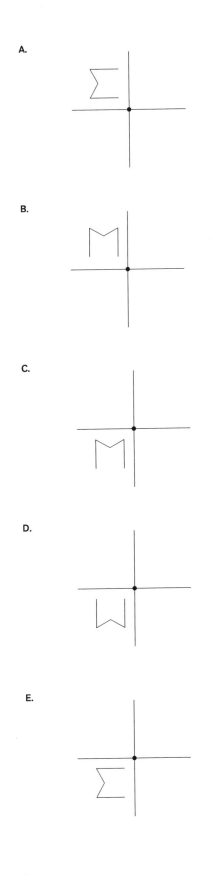

A.

B.

C.

D.

E.

32 Point A in the xy-coordinate system is shown below. Given two other points B $(4a, b)$ and C $(2a, 5b)$, what is the area of triangle ABC in terms of a and b?

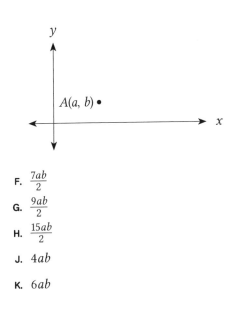

F. $\frac{7ab}{2}$

G. $\frac{9ab}{2}$

H. $\frac{15ab}{2}$

J. $4ab$

K. $6ab$

33 Students in an 11th grade history class are randomly divided into three teams of five students for a history trivia contest. Each student takes a trivia test with 100 total points available, and their scores are posted below. The team with the highest average score (rounded to the nearest whole number) wins the contest.

	Team 1	Team 2	Team 3
	74	64	77
	80	76	91
	93	81	92
	94	85	90
	74	89	85
Average Score	83	79	87

Which of the following is closest to the percent of individual trivia test scores that are at or above 80 points?

A. 10%

B. 33%

C. 60%

D. 67%

E. 80%

34 The average (arithmetic mean) of two numbers is 4x. If one of the numbers is y, then the value of the other number is:

F. $x - 4y$

G. $4x + 4y$

H. $8x - 4y$

J. $4y - 8x$

K. $8x - y$

35 A survey of a high school track team asked the 40 members how many hours per week (rounded to the nearest hour) they spend running outside of team practices. The 40 responses are summarized in the histogram below.

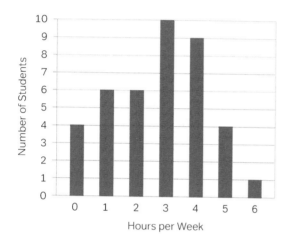

To the nearest hundredth of an hour, what is the average number of hours spent running for the 40 respondents?

A. 2.75

B. 2.90

C. 3.25

D. 3.40

E. 6.00

36 Suppose water was being pumped into a cistern, and the height of the water was rising at a constant rate. The height of the water was 23 cm at 9 a.m. and 72 cm at 4 p.m. What was the height of the water at noon (12 p.m.)?

F. 26 cm

G. 37 cm

H. 44 cm

J. 53 cm

K. 63 cm

37 In the standard xy-coordinate plane, what is the slope of a line that is perpendicular to $4x - 6y = 14$?

A. -4

B. $-\dfrac{3}{2}$

C. $-\dfrac{2}{3}$

D. $\dfrac{3}{2}$

E. 4

38 In the xy-coordinate system, line k passes through points $(-5m, 0)$ and $(0, 2m)$. Which of the following is a possible equation of line k?

F. $y = -\dfrac{5}{2}x + 2m$

G. $y = \dfrac{2}{5}x - 5m$

H. $y = \dfrac{5}{2}x + 2m$

J. $y = \dfrac{2}{5}x + 2m$

K. $y = -\dfrac{2}{5}x - 5m$

39 The microcurrent through the electrode in a delicate circuit is usually held constant at 3.6×10^{-8} amps. Because of a defect in another part of the circuit, the current was 1000 times smaller. What was the current, in amps, caused by this defect?

A. 3.6×10^{-8000}

B. 3.6×10^{-24}

C. 3.6×10^{-11}

D. 3.6×10^{-5}

E. $3.6 \times 10^{-\frac{8}{3}}$

40 A straight 16-foot-tall ladder is leaning against an apartment building at an angle of 50°, as shown in the figure below. Which of the following expressions gives the distance, in feet, from the base of the ladder to the building?

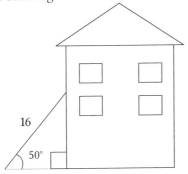

F. 16 cos 50°

G. 16 sin 50°

H. 16 tan 50°

J. $\dfrac{16}{\sin 50°}$

K. $\dfrac{16}{\cos 50°}$

41 In the standard xy-coordinate plane, when $a \neq 0$ and $b \neq 0$, the graph of $f(x) = \dfrac{2x+b}{x+a}$ has a vertical asymptote at:

A. $y = -a$

B. $y = a$

C. $x = -1$

D. $x = \dfrac{-a}{2}$

E. $x = -a$

42 If $g(x) = -\frac{1}{2} f(x)$, for all values of x, which of the following is a true statement describing the graph of g in comparison with the graph of f, shown below?

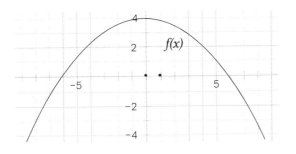

F. It is narrower and opens downward.

G. It is narrower and opens upward.

H. It is the same width but opens upward.

J. It is wider and opens downward.

K. It is wider and opens upward.

43 Which of the following angles has the same terminal side as 1,105°?

A. 15°

B. 25°

C. 45°

D. 105°

E. 335°

44 In the two-dimensional figure below, AB is parallel to ED, the measure of DCB is 44°, and the measure of ABC is 70°. What is the measure of EDC?

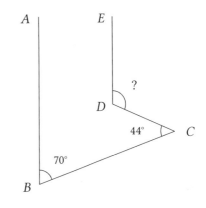

F. 100°

G. 114°

H. 118°

J. 124°

K. 136°

45 In the complex number system, what does i^{45} equal?

A. −1

B. 0

C. 2

D. i

E. $-i$

46 A bag contains x blue chips and y red chips. If the probability of selecting a red chip at random is $\frac{3}{7}$, then $\frac{x}{y} =$

   F. $\frac{7}{11}$

   G. $\frac{3}{4}$

   H. $\frac{7}{4}$

   J. $\frac{4}{3}$

   K. $\frac{11}{7}$

47 If $f(x) = 12 - \frac{x^2}{2}$ and $f(2k) = 2k$, what is one possible value for k?

   A. 2

   B. 3

   C. 4

   D. 6

   E. 8

48 The equation $y = x^2$ is graphed in the standard xy-coordinate plane. In which of the following equations is the graph of the parabola shifted 4 units to the left and 2 units up?

   F. $y = (x - 4)^2 + 2$

   G. $y = (x - 4)^2 - 2$

   H. $y = (x - 2)^2 + 4$

   J. $y = (x + 4)^2 + 2$

   K. $y = (x + 4)^2 - 2$

49 If $x^4 = y^{16}$, then $y = $?

   A. $\sqrt[4]{x}$

   B. $\sqrt{x}$

   C. x^2

   D. x^4

   E. x^{12}

50 A square in the standard xy-coordinate plane has vertices at $(1, 0)$, $(0, 2)$, $(2, 3)$, and $(3, 1)$. Where do the diagonals of the square intersect?

   F. $\left(2, \frac{3}{2}\right)$

   G. $\left(1, \frac{3}{2}\right)$

   H. $\left(\frac{5}{3}, \frac{5}{3}\right)$

   J. $\left(\frac{4}{3}, \frac{4}{3}\right)$

   K. $\left(\frac{3}{2}, \frac{3}{2}\right)$

51 *Note:* Figure not drawn to scale.

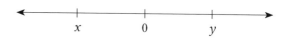

If x and y are numbers on the number line above, which of the following statements must be true?

I. $|x + y| < y$

II. $x + y < 0$

III. $xy < 0$

   A. I only

   B. III only

   C. I and II

   D. I and III

   E. II and III

52 If the circle with center O has area 9π, what is the area of equilateral triangle ABC?

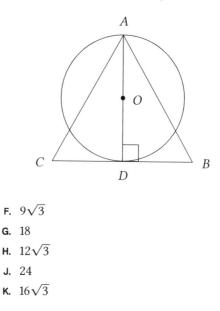

   F. $9\sqrt{3}$

   G. 18

   H. $12\sqrt{3}$

   J. 24

   K. $16\sqrt{3}$

53 In the equation $\log_4 256 - \log_3 9 = \log_2 x$, what does x equal?

A. 0

B. 1

C. 2

D. 4

E. 6

54 Bryce is building a ramp up to a platform in a skate park. The ramp is 11.5 feet long, and the end of the ramp that meets the platform is 3 feet above the level ground. Which of the following gives the angle of inclination of the ramp?

11.5 ? 3

F. $\sin^{-1}\left(\frac{3}{11.5}\right)$

G. $\cos^{-1}\left(\frac{3}{11.5}\right)$

H. $\tan^{-1}\left(\frac{3}{11.5}\right)$

J. $\sin^{-1}\left(\frac{11.5}{3}\right)$

K. $\cos^{-1}\left(\frac{11.5}{3}\right)$

55 The nth term (t_n) of a certain sequence is defined as $t_n = t_{n-1} + 4$.

If $t_1 = -7$, then $t_{71} =$

A. 273

B. 277

C. 281

D. 283

E. 287

56 A circle has an area of x. If the diameter is increased by 50%, what is the area of the resulting circle in terms of x?

F. $1.25x$

G. $1.5x$

H. $2x$

J. $2.25x$

K. $3x$

57 If $2^{2n} + 2^{2n} + 2^{2n} + 2^{2n} = 4^{24}$, then $n =$

A. 3

B. 6

C. 12

D. 23

E. 24

58 For quadrant 1 angles α and β, $\sin(\alpha) = \frac{3}{5}$ and $\cos(\beta) = \frac{12}{13}$.

Given that $\cos(\alpha + \beta) = \cos(\alpha)\cos(\beta) - \sin(\alpha)\sin(\beta)$, which of the following equals $\cos(\alpha + \beta)$?

F. $\frac{33}{65}$

G. $\frac{48}{65}$

H. $\frac{56}{65}$

J. $\frac{63}{65}$

K. $\frac{99}{65}$

59 The expression $\log_3 63 + \log_3 5 - \log_3 35$ equals which of the following?

A. 2

B. 3

C. 6

D. $\log_3 33$

E. $\log_3 56$

60 Which of the following complex numbers equals $(2 - i\sqrt{3})(\sqrt{2} + i)$?

F. $(2\sqrt{2} + \sqrt{3}) + i(2 - \sqrt{6})$

G. $(2\sqrt{3} - \sqrt{2}) + i(2 + \sqrt{6})$

H. $(2\sqrt{2} + \sqrt{6}) + i(2 - \sqrt{3})$

J. $(2 + \sqrt{2}) + i(2\sqrt{2} - \sqrt{6})$

K. $(2 - \sqrt{3}) + i(2\sqrt{2} + \sqrt{3})$

ACT Reading Test

35 Minutes | 40 Questions

The four passages in this test are accompanied by several questions. Read the passage, and then select the best answer to each question.

Note this answer on your answer sheet. You may go back to the passages as often as you need.

Literary Narrative

"Tiffany glass" refers to stained glass used in interior decorating, designed by Louis Comfort Tiffany or his studio, and known for its high cost.

1 Janet liked their new house. She really did. With its heavy oak door and its trellised north-facing wall covered in well-groomed ivy, it looked just like the
5 American one-bedroom equivalent of the mansions in a Jane Austen novel. The little lofted area above the bedroom was soon filled with bookshelves, sewing supplies, bookbinding equipment, and
10 even a little table for embossing. There was even a fireplace with a rustic bench at one end of the living room. It seemed like the ideal house, the one she always dreamed of throughout her suburb-
15 bound childhood.

Yet, the feeling of displacement persisted in the back of her head like the buzz of a tenacious fly. At first, she told herself that it was just the feeling
20 of life among boxes. So many boxes, all of them longing to be lovingly emptied. Every object had to find its own new home. It was overwhelming, that was all. Mind buzzing, Janet threw her
25 evenings and weekends wholeheartedly into unpacking every one. Once the task was over, she assured herself, she would love the place where she lived.

The kitchen and bathroom had fewer
30 cabinets than the young couple's first home, but there was space in the loft. But should the Tylenol go in the loft? If not the painkillers, then the toothbrushes might have to. At moments, she hated
35 the house, hated not having a pantry, hated the seven cabinets that ought to have been ten.

"Mama," Janet said over the phone three weeks into the move. "I'm just
40 not sure what I'm going to do. There's no place for my favorite lamp. I've got everything else in its home, but not that lamp."

"Janet, honey," her mama's voice
45 came through with some static. "It's just a lamp. If there isn't anywhere for it to go, it can just go in storage."

"No, it can't. It's that Tiffany lamp with beautiful glass. I don't own
50 anything I like more."

"Well, can't you just store a different lamp?" Mama asked.

"There isn't another one. It's not tall enough to be a floor lamp, but it's
55 too wide for the bedside table. I don't know where it's going to go. It's just sitting way up on the television cabinet now." Janet glanced up at the lamp as she spoke. It was a masterpiece of
60 stained glass, all gold and marble light. The crisscross pattern of the leading on

each face reminded her of the windows at her hometown library. A very generous wedding gift from an aunt, the lamp lent a solidity and peace to Janet's emotions, reminding her of Keats's famous poem "A Thing of Beauty is a Joy Forever."

But there was no place in her house for the thing of beauty. The furniture just fit perfectly in its place, and there was no surface both tall and wide enough for it, except its current high, uncomfortable perch.

"Honey, just remember you've got a great house," mama said. "It's a very, very nice place to be. You've got to learn to be grateful. Lots of folks out there would give an arm and a leg to have problems like where to put their Tiffany lamps."

Janet started to answer but realized that the call had dropped. There was hardly any cell signal this far out in the country. She began to dial her mother's number, and then set the phone aside instead.

She didn't mean to be ungrateful, although her mother wasn't the first to accuse her. Janet had been accusing herself of it ever since they moved in. The lingering, awful buzzing would not leave her alone: she simply didn't belong here. Maybe certain people just didn't have souls the right shape for certain houses. Deeper than her heart, she felt the strain of a city girl in a country home.

Taking the lamp down from its ungainly nest, Janet wrapped it carefully in packing material and settled it in a cozy box, as though it were a napping creature. She climbed into the loft with the box under her arm. With tenderness, she slipped it behind the bookshelf in the corner. Back down the ladder she went. Now, the house looked perfect. Everything had its place, and it fit beautifully. Resigned to the buzzing, Janet began to clean her lunch dishes. The sink really was nice. Twice as deep as the one in their old apartment. She could soak a whole meal's worth of dishes at once. That would leave more time for her crafts.

1 This passage as a whole is primarily about Janet's feelings of:

A. displacement.

B. loneliness.

C. anger.

D. despair.

2 The author describes Janet's favorite lamp primarily as:

F. a gaudy example of city life.

G. an expensive piece that could be stolen.

H. a reminder of beauty and a source of joy.

J. too fancy for their simple new home.

3 In lines 84–92, Janet finally comes to terms with:

A. her mother's tendency to accuse her.

B. the current placement of the lamp.

C. the number of cabinets in the kitchen.

D. her feelings toward the house.

4 In the final paragraph, the author uses which of the following literary devices to describe the lamp?

F. Simile

G. Alliteration

H. Onomatopoeia

J. Foreshadowing

5 Which of the following statements best captures how Janet's mother tries to help her daughter in the passage?

A. Although Janet's mother did not understand her daughter's problem, she did her best to listen.

B. When Janet's mother heard about her daughter's unwise decisions, she persuaded her to change her mind.

C. Discovering that Janet did not know information about the home, her mother supplied her with details.

D. Believing that Janet had a bad perspective on her situation, her mother reminded her of the importance of gratitude.

6 As it is used in line 91, the word *strain* most nearly means:

- F. force.
- G. effort.
- H. pleasure.
- J. difficulty.

7 In the context of the passage, the primary function of Paragraph 3 ("The kitchen and . . . have been ten.") is to:

- A. explain Janet's difficulty with her mother.
- B. indicate why Janet decided to move to the country.
- C. show factors that made Janet's transition challenging.
- D. represent a major shift in Janet's attitude toward the house.

8 As a child Janet regarded country homes as:

- F. desirable places to live.
- G. uncomfortable for her city-dwelling heart.
- H. mysterious and somewhat frightening.
- J. too small for her family.

9 The narrator describes all of the objects being placed into the lofted area EXCEPT:

- A. an embossing table.
- B. sewing supplies.
- C. a rustic bench.
- D. bookbinding equipment.

10 In the poem "A Thing of Beauty is a Joy Forever," the poet John Keats says that beautiful things "always must be with us, or we die." How does this line from the poem apply to Janet's feelings about the lamp expressed in this passage?

- F. It offers an ironic counterexample, showing how confused Janet's thinking is.
- G. It supports Janet's uneasiness with not having a place for the lamp.
- H. It proves that Janet's physical health is connected to the well-being of the lamp.
- J. It illustrates how important it is to remain grateful for the things one has.

Social Science

Passage A

1　Edmund Burke, the Irish writer of political
　theory, believed government had been
　improved by every preceding generation up to
　his own. He saw the successive effort of early
5　Greek democracies and Byzantine emperors
　and the rules set forth by the Magna Carta
　coalescing into a consummately effective—
　though far from perfect—society. In his eyes,
　the British Parliamentary system of his day
10　represented the realization of all of the efforts
　theretofore drawn together by the work of
　Enlightenment philosophers in the 18th
　century. It was the fullest expression of liberty
　balanced with order yet known to man. A deep
15　sense of gratitude to his forbears reigned in
　every word from his lips and from his pen.

　　Due to this national pride and patriotism,
　Burke's dismissal of the French Revolution
　brings little surprise to the student of history.
20　Yet, his positive attitude toward the American
　Revolutionaries, so uncommon in his time and
　station, was no less a natural expression of his
　political stance.

　　Years before the fateful July Fourth, Burke
25　addressed the British House of Commons
　regarding the trouble stirring far across the
　Atlantic. The British had treated the American
　Englishmen unjustly, he argued. Taxation
　without representation violated the principles
30　foundational to Parliament. Taking a long and
　careful view of history, Burke believed that
　the colonists had both tactical and ideological
　advantages; they wielded the two-edged sword
　of power and virtue. As long as the English
35　people exploited their overseas brethren,
　they could not hope to suppress the colonists
　with violence.

　　Burke's call to action went unheeded, and
　the American Revolution began. Still appealing
40　to his perennial belief in the superiority of
　the Parliamentary system of government, he
pled with the House: "As long as you have the
wisdom to keep the sovereign authority of
this country as the sanctuary of liberty, the
45　sacred temple consecrated to our common
faith, wherever the chosen race and sons of
England worship freedom, they will turn their
faces toward you. The more they multiply,
the more friends you will have; the more
50　ardently they love liberty, the more perfect
will be their obedience. Slavery they can have
anywhere. It is a weed that grows in every
soil. They may have it from Spain, they may
have it from Prussia. But, until you become
55　lost to all feeling of your true interest and
your natural dignity, freedom they can have
from none but you." Despite his wise words,
the English still sought to enslave the colonies,
thereby losing America.

Passage B

60　A refugee torn from the prisons of the French
Revolution, political philosopher Thomas
Paine ended his life without the slightest
loss of confidence in the beauty and value
of revolution. As he had stood with America
65　throughout his boyhood and early manhood,
Paine stood with France even as it sought to
kill him. For Paine, the world had been a
brutal, unjust place until the Enlightenment in
the 1700s. In the light of liberty and intellectual
70　freedom, the dusty thrones and inbred
monarchy that filled Europe's ruling class
seemed a matter for history books rather
than newspapers.

　　Paine championed these views and praised
75　the necessity of the American Revolution in
his famous pamphlet, *Common Sense*. Read in
bars and parlors throughout the colonies, the
straightforward, sometimes vulgar language of
Paine's writings provided the battle cry of an
80　Enlightened people against the old, cold ways
of King George III. It argued that ordinary
people had not only the ability and the right to
contribute to the structure of their leadership,
but even the duty.

85　What was true in America was doubly true
in France. A little over a decade after arguing the
American people into shuffling off the shackles
of the English monarchy, Paine joined what
he saw as a parallel effort in France. When the
90　peasants deposed the king and tore apart the
structure of their government, Paine lauded
the end of tyranny. The political philosopher
joined the effort in France with almost complete
accord, although he did try to argue against
95　the execution of King Louis XVI, who had been
an ally to the Americans in their own fight for
independence. Even after that execution, Paine
went on to write headstrong defenses of the
French Revolution until the tides turned. In
100　the unstable atmosphere of the French political
landscape, Paine soon found himself on the
wrong side of the ruling powers. Imprisoned and
sentenced to death, Paine relied on allies from
America and England to help him escape.
105　　Despite this accident of history, Paine refused
to speak against the French Revolution. To his
death, he continued to claim that individual
safety and stability ought to be sacrificed on the
altar of liberty.

11 The author's attitude toward Edmund Burke
in Passage A can best be described as:

　　A. interest and wariness.

　　B. skepticism and apprehension.

　　C. amusement and sentimentality.

　　D. reverence and fascination.

12 Lines 1–16 make it clear that Edmund
Burke believed that early Greek democracies,
Byzantine emperors, and the Magna
Carta were:

　　F. the result of Enlightenment philosophy.

　　G. influential in the formation of the British
Parliamentary system.

　　H. founded on outdated political science.

　　J. the fulfillment of all preceding
governmental models.

13 In lines 42–57, the author quotes Burke's
speech to Parliament primarily to emphasize
the fact that:

　　A. Burke still believed Parliament was an
inherently good institution.

　　B. Parliament had ignored Burke's previous
appeals.

　　C. the American colonies would find another
nation to govern them if Parliament pulled
away its support.

　　D. Parliament was too entangled in the slave
trade to maintain relations with America.

14 Passage A states that Edmund Burke's first
effort to change British treatment of the
American colonies was:

　　F. ineffective.

　　G. too emotional.

　　H. belated.

　　J. incoherent.

15 Passage B states that Thomas Paine made
some effort to defend:

　　A. King George III.

　　B. King Louis XVI.

　　C. Greek democracy.

　　D. the English throne.

16 One of the main purposes of lines 105–109 is
to show that:

　　F. Paine experienced a change of heart after
his persecution in France.

　　G. the French Revolution preserved safety
and stability.

　　H. liberty can only be achieved when
individual safety is upheld.

　　J. Paine did not allow negative personal
experiences to change his convictions.

17 As it is used in lines 92–97, the word *accord* most nearly means:

    A. proportion.

    B. acknowledgment.

    C. agreement.

    D. length of rope.

18 The author of Passage B most strongly implies that Thomas Paine was:

    F. uneducated.

    G. stubborn.

    H. timid.

    J. compliant.

19 Both Passage A and Passage B highlight the importance of which of the following in shaping attitudes toward the American and French Revolutions?

    A. Byzantine emperors

    B. The Enlightenment

    C. The British Parliament

    D. King Louis XVI

20 Based on the description of Edmund Burke in Passage A and Thomas Paine in Passage B, which of the following statements best summarizes the differences between these men?

    F. Burke had faith in existing government structures, while Paine believed that all good government systems had already died out.

    G. Burke expected the American Revolution to fail, while Paine was confident that it would succeed.

    H. Burke understood his government to be without fault, while Paine was skeptical about the idea of a perfect government.

    J. Burke believed that good governments give equal attention to liberty and order, while Paine believed that liberty was most important.

PASSAGE III

Humanities

1 In the Northern Sagas*, as in the heroic cycle of ancient Greece, a man's life is not fully ended till he has been laid in the ground, and the accident of death has been followed by the

5 sacred offices of burial.

That reluctance to end the story, to part with its hero until the funeral pyre was out and the last valediction over, was an attitude of mind which William Morris himself specifically loved;

10 and if we may believe that any sense of the last rites performed over them may touch the dead, [Morris] might find a last satisfaction in the simple and impressive ceremony of his funeral.

He was buried in the little churchyard of

15 Kelmscott on the 6th of October. "I have no hesitation," his family doctor writes to me, "in saying that he died a victim to his enthusiasm. I consider the case is this: the disease is simply being William Morris, and having done more

20 work than ten men."

The night had been wet, and morning lightened dully over soaking meadows, fading away in a blur of mist. As the day went on, the wind and rain both increased, and rose in the

25 afternoon to a tempest. The storm, which aged with great violence over the whole country, with furious south-westerly gales, reached its greatest force in the upper Thames valley. The low-lying lands were flooded, and all the little streams

30 that are fed by the Cotswolds ran full and deep brown. The voice of waters was everywhere. Clumps of daisies were in flower in the drenched cottage gardens, and the thinning willows had turned, not to the brilliance of their common

35 October coloring, but to a dull tarnished gold.

There was no pomp of organized mourning, and the ceremony was of the shortest and simplest. Among associates and followers of later years were the few survivors of that

40 remarkable fellowship which had founded the Oxford Brotherhood and the Firm of Red Lion Square; and at the head of the grave Sir Edward

Burne-Jones, the closest friend of all, stood and saw a great part of his own life lowered
45 into the earth. "What I should do, or how I should get on without him," he had once said when Morris's increasing weakness became alarming, "I don't in the least know. I should be like a man who has lost his back."

50 A great personality had ceased: yet the stronger feeling in the minds of the survivors was that it had returned to, rather than, in the customary usage, passed away from earth. Among the men and women through whom
55 he had so often moved as in a dream, isolated, self-centered, almost empty of love or hatred, he moved no more. It seemed natural that he should go out from among them, not really being of them.

60 "He doesn't want anybody," so his most intimate friend once said of him: "I suppose he would miss me for a bit, but it wouldn't change one day of his life, nor alter a plan in it. He lives absolutely without need of man or
65 woman. He is really a sort of Viking, set down here, and making art because there is nothing else to do." Far less easy to realize was his absence henceforward from the surroundings in which and through which he lived almost
70 as in a bodily vesture: from his books and manuscripts, from his [fabric-dyeing] vats and [weaving] looms, from the grey gabled house and the familiar fields, from the living earth which he loved with so continuous and
75 absorbing a passion.

"It came to pass," says the ancient forgotten author of the *Volsunga Saga*, when he tells of the death of the father of King Volsung, "that he fell sick and got his death, being minded
80 to go home to Odin, a thing much desired of many folk in those days." With no such desire had this last inheritor of the Viking spirit approached his end. To be, "though men call you dead, a part and parcel of the living
85 wisdom of all things," still to live somewhere in the larger life of this and no other world, such had been his desire, such his faith and

hope throughout the loneliness and fixedness in
90 which he had passed his mortal days. He might seem, now that the entanglement of life was snapped, to have resumed his place among the lucid ranks that, still sojourning yet still moving onward, enter their appointed rest and their
95 native country unannounced, as lords that are certainly expected, and yet there is a silent joy at their arrival.

*Northern Sagas are epic poems from the 12th–14th centuries written in Iceland, which describe the first settlers of Iceland in heroic fashion.

Adapted from John William Mackail, *The Life of William Morris*, Vol. II (New York, NY; Haskell House, 1970), Google Books, accessed April 13, 2018, https://books.google.ca/books?id=IhXdlf8yPy8C.

21 What is the most likely meaning of the word *mortal* as it is used in line 89 of the final paragraph?

- A. able to die
- B. living
- C. virtuous
- D. short-lived

22 Which of the following sentences best describes the main idea of the passage?

- F. William Morris's death came as a surprise to his friends and family.
- G. The funeral of William Morris was a lengthy, rainy ceremony.
- H. Even when William Morris died, there remained a sense that his work would live on in this world.
- J. William Morris maintained his beliefs in Viking religion to his deathbed.

23 In the third paragraph ("He was buried … than ten men."), the author probably includes the quotation from the doctor in order to:

A. convey a sense of the despair that surrounded William Morris's death.

B. tell the reader how much William Morris accomplished in his life.

C. indicate that the doctor had not done his best work to help heal William Morris.

D. suggest that William Morris despised his life.

24 According to the passage, who was William Morris's closest friend in life?

F. The author of the passage

G. Burne-Jones

H. Kelmscott

J. The Oxford Brotherhood

25 The funeral described in the fifth paragraph ("There was no … lost his back.") could best be characterized as:

A. solemn and plain.

B. well-attended and extravagant.

C. quiet and lengthy.

D. elaborate and sorrowful.

26 Where was William Morris buried?

F. Oxford

G. Kelmscott

H. Volsunga

J. Cotswolds

27 The author's tone in this passage could best be described as:

A. disapproving.

B. morbid.

C. admiring.

D. joyful.

28 The author suggests that the absence of William Morris will be noticeable in all of the following places, EXCEPT:

F. his library of books and manuscripts.

G. the places he created fabric.

H. his home and surrounding land.

J. the Kelmscott churchyard.

29 According to the first paragraph ("In the Northern … offices of burial."), the ancient epics presented the death of a hero as complete only when:

A. his heart stopped beating.

B. songs have been written about him.

C. his funeral was complete.

D. his children reached adulthood.

30 From clues in the passage, we can infer that William Morris was:

F. friendly but shy.

G. artistic but lazy.

H. outgoing but temperamental.

J. solitary but brilliant.

Science

1 After the discovery of Neptune in 1846, eager astronomers combed the solar system for signs of another planet that might lie beyond this gas giant. They had good reason to believe one
5 might exist: Neptune's discovery had directly resulted from French mathematician Urbain Le Verrier's hypothesis that perturbations in the orbit of Uranus were caused by the gravitational pull of a yet-undiscovered planet.
10 Le Verrier predicted the position of this new planet and sent his calculations to German astronomer Johann Gottfried Galle. With these coordinates, Galle discovered Neptune the very next day—exactly where Le Verrier
15 had predicted. But there remained some discrepancies in the gas giants' orbits even with the discovery of the blue planet, so the hunt for yet another distant planet in the solar system forged onward.

20 Percival Lowell, an early 20th-century astronomer, exhibited a particular obsession with this search for a ninth planet. Lowell christened this hypothetical new planet "Planet X," and, in his 1915 *Memoir on a Trans-*
25 *Neptunian Planet*, concluded that Planet X must have a mass roughly seven times that of Earth—about half that of Neptune—and a mean distance from the Sun of 43 AU.* When Lowell died suddenly in 1916, his observatory, led by
30 the efforts of his widow, persisted in the search for the elusive Planet X.

Fourteen years later, an ambitious budding astronomer from a Kansas farming family made the first major discovery in the search
35 for Planet X. In 1929, 23-year-old Clyde Tombaugh arrived at the Lowell Observatory and was given the task of systematically imaging the night sky. Tombaugh captured sections of the sky in pairs of images
40 taken two weeks apart. He then placed the paired images into a machine called a blink comparator, a microscope that superimposes two photographic plates, "blinking" rapidly between them and creating a time-lapse
45 illusion of the movement of any planetary body. In February 1930, after searching for almost a year and examining nearly two million stars, Tombaugh discovered a moving object on photographic plates taken in the
50 previous month. The object lay just six degrees from one of the two locations for Planet X that Lowell had suggested, and it seemed as though, at long last, Lowell had been vindicated.

This supposed new planet was named
55 Pluto, in part to honor Percival Lowell, as his initials make up the first two letters of the word. However, it did not take long before astronomers began debating Pluto's status as a planet. Observations showed that Pluto was
60 six times dimmer than Lowell had predicted. It also had a far more elliptical orbit than any other planet in the solar system. In 1978, Pluto was found to be too small for its gravity to affect the gas giants, a discovery
65 that resulted in a search for a 10th planet, which was eventually abandoned in the early 1990s when the Voyager 2 spacecraft found that irregularities in Uranus's orbit were actually due to a slight overestimation of Neptune's mass.

70 In 1992, the discovery of numerous small, icy objects similar in size and orbit to Pluto led to a more vocal debate over whether it should remain a planet or whether Pluto and its asteroid neighbors should be given
75 their own separate classification. In 2006, the International Astronomical Union ultimately reclassified Pluto and its friends as "dwarf planets," leaving the solar system, once again, with only eight planets. It is not likely that
80 Pluto will ever be called an official planet again, either. Mike Brown, who discovered Eris, a dwarf planet larger than Pluto, in 2005, speculates that there are likely thousands of other "rocks" like Pluto orbiting in the Kuiper
85 belt outside of Neptune.

Today, the astronomical community is largely in agreement that Planet X as it was

GO >

originally conceived does not exist, but Planet X as a concept has been revived by a number

90 of astronomers to explain other anomalies observed in the outer solar system. In popular culture, Planet X has become a stand-in term for any undiscovered planet in the solar system, regardless of whether or not it fits into Lowell's

95 original theory. Thus, real or not, Planet X remains a fixture in the astronomical universe.

An AU (astronomical unit) is roughly the distance from the Earth to the Sun.

31 The main purpose of the passage is to:

   A. describe how the gas giant Neptune and the dwarf planet Pluto were discovered and how they were classified.

   B. explain how Pluto's discovery resulted from the search for Planet X and how new findings about Pluto affected understandings of Planet X.

   C. analyze the opposing arguments in the debate over Pluto's status as a planet.

   D. interpret the meaning of Planet X from the perspective of 20th-century astronomers, modern-day astronomers, and popular culture references.

32 As it is used in lines 1–4, the word *combed* most nearly means:

   F. brushed.

   G. searched.

   H. smoothed.

   J. rolled over.

33 The "blue planet" referred to in lines 15–18 is intended to be:

   A. Pluto.

   B. Neptune.

   C. Uranus.

   D. Earth.

34 The passage devotes the LEAST attention to which of the following topics?

   F. Clyde Tombaugh's work at the Lowell Observatory

   G. The size and orbit of Pluto

   H. The process of Neptune's discovery

   J. Lowell's book, *Memoir on a Trans-Neptunian Planet*

35 Which of the following developments does the passage indicate occurred first chronologically?

   A. Clyde Tombaugh's discovery of Pluto

   B. Le Verrier's and Galle's discovery of Neptune

   C. The discovery of Uranus

   D. Percival Lowell's establishment of his Lowell Observatory

36 The author most likely chooses to describe Tombaugh as coming "from a Kansas farming family" in order to:

   F. imply that we might be surprised someone of Tombaugh's background discovered Pluto.

   G. emphasize the significance of Pluto's discovery by a Kansas-based observatory.

   H. foreshadow the eventual demotion of Pluto from a planet to a dwarf planet.

   J. indicate Tombaugh's close relationship with Lowell's family.

37 Within the passage, descriptions of findings concerning the size, brightness, and orbit of Pluto in lines 59–64 serve mainly to:

   A. support the idea that Lowell was correct in his assumptions about Planet X.

   B. discredit the original observations of Clyde Tombaugh when he discovered Pluto.

   C. provide evidence that casts doubt on Pluto's status as a planet.

   D. indicate the need for Voyager 2's mission to explore the outer solar system.

38 It can be inferred that Mike Brown's discovery of Eris was particularly damaging to Pluto's status as a planet because Eris was found to be:

   F. larger than Pluto.

   G. denser than Pluto.

   H. close enough to Neptune to have an effect on Neptune's orbit.

   J. a dwarf planet, unlike Pluto.

39 It can be inferred that the "friends" of Pluto referred to in line 77 are:

   A. supporters of Pluto's status as a planet.

   B. other orbiting objects that are similar to Pluto.

   C. the other eight planets in the solar system.

   D. astronomers and researchers at the Lowell Observatory.

40 The passage indicates that the most important difference between Planet X as it was conceived of by Lowell and Planet X as it is conceived of today is that:

   F. Planet X according to Lowell was Pluto and Planet X as it is used today is Eris.

   G. Planet X according to Lowell had a significant effect on Neptune's orbit and Planet X as it is used today does not.

   H. Planet X according to Lowell was a hypothetical entity and Planet X as it is used today refers to a concrete planetary body.

   J. Planet X according to Lowell had a specific location and specific characteristics and Planet X as it is used today is a substitute term for any undiscovered planet in the outer solar system.

ACT Science Test

35 Minutes | 40 Questions

Each of the seven passages in this test is accompanied by several questions. Read the passage, and then choose the best answer to each question. Note your answer on your answer sheet. You may return to the passages as often as you need. You may NOT use a calculator on this test.

PASSAGE I

Malaria is an infectious disease that kills more than 600,000 people every year. Several species of the genus *Plasmodium* cause malaria, with two of the most common being *Plasmodium falciparum* and *Plasmodium vivax*. Though both species cause a very similar illness, *P. falciparum* malaria is more likely to result in fatalities than *P. vivax* malaria, while *P. vivax* malaria is more likely to recur—to return after a period of time during which the patient is healthy and has no parasites present in the blood.

The two species of malaria parasites respond differently to antimalarial medications, but in many areas where malaria is common, testing to determine what type of malaria a patient has is not widely available. Therefore, malaria treatments are often tested against both species of the parasite, and first-line malaria treatments in these regions ideally should be effective against both parasites.

Experiment 1

For many years, public health professionals in Papua New Guinea have recommended a treatment regimen, Drug Combination A, as a first-line malaria treatment. Recently a new treatment regimen, Drug Combination B, has been proposed as a potential replacement for Combination A, and a study was conducted to compare their effectiveness.

Children entering a local health clinic with malaria symptoms were tested to determine which *Plasmodium* species they carried. The patients were then randomly assigned Drug Combination A or Drug Combination B, and their blood was tested periodically for the presence of parasites.

Figure 1 adapted from Laman, Moore, et al., "Artemisinin-Naphthoquine versus Artemether-Lumefantrine for Uncomplicated Malaria in Papua New Guinean Children: An Open-Label Randomized Trial," *PLOS Medicine* 11, no. 12 (2014), doi.org/10.1371/journal.pmed.1001773.

Figure 1

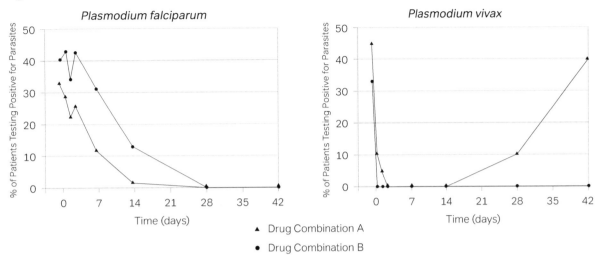

Plasmodium falciparum

Plasmodium vivax

▲ Drug Combination A
● Drug Combination B

Experiment 2

On rare occasions, patients have severe allergic reactions to a compound that is found in both Drug Combination A and Drug Combination B. In these cases, a second-line treatment must be used.
A second study was conducted to determine which of several drug combinations would be the best second-line drug to recommend for use in Papua New Guinea. Table 1 shows the treatment response to the second-line drug combinations.

Table 1

Response Measure	P. falciparum			P. vivax		
	Drug C	Drug D	Drug E	Drug C	Drug D	Drug E
% of patients free of parasites						
Day 1	0	25	90	62	87	55
Day 2	30	49	95	85	90	58
Day 7	75	51	100	99	97	76
Day 14	100	51	100	100	100	99
Day 42	100	52	100	20	100	89

1 According to Figure 1, the percentage of *P. falciparum* patients with parasites remaining in their blood on Day 14 was approximately:

   A. 1% for patients treated with Drug Combination A, and 12% for patients treated with Drug Combination B.

   B. 12% for patients treated with Drug Combination A, and 1% for patients treated with Drug Combination B.

   C. 7% for patients treated with Drug Combination A, and 14% for patients treated with Drug Combination B.

   D. 0% for both drug combinations.

2 Based on the data from Experiment 1, on which day of treatment could a patient expect to be free of parasites regardless of which species they were infected with or which drug combination they were given?

   F. Day 7

   G. Day 14

   H. Day 28

   J. There is no day that meets this criteria.

3 Recurrences of *P. vivax* malaria are known to be caused by hypnozoites, a form of the malaria parasite that can go dormant in the patient's liver for up to two weeks, and that remain alive following the initial treatment. Based on the data in Figure 1, which of the following conclusions is most likely to be true?

  A. Drug Combination A eliminates hypnozoites in all patients, but Drug Combination B eliminates hypnozoites only in some patients.

  B. Drug Combination B eliminates all hypnozoites, but Drug Combination A eliminates hypnozoites only in some patients.

  C. Drug Combination B eliminates all hypnozoites in all patients, but Drug Combination A does not eliminate any hypnozoites.

  D. Neither treatment kills hypnozoites.

4 If 1000 patients in the *P. falciparum* group were treated with Drug Combination B in Experiment 1, approximately how many of those patients remained infected on Day 7?

  F. 100

  G. 300

  H. 700

  J. 900

5 Suppose a patient is brought to the clinic with a life-threatening case of *P. falciparum* malaria. As the patient's condition is deteriorating quickly, it is essential that they be given the treatment that eliminates parasites from their blood within 7 days. Based on the data from Experiments 1 and 2, which treatment should they be given?

  A. Drug Combination A

  B. Drug Combination D

  C. Drug Combination E

  D. Drug Combination B

6 Drug treatments that are eliminated from a patient's body very quickly are likely to result in recurrence of *P. vivax* in the patient. Based on the information in the passage, which of the following drugs is likely NOT removed from the body quickly?

  F. Drug Combination A

  G. Drug Combination C

  H. Drug Combination D

  J. Drug Combination E

Gregor Mendel discovered the basic principle of independent assortment in genetics through selective cross-breeding of common pea plants (*Pisum sativum*). Table 1 lists the possible alleles of 4 of the genes Mendel discovered and the possible genotypes for each.

Table 2 lists *Pisum sativum* genotypes and the phenotype associated with each genotype.

Table 1

		Genotypes	
Gene	Alleles	Homozygous	Heterozygous
A	A, a	AA, aa	Aa
B	B, b	BB, bb	Bb
C	C, c	CC, cc	Cc
D	D, d	DD, dd	Dd

Table 2

Genotype	Phenotype			
	flower color	seed color	pod color	pod shape
AABBCCDD	purple	yellow	green	smooth
AABBCCDd	purple	yellow	green	smooth
AABBCCdd	purple	yellow	green	constricted
AABBCcDD	purple	yellow	green	smooth
AABBccDD	purple	yellow	yellow	smooth
AABbccdd	purple	yellow	yellow	constricted
AabbccDD	purple	green	yellow	smooth
AabbCCdd	purple	green	green	constricted
aabbccdd	white	green	yellow	constricted
aaBBccDD	white	yellow	yellow	smooth
aaBBCCDD	white	yellow	green	smooth
AaBcCcDd	purple	yellow	green	smooth

Table 3 lists 6 *Pisum sativum* crosses, the genotypes of each parent, and the percentage of offspring that displayed each phenotype for the traits listed in Table 2. Multiple matings of each genotype pairing were performed.

Table 3

Cross	Parent Genotype		Offspring Phenotype			
	Parent 1	Parent 2	flower color	seed color	pod color	pod shape
1	AABBCCDD	aabbccdd	100% purple	100% yellow	100% green	100% smooth
2	aaBBCcDd	aabbCcDd	100% white	100% yellow	75% green 25% yellow	75% smooth 25% constricted
3	Aabbccdd	aaBbCcDd	50% purple 50% white	50% yellow 50% green	50% green 50% yellow	50% smooth 50% constricted
4	AabbCcdd	AabbCcdd	75% purple 25% white	100% green	75% green 25% yellow	100% constricted
5	AaBbccDD	AaBbccDD	75% purple 25% white	75% yellow 25% green	100% yellow	100% smooth
6	aabbccdd	aabbccdd	100% white	100% green	100% yellow	100% constricted

7 Based on the information provided, a *P. sativum* plant that is heterozygous for each of the 4 genes will have which of the following phenotypes?

  A. White flowers, green seeds, yellow pods, smooth pods

  B. White flowers, green seeds, yellow pods, constricted pods

  C. Purple flowers, yellow seeds, green pods, smooth pods

  D. Purple flowers, yellow seeds, green pods, constricted pods

8 Based on the information provided in Table 3, $\frac{3}{4}$ of the offspring in which of the following crosses produced phenotypes expressing purple flowers and green pods?

  F. *AABBCCDD × aabbccdd*

  G. *aaBBCcDd × aabbCcDd*

  H. *AabbCcdd × AabbCcdd*

  J. *AaBbccDD × AaBbccDD*

9 Based on the information in Table 3, if Cross 5 produced 100 offspring, approximately how many would be expected to have white flowers?

  A. 25

  B. 50

  C. 75

  D. 100

10 Based on the information provided, all of the offspring of Cross 6 produced constricted pods because each received:

  F. allele *a* from Parent 1 and allele *a* from Parent 2.

  G. allele *B* from Parent 1 and allele *b* from Parent 2.

  H. allele *c* from Parent 1 and allele *C* from Parent 2.

  J. allele *d* from Parent 1 and allele *d* from Parent 2.

11 According to the information in Table 3, which of the following pairs of parental genotypes would produce offspring in which 50% presented yellow pea pods and 50% presented green pea pods?

  A. Parent 1: *CC*   Parent 2: *CC*

  B. Parent 1: *Cc*   Parent 2: *Cc*

  C. Parent 1: *Cc*   Parent 2: *cc*

  D. Parent 1: *cc*   Parent 2: *cc*

Sea turtles are often incidentally captured in commercial fishing operations in the Atlantic Ocean. The National Marine Fisheries Service (NMFS) records and reports incidents of sea turtle capture. The figures below show the seasonal distribution and relative abundance of leatherback (*Dermochelys coriacea*) and loggerhead (*Caretta caretta*) sea turtles caught by the US Atlantic longline fleet from 1992 through 1995.

Figure 1 shows a map of fishing areas in the Atlantic Ocean. Table 1 shows leatherback (Lb) and loggerhead (Lh) turtle captures by month in some areas shown in Figure 1. Table 2 shows captures by area. Table 3 shows CPUE (catch-per-unit-effort) values for the number of turtles caught per 1000 hooks fished, as well as whether longline fishing vessels were using chemical light sticks to attract fish at the time of capture.

Figure 1

1 – Caribbean
2 – Gulf of Mexico
3 – Forida east coast
4 – South Atlantic bight
5 – Mid-Atlantic bight
6 – North east coastal
7 – North east distant
8 – North equatorial
9 – Mid-Atantic Ocean

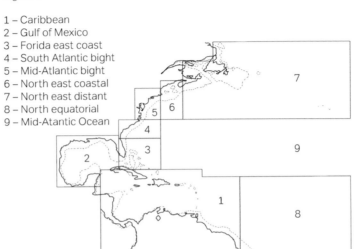

Table 1

	Area 1		Area 2		Area 3		Area 6		Area 7	
	Lb	Lh	Lb	Lh	Lb	Lh	Lb	Lh	Lb	Lh
Jan	16	12	4	6	4	2	0	0	0	0
Feb	17	7	12	1	2	3	0	0	0	0
Mar	13	24	8	4	6	2	0	0	0	0
Apr	4	4	7	3	2	1	2	1	0	0
May	5	1	1	4	1	1	5	3	0	0
Jun	1	1	3	9	2	1	35	49	40	39
Jul	2	0	10	5	0	0	48	62	170	233
Aug	3	0	10	7	1	0	48	14	152	212
Sep	0	1	0	1	1	1	30	4	167	310
Oct	1	1	2	5	1	1	12	6	56	123
Nov	3	1	3	2	0	0	0	4	8	19
Dec	4	4	3	1	3	3	0	0	0	0
Total	69	56	73	48	23	13	180	143	593	936

Leatherback (Lb) and loggerhead (Lh) turtle captures by the US pelagic longline fleet, by NMFS fishing area, by month, for 1992–95.

Table 2

	1992		1993		1994		1995	
Area	Lb	Lh	Lb	Lh	Lb	Lh	Lb	Lh
1	19	12	17	6	8	11	25	27
2	20	9	25	8	12	6	16	25
3	3	2	6	4	11	3	3	4
4	10	2	3	6	7	5	10	7
5	147	30	68	13	29	32	18	33
6	81	26	54	51	19	19	26	47
7	84	59	67	33	105	278	337	566
8	0	0	0	1	3	0	16	3
9	5	0	5	5	4	2	1	2
Total	369	140	245	127	198	356	452	714

Leatherback (Lb) and loggerhead (Lh) turtle captures by the US pelagic longline fleet, by NMFS fishing area, by year.

Table 3

Area	Lights	Lb Captures	Lh Captures	Lb CPUE	Lh CPUE
1	Y	66	54	0.0637	0.0521
1	N	3	2	0.0295	0.0197
2	Y	38	37	0.0147	0.0143
2	N	35	11	0.0112	0.0035
3	Y	23	13	0.0166	0.0094
3	N	0	0	0.0000	0.0000
7	Y	591	932	0.2832	0.4466
7	N	2	4	0.0362	0.0724
9	Y	15	9	0.0302	0.0181
9	N	0	0	0.0000	0.0000

Leatherback (Lb) and loggerhead (Lh) turtle incidental CPUE from 1992–95 logbooks, by area, with (Y) and without (N) chemical lightsticks. CPUE is turtle capture per 1000 hooks fished.

Tables and figures adapted from Wayne N. Witzell, "Distribution and Relative Abundance of Sea Turtles Caught Incidentally by the US Pelagic Longline Fleet in the Western North Atlantic Ocean," *Fishery Bulletin* 97, no. 1 (1999): 200–11, https://www.sefsc.noaa.gov//turtles/PR_Witzell_1999_FBull.pdf. ©1999 by the Southeast Fisheries Science Center.

12 According to the information provided in Figure 1 and Table 1, which of the following areas accounted for the greatest number of loggerhead sea turtles incidentally caught during the period studied?

   F. Caribbean

   G. Northeast coastal

   H. Northeast distant

   J. Florida east coast

13 According to Table 2, during which year was the number of loggerhead turtles caught greater than the number of leatherback turtles in Area 6?

   A. 1992

   B. 1993

   C. 1994

   D. 1995

14 According to Table 1, during which of the following months was the greatest number of sea turtles captured during the period studied?

   F. March

   G. July

   H. November

   J. December

15 Vessels fishing for swordfish generally work at night using chemical lightsticks to attract baitfish while vessels fishing for tuna generally fish during the day without lightsticks. Does the data presented in Table 3 for Areas 1–9 support the conclusion that fishing for swordfish is more harmful to endangered sea turtle populations than fishing for tuna?

   A. Yes, because Lb and Lh CPUE values were higher when lightsticks were used.

   B. Yes, because Lb and Lh CPUE values were lower when lightsticks were used.

   C. No, because Lb and Lh CPUE values were higher when lightsticks were used.

   D. No, because Lb and Lh CPUE values were lower when lightsticks were used.

16 Sea turtles migrate to different oceanic regions over the course of the year, and higher sea turtle capture numbers indicate a higher population of sea turtles in a given region. Which of the following observations about sea turtle migration is supported by Table 1? Some sea turtle populations:

   F. reside in Area 2 during January, February, and March and migrate to Area 3 during June, July, August, and September.

   G. reside in Area 7 during June, July, August, and September and migrate to Area 1 during January, February, and March.

   H. reside in Area 3 during June, July, August, and September and migrate to Area 6 during January, February, and March.

   J. reside in Area 1 during June, July, August, and September and migrate to Area 7 during January, February, and March.

PASSAGE IV

Ethylene glycol, a popular industrial chemical used in the manufacture of polyester fibers and in industrial applications like antifreeze, has the structure shown below:

$$HO-\underset{\underset{H}{|}}{\overset{\overset{H}{|}}{C}}-\underset{\underset{H}{|}}{\overset{\overset{H}{|}}{C}}-OH$$

Figures 1–3 each show how a property of solutions of ethylene glycol in H_2O varies as the concentration of ethylene glycol increases at 1 atmosphere (atm) of pressure. Concentration is given as the percent ethylene glycol by mass in H_2O. Figure 1 shows how the freezing point varies with % ethylene glycol. Figure 2 shows how the boiling point varies with % ethylene glycol. The surface tension is the property of the surface of a liquid that allows it to resist an external force due to the cohesive forces between molecules in the liquid. Figure 3 shows how surface tension varies with % ethylene glycol at 25°C.

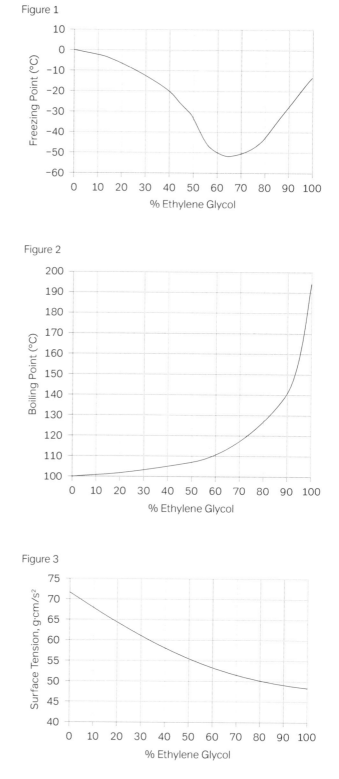

Figure 1

Figure 2

Figure 3

Tables and figures adapted from MEGlobal, *Ethylene Glycol Product Guide*, www.meglobal.biz/media/product_guides /MEGlobal_MEG.pdf. ©2008 MEGlobal.

17 According to Figure 1, at 1 atm, which of the following solutions has a freezing point furthest from the freezing point of pure H_2O?

   A. 15% ethylene glycol

   B. 40% ethylene glycol

   C. 65% ethylene glycol

   D. 90% ethylene glycol

18 At 25°C and 1 atm, as % ethylene glycol increases from 0% to 100%, the cohesive forces between molecules in aqueous ethylene glycol solutions:

   F. increase only.

   G. decrease only.

   H. increase then decrease.

   J. decrease then increase.

19 According to Figure 1, at 1 atm, the melting point of pure 100% ethylene glycol is closest to which of the following?

   A. 0°C

   B. −13°C

   C. −33°C

   D. −52°C

20 According to Figures 2 and 3, at 1 atm, an aqueous solution of ethylene glycol that has a boiling point of 130°C will have a surface tension closest to which of the following at 25°C?

   F. 50 g·cm/s²

   G. 53 g·cm/s²

   H. 60 g·cm/s²

   J. 63 g·cm/s²

21 Based on Figure 1, at 1 atm, how many gallons of pure H_2O would need to be added to 4 gallons of pure ethylene glycol to produce an antifreeze solution with a freezing point of −20°C ?

   A. 1 gallon

   B. 2 gallons

   C. 5 gallons

   D. 6 gallons

PASSAGE V

Electricity can be defined as the movement of electrons. Three of the most important concepts to understand in order to manipulate electricity to perform work are voltage, current, and resistance.

Voltage (measured in volts (V)) describes the amount of potential energy between two points on a circuit and is created by a difference in charge between those two points.

Current (measured in amperes (A)) is the rate at which electrons flow through a circuit. A rate of one ampere is equivalent to 1 coulomb (a standard unit of charge) per second.

Resistance (measured in ohms (Ω)) is a measurement of how much a material resists the passage of current through the material. Materials with high resistance are referred to as insulators, while materials with low resistance are referred to as conductors.

Students in a physics course conducted several experiments to investigate the relationship between these three electrical properties.

Experiment 1
Students were provided with a variety of batteries, resistors (electrical components that resist the flow of current), and an ammeter (a device to measure current flow), along with wire and connectors. The students constructed circuits based on the circuit diagram below and measured the current in each circuit. Table 1 shows their results.

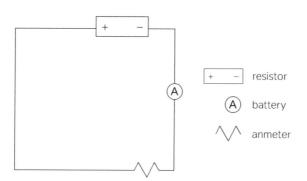

Table 1

Trial #	Battery Voltage (V)	Resistance (Ω)	Current (A)
1	6	3	2.000
2	9	3	3.000
3	12	3	4.000
4	6	6	1.000
5	9	6	1.500
6	12	6	2.000
7	6	9	0.667
8	9	9	1.000
9	12	9	1.333

Experiment 2
To further study the property of resistance, students replaced the resistor in their circuit with coils of nickel wire of various lengths. Students used a variable power supply to adjust voltage until the current was equal to 1 A. They then used the relationship between voltage, current, and resistance determined in Experiment 1 to calculate the resistance of the wire coil. Their results are graphed in Figure 2.

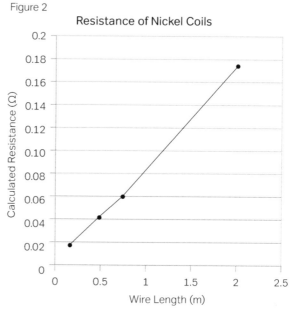

Figure 2

Resistance of Nickel Coils

Experiment 3

Students repeated the procedure from Experiment 2 using 1-meter wire coils of a variety of other metals. Their results are given in Table 2.

Table 2

Material	Calculated Resistance (Ω)
Copper	0.0214
Tungsten	0.0672
Aluminum	0.0338

22 Based on the data in Experiment 1, which of the following best describes the relationship between current, voltage, and resistance? Current:

    F. increases with an increase in voltage (V) and increases with an increase in resistance (Ω).

    G. increases with an increase in voltage (V) and decreases with an increase in resistance (Ω).

    H. decreases with an increase in voltage (V) and increases with an increase in resistance (Ω).

    J. decreases with an increase in voltage (V) and decreases with an increase in resistance (Ω).

23 In an additional experiment, the students set up a circuit similar to the one in Experiment 1, except that they used a 2V battery and a 5Ω resistor, and discovered that the current measured in this circuit is 0.400 A. What current should the students expect to measure in this same circuit if they doubled both the voltage and the resistance?

    A. 0.100 A

    B. 0.400 A

    C. 0.800 A

    D. 1.600 A

24 Silver is a slightly better conductor than copper. Considering the data from Experiment 3, which of the following could be the resistance of a 1-meter silver coil?

    F. 0.0202

    G. 0.0281

    H. 0.0414

    J. 0.0702

25 What would you expect to happen to the current in the circuit if the 2-meter nickel coil from Experiment 2 was used to replace the resistor in the Trial 1 circuit in Experiment 1?

    A. Current would decrease, because resistance in the circuit would increase.

    B. Current would decrease, because resistance in the circuit would decrease.

    C. Current would increase, because resistance in the circuit would decrease.

    D. Current would increase, because resistance in the circuit would increase.

26 The resistance of a length of wire is dependent on the material's conductivity: materials with high conductivities provide less resistance than materials with low conductivity. Based on the data in Experiments 2 and 3, which of the following lists metals in increasing order of conductivity?

    F. Copper, aluminum, tungsten, nickel

    G. Tungsten, nickel, aluminum, copper

    H. Copper, aluminum, nickel, tungsten

    J. Nickel, tungsten, aluminum, copper

27 Experiments 1–3 were completed in a classroom at 20°C. During the previous school year, the air conditioning was broken, so the same lab was completed at 28°C. It is known that conductivity of metals decreases as temperature increases. How would the higher classroom temperature have affected the voltage required to reach 1 A in Experiment 2?

   A. The same amount of voltage would be required.

   B. More voltage would be required.

   C. Less voltage would be required.

   D. It is impossible to determine from the information provided.

PASSAGE VI

Scientists concerned about significant long-term effects of global warming discuss a geoengineering proposal to cool the planet.

Scientist 1

Solar radiation management (SRM) could reverse global warming by seeding the stratosphere with sulfuric aerosols (SO_4), recreating past periods of global cooling caused by volcanic activity. Naturally reflective sulfate aerosols resulting from this seeding would be dispersed by atmospheric winds, forming a layer of fine particles that would reflect about 1% of sunlight back into space. On the basis of computer models, scientists have predicted that SRM would reduce the amount of sunlight entering earth's atmosphere, thereby reducing global average temperatures.

Atmospheric CO_2 levels were around 275 parts per million (ppm) prior to the Industrial Revolution. A level of 350 ppm is the critical threshold beyond which significant global warming occurs; current levels are around 400 ppm. Since CO_2 remains in the atmosphere for a very long time, even eliminating all CO_2 emissions immediately would leave global temperatures elevated far into the future. Reducing CO_2 emissions alone is not enough to preserve our climate; further action is needed. Preliminary research suggests SRM may be a way to stop or even reverse global warming.

Scientist 2

More research needs to be conducted before seriously discussing the injection of sulfate aerosols into the stratosphere. It will do nothing to affect CO_2 levels, and unintended consequences of SRM are so severe that it should not be considered as a possible "solution" to global warming. There is no way to experimentally predict the consequences of manipulating the atmosphere on a worldwide scale, as climate patterns simply cannot be isolated and manipulated on a local scale.

Injecting sulfate particles into the

stratosphere would increase acid rain and have a drastic impact on Earth's protective ozone layer. One study concluded that artificial injections of sulfates could destroy between one-fourth and three-fourths of the ozone layer above the Arctic.

This could affect a large part of the Northern Hemisphere because of atmospheric circulation patterns. The sulfates would also delay the expected recovery of the ozone hole over the Antarctic by about 30 to 70 years, or until at least the last decade of the century. A healthy ozone layer is critical for life on Earth because it blocks dangerous ultraviolet radiation from the sun.

Adapted from David Rotman, "A Cheap and Easy Plan to Stop Global Warming," *MIT Technology Review*, February 8, 2013, www.technologyreview.com/s/511016/a-cheap-and-easy-plan-to-stop-global-warming and National Science Foundation, "Injecting Sulfate Particles into Stratosphere Could Have Drastic Impact on Earth's Ozone Layer," news release, April 24, 2008, www.nsf.gov/news/news_summ.jsp?cntn_id=111467.

28 Which of the following statements best explains why Scientist 1 mentioned sulfuric aerosols?

   F. Seeding the atmosphere with sulfuric aerosols could increase global warming.

   G. Seeding the atmosphere with sulfuric aerosols could decrease global warming.

   H. Sulfuric aerosols help replenish ozone in the atmosphere.

   J. Sulfuric aerosols help replenish CO_2 in the atmosphere.

29 Scientist 1 would most likely state that the elevated atmospheric levels of CO_2 that are present in the atmosphere today were caused by:

   A. a prolonged period of global volcanic activity.

   B. injection of sulfate particles into the stratosphere.

   C. unintended consequences of solar radiation management.

   D. carbon dioxide emissions from industrial activity.

30 Scientist 2 would most likely agree with which of the following statements?

   F. Solar radiation management could cause atmospheric CO_2 levels to increase.

   G. Sulfuric aerosols from SRM would affect only the Northern Hemisphere.

   H. Between one-fourth and three-fourths of the ozone layer lies over the Arctic.

   J. Ozone levels are expected to rise over the course of the coming century.

31 Both scientists would likely agree that which of the following would NOT be affected if a large-scale solar radiation management program were implemented?

   A. The amount of radiation reaching the atmosphere

   B. The amount of ultraviolet radiation reaching earth's surface

   C. Global temperature levels

   D. The composition of the ozone layer

32 Both scientists would most likely agree that the distribution of fine particles throughout the upper atmosphere is largely maintained by:

   F. high levels of CO_2 in the air.

   G. global cooling caused by volcanic activity.

   H. circulation caused by wind.

   J. injection of sulfate aerosols into the stratosphere.

33 Scientists provided historical data of sulfuric aerosol concentrations near active volcanoes to a computer programmed to model global climate change. The model failed to accurately predict any long-term trends in global climate activity. Based on the information provided, if this information were true, it would most likely weaken the viewpoints of:

   A. Scientist 1 only.

   B. Scientist 2 only.

   C. both Scientist 1 and Scientist 2.

   D. neither Scientist 1 nor Scientist 2.

34 Scientist 2's objections to solar radiation management include all of the following EXCEPT:

F. it would destroy significant amounts of the ozone layer.

G. it would be difficult or impossible to thoroughly test before implementing.

H. it would adversely affect global atmospheric circulation patterns.

J. it would increase the amount of harmful radiation reaching earth's surface.

PASSAGE VII

One of the most common ways bacteria are grown in a lab is called batch culture. In batch culture, bacteria are added to a fixed amount of liquid growth media, a solution that contains nutrients for bacterial growth and allowed to grow under defined environmental conditions.

Bacterial growth in batch culture follows a predictable pattern of four phases:

1. **Lag phase:** Immediately after they are added to a new media, bacteria must adjust their metabolism to the new environment before they begin growing and dividing. The number of bacteria in the culture does not change during this phase.

2. **Log phase:** Bacteria actively grow and divide, and the number of bacteria in the culture grows exponentially.

3. **Stationary phase:** When an essential nutrient in the media is depleted, growth slows substantially, such that growth rate in the culture becomes equal to death rate. The number of bacteria in the culture is unchanged.

4. **Death phase:** When culture conditions can no longer sustain any growth, bacteria die off exponentially.

Phases 2–4 will happen in every batch culture, given enough time. However, it is possible for no lag phase to be observed if little or no adjustment of metabolism is needed for the bacteria to begin reproducing in their new environment.

The following experiments were conducted to investigate the variables that affect bacterial growth in batch culture.

GO >

Experiment 1

A batch culture of *E. coli*, a common bacterial species used for lab studies, was grown in a nutrient-rich media called LB. When this culture reached log phase, 0.5 ml samples of the liquid media was removed and used to inoculate each of two 1L flasks. Each of these flasks contained a different type of liquid growth media. The new cultures were then allowed to grow at 37℃.

Growth of the cultures was monitored by taking periodic measurements of the optical density, or OD_{600}, of the growth media. Optical density is a measurement of how easily light is able to pass through the media, and it is directly related to the concentration of living bacteria in the media. The resulting measurements are graphed in Figure 1.

Figure 1

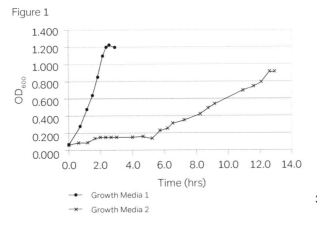

— Growth Media 1
—✕— Growth Media 2

Experiment 2

Eight 1L flasks of minimal growth media were inoculated with bacteria: four with *E. coli*, and four with *P. aeruginosa*. The flasks were then incubated at 37℃ under one of two conditions—either with or without oxygen—and OD_{600} measurements were taken every hour to monitor growth.

After OD_{600} measurements stopped rising, the bacteria was separated from the media and weighed. These measurements were used to calculate growth yield, or the percentage of carbon source(s) in the growth media that was converted to biological material. Growth yield can be used to determine how efficiently the bacteria are able to use energy during a given set of growth conditions. The results of these calculations are shown in Table 1.

Table 1

Species	Condition	Food Source	Growth Yield (%)
P. aeruginosa	with oxygen	glucose	25.2
P. aeruginosa	with oxygen	pyruvate	39.1
P. aeruginosa	without oxygen	glucose	0
P. aeruginosa	without oxygen	pyruvate	0
E. coli	with oxygen	glucose	37.7
E. coli	with oxygen	pyruvate	45.2
E. coli	without oxygen	glucose	12.6
E. coli	without oxygen	pyruvate	12.0

35 Which of the following is true of the relationship between OD_{600} values and bacterial growth?

   A. OD_{600} levels may increase, decrease, or remain stable during stationary phase.
   B. OD_{600} levels always increase when culture is in stationary phase.
   C. OD_{600} levels always stay stable when culture is in stationary phase.
   D. OD_{600} levels always decrease when culture is in stationary phase.

36 Three hours after the media in Experiment 1 was inoculated, which stage was each culture in?

   F. Medium 1: log phase;
      Medium 2: stationary phase
   G. Medium 1: stationary phase;
      Medium 2: log phase
   H. Medium 1: stationary phase;
      Medium 2: lag phase
   J. Medium 1: lag phase;
      Medium 2: stationary phase

37 Growth media can be minimal or nutrient rich. Minimal media contains only the bare minimum necessary to support growth. Nutrient-rich growth media contains a wide variety of compounds used in growth, such as amino acids and vitamins. Of the two types of media tested in Experiment 1, which is more likely to be a minimal media?

   A. Growth Media 2 because the long lag phase suggests the bacteria needed to turn on new metabolic pathways before they could begin dividing.

   B. Growth Media 2 because bacteria divide more quickly in minimal media.

   C. Growth Media 1 because the long lag phase suggests the bacteria needed to turn on new metabolic pathways before they could begin dividing.

   D. Growth Media 1 because bacteria divide more quickly in minimal media.

38 Bacteria that require oxygen for growth are called obligate aerobes, while bacteria that cannot grow in the presence of oxygen are called obligate anaerobes. Facultative aerobes can grow with or without oxygen, though they may grow better in one condition than in the other. Considering the data in Table 1, which of the following is most likely to be true?

   F. *P. aeruginosa* is an obligate anaerobe, while *E. coli* is an obligate aerobe.

   G. *P. aeruginosa* is an obligate anaerobe, while *E. coli* is a facultative aerobe.

   H. *P. aeruginosa* is an obligate aerobe, while *E. coli* is a facultative aerobe.

   J. *P. aeruginosa* is an obligate aerobe, while *E. coli* is an obligate anaerobe.

39 *P. aeruginosa* uses the ED metabolic pathway to convert glucose to pyruvate, while *E. coli* uses the EMP metabolic pathway to convert glucose to pyruvate. In the presence of oxygen, both bacteria use the citric acid cycle (CAC) to convert pyruvate to energy. Based on this information and the data in Table 1, which of the following lists the three pathways in increasing order of their efficiency at converting food sources to energy?

   A. ED, EMP, CAC

   B. EMP, ED, CAC

   C. CAC, ED, EMP

   D. CAC, EMP, ED

40 An *E. coli* culture in LB media growing in aerobic conditions was used to inoculate a new flask of LB media, which was then allowed to grow in anaerobic conditions. Given that in *E. coli*, different metabolic pathways are used for growth in anaerobic conditions than aerobic conditions, which of the following could be a growth curve for the the culture grown in anaerobic conditions?

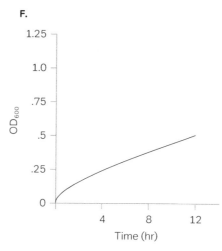

G.

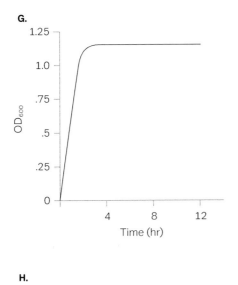

H.

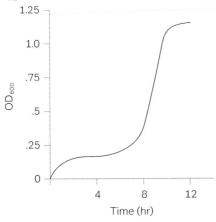

J.

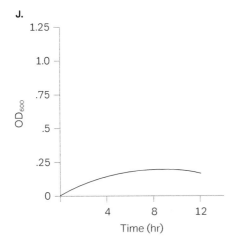

5

ACT Writing Test

40 Minutes

The following test assesses your writing skills. You have 40 minutes to read the prompt, plan, and write your essay in English. Before you start, read all of the information carefully and be sure to understand what the assignment is asking you to do.

Your essay will be graded based on the evidence it provides of your ability to:

- Clearly communicate your personal position on a complex issue and analyze the relationship between your perspective and at least one other perspective.
- Develop and support your position with reasoning and examples.
- Organize your ideas in a clear and logical manner.
- Successfully state your ideas in standard written English.

Note: On the ACT Writing Test, you will write your essay on the lined pages in the answer document. All writing on the lined pages will be scored. You will be able to use the unlined pages in the test booklet to plan your response. Your work on the unlined pages will not be scored. You will wait to open the writing booklet until told to do so, and will put your pencil down immediately when time is called.

Censorship

Almost since human beings first began sharing ideas, the issue of censorship (officially suppressing ideas or writing) has been debated. Proponents of censorship argue, for example, that offensive material might morally corrupt children or that governments have the right to protect their national secrets. Opponents argue that censorship infringes on individual freedom and hinders progress. Censorship has long been an issue regarding books and papers; now, it has become a critical issue concerning the seemingly infinite amount of information on the internet. Given the continued impact of censorship on various aspects of our lives, it is an issue worth examining.

Read and carefully consider these perspectives. Each suggests a particular way of thinking about the impact of censorship.

Perspective 1	Perspective 2	Perspective 3
Selective censorship prevents children from being exposed to offensive material. It allows parents and caretakers to determine what material children are ready for and when, based on their maturity level, they are ready for such material.	Censorship intrudes upon freedom of the press and freedom of speech. Individuals have the right to learn about their world—both its positive and negative aspects—and to express their ideas on it.	Censorship should not be condoned, because it places too much power in the hands of a few: no government or leadership system should be allowed to decide what information should reach the public.

Essay Task

Write a unified, coherent essay in which you evaluate multiple perspectives on the impact of censorship on society. In your essay, be sure to do the following:

- Analyze and evaluate the perspectives given.
- State and develop your own perspective on the issue.
- Explain the relationship between your perspective and those given.

Your perspective may be in full agreement with any of the others, in partial agreement, or wholly different. Whatever the case, support your ideas with logical reasoning and detailed, persuasive examples.

You have completed the test!

Answer Key

Congratulations! You finished a full-length ACT Practice Test. Now it's time to see how you scored.

Test 1: English

1. A	20. H	39. D	58. J
2. F	21. B	40. F	59. C
3. C	22. H	41. B	60. H
4. G	23. B	42. J	61. A
5. D	24. H	43. B	62. G
6. J	25. D	44. G	63. A
7. B	26. G	45. A	64. H
8. G	27. C	46. J	65. C
9. C	28. G	47. D	66. F
10. H	29. D	48. H	67. D
11. B	30. F	49. C	68. F
12. H	31. C	50. F	69. D
13. A	32. G	51. D	70. H
14. F	33. D	52. G	71. B
15. C	34. J	53. C	72. H
16. H	35. B	54. J	73. B
17. B	36. H	55. B	74. F
18. F	37. B	56. G	75. D
19. B	38. H	57. D	

Test 2: Math

1. E	16. H	31. D	46. J
2. J	17. D	32. K	47. A
3. B	18. F	33. D	48. J
4. K	19. C	34. K	49. A
5. D	20. F	35. A	50. K
6. F	21. D	36. H	51. B
7. A	22. G	37. B	52. H
8. G	23. D	38. J	53. D
9. B	24. J	39. C	54. F
10. K	25. D	40. F	55. A
11. B	26. G	41. E	56. J
12. J	27. C	42. K	57. D
13. D	28. K	43. B	58. F
14. K	29. C	44. G	59. A
15. C	30. G	45. D	60. F

Test 3: Reading

1. A	11. D	21. B	31. B
2. H	12. G	22. H	32. G
3. D	13. A	23. B	33. B
4. F	14. F	24. G	34. J
5. D	15. B	25. A	35. C
6. J	16. J	26. G	36. F
7. C	17. C	27. C	37. C
8. F	18. G	28. J	38. F
9. C	19. B	29. C	39. B
10. G	20. J	30. J	40. J

Test 4: Science

1. A	11. C	21. D	31. A
2. J	12. H	22. G	32. H
3. B	13. D	23. B	33. A
4. G	14. G	24. F	34. H
5. C	15. A	25. C	35. C
6. H	16. G	26. J	36. H
7. C	17. C	27. B	37. A
8. H	18. G	28. G	38. H
9. A	19. B	29. D	39. A
10. J	20. F	30. J	40. H

Are you into watching videos to learn more about the questions you missed? We offer text and video explanations for all of these practice questions in our online ACT prep. You can also email us at help@magoosh.com to get help on any of the questions you just answered.

Chapter 11

It's Test Day!

Test Day Tips

After all this time, ACT test day is fast approaching. You've put in the work to ace the questions—but what about the day itself? Here are some tips to make sure it goes as smoothly as possible!

1. **Pack the day before.** The last thing you want to worry about as you shake yourself awake on test day is what you need to bring with you to the test center. Here's a complete list:

   - Admissions ticket printed from the official ACT website
   - Photo identification (This is crucial! You will not be admitted without it. Check acceptable forms of identification on the official ACT site.)
   - Several sharpened No. 2 pencils (These must be the old-fashioned soft-lead, wooden kind, NOT mechanical pencils.)
   - A permitted calculator (Did you know that using a TI-89 is the most common reason students are dismissed from the ACT? Check the list of prohibited calculators on the ACT website.)
   - Extra calculator batteries
   - A watch to pace yourself (You can't rely on the test room to have a clock. And for the sanity of all involved—and to comply with ACT rules—please use a watch that doesn't beep.)
   - Good eraser
   - Pencil sharpener
   - Healthy snacks
   - Water bottle
   - Gum (This isn't required, but did you know chewing gum improves accuracy and reaction times? Snapping your gum, on the other hand, increases the

annoyance of those around you, so if you're in the habit of doing this, maybe save the gum for breaks.)

- ○ Outfit with layers (Your test room may be too hot or too cold. It's rarely just right, Goldilocks.)

2. **Go to bed early.** Make sure you give yourself a solid night of sleep. For most teenagers, this is eight to nine hours. Figure out when you need to get up to be completely ready and at the test center stress-free, and work backward from this time to figure out when you need to go to bed. If you can't sleep, though, don't force it. Get up and do something relaxing and try again in a half hour. Don't lie there agonizing.

3. **Wake up early and do some physical and mental exercise.** Go for a jog; do some jumping jacks. Waking up both your body and mind is crucial. Read some articles from the newspaper and focus on finding the main idea. Try a couple math problems, or play around with some mental math. It's important that your brain be warmed up for the test, but avoid the urge to do any last-minute ACT prep. At this point, it won't help.

4. **Eat a healthy, long-sustaining breakfast.** We recommend granola, fruit, eggs, and veggies. Drink coffee only if you're used to it. Don't try it now if you're not in the habit of drinking coffee—you might get crazy jitters.

5. **Bring a cheat sheet.** Not THAT kind of cheat sheet. But we *do* recommend bringing an "ACT strategy cheat sheet" that you can review before the test and then tuck safely away in a bag. This should include the most important reminders you've learned from your test prep such as "Watch out for comma splices!" and "Make sure to stick to a pace of five minutes per passage on the ACT Science Test." Having a last-minute review list can help you remember that you are, in fact, prepared and that you have, in fact, got this. You can use the following for a template for your cheat sheet:

General reminders:		
English	Pacing:	
	Watch out for:	
	Remember:	
Math	Pacing:	
	Watch out for:	
	Remember:	
Reading	Pacing:	
	Watch out for:	
	Remember:	
Science	Pacing:	
	Watch out for:	
	Remember:	

6. **Don't lose your cool before the test.** Libraries or cafeterias full of arriving test-takers aren't exactly spa-like places in terms of their Zen levels. You could cut the nervous energy with a knife. There are too many anxious students fretting about whether or not there will be a comparison reading passage (there always is) or quizzing each other on logarithms (a topic that shows up only rarely). There could be a group of your friends pulling you into some Homecoming Dance drama that distracts you from the task at hand. Or the worst person in the world: the kid leaning up against the wall, looking like he couldn't care less.

   Of course, eventually you need to check in, but if you get to the test center early, by all means pull out your headphones, blast your favorite pump-me-up music, and hang out outside. You've done too much preparation to let these other students shake your confidence.

7. **Keep your focus during the test.** A surefire way *not* to get the score you want is to pay constant attention to the test-takers around you. How does that girl in front of you answer math problems so fast (maybe she's guessing)? Why can't that kid stop tapping his foot (maybe he's understudying for *Hamilton*)? Doesn't matter. Stay in the zone and focus on your strategies. Everyone is different, and what these other students are doing is irrelevant. And it should go without saying that you should avoid any temptation to peer at your neighbor's answer sheet, even if it's just to figure out how the heck he's reading so fast. Cheating is not a risk you want to run here. And he's probably wrong anyway.

8. **Eat on your breaks, even if you aren't hungry.** Your brain needs fuel just like the rest of your body, even if your nervous stomach doesn't think so. And the last thing you want is to let a perfectly good snack break go to waste only to regret it later, when your stomach is howling halfway through the ACT Science Test. Fruit is great test fuel: the natural sugars help give you energy. Make sure to have something with protein, too, like a handful of nuts. Many of our students swear by peanut butter and jelly sandwiches or trail mix with chocolate for the perfect combo of sugar and sustenance. Don't forget the water!

9. **Reward yourself.** You worked hard for this, and no matter how you think the test went, treat yourself to something you enjoy afterward. You need the mental break and relaxation. But as important as an after-test reward is, what is even more important is rewarding yourself during the exam. No, you can't whip out a cookie in the middle of the ACT English Test, but don't forget to give yourself mental pats on the back when you catch yourself doing something right. So many students beat themselves up during a test for what they think they're doing wrong. Put a stop to this destructive mentality and instead congratulate yourself when you find yourself doing something right, such as sticking to your pacing or recognizing a grammar error you've missed before. Practice this during your practice tests if you can. It's a long exam and a positive attitude is crucial!

There are a lot of things you can do to prepare for the big exam—but once test day rolls around, the strategies at hand are much more limited. So take this opportunity to relax. Yep, relax! At this point, control what you can control and let the rest of it go. You've worked hard; you've got this. Trust yourself, and cheers to a fantastic test day!

Acknowledgments

This book wouldn't be available without the help of an incredible team of high school students, parents, tutors, and designers who provided incredible feedback along the way. These amazing fans and educators dedicated their time and brainpower to help edit, refine, and perfect the pages of the book you now hold in your hands.

Dylan Astrup

Bahar Baniasad

Nadira Berman

Ori Cantwell

Carol Chen

Catrina Coffey

Derek E.

Paula Fuhrman

Allen Glazer

Meredith Hoppe

R. Jennings

Michelle Lee

Mark Lehner

Leah Maassel

Raymond Ruscoe

Suzanne S.

Vinit Jatin Shah

Taylor Valentine

Aleksandra Voitcekhovskaia

Andros Williams

We'd also like to give a big shout-out to the entire Magoosh team for their collaboration and support! Meet everyone at magoosh.com/team.

Answer key to the puzzle on page 34:

ACROSS

1. Where you'll live freshman year (abbr.): **Dorm**
5. A group of atoms that are bonded together, like H_2O: **Molecule**
7. A course you must complete before signing up for the next level: **Prerequisite**
9. You dissolve a solute in this to form a solution: **Solvent**
12. Sin, cos, and tan are all part of this branch of math: **Trigonometry**
15. What you submit to potential colleges: **Application**
16. A special quality of a person, thing, or group: **Characteristic**
17. To intentionally leave something out: **Omit**
18. College _____: process of getting into college: **Admissions**
19. ACT Math subject involving lines and shapes: **Geometry**

DOWN

2. What you'll call most of your teachers in college: **Professor**
3. For the ACT, it's on a scale from 1–36: **Score**
4. _____ activities: Ex: volunteering, student government, or the debate team: **Extracurricular**
5. Your main academic focus in college: **Major**
6. What you need to do before the ACT so you don't get too anxious: **Relax**
8. Money awarded based on your academic achievements: **Scholarship**
10. The official record of all your high school grades: **Transcript**
11. Ex: "raining cats and dogs" or "hit the road": **Idiom**
13. When you _____ high school, you will become a high school _____: **Graduate**
14. Optional courses that you will take for college credit: **Electives**